Philosophy of Science Complete

A Text on Traditional Problems and Schools of Thought

SECOND EDITION

EDWIN HUNG
University of Waikato, New Zealand

WADSWORTH
CENGAGE Learning·

Australia • Brazil • Japan • Korea • Mexico • Singapore • Spain • United Kingdom • United States

***Philosophy of Science Complete: A Text on
Traditional Problems and Schools
of Thought,* Second Edition**
Edwin Hung

Editor-in-Chief: Lyn Uhi

Publisher: Clark Baxter

Senior Sponsoring Editor: Joann Kozyrev

Assistant Editor: Joshua Duncan

Editorial Assistant: Marri Straton

Media Editor: Katie Schooling

Brand Manager: Jennifer Levanduski

Market Development Manager: Joshua I.
Adams

Senior Marketing Communications Manager:
Linda Yip

Rights Acquisitions Specialist: Ann Hoffman

Manufacturing Planner: Sandee Milewski

Art and Design Direction, Production
Management, and Composition:
PreMediaGlobal

Cover Image: © Superstock/Superstock/
Corbis (RM)

For product information and technology assistance, contact us at
Cengage Learning Customer & Sales Support, 1-800-354-9706

For permission to use material from this text or product, submit all
requests online at **www.cengage.com/permissions.**
Further permissions questions can be emailed to
permissionrequest@cengage.com.

Library of Congress Control Number: 2012954118

ISBN-13: 978-1-133-94303-7

ISBN-10: 1-133-94303-9

Wadsworth
20 Channel Center Street
Boston, MA 02210
USA

Cengage Learning is a leading provider of customized learning solutions with
office locations around the globe, including Singapore, the United Kingdom,
Australia, Mexico, Brazil and Japan. Locate your local office at
international.cengage.com/region

Cengage Learning products are represented in Canada by
Nelson Education, Ltd.

For your course and learning solutions, visit **www.cengage.com**

Purchase any of our products at your local college store or at our preferred
online store **www.cengagebrain.com**

Instructors: Please visit **login.cengage.com** and log in to access
instructor-specific resources.

Printed in the United States of America
1 2 3 4 5 6 7 16 15 14 13 12

To my mother, Mrs. Hung Lee Fung-Sang,
wishing her peace,
health, happiness, and longevity.

For Suwei, recommending the five noble subjects:
Philosophy, Mathematics, Physics, Architecture, and Music,
which few, if any, can surpass in beauty, greatness, and delight.

About the Author

E dwin Hung is a recently retired Reader* of Philosophy at the University of Waikato, New Zealand. He studied philosophy at Oxford University, where he obtained his doctoral degree (DPhil). He has been an honorary fellow of Linacre College (Oxford), a research associate at the Boston University Center of Philosophy and History of Science, and a visiting scholar at Harvard University, MIT, and the Minnesota Center for the Philosophy of Science. He has written three books and has also published widely in the fields of philosophy of science, philosophy of mathematics, philosophy of logic, and philosophy of language.

*Readers in the British system are equivalent to full professors in the United States.

Brief Contents

---

*Chapters with asterisks are more advanced and may be omitted.

Detailed Contents

---

*Chapters with asterisks are more advanced and may be omitted.

Preface

After 15 years in the international market, it seems an appropriate time to produce this **second edition**.

This book is intended both as an **all-purpose textbook** and as an **encyclopedic reference** in the philosophy of science.

To this end, the book is specifically designed to be both **complete** and **simple**:

(i) The scope of the book is so complete that it can serve both the novice and the sophisticated, and with few topics left untouched.

(ii) The language of the book is so simple that both students and educated laypersons can follow the text without guidance.

However, it is not a survey, for surveys are usually superficial. They touch upon topics without going into them. In contrast, this book deals with each issue patiently and in detail. Thus the book is **unique** in the market. It can be called an **encyclopedic primer**.

COMPLETE

This book covers all the major topics in the philosophy of science, hence it is comprehensive. It consists of two divisions, known as Book I and Book II.

Book I deals with traditional problems in the philosophy of science:

- How are scientific hypotheses to be discovered and evaluated? (Problems of Truth)

- How are empirical data and laws to be scientifically explained? (Problems of Explanation)

- What are laws of nature? (Problem of Natural Necessity)

- What are scientific theories? (Structure of Theories)

- How should scientific theories to be interpreted? (Realism versus Antirealism)

Thus Book I is thematically oriented. It comprises what can be called "microphilosophy" of science.

Book II steers through the major milestones in the subject—all the major schools of thought, with their key thinkers, in their historical relationships to one another:

- Rationalism, starting with Plato and Euclid

- Empiricism, starting with Galileo and Bacon

- Hume's Problem, Goodman's and Hempel's Paradoxes

- Logical Positivism

- Popper

- Kuhn

- Lakatos

- Laudan

- Sociology of Knowledge: the Strong Program

- Constructivism

- Artificial Intelligence and Scientific Discovery

These topics are presented historically as evolving views and perspectives. Book II comprises what can be called "macrophilosophy" of science.

Happily, nowhere does the book repeat itself even though it covers the topics both horizontally (thematically) and vertically (historically).

SIMPLE AND ACCESSIBLE

In providing both breadth and depth, this book has not, however, sacrificed on simplicity or accessibility. The language is simple—even when dealing with rather complex ideas—and progress is gradual. Lots of examples for illustration help—there are many, many more than one would expect from a textbook of this type.

SUBSTANTIAL

This book attempts to offer not only breadth but depth as well. For example, the notion of hypothesis testing is first introduced in Chapter 1 almost as a common-sensical concept. Later on in Chapter 6 the role played by auxiliary hypotheses is explained. This is then followed in Chapter 7 by an in-depth discussion of

Popper's philosophy on ad hoc revision. Finally, the topic of testing ends with the controversial thesis of conventionalism in Chapter 9.

INTERESTING

Analytic philosophy by nature is abstract and thus tends to be dry. To write an interesting textbook in philosophy is therefore not easy. This book takes the need to motivate the reader seriously. In introducing a topic, I always attempt to make the student see the relevance as well as the exciting nature of the subject matter first. Examples are then employed to hold the student's interest because examples are essentially stories, and everyone loves a story. Occasional humour provides light-hearted breaks. And I find cleverly designed exercises can keep philosophical problems alive in students' mind even in their sleep!

Methods of science are learned from successes and failures of the past. The gradual development of science in its 2,500 years of history is where the treasure lies. Thus I employ a large number of examples from the history of science. As a consequence, students will come to learn quite a significant amount of science— mostly the more interesting and exciting episodes—as they do their philosophy. For instance, one reviewer wrote: "The inclusion of **historical examples** is praiseworthy and useful."

NEW TO THIS EDITION

- In this edition, I have adopted a new book title—*Philosophy of Science Complete: A Text on Traditional Problems and Schools of Thought*. The old title, *The Nature of Science: Problems and Perspectives*, is misleading. It tends to suggest that the book is a monograph rather than a textbook. Many people think that it is a work of science. Moreover, the phrase "Problems and Perspectives", though poetic, is rather opaque, and the absence of the term "philosophy of science" in the old title makes electronic search difficult.

- Years of feedback from readers have exposed to me numerous minor errors throughout the book. For instance, my explanation of the term "primary quality" in Section 17.2 was plainly incorrect. I am happy to report that all these mistakes have now been fixed.

- According to feedback from instructors, the book's structure is good. The two divisions, Book I and Book II complement each other. The chapters interlock into each other to form a unitary whole. Hence, no structural change has been made.

- An **electronic version** of this new edition is available over the Internet. Instructors and students are now able to purchase online just the chapters they need or the entire textbook at a significantly reduced cost. As the work is rather lengthy, this kind of **custom publishing** should work well. The electronic version of this edition is available at the online store front for Cengage Learning, www.CengageBrain.com. In www.CengageBrain.com, search for "Hung, Philosophy of Science" under the option "college faculty" or under "college student" should lead you to this book. Alternatively, you can go to www.CengageBrain.com/shop/search/.[1]

- The author's name has been simplified to "Edwin Hung" from "Edwin H.-C. Hung," which is rather clumsy for both memory and electronic search.

USE OF THE BOOK

This book is a self-contained textbook and a general reference for universities and colleges.

(A) To cover the entire book in detail would require a double-semester sequence of teaching. For a single-semester introductory course, one can select the easier chapters, which in general are the early chapters of each Part. Such selections shouldn't be difficult as the Parts and Chapters are rather self-contained even though they are all related. For a second single-semester course, one can select those chapters that complement what the students have already covered. The addition of materials from primary sources is optional. (As said earlier, **electronic custom purchasing** should make this practise both easy and affordable.)

(B) This book is also suitable for graduate students in three ways:

- Often graduate students from other disciplines (e.g., students from the sciences) wish to do a graduate-level course in philosophy of science. Usually they have little or no philosophical background. This book will serve very well for such students.

- As the book provides an encyclopedic summary of all the major fields in the philosophy of science, it will be suitable for those Phd students who want to brush up for their general qualifying examination in the subject.

- Philosophy graduate students who have not previously studied philosophy of science will also find this book useful as a text.

(C) As hinted earlier, this book is also suitable as a general reference for the professional philosopher as well as for the layperson. On account of its scope and accessibility I think it can very well serve as an encyclopedia.

For more details on the use of this book, you are invited to consult "A Word to Instructors" next to this Preface. Those who are really keen on advanced philosophy of science should enjoy reading Hung (2006).

---

1. Wadsworth Publishing is an imprint of Cengage Learning.

ACKNOWLEDGMENTS

First and foremost, I would like to thank most warmly the late Emeritus Professor Rudi Ziedins and Dr. Kai Jensen of the University of Waikato, the former for his philosophical comments, and the latter for his literary advice and secretarial assistance. Both had scrutinized the manuscript of the first edition from cover to cover, and both did it as a labour of love. Second, I am deeply indebted to my friend, Emeritus Professor Charles Dunlop of Michigan University, for his contribution in the production of this book and elsewhere. His wisdom and generosity are most touching. This is a good opportunity to express my profound gratitude. Many of my colleagues here in Waikato have given me both encouragement and advice. Among them I would like specifically to name Dr. Murray Jorgensen, Dr. David Lumsden, Dr. Don Smith, Dr. Mane Hajdin, and Dr. Gary Kemp.

My deep gratitude goes to Professor Ray Perkins, Jr. of Plymouth State University and Associate Professor Seungbae Park of Ulsan National Institute of Science and Technology (South Korea) for their detailed comments on the book. My thanks also go to the nine reviewers of the draft of the first edition. They are Professors Joseph Bessie, University of Central Oklahoma; Michael Bishop, Iowa State University; Brian B. Clayton, Gonzaga University; Malcolm Forster, University of Wisconsin-Madison, Ronald J. Glass, University of Wisconsin-La Crosse; John L. King, University of North Carolina at Greensboro; Robert Klee, Ithaca College; Eugene Lashchyk, La Salle University, and Morton L. Schagrin, State University of New York College at Fredonia. The same goes to the reviewers for this second edition. They are Professors Leslie Burkholder, University of British Columbia; William Devlin, Bridgewater State University; Theodore Everett, SUNY Geneseo; William Jones, Old Dominion University; Clayton Littlejohn, King's College London, and Michael Smith, College of the Desert. Their comments and suggestions were most valuable.

I would also like to thank most warmly my editors, Kenneth King, Peter Adams, Joann Kozyrev, Daisuke Yasutake, and Joshua Duncan for their advice and work.

Finally, my wife Priscilla and my daughter Estella deserve a warm expression of gratitude for being so patient, so understanding, and so supportive throughout the long days when I deserted the family to concentrate on this project.

Edwin Hung
June, 2012

A Word to Instructors

In teaching the philosophy of science, we are often frustrated at having to explain the most fundamental concepts to the students. This is one of the reasons behind the writing of this book.

This is a student-oriented text. It is self-contained and can be read by students without guidance. It is meant to provide them with an adequate foundation in all the major fields in the philosophy of science so that they can engage in more advanced and more interesting philosophical studies. You will find that the level of detail and technicality of this book is appropriate for the overwhelming majority of students. The book covers the major alternative views on each subject without descending to the level of "diminishing fleas" that can really put undergraduates off for life.

I take motivation seriously. Students must see the relevance and significance of what they study. To this end I make use of the introductions to each of the eight Parts and also those at the beginning of each chapter.

Teachers of philosophy of science are often hampered by the mixed background of their audience. Some are philosophy majors, some science majors, and some major in neither philosophy nor science. The simplicity of our presentation partly remedies the situation. The enormous number of examples helps. Students with little science background should enjoy and benefit from our mini-case histories as examples.

ORGANIZATION OF THE BOOK

As I pointed out in the Preface, the book consists of two divisions. **Book I** consists of four parts:

> **Part I** introduces the basic idea of hypothesis, deductive and inductive logic, probability and statistics.

Part II studies the traditional logic of hypothesis testing and its critique in the form of conventionalism.

Part III presents the classical covering-law thesis of scientific explanation and three contemporary alternatives. In the course of the presentation, we study the notion of law of nature, probabilistic causality, and some philosophies of mind.

Part IV studies the classical view of scientific theories and its difficulties as well as the empiricist challenge to realism.

Even though the classical tradition has largely been discredited, it is still arguably the best place to start the philosophy of science. First, it is a relatively clear and precise doctrine. Second, it is intuitively acceptable. Third, it is methodologically fruitful in many ways. Fourth, the classical tradition, despite its defects, is a useful first-order approximation. Finally, the more sophisticated views since 1962 can be properly understood only in contrast with it. I can think of an analogous case: the case of Newton's mechanics in relation to Einstein's mechanics.

The problems we study in Book I belong to the micro-philosophy of science. We study its complement—the macro-philosophy of science—in Book II. The appropriateness of answers offered to the problems of micro-philosophy depend very much on the schools or systems of thought that one presupposes. Book II studies these schools. It consists of four parts:

Part V introduces empiricism in contrast to rationalism, which is then followed by detailed discussions of the problems and objections that empiricism faces.

Part VI covers logical positivism and Popper's falsificationism. The two together form the classical tradition.

Part VII studies the Kuhnian revolution in detail.

Part VIII describes other post-positivist developments up to the present, including the impact of artificial intelligence on the philosophy of science.

Each Part in Book I concludes with a **summary**, and each chapter with a set of **exercises** and **references**. These exercises perform four functions: (i) to force students to clarify their understanding of the concepts and issues concerned, (ii) to provide a taste of philosophical problems in general, (iii) to stimulate students' interest further, and (iv) to test comprehension.

There is a rich **bibliography** located toward the end of the book.

USE OF THE BOOK

This book can be used on its own or with materials from primary sources. Here are some good anthologies of primary material on the market: Kourany (1987), Brody and Grandy (1989), Boyd et al. (1991), Fetzer (1993b), Curd and Cover (1998), Balashov et al. (2002), Lange (2007), and McGrew et al. (2009). Kourany contains mostly abridged materials and is therefore the simplest. It also has helpful introductions for each part. Books on scientific case histories should also be useful as supplementary aids Lastly, I would like to recommend Newton-Smith (2000), which provides a good survey of all the major topics in the field.

There are several ways to use our book:

A. For a One-Semester Course

(i) Book I should serve those who are mainly interested in micro-philosophy. No philosophical or scientific background is presupposed.

(ii) Book II is philosophically more sophisticated and should suit those who are more interested in macro-philosophy.

(iii) However, probably most of us would like to offer a course covering both micro- and macro-philosophy of science. In such a case a selection of topics from both Book I and Book II can be made. This should not be difficult, since the Parts—and many of the chapters within the Parts—are relatively self-contained though they are all related. For instance, instructors can choose one or more of Parts II to IV, and combine them with Chapter 19, Chapter 22, Part VI and Part VII to form a one-semester syllabus. The starred chapters are more advanced. For an elementary course, they can be the first to omit. Indeed a one-semester course composed of just the unstarred chapters is quite viable.

(iv) For a one-semester course as a second course in the philosophy of science, there should be enough material in this text to complement whatever the students have already covered in their first course.

B. For a Two-Semester Sequence

The book as a whole would be excellent for this purpose. Topics, however, need not be covered in the order presented. Omissions have been allowed for.

C. For Seminar-Style Classes

Since this book explains matters simply and in detail, it should serve well for seminar-style classes. Students can be asked to read the relevant passages beforehand, perhaps together with some chosen materials from primary sources. In class they are then asked to discuss certain set questions or topics. For this purpose some of the exercises in the book can be used.

D. As a Text for Science Students

For those who delight in practical matters but have little interest in philosophy, a syllabus made up of the following is recommended: Part I, Part II without Chapter 9, Chapters 15, 19, 22, 24, Part VII, Chapter 28, and perhaps Chapters 29 and 32.

E. As a General Reference

Because of its encyclopedic nature the book should serve well as a reference, especially since the materials are so simply presented.

If you should have any suggestions for the improvement of this book, please contact me. My e-mail address is **edwinspost@yahoo.com** Thank you.

An electronic version of this new edition is available over the Internet. Instructors and students are now able to purchase online just the chapters they need. For details, please read Preface.

A Word to Students

Here is a book on the **philosophy of science** that you can read without guidance. It is basically a digest. You will find that the materials in it are explained in very simple language, and there are many many examples for illustration (as well as for your enjoyment). Philosophy should be fun. I hope this book is going to convince you of that.

Having said this, as in any technical subject you have to learn some basic vocabulary and concepts before you can really get into the subject. Part I provides you with the necessary vocabulary. Chapter 4—which is on probability and statistics—may be a bit difficult. You might like to skip it if you find it tough going.

Beginning piano students have to practice lots of "finger exercises," which are typically boring. Part I is not like that. You will find a certain amount of delight even here. As you progress through the book you should experience flashes of insight. You will become aware of points that you have never dreamed of. If I may use a big word, you may get enlightened. It will dawn on you that your commonsense view of science is not quite right. You have been too trusting (or distrusting). You will become more reflective, more skeptical, and certainly more analytic. You will see old things in a new light. You will adopt a new interpretation of science. Science is no longer a set of facts to be learned. It is rather a set of viewpoints that allow for alternatives. The mind gets liberated.

You will learn quite a bit about the procedures of scientific reasoning. Most of these are "distilled" from actual scientific practice. You will be invited to evaluate these procedures. It's like being shown the mechanism under the hood of a car so that we can understand how cars work.

When you read this book—or for that matter any technical book—you may occasionally get bogged down in a particular passage. My advice is to skip it and carry on. Complete the section or chapter and then return to that opaque passage. You will probably find that passage more comprehensible because now you are studying it as part of a more complete picture. Often points are difficult to grasp in isolation. They have to be viewed in context. That's why you should proceed to acquire a wider view before you return to that difficult passage. Always re-read a chapter when you come to the end of it. In your first reading you are bound to have misunderstandings and are likely to miss a number of points. You learn much more through re-reading.

At the end of each chapter try some of the exercises collected there. Exercises are important for checking your understanding. They can in fact further your understanding. This is not to say that they are nothing other than training tools. Exercises can be fun. You will find most of the exercises in this book challenging, rather like puzzles.

Finally, do discuss and debate the issues you have studied with your teachers and friends. If you don't you could be miles off without realizing it. Only through discussion can you be sure that you have really understood. Discussion is the key to philosophical understanding.

HOW TO USE THIS BOOK

The **Introduction** should give you an idea of what philosophy of science is. **Chapter 0** is a fun chapter. It is about the investigation of the nature of light by scientists such as Newton and Huygens. It is meant to provide some background to students not well versed in science. Nevertheless, if you do find the chapter heavy going, do not hesitate to pass it over. It is not part of the book proper. However, **Part I** (with the exception of Chapter 4) should be studied thoroughly unless you have already had some exposure to deductive and inductive logic.

This book is meant to be read in its order of presentation. However, you may find certain topics boring—not all philosophical topics are equally exciting, you know. In most cases, it does no harm to skip them. You will find all the Parts—and most of the chapters—rather self-contained.

The **starred chapters** are more advanced and usually more "philosophical"; they can be omitted for starters. On each topic many **examples** are usually offered. You are not expected to understand them all. Students of the philosophy of science are often from a variety of backgrounds. Different examples suit different types of students. And there should be enough examples to satisfy everyone.

You will find lots of **cross-references** in the text. For example, following a sentence you may find something that reads like "(Section 11.5)." This means that you should find materials in Section 11.5 (of Chapter 11) relevant to what we are discussing. The cross-references may refer you forward or backward.

Toward the end of the book there is a **bibliography**. It contains a large number of titles of books and journal articles to which you can refer for further material. A book title may read like this:

Kourany, Janet A. (ed.), 1987, *Scientific Knowledge: Basic Issues in the Philosophy of Science*, Belmont, Calif.: Wadsworth.

The first item is the name of the author or the editor. In this case Janet A. Kourany is the editor. The next item is the date of publication, followed by the title, which is in italics. The last item is the name of the publisher, preceded by its location.

Among the references are some journal articles. For instance:

Koertge, Noretta, 1992, "Explanation and its Problems," *British Journal for the Philosophy of Science*, 43:1, pp. 85–98.

Here "Explanation and its Problems" is the title of the article, which is published in *British Journal for the Philosophy of Science*, Volume 43, Issue Number 1, pages 85–98.

In the text, these two publications would be referred to respectively as "Kourany (1987)" and "Koertge (1992)." A referring phrase such as "Kourany (1987, pp. 234–237)" means that the relevant passage occupies pages 234–237 of Kourany (1987).

In the book you will come across a large number of **footnotes**. They mainly perform the following two functions: (i) to provide further detail on the topic (usually you are not required to be acquainted with such additional information in order to move on in the text) and (ii) to refer you to further materials available from some other sources. Sometimes authors make use of footnotes to make passing remarks or express personal opinions on the topic, which are not supposed to be part of the text. In these cases, the reading of footnotes is obviously optional.

I think we are now ready to start reading the text proper. Let us therefore move on to the Introduction.

An electronic version of this new edition is available over the Internet. Instructors and students are now able to purchase online just the chapters they need. For details, please read Preface.

What Is the Philosophy
of Science?

Some years ago at a dinner party, I sat next to a neurosurgeon from California who asked about my area of specialization. On hearing that it was the philosophy of science, he expressed amazement and disbelief. I certainly did not look or behave like a philosopher, but this was not what caused his doubts. What he was amazed about was that there could be such a subject as "the philosophy of science"!

According to him philosophy is similar to religion, consisting mainly of claims about the abstract, the supernatural, and the incredible—usually wrapped up in fancy words that are woolly and muddled. He certainly had a "high" opinion of religion! In a word, philosophy, for him, is mumbo-jumbo. On the other hand, again according to him, science is clear, precise, and truthful, and, of course, terribly useful. It represents the best of our knowledge about the universe. (Quite an understandable belief for a neurosurgeon!) So how can there be a hybrid such as the philosophy of science? Hence his puzzlement.

I am not attempting to explain here what the philosophy of science is in a few words. It suffices, for now, to say that philosophy (contemporary Anglo-American philosophy) is not a set of claims about the material universe nor is it about the supernatural. Rather it is, crudely put, a set of advice, means, and practices to help us see things clearly and to evaluate claims, principles, arguments, and inferences carefully and critically. Hence we often refer to contemporary philosophy as analytic philosophy.[1]

---

1. To be accurate, Western contemporary philosophy is divided into two camps: What is known as continental philosophy finds its practitioners in continental Europe, whereas philosophers of the English-speaking world generally practice analytic philosophy.

The **philosophy of science**, in simple terms, is, therefore:

(i) A study of the claims of science, making it clear and precise what exactly these claims are.[2]

(ii) A study of the methods of science: isolating, analyzing, and evaluating the methods used and practiced in science, and perhaps suggesting new ones.

(iii) A study of the structure of science.[3]

(iv) A study of the way(s) science evolves and grows and, perhaps, the way(s) science should and could have evolved and grown.

We can, for example, ask the following sorts of questions in the philosophy of science:

(a) In science, we often come across claims such as "Space is curved," "The earth moves," "Absolute, true, and mathematical time, of itself and from its own nature, flows equably without regard to anything external … ," "Plants grow upward to seek sunlight," "Water is a collection of H_2O molecules," and "Smoking increases the probability of contracting lung cancer." What do such statements really mean? When and under what conditions can we reasonably accept them as true?

(b) Newton discovered the law of gravitation. What methods did he employ? Are these methods good? Are there better methods?

(c) What are scientific theories? What are laws of nature? What counts as a good scientific explanation?

(d) How was Aristotelian science replaced by Newtonian science? How was Newtonian science replaced by Einsteinian science? Were these replacements for the better or the worse?

The philosophy of science has its practical side in addition to making its intellectual contributions because, in a nutshell, the philosophy of science asks the simple question: "*How does science work?*" Obviously, knowing how science works will enable us to do better science: to employ better methods and better formulations. It should be helpful if you bear this question in mind when you read this book. Return to this simple question whenever you feel you are getting lost in the occasional complexities of the text.

The book has two divisions. **Book I** (the first division) studies the three central problems in the philosophy of science: truth, explanation, and reality. The views, theories, and critiques presented are based mainly on the classical tradition. Even though this tradition is by no means perfect, it is still the standard framework for the philosophy of science. All beginners should acquire a good knowledge of this tradition.

Book II surveys the four major milestones in the philosophy of science: rationalism, empiricism, positivism, and constructivism. The intention of this survey is:

(a) To give you a realistic picture of the subject so you will realize that the philosophy of science is not a static subject, not a subject that can be termed as closed, and surely not a subject that commands unanimity among philosophers.

(b) To provide a historical setting within which you can place the classical tradition, which you learned from Book I, and most importantly,

(c) To introduce you to the most recent views in the philosophy of science, most of which can be taken as disputations and revolts against the classical tradition.

You will eventually be introduced to a large number of historical examples as illustrations. Among them are: the geocentric theory versus the heliocentric theory of the universe, the caloric versus the kinetic theory of heat, and the phlogiston versus the oxygen theory of burning. Nevertheless,

---

2. And also establishing general ways and means of clarification.

3. This is a rather abstract notion, and I am leaving the details till later for clarification. At present it is sufficient to imagine that building science is comparable to building a house. Both science and houses have structures.

I think it is appropriate to provide one example right now so you can use it as a reference point when you read this book. It is useful to check philosophical views and claims against real examples. Chapter 0, which is coming up next, tells the memorable story of the historical study of light. Apart from enjoying it as a story, you may want to refer to it from time to time for a better understanding of the various contending philosophical views presented in this book.

Chapter 0

A Tale of Two Theories: The Story of Light

[*This is an oversimplified and quite nontechnical story about the contest between two theories of light over the last 300 years: the wave theory and the particle theory. Read it if you feel like enjoying a fascinating story; leave it if you are in a hurry to do philosophy of science proper.*]

0.1 THE THREE LAWS OF OPTICS

That brilliant, that colorful, that life-giving thing called light: What is it? What is it *really*? What is its *real* nature?

That light travels in straight lines[1] (law of rectilinear propagation) has been known since antiquity. The ancient Greeks, moreover, knew of the law of

---

1. Strictly speaking, this holds only for light traveling in a homogeneous medium.

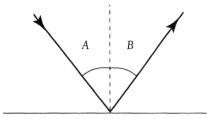

FIGURE 0.1

reflection and the law of refraction (though not in their exact forms). The former says that when a light ray strikes a smooth and opaque surface, it reflects in such a way that the angle of incidence is equal to that of reflection[2] (Figure 0.1). The latter says that when a light ray moves from one medium into another, it refracts (bends), as illustrated in Figure 0.2. Willebrord Snell (1591–1626) specified that the angle of incidence is related to the angle of refraction as[3]

$$\frac{\sin A}{\sin B} = \text{constant}$$

We can see an example of the law of reflection when sunlight strikes the surface of a mirror. The law of refraction can be demonstrated by half submerging a pencil at an angle into a glass of water. Or to take a different example, Aristotle (384–322 B.C.) observed that an oar when dipped into water looks bent. The three laws together are often referred to as the three laws of optics.

These laws are powerful indeed, so powerful that up to the end of the 19th century, most technology involving the use of light—including the making of telescopes and microscopes—required no knowledge other than these three laws. We can ask ourselves the following question: Having become aware of the three laws, why did so

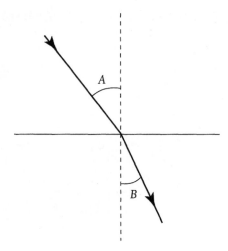

FIGURE 0.2

many scientists still expend so much effort in the study of light? They must have been searching for something more than technology! Is this the something that science is after? Is it what we call knowledge of the true nature of things, or is it what we call the ultimate explanation of the universe? Keep these questions in mind. Now, without further ado, let us begin our story.

0.2 WAVES VERSUS PARTICLES

This is the story of the contest between two theories: the wave theory and the particle theory of light.[4] Is light made up of a sort of waves or a sort of particles? From the time of the ancient Greeks to the beginning of the 20th century, there were two schools of thought. One school held that light was a sort of impulse (wave) transmitted through a transparent medium. Another thought that light

---

2. This is a simplified version. The more exact version should have allowed for reflection on nonopaque surfaces and also should have stated that both the incident ray and the reflected ray are in the same plane.

3. As I said before, you are not required to understand all the examples. Skip the following formula if you find it baffling.

4. What follows are adapted from McKenzie (196) and Holton and Roller (1958).

consisted of particles coming from the luminous objects and impinging on our eyes. Our story begins with the 17th century, even though a host of prominent scientists were studying light long before then—for example, Ptolemy, Kepler, Descartes, Snell, Fermat, Grimaldi, Hooke, and Roemer.

0.3 HUYGENS (WAVES)

Let's start our story with the Dutch scientist Christiaan Huygens (1629–1695). Huygens saw the close resemblance between light and sound and reasoned that since sound consists of waves through air or other media, light must be similar. [*What kind of reasoning is this?*] His main contribution was what is now known as Huygens's principle, which gives a method of working out how successive light waves would move forward. With this principle, Huygens could explain why and how light rays reflect, much as water waves are reflected when they meet the shore. He could also explain the refraction of light with the same principle.

However, if light consists of waves resembling sound, it should be able to turn corners, because sound after all turns corners. (That's why you can hear people talking in the next room if you leave your door open.) In other words, the law of rectilinear propagation is not explainable in terms of Huygens's wave theory. This led Newton to develop his particle theory of light. [*Note the role that is expected of theories in scientific explanation.*]

There is another problem, though it was not taken seriously at that time. If light consists of waves and can travel through space, there must be something invisible and intangible in space to support these waves. Waves have to be waves of something, such as water, because what we call waves are not really distinctive entities themselves. They are only regular and periodic distortions of something—again, for example, water. People at

that time called the medium for light waves *ether*. [*Note this notorious 'ether.' Under what circumstances can we have sufficiently good reasons to believe that something exists?*]

0.4 NEWTON (PARTICLES) AND THE THREE LAWS

Isaac Newton (1642–1727), for many, the greatest scientist ever, was not only the author of the theory of gravitation and the theory now known as Newton's mechanics, but also contributed monumentally to the study of light. He proposed that light rays are streams of minute corpuscles (particles) that travel at great speed. That's why light rays are straight lines. Moreover, on meeting a hard surface these corpuscles would rebound like elastic balls, thus satisfying the law of reflection. Finally, according to Newton's reasoning, when a beam of these corpuscles moves from a less dense medium (say, air) into a denser medium (say, water), the latter, because of its stronger gravitational pull, should bend the beam as prescribed by the law of refraction. We can see the explanatory power of Newton's theory.

0.5 NEWTON AND COLORS I

The three laws belong to what is known as **geometrical optics**, which is roughly about how light rays "draw" lines. In that field, nothing is said about colors. Many of you have probably heard of the story of how Newton, having had his room darkened, let in a single beam of sunlight through a small hole in the window shutters. Noting that the beam cast a white spot on the opposite wall, he placed a glass prism[5] across the beam. Since the prism was made of glass, a denser material than air, the beam of light was refracted (bent) as expected. But to Newton's great surprise, the single

---

5. A triangular slab of glass.

spot of white light on the opposite white wall now turned into an oblong shape with a series of colors, resembling the spectrum of an inverted rainbow, with violet and blue at the top and red and orange at the bottom. [*Have you ever wondered why rainbows have seven colors?*] When Newton interposed another similar but inverted prism across this multicolored beam, the oblong on the wall collapsed into a white spot again. From this he reasoned that the light corpuscles were not of one kind as he previously thought. They were *not* white corpuscles at all. There were in fact seven kinds of light corpuscles; each kind was one of the seven rainbow colors. When these colored corpuscles were combined, the result was white. The glass prism must have had the ability to separate out this mixture into its components, the rainbow colors. [*Note how theories are modified and refined to cope with new phenomena.*]

0.6 NEWTON AND COLORS II

Let's continue the story of colors. Most of you would have noticed soap bubbles or thin films of oil floating on water and displaying rainbow colors.[6] Newton, as a good scientist, reasoned that if his corpuscular theory was correct, it should be able to explain this phenomenon as well. But these thin films were not prisms, and they seemed to produce the colors not by refraction but by reflection. The idea that prisms could separate out the colored corpuscles was not applicable here. At this point, opposed to Huygens's wave theory as he was, Newton nevertheless postulated that his corpuscles did produce waves of a sort. These waves, however, were not light waves but "shock" waves, and the waves determined which kind (color) of light corpuscles at a given point would be reflected and which transmitted. The rays we see were thus

colored, being the colored corpuscles reflected. Note that in introducing the mechanism of "shock waves" Newton had to postulate a kind of ether to support them, quite analogous to Huygens's ether. [*The modification of a theory by the invention of certain mechanisms or entities solely for the sake of enabling the theory to explain certain otherwise unexplainable phenomena is said to be ad hoc. Are ad hoc moves acceptable to you? Aren't they a sort of excuse?*]

0.7 NEWTON AND DIFFRACTION

Another phenomenon involving light is known as **diffraction**. In a darkened room, a beam of sunlight let in through a tiny hole through the window shutters will cast a white spot on the opposite wall, as we saw in Newton's experiment. Francesco Grimaldi (1618–1663) discovered that if a tiny obstacle is put across the path of the beam, the shadow of the obstacle is smaller than it should be if light were to travel strictly according to the law of rectilinear propagation. In other words, light rays diffract round corners, albeit in a minute amount and only under certain circumstances.[7] Another mystery and another challenge to Newton! This time Newton proposed that his ether changed density as it approached material objects, so that diffraction was really a kind of refraction. (Remember that refraction occurs when light crosses media of different densities.)[8] You can see that to explain the phenomenon of diffraction Newton not only conceded the existence of a substance like Huygens's ether, but further postulated that this substance can change its density. [*Another ad hoc move or simply a*

---

6. This phenomenon is associated with the phenomenon known as Newton's rings.

7. Moreover, if the shadow is examined minutely, one can find rainbow-colored bands *inside* the shadow, hence light in this case at least does not travel in straight lines.

8. See McKenzie (1960, pp. 151–152).

brave move on Newton's part, making use of whatever he could think of?]

It is one thing to say that the phenomena are such that light travels in straight lines, that it reflects, that it refracts, and so on. It is another thing to claim that the *true nature* of light is such and such. Claiming, for example, that light consists of particles as Newton did makes it necessary to show that *all* the phenomena of light—including well-established ones, new ones, and those yet to be discovered—are explainable and accountable by that claim. Such claims are known as *theories*. Theories come and go in science. It is one of the central problems in the philosophy of science to work out when we can trust a theory as true or at least as close to the truth. Is Newton's corpuscular theory of light true? Let's see how it copes with the phenomenon of polarization.

0.8 NEWTON AND POLARIZATION

The problem of the true nature of light is becoming more and more complicated. Polarization is observable with certain transparent crystals—for example, tourmaline crystals. We can get a similar effect with Polaroid sheets from sunglasses. Look through two thin sheets of the crystal against a light source. If one of the sheets is rotated a full circle, we will find that at two positions 180° apart practically no light comes through, whereas at the other two in-between positions we get maximum transmission of light. In other words, as we rotate one of the sheets, the intensity of the light changes from dark to bright, then to dark, and then back to bright at every 90° of rotation. Is it possible to explain this phenomenon in terms of corpuscles? [*Newton did make another ad hoc and not very successful move to try to explain it.*]

Any theory of light must explain other phenomena as well. But I will not go into them here because I think you have had a sufficient sample already. This sample shows you the kind of difficulty a theoretician in science faces in trying to

fathom the true nature of certain phenomena such as those of light.

0.9 YOUNG (WAVES) AND THE THREE LAWS

I'll now move on to two other brilliant scientists, Thomas Young (1773–1829) and Augustin-Jean Fresnel (1788–1827). They improved on Huygens's wave theory along similar lines independently of each other, and the improved theory explained the various phenomena of light so well that later Sir John Herschel wrote: "[The theory] … , if not founded in Nature, is certainly one of the happiest fictions that the genius of man ever invented …" (McKenzie (1960, p. 161)).

If light did consist of corpuscles, Young asked why these particles should have a constant velocity irrespective of the nature and temperature of the light source. On the other hand, the constancy of velocity was *expected* of waves (because it is the medium of transmission, not the source, that determines the velocity). There were other puzzles with Newton's corpuscular theory. For instance, why should some of the corpuscles be reflected and some be refracted when a light beam struck a transparent surface like water? What mechanism was there to determine which particular corpuscle was to be reflected and which to be refracted? For waves, however, partial reflection and partial refraction were again expected phenomena. These gave Young great confidence in the wave theory.

0.10 YOUNG (INTERFERENCE) AND NEWTON'S RINGS

Young's greatest contribution was his principle of interference. A train of waves is a sequence of crests and troughs with regular spacing. The distance between consecutive crests is called the wavelength of the train, whereas the distance between the top

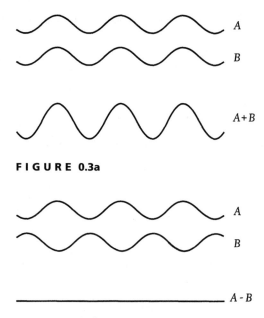

FIGURE 0.3a

FIGURE 0.3b

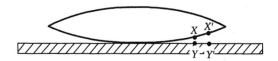

FIGURE 0.4

of the crests and the bottom of the troughs is known as the amplitude. When two trains of waves of the same wavelengths and same amplitudes meet, three things may happen: (1) The two are in phase (that is, in step): crests match crests and troughs match troughs. Under such circumstances, the amplitude of the resultant waves will be doubled, and so the crests will be twice as high and the troughs will be twice as deep. We say that this is a case of constructive interference (Figure 0.3a). (2) The two are completely out of phase: crests match troughs, and troughs match crests. In such a case, the waves from the two trains will cancel each other out, resulting in no waves at all. This is a case of destructive interference (Figure 0.3b). (3) The two may partially interfere with each other.

The principle of interference has proven to be very useful in the explanation of many phenomena of light, including what is now known as Newton's rings. If a very thin convex lens[9] is placed on a flat reflective surface (the narrow air space between the lens and the flat surface will form a thin "air film"),

and a beam of white light is focused directly onto it from above, you will find concentric rings of rainbow colors surrounding the center of the lens. And if a monochromatic beam of light—for example, red light—is used, the rings will be of that monochromatic color, alternating with black rings. These are known as Newton's rings.

Ironically these rings of Newton undermined the pet theory of their discoverer, instead, lending support to its rival, Huygens's wave theory. The principle of interference can easily explain these alternate rings of red and black, whereas the corpuscular theory cannot.

As the red light passes through the lens and emerges from the bottom surface (for instance, at point X in Figure 0.4), part of it is reflected back, while part is transmitted (that is, passes straight through). In other words, the light ray is split into two trains, one reflected and one transmitted. Let's call these two the *A-train* and the *B-train*, respectively.

The B-train on meeting the flat surface at point Y will be reflected as well, thus turning back to meet the A-train at point X. It is here that the two trains interfere, according to the principle of interference. The amount of interference will depend on how out of phase or in phase they are. If the distance between X and Y is that of a quarter of a wavelength of red light, the distance covered by the B-train will exceed that of the A-train by twice one quarter of a wavelength—in other words, by half a wavelength. Under such circumstances, they will interfere destructively: the waves will cancel each other out, and what we see will be blackness (Figure 0.3).

Next let us consider points X' and Y' where the distance $X'Y'$ is half a wavelength. The separation of the two trains in this case is one wavelength. This means that the two trains are now in phase. They

---

9. Meaning a lens with a very small curvature.

therefore reinforce each other, resulting in waves twice as high. To the observer, *X'* will thus be red. You can now see how alternate rings of black and red are formed as we move out from the center. Each time the distance between the lens and the flat surface (that is, the thickness of the air film in between) increases by a quarter of a wavelength the ring changes its color: from black to red or from red to black.[10] A spin-off is obvious: wavelengths of light of different colors can now be measured via Newton's rings.

Thus Huygens's waves became more real than ever. (If you could measure their wavelengths, the waves must be real!) There was a kind of naturalness to interpreting light as waves. As had been known for a long time, sound consists of waves. The pitch of sound corresponds inversely to the magnitude of the wavelength. The shorter the wavelength the higher the pitch. Sometimes you will hear people say that the pitch corresponds to the frequency. This is because the frequency is inversely proportional to the wavelength. Loudness, on the other hand, corresponds to the amplitude. Similarly for light. Colors correspond to wavelengths. Red light has a wavelength of about 7×10^{-5} cm, and blue light has a wavelength of about 5×10^{-5} cm. You can see that light waves are very short, in fact much less than the thickness of a hair. On the other hand, intensity (brightness) corresponds to amplitude: the "taller" the waves are, the brighter the light ray is.

White light is a mixture of all the (optical) wavelengths, from red to violet. Because waves of different wavelengths refract differently, Newton's prism was able to scatter them, thus producing a rainbow from the white sunlight. How naturally the wave theory explains the occurrence of colors! The colors of Newton's rings are explained in an equally natural manner, albeit differently. Whereas the prism sorts out wavelengths corresponding to the colors—red, orange, and so on—by "selecting" them directly,

the thin air film below the lens *subtracts* the colors—red, orange, and so forth—from the white mixture by interference. That's why even though the spectra produced by both the prism and the air film have a variety of colors, their patterns are different.

0.11 YOUNG AND DIFFRACTION

Again, diffraction (spreading around corners) is a natural phenomenon for all waves: water waves, sound waves, and so on. The amount of diffraction is noticeable only when the size of the opening through which the waves pass is of the same order of magnitude as the wavelength or smaller (Figures 0.5a and 0.5b). Since the wavelengths of sound (in air) can be as long as 16 meters, sound will bend around openings 16 meters wide or less. Now you can see why we can hear people talking even though they are around the corner from the doorway: because doorways are usually much less than 16 meters wide! The case is

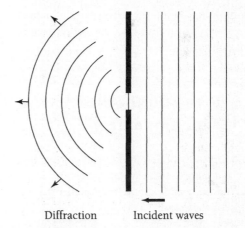

Diffraction   Incident waves

FIGURE 0.5a

---

10. You may remember how Newton tried to explain colors on thin films, such as soap bubbles, in terms of "shock waves" produced by his corpuscles. One of the distinctive characteristics of waves is their periodicity—that is, they repeat themselves at regular intervals in space and time. The main reason for Newton to "graft" shock waves onto his theory was to make use of the periodicity of waves. You have just seen how periodicity was employed to explain Newton's rings. However, this time the desired periodicity came naturally. It was no longer an ad hoc device grafted onto something that was by nature nonperiodic—that is, corpuscles.

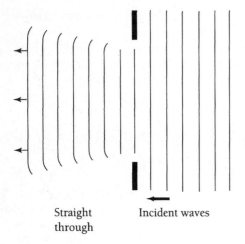

Straight   Incident waves
through

FIGURE 0.5b

same place. This is what I meant when I said that the direction of vibration of the water (indicated by the leaf) was perpendicular to the direction of propagation. When these two directions are perpendicular to each other, we say that the waves are transverse. However, sound waves are not transverse; they are longitudinal, in that the vibration of the medium (such as air) is in the direction of the propagation. Young at first thought that light, since it resembled sound, consisted of longitudinal waves, and it was hard to imagine how longitudinal waves could yield polarization.

But then it struck Young that light waves could be transverse! [*Is this what is commonly called lateral thinking? Does this have to do with creativity?*] You should be able to work out for yourselves how

similar for waves passing around obstacles: diffraction occurs only when the size of the obstacle is not much bigger than the wavelength of the waves.

The wavelengths of light are much smaller than those of sound. They are of the order of 10^{-5} cm. That's why we require very small openings or obstacles to bring about the effect of diffraction. You can see why Grimaldi's discovery of diffraction by light is commendable!

0.12 YOUNG AND POLARIZATION

At first Young was not able to explain polarization with his wave theory. With water waves, the actual vibrations of the water are perpendicular to the direction of propagation. Let's take an example. Imagine yourself standing at the edge of a pond. A friend on the other side of the pond drops a stone into the water. Now a train of ripples (waves) travels toward you. The direction of propagation can be seen to be from your friend to you, horizontal and along the surface of the pond. As the train of waves passes a fallen leaf on the pond, the leaf bobs up and down. Note that the leaf does not travel toward you; it just bobs up and down in the

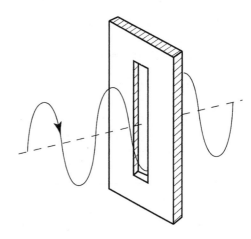

FIGURE 0.6a

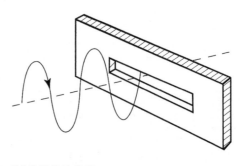

FIGURE 0.6b

transverse waves can become polarized. Get a cardboard sheet, say 10 inches by 10 inches. Make a slot, 1 inch by 7 inches, in the middle of the board. This cardboard now forms a sort of gate. Hold this gate with the slot vertical to the surface of the water in a bucket. You can imagine how (transverse) water waves can pass through, because the vibrations of the water, up and down, are not restricted by the slot (Figure 0.6a). However, if the cardboard is placed sideways, with the slot horizontal, the vertical vibrations cannot get through (Figure 0.6b).

0.13 FRESNEL, POISSON, AND FOUCAULT

Not knowing Thomas Young's work on light waves in Britain, Fresnel in France independently proposed the concept of interference some 15 years later. Based on this concept, he worked out a beautiful mathematical theory of diffraction and Newton's rings. Siméon Poisson, a prominent French mathematician, pointed out that Fresnel's wave theory implied that there should be a bright spot at the center of the shadow cast by a small circular obstacle. An experiment was carried out, and such a spot was in fact found. Imagine, a bright spot in the middle of a dark circular shadow! [*Light cannot be traveling in a straight line in this case, can it?*]

You may remember that, according to Newton, the reason light rays are refracted on entering water from air was that water, being denser than air, attracted the light corpuscles downward, hence the bending. If this theory were correct, light should travel at a higher speed in water than in air. The wave theory, however, predicted the opposite, that light should travel faster in air than in water. At the times of Huygens, Newton, Young, and Fresnel, no technique was available to measure the speed of light in water with sufficient accuracy to decide the issue. The scientific world had to wait until 1850, when J. L. Foucault, another Frenchman, did the crucial experiment. The outcome was that the speed of light is greater in air than in water. Another victory for the wave theory.

The bright spot in the middle of a dark shadow, Foucault's experiment, Young's interference experiments (including his famous double-slit experiments), and many others all supported the wave theory. In spite of Newton's authority, it was the wave theory that ruled the scientific world of light until the beginning of the 20th century.

The story of light is remarkable, but what is mentioned earlier is only the beginning of the story. The most remarkable part is still to come. However I don't think this is the place to develop the story much further. Those who are interested can always consult books on the history of light, and there is no shortage of these. I will end my part of the story with the historical search for the substance called 'ether.'

By the end of the 19th century, it was taken for granted that light had been proven beyond doubt to be constituted of waves. But waves must be waves of some substance (medium). There had to be a substance characteristically supporting these light waves. That substance could not be air, or water, or anything we are familiar with, because light can travel in a vacuum, so the substance had to be present even in a vacuum. They called this substance 'ether.'

If you pluck a violin string it will vibrate transversely. You can send a transverse wave down a nylon rope by waving it at one end. But can you get transverse waves down a long piece of damp clay? The answer is no. Damp clay is too soft. It does not have the elasticity required to transmit transverse waves. The study of elasticity was quite advanced in the 18th and 19th centuries. It was known that the speed of a train of transverse waves down a medium is proportional to the square root of its elasticity. Since the speed of light is extremely high, the ether would have to be extremely elastic; in fact, it had to be more elastic than steel! Such a medium could only be a highly rigid solid. But then how could we and the planets move smoothly across this all-pervading solid? Perhaps the density of this ether was very low, so low that it offered practically no resistance to any motion, which was why it was imperceptible. [*Is ether a credible entity? But then contemporary science postulates even more incredible entities.*]

0.14 RELATIVITY AND QUANTUM MECHANICS

So the search was on: to find this imperceptible ether! It was this search that brought about the famous special theory of relativity, which replaced the theory of ether.

The beginning of the 20th century saw the rise of two epoch-making, revolutionary theories in physics: the theory of relativity and quantum mechanics. They replaced the whole of the old physics, including the much-revered and well-established Newtonian mechanics. These two theories which were revolutionary in another sense, proposed radically different views of the world, weird, strange, and incomprehensible. The amazing thing is that both theories had their origin in puzzlement over the nature of light, and both, eventually, led to a very different understanding of light phenomena. According to them, light is neither purely waves nor purely particles. It is a sort of hybrid of both, half-wave and half-particle. Some people call these entities "wavicles." A more recognized term is 'photon.' Photons are matter of a sort, but then they do not have mass, and the amazing thing is that they play a definitive role in the structure of spacetime.

Are these theories fictions or facts? How are we to judge? Can we trust the scientists? How should we interpret their claims anyway? What is the difference between science and fairy tales? Questions like these motivate us to do philosophy of science.

(References: All general histories of science will have sections on light. For details, see the following works: McKenzie (1960, Chapter 12), Holton and Roller (1958, Chapter 30), and Ronchi (1970)).

Traditional Problems
Truth, Explanation, and Reality

The philosophy of science has a long history dating back to Aristotle (384–322 B.C.). Since then there has been no shortage of contributions to this subject. Philosophical giants such as Bacon, Descartes, Leibniz, Hume, Kant, Whewell, Comte, and Mill have all left their mark. However, these are just individual efforts. Large-scale, systematic, and coordinated research in the philosophy of science had to wait until the early 20th century, when logical positivism was launched around 1920. This school of thought, amended and improved on from time to time, has provided a basic platform—a foundation[1]—for the modern philosophy of science. Even though there are now few adherents of logical positivism in its original form and there was a major change of philosophical direction in the 1960s, every student of the philosophy of science should be acquainted with the classical tradition, which roughly covers the period from 1920 to 1960. Many terms have been used to designate this tradition. They include the positivist tradition, the logico-empirical tradition, the received view, the orthodox view, and the standard view.[2]

You will be able to find out more about the place of this classical tradition in history in Part VI. For now you are invited to study the problems of truth, explanation, and reality, formulated and discussed within this tradition as if it is *the* philosophy of science.

---

1. 'Foundation' is not used here in the same sense as the 'foundation' in 'foundations of mathematics.'

2. I have dropped the quotation marks around these terms to enable easy reading.

Book I is divided into four parts. **Parts II** and **III** deal respectively with what are commonly taken as the twin aims of science: the search for truth and the quest for explanation.

The search for truth, in general, takes two steps: the search for plausible hypotheses (for example, plausible laws of nature) and then the evaluation and justification of these hypotheses. We will also see how theoretical considerations can strengthen our faith in hypotheses. This is the content of Part II.

It is one thing to know that something such as a lunar eclipse has happened. It is, however, quite another thing to be able to *explain* why that something happened—for instance, the cause of that lunar eclipse. Some scientists believe that explanation plays the central role in science, and that explanation is much more important than the discovery and collection of facts. Part III deals with various theories of explanation, detailing how explanation is and should be carried out.

Whereas Parts II and III are, more or less, on scientific methods (methodology), **Part IV** covers a different kind of philosophy. In science, we often postulate (invisible) entities to explain (visible) phenomena. For example, we postulate electrons and atoms to explain changes in color, smell, and taste in things; we postulate genes to explain inheritance of characteristics by offspring and we postulate gravitational force to explain why things usually fall downward when unsupported. This chapter discusses what philosophers call the ontological status of these entities: whether they are real or not. Most of us are realists, believing in general the reality of the things that have been so successfully postulated in science. However, there are also good reasons for doubting their existence.

Lest we rush into these exciting topics ill-prepared, we should equip ourselves with some basic conceptual tools first. Let's begin with the various basic types of reasoning used in science. These form the subject matter of **Part I**.

Basic Types of Reasoning
in Science

This part has four chapters. **Chapter 1** introduces some basic terms commonly used in the philosophy of science. **Chapters 2** and **3** provide an overview of the two types of logic employed in scientific reasoning: deductive and inductive logic. Basic statistical concepts are presented in **Chapter 4.** Most of you probably already have some acquaintance with this material. Nevertheless, you may find it useful to read through the following chapters (carefully or casually as you see fit).

These basic terms and concepts are tools for future use in this book and thus are not meant for your "entertainment." However, they are not like finger exercises in piano lessons, either. You should find some of them enlightening and delightful to grasp. You might say to yourself, "Ah, I have always wanted to know more about this. It helps me clarify my thoughts."

So without more ado, I invite you to start Chapter 1.

Chapter 1

Hypotheses

1.1 INTRODUCTION

The history of Western civilization is full of interesting hypotheses. These hypotheses often contradict each other, and some are plainly incredible. For example, Thales (circa 600 B.C.) said that everything is made of water, whereas Aristotle (384–322 B.C.) said that there are four and only four elements—air, fire, earth, and water. Democritus (circa 400 B.C.) (and 19th-century scientists) asserted that atoms are the ultimate building blocks of the universe, whereas Descartes (1596–1650) thought that matter is continuous and infinitely divisible. Ptolemy (circa 100–178) thought that the earth is fixed at the center of the universe, whereas Copernicus (1473–1543) believed that the earth moves around a stationary sun. Newton (1642–1727) thought that light is made up of little particles. In contrast, Huygens (1629–1695) proposed that light is really made up of waves. Contemporary scientists, however, believe that a sort of compromise seems to be nearer the truth and that light is both particle-like and wave-like.

Science is exciting and fascinating. It is full of fantastic claims, some of which do not seem to make sense. Examples include Einstein's claim that space is curved and Pythagoras's famous theory that all things consist of numbers.

In science and philosophy, all these claims are known as hypotheses. Obviously, not all of them are true. How should these hypotheses be assessed as to their truth or falsity? This is our main concern in the present chapter.

The notion of hypothesis came from the ancient Greeks. They meant it as a statement that served as the starting point of a debate; it had to be acceptable to both the speaker and the audience. In this book, however, we will take a statement as a **hypothesis** in relation to someone who has grounds to doubt its truth status, so that the same statement could be a hypothesis to some but not to others. So 'hypothesis' is relativized to persons. There is no reason why we shouldn't relativize it to scientific communities as well—so that a hypothesis for a scientific community is a statement, the truth of which that community has good reason to question. When a statement has been accepted as definitely true, people call it a **statement of fact** (sometimes a **fact** for short).[1] Here are some examples:

(1) "It will rain tomorrow."

(2) "It rained last night."

(3) "It is raining now."

(4) "All swans are white."

(5) "The earth is flat."

(6) "For a fixed amount of gas under constant temperature, its volume will be inversely proportional to its pressure."

(7) "The probability of contracting lung cancer is higher for smokers than for nonsmokers."

(8) "Halley's comet will reappear in the night sky in 2061."

There are usually good grounds for doubting our ability to predict the weather, hence (1) is certainly a hypothesis for most of us.[2] We probably have more evidence for (2). Nevertheless, I, for one, still consider it to be only a hypothesis. Few people would consider (3) a hypothesis if they are actually experiencing the downpour, hence we say that it is a fact (a statement of fact) for them. As far as I know, (4) is false, and we usually take it as conclusively refuted by the existence of black swans in Australia. We can, therefore, say that, for most of us, the denial (or negation) of (4) is a fact. However, what is taken as a fact one day may turn out to be false after all. This is true of (5). At one time it was taken as an obvious fact that the earth is flat. Now we are all taught that (5) is not a statement of fact. Statement (6) is the famous Boyle's law, (7) is a well-publicized statistical statement, and (8) is a well-known astronomical prediction. You may wish to debate whether they should be taken as hypotheses or as facts.

So hypotheses are statements of a particular kind. What are statements then? **Statements** are sometimes called assertions or judgments. Their essential characteristic is that they are either true or false. (In philosophical jargon, we say that they have a **truth value**—either the truth value **TRUE** or the truth value **FALSE.)** Usually they are expressed by declarative sentences.[3]

In this book, we are interested only in **empirical hypotheses**—hypotheses whose truth or falsity would make a difference in what we should expect in our experience.[4]

---

1. Strictly speaking, a fact is different from a statement of fact. Roughly, facts are the "things" represented or spoken of by statements of fact.

2. We are taking (1)—and (2) and (3)—as uttered on a certain specific date and at a certain specific place, for example, today in New York.

3. Questions such as "Where is London?" are not statements. Neither are commands such as "Keep quiet!" Philosophers also make fine distinctions between statements and propositions, which need not worry us here.

4. The word 'empirical' is derived from the Greek word 'empeiria,' meaning (sense) experience. Here is an example of a nonempirical hypothesis: 24,174,948,204, 737,857 is a prime number.

1.2 MOTIVATIONS FOR THE PROPOSAL OF HYPOTHESES

In science, hypotheses are often proposed as **predictions**. Statements (1) and (8) in the previous section are typical cases. Statement (2) is a case of **postdiction**.[5] Both are cases of projection.

Sometimes hypotheses are invented to **explain** things. Newton invented the hypothesis that matter attracts matter, in order to explain why his apple fell downward rather than upward (so the story goes). He also invented the hypothesis that light rays are made of little particles in order to explain the phenomena of reflection and refraction and the phenomenon of colors (Chapter 0).

Sometimes scientists propose hypotheses to **unify** a group of phenomena. The hypothesis that Mars moves in an ellipse around the sun was proposed by Kepler (1571–1630) 400 years ago to unify the thousands of apparent positions of the planet across the night sky recorded by Tycho Brahe. The atomic theory of matter was designed to unify the diversity of millions and millions of kinds of material substance.

1.3 THE PROBLEM OF DISCOVERY

The history of science is a book of wonder and fascination. Aristotle thought that the earth is at the center of the universe, immobile and stationary, while the stars, the planets, the sun, and the moon all move around it. You might think that such a hypothesis is obvious. Its discovery or invention is no great wonder. But then Copernicus proposed quite a different hypothesis in the 16th century—that the sun is stationary while everything else, including the earth, moves around the sun in circles. Kepler improved on Copernicus with his hypothesis of elliptical orbits.

You might wonder how these great hypotheses are discovered. Are there methods individuals can learn to enable them to arrive at these powerful as well as fascinating hypotheses? Huygens thought that light rays are composed of waves. Franklin (1706–1790) conjectured that lightning is an electrical phenomenon. Rutherford (1871–1937) suggested that atoms are miniatures of the solar system. Then Einstein (1879–1955) early in 20th century asserted that space is curved and that time is somehow dependent on space.

The study of how hypotheses in science were discovered, and how in general they can be discovered, is known as the **problem of discovery**. It has been a major branch of the philosophy of science since the time of Aristotle. The advance of science depends on the discovery of correct and powerful hypotheses, and surely such an enterprise cannot be left to chance. Philosophers, therefore, prefer to have some sure methods in this direction. We will study this fascinating topic in Chapter 5 (and Chapter 32).

1.4 THE PROBLEM OF EVALUATION

Once a hypothesis is discovered and proposed as plausibly true, the world of science is faced with the problem of evaluation or assessment. Should the hypothesis be accepted as true, as a reasonable belief, as workable, and/or as useful? How should such a decision be made? What grounds should such a decision be based on? If the verdict of evaluation is positive, we can say that the hypothesis is justified. That's why traditionally this field of study has been known as the **problem of justification**. However, I think it would be more helpful to the beginner if we call it the **problem of evaluation**. This problem and the problem of discovery have been two of the most prominent problems in the philosophy of science since Aristotle.

The bulk of our discussion of the problem of evaluation, like that of the problem of discovery, will be delayed till Part II. However, in the rest of this chapter I will sketch two methods of evaluation as a way of introducing you to some key

---

5. 'Postdiction' means predicting about the past. Sometimes the term 'retrodiction' is used.

concepts of logic and reasoning often used in the philosophy of science. They are the methods of direct and indirect tests.

1.5 DIRECT TEST

Some hypotheses can be tested directly. The hypothesis "The Tower of Pisa is red" can be directly assessed with the senses. We can look at the tower to see if it is red. Looking at an object is supposed to be sufficient to determine its color. Similarly, to test whether the glass of water in front of me is hot, I need to only dip my finger in the water.

The method of direct test seems to be a matter of matching the given hypothesis with reality (the world). In the first example, we "line up" the expression "Tower of Pisa" with the famous tower in Italy and check whether the word 'red' corresponds to the color of the tower. The matching is done with one or more of the senses. The sense of sight is most often used, but not always, as the second example shows. Since the matching is between the hypothesis and reality, and it is done with the senses (without the help of instruments), it is appropriate to call such tests **direct tests**.

1.6 INDIRECT TEST

The hypothesis that the earth is round can be tested directly by checking the shape of the earth from outer space with the help of sight. But such a test could be carried out only with modern technology. Nevertheless, long before the present century, scientists were convinced on empirical grounds that the earth was round. How was that done?

In the 4th century B.C., Aristotle argued that since the shape of the shadow cast by the earth on the moon during a lunar eclipse is round, the earth must be round. This is a case of an indirect test. The senses are not attempting to match the hypothesis

with reality. They seem to be directed toward something else: the shadow. The matching is between the statement "The shadow is round" and reality. (Note that the shadow is not even mentioned in the hypothesis "The earth is round.") Another well-known test of the hypothesis is by watching sailboats come in from the horizon. It is said that since we see the top of the mast before the hull, the round-earth hypothesis is empirically confirmed. Again the senses seem to be directed toward something other than the earth. Sailboats are brought in from outside the hypothesis, so to speak.

"The shadow of the earth is round" is said to be a **logical consequence** of "The earth is round."[6] An **indirect test** is a matter of comparing a logical consequence of the hypothesis (rather than the hypothesis itself) with reality. Again, "The mast of a sailboat coming in from far away is visible before the hull" is a logical consequence of the hypothesis. And it is this logical consequence that is compared with reality.

I know that the notion of logical consequence may be new to you. Possibly an alternative definition of 'indirect test' would be useful. Let's try the idea of an instrument. For example, we can take the sailboat as an **instrument** for measuring the shape of the earth. The shadow also can be taken as an instrument. In a more obvious case, to check whether the glass of water is 70°C, we use a thermometer. The thermometer is an instrument. Again, to test whether a metal bar is magnetic, we can sprinkle iron filings near it to see if the filings move toward the bar. The filings are indicators of magnetism. They are instruments. The test is indirect because the experimenter "looks" at the instrument rather than the original object. (In the previous formulation, the person matches a logical consequence rather than the original hypothesis with reality.) So an **indirect test** can also be said to be a test where the hypothesis is compared with reality through the use of instruments.

The two formulations of indirect tests will be shown to be equivalent when we learn more about

---

6. Strictly speaking, it is a logical consequence only if additional premises are present. Such premises are known as *auxiliary hypotheses*, which will be discussed in detail in Chapter 6.

indirect tests in Chapter 6. For the present it suffices to point out that the general intention of using instruments is to bring about observable effects, so that we can check the original hypotheses through the verification of these effects. The bringing about of these effects is closely bound up with the notion of logical consequence, hence the two formulations are really different ways of saying the same thing.[7]

1.7 DIRECT TEST VERSUS INDIRECT TEST

The distinction between direct and indirect tests is helpful to an understanding of empirical evaluation in scientific practice. Nevertheless, such a distinction is neither strict nor philosophically clear. Take the hypothesis "There is a dog next door." It may seem obvious that to directly test it, we need only open the adjoining door and look through. What if the door is locked? Would listening through the wall be counted as a direct test? After all, the difference is only between the use of the faculty of hearing and the faculty of sight. But somehow we feel that the use of sight is more direct, especially if we can only hear scratching noises and not barking. The intuition seems to be that direct tests are veridical (amounting to certainty), whereas indirect tests yield only probable results. It seems that if we see a dog, there has to be a dog, whereas if we only hear barking, there need not be a dog that does the barking.[8] This analysis is, on closer examination, incorrect. If we see what looks like a dog, there need not be a dog. It could be a "lamb in a dog's clothing," as in a muppet show. Anyway, seeing requires the use of light, especially when we are trying to ascertain

color. The light used is a kind of instrument. The barking we hear depends on the medium (for example, the air between the observer and the dog), on its temperature, its density, and so on. We can only say that should there be a dog next door, and should it bark, and should the medium be such and such, we would hear sounds of such and such quality. The sound quality we expect to hear is not in the original hypothesis, but rather is an inferred consequence of it. The same applies to the light image the observer expects to have. That light image is only an inferred consequence of the original hypothesis. So strictly speaking, there are no such things as direct tests. All tests are indirect, but we can say some are less indirect than others. Therefore, it is closer to the truth if we take the terms 'direct' and 'indirect' in a relative sense.[9]

1.8 LOGIC OF INDIRECT TESTS

Indirect tests involve two kinds of reasoning: deductive reasoning and inductive reasoning. From the given hypothesis, H, we reason **deductively** to an **implication**, I, and compare I with reality. To reason deductively is to make one or more (valid) **deductions**. The implication we arrive at is the **logical consequence** of the premise, which in this case is the given hypothesis. We will have more opportunity to study deductive logic together with its technical terms in Chapter 2.

When we compare I with reality through the use of our senses (such as sight), we may discover that I is in fact false. Here is an example. Let H be the hypothesis that the figure on the blackboard is a

---

7. Note that the use of the idea of 'instrument' here has nothing to do with the philosophy of instrumentalism (Chapter 16). The formulation of the indirect test in terms of logical consequence, in philosophical jargon, belongs to the formal mode of speech, whereas the formulation in terms of instruments belongs to the material mode of speech.

8. Similarly, it seems that the earth has to be round if it is seen to be round. On the other hand, it is only probably round if its shadow on the moon is round, or if the mast is visible before the hull.

9. In Chapter 22, we will discuss the nature of observation—whether we see things as they really are at all. This problem is related to what is usually known as the observational-theoretical distinction, which is also discussed in Chapter 17.

square. One implication of this hypothesis is that the figure has four corners. However, as a matter of fact, the figure on the board has only three corners. So *I* is false. Since *I* is false, we can conclude definitely that *H* is false. This mode of reasoning is known as **modus tollens**, a type of deductive reasoning. It can be schematized as follows:

If *H*, then **I**. But Not-**I**. Therefore Not-**H**.

or as

If **H** is true, then *I* is true. But *I* is found to be false. Therefore, *H* is false.

The other possibility is that *I* turns out to be true. Can we in such a case conclude that *H* is definitely true? Let's take the case of the square figure again. Suppose it is discovered that it does have four corners. Can we conclude that it must be a square? Obviously not. We can, however, conclude that now there is some basis for believing it is a square. So the logic is that:

If **H**, then **I**. And indeed **I**. Therefore there are some grounds for **H**.

(Alternative 1) If **H** is true, then *I* is true. *I* is indeed found to be true. Therefore there are some grounds for the truth of *H*.

(Alternative 2) If **H** is true, then *I* is true. *I* is indeed found to be true. Therefore the credibility (probability) that *H* is true has increased.[10]

From these formulations, we can see that, as more and more implications of *H* turn out to be true, it becomes more and more likely. For example, from the hypothesis that *M* is copper, we can infer that (i) *M* is a metal, (ii) *M* is rosy-pink, (iii) *M*

is malleable, (iv) *M* conducts electricity, and (v) *M*'s density is 8.95. As more and more of these properties of *M* are found to be true, it becomes more and more apparent that *M* is really copper.

The kind of reasoning we have been considering is known as **inductive reasoning** or **induction**. In induction, the conclusion is never conclusively established. The argument, however, can render the conclusion more credible (more probable).[11] We will study induction in detail in Chapter 3.

1.9 PHILOSOPHY OF TESTS

Descartes (1596–1650), the father of modern philosophy, was renowned for his search for certainty. For him, only that which is certain is knowledge. Anything that is even slightly doubtful is not true knowledge. From what we have covered so far, it looks as if we would never have certainty; at least we would not have certainty about empirical hypotheses.[12] First, there are no such tests as (absolutely) direct tests. Second, in an indirect test, if we discover that the implication is true, we can only say that the hypothesis has become more likely to be true.

Empirical testing, whether directly or indirectly, is an important means of evaluating hypotheses. In the philosophy of science, we have special terms to describe various possible "verdicts" of evaluation. They are as follows:

1. A hypothesis *H* is said to be **verified** by evidence *E*, if *E* provides conclusive grounds for the truth of *H*.[13]

---

10. We will deal with probability in detail in Chapter 4.

11. Some philosophers dispute this, however. See Chapter 20.

12. An empirical hypothesis is one whose truth or falsity can be assessed only through experience. In contrast, it is said that mathematical statements like $2 + 2 = 4$ are not empirical. Neither are tautologies like "Either today is Monday, or today is not Monday."

13. The term 'verification' is sometimes used in a more general manner, meaning partially verified rather than conclusively verified as we have done here.

2. A hypothesis *H* is said to be **falsified** (or **refuted**), if *E* provides conclusive grounds for the falsity of *H*.

3. A hypothesis *H* is said to be (partially) **confirmed** by evidence *E*, if *E* provides some grounds for the truth of *H*.

4. A hypothesis *H* is said to be (partially) **disconfirmed** by evidence *E*, if *E* provides some grounds for the falsity of *H*.

5. When a hypothesis is either verified or confirmed, we can say that the hypothesis has been **empirically justified**.

6. The study of reasoning behind verification and confirmation is often known as **confirmation theory**.

7. Often we say 'empirically verified,' 'empirically falsified,' and so on, instead of 'verified,' 'falsified,' and so forth.

As you can see from the logic of indirect tests, we require the notion of logical consequence. So let us now turn to the exciting subject of deductive logic.

KEY TERMS INTRODUCED IN THIS CHAPTER

hypothesis	postdiction	deductive	falsified
statement of fact	explain	implication	refuted
fact	unify	deduction	confirmed
statement	problem of discovery	logical consequence	disconfirmed
truth value	problem of justification	modus tollens	empirically justified
TRUE	problem of evaluation	inductive reasoning	confirmation theory
FALSE	direct test	induction	
empirical hypotheses	logical consequence	instrument	
prediction	indirect test	verified	

REFERENCE

Hempel (1966, secs. 2.1 and 2.2) and Copi and Cohen (1994, chap. 13) are good introductions to the subject.

EXERCISES

1. Give an example for each of the following:
   (a) a commonly known true hypothesis
   (b) a commonly known false hypothesis
   (c) a hypothesis proposed for explanation
   (d) a hypothesis proposed for prediction
   (e) a hypothesis proposed for postdiction
   (f) a hypothesis proposed for unifying a number of facts

2. Find a hypothesis from the history of science. How was it discovered? How could it have been discovered? Is the discovery of plausible and fruitful hypotheses easy? (You might like

to make use of the historical materials on the study of light in Chapter 0.)

3. Give an example of a hypothesis and a direct test of it. Is the hypothesis also indirectly testable?

In the next three exercises, specify the logical consequences and the instruments employed.

4. Give an indirect test of the hypothesis that wood floats in mercury.

5. Find a hypothesis from the history of science. Suggest or locate some of the indirect tests that have been performed on it.

6. Concoct a hypothesis of your own and suggest an indirect test for it.

7. Illustrate the use of modus tollens with one or more of the tests so far discussed.

8. Do you think we can ever verify an empirical hypothesis?

9. Do you think we can ever falsify an empirical hypothesis?

Chapter 2

Deductive Reasoning

2.1 INTRODUCTION

In the last chapter, we discussed the logic of indirect tests. In indirect tests, we *deduce* an implication from the given hypothesis and compare this implication (instead of the hypothesis itself) with reality. The study of the notion of deduction and associated notions such as logical consequence, consistency, and contradiction belongs to the discipline known as **deductive logic**, to which we now turn.

2.2 ARGUMENT

Deduction is a kind of argument.[1] An **argument** has two components: the **premises** and the **conclusion**. There is at least one premise, usually more. Each premise is a statement. The conclusion is also a statement. In an argument, there is always only one conclusion statement. We argue from the premises to the conclusion. Hence we can represent an argument as follows:

$$P_1, P_2, P_3, ..., P_n \rightarrow C$$

There are n premises where n is a natural number, and there is one conclusion, C. We can read the arrow as "therefore." When we make an argument, we try to establish the conclusion on the strength of the premises. In other words, the

---

1. Some books employ the term 'inference' instead of 'argument' for the explanation of deduction. In this book, I will use the two terms interchangeably according to context, because you will find that in certain contexts, especially in connection with scientific predictions, 'inference' will sound more natural and more appropriate than 'argument.'

conclusion is drawn from the premises; the conclusion is reached and affirmed on the basis of the premises.

2.3 ASSESSMENT OF ARGUMENTS

Let's consider the following examples:

Argument I

Apple A_1 when unsupported falls downward.

Apple A_2 when unsupported falls downward.

Apple A_3 when unsupported falls downward.

∴ All apples when unsupported fall downward.

Argument II

Matter attracts matter.

Apples are matter.

The earth is matter.

∴ All apples are attracted by the earth.

Argument III

Angle A_1 contained in semicircle K_1 is a right angle.

Angle A_2 contained in semicircle K_2 is a right angle.

Angle A_3 contained in semicircle K_3 is a right angle.

∴ All angles contained in semicircles are right angles.

Argument IV

All isosceles triangles have equal base angles.

The angle sum of any triangle is two right angles.

∴ All angles contained in semicircles are right angles.

Here are four arguments. The first has three premises and a conclusion, separated by a line that can be taken as a symbol for the word "therefore." Intuitively, arguments I and III fall into one class, while II and IV fall into another. Argument II seems to be a better kind of argument than I. Argument IV, however, is opaque. What are the proper ways to *assess* arguments? Since arguments play a central role in

science (and in daily life), we must know how to assess them; otherwise we may employ the wrong kind of argument in planning and prediction.

In philosophy, we classify arguments into deductive arguments and inductive arguments. In putting forth a **deductive argument**, the arguer claims that the premises provide conclusive grounds or reason for the acceptance of the conclusion. Thus a deductive argument involves a claim—a claim that if the premises are true, the conclusion has to be true. When the claim is correct, we say that the deductive argument is **valid**; otherwise it is **invalid**. Deductive arguments are usually known as **deductions**. Deductions are thus either valid or invalid. If the deduction "A, therefore B" is valid, we say that from A we can **deduce** B, or B is **deducible from** A, or B is a **logical consequence** of A, or B is a **logical implication** of A, or A **(logically) entails** B.

Let us study arguments I to IV listed earlier. Suppose they were made as deductive arguments. Are any of them valid? Obviously I and III are invalid, whereas II is valid. What about IV? Some arguments are not as transparent as others in their validity, and IV is an example. However, when the intermediate links of a rather "opaque" argument are supplied, its validity can become obvious. Such a process is often called a **proof**. To illustrate, let us try to prove the conclusion of IV from its premises.

Let the radius OC partition the contained angle into m and n, as illustrated in Figure 2.1.

Proof:

(1) $a = m$ — (because of the first premise)

(2) $b = n$ — (because of the first premise)

(3) $a + b + m + n = 2$ right angles — (because of the second premise)

(4) $m + n + m + n = 2$ — (because of lines 1, 2, 3)

(5) $2 \times (m + n) = 2$ right angles — (because of line 4)

(6) $m + n = 1$ right angle — (because of line 5)

Q.E.D.

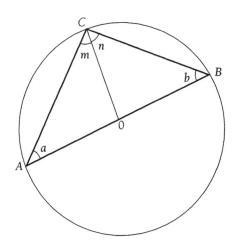

FIGURE 2.1

So we can see that both II and IV are valid, whereas I and III are invalid. Should we then restrict ourselves to arguments such as II and IV?

Invalid deductions are faulty, and I and III are certainly invalid. Yet in science as well as in daily life, we seem to use arguments such as I and III all the time. For example, the reason the ancients (like most of us today) expected the sun to rise roughly every 24 hours in the east is not because they could deduce this statement from some true premises. They believed it because they had seen the sun rise so often in the past. The same reasoning operates, for example, when we avoid restaurants that, in the past, have often served lousy food.

When we pass judgment on a certain argument, it all depends on the claims the arguer has made. What if in putting forth arguments I and III the arguer only claims that the premises provide *some* grounds for the conclusion? Note that the person is not saying that the premises will guarantee the conclusion. The arguer only modestly claims that the premises have made the conclusion more credible. Surely in such a case we can accept the claims. In argument I, that three apples have been observed to have fallen downward should provide us some grounds to expect that all other apples will behave likewise. These sorts of arguments

are known as inductive arguments. **Inductive arguments** are arguments that involve the claim that the premises provide *some* grounds for the acceptance of the conclusion. An inductive argument is also known as an **induction**. We do not employ terms like 'valid' or 'invalid' to assess inductions because these are reserved for deductions. For inductions we can say whether they are **reasonable** or **unreasonable**. Unlike 'validity,' 'reasonableness' is not an absolute term. A deduction is either valid or invalid; there is no in between. However, reasonableness is a matter of degree. Some inductive arguments are very reasonable, some less reasonable, while others are totally unreasonable. Do you think argument I is reasonable or not? Perhaps you would find it more reasonable if more apples, say 100, had been observed falling downward instead of just three.

Sometimes inductions are formulated in terms of probability. We can say that an argument is an induction if it involves the claim that the premises (if true) provide information that will increase the likelihood (probability) of the conclusion being true.

We will study various kinds of induction in detail in Chapter 3. In this chapter, we will concentrate on deductions.

2.4 VALID ARGUMENTS

Beginners often confuse the notions of validity and truth. To start with, we must not use the term 'valid' as it is commonly used in daily life. It is a technical term in philosophy. We must take it exactly as it has been defined: (i) Validity applies to arguments and only to arguments. So, for example, it does not apply to statements. (ii) Validity signifies a certain relationship between a group of statements (the premises) and one other statement (the conclusion), and this relationship depends on the contents of the premises and the conclusion rather than on their truth or falsity. What is said in the premises determines what can be drawn out of them as a conclusion, independent of whether what is said happens to be true or false. Let me illustrate:

Argument V	**Argument VI**
All humans are mortal.	All humans are lions.
All Greeks are humans.	All Greeks are humans.
All Greeks are mortal.	All Greeks are lions.

Argument VII	**Argument VIII**
All tigers are mortal.	
All Greeks are tigers.	?
All Greeks are mortal.	

We can see that arguments V to VII are all valid, and yet

(i) V has true premises as well as a true conclusion.

(ii) VI has two premises, one true and one false, and its conclusion is false.

(iii) VII again has two premises, one true and one false, but its conclusion is true.

It can thus be seen that false premises (whether one or more) do not necessarily bring about false conclusions. The validity of an argument depends on what is said in the premises and what is said in the conclusion. Whether things so said happen to be true or false does not affect the validity of the argument at all. We see that V is valid, not because we know that it is true that all humans are mortal and so on. We are convinced of its validity because we know that should humans be mortal, and should Greeks be humans, then Greeks must be mortal. It might turn out that not all Greeks are humans (some of them are said to have been gods, according to mythology). Such a discovery would not, however, affect the validity of the argument. In fact, we can judge the validity of an argument without knowing the meaning of some of the words. The argument could have been presented to us as:

Argument IX	**or as Argument F**
All H are M.	All Y are Z.
All G are H.	All X are Y.
All G are M.	All X are Z.

We can see the validity of such an argument, even though we have no idea whether the premises or conclusion are true. We can use IX to represent a *type* of argument. In logic, we call it a **form of argument**. Indeed, V–VII all belong to this type. They all have the same form. That's why they are all valid. In philosophical jargon, we say that the validity of an argument usually comes from its form rather than from its content.[2] The form we have been considering is one of the most important forms of argument; logicians have given it the name BARBARA.

We said that the validity of an argument usually depends on its form, not on its content. To dissociate ourselves from contents altogether, it would be more appropriate to represent the form BARBARA as argument F, where X, Y, and Z are said to be **variables**. This form becomes an argument if we replace these variables with terms (known as **constants**) such as 'human' and 'Greek.'

We have seen from the preceding examples that valid arguments allow the following possibilities:

(i) True premises and true conclusion.

(ii) (One or more) false premises and false conclusion.

(iii) (One or more) false premises and true conclusion.

Let's now ask whether it is possible to have a valid argument where

(iv) The premises are all true and the conclusion false.

---

2. I qualify the statement with 'usually' because in this book we assume the view that some arguments' validity does not come from their forms. An example might be "Peter is a bachelor, therefore he is an unmarried man." This assumption is by no means acceptable to all philosophers.

Think it through for yourself. The definition of validity should be clear enough to provide a definite answer. That's why I have left the space under 'Argument VIII' blank.

2.5 DEDUCTIVE LOGIC

There are two kinds of logic: deductive logic and inductive logic. **Deductive logic** is the study of forms (or rules) of valid deductive argument—for example, BARBARA. **Inductive logic**, on the other hand, is the study of forms (or rules) of relatively reasonable inductive arguments. Leaving inductive logic for the next chapter, let us consider some valid forms of deduction.

Besides BARBARA, there are many, many other valid forms. Here are a few with their traditional names:

DARII	**CELARENT**	**BOKARDO**
All Y are Z	No Y are Z	Some Y are not Z
Some X are Y	All X are Y	All Y are X
Some X are Z	No X are Z	Some X are not Z

MODUS PONENS

If p, then q

p

q

MODUS TOLLENS

If p, then q

Not-q

Not-p

SIMPLIFICATION

p and q

p

If terms such as 'Greek,' 'tiger,' and 'red' are substituted for the variables X, Y, and Z, we get valid arguments from the first three forms. If we replace p and q with sentences such as "This bar is made of copper" and "This bar conducts heat," we get valid arguments out of the last three forms. Thus valid forms are very useful. Knowledge of such forms enables us to draw all kinds of conclusions from the given premises. Since the time of Aristotle, logicians have been engaged in the discovery of such forms, knowing that such forms are tools for the advancement of science and knowledge in general.

Deductive logic is often known as **formal logic** or just **logic**. It is a field in its own right, very important for philosophy, mathematics, and artificial intelligence. There are many branches, of which predicate calculus is the most useful and best known. Other common branches include modal logic and many-valued logics. All of us, whether we are scientists, mathematicians, lawyers, detectives, doctors, business-people, or store clerks, make deductive arguments every day. That's why logic is an important subject.

KEY TERMS INTRODUCED IN THIS CHAPTER

argument	deduction	proof	deductive logic
premise	deduce	inductive argument	inductive logic
conclusion	deducible from	induction	formal logic
deductive argument	logical consequence	form of argument	logic
valid	logical implication	variable	
invalid	logically entail	constant	

REFERENCES

Most elementary logic texts give good introductions to deductive logic, and there is no shortage of them. Kahane (1995), Copi and Cohen (1994), and Harrison (1992) are typical.

EXERCISES

1. (a) Which of the following 12 arguments are valid if taken as deductions?
    (b) Of the invalid arguments, which are reasonable if taken as inductions?

    (1) All copper conducts heat.

    This is a piece of copper.

    This conducts heat.

    (2) All copper conducts heat.

    Copper is a metal.

    Iron is a metal.

    Iron conducts heat.

    (3) All metal conducts heat.

    Copper is a metal.

    Copper conducts heat.

    (4) A, B, and C are swans.

    A and B are white.

    C is black.

    All swans are white.

    (5) A, B, and C are swans.

    They are all white.

    All swans are white.

    (6) A is a swan.

    A is white.

    All swans are white.

    (7) If Albert wins, then Bill loses.

    If Bill loses, then Mary is unhappy.

    If Albert wins, then Mary is unhappy.

    (8) If Albert wins, then either Bill or Charles loses.

    If Bill loses, then Mary is unhappy.

    If Albert wins, then Mary is unhappy.

    (9) If Albert wins, Albert gets the prize.

    Albert wins.

    Charles is unhappy.

    (10) Wood conducts heat.

    This is wood.

    This conducts heat.

    (11) Wood conducts heat.

    This conducts heat.

    This is wood.

    (12) Either copper or wood conducts heat.

    Copper does not conduct heat.

    Wood conducts heat.

2. (a) Give an example of a valid argument whose premises are all false and whose conclusion is also false.
    (b) Give an example of a valid argument with some false premises and a true conclusion.
    (c) Is it possible to have a valid argument with true premises but a false conclusion?

3. Give an example of a valid deductive form.

4. Why don't logicians confine themselves to the study of valid arguments that are sound? (A sound argument is a valid argument that has true premises.)

5. What are the (logical) forms of the 12 arguments in Exercise 1?

6. Give two real-life examples to illustrate the use of valid deductions in everyday reasoning (in the course of predictions, explanations, arguments, or other contexts).

7. Find an example of the use of deductive argument from the history of science. (You might like to make use of the historical materials on the study of light given in Chapter 0.)

Chapter 3

Inductive Reasoning

3.1 INTRODUCTION

We have just examined deductive logic; inductive logic is the other branch of logic. It studies forms of reasonable inductive arguments.

Both deduction and induction are essential for scientific growth. Each has its own role to play. Science cannot advance on deductions alone. It needs inductions as much as deductions.[1] The two are complementary.

The complementary nature of induction can be seen clearly from arguments I–IV in the last chapter. Arguments I and III are inductions, which we often make. We go back to the same restaurant again and again because it has served us good food in the past. We trust a particular person because she has always been faithful to her promises. Predictions in general are often based on inductions from past experience.

The reason we need induction in science is obvious. Valid deductions are non-ampliative. By this, I mean that the content of the conclusion cannot exceed that of the premise. In other words, what is said in the conclusion is already present in the premises. Sometimes this is explicit, as in the case of *simplification*. If we are told that Tom is a black dog, we can conclude that Tom is a

---

1. Karl Popper is one of the few philosophers who think otherwise. We will have more opportunity to study Popper's famous thesis of falsificationism, which claims that science does not require inductions (see Section 7.2).

dog. It is obvious here that the conclusion is part of the premise. What is said in the conclusion is already present explicitly in the premise. Sometimes, however, the presence of the conclusion in the premises is not so explicit. BARBARA is such a case. Given that all Y are Z, and that all X are Y, by BARBARA we infer that all X are Z. Here we can see that "all X are Z" is there, though not explicitly in the premises. The argument seems to be an act of combining the two statements to form the conclusion. So we can see that an argument is valid if and only if it is non-ampliative. It is no wonder that, for valid arguments, whenever the premises are true, the conclusion has to be true.[2]

If we are to extend our knowledge in science, we need to make inductive inferences. This I think should be obvious. We would like to extend what we know of today to what we could know of tomorrow. Our knowledge of one place should be applicable to other places. Information on cats should be useful on dogs. All these are inductive inferences. Newton supposedly inferred the law of gravitation from his observation of falling apples. The inference is a sequence of two inductive arguments.[3] He first inferred that all apples, whether past or future, whether in England or elsewhere, resemble the few apples he actually saw, in that they all fall downward when unsupported. He then inferred inductively that there must be a force—which he called the force of gravity—that pulls the apples toward the earth.

What we have just said about Newton and his apples demonstrates an important insight attained by Aristotle more than 2,000 years ago. He observed that in daily life, we encounter only particular events (singular facts), such as the falling of a specific apple from a specific tree. However, we can induce general principles (universal facts) like the law of gravitation (which applies to *all* matter) from these particular events. In turn, these principles can be used to explain other kinds of occurrences, such as why pendulums have a regular period, why the moon circles the earth about once every 27 days, why

heavier things do not fall faster than lighter things, and so on. Furthermore, according to Aristotle, such explanations take the form of deductions such as arguments II and IV in the last chapter. In sum, we *ascend* to general principles from particular occurrences through induction, and we *descend* from those general principles to the particular occurrences through deduction. This illustrates the complementary natures of the two types of argument.

In this chapter, we will study some of the more common forms of induction.

3.2 INDUCTION BY ANALOGY AND INDUCTION BY SIMPLE ENUMERATION

Induction by analogy can be illustrated by the following example. My neighbor's four-year-old child was afraid of dogs. When a furry thing that looked like a dog appeared, she would scream or run to her mother. Why was she afraid of dogs? In the past, she had the experience that things that were furry, ran on four legs, and had a wide mouth full of sharp teeth could suddenly bark. From her past encounters, she expected that the next thing that was furry and so on could also bark suddenly.

This kind of induction can be seen to have the following form:

A_1 has properties $P_1, P_2, \ldots, P_k$, and F.

A_2 has properties $P_1, P_2, \ldots, P_k$, and F.

....

A_n has properties $P_1, P_2, \ldots, P_k$, and F.

A_{n+1} has properties $P_1, P_2, \ldots, P_k$.

A_{n+1} has property F.

The reasoning is based on the principle that things that are similar in one or more aspects are likely to be similar in other aspects. This is the commonest kind of induction. According to

---

2. We can see that in a valid deduction the conclusion is only psychologically new, but not new in terms of content. See Salmon (1966, p. 8).

3. Some, like Popper, would deny that it is an act of induction.

common sense, the reasonableness of the argument is proportional to the size of n and that of k. In Chapter 20, we will have an opportunity to consider whether this is indeed the case.

Induction by simple enumeration (also known as **universal generalization**) is similar. It has the following form:

A_1 has properties $P_1, P_2, \ldots, P_k$, and F.

A_2 has properties $P_1, P_2, \ldots, P_k$, and F.

....

A_n has properties $P_1, P_2, \ldots, P_k$, and F.

All things which have properties
$P_1, P_2, \ldots, P_k$ have F.

Thus we can see that induction by simple enumeration makes a stronger claim than induction by analogy. Whereas the latter only claims that the next one (that is, A_{n+1}) resembles the items in the data, the former extends the claim to "all." The ampliative nature of these two kinds of argument is obvious. In both cases, the conclusion exceeds what is given in the premises.

Arguments I and III in Section 2.3 are examples of induction by simple enumeration. Science is full of empirical laws such as Boyle's law,[4] the law that metals expand when being heated, and the commonsensical law that ice floats on water. All these laws seem to have been arrived at through induction by simple enumeration.

3.3 MILL'S METHODS
OF INDUCTION

Four medieval philosophers (Robert Grosseteste, Roger Bacon, John Duns Scotus, and William of Ockham) noticed that, for the advancement of science, we need methods other than the two simplistic types of induction just discussed. They made a number of proposals that were later perfected and systematized by Francis Bacon (1561–1626) and John Stuart Mill (1806–1873). Hence these methods are now known as Mill's Methods. There are five of them: Method of Agreement, Method of Difference, Joint Method of Agreement and Difference, Method of Concomitant Variation, and Method of Residues.

3.4 METHOD OF AGREEMENT (MA)

Let's illustrate this with an example.[5] Suppose a number of students in a dormitory became sick. They suffered from nausea and diarrhea. A doctor was called. She questioned six of them about what they had eaten in the cafeteria just before they got sick. She found that they had consumed a variety of foods. Some had potatoes, others had rice, and so on. The one thing they all had was soup. The doctor then suspected the soup of having caused the illness and sent a sample to a laboratory for analysis.

In searching for the cause of the sickness, the doctor has used the Method of Agreement (MA for short). She mentally constructed a table such as Table 3.1.

The six students are coded 1 to 6 in the Instances column of the table. The kinds of food they ate before becoming sick are recorded in the Antecedent Circumstances column. These are represented by letters A to F. The last column records the resulting phenomenon, which is the phenomenon of sickness, represented by S. The **Method of Agreement (MA)** can be stated as follows:

If two or more instances of the phenomenon under investigation have only one antecedent circumstance in common, the circumstance in which alone all the instances agree is the cause of the given phenomenon.[6]

Since C—the soup—fills the bill, the doctor concluded that C is the cause.[7]

---

4. That the volume of a given amount of gas varies inversely with its pressure, provided its temperature is kept constant.

5. This example is adapted from Copi and Cohen (1994, p. 487).

6. Adapted from Mill (1843, p. 255).

7. A more reasonable conclusion would be that C is *plausibly* the cause. See the subsequent discussions of MA.

T A B L E 3.1   **Table of Agreement**

Instances	Antecedent Circumstances	Consequent Phenomenon
1	A B C E F	S
2	A B C E	S
3	A C D F	S
4	B C D E F	S
5	A C E F	S
6	B C E	S

As can be seen, this method is often used in daily life, whether consciously or unconsciously.

Popular as it is, MA can lead to erroneous conclusions. The most famous and vivid example is perhaps the story of Pavlov and his dogs. Pavlov, a renowned Russian physiologist of the 19th century, performed a number of what are now known as *conditioned reflex* experiments. He would give a dog food and at the same time ring a bell. At the sight of the food the dog salivated. After a number of such pairings of "bell and food," Pavlov discovered that the dog could not help but salivate on the sound of the bell alone. It is as if the dog had made an inference based on MA. He inferred that the ringing of the bell was causal to the appearance of the food.[8]

MA can lead to error for the following reasons:

(i)   The "agreement" between the circumstances and the phenomenon could be merely coincidental. Suppose all six students coincidentally have names starting with the letter *P*. MA would prescribe that the letter *P* in the names had caused the illness.[9]

(ii) The cause may not be among the listed antecedent circumstances. For example, the lecture on philosophy of science the students attended earlier that afternoon might be the cause of the illness.

(iii) It may be a case of multiple causes. For example, the effect is produced only when two of the antecedent circumstances occur simultaneously—say, *C* and the vitamin pills the students took after the meal.

(iv) It may be a case of nonuniform causes. That is, the phenomena manifested by two of the distinct instances may be the same yet their underlying causes may differ. For example, the sickness of instance 1 can be caused by *E*, whereas that of instance 3 can be caused by *D*.

Let's put these four considerations differently. When we make an inference according to MA, we implicitly assume that none of the four possibilities listed here is the case. In other words, we take the negation (that is, denial) of each of the four possibilities as implicit assumptions. Should those assumptions be made explicit, the inference would become a (valid) deduction. Thus MA can be taken as a kind of valid deduction with hidden assumptions (which are often false).

Before we move on to the next method, let me alert you to another possible misuse of MA. Often when two types of events "agree" (occur together or sequentially), neither is in fact the cause. An example is the case of thunder and lightning. Thunder (phenomenon) is always preceded by lightning (antecedent conditions). Hence, according to MA, we should conclude that thunder is caused by flashes of light, but this conclusion is wrong. What is in fact the case is that thunder and lightning have a common cause, which is the discharge of electricity from the clouds to the ground. In view of this, MA should be stated as:

If two or more instances of the phenomenon under investigation have only one antecedent circumstance in common, the circumstance in which alone all the instances agree, is *causally connected* to the given phenomenon.

---

8. Pavlov paired flashes of light with the presentation of food as well and obtained similar results.

9. This is a true story: A little boy living in a big city with little opportunity to enjoy bright sunshine was occasionally taken to the beach in the summer for a swim. After a few trips, the little boy concluded that seawater tans the skin.

3.5 METHOD OF DIFFERENCE (MD)

The **Method of Difference (MD)** is more sophisticated than MA in that the latter makes use only of positive instances—instances where the phenomenon in question actually occurs. In the case of the sick students, only those who became sick were interviewed. MD, however, makes use of both positive and negative instances. Let's illustrate with the example of the sick students. According to MD, the doctor investigating the cause of the illness should interview two students and then compose a table such as Table 3.2. From the table, the doctor can conclude that *C* is the cause of the illness. The reasoning is that the cause of *S* must be among the five antecedent circumstances in which student 1 is involved. However, student 2 did not become sick even though she also consumed *A, B, E,* and *F*. Circumstances *A, B, E,* and *F* cannot therefore be the cause. That leaves *C* as the only possible candidate.

MD looks simple to use because it requires only two instances. There is a catch, however. The two instances must match exactly except for one factor, but in reality this kind of matching is difficult to obtain. For example, think of the case of finding the cause of lung cancer. Is it easy to find two people who agree in every respect (age, height, habits, and so on) except for one factor (for example, one smokes while the other does not)?

MD can be summarized as follows:

If an instance in which the phenomenon under investigation occurs, and an instance in which it does not occur, have every circumstance in common except one, and that one occurs in the former, then the circumstance in which alone the two instances differ is causally related to the phenomenon.[10]

Is this method liable to the same four types of error as MA? The answer is yes.

TABLE 3.2   Table of Difference

Instances	Antecedent Circumstances	Consequent Phenomenon
1	A B C E F	S
2	A B E F	–S

3.6 JOINT METHOD OF AGREEMENT AND DIFFERENCE (MAD)

In order to make MD more reliable, we can improve on it in the form of **Joint Method of Agreement and Difference (MAD)**. Here a number of positive and negative instances are taken. From our study of MA and MD, we can see that the essential step in reasoning with these two methods is that of *elimination*. Taking the example of the sick students, at the beginning we have a list of six possible causes: *A, B, C, D, E,* and *F*. Anything a sick student has not eaten can be eliminated as a possible cause. Similarly what is eaten by a nonsick student can also be eliminated. As its name suggests, MAD is the combination of MA and MD—that is, the taking of a number of positive instances as well as a number of negative instances. Using the mechanism of elimination, we can conclude that the only antecedent circumstance that occurs when the phenomenon occurs, and that does not occur when the phenomenon does not occur, is the cause.

3.7 METHOD OF CONCOMITANT VARIATION (MCV)

The **Method of Concomitant Variation (MCV)** can be introduced with the following illustrations. A child soon discovers, without being told, that the image in the mirror is herself. How does she do it? She can easily tell which shadow is hers and which is her brother's, when they play together in the sun. Children have no knowledge of optics, yet they inevitably correctly identify their own shadows. MCV says that when two types of events vary together, they are causally connected. The child looks at the little girl in the mirror. She finds that the mirror-girl somehow mimics her own actions, the girl smiles as she smiles, the girl

---

10. Adapted from Mill (1843, p. 256).

makes a face as she makes a face, the girl waves as she waves, and so on. She unwittingly applies MCV and concludes that the "mirror-girl" is caused by herself. The same with her shadow. As she skips along, the shadow also skips along, and so forth. On the contrary, her brother's shadow does not mimic her actions. So, again applying MCV, she draws the correct conclusion.

MCV states that:

Given two variables, *X* and *Y*, if *X* varies (roughly) in direct proportion to *Y*, or varies (roughly) in inverse proportion to *Y*, then *X* and *Y* are causally related.

Corresponding to Tables 3.1 and 3.2, there would be a graph such as Figure 3.1. For instance, as the temperature (*X*) rises, the length (*Y*) of a copper bar increases, and as the temperature sinks, the length decreases. By means of MCV we can conclude that the temperature and the length of the copper bar are causally related in that either the rise in temperature causes the increase in the length of the bar, or the increase in length causes the rise in temperature, or they have a common cause. Note that by this method alone we cannot tell which is the cause and which is the effect. Should the variation in *X* always precede that of *Y*, it is most likely that *X* causes *Y* because effect never precedes cause. However, it could be a case where neither is the cause of the other. Take the case of the barometer. As the mercury column of the barometer drops in height, the amount of cloudiness in the sky gradually increases. It would be wrong for us to conclude that the gathering of the clouds is brought about by the movement of the mercury column. As a matter of fact, the two have a common cause: the change in atmospheric pressure. We have discussed a similar case in considering thunder and lightning in Section 3.4.

Jacques Charles (1746–1823) discovered that the volume of a given amount of gas varies in direct proportion to its temperature, provided that its

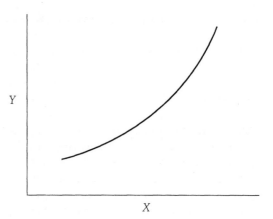

FIGURE 3.1

pressure is kept constant. Robert Boyle (1627–1691), a century before Charles, discovered that under constant temperature, the volume of a gas varies in inverse proportion to its pressure. In both cases, whether it is a case of direct proportion or a case of inverse proportion, we can conclude by MCV that the two variables are causally related. MCV is widely applied in science. Indeed, this is how scientists came to the conclusion that smoking can cause lung cancer.

It can be seen that MCV is a generalization of MAD. We can view the latter as a case where the two variables (circumstance and phenomenon) take only the values of 0 and 1 (presence and absence), whereas in the case of MCV, the two variables can take a range of values. MAD obviously cannot be applied to a case like Boyle's law. It is not a case where you have either full volume or no volume. The volume of the gas can take all sorts of values. In the case of the child and her image in the mirror, the two variables, besides taking on a range of values, span multidimensional spaces. The body of the child moves in three-dimensional space, while her image "echoes" this movement in a two-dimensional space.[11]

---

11. We have ignored the roles color plays.

Concomitant variation is a special case of statistical correlation. We will take up statistics and probability in Chapter 4.

3.8 METHOD OF RESIDUES (MR)

The **Method of Residues (MR)** is the last of Mill's five methods. It differs from the previous four in that it assumes a principle of additivity of causes and effects. MR can be stated as follows:

If C is known to cause E, and if C' is a component of C and is known to be the cause of E', then we can conclude that (C – C') is the cause of (E – E').

A simple example of the application of MR is the way we find out the weight of a baby. First we weigh an adult holding the baby. Then we weigh the adult herself. The difference in weight should be that of the baby. We can put this in terms of cause and effect: The weight of the adult plus that of the baby causes the scale pointer to shift E points, whereas the weight of the adult alone causes the pointer to shift E' points. Hence we conclude that the weight of the baby will shift the pointer by $(E - E')$ points. We can apply the method repeatedly, subtracting one causal factor at a time until we isolate the last residue as the cause of the remaining effect.

As I observed earlier, this method relies on the additivity of causes and effects. What does additivity mean? Let us say that A is independent of B in effect, if A produces exactly the same effect irrespective of B's presence or absence. Usually light switches are independent of each other in effect. However, occasionally we could have two or more switches on one circuit. In such a case, they would not be independent. We say that two causes F and G are additive, if E and G are mutually independent of each other in effect. But causes are not often additive. In such cases, MR would lead to error.

Let's take an example. Chlorine, at room temperature, is a greenish-yellow gas with a suffocating smell and is very toxic, whereas sodium is a soft metal that shows a bright silvery surface when scraped with a knife. Yet when they combine to form sodium chloride, which is popularly known as table salt, neither is gaseous, nor greenish-yellow, nor "smelly," nor bright silvery, and certainly not toxic (otherwise we would not use it in cooking). This is an obvious case where MR cannot be applied. In general, the properties of chemical compounds are not the sums (or averages) of their component parts. Medicines should often not be taken together. Two kinds of pills can each be taken by itself for its own purposes; however, if taken together, they may bring about harmful effects, sometimes even death.

Let me add, without going into detail, that in mathematics and science we distinguish between two kinds of additivity: scalar (linear) and vector addition. Weight addition is typically scalar, whereas force addition is typically vectoral. When we apply MR, obviously we should select the appropriate kind of addition to do our "sums."[12]

3.9 INDUCTIVE LOGIC

As pointed out in Chapter 2, there are two kinds of logic: deductive and inductive logic. Inductive logic deals with types of reasonable inductive arguments. In Section 3.2, we introduced two types: induction by analogy and induction by simple enumeration. These types of induction do not have a fixed number of premises, as can be seen from the two schemas in Section 3.2. Mill's five methods of induction were introduced in the rest of the chapter as methods rather than as arguments. However, they can easily be taken as arguments. For example, Table 3.1 contains the set of premises for the MA argument resulting in "C is

---

12. Vector addition was first introduced by Galileo and then developed by Newton when they studied velocities and forces. J. S. Mill, the author of MR, nonetheless seemed to be unaware of this some 200 years later. An example of MR employing vector addition is the case of the discovery of Neptune. The irregular motion of the planet Uranus could not be explained in terms of known forces. So U. J. J. Leverrier and J. C. Adams independently conjectured that there was a 'residual force' from an unknown planet acting on it. That planet was later found and named Neptune.

the cause of the illness" as the conclusion. The premises of MD and MAD are also usually formulated as tables, while graphs are often used in MCV.

How many kinds of inductive arguments are there? This is the main problem that inductive logic is concerned with. We could classify inductive logic into **qualitative inductive logic** and **quantitative inductive logic**. The types of inductive arguments we have studied in this chapter are qualitative, whereas what are commonly known as statistical arguments (statistical inferences) are quantitative. Statistical arguments are the subject of the next chapter.

If this classification is acceptable, we can ask: How many kinds of *qualitative* inductive arguments are there?

Aristotle, more than 2,000 years ago, classified qualitative inductions into induction by simple enumeration and intuitive induction. Here is an example of what Aristotle took as a case of intuitive induction. From the observation, on several occasions, that the bright side of the moon always faces the sun, one can conclude that the moon shines by reflected sunlight. Unlike the case of induction by simple enumeration, there seems to be no rule that can take us from the premises to the conclusion here. Hence Aristotle called it 'intuitive induction.'

After Aristotle's time, philosophers like Mill were able to formalize[13] a number of inductive arguments. I am quite sure more and more of what Aristotle called intuitive inductions will become formalized in the future. Intuitiveness is the polar opposite of rule-governedness. It is one of the tasks of logicians to reduce the intuitive to something explicit, learnable, and objective in the field of arguments. In Chapter 32, we will discuss the idea of formalization of inductive reasoning in the context of artificial intelligence.

Now let us move on to statistics and probability, where quantitative inductive logic is studied.

KEY TERMS INTRODUCED IN THIS CHAPTER

induction by analogy

induction by simple enumeration (universal generalization)

Method of Agreement (MA)

Method of Difference (MD)

Joint Method of Agreement and Difference (MAD)

Method of Concomitant Variation (MCV)

Method of Residues (MR)

qualitative inductive logic

quantitative inductive logic

REFERENCES

Most elementary logic texts have a part on inductive logic—for example, Copi and Cohen (1994, chaps. 11 and 12), Kahane (1995, part IV), and Bonevac (1990, part IV). Skyrms (1975, chap. IV) provides a clear and simple exposition of Mill's methods.

---

13. 'Formalization' is a technical term in philosophy. For present purposes, we can take "to formalize an argument" as meaning "to make the argument explicit in terms of rules and symbols so as to enable people to evaluate it as well as to learn how to use it precisely."

EXERCISES

1. Imagine that you have been presented with a radio, the controls of which are labeled in a foreign language. Which of Mill's inductive method(s) would you use to discover the functions of these controls? Explain why the method(s) should work. What if the radio is faulty?

2. Corresponding to each of Mill's five methods of induction, recall one episode from your past when you had employed or could have employed that method to try to discover causal connections between (types of) events. Think of episodes such as trying to find out why your favorite potted plant died, why your cat got sick, or why your car (or motorbike) refused to start.

3. (a) Take 20 objects. Record their (approximate) colors, shapes, sizes, and weights. Now place them one at a time in a trough of water and note down which of them float and which sink. Construct a joint method of agreement and difference (MAD) table out of these data. From the table, are you able to discover any causal principles or laws that underlie the phenomenon of flotation? Discuss the efficiency and limitations of MAD in terms of this experiment.

   (b) It is said that Archimedes (287–212 B.C.) discovered the principle of flotation in his bath. What is this principle, which tells us what sort of objects will float and which will not? Is it possible for this principle to be discovered through any of Mill's five methods?

4. In his *Animal Intelligence* (1911), E. L, Thorndike—a pioneer psychologist—reported on a large number of his experiments with cats. The following story is *inspired* by his findings: A cat is placed inside a "puzzle box" with a door, which can be opened only by pulling at a loop hanging from the ceiling of the box. Trying to get out, the cat meows, paces, claws, and bites, but the door remains shut. Finally, quite exhausted, he rolls over on the floor. As he does so, his tail unwittingly hits the loop. Lo and behold, the door opens. When the cat is returned to the box (after being rewarded with food, of course), the cat starts rolling on the floor once more. But this time the door does not open. After he rolls around a few more times, lo and behold, the door opens again.

5. What inductive method or methods can you attribute to the cat's attempt to discover the way to open the door? Assess the efficiency and limitations of these methods in terms of the experiment of "Thorndike's cat."

6. Are Mill's methods applicable in the diagnosis of diseases?

7. Are Mill's methods applicable in finding one's way out of a maze?

8. Can you discern the use of any of Mill's methods in the story of light told in Chapter 0? Can you draw any morals from your findings?

9. In Section 3.4, the doctor made an inference about the cause of the sickness of the six students. Identify the premises and conclusion of the inference.

Chapter 4*

Statistical and Probabilistic Reasoning

4.1 INTRODUCTION

A common misconception in science is that data are presented to us neatly and tidily, so that, with a bit of patience, we can come to straightforward and neat conclusions such as "all ravens are black" and "all stones sink in water." At least, this seems to be in the mind of inductivists like Bacon and Mill. However, the common saying that every rule has its exceptions appears to be more correct. The universe is perhaps basically orderly and simple, but the empirical data we encounter (through our five senses) are usually not. Not all ravens are black; there are mutant ravens that are nonblack! Even "all stones sink in water" has exceptions. (Try to sink some of the pumice stones on the shore of Lake Rotorua!)

We have not touched on the more untidy areas like the weather, the economy, and health. Smoking has been suspected of causing lung cancer, yet there are people who live to a good old age though they smoke like a chimney. On the other hand, there are nonsmokers who contract lung cancer in their prime. The rate of lung

---

*This chapter is more advanced and is optional.

cancer contraction is by no means proportional to the amount of smoking a person indulges in.

The general conclusion is that even though the universe may be ruled by simple causal laws, since there are so many of these causal laws criss-crossing one another and such a multitude of causally potent events colliding with each other, we can get very untidy phenomena. This is why induction by simple enumeration and Mill's methods are limited in scope.[1] **Statistics** is the study of methods for the analysis of untidy phenomena, revealing and sorting out causal relationships criss-crossing the available empirical data. In other words, qualitative inductive logic has to be supplemented by quantitative inductive logic.

Some of us are "allergic" to numbers and symbols. The term 'statistics' can put us off. I will attempt here to present the *essence* of statistics without the use of any formulas, much as I presented deductive and inductive logic earlier.

Knowledge of statistics is not necessary for most areas of the philosophy of science. So if you are feeling a bit apprehensive at this stage, there is no harm in your skipping this chapter. (After all, this is a starred chapter.)

4.2 WHAT IS STATISTICAL INFERENCE?

According to induction by simple enumeration (which we will call *universal generalization* from here on), the observation of 10 white swans might lead us to conclude that "All swans are white." What, however, should we conclude if we should observe 7 white swans and 3 nonwhite swans? I suppose it would be reasonable to conclude that 70 percent of all swans are white.

Let us introduce two key terms used in statistics: 'population' and 'sample.' When we are investigating certain characteristic distributions of a collection of things, that collection is known as the **population**. In the present case, the collection of all the swans, past and present, is the population, and we want to know about the distribution of the color of the population.

Obviously we cannot survey each and every member of this population. So we take a **sample**, which is part of the population. Here the 10 observed swans make up the sample.

Statistical inference is a kind of reasoning from samples to populations, trying to find out what the population is like from the available data obtained in the sample. Political polls are typical statistical inferences. Often we would like to predict who is going to win the American presidency and by how much. So we survey a sample—say 10,000—of American voters. From that survey, using statistical technique, we infer that *XYZ* is going to win the election by a margin of so much. (When the actual votes are cast, the collection of all the voters makes up the population.)

The inference from a sample of 10 white swans to "All swans are white" has been called a **universal generalization**.[2] Let's call the inference from a sample of 10 swans, of which only 7 are white, to "70 percent of swans (in the universe) are white" a **statistical generalization**. It can be seen that universal generalizations are really limiting cases (special cases) of statistical generalizations since to say that all swans are white is no more and no less than saying that 100 percent of all swans are white. You should see that the present chapter is just an extension and continuation of the previous chapter on inductive logic where, among others, we dealt with universal generalizations (that is, induction by simple enumeration).[3]

It is one thing to make statistical generalizations. It is another to trust them. For example, how credible is our generalization that 70 percent of swans

1. Recall that the Method of Agreement and so on work on certain assumptions, one of which is that there is *only one* cause for the effect (Section 3.4).

2. We often use the term 'universal generalization' for both the inference and the conclusion of the inference.

3. You will find that Mill's five methods also involve universal generalizations if we deal in general cases of cause and effect. For example, we might be interested in the general cause of sickness (not just the sickness those six students suffered).

(in the universe) are white? Some of you might say that the sample of 10 is too small. Some might notice that all members of the sample are taken from a certain site, say a zoo in California. Statistics studies not only the kind of statistical inference that can reasonably be made but also various measures of credibility that can be attached to the conclusions of such inferences. Credibility in the present context is also known as probability. "How credible (probable) is the hypothesis that 70 percent of all swans (in the whole universe) are white?" we can ask. Would the hypothesis (based on the same data) that "80 percent of swans (in the whole universe) are white" have the same credibility (probability)?

So statistics studies both statistical inferences and the probabilities (credibilities) of these inferences.

Because of the numerical nature of probabilities, I think we are justified in dividing up inductive logic into **qualitative inductive logic** and **quantitative inductive logic**.[4] Statistical inference is obviously inductive and, since it is quantitative in nature, it belongs to quantitative inductive logic, whereas what people normally call inductions belong to qualitative inductive logic.

4.3 DESCRIPTIVE STATISTICS

Let's start with an example. Suppose there are 70 people in a room. We can then ask what their average age is. How is this to be calculated? First, we go around the room, taking down the age of each person. We then record the ages in a table, which may look like Table 4.1.

This table, known as a **frequency distribution table**, indicates that there are three people of age 16, five people of age 17, and so on. To be more exact, we are actually grouping people into age groups, the first group being those between 16 and 17, the second group being those between 17 and 18, and so on. We call these entries **data**. Since we are not interested in the persons' names, we do not record them as part of the data. There are other

TABLE 4.1

Age	Frequency
16	3
17	5
18	4
19	6
20	12
21	10
22	10
23	9
24	8
25	3
Total	70

ways of presenting the data—for example, in bar charts, which are more correctly known as **histograms**. Figure 4.1 shows a histogram corresponding to the frequency distribution table (Table 4.1).

Both the frequency distribution table and the histogram give us the same information: the **frequency distribution** of the ages of the people in the room. From this distribution, the average age can now be calculated as follows:

$$\frac{(16 \times 3) + (17 \times 5) + (18 \times 4) + \cdots + (25 \times 3)}{70}$$

This merely means that the average age is obtained by adding up the ages of all persons present and dividing it by the total number of persons present. In statistics, we quite often use the term 'mean' instead of the term 'average.' The mean age of the group can be seen to be 20.9. Note that the mean, 20.9 years of age, is not meant to be a description of any one particular person in the room. It is rather a description of the collection of persons as a whole.

We say that the mean is a **parameter** of the frequency distribution. Parameters are features of the distribution that planners and scientists are interested in. Another common parameter is the **mode**. The mode is the age that has the highest

---

4. These are *my* terms. See Section 3.9.

FIGURE 4.1

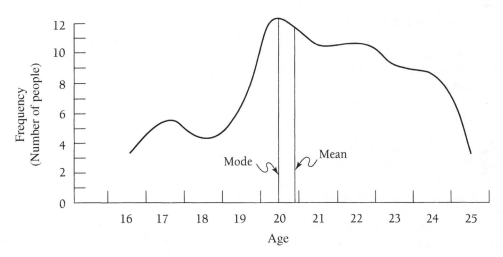

FIGURE 4.1a

frequency. In our example, 20 is the mode. This means that there are more 20-year-olds in the room than people of any other age, and yet this is not quite the mean age. The mean age is in fact 20.9. The difference between the mode and the mean can be much more than this small amount. Let me illustrate by evening out the "bars" in Figure 4.1 and representing that figure as a smooth curve (graph), Figure 4.1a.

You can see that the curve, though not quite symmetrical, is "balanced" enough to yield a value of the mean close to the mode. However, let us consider Figure 4.2.

Here the mode and the mean are quite far apart and we say that the frequency distribution is right-skewed (tailing off to the right).

There is another common parameter used in statistics—the **median**—which is the line dividing the area under the frequency distribution curve into two equal halves. In other words, there are as many items below the median as above it. In our present example, the median is 21.5. This means that half

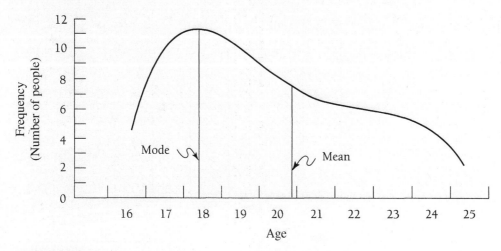

FIGURE 4.2

the people in the room are under 21.5 and half are above it.[5]

For a perfectly symmetrical graph, the mean, the mode, and the median will coincide, as in Figure 4.3. In a skewed graph, they will have separate values, as in Figure 4.4. We say that these parameters are features of the frequency distribution curve (the graph). However, they are far from determining its shape. Compare, for example, the graphs in Figures 4.5a and 4.5b. They are both symmetrical about the mean (mode and median) 7, yet all the occurrences are heaped toward the middle for one, whereas the occurrences are spread out almost throughout the whole range for the other. A common measure of the spread is known as the **standard deviation**. I will not define it here; what we need to know for our purpose is that the larger the standard deviation, the bigger the spread. Figure 4.5b, for example, has a much bigger standard deviation than Figure 4.5a.

There are other parameters for the description of frequency distributions (graphs), which we need not go into. I think we now have a good idea of what **descriptive statistics** is all about. Descriptive statistics deals with the description of statistical data about groups of things.

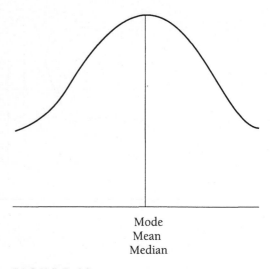

Mode
Mean
Median

FIGURE 4.3

4.4 STATISTICAL INFERENCE I: STATISTICAL GENERALIZATION

Let's suppose that we lack the time and resources to ask each and every one of the 70 people in the room his or her age. (Imagine trying to have an

---

5. Of course we should also allow for the possibility that members of the collection may be located exactly at the median.

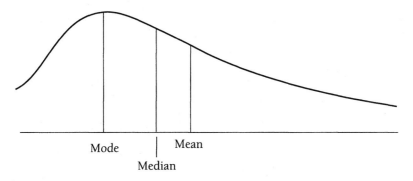

FIGURE 4.4

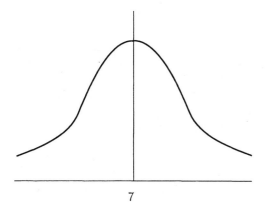

FIGURE 4.5a

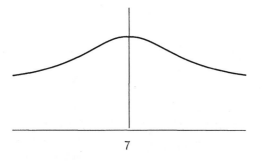

FIGURE 4.5b

accurate picture of the age distribution of all New Yorkers.) What we can do is to take a sample from this population of 70 people and analyze the sample instead. The data from the analysis of the sample can be tabulated as a frequency distribution table (Table 4.2).

TABLE 4.2

Age	Frequency
16	1
17	0
18	1
19	0
20	3
21	2
22	1
23	0
24	2
25	0
Total	10

The question is: From this sample of 10, what can we conclude about the population? The idea of statistical inference is to infer the (unavailable) features of the population from the (available) features of the sample. Let us calculate the mean, mode, and median of this sample: mean = 20.6, mode = 20, and median = 21.5. Should we conclude, therefore, that the population also has these values for the three parameters? (Of course in this artificial example, we know the answer: the population has a mean of 20.9, a mode of 20, and a median of 21.5. The two sets of figures are very close indeed!)

However, there is no guarantee that the sample will resemble the population even remotely. It is not an impossibility that we might obtain a sample where all 10 come from the upper end of the age group, say three 25-year-olds and seven 24-year-olds. In such a case, we would have concluded that the mean is 24.3, the mode is 24, and the median is 24.7. Of course, you would say, "Such an unusual sample is highly improbable!" Why is it improbable, and what does 'improbable' mean?

You see now that statistical inferences are based on the notion of **probability**. In a statistical inference, we estimate how well a sample resembles the population and we calculate how probable this estimate is. Contrast it with the method of universal generalization, which concludes from 10 (observed) white swans to "All swans are white"—*without* attaching a probability to the conclusion to qualify its credibility!

Statistics is a branch of mathematics that provides us with probabilities for conclusions (about the population) that are inferred from samples.

What is probability? An example of a probability statement might be as follows. With the surgical operation over, the doctor says to the patient, "Good news! You now have a 60 percent chance (probability) of surviving the next three years." What can the doctor mean? How is the probability of an event calculated?

Consider the case of throwing a die. Suppose the die is perfectly symmetrical—that is, its six faces are all the same, the edges are all straight, the corners are all the same, the weight of the die is evenly distributed, and so on. We call such a die, a fair die. What is the probability of throwing a 1? I think most of us would say that it is 1 in 6. (1 am not being careful here in using the qualifying word 'most,' for philosophers, and that may include you, are typically skeptics and sometimes disagreeable skeptics.) What about throwing a 2? You would say, "Obviously the same—that is, the probability is 1/6. In short, the probability of throwing any one of the six numbers is 1/6."

Can you justify your claim? (A typical philosophical challenge!) The usual justification is: since

the six faces are all identical, they must have the same chance of being thrown. However, they are not quite identical, are they? There is only one dot on the face of the 1, whereas there are six dots on the face of the 6. "Ah," comes an instant rejoinder, "these dots are irrelevant."

We can see that the understanding of the notion of probability here is based on the notion of **equiprobable** event.[6] (Two mutually exclusive types of events are equiprobable if they have the same probability of occurring.) In our present case, the six possible ways for the thrown die to land are taken as equiprobable. Once this is assumed, other probabilities can be calculated. For example, the probability of throwing an even number is $3 \times 1/6$, which is 1/2; that of throwing an odd number is the same; that of throwing a non-6 is $5 \times 1/6$, which is 5/6; and so on. We can also calculate the probability of throwing a double 6 with two fair dice, which is $1/6 \times 1/6$, which is 1/36, because the chance of throwing a 6 with the first die is 1/6, and having succeeded in doing that, there is still only 1 in 6 chances of throwing a 6 again. The point to note is that these numerical calculations belong to the field of deductive logic (Chapter 2). In a (valid) deductive argument, provided the premises are true, the conclusion is true. In other words, simply by assuming the equiprobability of certain types of events, we can *deduce* a whole host of probability statements. That is how credibility estimates of statistical conclusions are arrived at.

Let's return to the example of a few paragraphs back, where the sample of 10 people from a room of 70 people has a mean of 20.6. We asked the following question: Would it be reasonable to infer that the population would have a similar mean? If so, how probable is this conclusion? Taking the sample to be a random sample, the answer is that the probability of the population having a mean of 20.6 ± 1.76 is roughly 95 percent. In other words, we can expect the mean of the population to be between 18.84 and 22.36 with a

---

6. Some texts use the term 'equipossible' instead.

probability of 95 percent.[7] This result is actually mathematically deducible from the assumption of random sampling. What is random sampling? A sample is randomly chosen if our method of selecting the persons for the sample is such that each person in the room has the same chance of being selected—that is, they are equiprobable for selection. To sum up, we have just made the following **statistical inference**:

(a) Premise: The mean age of a random sample of 10 people is 20.6.

(b) Conclusion: The mean age of the population is 20.6 ± 1.76.

(c) The probability (credibility) of the conclusion given the premise is 95 percent.

As mentioned in Section 4.2, the inference from the data of 10 observed white swans to the conclusion that all swans are white is a case of **universal generalization**. In this chapter, we have studied the inference from the mean and other parameters of a sample to the mean and other parameters of the population. To emphasize its similarity and relationship to universal generalization, I have proposed in Section 4.2 to call the kind of inference we have studied here **statistical generalization**.

4.5 STATISTICAL INFERENCE II: STATISTICAL CORRELATION

Besides inferring the mean and other parameters of a population from a sample, we can also statistically infer the correlation of two variables. For example, we might be interested in the relationship between age and income of people, between age and height, and between age and weight. We might even be interested in the relationships between income and weight or between income and height. Of course, in many cases we may not find any relationships. When there is a relationship in the sense that the two quantities (we usually call them **variables**) vary together, we say that they are **correlated**. Intuitively, we can see that, for example, age is correlated with income, but income does not seem to be correlated with height. Is income correlated with weight?

This exposition sounds somewhat familiar, doesn't it? Yes, you are right. We had this before in Section 3.7, where we introduced the method of concomitant variation (MCV).

I said that inductive logic can be classified into two main types: qualitative inductive logic and quantitative inductive logic. MCV belongs to qualitative inductive logic. Why qualitative? Because, by that method, we can only learn that the two variables are causally related, but what we do not know is how "tightly" and "variably" they are tied together. Statistics gives us quantitative measures of such correlations, hence statistics belongs to quantitative inductive logic.

I'll give an example. Robert Boyle (Section 3.7) was interested in knowing how the volume of a gas varies with its pressure (or the pressure exerted on it, if you like). All of you have the experience of pressing on an inflated balloon: The harder you press on it, the smaller it gets. MCV will thus tell us the two are causally related, but it leaves unanswered the question of how exactly they are related. Suppose we performed an experiment and obtained the results given in Table 4.3. We can see at once that volume and pressure are related. But in what manner are they related? Should we say that pressure is inversely proportional to volume?

---

7. In statistics, we do not try to assess the probability of a certain definite answer like "mean = 20.6." The reason is that such definite answers are "points," which do not occupy any area. The probability of hitting an exact point with an arrow is, strictly speaking, zero, because the point is nothing, spatially. Putting it differently: Within the line segment between 16 and 25 (the range of ages), there are infinitely many points. The chance of the mean being the point 20.6 is zero. Hence, in statistics, we always use intervals to make estimates: mean = 20.6 ± 1.76. This means that we conjecture that the mean is between (20.6 − 1.76) and (20.6 + 1.76).

TABLE 4.3

Volume	Pressure
1	1 + 0.00
2	1/2 + 0.02
3	1/3 + 0.01
4	1/4 − 0.03
5	1/5 + 0.02
6	1/6 − 0.05
7	1/7 − 0.01
8	1/8 + 0.04
9	1/9 + 0.01

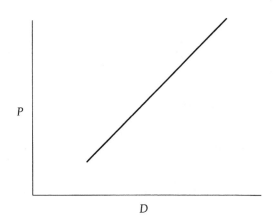

FIGURE 4.6b

$$P = 1/V$$

If we define D to be $1/V$, we can write the previous equation as:

$$P = D$$

This suggests the graphs in Figures 4.6a and 4.6b.

If we ignore the decimal adjuncts in the Pressure column (0.00, 0.02, 0.01, 0.03, and so on) as "perturbations" or "noises," we can see that the two equations fit the data in Table 4.3 perfectly. But what counts as perturbations? Are we justified in ignoring them? MCV has not addressed this problem. Table 4.3 represents a relatively "neat"

case, but such "neat" cases seldom occur in nature or in experiments. What should we conclude about the relationship of X and Y if the available data are as in Figure 4.7a? I suppose we can say that they are related, but is the relationship a straight line as in Figure 4.7b? Or is it a curve as in Figure 4.7c?

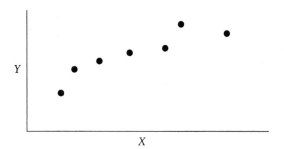

FIGURE 4.7a

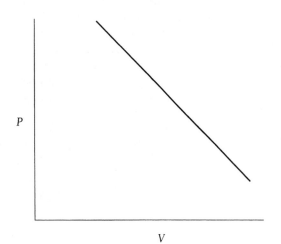

FIGURE 4.6a

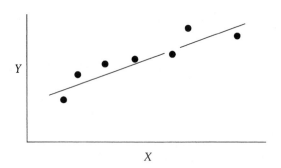

FIGURE 4.7b

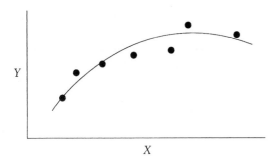

FIGURE 4.7c

If we hypothesize that it is a straight-line relationship (linear relationship), how credible is this hypothesis? Alternatively, how credible is the rival hypothesis that the relationship is a curve? (We have to take into account that the measurements of X and Y may not be accurate and there may be other uncontrollable factors.) In statistics, these types of problems are studied and dealt with in **regression analysis** and **correlation analysis**.

TABLE 4.4

Volume Pressure	Observed Pressure	Predicted
48	29.12	29.13
46	30.56	30.37
44	31.93	31.75
42	33.50	33.14
40	35.31	35.00
38	37.00	36.79
36	39.31	38.87
34	41.62	41.11
32	44.18	43.68
30	47.06	46.60
28	50.31	50.00
26	54.31	53.77
24	58.12	58.25
22	64.06	63.54
20	70.68	70.00

Source: Adapted from Wolf (1962a, p. 241).

4.6 STATISTICAL METHODS
OF CREDIBILITY
ASSIGNMENT

A third area of study in statistics is that of hypothesis testing. In the last two sections, we discussed methods of *generation* of hypotheses. Here we deal with a different problem: When confronted with a hypothesis, how is it to be empirically *tested* so that we can assess its credibility?

The relationship between pressure and volume for a gas is usually summarized as Boyle's law: For a given quantity of gas, under constant temperature, its volume varies in inverse proportion to its pressure—that is, $V = r/P$, where r is a numerical constant.[8] Historically Boyle did not *induce* the law from experimental data, in the manner we presented in the last

subsection. It was *not* that Boyle first did his experiments with no idea of what the relationship was going to be, and then from the data read off the relationship. According to records, it was Richard Towneley who proposed the hypothesis to Boyle, who then went on to test it with experiments.[9]

In one of his experiments, Boyle obtained the results presented in Table 4.4. The first column gives the various volumes into which an enclosed amount of air was successively compressed, the second gives the corresponding pressures observed, and the third gives the corresponding pressures calculated according to Boyle's law based on the volumes of the first column.

The question now is whether we should take these results of the experiment as *confirming* or *disconfirming* the hypothesis (Section 1.9). The observed pressure does not quite agree with the theoretically predicted pressure. For example, the second value

---

8. The law is only approximately true.

9. See Wolf (1962a, p. 239).

for Observed Pressure is 30.56, whereas the second value of Predicted Pressure is 30.37. However, the other values seem to agree better.

Most of you would probably say that the agreement is good enough, so that we should take Boyle's hypothesis as confirmed and confer the title 'law' on it. However, is the agreement *really* good enough? How do you know? Shouldn't there be objective (nonintuitive) criteria for the measurement of its goodness?

Shouldn't these criteria be backed up by rational arguments? For example, if corresponding to Volume 38, the value for the Observed Pressure is 50 instead of 37, should we still take the hypothesis as having been confirmed? What if all the observed values were either higher or lower than the actual observed ones by one unit? As the discrepancy between the observed values and the expected values increases, disagreement between scientists would proportionally increase. We surely need some sort of rational criterion to guide us in making decisions on such issues. We cannot rely on our intuition as if we were passing judgment on works of art!

This may be your first encounter with questions of rational criteria that philosophers have been asking for in the past two and a half thousand years of Western civilization. We can safely say that on all matters of acceptance or rejection, philosophy demands rational criteria. Every decision we make, as far as acceptance or rejection of claims is concerned, must be based on rationality, over and above (subjective) intuition or feelings. Science has been taken as a model of rationality, in contrast to the arts. Moreover, the acceptance or rejection of a scientific hypothesis can have serious political, financial, and social implications. (Think of the invention of the atomic bomb.) Hence it is even more important that we secure rational criteria for the assessment of hypotheses.

We can see that the methods we studied in Chapter 3 (induction by simple enumeration and Mill's five methods) have nothing to say in this field. Statistics (based on the notion of probability) is the field that furnishes the scientific world with the criteria we have been talking about. According

to the statistical theory of regression, the values observed by Boyle indeed showed that Boyle's hypothesis (or more accurately, Towneley's hypothesis) has a high credibility, and so the hypothesis should be accepted as *confirmed*! (In statistics, the term '**probability**' is usually employed instead of '**credibility**.' Thus we say that Boyle's hypothesis is highly probable.)

We have, by this example, illustrated the third area of statistics: the study of statistical measures of probability (credibility) of hypotheses based on empirical data. But what is probability? You will find that this is not such a simple question to answer.

4.7 THE CLASSICAL INTERPRETATION OF PROBABILITY

You often hear people say things like the following: "The chances are that it will rain tomorrow," "Most likely it will rain," "Probably it will rain," and "There is a high likelihood that it will rain." We generally take these as merely different ways of expressing probability of some sort. For the layperson there is only one notion of probability. Remember that we asked the question "What is probability?" in Section 4.4. There we assumed that there is only one notion of probability too.

Mathematicians and philosophers have been puzzled by the notion of probability for a long time. When the doctor said that Peter had a 60 percent chance of surviving the next three years, what could he mean? If Peter were to die within six months, would the doctor have been wrong? If he died on the last day of the third year, would the doctor have been right? This shows that we need a better understanding of the notion of probability. What are we claiming when we say that the probability of event E occurring is P? You will find that the meaning of probability that a person has in mind can be discerned by the ways she computes the probability in question. In other words, the methods of computation of probability underlie the meaning of probability.

In Section 4.4, we based the notion of probability on equiprobability. When a die is thrown, there are six possible outcomes. Since there is no reason to prefer one of the faces of the die over another, we say that the faces are equiprobable—that is, we assign the same probability to each of the faces (1/6). This is an application of the famous principle of indifference, which states that two alternative possibilities are equally probable if there is no reason for preferring one over the other. There is more than one way of reading this principle, however.[10] Here we take the following: Let the type of event, the occurrence of which we are interested in, be called A_1. Let there be other possible alternatives: A_2, A_3, …, A_k. Suppose these k alternatives (including the one we are interested in) are all the possible alternatives. Let H be the statement, "A_1 will occur (rather than the other alternatives)." Let E be the available information on the setup. Then the **principle of indifference** says: If according to E there is no reason why one of the alternatives is preferable over the others, the k possibilities are then taken as equiprobable, and thus the probability of the truth of H based on information E is $1/k$. We say:

(1) $\Pr(H \text{ given } E) = 1/k$

The use of the principle of indifference for the calculation of probability is known as the **classical interpretation**, which dates back to Jacob Bernoulli (1654–1705), Thomas Bayes (1702–1761), and Pierre Simon de Laplace (1749–1827).

This interpretation, however, suffers from two major defects. (i) There may be no way of calculating equiprobable probabilities. The actual universe is a rather messy universe. More often than not, the information E alone will not enable us to tell which types of events are equiprobable. For example, suppose the available information E is "The die is slightly loaded toward face 1." How are we to calculate the probability of H, that the die will land on face 1? In other words, how is the total probability

1 to be divided into a number of equiprobable possibilities, from which the probability of H can be calculated? In real cases, most of the probabilistic situations we encounter are similarly "vague." (Think of cases like weather prediction or the prediction of a person's behavior. Remember that neither the atmosphere nor a person is a die with regular faces!) (ii) There may be more than one reasonable way of deciding which types of events are equiprobable. (More on this later.)

4.8 THE LOGICAL INTERPRETATION

The classical interpretation is only one among many interpretations. The next one that we ought to know is the **logical interpretation**, which can be taken as an extension and refinement of the classical interpretation. The development of this interpretation in the 20th century has mainly been due to J. M. Keynes, F. Waismann, R. Carnap, and J. Hintikka.[11] The idea is to treat probability as a relationship between statements, as in (1) in Section 4.7. In Chapter 2, we studied deductive logic. An argument is said to be (deductively) valid if the premises guarantee the conclusion. We also say that P entails C if the argument 'P, therefore C' is valid. So we can see that P entails C if and only if whenever P is true, then C is true. Here are two examples:

(2) "John is tall and heavy" entails "John is tall."

(3) "Peter is a student, and all students are clever" entails "Peter is clever."

However,

(4) "1,000 observed swans are white" *does not* entail "All swans are white."

Nevertheless, intuition tells us that in case (4), even though the relationship is not one of entailment (strict guarantee), the premise still bears some

---

10. See Cohen (1989, pp. 43–44).

11. See Cohen (1989, pp. 74–80).

weight on the conclusion. It makes the conclusion more likely to be true. To say that some statement is more likely to be true, as the conclusion of an argument, is the same as to assign it a higher probability on the evidence of the premise. This is the intuition that leads to the logical interpretation of probability. According to this interpretation, given any pair of statements E (the premise), and H (the conclusion), we should always be able to assign a probability-relationship to the pair, and we write

(5) $\Pr(H \text{ given } E) = \boldsymbol{p}$

where 'Pr' stands for 'probability' and p is a number varying from 0 to 1. The probability relationship should have three features:

(i)   If E is such that E entails H, the probability p is 1.

(ii) If E is such that E entails not-H (sometimes called the negation of H), then p is 0.

(iii) In all other cases, p is between 0 and 1.

"$p = 1$" implies certainty. In case (i), since E entails H, given that E is true, it is clear that the truth of H is a certainty. On the other hand, "$p = 0$" implies impossibility (that is, certainly not). In case (ii), since E entails not-H, given that E is true, it is clear that the truth of H is an impossibility (since the truth of not-H is a certainty), (iii) covers the "middle ground." When $0 < p < 1$, the truth of H, given E, is neither certain nor impossible and has a certain probability.

Let's illustrate. Let

$e_1 = 1,000$ swans have been observed to be white.

$e_2 = 10,000$ swans have been observed to be white.

$e_3 = 1,000$ ravens have been observed to be black.

$h_1 = $ All swans (anywhere at any time) are white.

$h_2 = $ There is at least one white swan.

$h_3 = $ No swans are white.

Then intuition prompts us to say: $\Pr(h_1 \text{ given } e_1)$ should be smaller than $\Pr(h_1 \text{ given } e_2)$, and $\Pr(h_1$

given e_3) should be smaller than $\Pr(h_1 \text{ given } e_1)$. Indeed $\Pr(h_1 \text{ given } e_3)$ should be close to zero because information about ravens, intuitively, has no bearing on swans. The reason why we have chosen letters h and e for our illustrations should now be clear. h comes from 'hypothesis' and e comes from 'evidence.' '$\Pr(h_1 \text{ given } e_1) = p$' then says, 'Given evidence e_1 the probability of h_1 being true is p.' We can also see that $\Pr(h_2 \text{ given } e_1) = 1$, because e_1 entails h_2. This agrees with the intuition that should e_1 be true, the probability of h_2 is 1— that is, a certainty. Further, that $\Pr(h_3 \text{ given } e_1) = 0$ should also be obvious.

How is Pr to be worked out for various cases of (iii), though? Carnap suggests a number of alternatives. Here is one, and I'll call it **system C**. The best way to introduce it is in terms of a simple example. A blocks world is a world made up of blocks and blocks alone. To keep matters simple, let us define a B-world as one in which all blocks are cubes, identical in shape and size, colored in either red or green, and there are exactly three such blocks.

Let's see how many possible B-worlds there can be. Suppose the three blocks are called a, b, and c. Then it is obvious that there can be only eight possible B-worlds:

W1: $Ra \ \& \ Rb \ \& \ Rc$	W5: $Ga \ \& \ Rb \ \& \ Rc$
W2: $Ra \ \& \ Rb \ \& \ Gc$	W6: $Ga \ \& \ Rb \ \& \ Gc$
W3: $Ra \ \& \ Gb \ \& \ Rc$	W7: $Ga \ \& \ Gb \ \& \ Rc$
W4: $Ra \ \& \ Gb \ \& \ Gc$	W8: $Ga \ \& \ Gb \ \& \ Gc$

(where W1 is the world where a is red and b is red and c is red, and W2 is the world where a is red and b is red and c is green, and so on).

Suppose God made a B-world and you were asked to guess which of the eight possible worlds had been created. Which would you pick?[12]

You probably would have recognized that the present case is similar to the case of the fair die with its six faces. There we assigned 1/6 probability to each face. Here I think most of you would say that

---

12. Leibniz (1646–1716) once argued that the world created by God must be the best of all possible worlds. If that were the case, the theory of probability would be of little relevance here.

the eight possible worlds are equiprobable, and the probability of each is, therefore, 1/8. Indeed this is Carnap's recommendation.

If so, we can work out the probabilities of the following statements e, f, h, and k where

e = a is red.

f = a is red and b is red.

h = All things (in the B-world) are red.

k = b is red.

Their probabilities should be:

$$\Pr(e) = 4/8$$
$$\Pr(f) = 2/8$$
$$\Pr(h) = 1/8$$
$$\Pr(k) = 4/8$$

Why is it that $\Pr(e) = 4/8$? Because, out of the eight possible cases, four of them are favorable (the first four cases and only these four cases are such that a is red). The other cases are similar. So what is the likelihood that God has created the B-world in which all things are red (that is, h)? The answer is one chance out of eight. If we are to bet on it, odds of 7 to 1 would be fair. This betting ratio is fair if we know nothing other than the fact that God has created a B-world. Now suppose we are further told that in that world e is true (that is, that block a is red). What sort of odds would then be fair?

Let's reason this way: We know that e is true. That means that the world that God has created can only be among worlds W1 to W4. Out of these four worlds, h is true only in W1. Therefore the probability of h relative to e must be 1 out of 4. Let's present our method of calculation as a formula:

$$\Pr(h \text{ given } e) = \frac{m(h \ \& \ e)}{m(e)} = \frac{1}{4}$$

where $m(h \ \& \ e)$ is the number of cases where both h and e are true, and $m(e)$ is the number of cases where e is true. We can see that evidence e increases the probability of h from the initial probability of 1/8 to 1/4. What is $\Pr(h \text{ given } f)$? It should be $m(h \ \& \ f)$ divided by $m(f)$, which is 1/2. Statement f is more favorable to h than e, because f says that *both*

a and b are red. Hence the likelihood of h being true should further increase, and indeed it does (from 1/4 to 1/2). The system works well, so far, with our intuition.

However, it does not work in the following case. The probability of $\Pr(k)$ is 4/8, as shown earlier. We should expect $\Pr(k \text{ given } e)$ to be higher. In daily life, a child bitten by a dog once would be wary of the next dog. The evidence e (that block a is red) should increase our expectation that the next block would also be red (that is, k). However, according to the present system you would find that $\Pr(k \text{ given } e)$ is 2/4, which is the same as $\Pr(k)$. In general, given a hypothesis H, '$\Pr(H)$' represents what is known as the **prior probability** (initial probability) of H. The prior probability H represents its likelihood *before* the evidence, E, is collected. '$\Pr(H \text{ given } E)$' represents the **posterior probability** of H, which is the probability of H *after* the additional information E has been obtained. If E is relevant to H, $\Pr(H \text{ given } E)$ should be greater or smaller than $\Pr(H)$, depending on whether E is favorable or unfavorable to H. In the cases we have just discussed, both e and f are favorable to h. That's why $\Pr(h \text{ given } e)$ and $\Pr(h \text{ given } f)$ are both greater than $\Pr(h)$. However, since e is also favorable to k, we should expect $\Pr(k \text{ given } e)$ to be greater than $\Pr(k)$. But system C gives both $\Pr(k \text{ given } e)$ and $\Pr(k)$ the same value. So system C has failed our intuitive expectation, and we say that this system is **evidence-insensitive**.

Because of this, Carnap proposes a second system. I'll call it C★. In system C, the eight possible B-worlds, W1–W8, are taken as equiprobable. In contrast, C★ groups these eight worlds into four classes:

T1: One cube is red (two green).

T2: Two cubes are red (one green).

T3: All three cubes are red.

T4: None of the cubes are red (three green).

And C★ takes these four classes as equiprobable to each other. It seems reasonable to do so. Because, for example, even though there are three possible worlds falling under T1—W4, W6, and W7—these three are actually **qualitatively identical**. (You can say that if God should show us the three worlds without the labels *a*, *b*, and *c* attached to the cubes, we cannot tell which world is which. As far as qualities are concerned, they are the same.) In philosophy, we say that they are **indiscernible**. According to the great 17th-century philosopher Leibniz (1646–1716), indiscernible possible worlds are really identical.[13] So if God should be contemplating the creation of a B-world, there would be only four choices—T1–T4—not eight. Thus it is reasonable to assign the probability of 1/4 to each of these four cases. Now you might ask what the chance is of W2 (out of W1–W8) actually being chosen by God for creation. The answer can be reasoned out as follows: (i) W2 belongs to T2, (ii) W3 and W5 also belong to T2, (iii) these three worlds should be equiprobable within T2, therefore (iv) they should share the 1/4 probability of T2, and therefore (v) W2 has a probability of 1/12. Contrast this with system C, under which W2 has a probability of 1/8 of being selected. So C⋆ and C do have different consequences!

It can be shown that system C⋆ is superior to system C in that C⋆, unlike C, is evidence-sensitive in all cases.

Carnap was the main exponent of the logical approach to probability. As a philosopher of science, one of the main problems that he set himself to solve was the problem of evaluation (Chapter 1). Every proposed hypothesis should be weighed against empirical evidence. That's why scientists design tests (whether direct or indirect). In Chapter 1, we saw how tests work. If a hypothesis fails a test, we can conclude that the hypothesis is false. On the other hand, if it passes a test, the hypothesis need not be true, even though there are now more grounds for believing that it is true. In other words, the probability that the hypothesis is true has increased. The question is: Increased by how much? Carnap attempted to give an answer. Under his system, C⋆, for example, given a hypothesis, *H*, and a piece of evidence, *E*, the probability of the truth of *H* relative to *E* can be calculated as Pr(*H* given *E*). He calls this a **confirmation function**, and it is denoted as "*c*⋆(*H* given *E*)" under system C⋆. (The corresponding function under system C is denoted as "*c*(*H* given *E*).") You can now see how the credibility of hypotheses can be calculated, and this was what we were after in Section 4.6. We will have more on Carnap in Chapter 23.

4.9 OTHER INTERPRETATIONS

The logical interpretation is a great improvement on the classical interpretation. However, it is not without its own defects, even though many of these have been dealt with (satisfactorily or unsatisfactorily).[14] The most serious defect is that there are so many ways of constructing equally reasonable confirmation functions; in fact, Carnap himself pointed out that there are infinitely many of them. Systems C and C⋆ are just two out of this infinitude. Why are there so many equally reasonable confirmation functions? The notion of equiprobability is vague and elusive. Different intuitions on equiprobability imply different confirmation functions. Because there seem to be no objectively rational criteria to choose among these infinite numbers of confirmation functions, the project of the logical approach is not generally thought to be very promising.

A number of other interpretations have been proposed. Among these are the **frequency interpretation** and the **propensity interpretation**. We will have an opportunity to study these in Chapter 12.[15]

From now on, let us take **induction** to cover both inductive inferences and statistical inferences.

---

13. This is one interpretation of the well-known principle of indiscernibles.

14. See Cohen (1989, pp. 120–130).

15. See Salmon (1966), Skyrms (1975), O'Hear (1989), and Cohen (1989) for various other interpretations.

KEY TERMS INTRODUCED IN THIS CHAPTER

statistics

population

sample

universal generalization

statistical generalization

qualitative inductive logic

quantitative inductive logic

frequency distribution table

data

histogram

frequency distribution

mean

parameter

mode

median

standard deviation

descriptive statistics

probability

equiprobable

statistical inference

universal generalization

statistical generalization

variable

correlated

regression analysis

correlation analysis

credibility

principle of indifference

classical interpretation

logical interpretation

system C

prior probability

posterior probability

evidence-insensitive

qualitatively identical

indiscernible

confirmation function

frequency interpretation

propensity interpretation

induction

REFERENCES

On statistics: There are many useful elementary texts on statistics, among which I mention two. Wonnacott and Wonnacott (1982) will do for those who want to make use of statistical results without going into the reasons behind them, whereas Bhattacharyya and Johnson (1977) is a better text if you are not put off by a bit of mathematics.

On interpretations of probability: Copi and Cohen (1994, chap. 14), Kahane (1995, part IV), M. H.

Salmon et al. (1992, pp. 66–89), and Skyrms (1975, chap. VII) provide brief introductions. Salmon (1966, chaps. IV and V) is more detailed and very well written. Cohen (1989, chap. II) is slightly advanced. O'Hear (1989, chap. 7) is more philosophically oriented.

On the application of statistics in science, see Giere (1991, part II).

EXERCISES

1. Measure the pulse rates of 10 people in terms of the number of pulses in 15 seconds. Construct a frequency distribution table and a histogram on the data. Work out its mean, mode, and median. What do these three numbers mean? Explain their significance in common-sensical terms.

2. Measure the heights of 30 books (preferably in millimeters). Record them in a frequency distribution table. Take a random sample of 10 out of these 30 books. Make a frequency distribution table of their heights. Now calculate the

mean, mode, and median of the sample and those of the population. Compare the two sets of results. (The sample of 10 could be chosen according to their colors, or according to their subject matter, but should not be chosen on the basis of their widths or their publishers. Why?)

3. Measure the heights and weights of 10 people. Record your findings both in the form of a table and in the form of a graph. Are the two variables, height and weight, correlated? Is it possible to capture the correlation in terms of a mathematical formula? (If you find it hard to

get the cooperation of 10 people in doing this exercise, you can compare the thickness of books—in terms of number of pages—with their prices instead.)

4. Find a gambling game, other than dice throwing and coin spinning, where the principle of indifference is applicable. Are there any common gambling games where the principle is inapplicable?

5. Let there be a blocks world with two objects, *a* and *b*, which can have one of the three colors, red, yellow, and green. Let statements *e, h, k, f,* and *g* be as follows:

e = *a* is red.
h = All things are red.
k = *b* is red.
f = *a* is green.
g = *b* is green.

6. Calculate Pr(*e*), Pr(*h*), Pr(*h* given *e*), Pr(*k* given *e*), Pr(*f* given *e*), and Pr(*g* given *e*) in terms of both systems C and C★. Comment on your findings.

PART I SUMMARY

These are "tools" chapters, introducing basic concepts and terms that we will be using over and over in the book. In **Chapter 1**, we introduced the concept of a **hypothesis**. A hypothesis is a statement of which we are not sure whether it is true or not. Given a set of empirical data, are there reliable methods to infer plausible hypotheses from these data? If so, what are these methods? This is known as the **problem of discovery**. After the discovery of some plausible hypotheses, the next step is to evaluate them. What are the reasonable methods to be employed here? This is known as the **problem of evaluation**. In Chapter 1, we studied the method of direct and indirect tests. In an indirect test, a logical implication I is deduced from H, the hypothesis to be tested. If I is found to be false, we can conclude that H is false, and if I is found to be true, we can induce that H is now more likely to be true. Logic is the study of correct reasoning and inference, and we can see that logic plays an essential role in both the problem of discovery and the problem of evaluation.

Chapter 2 introduced the basic ideas behind **deductive logic**. An argument is valid if and only if its premises (when true) are strong enough to guarantee (the truth of) the conclusion. Deductive logic studies forms (rules) of valid arguments.

Chapter 3 introduced **inductive logic**. An argument is a reasonable induction if the premises (when true) provide some grounds that increase the credibility of the conclusion. Here we presented the subject in terms of rules and methods, rather than forms as in Chapter 2. The methods introduced are **induction by analogy**, **induction by simple enumeration**, **method of agreement**, **method of difference**, **joint method of agreement and difference**, **method of concomitant variation**, and **method of residues**. These seven methods are mainly used for the discovery of hypotheses. They belong to what I call **qualitative inductive logic**. These methods are rather naive in that they assume that empirical data (data obtained by observation) about the universe would come in neat forms. For example, induction by simple enumeration

works on the assumption that the data are uniform without exceptions: *All* the observed X are Y. If there is even one observed X that is not also a Y, the method does not work. Similarly, for the method of agreement and difference and others to work, the suspected cause must be present (*without exceptions*) whenever the phenomenon is present and must be absent (*without exceptions*) whenever the phenomenon is absent. Such neat correlations are rare in nature. Hence the methods are limited in application.

Every point in space and time is a crossroad of countless causally potent events. They all affect each other, some significantly and others insignificantly. The clever experimenter usually designs "screens" to isolate causal factors that she is interested in. Nevertheless, there are always background "noises." Statistics is the tool that enables us to deal with "noisy" backgrounds and, in general, to extract relevant information out of messy or distorted empirical data, which are the resultants of known and unknown, relevant and irrelevant causal factors. Thus in **Chapter 4** we studied statistics.

Statistics can be called quantitative inductive logic. Statistical generalization is an extension of universal generalization (that is, induction by simple enumeration), and statistical correlation is an extension of the method of concomitant variation. These two types of statistical methods are for the discovery of hypotheses, especially useful in a "noisy" world. In addition, statistics provides measures of probability (credibility) of hypotheses in relation to available empirical data. Thus in addition to traditional inductive methods, statistical inductive methods are now available. These have greatly strengthened the methodology of induction.

Statistics claims to enable us to know about the whole **(population)** based on (usually meager) knowledge about a part **(sample)**. Thus it seems rather magical. It is comparable to palmistry, which claims that a person's life, past and future, can be "read off" her palms. Yet statistics is widely used in fields ranging from everyday economic and political predictions to highly sophisticated space and nuclear technologies. Most people, so far, are satisfied with this kind of magic in that it usually gives good and reliable results. How does this magic work? Why does it work?

The answer lies with the notion of **probability**, which is the fundamental concept underlying statistics. The whole of statistics is built on the concept of probability, yet we do not seem to understand the notion very well, for there are many interpretations of this notion.

Toward the end of Chapter 4, we studied two such interpretations: the **classical interpretation** and the **logical interpretation**. The former can be taken as a special case of the latter. It is tempting for those who take **confirmation theory** as the central problem in the philosophy of science to advocate the logical interpretation. In this view, deductive and inductive logic differ only by a matter of degrees. In deductive logic, one studies the relationships that obtain in order that the premises, if true, raise the probability (credibility) of the conclusion to 100 percent. In inductive logic, one studies the relationships that obtain in order that the premises, if true, raise the probability (credibility) of the conclusion to a percentage that is short of 100 percent. In other words, both kinds of logic study the weights of arguments (independent of whether the premises are actually true or not).

Now, with your newly acquired "tools," you are ready to enter into the philosophy of science proper, beginning with the topic "In Search of Truth" (Part II).

The Search For Truth

After a brief excursion into logic and statistics where we brought out some of the more important tool concepts and tool ideas for the understanding of science, let us return to the twin aims of science: truth and explanation.[1] In this part we will deal with truth, leaving explanation to Part III.

How is truth acquired in science? There are two levels of acquisition: the phenomenal level, which is the primitive level, and the theoretical level, which is the sophisticated level.

At the phenomenal level, the acquisition of truth takes two steps: the discovery of plausible hypotheses **(Chapter 5)** and the evaluation and justification of these hypotheses **(Chapters 6 and 7)**. What we have learned from Part I will be found relevant here. Both qualitative and quantitative inductive methods—that is, statistical reasoning **(Chapters 3 and 4)**—are methods of discovery. The statistical methods of credibility assignment we studied in Section 4.6 are methods of evaluation. And you will find that deductive reasoning **(Chapter 2)** is used throughout **Chapters 5 to 8**.

At the theoretical level, we employ theories both for the justification and for the discovery of plausible hypotheses. This is the advanced way of doing science **(Chapter 8)**.

Chapter 9 is slightly abstract and "philosophical." Though it is not directly about the nature of truth, it is about how the methods for the acquisition of truth earlier discussed can be problematic, and can, in a sense, lead us to quite arbitrary results. In view of this, the nature of truth, as traditionally conceived, is itself questionable.

---

1. Not all philosophers subscribe to truth and explanation as the twin aims of science.

Chapter 5

Empirical Discovery of Plausible Hypotheses

5.1 Introduction

5.2 Mechanical Methods

5.3 Mechanical Methods for the Generation of Plausible Hypotheses

5.4 Limitations of the Simple Inductive Method

5.5 Mechanical Methods for the Generation of Plausible Hypotheses for Specific Problems

5.6 Mechanical Methods for the Evaluation of Hypotheses

5.7 Partially Mechanical Methods

5.1 INTRODUCTION

It is the deep belief of humankind that the universe is governed by natural laws (laws of nature). Unlike laws made by human beings, natural laws are inviolable in that things in the world, without exception, conform. It is this aspect of natural laws that gives order to the world. Hence we have the perpetual cycle of the four seasons, the daily routine of the sun crossing the sky, the sequential phases of the moon, and so on. However, most laws are hidden. You will find few laws are as "obvious to the eye" as "Salt is soluble in water" or "Copper expands when heated." One of the main tasks of science is to discover these *hidden* laws of nature. (It is sometimes said that God hides these laws on purpose to test the ingenuity and perseverance of humankind.)

Some believe that laws can only be discovered through luck or by accident. It was supposed that Newton discovered the law of gravitation when an apple in his garden fell on his head, and that the law of flotation was "revealed" to Archimedes when he was taking his bath. Some would say that the discovery of laws is the domain of the genius. They often cite Einstein as an example. On the other hand, many philosophers, since antiquity, have believed that there are **methods of discovery**—that the ways to discover can be extracted from the great scientists, can be made explicit, can be systematized, and can be both taught and learned. They trust that the methods of science can be shared by ordinary people like you and me. With a bit of diligence we can all become competent scientists provided we possess average intelligence.

Why are methods of discovery important? Imagine that we are in a desert, and naturally it is important for us to find water. Would we blindly dig around hoping that luck will sooner or later bring us water? Oil is a valuable commodity. That's why scientists are at pains to design methods of discovery for the detection of oil. Laws of nature are even more valuable than either water or oil. Hence it is reasonable and understandable that we should strive for methods to discover laws.

As pointed out earlier, however, laws are usually hidden. Indeed they are so well hidden that, even on their discovery, we usually are not sure whether they are genuine laws or not. Take the "law" that light travels in straight lines (Chapter 0). For over 2,000 years we thought that it was a law, but now we are not so sure. According to Einstein's theory of relativity, this "law" is not quite true. Also, there are "facts" other than laws that we would like to discover—for example, the diameter of the earth, the timing of the next solar eclipse, a cure for lung cancer, and so on. So I think it would be more appropriate if we study methods of discovery of *plausible hypotheses* in general, not confining ourselves to methods of discovery of laws.[1]

In the literature, the study of methods of discovery is usually labeled the **problem of discovery**. We ask the following questions, among others:

(a) How can *plausible* and fruitful hypotheses be discovered?

(b) Are there any methods to improve the chances of such discoveries?

(c) Are there any *mechanical methods* that will inevitably lead to such discoveries?

Let's start with the third question.[2]

5.2 MECHANICAL METHODS

What does 'mechanical method' mean? A (fully) **mechanical method** consists of a finite sequence of operations, each of which is easy to perform. We can say that the operations are so clear, precise, and simple that no intelligence is required to perform each of them. Indeed every one of the operations can be handled by a machine. Since each operation can be mechanically handled, it is obvious that the full sequence of operations can be mechanized—that is, the task as a whole can be done mechanically. In a word, if a machine is programmed to perform each of these operations in sequential steps, then at the push of a button, so to speak, the job will be done after so many steps.[3]

Even though each operation is simple and clear to perform, the ultimate product of the sequence of operations can be impressive. A cooking recipe is a good example. Each step in the recipe is usually simple and straightforward, yet the final product could be something beyond our wildest imagination. Children learn to multiply (employing the multiplication table) and to divide mechanically. At first, they can only multiply one-digit figures. Then they extend their skills to two digits, then to three digits, and eventually they realize that in fact the method they have learned can be applied to figures of any number of digits.

Mechanical methods are sometimes presented as **algorithms**. The first-ever algorithm is probably Euclid's algorithm for the discovery of the greatest

---

1. Some philosophers prefer to employ the term 'invention' rather than 'discovery,' arguing that hypotheses are really free *inventions* of the mind, and that they are being employed by us to understand the world. For them, laws of nature should not be considered written in the world for us to discover. I have great sympathy with this point of view. You will appreciate it more when you have done topics such as instrumentalism, conventionalism, and constructivism later. However, at this early stage I think I should stick to the traditional employment of the term 'discovery.'

2. In this chapter, we only deal with empirical discoveries—discoveries based on information collected through our five senses. We will deal with other methods of discovery later in the book.

3. Some of the steps may have to be repeated, forming what are known as loops.

common factor (GCF) of two numbers.[4] To find the GCF of two whole numbers, A_0 and B_0 (where B_0 is greater than A_0), the algorithm specifies that we divide B_0 by A_0. Let the remainder be B_1. Then divide A_0 by B_1 with remainder A_1. In turn, divide B_1 by A_1, leaving B_2 as the remainder, and so on. In general, we always divide B_n by A_n, and divide A_n by B_{n+1}. The divisor that leaves no remainder is the GCF of the two original numbers.[5]

The beauty of mechanical methods is that anyone can employ them to gain the desired results. For example, one need not be a great mathematician to find the GCF of two numbers. All one needs to do is to follow those rules and steps laid down by Euclid. So, if there are mechanical methods of scientific discovery, then science should be both sure and simple. We need not rely on the ingenuity of great scientists to provide us with good working hypotheses. The rules and steps of those mechanical methods should eventually yield us results comparable to those of Newton or Einstein. Such are the prospects of mechanical methods. They may give us "pushbutton" science![6]

5.3 MECHANICAL METHODS FOR THE GENERATION OF PLAUSIBLE HYPOTHESES

Here is a mechanical method for the discovery of plausible hypotheses, which I'll call the **simple inductive method (SIM)**. It consists of the following steps:

(a) Choose an object in your field of vision.

(b) Classify it in accordance with the property terms[7] as listed in the *Oxford Dictionary*—for example, 'red,' 'round,' 'happy,' 'hot'—in alphabetical order.

(c) Repeat steps (a) and (b) for another object.

(d) Enter the results of the classification in a table.

(e) When the number of instances collected in your table reaches 100,000, make generalizations. These generalizations are your hypotheses.

A resulting table of classification may look like this:

Inst	A	B	C	D	E
1	0	1	0	1	0
2	1	0	1	1	1
3	0	1	1	1	0
4	1	0	0	0	1
5	0	1	0	1	0
6	1	1	1	1	0
7	0	0	1	1	1
8	0	1	0	1	0

The first column represents the instances encountered in step (a). Here we list only the first eight instances. The letters A, B, C, and so on stand for property terms in alphabetical order as listed in the *Oxford Dictionary*. The numeral 1 occurring under a property term signifies that the instance of that row has that property, whereas the numeral 0 indicates the lack of such. For example, instance 2 has property A but not property B. The table is the result of repeating steps (a) to (d) eight times. The generalization step (e) makes use of what we called induction by simple enumeration in Chapter 3, which is also known as universal generalization: If two property terms, X and Y, are such that whenever X has a

---

4. This algorithm was invented by Euclid (fl. 300 B.C.).

5. Here is an example: What is the GCF of 4,641 and 24,255? Try to find it by *your own* method first. Then try out Euclid's algorithm. You would find that $A_0 = 4,641$, $B_0 = 24,255$; $A_1 = 441$, $B_1 = 1,050$; $A_2 = 105$, $B_2 = 168$; $A_3 = 42$, $B_3 = 63$; and $A_4 = 0$, $B_4 = 21$. Hence the required GCF is 21. Now see if you can find a number bigger than 21 such that it divides both of the original numbers A_0 and B_0. I don't think you can.

6. The great philosopher Francis Bacon (1561–1626) had visions not too different from these. With the advent of artificial intelligence, the prospect of "mechanical" science becomes more realistic.

7. You can take property terms more or less as adjectives.

1, *Y* also has a 1 for the same instance, then conclude "All *X* are *Y*." It can be seen that "All *B* are *D*" and "All *C* are *D*" can both be concluded from the table. Further, if we take *X* and *Y* as covering not only property terms but also their negations,[8] then "All *E* are non-*B*" can be inferred as well.[9]

This method is tedious and lengthy, because we first have to classify each instance by checking through all the property terms in the dictionary, and second, step (e) involves the checking of each pair of property terms and their negations for each of the instances to discover any actual correlations. But then the computer can easily handle all these. The nice thing with this method is that it is fully mechanical.

It might be objected, however, that step (a) is not really mechanical, because choice always requires intelligent deliberations. This is certainly true in general. However, in the present case, we can always "mechanize" the step by stipulating "narrowly" how the choice is to be made—for example, "choose the object that first catches your attention." Step (e) is a relatively complex step, which, nevertheless, is mechanical. In the not-too-distant future, an artificial intelligence with adequate eyesight and categories of classification can probably be programmed to use this method with great efficiency.

Naive as it seems, SIM has been widely used by us, and not without results. I conjecture that the following commonsensical beliefs were obtained by SIM:

(1) Wood floats in water.

(2) Ice melts when it is heated.

(3) Lions are carnivorous.

Our ancestors, through repeated observations and classifications (not in terms of the *Oxford Dictionary*, but in terms of their own vocabulary), came to these conclusions. I further suggest that animals such as cats and dogs also employ SIM. It seems to me that SIM is the first and most elementary of the scientific methods that have been employed consciously or unconsciously throughout human history and perhaps among animals as well. SIM results in a large collection of commonsense knowledge and a large number of rules of thumb.

5.4 LIMITATIONS OF THE SIMPLE INDUCTIVE METHOD

Successful as it is in providing science with basic generalizations, SIM is, however, quite limited. First, it can be seen to be a "blind search" method. The investigator's choice of objects for investigation and classification is undirected and random. Whatever she chances to see will be recorded and classified. Undirected search is highly inefficient. Suppose we are attempting to find the cause(s) of lung cancer. SIM may have us classifying pebbles on the beach instead of studying lungs, smoking, radiation, and so on, simply because the investigator happens to be at a beach. When plausible hypotheses are sought as solutions to specific requests, SIM is helpless. But science is mostly required to solve specific problems, such as: Why does grape sugar turn into wine when yeast is added? (This was Pasteur's concern.) Why do apples and other things fall downward? (Recall Newton.) What is the cure for the common cold? What causes people to steal? What brings about (political) revolutions? To solve such specific problems, we can't rely on the random collection of empirical data. We must operate on some working hypothesis to guide our study and data collection. This is the main shortcoming of SIM. The reason why (1), (2), (3), and others (last section) have been successfully discovered, in spite of this shortcoming, is simply due to the combined effort of hundreds of generations of our ancestors.

The effectiveness of SIM also depends on the list of "property terms" available. To be more precise, we use terms other than property terms to

---

8. For example, the negation of property term *A* is non-*A*.

9. According to the table, whenever *E* is 1, *B* is 0. This means the same as "whenever *E* is 1, non-*B* is 1." Hence the generalization: All *E* are non-*B*.

classify. We classify things in terms of 'man,' 'woman,' 'table,' 'chair,' and so on. These are strictly speaking not property terms. We also use verbs to classify—for example, 'can swim,' 'will die,' and so on. Relations such as 'love' are also used to classify. Philosophers, therefore, employ the term 'predicate' to cover all these varieties. It is obvious that the availability of predicates is a precondition to generalization. For example, if, in our example in Section 5.3, predicate *B* is not available, then we cannot possibly have arrived at the generalizations "All *B* are *D*" and "All *E* are non-*B*."

SIM does not provide us with a mechanism for the generation of new terms. Yet new terms (novel concepts, to be more technical) are important in science. They play an essential role in the advancement of science. Think of terms like 'electron,' 'atom,' 'wavelength,' 'gene,' and 'mammal.' All of these were invented in the course of scientific investigations. And what important roles they have played and will play in science! SIM is limited to the correlation of existing predicates. With SIM, science can only crawl, whereas we would like to see science leap and even fly. The notion of gravitation is an outstanding example. Its invention by Newton and others took 17th-century science to a new stage. Another idea that had a comparable effect in the field of chemistry is Dalton's notion of the atom. It revolutionized the chemistry of the 18th century. No application of SIM could bring about these novel concepts. You will find in Chapter 8 that all high-level theories involve the use of novel concepts.[10] Hence, for the advancement of science, we require methods other than SIM.

Let's return to question (c) raised in Section 5.1: Are there any mechanical methods that have a good chance of leading to the discovery of plausible hypotheses? The answer is yes—there is at least one such method (SIM). However, we must not be too optimistic about this prospect because, as we saw earlier, SIM is highly inefficient. Employing it, we can find ourselves recording and classifying instances in a totally unproductive area; it is almost useless in the search for answers to specific problems; moreover, it cannot generate novel concepts, which are so vital for the advancement of science. Let's see if there are superior methods of discovery.

5.5 MECHANICAL METHODS FOR THE GENERATION OF PLAUSIBLE HYPOTHESES FOR SPECIFIC PROBLEMS

If SIM is limited, why not employ Mill's five methods of induction as well? In Chapter 3, we saw how these methods can be used for the discovery of causal relationships. They should be employable in dealing with specific problems such as "What causes the common cold?" Indeed both Bacon and Mill saw the superiority of these methods over SIM, so much so that they thought these five methods plus induction by simple enumeration were sufficient for the practice of science!

In reality, however, these methods are themselves limited. We saw in Chapter 4 how they were superseded by statistical methods. In Chapters 8 and 15, we will study how theoretical science works, as exemplified by Newton's physics and Dalton's atomic chemistry. In comparison with the method of theories, Mill's methods will look simplistic.

Anyway, unlike SIM, Mill's methods are only *partially* mechanical. The method of agreement (MA), for example, requires the scientist to enumerate a number of antecedent circumstances, from which the one that agrees with the phenomenon is taken as the cause. Obviously, we cannot enumerate *all* the circumstances. We must make a selection. In the case of the students getting sick, the doctor enumerated the foods they ate just before they became ill. In doing so, she made several judgments. She judged that the sickness was

---

10. Later, in Section 17.6, we will find that novel concepts do not come about simply as individual terms. They are linked to other concepts (novel and existing) through a network of laws, forming what are known as theories. It is these laws and theories that give "life" to the novel concepts.

food-related (not caused by the weather, or by class tests, or by people performing raindances 10,000 kilometers away, or by what happened on the moon three days ago, and so on). Further she conjectured that only foods eaten *recently* were relevant. Such judgments require intelligence and knowledge. None of the rules of MA specify a mechanical choice of antecedent circumstances. However, once a choice of *relevant* circumstances is made, the table of agreement can be completed mechanically. Hence MA is highly mechanical, though not fully so. Similarly, statistical methods (Chapter 4) are only partially mechanical.

In summary, we have one fully mechanical method of discovery (which is, however, both inefficient and limited in application) and a number of partially mechanical methods (which are more powerful but still limited).

5.6 MECHANICAL METHODS FOR THE EVALUATION OF HYPOTHESES

After their discovery, hypotheses should be evaluated for their credibility. Thus, parallel to the problem of discovery we are faced with the **problem of evaluation (justification)**, where the following questions, among others, are asked:

(a) How can hypotheses be evaluated (justified)?

(b) Are there any methods that can be used to evaluate hypotheses?

(c) Are any of these methods mechanical in nature?

In Chapter 1, we saw how hypotheses can be tested directly or indirectly. The logic of indirect test is as follows. Let H be the given hypothesis for testing. (a) An implication I is deduced from H, and (b) I is then compared with the world (instead of H). If I turns out to be true, we can claim that H is plausibly true. To be more accurate, the probability (credibility) of H is increased by the truth of I. This method of testing is often called the **hypothetico–deductive method (HDM)**. Is HDM a (fully) mechanical method of assessment? In other words, can steps (a) and (b) be carried out mechanically? The answer is unfortunately no: neither step can be carried out mechanically.[11]

For any hypothesis (statement), an indefinite number of implications can be drawn. We certainly cannot and should not try to deduce all the possible implications and test each of them. Nor should we simply choose a number of them at random. Some implications are more significant than others. Some are easier and more economical to handle than others. For example, to test whether a figure F (about one square kilometer in area) is a square or not, we can make use of any one of the following implications: (i) F has four sides, (ii) all the sides are equal, (iii) F has four angles, (iv) at least one of the angles is a right angle, (v) all four angles are right angles, (vi) the diagonals are equal, (vii) the diagonals intersect at right angles, and (viii) if it takes one unit of time to walk the distance of one of the sides, it will take about 1.4 units of time to cover one of the diagonals. You can be assured that these eight are not the only possible implications. Which of these should be chosen for testing? Can this choice be made mechanically? Can these eight implications be generated mechanically? Note that the example in question is only a very simple hypothesis. Think of more complicated ones such as "This crown is made of pure gold."[12]

On the other hand, often the difficulty lies not with having to choose from among a large number of possible implications for testing. It lies with the difficulty of obtaining any. I'll give an example: According to the theory of general relativity, light bends when it travels close to matter. It is not at all

---

11. In fact, there is a third step in the process of evaluation: Ideally, the increase in probability of H by the truth of I should be calculable. However, except in relatively simple cases such as those that can be handled by ordinary statistics, mathematical functions for such calculations do not exist (Chapter 4).

12. Archimedes was asked by his king to test this very hypothesis.

simple to design an experiment to test this hypothesis, because the amount of deviation is undetectably small unless the mass of the nearby matter is immense. The sun is in fact massive enough for this purpose but, unfortunately, it is normally too bright to allow any observation of the bending of light rays in its vicinity. In 1919, however, Arthur Eddington reasoned that during a total solar eclipse, the glare of the sun would be blacked out by the moon, and therefore if light rays are indeed bent by the sun, certain stars behind the sun's disk should be observable. This is a testable implication. The experiment was carried out, and, to the world's astonishment, he did see stars behind the sun. The general theory of relativity was thus empirically confirmed.[13] Experimental scientists with such ingenuity are rare. Galileo was another one of them. To test his theory of free fall, he designed the inclined plane to slow down the rapid motions of falling objects so as to make them measurable. He has since been hailed as the father of empirical science.

We can now see why step (a), the deduction of testable implication from the hypothesis, is not mechanical. Indeed, step (b), in most of the ordinary cases, cannot be made mechanical either. In Chapter 22, which discusses the theoretical nature of observation, we will find that observation, unlike the taking of photographs, is far from being mechanical. So it seems that there are no mechanical methods of evaluation of hypotheses. Perhaps common sense is right: science requires effort and ingenuity. Would the advance of artificial intelligence change the situation? (See Chapter 32.)

5.7 PARTIALLY MECHANICAL METHODS

Since the philosopher's stone does not seem to exist, are there any worthwhile "partial stones" then?

In the old days, furniture, garments, shoes, and indeed most things were made by hand. The idea of mechanization is, first of all, to save labor. Second, mechanization can save costs, increase production speed, and guarantee quality. Hence the 19th-century industrial revolution saw the beginning of mechanization of most industries. However, even now, there are few *fully* mechanized productions. (Otherwise there would be even more unemployment.) Human intelligence is still required for many types of work, and human interventions and directions are required at certain crucial "junctions." Yet these partially mechanized industries have brought enormous wealth and prosperity to the human race. So can't we have a *partially* mechanized science, which will bring in similarly impressive results?

There are pessimists and there are optimists on this issue. The pessimists think that we should not expect to be able to secure partially mechanized methods significantly more sophisticated than Mill's five methods of induction. The statistical inferences we studied in Chapter 4 are indeed partially mechanical methods, but then they are at the same level of sophistication as Mill's methods. Can there be mechanical methods, partial or full, for the production of high-level theories such as the chemical atomic theory, Newton's theory of mechanics, and Darwin's theory of evolution? For the pessimists, the answer is a definite no! There are neither mechanical methods of discovery of these theories, nor any mechanical methods of evaluation of such theories, nor even partially mechanical ones.

The optimists, on the other hand, think that partial mechanization can go far beyond both statistical inferences and Mill's methods. For them there are rules—and there must be rules—for both discovery and evaluation. After all, science is a profession that can be learned, and whatever can be learned is governed by rules, ranging from talking to driving. For example, the making of music was, for our ancient ancestors, an art belonging only to the very gifted. Now music is quite a (though not fully) mechanized discipline, both in its production through mechanical instruments such as the piano

---

13. See Section 1.9 for the meaning of 'confirm.'

and in its composition through well-worked-out rules and theories. With a cookbook, an ordinary mortal can make reasonable dishes simply by following instructions. It is certainly true that full mechanization is a long way off in both fields. Yet for the optimists, the preparation of a gourmet dish at the press of a button should be as realizable as the production of Coca-Cola down a factory assembly line, and computer composition of reasonable music should be just around the corner. Similarly a robotic Newton or Einstein should not be out of the question. The optimists think that science can be and will be progressively mechanized through the gradual uncovering of rules of discovery and evaluation. For instance, appropriate rules for the selection of relevant antecedent circumstances in the use of the Method of Agreement will, sooner or later, be found, and heuristics and strategies for the discovery of significant test implications for hypotheses should not elude us much longer.

Indeed, the advance of artificial intelligence has given much hope to the optimists. After all, the human brain is a sort of computer. Its ingenuity and creativity should, in theory, be reducible to computation. Don't we now have computer chess-playing programs that can beat masters? Isn't it that the computer can now reason in terms of the rules of various logics? It seems that both intelligence and creativity are mechanizable.

We will return to this interesting and hotly debatable subject in Chapter 32, where we will study the implications of artificial intelligence for the philosophy of science. For now, let us move on to the topic of evaluating hypotheses.

KEY TERMS INTRODUCED IN THIS CHAPTER

method of discovery

problem of discovery

mechanical method

algorithm

simple inductive method

problem of evaluation (justification)

hypothetico-deductive method (HDM)

REFERENCES

Hempel (1966, chaps. 2–4) provides a solid introduction to the subject, and Kourany (1987, part 3) presents a collection of original papers by some of the more influential philosophers with a helpful introduction.

Hempel (1966, sec. 2.3) presents a good introduction. Brody and Grandy (1989, pp. 398–429) provides more advanced analyses.

EXERCISES

1. Find the GCF of 301 and 413, using Euclid's algorithm.

2. Write out an algorithm for the method of agreement (that is, breaking the method down into small easy-to-carry-out steps).

3. Give a commonsense general belief that is probably based on the simple inductive method.

4. Imagine that in the last few days your cat, instead of curling up on the sofa after her evening meal, lay down underneath your bed instead. Work out how the method of agreement and difference could solve this "mystery." Discuss how mechanizable the method of agreement and difference is with respect to this example.

5. Why is it not possible for the hypothesis that water is made up of H_2O molecules to be discovered through one or more of Mill's methods?

6. Attempt to work out two test implications for each of the following three hypotheses. Then discuss whether there are any mechanical methods (full or partial) for the discovery of reasonable, technologically possible, and financially manageable test implications for hypotheses in general. The three hypotheses are: (i) John is heavier than Peter, (ii) New York is further away from Los Angeles than Chicago, and (iii) There is a huge creature (known as the Loch Ness Monster) living at the bottom of the lake Loch Ness.

7. Could any of the hypotheses in Chapter 0 be discovered by mechanical methods?

Chapter 6

Empirical Evaluation I: Indirect Tests and Auxiliary Hypotheses

6.1 Introduction

6.2 Singular Versus Universal Hypotheses

6.3 Conditional Test Implications

6.4 Auxiliary Hypotheses

6.5 Direct Versus Indirect Tests

6.1 INTRODUCTION

Given that a certain hypothesis has been discovered (proposed), how can it be empirically evaluated? In Chapter 1, we introduced the notion of an indirect test. Here we investigate the notion further. We will see that auxiliary hypotheses play an important role in the logic of indirect tests.

6.2 SINGULAR VERSUS UNIVERSAL HYPOTHESES

Statements can be roughly classified into two types: singular and universal.[1] Singular statements are about particular objects, things, or events. Thus the following are all singular:

(1) "The sun is made of gases."

(2) "Newton loved horses."

(3) "If this piece of ice is heated, it will melt."

(4) "All people in New Zealand love horses."

---

1. There are exceptions to this classification—for example, existential statements such as "There are oxygen atoms."

(5) "Seventy percent of all people in New Zeal-
and love horses."

(6) "The sun and the moon are both round."

You can see that most of them are about one particular object. Statement (6), however, is about two
particular objects. The singularity of statement (4)
does not come from 'people.' It comes from the
particular object, New Zealand. It can be seen
that some of the statements are true, while others
are false.

In contrast, universal statements are about
things, objects, or events in general (unrestricted
in space and time). Thus the following are
universal:

(7) "All stars are made of gases."

(8) "Humans love horses."

(9) "If a piece of ice is heated, it will melt."

(10) "All people anywhere in the world love
horses."

(11) "Seventy percent of all people love
horses."

(12) "All celestial objects are round."

A useful rule of thumb for the distinction between
singular and universal statements is that singular
statements in general contain proper names, or
expressions equivalent to proper names, whereas
universal statements do not.[2]

Since hypotheses are statements, they are also
classifiable into two types: singular and universal.
Universal hypotheses dominate the pure sciences,
such as physics, chemistry, and biology, whereas
singular hypotheses are common in the applied
sciences, such as earth science and astronomy.
Universal hypotheses are about the nature of
things in accordance with their kinds, whereas
singular hypotheses are about properties and relationships of things located in particular places and
times. Either type has its own roles to play in
science.

6.3 CONDITIONAL TEST IMPLICATIONS

Most test implications derived from hypotheses are
conditional in form, irrespective of whether the
hypotheses are universal or singular. Take the
hypothesis "All swans are white." You cannot
infer from it that John is white. However, you
can say that *if* John is a swan, then John is white.
In other words, the following is valid.

(13) $\dfrac{\text{All swans are white.}}{\text{If John is a swan, John is white.}}$

The next one is also a valid deduction. Its
premise is, however, a singular hypothesis.

(14) $\dfrac{\text{It is raining outside.}}{\text{If you should step outside, you would get wet.}}$

Both (13) and (14) are of the following logical
form:

(15) $\dfrac{H}{\text{If } C, \text{ then } E.}$

The implication (denoted by the symbol I in
Chapter 1) has the form: "If C, then E." We call
it a **conditional statement**, with C as the condition part such that, if C is realized, then E would be
the case. A test based on such an implication would
consist of the implementation of C, and the waiting
for E to occur. If E does occur, then we say that
the test has confirmed the hypothesis. If it doesn't,
the hypothesis is said to have been refuted. Thus if
you should step outside and subsequently get wet, it
would be reasonable to conclude that it is raining
outside. On the other hand, if you do not get wet,
the hypothesis should be rejected.

Here is a more "mature" example:

(16) $\dfrac{\text{Salt is soluble in water.}}{\begin{array}{l}\text{If this is salt, and that is water, and this is}\\ \text{placed into that, then this will disappear}\\ \text{in that.}\end{array}}$

---

2. Usually universal statements are of the form: "All X are Y" where both X and Y are what philosophers call 'purely qualitative
terms.'

This is a common implication people would draw. It has the following logical form:

$$(17) \quad \frac{H}{\text{If } C_1, C_2, \text{ and } C_3, \text{ then } E.}$$

We can see that there can be more than one condition to fulfill before the expected outcome will occur.

To carry out a test of the form "If C, then E," one is required to realize condition C and ascertain whether E does occur as predicted. Usually E is a sort of happening, an event, being brought about by C.[3] Hence we can take C as designating the cause(s), and E the effect.

In case (16), the conditions C_1, C_2, and C_3 are easily realizable. Our technology is quite adequate to enable us to put some salt into some water. Hence we can call the condition part of the conclusion of (16) a set of **technologically realizable conditions** and the test implication a **technologically realizable test implication**. However, not all hypotheses have such implications. Consider the following example:

(18) Showers in late afternoon are always followed by the appearance of a rainbow in the east.

Showers cannot be improvised at will, despite all the technology at our disposal. To test this hypothesis, we would have to wait for showers to occur in late afternoon on a number of days. I doubt if (18) has any technologically realizable test implications. In science, securing technologically realizable test implications for certain hypotheses can prove very challenging. An example is the hypothesis that light travels faster in water than in air (Chapter 0).

6.4 AUXILIARY HYPOTHESES

(A) It is well known that Christopher Columbus was convinced that the earth is round. He observed that when a ship sails away toward the horizon, the masthead of the ship remains in sight from the shore long after the hull of the ship has disappeared under the horizon. This he claimed demonstrates the truth of the hypothesis. The argument involved is as follows:

$$(19) \quad \frac{\text{The earth is round.}}{\begin{array}{l}\text{If a ship should sail away over the hori-}\\ \text{zon, then its hull will disappear below the}\\ \text{horizon before the masthead does.}\end{array}}$$

However, as it stands, the argument is invalid. To make it valid, we have to add extra premises such as "Light travels in straight lines." For instance, if the light from the ship should curve with the earth's surface as it travels toward the observer on the shore, neither the hull nor the masthead would disappear from sight under the horizon (Figure 6.1).

"The earth is round" is said to be the **main hypothesis** (that is, the hypothesis to be tested). "Light travels in straight lines" is an **auxiliary hypothesis**. Together, they imply the test implication, "If a ship should sail away over the horizon, then its hull will disappear below the horizon before the masthead does." Most test implications require auxiliary hypotheses. Often such auxiliary hypotheses are omitted because the scientific world takes them for granted as too obvious and too mundane to warrant explicit mention. Thus a majority of the arguments used for the derivation of test implications are what logicians would call **enthymemes** (arguments with hidden premises). Usually such practices are quite acceptable, and, for pragmatic purposes, to be encouraged.

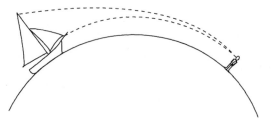

FIGURE 6.1

---

3. The case of the white swan is an exception.

However, there are occasions when such practices could mislead the scientist. In Chapter 1, we pointed out that if the test implication is found to be false then, by modus tollens, we can conclude that the hypothesis is false. For instance, if ships did not disappear under the horizon gradually (first the lower part, then the upper part), scientists who are unaware of the existence of the auxiliary hypothesis would conclude that the earth is not round. The proper conclusion, however, should have been that *either* the earth is not round, *or* light does not travel in straight lines, *or* both. It is well known in logic that if the conclusion turns out to be false, one can only conclude that *at least one* of the premises is false. The auxiliary hypothesis may prove false just as easily as the main hypothesis. On the other hand, a stubborn scientist, when faced with a falsified test implication, can always shift the blame to the auxiliary hypothesis, and thus keep his main hypothesis intact. This strategy was much discussed by Pierre Duhem (1861–1916) (Chapter 9) and Karl Popper (Chapter 7).

(B) Here's another example of a (hidden) auxiliary hypothesis. Our present theory of the solar system came from Nicolaus Copernicus (1473–1543). It is a heliocentric theory because the sun is taken to be the center of the universe, in contrast to the geocentric system of Ptolemy (circa 100–178), with the earth taken as the center of the universe.[4] Copernicus's system is also said to be heliostatic, because the sun is said to be stationary, whereas Ptolemy's system is geostatic. When Copernicus first proposed his theory in the 16th century, there was a lot of opposition to it. One main objection was that if the earth does move around the sun, the apparent position of the fixed stars with respect to the sun should change as the earth moves. The maximum amount of change we can expect could be obtained by measuring the angular position of the star relative to the sun at half-year intervals. This expected angular change was known as the annual parallax of the star. But no such parallax was ever observed (Figure 6.2).

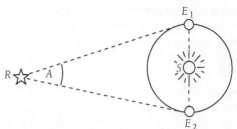

FIGURE 6.2

S stands for the sun. E_1 and E_2 are two positions of the earth separated by six months. R is a chosen star. Angle E_1RE_2 is the annual parallax and should be measurable by subtracting the angles SE_1R and SE_2R from 180°. (Note that some authors take only half of E_1RE_2 as the parallax.)

Copernicus explained away the absence of parallax by supposing that the stars are at a great distance from us, a distance far greater than the distance of the sun from the earth. When the distance is sufficiently great, the expected parallax would be too small for detection.

We can recast Copernicus's defense of the heliocentric theory as follows, employing the notion of test implication.

(20) The earth moves around the sun.

If a star's position with respect to the sun is measured at a half-year interval, an angle known as the annual parallax of the star would be observable.

Copernicus pointed out that (to be valid) this inference is assuming the hidden premise that the distance of the star from us is not immensely great when compared to the distance of the sun from the earth. He challenged this hidden premise, suggesting that it is in fact false. In other words, according to Copernicus, the test implication is not deducible from the main hypothesis by itself. At least one auxiliary hypothesis is necessary for the deduction.[5] When the test implication does not match with reality, it could be due to a faulty auxiliary hypothesis. If so, the main hypothesis can be retained.

---

4. 'Helio' refers to the sun, whereas 'geo' refers to the earth.

5. In fact, there is at least another hidden premise—that light travels in straight lines.

It was difficult to assess Copernicus's defense. In the 16th century, the available astronomical instruments were crude and there were no telescopes. Was Copernicus hiding behind an excuse? After all, the distance of the stars from the earth can be made indefinitely great as required to account for the non-observability of the parallax. Defenses that are mere excuses are said to be *ad hoc*. Intuitively, ad hoc defenses should not be admissible in science. However, we should not rely on intuition, which can be faulty. We should have an objective criterion of ad hocness. This we will study in detail in Chapter 7.[6]

(C) There was another serious objection to Copernicus's theory. According to him, the earth not only moves around the sun once a year, it also spins on its own axis once a day. If the earth does spin in this way, a stone dropped from a tower should land somewhere west of its foot, because as the stone leaves the top of the tower and travels downward, the earth would have moved a distance toward the east. The faster the earth moves, the greater the distance by which the stone is left behind.[7] But we all know from our own experience that no such "westward displacement" has ever been observed. (See for yourself by dropping a stone from your window. Of course you should make sure that no one is passing by below!) This argument, by the way, was first raised by Aristotle against any "moving earth" hypothesis.

However, neither Copernicus nor the great astronomer Galileo (1564–1642) accepted this argument. Copernicus claimed that the air surrounding the earth is somehow "linked" to the earth so that stones falling from a tower are being carried along with the earth by the air, instead of being left behind in the west. Galileo was more sophisticated but more difficult to comprehend. He reckoned that stones and indeed any other objects are "inert." It is obvious that a stone shares the motion of the earth if it is held at the top of a tower. Galileo, however, claimed that due to its inertness, the stone still shares this same motion even after it has started falling away from the top of the tower.[8] In other words, both Copernicus and Galileo thought that the test implication that a falling stone from a tower should land somewhere west of the tower presupposes an auxiliary hypothesis that is in fact not true. This hypothesis is that the motion of the earth shared by an object would not be wholly or partially shared by it, once the object is falling freely.

(D) Often when the results of an experiment are not what is expected, the scientist blames the accuracy or reliability of the instruments used. This is another case of rejecting an auxiliary hypothesis instead of accepting the falsification of the main hypothesis. The expected would occur only if the instruments are sound. In other words, the soundness of the instruments is also a hidden premise for the deduction of the conclusion. Hence it could always take the blame when things go wrong. In Chapter 7, we will examine such rejections and try to discover some reasonable and practical criteria for the apportionment of blame. When should an auxiliary hypothesis be blamed instead of the main hypothesis?

So the full schema for the derivation of test implications is as follows:

(21)

Main hypothesis:	H
Auxiliary hypotheses:	$A_1, A_2, ..., A_n$
Test implication:	If C, then E.

This form, of course, is equivalent to the following:

(22)

Main hypothesis:	H
Auxiliary hypotheses:	$A_1, A_2, ..., A_n$
	C
Test implication:	E

---

6. Stellar parallax of a minute order was finally observed in certain stars in the 19th century.

7. The earth spins from the west to the east. That's why, to us, the sun rises in the east. The circumference of the earth is roughly 24,000 miles, and it revolves once every 24 hours. Hence the surface of the earth moves at roughly the speed of 1,000 miles an hour from west to east at the equator, which is more than a quarter of a mile in a second. This means that if a stone dropped from a tower takes one second to reach the ground, it should land about one quarter of a mile to the west of the foot of the tower.

8. Newton later developed this idea of inertness, resulting in his famous first law of motion.

To put it in a more general form, we have:

Main hypothesis: H
Auxiliary hypotheses: $A_1, A_2, ..., A_n$
(23) $C_1, C_2, ..., C_m$
_____
Test implication: E

In other words, we can take the test conditions, $C_1, C_2, ..., C_m$, as additional auxiliary hypotheses so that the test implication becomes a straightforward, unconditional statement. Since E is to be compared to the world, the simpler E is, the better. E may, for example, be the simple statement that the color of the flame is yellow (in testing for the presence of sodium), or that the pointer points at a certain mark on a scale, say the seventh mark (meter reading—for example, voltmeter, thermometer), or that event A occurs before event B (Galileo's tower experiment to test whether heavier objects fall faster than lighter objects). These E's are all simple in the sense that a normal observer can easily and quickly decide whether they are true. In addition to being simple, E should be **intersubjectively decidable**. By this, I mean that it should be such that any two normal observers should come up with the same answer (yes or no) when they are asked to judge whether E has actually occurred or not. So, though each observer's judgment is subjective, intersubjectiveness seems to be the closest one can get to the objectivity of empirical evidence.

You can see that the art of testing rests on the ingenuity of the experimenter to be able to reduce a complex and often abstract hypothesis (such as that space is curved) to a simple E, through the use of auxiliary hypotheses. But then, when E does not correspond to reality, it is often difficult to ascertain whether the main hypothesis or one or more of the auxiliary hypotheses is at fault, especially when a large number of auxiliary hypotheses exist.

6.5 DIRECT VERSUS INDIRECT TESTS

In Chapter 1, we defined an indirect test as a test where the hypothesis is compared with reality through the use of instruments. We can now refine this idea. We can take the auxiliary hypotheses necessary for the deduction of the test implication E as specifying the physical circumstances and instrumental setups for the realization of the outcome E. We would find that whenever instruments are used, whether they be thermometers, telescopes, pieces of wire, or chemical solutions, auxiliary hypotheses are implicitly assumed. Conversely, whenever auxiliary hypotheses are employed for the deduction of the test implication E, some sort of physical instruments will be used. These physical instruments need not be instruments in the conventional sense, such as thermometers. They can be sailing ships, as in the case of the indirect test on the roundness of the earth. They can be stars, as in the case of using stellar parallax to test the annual revolution of the earth around the sun. They can be stones dropped from a tower, as in the tower experiment of Galileo.

So a more generalized definition of indirect test would be: An **indirect test** of a hypothesis H is one based on a test implication (that is, logical consequence), E, derived from H with the help of at least one auxiliary hypothesis, E being an unconditional statement that can be empirically compared with reality.[9]

Let's apply this definition to the testing of the hypothesis H, "S is a square." We might draw the test implication I, "Angle A (which is one of the angles of S) is a right angle." This follows from H without the necessity of any auxiliary hypotheses.[10] Hence if we should empirically evaluate I, the test would, by our present definition, be a **direct test**. However, I is *not* a statement that can

_____

9. Since the auxiliary hypotheses play an instrumental role, they can be called instrumental hypotheses.

10. Let's ignore the sophisticated point that I follows only if we assume the auxiliary hypothesis that space is Euclidean rather than non-Euclidean.

be directly assessed with our senses. We need to employ instruments such as protractors for the measurement of angles. In other words, we *do* need auxiliary hypotheses (which are statements about protractors or such) to deduce some logical consequence such as "Lines *M* and *N* on the protractor would fall along the two sides of angle *A*, one on each side." You can now see why most tests are indirect tests.

To see if a hypothesis is true or not, the fundamental idea is to compare it with the world. However, it is usually impossible to do so directly. Nature is like a cunning criminal who always cleverly covers up misdeeds. The scientist can be likened to an interrogator, who has to design equally clever questions to confront the suspect so as to extract the truth. By borrowing the correct auxiliary hypotheses (instruments), the scientist reasons out, using deductive logic (Chapter 2), some observable consequences that are easy to detect. If these consequences do not materialize, the scientist then claims that the hypothesis has been refuted. On the other hand, if the consequences do materialize, the scientist can then claim that the hypothesis is confirmed (Section 1.9). That is, the new evidence has now given the hypothesis more credibility.

However, there are two problems. First, for most cases, there is no unique and well-justified way to work out exactly how much weight to assign to the new evidence (Section 4.8). Second,

the test is as good as the reliability of the auxiliary hypotheses. If the auxiliary hypotheses are false, the test is not valid.[11] That's why it is a common practice in science to discredit a test when the outcome is against the hypothesis by claiming that some of the auxiliary hypotheses are suspect. Actually there is a third problem. But we have to delay the discussion of it until Chapter 27, when we introduce the view that claims that paradigms can influence the designs and interpretations of indirect tests.

Confirmation theory (Section 1.9) deals with these problems. Traditionally these concerns belong to the field known as the **problem of justification**: how hypotheses can be justified. The short answer is that these hypotheses are evaluated by empirical tests, and if they pass these tests, we say that they are empirically justified. Nowadays, we say that they are confirmed, hence the term 'confirmation theory.' The term 'problem of justification' is archaic. I think a better term is '**problem of evaluation**.' There are influential philosophers who think that the process of science is not a matter of justification, and we should not aim at justification.[12] Whether we go along with this line of thought or not, we should not prejudge the situation. We should approach a hypothesis with an open mind, not to justify it, but to evaluate it. Should the evaluation assign a low credibility to the hypothesis, we should relinquish it altogether.

KEY TERMS INTRODUCED IN THIS CHAPTER

conditional statement	main hypothesis	indirect test
technologically realizable conditions	auxiliary hypothesis	direct test
technologically realizable test implication	enthymeme	confirmation theory
	intersubjectively decidable	problem of justification
		problem of evaluation

---

11. The term 'valid' here is used in its nontechnical sense, quite different from its use in Chapter 2, where only deductive arguments can be valid (or invalid).

12. Karl Popper is a leading figure in championing this line of thought (Chapter 24).

REFERENCES

Hempel, (1966, secs. 3.1–3.2) and M. H. Salmon et al. (1992, pp. 42–48) provide good introductions. Duhem (1982, reprint) discusses in detail the role of auxiliary hypotheses in indirect tests. For materials on the implications of the observability of annual stellar parallaxes by Copernicus's theory, consult Cohen (1985, pp. 45–50).

EXERCISES

1. Give two examples of a universal hypothesis, preferably from the history of science. For each hypothesis, work out one or more tests which take the form of a conditional statement. Make explicit any auxiliary hypotheses employed.

2. "The surface temperature of the planet Jupiter is between 100°C and 200°C." Give some technologically realizable test implications for this hypothesis.

3. Locate some auxiliary hypotheses that would have to be employed other than those pointed out in the text (Section 6.4) for the discussed indirect tests of the following hypotheses:

   (a) The earth moves around the sun.
   (b) The earth spins on its own axis once a day.

4. Are there any hypotheses that can be directly tested (that is, can be tested without the use of auxiliary hypotheses)? What about the hypothesis that all flames are green in color?

5. Draw one or more test implications from the hypothesis that ice is lighter than (less dense than) water. Do the test implications depend on any auxiliary hypotheses?

6. Compare and contrast the three definitions of indirect test (the first two in Section 1.6 and the last in Section 6.5). Are they equivalent? Which do you prefer? Which is more helpful in understanding the practice of science? Discuss.

7. Select one or more of the hypotheses given in Chapter 0. Find out some indirect tests that have been performed on them. Locate the auxiliary hypotheses assumed in these tests. In your opinion, were the conclusions drawn from the results of those tests reasonable?

Chapter 7

Empirical Evaluation II: Crucial Tests and Ad Hoc Revisions

7.1 INTRODUCTION

In the last chapter, we talked as if hypotheses are tested one at a time. This is not always the case, for often two alternative hypotheses are proposed to deal with the same set of phenomena, competing with each other for acceptance. Under such circumstances, scientists may design what is known as a crucial test to enable them to make a choice between them. The idea of a crucial test came from Francis Bacon (1561–1626), who meant it to be a test that will settle the rivalry once and for all, decisively and unambiguously. However, because of the inevitable use of auxiliary hypotheses in tests, few, if any, such tests are crucial in Bacon's original sense, for scientists can always revise their auxiliary hypotheses so as to protect the main hypothesis under test. This we have discussed in the last chapter. Our present problem is: Can anything be done to improve on the situation? Can reasonable criteria be given so as to prevent scientists from using "excuses" in order to hold on to their pet hypotheses in the face of unfavorable evidence? In other words, can the use of logic and other devices help us to restore the possibility of crucial tests, so that decisive rulings can be made with regard to competing hypotheses—both claiming that they possess the truth of the matter?

At this point I can think of the biblical story of King Solomon's judgment. There were these two women. Both claimed to be the mother of the newborn baby. Solomon conducted a "crucial test"; sure enough, the test was decisive and the true mother was identified.

Can Solomon's wisdom be repeated in science? Are crucial tests in Bacon's sense available in the process of scientific investigations? According to Karl Popper (1902–1994), we can at least improve the situation if we limit the allowable kind of revision of our hypotheses to what he termed *non–ad hoc revisions*.

7.2 CRUCIAL TESTS

Two hypotheses are said to be in competition if they are contrary to each other. In logic, two statements are said to be **contrary** to each other if they cannot both be true, but can both be false. For example, the following are two pairs of contrary statements:

(1a) This piece of paper is (totally) white.

(1b) This piece of paper is (totally) red.

(2a) Albert Einstein in 1910 was six feet tall.

(2b) Albert Einstein in 1910 was five feet tall.

When two statements are such that they cannot both be true and cannot both be false, they are said to be **contradictory** to each other. In other words, if one is true, the other would be false, and if one is false, the other would be true. The following are such a pair:

(3a) This piece of paper is (totally) white.

(3b) This piece of paper is *not* (totally) white.

Contradictory hypotheses are not really in competition with each other, because essentially there is only one statement involved. The two hypotheses simply represent the affirmation and the denial of that one single statement. For example, (3a) represents the affirmation of one statement, while (3b) represents the denial of the same. Contrary hypotheses, on the other hand, are in true competition. For example, (1a) and (1b) involve two distinct statements that exclude each other. They are about the same subject, and both are about color. Had one statement been about color and the other about shape, they would not be in competition. In such a case, the two can be both true. But since (1a) and (1b) are about the (total) color of the same object, when one is true the other has to be false. However, obviously they can be both false. For example, the piece of paper can be green in color.

In the history of science, there are many occasions when hypotheses compete in this sense. In the 19th century, the caloric theory of heat competed with the kinetic theory. In the 18th century, the phlogiston theory competed with the oxygen theory. In the 16th and 17th centuries, the geocentric theory competed with the heliocentric theory. We will deal with these in detail later. Here let's consider a simple example to illustrate the logic of crucial tests.

Suppose there are two contrary claims:

(4a) This heap of granules is sugar.

(4b) This heap of granules is salt.

How are we to settle the dispute? From the look of the granules, we cannot tell. We can, of course, try to taste them. However, such a test is subjective. The sense of taste differs significantly from person to person. Are there any objective tests that can be employed to settle the dispute? A test that favors one of two competing hypotheses and definitely rules out the other is known as a **crucial test**.[1] Can we think of any crucial tests for the two competing hypotheses (4a) and (4b)? Let us consider the following two inferences:

(5a)   This heap of granules is sugar.

If this heap is strongly heated, it will turn black.

---

1. Also known as 'crucial experiment.'

(5b) This heap of granules is salt.

   If this heap is strongly heated, it will not turn black.

We can take the conclusions of these inferences as test implications. To test which of the hypotheses is true, we need only heat the heap strongly, and see if it turns black or not. If it does turn black, the test favors (4a) and rules out (4b), whereas the opposite is the case should the heap resist turning black.

In abstract, the two inferences are as follows:

(5a) $\dfrac{H_1}{\text{If } C, \text{then } E_1.}$ (5b) $\dfrac{H_2}{\text{If } C, \text{then } E_2.}$

The point to take note of is that, whereas the condition C is common to both inferences, the consequents, E_1 and E_2 are different. Indeed we require that E_1 and E_2 be either contradictory or contrary to each other. In other words, E_1 and E_2 are mutually exclusive. It is because they are mutually exclusive that the test is a *crucial* test. The outcome cannot favor both hypotheses. I use the rather modest word 'favor' intentionally. The test cannot say which of the two hypotheses is definitely true. No empirical test can ever do that. We have covered this point in both Chapters 1 and 6. The heap's turning black on being heated is only a sign that it is sugar. It could, of course, be something else.

The inferences (5a) and (5b), strictly speaking, are invalid. We need the extra premise, 'All sugar turns black when strongly heated' for (5a), and a similar one for (5b). These, as we pointed out in Chapter 6, are auxiliary hypotheses and are often omitted in test inferences. So the full schemas of inferences for crucial tests are as follows:

(6a) $\dfrac{\begin{array}{c} H_1 \\ (A_1, A_2, \dots, A_n) \end{array}}{\text{If } C, \text{then } E_1}$ (6b) $\dfrac{\begin{array}{c} H_2 \\ (B_1, B_2, \dots, B_m) \end{array}}{\text{If } C, \text{then } E_2.}$

$A_1, A_2, \dots, A_n$ are auxiliary hypotheses for (6a) and $B_1, B_2, \dots, B_m$ are for (6b). The two sets of auxiliary hypotheses need not be the same. However, the two deductions must share the same C, and E_1 must either be contrary or contradictory to E_2.

7.3 HISTORICAL EXAMPLES OF CRUCIAL TESTS

"Philosophy of science without history of science is empty; history of science without philosophy of science is blind" (Lakatos, 1971, p. 91). In this book, we will as far as possible provide historical examples to illustrate and support our philosophical discussions. In the present section, two historical examples of crucial tests are presented.

In the 19th century, there were two competing schools of thought as to the nature of heat. The older school advocated the caloric theory, whose main exponent was Joseph Black (1728–1799). The newer school, led by Count Rumford (1753–1814), advocated the kinetic theory. According to the former, heat is a substance. Indeed it is a fluid, much like water. It flows, hence it can redistribute itself. But it cannot be created (out of nothing or out of other things), and it is indestructible. This fluid was given the name 'caloric fluid.' Caloric fluid is said to be invisible, but not imperceptible, for it manifests itself as "hotness." When caloric fluid enters into an object, it will raise its temperature. The rise in temperature is directly proportional to the amount of caloric fluid that has entered. On the other hand, should caloric fluid leave an object, the object will get cool. This theory was very popular in the 18th century. It explains why things get hot and why things get cold.

The kinetic theory of heat, on the other hand, asserts that heat is not a substance (not a kind of stuff) at all. An object gets hot, not because a certain fluid has entered into it, but because the minute particles that make up the object get agitated, increasing their motions. Heat, therefore, is simply micromotion. According to this theory, there is no such thing as caloric fluid. All objects are made of fine particles. These particles are always in motion, usually vibratory. The faster they move, the hotter the object becomes.

Thus the two theories are in stark contrast. Here is a simplified version of a crucial test performed by Rumford. He had two pieces of metal rubbed together at high speed and observed that the temperature of both pieces of metal rose with the rubbing, eventually becoming intensely hot. He reasoned that since rubbing is a form of motion, heat should be produced by rubbing if the kinetic theory holds, and in fact that was what was observed. On the other hand, since the caloric theory asserts that heat arises from caloric fluid, and caloric fluid is uncreatable, the two pieces of metal should not become hot at all. As heat was in fact produced, Rumford concluded that the caloric theory had to be false.

In this test, the condition C is the rubbing together of two pieces of metal. E_1 is that the two pieces of metal get hot, whereas E_2 is that they do not get hot. E_1 and E_2 are mutually exclusive in that they are contradictory to each other.

Our second example is derived from the debate between the phlogiston theory and the oxygen theory of combustion. According to the phlogiston theory, when an object burns, a substance known as phlogiston is given off. This theory was popular in the 17th and 18th centuries. Lavoisier (1743–1794), however, proposed in the late 18th century that, in burning, a substance is taken in rather than given off, and that substance he named 'pure air' (later called oxygen). Here is a typical case of two hypotheses in competition. They could both be false, but they cannot both be true.

Lavoisier designed a crucial experiment. He burned mercury in an enclosure of air and found the resulting calx heavier than the original mercury. He argued that if the phlogiston theory were correct, the calx should certainly have been lighter. In this experiment, the condition C is the burning of mercury in an enclosure of air. E_1 (from the phlogiston theory) states that the calx should be lighter than the original mercury. E_2 (from the oxygen theory) asserts the opposite. We will study more of this crucial test and related issues in Chapter 25.

The history of science is full of the kind of debates illustrated here. To settle such debates, inevitably (clever) crucial experiments are designed.

Thus crucial experiments play an important role in the progress of science, and they certainly provide exciting stories to read. Can you spot any crucial tests in Chapter 0?

7.4 FURTHER EXAMPLES (PTOLEMY VERSUS COPERNICUS)

For the illustration of the logic of crucial tests for competing hypotheses, few examples in the history of science surpass the debate between Ptolemy's geocentric system and Copernicus's heliocentric system of the universe. (We covered part of the debate in Section 6.4.) Both systems aimed at explaining the movements of the stars, the sun, the moon, and the five planets[2] across the sky. Ptolemy (2nd century B.C.) postulated that the earth is stationary at the center of the universe with the sun, moon, stars, and planets revolving round it. Hence it is a geocentric system. Whereas the observed paths traced by the sun, moon, and stars are rather regular, those of the planets are not. For example, the observed mutual distances between the stars seem fixed (hence they appear to us as constellations). On the other hand, the planets seem to wander among these stars.[3] Moreover, though their general directions are, like those of all other heavenly bodies, from east to west, they sometimes move backward or perform loops. These are known as retrograde motions (Figure 7.1). These retrograde motions appear strange and are difficult to explain. So Ptolemy proposed his famous device of the epicycles. He postulated that a typical planet, like Mars, does not move in a circle directly around the earth. It rather moves on a circle, known as an epicycle, whose center moves on a circle around the earth. The latter circle is known as the deferent of the planet (Figure 7.2a).

---

2. The known planets in those days were Mercury, Venus, Mars, Jupiter, and Saturn.

3. 'Planet' was derived from the Greek word for wanderer.

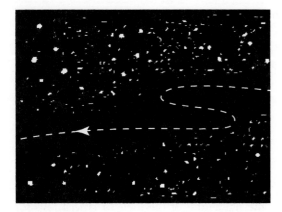

FIGURE 7.1

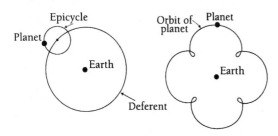

FIGURE 7.2a   **FIGURE 7.2b**

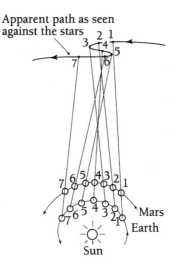

FIGURE 7.3

This combination of two circular motions produces the observed retrograde motion (Figure 7.2b).

The heliocentric system was first proposed by the Greek philosopher Aristarchus in the 3rd century B.C. It was revived and refined by Copernicus (1473–1543). According to Copernicus, the sun is stationary at the center of the universe. The earth is but one of the planets, and all planets move around the sun. Retrograde motions are not real. The planets do not move in loops as Ptolemy's system suggested. Retrograde motion is merely an *apparent* motion. The reason why a typical planet like Mars displays such motion is because the earth moves faster around the sun than Mars. When it overtakes Mars, the latter would appear as if it were going backward (Figure 7.3).

Thus both systems explained the strange phenomenon of retrograde motion rather satisfactorily, but in quite different manners. For Ptolemy, the planets really move backward at times, whereas,

for Copernicus, the backward motion is only an "illusion" because the observer is moving.

Another phenomenon that the two systems handled well was that of the observed relative positions of Venus to the sun. Venus was called the morning star and the evening star by the ancient Greeks. The reason was that it is only visible either just before sunrise or just after sunset. Moreover, it is never seen far away from the sun, never more than 45° away. Thus it is as if the sun somehow carries the planet along as it moves across the sky. This phenomenon is true of Mercury as well but is not true of the other planets. Mars, for example, is often seen at the zenith at midnight (180° from the sun). It is also often observed in the west when the sun is just about to rise in the east, and in the east, when the sun has just set in the west.

Ptolemy explained the phenomenon by postulating that the centers of the epicycles of Mercury and Venus are somehow fixed on the straight line linking the sun and the earth (Figure 7.4a). In other words, these centers move once a year around the earth exactly in step with the sun. Thus the observed phenomenon of Mercury and Venus being carried along by the sun is taken as literally true by Ptolemy. Copernicus explained it rather differently. He suggested, as before, that the phenomenon is an "illusion." According to him,

Mercury and Venus are inner planets—planets inside the orbit of the earth—whereas all the other planets are outer planets. For Copernicus, the order of the planets from the sun is as follows: Mercury, Venus, Earth, Mars, Jupiter, and Saturn. The sun does not carry Mercury and Venus along as the sun is stationary. The reason Mercury and Venus are never observed far from the sun is simply that they are inner planets (Figure 7.4b).

Here are two competing hypotheses, the geocentric and heliocentric theories. They cannot both be true, but they can both be false. Both satisfactorily explained the motions of the sun, moon, and stars. Both explained the retrograde motions of the

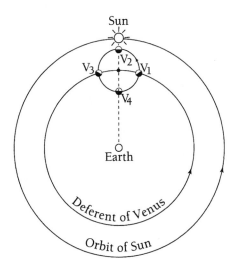

FIGURE 7.4a

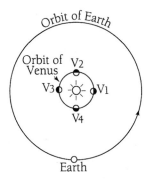

FIGURE 7.4b

planets and the constant proximity of Mercury and Venus to the sun. As was pointed out in Chapter 1, hypotheses are often proposed to explain observed phenomena. For this purpose, both the geocentric and the heliocentric systems were successful. Nevertheless they cannot both be true. So crucial tests have to be brought in to settle the dispute. In what follows, I will reconstruct the history of competition between the two systems as three crucial tests.

Crucial Test 1

In Section 6.4, we mentioned the experiment of the stone falling from a tower. If a stone is dropped from a tower, the heliocentric theory would expect it to land somewhere west of the tower, whereas the geocentric theory would predict that it would land at the tower base. We can take this experiment as a crucial test. The test condition is the dropping of the stone from a tower. One theory predicts E_1 whereas the other predicts E_2, and the two are contrary to each other. The facts, as we all know, favor the geocentric theory. However, as we saw in Section 6.4, Copernicus and Galileo defended their heliocentric theory by changing some of the implicit auxiliary hypotheses.

Crucial Test 2

According to the heliocentric theory, annual stellar parallax should be observable, whereas the geocentric theory predicts the absence of such annual parallax (Section 6.4). Again the outcomes favored the geocentric theory. Again, Copernicus and Galileo blamed some of the hidden auxiliary hypotheses, and hence the unfavorable implication of the test was diffused.

Crucial Test 3

So far the heliocentric theory was on the defensive. Its eventual triumph over the geocentric theory was due to the invention of the telescope. According to the Ptolemaic system, Venus's epicycle moves in step with the sun so that it is always in the straight line linking the sun to the earth. From the earth, therefore, we should never see Venus as a "full moon" (that is, as a round disk) because Venus is always somewhere between the sun and the earth. The expected phases of Venus are "half moon," "no moon," "half moon," and "no moon" (Figure 7.4a). On the other hand, the heliocentric system does expect a full moon to occur when Venus goes behind the sun. The phasal sequence expected is "half moon," "full moon," "half moon," and "no moon" (Figure 7.4b). However, Venus is too far away for the naked eye to discern its phases. We can appreciate the triumphal feeling that overcame Galileo when, in pointing the newly invented telescope toward the planet, he witnessed the sequence of phases exactly as predicted by the heliocentric system, the system he had been defending all his life.

These three crucial tests illustrate how such tests can be used to arbitrate between competing hypotheses. However, since auxiliary hypotheses are almost always employed for the deduction of test implications, no crucial test is ever crucial in the strict sense. Clever modifications of the main hypotheses or the auxiliary hypotheses can always be devised to evade any refutation of our chosen beliefs. This should be apparent from the examples listed previously. It seems that, in science, any belief is defensible. You can somehow always stick to your favorite hypothesis, even in the face of obvious empirical evidence. You can, for example, reject the observed phases of Venus through the telescope as due to a faulty instrument, which does not always give a true image. Indeed, that was how the cardinals of the Church defended the geocentric theory, so the story goes.

But then there must be legitimate ways of defending a hypothesis as contrasted with illegitimate ways. If science is to be objective, we should have ways of settling disputes of this sort rationally. There must be objective and reasonable rules we can apply to rule out defenses that unreasonably protect false hypotheses from refutation. How otherwise can we work toward the truth?

7.5 AD HOC REVISION OF MAIN HYPOTHESES

Popper, a prominent philosopher of science of the 20th century, proposes that in defending a hypothesis against empirical refutation, ad hoc revisions should not be allowed.[4] Intuitively, an ad hoc revision is one that is done for the sole purpose of protecting the hypothesis under test from unfavorable experimental results. It is an evasive move, a move not for the advancement of knowledge but rather for the sake of keeping a hypothesis irrespective of its real worth. It is usually a clever move based on some ingenious arguments. If such moves are permitted in science, empirical tests would not be able to function as arbitrators between truth and falsity, according to Popper.

The idea of disallowing ad hoc revisions is laudable. However, you'll find that it is not simple or straightforward to turn this vague idea into an objective and usable criterion. Let us start with the study of ad hoc modification of main hypotheses.

Often when the results of a test are unfavorable, the scientist modifies the main hypothesis (the hypothesis under test). For example, Lavoisier burned mercury in air and found that the calx was heavier than the mercury metal (Section 7.3). This result contradicted the phlogiston theory, which says that, in combustion, phlogiston escapes from the burnt object. Nevertheless, quite a few defenses of the phlogiston theory were proposed. A well-known one suggested that phlogiston has negative weight. This can be seen as a modification of the original phlogiston theory, which assigns a positive weight to phlogiston. Shall we say that this move is ad hoc? Surely it was proposed solely for the sake of keeping the phlogiston theory. But can we reject a hypothesis on account of the *motives* of its proposer? Motives vary from person to person. The same hypothesis, modified or not, can be proposed by more than one person, for a variety of purposes. Motives are, anyway, difficult to ascertain.

---

4. See Popper (1959, pp. 81–84). We will cover his philosophy in detail in Chapter 24.

Popper thinks that science should not aim at truths per se, but should aim at truths with high contents.[5] Science should progressively move from statements of low content to statements of high content in the general direction of truth. Thus Popper sees that in science hypotheses are constantly proposed and then regularly replaced by better ones. The growth of science can be pictured as a sequence of progressively better hypotheses. When is a hypothesis better than its rivals? For Popper, a better hypothesis is not just one nearer the truth, but one that has higher content as well. Otherwise the move from the hypothesis that it will rain tomorrow, to the hypothesis that it will either rain or snow tomorrow, would be considered good, because the latter cannot be less true than the former, since the former entails (logically implies) the latter. For Popper, a move that lowers the content of a hypothesis is unacceptable. The statement that it will either rain or snow tomorrow has less content than the statement that it will rain tomorrow, because the former claims less. If you should say that it will either rain or not rain tomorrow, you are saying even less. In fact, you would be saying nothing; the content of such a hypothesis is zero.

Let us therefore try the following definition:

D_1: In the face of unfavorable results from a test, a modification of the (main) hypothesis is ad hoc if the modified hypothesis has no novel (new) predictions other than predictions of those same or similar unfavorable results that prompt the modification.

Consider the hypothesis:

H: All swans are white.

The discovery of black swans in Australia in the 19th century contradicted this hypothesis. To salvage H, one might modify H to

H':   All swans are either white or black.

However, such a modification would be ad hoc according to D_1, for H' has no novel predictions. It can be seen that H' has less content than H in the sense that it claims less. In Popperian jargon, it is less refutable. Even though H' is nearer to truth, it nevertheless represents a retrograde step, a retreat from a statement of high content to a statement of relatively low content. For science to progress, Popper recommends that the replacing hypothesis should always provide novel or fresh predictions, predictions not given by the original hypothesis. Novel prediction is a sign of increase in content,[6] and non-ad hocness.

The hypothesis,

H'':   All swans, except those in Australia, are white,

is a slight improvement. Its content is not lower than that of the original, because it predicts something that H does not predict—that Australian swans are not white. However, the modification of H to H'' is still ad hoc, because H'' has no novel predictions other than the prediction of the kind of empirical findings that prompted the modification.

Finally, let us consider

H''':   All swans are white except for those that feed on eucalyptus leaves.

Unlike the previous two, this last hypothesis has novel predictions other than predictions of findings that prompted the revision. It predicts, for example, that white swans do not feed on eucalyptus leaves. It also predicts that if a swan should feed on eucalyptus leaves (eucalyptus trees abound in Australia), the swan would be nonwhite. Popper sees the modification of H to H''' as a good move. The availability of novel predictions is always a sign of higher content, and thus of growth.

What about the modification of the phlogiston theory to the effect that phlogiston has negative weight? Is that an ad hoc revision? It seems so according to our definition, for it does not seem to have any novel predictions.

---

5. A detailed account of Popper's theory of content will be given in Section 24.5.

6. At least not a decrease in content.

In Section 7.3, we saw how the caloric theory was empirically refuted by the rubbing of two pieces of metal together. To save the caloric theory from such a refutation, we can modify it by revising the clause that caloric fluid is uncreatable by allowing for an exception—that friction can produce caloric fluid. However, this revision can be seen to be ad hoc, very similar to the postulation of negative weight. Thus for Popper, this revision should not be allowed.

7.6 AD HOC REVISION OF AUXILIARY HYPOTHESES

The absence of annual parallax of the stars is an empirical refutation of the heliocentric system. To salvage his system, Copernicus claimed that the stars are at an immensely great distance away. This is not a modification of the main hypothesis itself. Rather, it is a modification of one of the auxiliary hypotheses required for the derivation of the presence of annual parallax. The modification is from the assumption that the stellar distances from earth are relatively small to the assumption that they are great. Is this revision of auxiliary hypothesis ad hoc?

In regard to this, here is Popper's proposal: "I call a [hypothesis] 'ad hoc' if it is introduced … to explain a particular difficulty, but if … it cannot be tested independently."[7] So let's consider the following definition:

D_2: A modification of an auxiliary hypothesis to nullify an empirical refutation is ad hoc if the modified auxiliary hypothesis is not independently testable.

Let's illustrate this definition with a simple example. Suppose Peter claimed that water is nonpoisonous. However, the water from John's well made John sick. One way to save his hypothesis was for Peter to introduce the auxiliary hypothesis that the well water was impure. You can see that Peter explained away the unfavorable phenomenon

as due to some sort of foreign objects in the well water. In other words, he changed the original implicit auxiliary hypothesis that what was in the well was pure water to the hypothesis that it was water plus something else. Now if that something else is independently detectable—for example, by some chemical tests—then this revision is non–ad hoc. However, if the impurity produced only one kind of detectable effect—that of making people sick—then the revision would be ad hoc by definition D_2, because now it is not independently testable, not testable independently of the very phenomenon that the revision is meant to explain.

We say that an auxiliary hypothesis is **independently testable** if and only if there is a type of test for the hypothesis, of which the unfavorable phenomenon (that is, the refuting phenomenon) is not an instance. This criterion of independent testability will prevent people from pointing at John's getting sick as evidence of the impurity of the water (and, circularly saying that the water's impurity explains why John fell sick). In fact, the criterion will bar the employment of any instance of sickness from drinking the water as evidence of the water's being impure, be the sick person Tom, Dick, or Harry.

(A) Let's apply D_2 to a real case in science. Copernicus explained away the absence of stellar parallax by claiming that the stars are very far away compared to the distance of the sun from the earth. Is this move ad hoc? If the absence of stellar parallax is the only evidence of the immense distance, then it is by D_2 ad hoc. The revision was quite ad hoc at the time of Copernicus, since there was no evidence other than the absence of annual parallaxes. With modern technology, however, distances of the stars from the earth can be measured quite accurately by various means. In fact, they all confirmed Copernicus's speculation. Thus ad hocness is time-dependent. A modification can be ad hoc at one time without being ad hoc at another.

(B) Let's apply D_2 to another real case. If the earth spins on its own axis, objects dropped from a

---

7. Popper (1974a, p. 986).

tower should fall westward. Galileo explained away the absence of western motion of freely falling objects by suggesting that falling objects share the motion of the earth. He called this sharing 'inertia.' As if anticipating Popper's objections, he offered an independent test of the existence of inertia. He predicted that if a heavy object is dropped from the top of a ship's mast, it would land at the foot of the mast because of inertia even though the ship might be moving forward—that is, provided the motion of the ship is even and smooth. Obviously, we cannot expect sailing ships of the 17th century to be able to make even and smooth speed in the open sea (to give them sufficient speed) for the experiment to be done. Thus at the time of Galileo, this was not really a technologically possible test. Nowadays such an experiment can easily be carried out, and it has been done many times. Of course you all know the results.

(C) Finally, to explain away the observed phases of Venus by blaming the telescope as an instrument that does not give a true picture of things can be seen to be ad hoc unless the explanation is accompanied by substantiations other than the claim that the telescope gives a false picture of Venus.

The practice of ad hoc revisions of auxiliary hypotheses would obviously make empirical tests meaningless. You can defend any hypothesis whatsoever in the face of adverse empirical evidence. For Popper, this is not acceptable.

7.7 ASSESSMENT OF POPPER'S PHILOSOPHY ON AD HOC REVISIONS

Philosophy is not a set of doctrines, nor is it a list of facts. I hope you will get into this perspective gradually as we progress through this book. Philosophy can be characterized (in one of many ways) as a series of debates over the nature of certain conceptual and methodological problems and debates over various proposed solutions to these problems.[8] We have on hand a methodological problem—how to handle ad hoc revisions, which seem to impede the growth of science. Popper proposes a solution, and, as philosophers, we should assess it. Usually in philosophy there are many ways to formulate a problem and many views on the same problem, and most of these views are worth studying, though it is unlikely that any of them will give you the so-called *correct* answer.[9] Philosophy, unlike mathematics, does not provide or attempt to provide correct answers in the ordinary sense. What it does is to provide perspectives and understanding, so that we can rise above our traditional (entrenched) ways of thinking to see things more clearly and thus become wiser.

We have just studied Popper's idea of ad hocness and his recommendation that such ad hoc revisions be barred from science. In this section, as philosophers, let's assess this recommendation. Is it reasonable? Is it practical? Can it be improved on? Can it be superseded by a better approach or a more sophisticated perspective?

Before we start the assessment, I think it proper to make clear that it is usually unfair to any philosophy to have it assessed out of context. Popper's philosophy on ad hocness is only a small part of his total philosophy, which we are going to study in detail in Chapter 24. Under such circumstances, perhaps it is wise to take what follows as a provisional assessment. Anyway, as we progress through this text, we will come into contact with a variety of views. Your opinions, on this issue or on any other issues, will, I'm sure, change accordingly. It is essential to keep an open and pliable mind in the study of philosophy.

---

8. The question "What is philosophy?" is rather philosophical itself. It has aroused numerous replies. Here I am certainly not trying to give my version of what philosophy is. My only intention is to introduce you to the phenomenon of philosophical debates so that you will know how to appreciate and handle such debates.

9. For example, Laudan (1977, pp. 114–118) presents another theory of ad hocness, which is in terms of increase in conceptual problems.

(A) Let's start with D_1. Popper's case is convincing with the simple hypothesis H, and simple revisions such as H', H'', and H''' which I used for illustration. However, if we look at some of the more realistic (historical) cases, D_1 can be seen to be simplistic.

Let's take the case of the phlogiston theory, which we discussed earlier. To defend the theory from refutation, it was proposed that the theory be modified so that phlogiston, instead of having positive weight, has negative weight. Does this modified phlogiston theory really have no novel predictions? How are we supposed to *demonstrate* that it has no novel predictions? I'm sure you will agree with me that the lack of imagination on our part does not *prove* it has no novel predictions. This is similar to the argument that the failure to solve a mathematical problem does not prove that such a solution does not exist.

If you carefully consider the hypothesis that phlogiston has negative weight, you should find that there can be many novel predictions. To start with, all the old results concerning weight changes in combustion that had been so admirably explained by the *positive* weight hypothesis have to be reinterpreted. For example, when a piece of wood burns away, what is left is a heap of ashes much lighter than the original piece of wood. The old explanation is straightforward: phlogiston with its positive weight has left the wood. The negative-weight hypothesis has to deal with this phenomenon somehow. I think this amounts to a kind of novel prediction. Some of you would probably say that this is not really a case of novel predictions, but a case of re-explanation of some old facts. I think you have a point here. However, what about the following cases?

Have you considered what would happen to things with negative weight when they move at high speed, say, almost as fast as light? What would happen if such objects are frozen to a temperature near absolute zero? What if there are substances other than phlogiston that have negative weight, and those substances are present only on Mars? One thing we have learned from the present chapter and the last is that test consequences from a (main) hypothesis are almost always obtained through the use of auxiliary hypotheses. These auxiliary hypotheses are usually well known and thus taken for granted. We say that they are part of our *background knowledge*. An example is the claim that, if the earth is round, we should see the mast of a sailing ship disappear before its hull (Section 6.4). Here we assume that light travels in straight lines, which is part of our background knowledge. Now background knowledge is not static. It changes as we correct our views, and, moreover, it increases with time. You can see that even if no novel prediction can be made from a hypothesis now (based on our present background knowledge), it does not mean that no such predictions can be made in the future. I think it is foolhardy to assume that the negative-weight modification of the phlogiston theory has no novel predictions, and thereby conclude that it is ad hoc.

In Section 0.11, we saw how Young modified his wave theory of light to accommodate the phenomenon of polarization. Was that modification ad hoc? It was initially believed that light consists of longitudinal waves, but such waves cannot possibly polarize. So Young proposed that the waves are in fact transverse. If at that time no one could think of any novel predictions that the modification would lead to, should Young have dropped his proposal according to Popper's recommendation?[10]

You will remember how Copernicus's heliocentric theory postulates that the planets move around the sun in circles. But there were many data that did not square with this hypothesis. This led Kepler (1571–1630) to a modification: that the orbits of the planets are ellipses, even though their eccentricities are so small that they are very close to being circles. Is this modification ad hoc? I'll leave

10. That light consists of transverse waves implies that the medium—ether—has to be a solid of high elasticity, which can be taken as a sort of novel prediction.

this as an exercise for you to solve, even though it could be difficult.

My general point is that, other than those simplistic cases that I used as examples of ad hocness, few real cases are such that they are ad hoc in Popper's sense. The worst feature of the criterion is that a modification can *look* ad hoc at the time of the proposal (because no one can think of novel predictions), and this appearance of ad hocness can kill a worthy modification in its infancy. We will consider this issue further in Parts VII and VIII.

(B) Let us now turn to the other definition of ad hocness, D_2, which is on the ad hoc revision of auxiliary hypotheses (rather than on the main hypothesis). Consider this simple case first. Suppose we want to test the following hypothesis:

(7) Rain dance of type K if performed for seven consecutive days will bring rain on the eighth day.

Suppose the rain dance was performed for seven days and yet on the eighth day there was not a cloud on the horizon. I think most of us will probably give up the hypothesis (even though they might still keep on dancing for the fun of it). However, the logic of indirect tests is such that we need not give up the hypothesis, for a test implication follows only if certain auxiliary hypotheses are true. One of these is:

(8) The dancers performed the K-dance correctly—that is, no mistakes were made in the dance steps.

If (8) should be false, (7) would not imply the occurrence of rain on the eighth day (for what were performed were not genuine K-dances). To replace (8) with its negation (denial) amounts to a revision, and is this revision ad hoc? You might say that making the wrong dance steps is certainly independently testable, because we can examine the video record of the dance frame by frame to check the dance steps. Hence this revision, according to D_2,

should not be ad hoc. I am not so sure of this judgment, however. Even in the present high-tech age, our videocameras may not be sophisticated enough to detect minute deviations in dance steps. (It is said that the rain god has excellent vision and could be very fussy and demanding on the exactitude of the dance steps.) The claim that wrong steps were made in the dance may not be independently testable (at least not at present).

(C) You may remember how Newton attempted to explain diffraction in terms of variation of ether density near material objects, so that diffraction is really a kind of refraction (Section 0.7). This is another example of revision of auxiliary hypotheses. Originally Newton assumed, as everyone else in his time did, that ether is a homogeneous substance permeating the whole universe. To accommodate the phenomenon of diffraction, he altered it to a substance of varied density. Is this ad hoc? Can we test the variation in the density of ether other than by invoking the observation that light bends around corners when obstructed by tiny objects, which, of course, was what prompted the revision itself? Since at the time of Newton nobody could say much about what ether is in fact like, the search for independent tests probably would not succeed. But that does not mean that independent tests are in principle unavailable.[11]

(D) Finally, there was the case of the neutrino. When the nucleus of an atom disintegrates, it may emit an electron known as a beta particle. (The process is known as a beta decay.) After Einstein's discovery that energy and mass are interchangeable, the principle of conservation of mass was replaced by the principle of conservation of mass-energy. During a beta decay, the sum of the mass-energy of the beta particle and the remnants of the nucleus should be equal to that of the original nucleus. However, in the case of the disintegration of a bismuth nucleus (and others), the actual sum was found to be far less than expected! Where had the

---

11. I don't see why tests of density variation of ether cannot be designed along the line of Michelson-Morley's experiment, which attempted to measure the speed of the ether drift around earth during the end of the 19th century.

mass-energy gone? We can, and perhaps should, interpret this phenomenon as a falsification of the principle of conservation of mass-energy, because according to it the mass-energy of the two fragments of a disintegrated nucleus should be equal to the mass-energy of the original nucleus if the principle holds.

However, two eminent physicists in the 1930s, Wolfgang Pauli and Enrico Fermi, chose to revise some of the auxiliary hypotheses involved. One such auxiliary hypothesis says that the nucleus breaks into *two* fragments. They revised the number 'two' into 'three.' According to them, in that beta decay, an undetected particle so small and light that its mass is near zero has been simultaneously emitted. Moreover, the speed of the emission of this particle is so extremely high that its kinetic energy, in spite of the particle's near zero mass, is sufficient to make up for the "lost" mass-energy. Fermi gave it the name "neutrino."[12]

What is the difference between this case and the case of the rain dance? Remember that neutrinos are supposed to be so minute (far smaller than even an electron) and to be moving so fast that the chance of "capturing" them is remote. In the 1930s, certainly our background knowledge and technology were not adequate to design independent tests for this new hypothesis. Should we have given it up according to Popper's ruling on ad hoc hypotheses? (As a matter of fact, in 1956, some 20 years after the proposal of the hypothesis, the conscience of the scientific world was set at ease with the unambiguous "capture" of the neutrino.)[13]

We have considered both definitions of ad hocness in terms of a number of historical examples. It seems that taking ad hocness as a pragmatic concept (in terms of novel predictions or independent testability) is not helpful, for there is no logical difference between the case of the rain dance and the case of the neutrino. Either they are both ad hoc or neither of them are. I personally favor the latter. In fact, as I argued in the case of the hypothesis that phlogiston has negative weight, the availability of novel predictions depends on our background knowledge (and our imagination), and most of the modifications and revisions made in actual history would not be ad hoc if we could only provide them with sufficiently rich background knowledge. I think we should relativize the notion of ad hocness to background knowledge and (therefore indirectly to time). That is, you often hear people say: "The hypothesis was ad hoc (in the time of Copernicus) but it is not ad hoc now." Such a relativization is, however, not helpful in methodology, for we would like to establish a notion that can help the scientist accept or reject a certain proposal on the spot at the time of the proposal. Should we then reject hypotheses that are ad hoc in the sense of Popper at the time of the proposal? If the answer is yes, then we would see Copernicus's heliocentric theory, Young's transverse wave theory, the neutrino theory of Pauli and Fermi, and many more rejected at the moment of their birth. However, all these theories were later proved to be (largely) correct and are still respectable theories in the community of science today.

The general contemporary opinion is that Popper's analysis of ad hocness is innovative but unrealistic. Its associated methodology does not agree with the actual practices in (progressive) science. We will return to this issue in Parts VI, VII, and VIII. In the meantime, it suffices to point out that there was an earlier philosophy that dealt with the same issue, and it is known as conventionalism. Conventionalism originated at the turn of the century (before Popper) and has had great influence on contemporary philosophies such as those of Kuhn, Feyerabend, and Lakatos. In Chapter 9, we will see how conventionalism proposes to handle the problem of ad hocness.

In this chapter and the last, we have spent quite a bit of time on the role auxiliary hypotheses play in

---

12. An auxiliary hypothesis that asserts that there are no other factors in play except for those that have been mentioned explicitly in the main hypothesis and in the auxiliary hypotheses is often known as a *ceteris paribus* clause. The presence of such a clause is usually taken for granted. So here Pauli and Fermi's revision is tantamount to a rejection of the *ceteris paribus* clause.

13. See Holton and Roller (1958, pp. 711–713) for details.

indirect tests. This, as I pointed out before, belongs to the field of **confirmation theory**,[14] which we called the problem of empirical evaluation and justification. Let's move on to a related field, the role played by theories (rather than by empirical data) in the justification of hypotheses.

KEY TERMS INTRODUCED IN THIS CHAPTER

contrary

contradictory

crucial test

ad hoc revision of main hypotheses

ad hoc revision of auxiliary hypotheses

independently testable

confirmation theory

REFERENCES

On crucial tests: Hempel (1966, secs. 3.3–3.5) and Copi and Cohen (1994, sec. 13.6). On theories of heat and the neutrino: Goldstein and Goldstein (1978, chap. 4) and Holton and Roller (1958, chaps. 19, 25, and 38).

On the phlogiston theory: Gale (1979, chap. 5), McKenzie (1960, chap. 8), and Wolf (1962, chap. 13).

On Ptolemy and Copernicus: Cohen (1985, chap. 3), Holton and Roller (1958), and Wolf (1962, chap. 2).

On ad hoc revisions: Chalmers (1976, sec. 5.2) provides a good introduction. Popper gives the original statement of his thesis in two works (Popper 1974, 1957). Newton-Smith (1981, pp. 70–76) briefly discusses the subject. For a critique, see Bamford (1993). To anticipate Chapter 28, Lakatos (1970b), a rather advanced text, provides a critique as well as suggested improvements on Popper's thesis.

EXERCISES

1. Give an example (historical or otherwise) of a crucial test. Try to illustrate Popper's notions of ad hoc and non–ad hoc revisions in terms of that example.

2. Give an example of an intuitively undesirable revision of a main hypothesis which is ad hoc according to Popper's D_1.

3. Give an example of an intuitively undesirable revision of certain auxiliary hypotheses which is ad hoc according to Popper's D_2.

4. Find out some of the historical defenses of the phlogiston theory against Lavoisier's experimental results. Were these defenses ad hoc

according to Popper's criteria? Should they be condemned?

5. Should the defense of the rain dance hypothesis (Section 7.7) be that some of the dancers are impure in spirit? What sort of defense is this? Is it a modification of the main hypothesis, or is it a revision of some of the auxiliary hypotheses? Is this defense ad hoc? Is it acceptable?

6. To explain the occurrence of rainbow colors on thin films of oil, Newton postulated that his light corpuscles produced "shock waves" that brought about these colors indirectly (Section 0.6). Is this a modification of the main

---

14. See Chapter 21 for more on confirmation theory.

hypothesis (his theory of light corpuscles) or is it a revision of auxiliary hypotheses? Is this move ad hoc? Is it acceptable?

7. Perform the following experiment. Place some sugar on tinfoil and heat it over a candle flame. Observe whether it turns black or not. Suppose it did not. Think of some revisions of auxiliary hypotheses that can be employed to protect the main hypothesis that the stuff you placed on the tinfoil is sugar. (Consult (5a) of Section 7.2 and you might like to make use of the fact that you heated the sugar on a piece of *tin* foil, with a *candle* flame and in *air*.)

Chapter 8

Theoretical Justification: Theories and Their Uses

8.1 INTRODUCTION

In the last two chapters, we saw the role played by empirical data in the justification of hypotheses. Here we will study the role played by theories.

Science grows in two stages: the **phenomenal stage** and the **theoretical stage**. The phenomenal[1] stage is characterized by the use of inductive methods (Chapter 3), implying that the acquisition of knowledge is a matter of collection, elimination, and correlation, as respectively exemplified by the method of induction by simple enumeration, Mill's method of difference, and the method of concomitant variation. Such a procedure is a bottom-up approach in which observation plays the major role. All civilizations seem to possess this kind of science, and that, I think, is how our ancestors arrive at such generalizations as "Wood floats on water." In addition to passive observation, active experimentation slowly came onto the scene. For example, it was reported that Petrus, a medieval scholar, performed a number of experiments with magnets, one of

---

1. The term 'phenomenal' used here does not carry the suggestion of the unusual or the unexpected. It refers to what is observable and detectable.

which involved the breaking of a magnetic bar crosswise to produce two distinct magnets. Later both Roger Bacon (13th century) and Francis Bacon (16th century) preached the importance of experiments. Whether through passive observation or active experimentation, the idea is to accumulate empirical data at the base so as to enable inductive ascent to more general statements made earlier.

The wider the empirical base the more accurate and more precise the empirical generalizations so induced, as Francis Bacon observed.

The phenomenal stage was historically the first stage of science, which was a stage of common sense on two counts. First, the inductive methods used are essentially commonsense methods. Second, the empirical generalizations thus arrived at are usually formulated in commonsense terms. In spite of the contributions of Grosseteste (12th–13th centuries), Bacon, and Mill toward improvement and refinement, phenomenal science was intrinsically limited because the methods of induction can advance science only when the data are rather simple, regular, and pure. It was the second stage, the theoretical stage, that brought about significant advances in science.[2]

Let's call the science of the phenomenal stage **phenomenal science** (or purely empirical science), and the science of the theoretical stage **theoretical science**.

Theoretical science is characterized by the use of (abstract) theories[3] that not only can explain observed phenomena in a unified manner, but also can yield predictions far beyond the reach of inductive methods. Theories are produced by the mind just as empirical data are obtained through the senses.[4] The scientists who create such theories are often called theoreticians, and the history of science since the 17th century is full of them: Newton, Dalton, Franklin, Maxwell, Rutherford, Bohr, Einstein, Schrödinger, and Heisenberg, to name just a few. The use of theories is a top-down approach in that one starts with a theory at the top, and, via deduction, arrives at empirical predictions at the bottom. On the other hand, as I pointed out before, the use of inductive methods is a bottom-up approach because these methods start with empirical data and ascend, via induction, to generalizations higher up.

Each branch of science seems to have gone through these two stages. The case with psychology, albeit a social science, is no exception. In this chapter, we will study two topics: how empirical generalizations require the support of theories, and how theories are able to advance science far beyond formal induction. Together they can be taken as arguments for the superiority of theoretical science over phenomenal science.

8.2 THEORETICAL SUPPORT

Let's consider the empirical generalization that iron conducts heat, which has had millions of confirming instances.[5] Does the generalization require anything else to justify its worth? A layperson would probably say "No, it doesn't." For a layperson,

---

2. The picture I have painted has been made slightly more complicated by the rise in the use of statistics (that is, quantitative inductive methods) in the 20th century, which has superseded qualitative inductive methods such as Mill's methods. However, it still remains true that science in general grows in two stages, the phenomenal and the theoretical, although the former now is more sophisticated, being enriched by powerful statistical methods to deal with complex and "noisy" phenomena.

3. The term 'theory' is ambiguous. Often people use the term 'theory' in contrast with the term 'fact,' referring to guesswork. I use it here rather as a term in contrast to 'empirical data,' so that the derived term 'theoretical' in the present context should be contrasted with the adjective 'empirical,' *not* with the term 'factual.'

4. This is an oversimplified picture of the roles played by the mind and the senses. See Chapter 22 for a more accurate picture of their roles in perception.

5. 'Iron conducts heat' is an empirical generalization because it has been arrived at through *generalizing* over a number of *empirical* data such as "*A* is a piece of iron and it conducts heat," "*B* is a piece of iron and it conducts heat," and so on.

experience, in the form of the millions of confirming instances, has "demonstrated" its truth. However, scientists think that empirical confirmation is not enough. The generalization is not trustworthy unless it has theoretical support as well. What is required is a theory that explains *why* iron conducts heat, whereas, for example, wood does not.[6] Without a theory the phenomenon of heat conduction seems to be a matter of (mysterious) coincidence, and not a case of rational necessity. If the environment changes, iron may not conduct heat.[7] A clear case is that of acupuncture. Acupuncture works in many areas, notably in anesthesia. However, without a supporting theory, acupuncture lacks the kind of credibility that most conventional scientific hypotheses enjoy. In this chapter, we are not going into philosophical debate about whether the scientist is behaving rationally when she requires theoretical support for her hypotheses. I am only pointing out a common practice of present-day science. Since Newton, most scientists have reserved a place of honor for theories, without which science for them is but a collection of brute facts, irrational and blind. Theories make science rational and, in addition, aesthetically pleasing.

What is a theory like? Let's consider some examples. A theory that supports the generalization that iron conducts heat can be a "story" about the molecular structure of iron, and how such a structure handles heat, whereas wood, for example, has a different kind of structure. A theory as such is usually invented freely by the mind. The scientist makes it up, so to speak, out of the blue.[8]

Let's consider another example. The rainbow is a common phenomenon. We can say a lot about rainbows: their colors, their shapes, their positions, and so on. We all know, for example, that rainbows have seven colors. Such knowledge is supported by many, many past observations, ours as well as those of our ancestors. Yet scientists were not happy with mere empirical support. They looked for theories that can explain the seven colors, their round shapes, their positions, and so on. Theodoric of Freibourg in the 14th century was among the first to theorize about rainbows. He proposed that rainbows are made of rain droplets that, when lit up by the sun, yield the seven colors by refraction.

Here is another example. Boyle's law states that, for a fixed amount of gas sealed in a container of variable size, any increase in pressure will decrease the volume of the gas proportionally, and vice versa, provided that the temperature of the gas is kept constant. In other words, $P \times V =$ constant (with temperature kept constant). Robert Boyle, in the 17th century, obtained an impressive amount of empirical data in support of this law by measuring the volumes of trapped air under different pressures (Section 4.6). However, the scientific world was not satisfied with mere empirical support. Roughly 200 years later, *theoretical* support finally came in the form of the kinetic theory, which postulates that gas is made of a large number of minute particles in rapid motion. The impact of these particles on the container wall produces the gas pressure. From this theory, Boyle's law can be deduced as a logical consequence. Amazingly, the same theory also explains the law of Charles and Gay-Lussac, which says that, for a given amount of gas, its volume is directly proportional to its temperature, provided that the pressure of the gas is kept constant.

---

6. At least not as much.

7. Here is a simpler case. Consider the generalization that iron sinks in water. We all "know" that this is true. Do we really *know*? Archimedes produced his now famous theory of floating objects. From this theory, we can actually deduce that iron sometimes does float. Have you ever considered the metal hull of a ship?

8. Theories are often borrowed from another branch of science through a type of reasoning known as reasoning by analogy. Researchers in artificial intelligence hope that these so-called "free inventions of the mind" can be captured through algorithms, and thus be mechanized. See Chapter 32.

8.3 THE NATURE OF THEORIES

We can look at science as organized in levels. At the lowest level, we have what are known as **empirical data**. Here are some examples of empirical data:

(1) Rainbow A, seen on Monday, had seven colors.

(2) Rainbow A was round in shape.

(3) The top of Rainbow A was 20° above the horizon.

(4) Rainbow A was in the east, facing a setting sun.

(5) Rainbow B, seen on Friday, had seven colors.

(6) Rainbow B was round in shape.

(7) The top of Rainbow B was 25° above the horizon.

(8) Rainbow B was in the west, facing a rising sun.

It can be seen that empirical data are about specific things. Therefore they are singular statements (Section 6.2). In this list, some are about Rainbow A, and some are about Rainbow B. Usually, scientists collect hundreds of such data.

The next level is that of **empirical generalizations**. Such generalizations are usually obtained from the data by methods of induction. As a result of our many, many observations of rainbows, we have arrived at the following generalizations:

(9) All rainbows have seven colors.

(10) All rainbows are round.

(11) All rainbows are situated opposite the sun.

These empirical generalizations can be seen to be universal statements, which are about things in general—for example, about any rainbows (Section 6.2).

Even though, strictly speaking, both empirical data and empirical generalizations are hypotheses, in practice, scientists usually treat empirical data as given and veridical. Only empirical generalizations are treated as hypotheses. It is these empirical generalizations that require theoretical support.

In the case of generalizations about the rainbow, the current theory is the water droplet theory. Water droplets in the atmosphere (usually left behind by a shower) refract white light from the sun to produce the seven colors. From this, the empirical generalizations (9), (10), and (11) can be deduced. We say that these generalizations are now supported (suspended) from above by a theory. We also say that the theory *explains* the empirical generalizations (Part III). It can be seen to be a rather symmetrical picture in that generalizations like (9), (10), and (11) are now supported both from above and from below. They are deducible from the water droplet theory and are "inducible" from the empirical data—for example, (1) to (8).

The theory itself is, of course, a hypothesis. We can call it a **theoretical hypothesis**. In contrast to empirical generalizations, theoretical hypotheses are not obtained by methods of induction from below. They are said to be free inventions of the mind.[9] For example, to explain why objects, when unsupported, fall downward, Newton concocted (conjured up) the theory of gravitation, which, ironically, he also employed to explain why the moon does *not* fall downward (toward earth).[10] Dalton devised the theory of the atoms to explain why certain things can combine to form other things, and why certain things dissociate into other things under certain conditions (for example, when they are heated), why certain things are combustible and others are not, and so on. Dalton had no direct access to the atoms, which are too small to

---

9. The notion of free invention is slippery. See Chapter 32 for discussions of creativity and its relationship to the techniques of artificial intelligence. Aristotle distinguished between what we call formal induction (that is, inductive methods) and what he called intuitive induction, which is not regulated by rules. What is intuitive induction? Is it what creativity is about? What are *free* inventions?

10. This is a simplification of the story of the invention of the theory of gravitation. The credit for its invention cannot be attributed to just one person.

be visible. He had little more than his own imagination to guide him to this amazingly wonderful theory of the "microworld."[11]

Since theories are (supposedly) free inventions of the mind, what prevents them from being mere "tall tales"? After all, we could say that apples fall toward the earth when released because they are in love with the latter. We could say that the reason iron conducts heat is that it is minutely porous, so that it is relatively easy for heat to flow along its length (whereas wood is not minutely porous, hence does not conduct heat so well). Descartes, for example, did not explain the motions of the planets in terms of gravity as Newton did. He claimed, on the contrary, that the planets move as they do because they are caught in cosmological vortices. Such theories are (now) said to be bad, whereas the theory of gravitation and the theory of the atoms are classified as good. Are there any rational criteria for such judgments?

One such criterion is of course the criterion of empirical adequacy. For example, the caloric theory of heat, that heat is a kind of fluid, has been rejected as unacceptable (Section 7.2). The phlogiston theory has also been rejected (Section 7.2). The reason for these rejections is that they both failed certain empirical tests. So it seems that the goodness of a theory depends on whether it agrees with observations. A theory that agrees with observation is said to be **empirically adequate**, and empirically adequate theories are commonly recognized as good.

However, empirical adequacy is just one criterion of assessment. Theories can also be assessed in terms of logic. Every theory has certain logical features, from which we can often sort out the good from the bad. Naturally such logical assessments should be carried out before any empirical tests are done since they are much simpler and cheaper. We will study such assessments in the remainder of the chapter.

8.4 LOGICAL CHARACTERISTICS OF A GOOD THEORY

To discover these logical characteristics, let's ask what theories are for. What are the functions of theories? If the function of theories is merely to explain, then for any empirical generalization, satisfactory theories are not hard to find.

To illustrate, let us consider the empirical generalization,

H: Chalk is white.

(**H** has ample empirical support in that every white piece of chalk encountered is an empirical datum in support of *H*.) To explain *H*, let the theory, *C*, be invented.

C: Chalk is made of cheons. Cheons are small and white.

It can be seen that *H* is deducible from *C* and explained by *C*. However, intuitively we do not think that *C* is a good theory, not because it has failed certain tests, and not because it contains the unfamiliar word 'cheon,'[12] but because of something else too difficult to put into words. Roughly, we can say that such an explanation *does not advance our understanding*. It is like the story that runs as follows: Why doesn't the earth fall downward? Because it is supported on the back of an (invisible) tortoise. Why doesn't the tortoise fall downward? Because it is resting on the back of an (invisible) elephant. And so on.

Consider this example as well. Why did it rain last night? Because God willed it. Why was there an earthquake in Java? Because God willed that it occur. Why did my apple fall downward? Because God willed my apple to fall downward. Why does copper conduct heat? Because God wills that copper conduct heat. We can see that, with this device,

---

11. The atomic theory originated with the Greeks, dating back to the 5th century B.C.

12. In physics and chemistry, unfamiliar words abound—for example, 'electron,' 'positron,' 'valence.'

any phenomenon *P* can be explained. *P* would follow logically from GW1 and GW2:

GW1: Whatever God wills to happen does happen.

GW2: God wills that *P*.

There is something wrong with this explanatory schema, GW. It seems that explanation is too easy to come by. We can see that the unacceptability of GW is similar to that of the cheon theory.[13]

Perhaps being able to explain things is not enough for a theory to be acceptable. One might insist that acceptable theories must be true as well—that is, true theories are good, and false theories are bad. This goodness criterion is certainly appealing as well as commonsensical. After all, in science we are looking for truths, aren't we? But truth is an elusive notion. We have no way of knowing whether the cheon theory of chalk is true or not except by testing it empirically. Indeed such empirical tests have in fact been carried out many, many times in the two cases discussed earlier. Each piece of white chalk encountered bears testimony to the truth of *C*. But we don't think the theory is a good one. The GW theory is apparently true, too. The fact that it rained last night, the fact that there was an earthquake in Java, the fact that my apple fell downward, and the fact that copper conducts heat all seem to be testifying to the manifestation of the will of God and thus to the truth of the theory. But is the theory a true theory? Is it a *good* theory?

8.5 UNIFYING POWER OF THEORIES

Let's try a pragmatic approach to justify the use of theories. A theory like Newton's theory of gravitation (in the context of his mechanics) explains a large number of phenomena: why terrestrial objects fall downward, why they fall with (nearly) uniform acceleration, why pendulums swing with a regular pace, why projectiles move in parabolas, why there are tides, why the moon perpetually encircles the earth, why the planets move in ellipses, and hundreds of thousands of other kinds of phenomena. Even though the theory of gravitation consists of only one law, its explanatory power is immense.[14] I think Newton's theory of gravitation has achieved what Ernst Mach (1838–1916) called economy of thought. It is as if these hundreds of thousands of kinds of phenomena are all "stored" in his single law of gravitation in spite of their diversities. All these hundreds of thousands of kinds of motion are nonetheless derivable from the single law of gravitation. We can say that this single law **unifies** them all. To be able to reduce the many to the few, in particular to the one, is an achievement of economy. That's why Newton's theory has been hailed as the greatest achievement in science. Benefiting from this piece of history, we can see that one of the characteristics of a good theory is that it should have high **unifying power**, the higher the better. This is another way of saying that a good theory explains widely and thus promotes deep understanding. For what is understanding? It is but the ability to relate the apparently unrelated or to see the diverse as different manifestations of the one and the same underlying principle. In short, unifying power is explanatory power, and explanatory power is proportional to the depth of understanding. At least this is the opinion of a section of the philosophical community.[15]

A similar story can be told of the kinetic theory. The theory not only explains Boyle's law, and the law of Charles and Gay-Lussac, it also explains

---

13. A similar example was employed by Kitcher (1981). Mine dates from before his, when I employed it in lectures.

14. The theory of gravitation is built on Newton's mechanics, which consists of three laws of motion. To explain the phenomena mentioned, both the theory of gravitation and the three laws of motion are actually required.

15. This notion of explanation is different from the deductive notion of explanation to be discussed in Chapter 10. Rather it is related to the unificatory notions of Friedman and Kitcher (Sections 14.6 and 14.7).

the law of partial pressures, Graham's law of diffusion, the various specific heat capacities of gases, and many others.

The droplet theory of rainbows explains the seven colors, their order of appearance, the existence of secondary rainbows (which have a reversed color spectrum), the positions of rainbows relative to the position of the sun, the round shapes of rainbows, the angular radii of rainbows', and many others.

Thus we can see that all the three theories have impressive explanatory and unifying power, an indication that they are all good.

In contrast, the explanatory power of the cheon theory of chalk is absolutely at a minimum, because it explains one and one thing only—why chalk is white. For example, it cannot explain the "sister" phenomenon that rubies are red. Of course we can invent the reon theory to explain this second phenomenon, according to which rubies are made of reons, and reons are red. But this proves my point. From the phenomenon of white chalk to the cheon theory, there is no "economy of thought." The cheon theory unifies nothing. Neither does the reon theory.

The GW theory is also poor in unifying and explanatory power. To explain different phenomena P, different clauses have to be substituted for P in GW2. Thus there are as many GW2 statements as there are P phenomena. The case is obviously parallel to that of the cheons and the reons, where a distinct kind of particle has to be concocted to account for a distinct color. There is no economy of thought whatsoever.

The unifying power of a theory is a logical feature, for it is based on the logical relationship of deduction between the theory and what it can explain.

8.6 IN-BREADTH PREDICTIVE POWER OF THEORIES

Another pragmatic measure can be adopted for the assessment of theories. Apart from explanation and economy of thought, science also aims at (correct) predictions, and theories can be powerful predictive instruments. The invention of a theory is usually motivated to explain certain phenomena, but it would be a poor theory if it is "tailor-made" to fit these phenomena and these only. What is wrong with the cheon theory is that it is tailor-made to fit exactly the fact that chalk is white. The same is true of the reon theory. Such theories carry no (surplus) predictive power. For example, the cheon theory predicts nothing other than that chalk is white. The reon theory predicts nothing other than that rubies are red. Popper calls such theories *ad hoc*.[16] The GW explanatory schema has no predictive power either. To fill out the variable P, we need to know what has already happened. Thus it can explain everything but can't predict anything.

Good theories should possess high **predictive power**. Even though the kinetic theory of heat (and of gases) was first proposed mainly to account for Joule's equivalent of heat, Boyle's law, and the observed specific heat capacities of various gases, its scope of prediction far exceeds these. It predicts, for example, what is now known as the law of Charles and Gay-Lussac, and a whole host of others in the hands of Helmholtz, Maxwell, Boltzmann, and Gibbs.

The droplet theory of rainbows was first proposed by Theodoric of Freibourg in the 14th century, then correctly worked out in its details by M. A. de Dominis in 1611, and then further developed by Descartes in 1637 (Figure 8.1). Other than being successful in the explanation of the various phenomena associated with the rainbow in those days, it has numerous novel predictions. For example, it predicts the existence of tertiary rainbows and quaternary rainbows with their respective color orders. It predicts the occurrence of rainbows over waterfalls, and over the humble garden sprinkler. It also predicts the possibility of rainbows generated by oil droplets, rainbows by moonlight, rainbows by reflected lights on the ocean, and so on.

---

16. This notion of ad hocness is obviously related to those we discussed in Chapter 7.

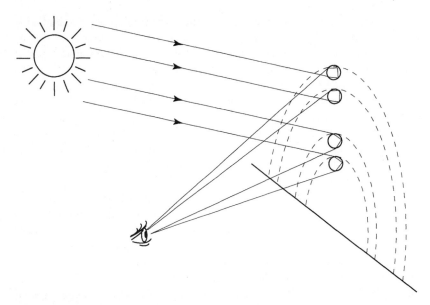

F I G U R E 8.1   Formation of the primary rainbow (lower one) and the secondary rainbow (upper one) by refraction and internal reflection in rain droplets.

It can be seen that the predictive power of both the kinetic theory and the droplet theory is high. That is what we expect of good theories.

8.7 IN-DEPTH PREDICTIVE POWER OF THEORIES

The kind of predictive power we have been studying is an **in-breadth predictive power**. The theory spreads itself laterally to cover many items and fields. For example, the kinetic theory spreads from the area of pressure (Boyle's law) to the area of temperature (the law of Charles and Gay-Lussac). The droplet theory of rainbows covers not only the phenomena of primary and secondary rainbows but also predicts the phenomena of tertiary and quaternary rainbows. In addition to rainbows caused by showers, it covers rainbows caused by waterfalls, sprinklers, and oil drops. In this section, we study another kind of predictive power: **in-depth predictive power**.

Observation tells us that rainbows are round, but how round are they? The observer has only a rough idea. In the days of de Dominis and Descartes, only crude measurements could be made to determine the angular radii of rainbows. The droplet theory, however, enables the mathematician to work out, from the laws of reflection and refraction, precisely these angular radii. The red border of the primary rainbow should have an angular radius in the vicinity of 42°, and the value for the violet border of the secondary rainbow should be about 54°. Such precise predictions could not have been made before the invention of the droplet theory. Thus the droplet theory improves on the precision of those observational generalizations.

The droplet theory also corrects observations. For example, the pretheoretical observer would think that the bow of the rainbow is an arc vertical to the horizon. The theory corrects this observation, for, according to the theory, the plane of the arc is perpendicular to a line linking the sun and the eyes of the observer. From these we can see the in-depth predictive power of the droplet theory.

A more striking kind of in-depth predictive power can be illustrated with the following example. If we combine Boyle's law and the law of Charles and Gay-Lussac, we have what is known as the equation of state of a gas: $PV = rT$. In 1873, from the kinetic theory of gases, J. D. van der Waals derived a refined version of this law, now known as van der Waals's equation: $(P + a/V^2)(V-b) = rT$.[17] It can be seen that this equation coincides with the equation of state when V (volume) is large compared to the two constants a and b. Experiments later confirmed van der Waals's equation.

Often in science, observation can only give us a rough idea of how nature behaves. The equation $PV = rT$, based purely on empirical findings, is only approximately correct. The kinetic theory yields a more exact version—van der Waals's equation. We can say that the kinetic theory possesses high in-depth predictive power. In fact, it improves and corrects the empirical generalization that the theory is meant to explain. The theory is non–ad hoc in a strong sense for it cannot be a mere case of tailor-made explanation to fit an empirical generalization, since the former is in fact inconsistent with the latter.[18]

We can now see why theories with high predictive power are desirable, whether they are of the in-depth kind or of the in-breadth kind. Formal induction as a means of projection cannot move across fields. For example, from a finite number of observations of white swans, formal induction predicts that all swans are white, yet it has absolutely nothing to say about the colors of ducks, of sparrows, or of cats. If one makes an ascent to a theory, however, such as the theory of genes, such predictions can be made. Thus the power of theories as predictive machines is obvious, and it is not an arbitrary requirement for good theories to have high predictive power. We can call the invention of (good) theories to support (explain) empirical generalizations the **method of theories**, which as you can see is far superior to the **method of induction**.[19]

8.8 SUMMARY AND DISCUSSION

Through observation, and then by formal induction, we can arrive at very useful generalizations such as "Wood floats in water," "Ice melts when heated," "Salt is soluble in water," and "Metal conducts heat." These findings belong to the stage of phenomenal science, which is then usually followed by the stage of theoretical science, where theories are invented to explain empirical generalizations. Theories can be good or bad. The empirical criterion of a theory's goodness is, of course, that it makes correct (empirical) predictions and passes (empirical) tests—that is, that it should be empirically adequate. However, apart from this, a good theory should also satisfy the following three logical criteria:

(a) It should have high unifying power in that it explains and unifies a large number of diverse phenomena and generalizations.

(b) It should have high in-breadth predictive power in that it makes novel predictions over and above the phenomena and generalizations that first prompt the invention of the theory, thus covering new fields and areas.

---

17. Here a and b are constants characteristic of each gas, a/V^2 is a correction term that takes into account the attraction between molecules, and b allows for the fact that molecules have finite volumes.

18. This notion of ad hocness is also related to those we discussed in Chapter 7. Another example of in-depth predictive power is that of Newton's theory of gravitation in that it corrects (albeit by small amounts) both Galileo's law of free fall and Kepler's laws of the revolutions of the planets.

19. Karl Popper's methodology is based on the contrast he draws between the method of induction and his favored hypothetico-deductive method (Chapter 24). 1 think it more fruitful to contrast the method of induction with the method of theories sketched here, especially in light of Thomas Kuhn's critique (Part VII).

(c) It should have high in-depth predictive power in that it improves, refines, and corrects those predictions embodied in the generalizations that motivate the invention of the theory.

When a theory lacks predictive power as described in (b) and (c), Popper calls it ad hoc, so that we can say that a good theory should not only be empirically adequate, it should also have high unifying power and should be non–ad hoc.

'Unifying power' and 'predictive power' are closely related pragmatic notions that play central roles in the philosophy that science aims at the economy of thought (Section 9.5). According to one version of this philosophy, science should be organized as a pyramid, at whose apex are a few very general principles from which all scientific truths can be derived and thus unified. Such a vision of organized science was first conceived by Aristotle (Chapters 15 and 19).

On the other hand, theories with low unifying power are uneconomical, whereas ad hoc theories are barren and infertile. There is little pragmatic gain in having such theories.

From our discussions so far, it looks as if the choice between theories is simple and straightforward. The "good guys" are those that are empirically adequate, highly unifying, and non–ad hoc. The "bad guys" are those that have none of these "virtues." But life in philosophy is never this simple and straightforward. We saw in Chapter 7 how difficult it is to develop an adequate notion of ad hocness for the revision of hypotheses, and how Popper's definitions fail in many ways. Similar difficulties face the present notion of ad hocness of theories. Popper would say that:

(12) A theory is ad hoc if it lacks either in-breadth predictive power or in-depth predictive power. In other words, a theory is ad hoc if it cannot generate novel predictions.

This definition can be seen to be in the same line of thinking as D_1 and D_2 of Sections 7.5 and 7.6. It looks reasonable enough. Definition (12), in commonsense terms, says that a theory is ad hoc if it can only explain the given empirical data and nothing more. In other words, the theory is cut to size to fit the data. Such ad hocness was amply illustrated by the chalk-cheon example of Section 8.4. It seems indisputably obvious that such theories are unacceptable.

However, even though (12) looks simple, straightforward, and reasonable, it has hidden difficulties. Let me explain. Usually in predictions (such as those in tests) we require the employment of auxiliary hypotheses (Chapter 6), and auxiliary hypotheses typically come from fields other than the one we are concerned with. For example, to test the rain dance hypothesis (hypothesis (7) of Section 7.7), we may invoke auxiliary hypotheses belonging to the field of videocamera technology. You can see from this that since most predictions require auxiliary hypotheses from other fields, the availability of auxiliary hypotheses from other fields determines the number of novel predictions that can be made. A theory standing on its own may not furnish any novel predictions, but in combination with other fields of study it may provide plenty. The chalk-cheon theory, on its own, may not have any predictive power, but, who knows, when coupled with other theories it may have high predictive power. A clear example is the theory that magnets are aggregates of tiny magnets. This theory is parallel to the chalk-cheon theory, yet, when coupled with other theories, it yields many novel predictions, and in fact this is the current accepted theory of magnets.[20]

Since I spent some time in Section 7.7 on this point—the dependency of novel predictions on background knowledge (accepted theories and data of other fields)—I will not repeat myself here. I would simply make two further remarks: (i) the unifying power of a theory also depends on the nature of our background knowledge, and (ii) the notion of ad hocness as in (12), and indeed in D_1 and D_2 of Chapter 7, is a local concept. What is required is a global concept, which covers not just one theory at a time, but covers globally a

---

20. Exercise 2a for this chapter gives you further opportunity to discuss this example.

collection of theories in related fields. This can probably be developed out of the notion of simplicity that we will study in Chapter 9.

Besides empirical adequacy, unifying power, and non–ad hocness, other "virtues" have been proposed for good theories—for example, coherence with other theories, simplicity, consistency, and progressiveness. We will explore these as we move into deeper and wider issues (Chapters 9 and 24, and Part VIII), and we will further our study of the nature of theories in Part IV.

We began this chapter by asserting that all branches of science progress in two stages: the phenomenal and the theoretical. I would like to close with a word of "wisdom": the idea of the two stages is only a description of science up to the present. We should not rule out the possibility of a third stage yet to come. Theories have been making their mark in science since Newton. With the advance of artificial intelligence and cognitive science (Chapter 32), who can foresee the future shape of the development of science? Techniques and methods more powerful than the use of theories, I think, are real possibilities. (Fortunately we teachers and students are not required to deal with these in examinations yet!)

KEY TERMS INTRODUCED IN THIS CHAPTER

phenomenal stage	empirical generalizations	unifying power	in-depth predictive power
theoretical stage		predictive power	
phenomenal science	theoretical hypothesis	in-breadth predictive power	method of theories
theoretical science	empirically adequate		method of induction
empirical data	unifies		

REFERENCES

Hempel (1966, secs. 4.3–4.4), Carnap (1966, partly reprinted in Kourany (1987, 122–138)), and Holton and Roller (1958, sec. 8). For further references, see Section 4.1 and its references.

EXERCISES

1. Give an example of an empirical generalization (preferably from the history of science) that has theoretical support, and give one which as yet has no theoretical support.

2a. It is a well-known "hypothesis" that iron bars when stroked with a magnet a large number of times will become magnetic. The generally accepted explanation is as follows: (i) Each iron bar consists of numerous tiny magnets, which are randomly orientated, thus nullifying one another's magnetic effects, (ii) When an iron bar is stroked by a magnet, the stroking realigns those tiny magnets, so that all the north poles are now in the same direction. This realignment yields the observed magnetic effect.

Is this theory a good theory? How does this theory compare with the theory that chalk is made of white particles (and hence chalk is white)?

2b. Repeat Exercise 2a with the following theoretical explanation: When water boils, it disappears into the atmosphere as what we call steam. The reason for the disappearance is that water is made up of tiny particles packed tightly together. When heated, these particles disperse forming what we call steam. Their invisibility soon after becoming steam is due to the small size of the particles.

2c. Repeat Exercise 2a with the following theoretical explanation: Salt dissolves in water but not in oil. This is because water is a substance that is interspersed with tiny cube-shaped pores. Salt, being made up of tiny cubical particles, "slips" into these pores in the act of dissolving. The reason why salt does not dissolve in oil is because the pores in oil are round. (That sand does not dissolve in either water or oil is because its particles are too big for either.) (This is adapted from the ancient Greeks.)

2d. Repeat Exercise 2a with the following theoretical explanation: The spider, without education, builds complicated webs. The swallow migrates thousands of miles without guidance or foreknowledge of its ultimate destination. The reason is because the spider is born with a web-building instinct, whereas the swallow possesses a migration instinct. (This is how the "instinct" school of motivation in the 19th century attempted to explain characteristic animal behaviors.)

3. Can you think of a theory which has high unifying power but low predictive power? Low unifying power but high predictive power? Check in the history of science whether these two "virtues" regularly correlate. If so, explain why it is so.

4. Scrutinize a fringe science such as astrology or palmistry. Assess its theories with our criteria of empirical adequacy, explanatory power, in-breadth predictive power, and in-depth predictive power.

5. Choose a field of study from the history of science or from the history of the social sciences. Check whether its development follows the two stages: the phenomenal stage and the theoretical stage. (You might like to make use of the materials in Chapter 0. Or you might like to study the development of psychology, which should be comparatively easy for the nonscientist student to handle.)

Chapter 9*

Conventionalism and the Duhem-Quine Thesis

9.1 Introduction

9.2 Conventionalism

9.3 Duhem-Quine Thesis

9.4 Simplicity

9.5 Phenomenalism and Conventionalism

9.6 Instrumentalism and Conventionalism

9.7 Critique of Conventionalism

9.1 INTRODUCTION

We saw, in Chapters 6 and 7, how the employment of auxiliary hypotheses in indirect tests poses a predicament for science. To test a hypothesis, *H*, the normal practice is to deduce an *observable* consequence, *C*, from *H* with the aid of a number of auxiliary hypotheses, *A*. Then through observation we check whether *C* is true or not. However, the predicament is that neither can we say definitely whether *H* is true when *C* is true, nor can we say definitely whether *H* is false when *C* is false. However, you might say that even though we cannot make *definite* conclusions, we can still make *probable* conclusions. Carnap tried to work out how much the probability of *H* would be increased by the truth of *C*, and how much it would be decreased by the falsity of *C* (Section 4.9). But his program, so far, is not promising. For one thing, we do not know whether the auxiliary hypotheses, *A*, are true or false. If they should be false, the test would be of little value, irrespective of whether *C* eventually turns out to be true or false. You might suggest that, before we do the test, we should first ascertain the truth of *A*, or, at least, its probability. This appears the right thing to do. However, in trying to ascertain the truth of *A*, we need to design a test, and this test most likely would require its own auxiliary hypotheses. Now we are stepping into an infinite regress. Let us call this predicament, the **auxiliary-hypothesis predicament**.

---

*This chapter is more advanced and is optional.

Popper tries to overcome the predicament by introducing the methodological rule: that no ad hoc revisions of either the main hypothesis or the auxiliary hypothesis are allowed. But, as we saw in Chapter 7, this does not work.

So what are we going to do with the predicament? Should we give up the search for truth? This is, in a sense, precisely what conventionalism recommends!

9.2 CONVENTIONALISM

The chief exponents of conventionalism were Henri Poincaré (1854–1912), mathematician-cum-philosopher, and Pierre Duhem (1861–1916), physicist-cum-philosopher, both of whom were from France. According to them, statements can be classified *roughly* into **observational statements**[1] and **theoretical statements**. Observational statements are roughly those whose truth or falsity can be checked by direct observation, whereas theoretical statements are those that cannot be so checked.[2] For example, 'This tabletop is round' is said to be observational, whereas 'The earth is round' is said to be theoretical. 'Rainbows have seven colors' is observational, whereas 'Rainbows are produced by rain droplets' is not. Other theoretical statements, for example, include 'Heat consists of micromotion' and 'Oxygen is entering into the burning candle.' Plenty of controversy surrounds the observational-theoretical distinction, and no one seems to be able to agree to the boundary line between the two.[3] In Chapter 1, we raised the question whether any statements are directly testable. We will have more opportunity to enter into detail about this issue in Chapters 17 and

23. Fortunately, to understand conventionalism, it is not necessary for us to go into all sorts of niceties.

Here is Conventionalism 1:

Any *theoretical* statement can be held to be true, irrespective of (unfavorable) empirical evidence.

The argument for this thesis is simple. Let T_1 be any theoretical statement. To refute it empirically, it is necessary to check it with an indirect test. But, in practice, any indirect test will involve the use of one or more theoretical statements, T_2, as auxiliary hypotheses. Should the test turn against T_1, we can always lay the blame on T_2, unless T_2 can be independently affirmed. This will involve one or more further indirect tests, which again will involve one or more theoretical statements, T_3.[4] This can carry on ad infinitum. You can see that this is simply an elaboration of the auxiliary-hypothesis predicament, which was discovered by Poincaré and Duhem.

Let me argue the case differently. In indirect tests, we need to use instruments ('instrument' being understood in a wide sense). For example, to test whether the earth is round by watching sailing ships going out into the horizon (Section 6.4), we require the use of light to look at the boat. Light is an instrument for our test. The use of *any* instruments involves theories about them. Here we assume that light travels in straight lines, which may not be true. This is a very simple test compared with most tests used in modern-day scientific experiments. Think of the use of the optical microscope. The theories involved are far more complicated and sophisticated than the use of light rays without modification. If you are not convinced, think of the use of the electron microscope then, and think of the use of all sorts of meters in the laboratory.

---

1. This classification of theirs is implicit rather than explicit, and you will find that 'observation statement' is often used instead of 'observational statement.'

2. The use of the word 'theoretical' here is different from our use of the word in Chapter 8, though the two uses are related.

3. We have so far ignored the complexity brought in by the use of logical terms like 'all' as in "All rainbows have seven colors" as opposed to 'This rainbow has seven colors.'

4. Whether this test turns out to be positive or negative, the involvement of further auxiliary hypotheses, T_3, means that we cannot say anything about the truth of T_2. (We also have to allow for the possibility that T_1 may be part of T_3.)

Poincaré and Duhem's conventionalism takes empirically confirmed observational statements as given. In contrast, theoretical statements are conjectures. According to Conventionalism 1, while you cannot do much about the given observational statements, usually called empirical data, you can propose *any* theoretical statements to "cope" with these data. The term 'any' might be too strong for some. (At least it appears as if anything goes.) **Conventionalism 1a** is a weaker version of the philosophy, which is intuitively more acceptable:

Given a set of empirical data (in the form of true observational statements), many possible theories are available to "cope" with them.[5]

You can see that I use the loose term 'to cope with' on purpose. You may like to employ the term 'to explain' instead. Unfortunately 'explanation' is not a term that Poincaré and Duhem would use. We will hear more about this later.

Poincaré gave a convincing parable in terms of geometry. However, since this parable is slightly technical, let me help out with a much simpler but less elegant and less accurate example, to set you on the way. Suppose you are given a clock. The three clock hands go around the clock face, which has the traditional 12 numerals on it. You, being a scientist, take note of the movements of these clock hands and record the hands' positions accurately and minutely at certain fixed intervals. You may have these positions listed as three separate tables, one for each hand of the clock. These are your empirical data. Now you might like to invent a theory to explain these data (even though Poincaré and Duhem would not recommend the use of the term 'explain'). Your theory might be based on the postulation that the clock works on a spring, a pendulum, and a set of cogwheels, all hidden behind the clock face. Let's call this type of theory ST. Please take note that there can be

as many theories belonging to ST as your imagination can allow. For example, one theory may make use of 5 cogwheels, and another may make use of 50 cogwheels. However, a friend of yours does not like the idea of pendulums and springs at all. So she postulates that the clock is driven by an electric motor. Let's call this second type of theory ET. Again many theories can belong to ET. Of course there are many other possible types of theory. "Which is the *true* theory for this clock then?" one might ask. Obviously, one way to find out the correct theory is to open up the clock and take a look. But what if the clock cannot be opened? We will then never know which is the *correct* theory.[6] Perhaps the terms 'true' and 'correct' have no meaning here if we *in principle cannot* open up the clock and examine the inside. This is the position of Conventionalism 1a.

For conventionalism theories are not meant to yield truths. They are invented to "cope" with given empirical data. We will later spend a bit more time on this elusive term "to cope." In our present example, there are an infinite number of theories, each able to "cope" with the given data. You can attempt to eliminate some by requiring them to "cope" with more data. For example, you might put your ear to the clock and find that the clock gives out loud ticks. You may then argue that the loud ticking noise should rule out all theories of the ET type. This may sound intuitively correct even though, according to conventionalism, you can always protect the ET theories by revising some of the auxiliary hypotheses. For example, you might claim that the air medium between your ear and the clock has distorted the sound from the clock, or that the ticking comes from somewhere else. On the other hand, even if all the ET theories were forced to be withdrawn, an infinite number of other possible theories would still be left. The thesis of conventionalism is certainly not easy to refute!

---

5. There is more than one way to skin a cat!

6. The impossibility of the clock being opened up corresponds to the unobservability of theoretical entities.

Let's now proceed to Poincaré's parable.[7] Imagine a two-dimensional Euclidean world in the form of a flat circular disk of diameter, say, one meter in length. Imagine that it is inhabited by some two-dimensional beings. Since it is difficult to imagine two-dimensional beings, let's think of some antlike creatures living on the circular flat disk. Suppose the center of the disk is hot (not so hot that the antlike creatures feel uncomfortable), and the temperature gradually drops off to absolute zero at the perimeter. Suppose further that everything (including the antlike creatures and their measuring rods) expands and shrinks with increases and decreases in temperature, in such a way that the length of anything will shrink to zero if it were placed at temperature absolute zero. What is this world like *as far as* these antlike creatures are concerned?

First, they will never be able to reach the rim of the disk, because as they walk (crawl?) toward the rim, they gradually shrink, and their steps get proportionally smaller. As far as they are concerned, their world is infinite in all directions.

Second, when they draw a circle anywhere, they will find that its circumference (as measured by standard measuring rods, which, unknown to the scientist, vary their lengths according to the temperature of their positions) is more than 2π times that of its radius. You can easily see this to be the case for circles drawn concentric with the disk itself. Given such a circle, its circumference would be colder than anywhere inside the circle, hence it takes more spans of the standard measuring rod to go round the circumference than are normally required.

Third, it can be shown that triangles drawn on such a disc will be such that their angle sums will be less than two right angles (180°) (again as measured by their measuring rods whose lengths are susceptible to temperature variations).

There are at least two different ways to "cope" with such strange experience. One way is the way

I have just told the story: postulating a mysterious force (such as heat) that distorts our measuring rods (and all other objects) in such a way that they yield the three types of phenomena discussed earlier. However, this is not the only way, and certainly not the most aesthetically pleasing way. The second way is to assume that the space in which these creatures live is non-Euclidean (that is, does not obey the laws of Euclidean geometry). In fact, a two-dimensional space obeying Lobachevskian geometry can be shown to have the three properties listed. We can, therefore, say that the empirical data can be *reinterpreted* so that the effects of the distortions of the measuring rods are now "transferred" to the "crookedness" of space. Under either interpretation, the antlike creatures can say that the three phenomena listed are exactly what they would expect.[8,9]

Conventionalism 1a can be illustrated in terms of other examples: (a) The same empirical data on the specks of lights in the night sky can be "coped" with in terms of either the geocentric theory or the heliocentric theory (Section 7.4). (If we are willing to sacrifice the authenticity of the telescope, the geocentric theory can handle even the phases of Venus.) (b) The phlogiston theory and the oxygen theory are merely two of many possible interpretations of data on combustion (Section 7.3), and (c) With a bit of ingenuity, even the caloric theory can cope with data that are supposedly in favor of its rival, the kinetic theory (Section 7.3).

An analogy might help: We can take true observational statements as islands, and theories as a network of bridges linking these islands. Conventionalism 1a simply states that there are many possible ways of building such networks. You can see that conventionalism is not taking (absolute) truth or (correct) explanation as the aims of science. Even though theory making is not arbitrary, there is an essential element of convention in the choice of theories, hence the name conventionalism. The purpose

---

7. If you should find this example difficult, please skip it, since I had advised you to do so in "A Word to Students." There are many other examples you can rely on. The policy of this text is to oversupply examples so that you will not miss out.

8. Einstein's theory of special relativity was published in 1905, the same year as the publication of Poincaré's *Science and Hypothesis*, where this parable was told. The similarity of the two works on the (conventional) interpretation of space is striking.

9. A more fully digested version of Poincaré's parable is available from Sklar (1974, chap. 2, secs. F and G).

of theory making is only to represent efficiently and to predict accurately. Poincaré has another analogy. Theories are likened to library catalogs. The purpose of these catalogs is to classify books for easy access. Thus theories, for Poincaré, are not statements attempting to make assertions about the world. They are, rather, means of classification of empirical data in such a way that these data are so systematically organized as to enable easy access. Needless to say, analogies should never be taken literally. We will hear more on this topic later.

9.3 DUHEM-QUINE THESIS

In 1951, Willard Van Orman Quine published his celebrated article "Two Dogmas of Empiricism" (Quine, 1951), which, among other things, developed the thesis of conventionalism further. For Quine, the element of convention is not confined to theoretical statements. In fact, according to him, there is no basic distinction between theoretical and observational statements.[10] Thus Quine proposes **Conventionalism 2**:

Any statement, be it what is traditionally called theoretical or observational, can be held immune from refutation by sense experience.[11]

Quine denies that "each statement, taken in isolation from its fellows, can admit of [empirical] confirmation or [disconfirmation]." His countersuggestion is that "our statements about the external world face the tribunal of sense experience not individually but only as a corporate body" (Quine 1951, p. 41). Thus Poincaré and Duhem's **holism**[12] is being extended to cover *all* statements.

Some of you might think that Quine's extension may be overstretched. You might object, claiming that simple observational statements such as 'This is a piece of red paper' should surely be refutable by sense

experience. We need only look at the object to ascertain whether the statement is true. However, the truth of the matter is not so simple. First, it takes more than just a look to ascertain that the thing is a piece of paper. Second, to ascertain whether it is red or not, we need to look at it through light. Light is here playing the role of an instrument, and it can be faulty (for example, the light used may not be white: it may be red). Even if we assume that the light is not faulty, we still have to assume lots of theories surrounding the use of this instrument—for example, that it will provide us with certain sensations if it is *reflected* by a red *smooth* surface after passing through *air* of certain *density*. When the expected sensations do not obtain, one can always lay the blame on one of these theories. (I have discussed this issue before in Section 1.7 and Chapter 6, and I will offer more discussion of it in Chapter 22.) Quine claims that as long as you are willing to sacrifice some other statements (no matter how dear and clear they are to you—for example, "$2 + 2 = 4$"), you can hold onto any statement you like come what may in terms of recalcitrant experience.

The formulation of Conventionalism 2 can be misleading. It is as if Quine recognizes the observational-theoretical distinction and then claims that both observational and theoretical statements can be held immune from empirical refutation. The truth of the matter is that Quine denies the observational-theoretical dichotomy altogether. So I think we should formulate his conventionalism as **Conventionalism 2a**:

All statements are theoretical, and any theoretical statement can be held immune from refutation by sense experience.

The thesis of conventionalism, in broad terms, is often known as the **Duhem-Quine thesis**, probably

---

10. This does not mean there is no *practical* distinction between the two. There can be distinctions prompted by convenience or other pragmatic values.

11. Quine's actual thesis is even stronger if we state it more accurately. Quine's conventionalism states that "any statement [be it theoretical or observational, analytic or synthetic] can be held true, come what may, if we make drastic enough adjustments elsewhere in the system" (Quine, 1964, p. 43). For the distinction between the analytic and the synthetic, see Chapter 11.

12. 'Holism' is sometimes spelled as 'wholism,' derived from the word 'whole.'

because Quine quoted Duhem as his source of inspiration. I, for one, think that the thesis should be called the **Poincaré-Duhem-Quine thesis**.[13]

9.4 SIMPLICITY

Conventionalism seems to have opened the way to pluralism, if not chaos, in science. Traditionally science aims at truth and explanation. Truth should be absolute in the sense that there cannot be two incompatible statements which are both true, and explanation should also be absolute as well in the sense that there cannot be two incompatible explanations that are both correct. Since conventionalism seems to claim that for any given set of sense experience we can have more than one satisfactory and yet mutually incompatible theories, it implies that either truth and explanation are not absolute or they are not the aims of science. Whereas Quine has little to say on this issue, Poincaré and Duhem choose the second alternative. For Poincaré and Duhem, theories are not meant to be truths, nor are they meant to be used to explain phenomena. They are invented to coordinate the observational statements which we find true. A theory is a sort of network, connecting and relating our observational data. Duhem uses the term 'representation.' A representation, in this sense, does two things. It helps to organize thoughts and it helps to generate predictions. Thus the first desideratum that a theory aims for is simplicity. The more simple a theory is the better it organizes thoughts. At least, this is intuitively the case. The second desideratum is elegance, in that some representations are more elegant than others. The third is consistency. An acceptable theory should be consistent in the sense that it does not contradict itself, even though Poincaré and Duhem do allow for the use of incompatible theories for different ranges of experience. The notion of elegance is obviously difficult to capture. It may even be subjective. The notion of consistency belongs to logic and has been quite fully and satisfactorily studied. But what is simplicity?

The notion of **simplicity** is not simple. Many attempts have been made to pin it down but without much success. Let me illustrate the problem in terms of hypotheses in general (taking theories as a special kind of hypothesis, as we have been doing here and in the last chapter).

Hypotheses are usually projections from what has been observed (empirical data) to what has not been observed. For example, having examined 500 swans and found them all white, you may project and claim that

(1) *All* swans are white.

This is a hypothesis. Another hypothesis can be:

(2) The 500 swans that have been observed are white but all other swans are black.

The question is, Which of these two hypotheses is simpler? You might say that (1) is definitely simpler. Why? Is it because (2) has more words in it? But what about (3)?

(3) Swan 1 is white, swan 2 is white, ..., swan 500 is white, and all other swans are also white.

Surely (3) says the same thing as (1), yet (3) has so many more words than (2). If (1) is simpler than (2), (3) should be simpler as well in spite of its long-windedness. Perhaps what counts toward simplicity is not the formulation but the content. But how to measure the content of a hypothesis? And how to measure its simplicity?

I'll give a more sophisticated example. In analytic geometry, a straight line is representable by a linear equation (a first-order equation):

(4) $ax + by = c$

A circle is representable by a second-order equation:

(5) $x^2 + y^2 = c^2$

An ellipse is representable by another second-order equation:

(6) $ax^2 + by^2 = c^2$

---

13. There are subtle differences between Poincaré's and Duhem's conventionalisms (see Gilles, 1993, Part II).

You may say that since the three equations are in increasing order of complexity, the straight line, the circle, and the ellipse are also increasing in complexity in that order. However, it is possible to represent a circle by a first-order equation:

(7) $r = c$

where r stands for the radius vector in polar coordinates and c is a constant. This equation is apparently simpler than (4)! So again it seems that the term 'simplicity' is about the content and not the representation. But what is this content? How is its simplicity or complexity to be measured?

You might say that (4) and (5) are representations of a straight line and a circle respectively, hence the straight line and the circle are the contents. Further you might claim that the straight line is simpler than the circle because the straight line is generated by a point that "carries on" in the same way—that is, in the same direction, whereas the circle is generated by a point that moves "around." But, of course, if you think a bit deeper, you will find that the circle is generated by a point keeping the *same* distance from a fixed point. By the same token the spiral of Archimedes should be equally simple, since it can be generated by a point keeping its distance increase from a fixed point the *same* as its angular increase from a fixed line. That's why it is representable in polar coordinate as:

(8) $r = \theta$

Karl Popper has an interesting theory of simplicity that relates simplicity to content rather than to forms of representation. Popper proposes two theses: (i) that the simplicity of a hypothesis is proportional to its content and (ii) that science aims at statements of high content. You can see that the two together justify our intuition that science prefers the simple rather than the complicated. I will be brief here because I will be presenting his philosophy in detail in Chapter 24.

It is a well-known fact that given *any* two points, a straight line can be drawn through them. But this is not so for an arbitrary set of three points. So in order to falsify the hypothesis that a certain relationship is a straight line, we require only three data points. However, to falsify a circle hypothesis (that a certain number of data points are related by a circular curve), we require four data points. Similarly, to falsify an ellipse hypothesis, we require a minimum of five points. For Popper, the easier it is to falsify a hypothesis, the higher the content it has. And since content is proportional to simplicity, we can see why the straight line is simpler than the circle, which, in turn, is simpler than the ellipse. At least this is Poppers argument.[14]

Unfortunately his theory of simplicity does not square with intuition. Let's take the following two hypotheses:

(9) All chairs are red.

(10) All the chairs in this room are red, and all other chairs are brown.

Intuitively (9) is simpler than (10), but each hypothesis requires only one "misbehaving" chair for its falsification. Hence according to Popper, the two should be equally simple.[15]

Is simplicity a logical concept, as Popper thinks? Is it an objective concept at all? I think it is a mixed concept, partly objective and partly subjective. I'll illustrate with an example. As you will remember, Ptolemy proposed a system of epicycles to account for the positions of the planets relative to the fixed stars (Chapter 7). This was a geocentric system. More and more epicycles had to be added to Ptolemy's system, as more and more data on the planets were collected. At the time of Copernicus—that is, about 1,400 years later—the number of epicycles required reached 80. Copernicus switched over to a heliocentric system and claimed that he needed only 34 epicycles. Kepler, following on the heels of Copernicus,

---

14. See the discussions on ad hoc revisions in Section 7.5.

15. Another objection to Popper's theory of simplicity is that, for any *specific* curve, be it a straight line, a circle, or an ellipse, it requires only one point (outside it) for its falsification.

replaced Copernicus's epicycles with six ellipses, one for each of the planets.

Which of the three systems is the simplest? If we count the number of closed curves used, Kepler's system obviously leads in simplicity, followed by Copernicus's system, and then by Ptolemy's system. This is the objective side of simplicity: that simplicity is inversely proportional to the number of "components" used. However, this conception of simplicity is not so convincing once we note that the ellipse was mathematically a very difficult figure to handle given the sort of mathematical techniques available to Ptolemy. Probably the circle is the only closed curve that Ptolemy could handle with relative ease. In other words, the choice of the circle is not really because the circle is the perfect figure, but is a choice based on the given technological circumstances. It was much easier for Ptolemy to construct his ever-increasing number of epicycles than to try to "capture" the planets with the unfamiliar ellipse.[16] You should note that the circle is a figure with only one variable (the radius), whereas the ellipse is governed by two variables: the eccentricity and the distance between the two foci. If we assess Ptolemy's choice in terms of the availability of mathematical techniques of his time, the epicycle is the natural and simpler choice. This seems to have illustrated the subjective side of simplicity, that simplicity is relative to, among other things, the mathematical techniques available.

Simplicity is an illusive notion, not at all easy to capture. Is it an objective concept or a subjective one, or is it a mixed concept? That's why neither Poincaré nor Duhem had much to say about it, apart from using expressions such as "good sense is the judge of hypotheses which ought to be abandoned."[17]

9.5 PHENOMENALISM AND CONVENTIONALISM

The exposition of conventionalism and the concept of simplicity will not be complete if we omit mentioning the great physicist-cum-philosopher Ernst Mach (1838–1916). His philosophy is often known as **phenomenalism** and also as **sensationism**, and it predated the conventionalism of Poincaré and Duhem. Mach claims that "properly speaking the world is not composed of "things" as its elements, but of colors, tones, pressures, spaces, times—in short what we ordinarily call individual sensations" (1960, pp. 48-49). Sometimes these "individual sensations" are known as **sense data**, to stress the *given* nature of sensations. So what Mach claims is that material objects such as tables and chairs, stones and sticks do not really exist. The only things that exist are our sensations—that is, sense data.[18]

A *vulgar* version of the argument for this thesis is that the scientist is confronted (directly) by a variety of sensations and *nothing else*. She can know, with more or less certainty, facts about particular pieces of sensation. For example, she knows what sort of color the piece of visual sensation has when she looks at a red table (under any kind of light). But she does not really know the table's true color. In order to know the latter, she has to *infer correctly* from the color of her piece of visual sensation to the color of the actual mind-independent material object, relying on the authenticity of auxiliary hypotheses such as the color of the light used to illuminate the object, theories of reflection of colored lights, physiological theories of sensation production, and so on. As pointed out earlier, these auxiliary hypotheses can themselves be false,

---

16. Note that Kepler's ellipses work only with the heliocentric system. If Ptolemy had adopted the use of the ellipse, he would have had to face the additional complexity of having to reproduce the apparent motions of the planets from a moving earth.

17. Duhem (1987, p. 168).

18. This is a simplified version of phenomenalism. The fuller version would have to recognize the existence of something like mind (unless you go for something like Bertrand Russell's neutral monism). Minds need to be there in order to "contemplate" or "receive" the sense data. This is most obvious in Berkeley's (1685–1753) writings. Because of this essential involvement of minds, his philosophy is known as a kind of idealism.

hence such inferences are not reliable. Hence the table does not exist.

For many this argument is fallacious and unacceptable. It is one thing to say that we do not know with *certainty* that material objects exist, but another thing to say that they certainly do not exist. Inferences can be unreliable and yet can (with a bit of luck) yield correct results. There is, of course, no guarantee that tables and chairs exist, but it is not foolhardy to conclude that they exist (based on good reasons).

I think Mach's argument is more refined. It is in line with Conventionalism 1a rather than with Conventionalism 1. The difference between Mach's thesis and Conventionalism 1a is that empirical data for Mach are not about material objects as we normally take them to be, but about sensations. Hence we can formulate Mach's thesis as **Conventionalism 3**:

Given a set of sense data (in the form of true statements about sensations), many possible theories are available to "cope" with them.

I would like to warn you that this is *not* Mach's own formulation. It is my digest of his thesis in light of conventionalism, which we have been studying. You may not, at this stage, see the difference between Mach's real argument and its vulgar version, as related at the start of this section. In brief, Mach claims that we are not *warranted* in claiming existence for material objects if Conventionalism 3 is true. I'll delay the details of this argument until Chapter 18, where we study scientific realism and antirealism. As far as we are concerned here, for Mach there is no intrinsic difference between macroscopic objects such as tables and chairs, and microscopic objects such as electrons and genes, and rather abstract objects such as absolute space, radio waves, ether,

phlogiston, oxygen, caloric fluid, and magnetic fields. They are all "products" of scientific theories. The function of theories, for Mach, is to coordinate the sense data that have been collected. Theories are not statements, making assertions, and they are not meant to explain the occurrence of events. They are, as the conventionalists would say, systems for the representation of data, albeit not data about material objects as Conventionalism 1a would have, but data about sensation.[19]

Mach coined the phrase 'economy of thought.' Theories are for economy of thought. They are economical representations of the actual. Sometimes Mach calls them *memoria technica* (technical memory aids) so that they are mere instruments[20] to help us to "cope" with (that is, to remember), in an economical fashion, the vast amount of sense data that "shower" on us day in and day out. For the same set of sense data, there can be numerous possible theories. Since the function of theories is the economical representation of the actual, it is obvious that the most economical theory should be adopted. His notion of the economical corresponds exactly to Poincaré's and Duhem's notion of the simple, although the former is based on utility whereas the latter seems to be based on aesthetics. Thus, in Mach's own words: "Science itself, therefore, may be regarded as a minimal problem, consisting of the most complete possible presentation of facts with the least possible expenditure of thought."[21]

9.6 INSTRUMENTALISM AND CONVENTIONALISM

You can see that conventionalism denies that theories and hence theoretical statements have truth values. In other words, the conventionalist thinks

---

19. A typical sense-data statement would be: "There is a piece of orange, round patch (of sensation) inside a piece of blue square patch (of sensation) here and now." It is claimed that this would be a true sense-data statement for someone looking at an orange against a blue wall.

20. The idea that theories are instruments is the central thesis of a school of thought known as instrumentalism, which we will study in Chapter 16.

21. Mach (1960, p. 51).

that theories and theoretical statements are neither true nor false.[22] For example, the following are generally recognized as theoretical statements:

(11) When an alpha particle collides with a nitrogen atom, the latter will turn into an oxygen atom with the emission of a proton.

(12) In 1887, Heinrich Hertz transmitted radio waves from one end of his room to the other end.

(13) The virus of rabies[23] on attacking the nervous system of animals can cause convulsions and paralysis.

According to conventionalism, these statements would be neither true nor false because they contain theoretical terms such as 'alpha particle,' 'radio wave,' and 'virus of rabies.' These terms, it is said, do not denote anything. Theories are mere instruments, as has been said in the last section, and, as instruments, they can only be classified as being useful or not, but not as being true or false. (For example, we would not apply the attributes 'true' and 'false' to items in our toolbox such as hammers, spanners, screwdrivers, and so on.) In a nutshell, this is what is known as **instrumentalism**.

For the layperson, however, when we say that a certain statement, S, is true, we mean that there is a "piece" of reality that corresponds to S, and it is this piece of reality that makes S true. For example, the statement:

(14) Edmund Hillary and Tenzing Norgay reached the top of Mt. Everest on May 29, 1953.

is true if and only if Edmund Hillary and Tenzing Norgay were *real* people, Mt. Everest was a *real* mountain, and the pair did reach the top of the mountain on May 29, 1953. Hillary and Tenzing Norgay's reaching the top of Mt. Everest is the piece of reality which makes (14) true.[24] So, according to the conventionalist, we must not equate the statement status of (14) with the status of any of (11)–(13). There is no reality meant to correspond to the latter. This is not because the latter three are false. It is simply because they are not, strictly speaking, statements at all. There are no claims of the existence and reality of alpha particles, nitrogen atoms, radio waves, viruses, and so on. We make and accept such "statements," not because they are true, but because of something else—for example, their usefulness. Theoretical terms such as 'alpha particle' are not meant to denote anything. There are no "hard" pieces of objects, big or small, supposedly to correspond to these terms. Thus, for the instrumentalists, alpha particles and so on are merely useful fictions.[25]

Instrumentalism comes in grades corresponding to the various shades of conventionalism. Let me explain. Conventionalism classifies statements into the observational and the theoretical, and claims that theoretical statements can, simply by convention, be held against the onslaught of all and every type of sense experience imaginable. Since the boundary between the observational and the theoretical depends very much on one's philosophical inclinations, there are arguably many acceptable demarcations, each of which results in a different corresponding instrumentalism. For example, some might say that (11) and (12) are theoretical while (13) is observational, and others might say

---

22. First, we are here taking 'theory' in a very general and loose sense so that what we say in this sentence covers all the three varieties of conventionalism discussed. Second, the term 'truth-value' is a technical term used in logic. There are two truth-values in classical logic: truth and falsity. When a statement is true, we say that it has the truth-value truth, and when it is false, we say that its truth-value is falsity (Section 1.1).

23. The virus is invisible to the naked eye.

24. This type of philosophy of truth is known as the correspondence theory of truth.

25. Though (12) and (13) do have denoting terms such as 'Heinrich Hertz' in (12) and 'convulsion' in (13), such statements are still not meant to correspond to reality because of the presence of theoretical terms in them. (12) would have been an observational statement had it been formulated as (12'), which reads: "In 1887, Heinrich Hertz switched on an induction ("spark") coil at one end of his room and found that the receiver coil placed at the other end of the room produced sparks across its gap."

that all the three are theoretical.[26] Phenomenalism, on the other hand, claims that even (14) is theoretical, and the only observational statements are sense-data statements. Thus you can see that there are grades of instrumentalism.[27]

The aims of science, as we said before, are usually taken as truth and explanation. If the conventionalists are right, then these two aims seem to need modification. First, truth now applies only to observational statements (which, according to phenomenalism, are confined to sense-data statements). Second, explanation in science is usually in terms of theories. Since theories are not meant to be statements, and their functions are not meant to be explanatory, this second aim of science requires revision as well. According to the conventionalists, theories are invented for the systematization or representation of the given—observational statements found to be true. The simpler and more economical these systematizations or representations are, the better. In sum, for the conventionalist, science aims at the collection and systematization (or representation) of true observational statements, and theories are instruments for the latter of these two aims.[28]

9.7 CRITIQUE OF CONVENTIONALISM

Let's close this chapter with a critique of conventionalism!

First, you will find that there are serious doubts about the so-called observational-theoretical distinction which forms the basis of conventionalism (except for Quine's version, which is Conventionalism 2 and 2a). Arguments for and against the distinction will be given in Chapter 17.

Second, the notion of simplicity (and the corresponding notion of economy of thought) is difficult to make rigorous and explicit. Intuitively, we seem to be quite clear what it is for a theory to be simple. It is quite a different matter when we have to write down objective criteria for the notion.

Third, to clear these two hurdles, we should and must understand the logical structure of scientific theories. As with atoms and molecules (and houses), theories have structures. At this juncture we are relying heavily on metaphors. We have been saying that theories provide a *network* that links up islands of true observational statements. Poincaré has likened theories to *library catalogs*. Others say that they are like languages. And I, in Section 9.6, used the terms 'systematization' and 'representation,' and, quite a while back, I said that theories, according to conventionalism, are employed to "cope" with empirical data. It is one thing to use metaphors, and another thing to say what we want to say clearly and precisely so that others can assess it objectively. Metaphors are useful, but they can only be taken as the first step toward the final stage of understanding.

What, then, are theories like, so that they can cope with and *systematize* empirical data? It is true that library catalogs do help to systematize the arrangement of books, and it is also the case that catalogs are neither true nor false just as theories are claimed to be neither true nor false. Also, catalogs are judged for their usefulness and simplicity, and so are theories. But theories are *not* catalogs. So what are they? Similarly, though the metaphor of language does help us to understand the working of theories, few would say that theories *are* languages. So, again, what are theories? How do theories "cope" with data? How do they *systematize* data? One last point, which is by no means the least, is that theories are supposed to be able to enable us to

---

26. See Section 17.2 for further details.

27. See Chapter 16 for more on instrumentalism.

28. This line of thinking, however, is not quite fully applicable to Conventionalism 2 and 2a, because, according to them, there are no observational statements (all statements being theoretical). If there are no observational statements at all, what can be the candidates for systematization?

make useful and true predictions. How can catalogs or languages manage to do that?[29]

I'll close this chapter on conventionalism. However, this is by no means the end of this fascinating philosophy. You will study (i) how instrumentalism and conventionalism take on scientific realism in Chapters 16 and 18; (ii) how Lakatos attempts to contain the "heresy" of conventionalism in Chapter 28; and (iii) how Quine's version of conventionalism resurfaces in Kuhn's philosophy in Chapters 26 and 27.

KEY TERMS INTRODUCED IN THIS CHAPTER

auxiliary-hypothesis predicament

observational statement

theoretical statement

conventionalism

holism

Duhem-Quine thesis

Poincaré-Duhem-Quine thesis

simplicity

phenomenalism

sensationism

sense data

instrumentalism

REFERENCES

On conventionalism (Poincaré and Duhem): The article "Conventionalism" in Edwards (1967) gives a good overview of conventionalism. Poincaré (1952, Part II) gives the full details of Poincaré's parable, whereas Sklar (1974, pp. 88–94) provides a helpful digest of the parable. Duhem (1987, pp. 158–169) is a readable excerpt from Duhem's writing. Oldroyd (1986, pp. 189–203) and Losee (1980, pp. 165–170) provide easy readings on both Poincaré and Duhem. Gilles (1993, Part II) is a detailed and slightly more advanced text on the subject.

On conventionalism (Quine): Quine (1951) is the classic that details his arguments for conventionalism. Gibson (1988) provides a digest as well as an appraisal of Quine's philosophy as a whole. Harding (1976) is a collection of essays by some of the most influential contemporary philosophers on the Duhem-Quine thesis.

On simplicity: For an introduction, see Hempel (1966, pp. 40–44). For Popper's analysis, see Popper (1959, chap. 7). For detailed general discussions, see Thagard (1988, sec. 5.4), Hesse (1974, chap. 10), and Bunge (1963).

On phenomenalism: Bakker and Clark (1988, pp. 47–54) and Oldroyd (1986, pp. 176–182) give good summaries of Mach's phenomenalism.

On instrumentalism: Consult Chapter 16 and its references.

EXERCISES

1. Three hypotheses and, following each, some refuting evidence are listed. Defend the hypotheses as best you can in the spirit of Conventionalism 1, taking the hypotheses as theoretical statements. Critically discuss Conventionalism 1 in view of your (successful or unsuccessful) defenses.

   (a) Hypothesis: The earth is flat (that is, is a flat disk).

---

29. See Hung (1981a) for my opinions on the subject.

Refuting evidence: pictures of the earth from space, your flying experience round the globe, and shadows of the earth on the face of the moon.

(b) Hypothesis: The theory of gravitation.
Refuting evidence: Moses parted the Red Sea (assuming this to be true).

(c) Hypothesis: The clock (in our clock parable of Section 9.2) is driven by a swinging pendulum.
Refuting evidence: The clock still works when it is placed upside down.

2. Find evidence from the history of science to support Conventionalism 1a: Find historical cases where the same set of experimental data is explainable in terms of more than one theory. (You may like to make use of materials in Chapter 0.)

3a. Taking the following hypothesis as an observational statement, defend it in the spirit of Conventionalism 2. In view of your defense, critically discuss Conventionalism 2:
The Statue of Liberty is taller than the twin towers of the World Trade Center (of New York).

3b. To minimize the chances of observational error, science has been attempting to reduce observations to the simplest forms. For example, many of the observations done in the laboratory are meter readings. Suppose the pointer of a certain meter has been acknowledged by all the colleagues of Quine to be pointing at 7. Do you think that Quine can reasonably argue for the hypothesis that the meter reading is 8 instead? Is Conventionalism 2 really defensible?

4. In the context of his phenomenalism, does Mach mean that we should not trust sitting on our favorite chair because according to Mach that chair does not exist? (Surely it is foolhardy to try to sit on patches of color sensations!)

5. Since sensations are private, in that your sensations are yours and my sensations mine, how can phenomenalism explain the public nature and objectivity of science?

6. Can theories always be compared in simplicity? How often can they be so compared? Discuss in terms of both our intuitive notion(s) of simplicity and Popper's. You may like to base your discussions on the following pairs of theories:

(a) The caloric theory of heat versus the kinetic theory of heat (Section 7.3).

(b) The phlogiston theory of combustion versus the oxygen theory of combustion (Section 7.3).

(c) The particle theory of light versus the wave theory of light (Chapter 0).

(d) Empirical data: the first two numbers of a sequence are 2 and 4.

Theory A: the sequence is an instantiation of the formula: $2n$ (where $n = 1, 2, 3, \ldots$)
Theory B: the sequence is an instantiation of the formula: 2^n (where $n = 1, 2, 3, \ldots$)
Predictions from A: the next number is going to be 6
Predictions from B: the next number is going to be 8
Which is simpler, A or B?

7. In Chapter 8, we said that a good theory should be high in explanatory power and also high in predictive power. Are the two notions, explanatory power and predictive power, related to the notion of simplicity? Discuss in terms of both our intuitive notion(s) and Popper's notion of simplicity.

PART II SUMMARY

This part is on scientific methods for the acquisition of truth. Such methods come at two levels: the phenomenal level and the theoretical level.

A.   At the phenomenal level:

1.   **Discovery (Chapter 5)**: After introducing the notion of **mechanical method**, we asked whether there are any mechanical methods of discovery. The answer is "yes, namely, the **simple inductive methods**." But SIM is highly limited and highly inefficient, because it is essentially a "blind search" method. Mill's methods and various statistical methods are improvements on SIM even though they are only partially mechanical. The development of artificial intelligence (Chapter 32) will probably bring about more methods of discovery.

2.   **Empirical evaluation and justification (Chapters 6 and 7)**: Here we studied the logic of indirect tests in detail. In any test, **auxiliary hypotheses** would always be employed in practice. The involvement of auxiliary hypotheses in a test situation would make it difficult to locate the place of fault should the result of the test turn out to be negative. The fault could lie with either the main hypothesis or with the auxiliary hypotheses, or with both. Then we proceeded to the study of **crucial tests**, tests for the purpose of choosing between two competing hypotheses. Since these tests usually involve the use of auxiliary hypotheses, they cannot be conclusive in their findings. Thus the term 'crucial' can be misleading. In order to remedy the situation, Popper suggests that scientists should make it a rule of practice that they would not seek **ad hoc revisions**: neither to their main hypotheses nor to their auxiliary hypotheses. However, Poppers suggestion does not work in real-life cases, as exemplified by the history of science.

B.   At the theoretical level:

3.   **Theoretical justification (Chapter 8)**: The credibility of empirical generalizations is believed to be enhanced by theoretical support. Whereas empirical data support empirical generalizations

from below through induction, theories support generalizations from above by deduction. However, not all theories are good theories. It is not sufficient for a theory to be **empirically adequate**. A good theory would have to share the following characteristics: **high unifying power, high in-breadth predictive power, and high in-depth predictive power**.

4.   **Conventionalism and the Duhem-Quine thesis (Chapter 9)**: The unavoidable employment of auxiliary hypotheses in empirical tests results in what I called the **auxiliary-hypothesis predicament**. Various interpretations of this predicament result in various philosophies, among which are three versions of conventionalism. Conventionalism assumes that there is a distinction between observational statements and theoretical statements. Observational statements found to be true through direct experience, generally known as empirical data, are taken by conventionalism as objective and veridical. However, because of the inevitable employment of auxiliary hypotheses in tests, there are indefinitely many possible theories that can cope with these data. According to conventionalism, choice among these theories can only be a matter of pragmatics, and it takes simplicity as the prime factor governing such choices.

Conventionalism faces three types of difficulty:

(1)   What is simplicity? Is it an objective concept or a purely subjective concept or a mix?

(2)   One of the underlying assumptions of Conventionalism is the observational-theoretical distinction, which is a highly controversial subject.

   (a)   One can take the observational as more or less what the term means in common usage. This is **Conventionalism 1** (and **1a**).

   (b)   One can confine 'observational' to cover only sense-data statements. This is **Conventionalism 3 (Phenomenalism)**.

   (c)   Finally, one can take all statements to be theoretical. This is **Quine's Conventionalism 2** (and **2a**).

(3) The third difficulty with conventionalism concerns theory structure. What is the logical structure of a theory so that it can "cope" with empirical data without claiming to be true or false? How do theories "cope" with such data?

5. **Instrumentalism** (Section 9.6): Conventionalism naturally leads to instrumentalism, according to which theories are not meant to be taken literally. The theoretical terms used are not to be understood as denoting real entities. Thus, for Conventionalism 1, electrons and radio waves are only useful fictions. Conventionalism 3 (phenomenalism) goes even further. It takes even tables and chairs as convenient fictions (for, according to it, only sensations are real). Finally, Conventionalism 2 (Quine's version) goes to the extreme. For it there are no observational statements. If we give this version of conventionalism an instrumentalistic interpretation, nothing seems to be claimed by science to be real. In other words, science does not seem to claim that anything is real, be it electrons or radio waves, tables or chairs, red sensations or blue sensations. This does not sound right. But then philosophy is meant, at least occasionally, to expose the folly of common sense and common intuitions. Perhaps science is not about any particular things, but is about the universe as a whole. Quine himself seems to opt for a philosophy known as *internal realism*,[1] which will be discussed in detail in Chapter 31. (Just as in detective stories, the solution of the riddle should always be left to the very end.)

Has conventionalism undermined the thesis that one of the main aims of science is the seeking of truth? The answer, I think, depends on which type of conventionalism we subscribe to. Conventionalism 1 limits the search for truth to truths about commonsensical, medium-size material objects. Conventionalism 3 takes truths to be truths about sensations. As for Conventionalism 2, internal realism has to be clever in trying to reconcile the traditional and well-testified idea of science as a truth-seeking enterprise with its nonrecognition of any particular kinds of objects that science is supposed to be about.

---

1. This term is not Quine's. It came from his Harvard colleague, Hilary Putnam, who employed the term to describe his own philosophical position.

The Quest for Explanation

Most people think that the discovery of truth is the sole aim of science. In their mind, the business of science is the collection and accumulation of truths rather like the practice of collecting stamps. Notions like testing and prediction, which have taken up a large part of Part II, are all truth-oriented notions. I think the time has come for us to study the other aim of science: explanation.

Science should not be thought of merely as a collection of "brute" facts. In science facts should be well organized and well understood. It is nice to know that salt is soluble in water. But it would be much better if we also know *why* salt is soluble whereas, for example, sand is not. Science should be able to promote understanding. The world cannot be a mere mess of brute happenings. On the contrary, each and every single event should occur with and only with a good reason. Such a "principle of sufficient reason" was proposed by Leibniz (1646–1716). Science is exciting because it is the business of science to find out these reasons. Our intellect has a natural yearning to understand things around us, and hence has an attraction to science.

People often take (correct) prediction as the pragmatic aspect of science whereas explanation is the theoretical aspect. Explanation is said to be non-pragmatic in that it has no practical value. At best it only satisfies the curiosity of the mind. We shall, however, show that prediction and explanation are in fact closely related. Usually when one is attained, the other is achieved as well. Good science has both high explanatory power and high predictive power, whereas bad science has neither. We have already touched on these points in Chapter 8.

What is explanation? Scientists and laypersons provide scientific explanations almost every day of their lives and yet, when you ask them what counts as an explanation, what conditions govern a good explanation, and why science should attempt explanations, you'll discover that answers to these questions are not so readily forthcoming.

There are quite a number of theses on the nature of scientific explanation. We will study four. The classical view put forth by Popper, Hempel, and Oppenheim in the early part of the century takes explanations as deductive arguments. It is a relatively simple thesis, but powerful, insightful, and useful. It will take up Chapters 10–13.

Chapter 10 gives a straightforward exposition of this thesis, which is known as the covering-law thesis. Since the notion of laws of nature plays a vital role in the thesis, we will spend **Chapter 11** on laws of nature, those "things" that "run" the universe! **Chapter 12** will be on the probabilistic variant of the thesis, and on a number of difficulties

it faces, including the problematic notion of probabilistic causality (causes that sometimes bring about effects, and at other times not, all according to a probabilistic preset pattern). **Chapter 13** studies the nature of human actions. Can actions be explained in terms of laws of nature as the covering-law thesis claims? Human actions are supposed to be free. It is the mind which decides what to do, not laws of nature. But then, what is mind? Thus the study of explanation leads us into the study of the philosophy of mind!

Simple and powerful as the covering-law thesis is, there has been widespread dissatisfaction with it. In **Chapter 14** we shall study three different proposals. Thus we are faced with four alternatives. Are they mutually exclusive views or are they complementary perspectives? You have to make up your own mind.

Chapter 10

Covering-Law Thesis
of Explanation

10.1 CANDIDATES FOR EXPLANATION

The term 'scientific explanation' covers all kinds of explanation distinctive of science and practiced by successful scientists. First we would like to know what kinds of "things" need explanation. The straightforward answer is that only facts require explanation. For example, it is a fact that the earth revolves round the sun once in approximately 365 days. This fact requires an explanation. Why around the sun? Why 365 days? However, it is not a fact that the earth revolves round Mars in a circle. Since it is not a fact, there is no way and no need to explain it. We cannot explain "things" which haven't occurred or "things" which aren't there. We can't explain, for example, why Newton had three legs (simply because it is not a fact that he had three legs).

A fact is usually represented by a true statement. For example, "The earth revolves round the sun in approximately 365 days" is one. Let P be a statement. What we are saying is, therefore, that P requires an explanation, should P be true. In philosophy, we find it simpler to talk about statements rather than talking about facts. The notion 'fact' is awfully elusive. One might, for example, be tempted to ask: Where is the fact that the earth revolves round the sun? Or where is the fact that salt is soluble in water? In trying to answer such questions, you would soon discover how mysterious and puzzling facts are. Hence let us avoid the use of the term 'fact' here.[1] We will say that only true statements (or sentences) require explanations.[2]

But not all true statements require explanations. To explain a true statement P is, broadly speaking, to locate some other statement, from which P "acquires" its truth. However, some statements are true by themselves, so to speak. They do not need something else to "bestow" truth on them. I am referring to statements such as: "All bachelors are unmarried," "All white swans are white," and "All triangles have three angles." In philosophy, we call such statements "analytic." Sometimes we say that they are true by definition—that is, that they are true solely because of the meaning of the words involved. We can see that such statements are necessarily true. Since we will have an opportunity to study statements of this kind further in the next chapter, here I would merely like to point out that such statements do not require scientific explanations.

Only statements which, though true, could very well be false require explanations. For example, the time it takes the earth to go round the sun could be 300 days. That's why it makes sense to ask, why 365 days instead of 300 days? Newton's apple could have fallen upward or sideways, but, as a matter of fact, it fell downward. Hence, again, it makes sense to ask why. It can thus be seen that only facts that can be conceived to be otherwise require explanation. Such facts are known as **contingent facts**, and statements stating such facts are known as **contingently true statements**. Here are a few more examples:

(1) This object floats in water.

(2) This bar conducts heat.

(3) All ice floats in water.

(4) All copper conducts heat.

Note that (1) and (2) are singular statements whereas (3) and (4) are universal statements (Section 6.2). In the following sections, we will study various forms of explanation concerning both singular and universal statements.

10.2 DEDUCTIVE-NOMOLOGICAL EXPLANATION OF SINGULAR FACTS

The statement that is to be explained is known as the **explanandum**. The set of statements that gives the explanation is known as the **explanans**.[3] What is the relationship between the explanans and the explanandum that must hold in order for the explanans to explain the explanandum? In other words, how does the explanans manage to explain the explanandum? For example, when asked, "Why does this block float in water?", would the statement that some birds are white be considered an adequate answer?

(I) Explanandum: This block floats in water.

     Explanans: Some birds are white.

"Certainly not!" one would say. Birds have nothing to do with this block, and whiteness has nothing to do with flotation. It seems that the explanans has at least to be *relevant* to the explanandum. But 'relevance' is a vague term. For example, I don't think one would accept the following explanation either:

(II) Explanandum: This block floats in water.

      Explanans: This block is cubical in shape.

Clearly the explanans is *relevant* in that the same thing is being talked about. But just as little does

---

1. Those who are intrigued by the notion of fact can read Chapter 1 of Bertrand Russell's (1956) famous essay, "The Philosophy of Logical Atomism," originally published in 1918 and reprinted in *Logic and Knowledge*, 1956.

2. In practice, it is only statements that we *believe* to be true that require explanations.

3. 'Explanans' is in the singular form; its plural is 'explanantia,' whereas the plural for 'explanandum' is 'explananda'. Some of the older texts might employ the terms 'explicans' (for explanans) and 'explicandum' (for explanandum).

the explanans explain the explanandum. Now what about the following:

(III)   Explanandum: This block floats in water.

      Explanans: This block is ice.

I don't think there is any difference between this case and the last. Being ice has nothing to do with flotation in water, *unless*, of course, ice is such that it floats in water. So let us have:

(IV) Explanandum: This block floats in water.

     Explanans: This block is ice.

                All ice floats in water.

Alternative (IV), unlike (III), is an acceptable explanation, at least intuitively.

As has been indicated earlier, true statements that could very well have been false require explanations. "This block floats in water" could have been false. It is conceivable that the block could sink. To explain a fact is to make out why the possible alternatives have not been "taken up." In our case, an alternative for the block is to sink, which, however, has not occurred, and so an adequate explanation must show why the block has not "chosen" to sink. Now the explanans of (IV) can be seen to be adequate because it logically implies the explanandum. "This block floats in water" would have to be true if this block is ice and all ice floats in water. In other words, (V) is a valid deduction.

(V)   Explanans: This block is ice.

               All ice floats in water.

     Explanandum: This block floats in water.

The explanans explains because the explanandum has been shown to have no "choice" but be true.

Let's take another example:

(VI) Explanans: This bar is copper.

               This bar is heated.

               Copper expands on being heated.

     Explanandum: This bar expands.

We can see that this intuitively acceptable explanation is again a valid deduction. Since the explanans guarantees the truth of the explanandum, the bar has no "choice" but to expand, provided that the explanans statements are true.

This relationship between valid deduction and scientific explanation has been pointed out by Karl Popper[4] and Carl Hempel.[5] According to them, the explanans explains in virtue of the fact that the statements of the explanans serve as premises of a valid deduction with the explanandum as the conclusion.

In Example V, the explanans consists of two statements. "This block is ice," in characterizing the block, says that it is ice, and not stone, not sugar, and so on. We say that this statement states the **initial condition** of the explanation. The term 'initial condition' comes from physics. It is not too appropriate here, as the term 'initial' has a temporal implication. I personally would prefer to call the expression 'the condition clause.'

The initial condition alone in general does not logically imply the conclusion. In the present case, we can see that the inference from "This block is ice" to "This floats on water" is invalid. For it to be valid, an extra premise is required, and this required linkage between "ice" and "flotation" is provided by "All ice floats in water." Without this linkage, 'ice' is irrelevant to 'flotation,' just as 'being cubical' is irrelevant.

"All ice floats on water" is a **law of nature**, which we shall deal with in detail in the next chapter. Here it suffices for me to say that laws of nature are both universal and (physically) necessary. The present law, for example, says that ice invariably floats, irrespective of space and time. It further says that ice floats, not as a matter of chance, but because of its intrinsic nature, hence it necessarily floats. It should now be plain why "This block is ice" together with "All ice floats on water" gives an adequate explanation of the explanandum: this floats because it is ice, and the intrinsic nature of ice is such that it floats.

Popper puts it this way: "To give a **causal explanation** of an event means to deduce a statement which describes it, using as premises of the deduction one or more **universal laws**, together with certain singular statements, the **initial conditions**."[6] Carl Hempel[7] presents a similar point in the form of the following schema:

(VII) $C_1, C_2, \ldots, C_m$ (initial conditions)

$$\frac{L_1, L_2, \ldots, L_n}{E} \quad \begin{array}{l} \text{(laws of nature)} \\ \text{(explanandum)} \end{array}$$

The initial conditions are all singular statements. They together characterize the actual situation. There may be more than one of them. The laws of nature, because they are laws of nature, "compel" the "conditions" in such a manner that E has to eventuate. Again there may be more than one law of nature.

Example VI is a slightly more complicated example than Example V. Here there are two initial conditions. As I said before, the term 'initial' implies that the condition somehow occurs earlier than the event to be explained. This does not apply to "This bar is copper," for the bar's being copper is not a happening that occurs just before the expansion. The bar has always been made of copper. Hence the term 'initial condition' for this statement is misleading. On the other hand, however, the term applies quite well to the second premise. That the

bar is heated can be seen to be a "proper" initial condition because the heating does occur before the expansion takes place.

It is helpful at this stage for you to conceive scientific explanations as causal explanations.[8]

We can, therefore, take the initial conditions as specifying causes, and the explanandum as specifying the effect.[9] To explain an effect E is to point out the causes $C_1; C_2, \ldots, C_n$. It is on account of these causes that E happens. Again, just as in the case of initial conditions, we do not usually say that the bar's being made of copper is a cause. However, for the sake of simplicity, it does no harm at present to stretch the use of 'cause' so that all the initial conditions can be called causes. This cause-effect formulation, I think, is easier to grasp than the initial condition–explanandum formulation. To explain E is to specify both the causes of E and the laws that link the causes to the effect.

Schema VII represents what Hempel calls a **deductive-nomological (D-N) explanation**. It is "deductive" because the explanation is a valid deductive inference; it is "nomological"[10] because laws of nature, being the link between the causes and the effect, play an indispensable part in the explanation. Both the initial conditions and the explanandum are singular statements, whereas laws of nature are always universal.

10.3 DEDUCTIVE-NOMOLOGICAL EXPLANATION OF LAWS

Not only singular statements are in need of explanation, universal statements also require explanation. For example, we can ask "Why should ice

---

6. See Footnote 4.

7. See Footnote 5.

8. This suggestion is meant to help the beginner gain an initial understanding of scientific explanation. Other concepts of causal explanation will be introduced in Chapter 14.

9. Strictly speaking, the initial conditions and the explanandum are *statements* that specify the causes and the effect respectively.

10. 'Nomological' is derived from the Greek word 'nomos,' meaning law.

float in water?" Note that the question is not about any particular piece of ice, but about ice in general.

True universal statements are usually laws of nature. Laws of nature are explicable in terms of other laws of nature. For example, the following would be an acceptable explanation:

(VIII) Explanans: Ice is less dense than water.

Anything less dense than water floats in water.

Explanandum: Ice floats in water.

Note that the explanation is again a valid deduction, and since laws of nature are indispensable components of the explanans, this type of explanation is a case of deductive-nomological explanation as well. We can summarize this type by the following schema:

(IX) $L_1, L_2, \ldots, L_n$ (laws of nature)

L (explanandum, which is also a law of nature)

L is the case because it is the case that L_1, $L_2, \ldots, L_n$.
The latter necessitate the former.

10.4 THE COVERING-LAW THESIS OF SCIENTIFIC EXPLANATION

According to Hempel, D-N explanation is the ideal and standard type of explanation for science. Hempel proposes that an acceptable explanation must satisfy two conditions: (i) The explanans must be relevant to the explanandum, in the sense that the former provides good grounds for believing that the latter has occurred and (ii) The explanans must be independently testable.[11]

D-N explanations satisfy the first condition admirably in that the explanans fully guarantees the explanandum, for, given that the explanans is true, the explanandum would have to be true. We can almost say that the explanans is relevant to such an extent that it brings about the occurrence of the explanandum.

The second condition is meant to rule out pseudoexplanation such as the following:

(X) Neptune is angry today.

Whenever Neptune is angry, the sea is rough.

The sea is rough today.[12]

This is a valid deduction and yet it is not acceptable as a genuine explanation, not because the premises are untrue, but because there is no *independent* means to ascertain whether they are true or not. If the only way to show that Neptune is angry is by pointing out the roughness of the sea, the premises are said to be not **independently testable**—that is, not testable other than by using the explanandum as a test phenomenon. Clearly a vicious circle has been created, for now, on the one hand, the conclusion is justified (explained) by the premises, and on the other, the premises are justified (empirically supported) by the conclusion.[13]

In contrast, (V) is an acceptable scientific explanation. Not only is the argument valid, its two premises are both independently testable—that is, tests not involving the use of the explanandum-fact are available. For example, we can test the first premise by measuring the object's temperature and seeing whether it is in the vicinity of 0°C. The second premise can be tested by taking ice blocks from, say, the Antarctic to see whether they float. In

---

11. In Hempel (1966, sec. 5.2), the second condition is, however, erroneously described as "the requirement of testability," not as "the requirement of *independent* testability."

12. This example came from Popper (1972, p. 192).

13. An independent test would be possible if it were, for example, true that whenever Neptune is angry then the sky will be covered with clouds. The reason is that one can test whether Neptune is angry or not, by examining the sky instead of looking at the sea.

either test, the explanandum-fact involving that particular piece of ice has not been employed. This is what is meant by "*independently* testable."[14]

The nice thing about valid deductions is that if the premises are true, the conclusion has to be true. The premises guarantee the conclusion. Used as an explanation, the valid deduction demonstrates why the explanandum has to be the case by virtue of the truthfulness of the premises. You can see the symmetry between explanation and prediction in Hempel's model. Take a deductive argument like (V). If the given is the conclusion (that is, 'This block floats in water'), then the argument is an explanation, the premises functioning as explanans. However, if the given is the premises, the argument can be taken as a predictive inference, the conclusion being the prediction. We can summarize this feature of symmetry between explanation and prediction as follows: a quest for explanation is a quest for as-yet-unknown premises to ensure the given conclusion; a quest for prediction is a quest for as-yet-unknown conclusions from the given premises.

According to Hempel, many acceptable explanations that do not seem to display the D-N form are D-N explanations in disguise. Let's consider the explanation: "This lump of butter melted because it had been placed in a hot frying pan." It is not in D-N form, for, as it stands, it is neither deductively valid nor nomological. Hempel calls this kind of explanation **elliptic explanation**. In an elliptic explanation, some obvious premises have been suppressed. In the present case, the suppressed premise is that butter melts when heated. Elliptic explanations can be seen to be genuine D-N explanations once such premises are restored.

Another case of seeming nonconformity to Hempel's ideal of D-N explanation is what Hempel calls '**explanation sketch**.' Explanation sketches are not full explanations in that they are only rough indications of where satisfactory explanations can be found. For example, one can say that John has blue eyes because of his genes. This is only an

explanation sketch. An area has been marked out as the likely area of the causes—that is, in the genes—and a research program is implied. But this is far from being a full explanation yet. In short, such "explanations" are not of D-N form, because they are not full explanations, but are only explanation sketches.

What about **historical explanations**?[15] When asked why Henry VIII divorced Catherine of Aragon in 1533, the historian might say that it was because Henry wanted a male heir, or she might say that Henry got tired of Catherine. Such explanations occur frequently in historical writings, and they do not seem to conform to the D-N pattern since they are not deductive and no laws of nature seem to be employed. Historians also from time to time attempt to explain "macro-events" like the French Revolution, and usually such explanations are not of the D-N form either. They might, for example, say that the French Revolution was due to the widespread dissatisfaction of the people with a weak government.

Hempel insists that, in the social sciences, D-N explanations should be used, and have actually been used, whether it is a case of "macro-events" or a case of "micro-events." Most historical explanations, according to Hempel, are based on commonsense psychological and sociological laws, which are usually suppressed because of their commonsense nature. Thus historical explanations are in general elliptic, and they can be seen to be D-N explanations once the missing premises are restored. In the case of Catherine of Aragon and Henry VIII, a plausible psychological law could be that when a man is tired of his wife, he tries to find a way to get rid of her. In the case of the French Revolution, a (not so plausible) sociological law could be that revolutions take place whenever there is widespread dissatisfaction with a government that happens to be weak.

Thus Hempel argues that D-N explanation is universally applicable, not only to the natural

---

14. We have discussed this notion in Section 7.6.

15. Sometimes known as *genetic explanations*.

sciences but also to the social sciences. Other than probabilistic explanation, which will be studied in Chapter 12, Hempel and his followers claim that it is the only acceptable kind of explanation.

This is Hempel's **covering-law thesis**, in essence: (i) To explain the occurrence of an event E is to show that E happens as a necessary consequence of one or more laws of nature. (ii) To explain a law of nature, L, is to show that L is a logical consequence of some other laws.

Hempel has produced good arguments for his thesis. First, he argues that only covering-law explanations satisfy the two requirements of adequate explanation: the requirement of relevance and that of independent testability. Second, he argues that all well-known cases of explanations in the history of science are covering-law explanations. It seems that this thesis has a theoretical justification as well as a factual justification. However, not all philosophers

are convinced by his arguments. In fact, in the last 30 years or so the philosophical community has become more and more skeptical of the thesis. We will survey the rise of other contending schools of thought in Chapter 14. For the present, however, we should study the topic of natural laws in detail because the covering-law thesis hinges on what sort of "animal" laws of nature are. What are these wonderful things called laws of nature, which can make things happen and which are so sought after by the scientists? We must, as philosophers, try to understand these fundamental building materials of the world because it is obvious that the covering-law thesis implies that all explicable events occur in accordance with laws. Thus laws are the keys to the secrets and mysteries of the universe.

"What are laws of nature?" This is our next problem.

KEY TERMS INTRODUCED IN THIS CHAPTER

contingent fact	initial condition	initial conditions	explanation sketch
contingently true statement	law of nature	deductive-nomological explanation	historical explanation
explanandum	causal explanation		covering-law thesis
explanans	universal law	independently testable	
		elliptic explanation	

REFERENCES

General References for Part III as a Whole

Introductions: Lambert and Brittan (1987, Part II), M. H. Salmon et al. (1992, chap. 1), and Trusted (1987).

Anthologies: Kourany (1987), Boyd et al. (1991, Part II), Brody and Grandy (1989, Part II), Pitt (1988), and Brody (1970).

Others: Nagel (1961) (chaps. 2, 3, and 4) and Scheffler (1963, Part I), offer a classical presentation of the subject.

Salmon (1989) gives a comprehensive survey and critique of four decades of research and controversies in this area.

Kitcher (1989) presents his unifactory theory of explanation as well as critiques of other three theories.

Koertge (1992) gives a fair and well-argued summary critique of the four main theories of scientific explanation in the course of reviewing Kitcher and Salmon (1989).

Specific References for this Chapter

There are numerous introductory texts on the subject: Hempel (1966, secs. 5.1–5.2) (reprinted in part in Boyd et al., 1991), Lambert and Brittan (1987, pp. 18-25), Bakker and Clark (1988, chap. 5), Kosso (1992, chap. 3), Trusted (1987, chaps. 11 and 12), M. H. Salmon et al. (1992, chap. 1), and Smart (1968, chap. 3).

For more detailed presentations, see Hempel and Oppenheim (1948), which is partly reprinted in Kourany (1987) and Hempel (1965, chap. 12).

EXERCISES

1. Is it reasonable to attempt to explain the following?

   (a) Triangles have three sides.
   (b) Space has three dimensions.
   (c) Most birds have wings.
   (d) Water turns into steam when strongly heated.
   (e) Magnets have two poles.

2. Imagine that there was a lunar eclipse last night. Construct a D-N explanation for the event.

3. Give one example of a D-N explanation (i) of an event and (ii) of a law of nature (preferably from the history of science).

4. Expand the following elliptic explanation into a D-N explanation: "This (particular piece of paper) caught fire because a lighted match had been placed to it." Identify the initial conditions and laws used.

5. Expand the following elliptic explanation into a D-N explanation: "Fish cannot survive when out of water for lack of oxygen."

6. Is the following an explanation sketch (of the Hempelian kind)? "Salt is soluble in water because water possesses the property of breaking up salt crystals into small invisible pieces."

7. Give a historical explanation for each of the following. Can these explanations be formulated as D-N explanations? What are the likely laws of nature involved?

   (a) On April 14, 1865, John Wilkes Booth assassinated Abraham Lincoln.
   (b) On July 4, 1776, the Congress (of the United States) passed the Declaration of Independence.

Chapter 11

Universal Laws of Nature

11.1 INTRODUCTION

That the story of science is often told in terms of the discoveries of laws of nature demonstrates the important role laws play in science. It is said that they govern the workings of the universe, that they *make* things happen, that they enable occurrences to be predictable, that they give rise to uniformities and regularities, and that they are the objects of discovery for science which, once discovered, cause great excitement and celebration throughout the world. The story of how Archimedes (287–212 B.C.) discovered the law of flotation is well known. It was said that the idea struck him while he bathed, and he, in great joy and excitement, ran naked through the streets shouting "Eureka"—that is, "I've got it."

In the previous chapter, we saw how, according to Hempel, laws of nature play an indispensable role in scientific explanation. They form the necessary link between the initial conditions and the explanandum. In other words, it is laws which enable causes to bring about their effects. Let us now look into these wonderful "things" called laws of nature.

11.2 CHARACTERISTICS OF LAWS OF NATURE

What is a law of nature? What do (expressions of) laws of nature look like? What forms do laws of nature assume? What are the characteristics of a law of nature? From now on, by 'law,' I will mean 'law of nature.'[1]

Let's consider the following three groups of statements:

Group A:
> All chimneysweeps are male.
> All diamond stones are less than 20 pounds in weight.
> All ruminants have cloven hooves.

Group B:
> All bachelors are unmarried.
> All triangles have less than four sides.
> If today is Monday, then tomorrow is Tuesday.

Group C:
> All copper conducts heat.
> All gold is soluble in aqua regia.
> Every material object attracts every other material object.

Which of these nine statements are laws of nature? Intuitively only those of group C are what can be so called, and yet, superficially, it is difficult to tell why statements from the other two groups are not. We certainly want laws of nature to be true statements, but then all the statements of the three groups are true. A second characteristic of laws of nature is that they are applicable everywhere and at all times. In other words, they hold universally throughout time and space, so that they are what we called universal statements (Chapter 6), having the form "All *X* are *Y*." But then the statements of all the three groups are universal.

Universality and truth cannot be the full story. Laws, in addition, seem to have an element of compulsion. For example, it is not a matter of chance that gold should dissolve in aqua regia. If a piece of gold should be placed in a glass of aqua regia, it would, with certainty, dissolve, whereas if it should be placed in water or gasoline it would, again with certainty, not dissolve. We can say that the nature of gold is such that it *has to* dissolve in aqua regia but not in water. It is this element of necessity that makes "Gold is soluble in aqua regia" a law of nature.

On the other hand there is no embedded necessity in the statements of group *A*. For example, even though as a matter of fact all chimneysweeps are male,[2] it is not in the nature of chimneysweeps that they have to be male. Even though most females would hesitate to take up that career, it is not physically impossible for them to sweep chimneys. Indeed I can envisage the possibility that some women can make a better job of it than men. It is a similar case with the possibility of diamonds of mammoth size. Even though, as a matter of fact, no diamonds are heavier than 20 pounds, there is nothing to prevent the occurrence of such huge stones. That, unfortunately, all diamond stones in the whole universe stay under this size is an accidental fact rather than a necessity of nature. The third statement is about ruminants and says that they have cloven hooves. Ruminants have a stomach of four compartments and chew their cud. Common examples of ruminants are deer, cattle, sheep, and goats. It seems that, even though, as a matter of fact, they all have cloven hooves, there is no causal connection between the peculiar structure of their stomachs and the shape of their hooves. The two co-occur only accidentally, not as a matter of necessity. It is possible to have a ruminant that does not have cloven hooves, and such a combination could have occurred if the

---

1. For simplicity of presentation (for the benefit of the beginner), I will not make the tedious distinction between laws of nature (which operate on the world) and the linguistic expressions of these laws (which usually take the form of sentences), since there is little risk of confusion.

2. I think that it is true that all chimneysweeps, past, present, and future, are male. If there have been female chimneysweeps, you are advised to replace the example with 'All sumo wrestlers are male.'

history of evolution in the animal kingdom had taken a different route. We can now see why statements of group A, though true and universal, are not laws of nature. They are quite different from those of group C in that they lack the element of necessity.

But then, even though statements of group B seem to embody an element of necessity they can hardly be said to be laws of nature. Let's investigate why. Laws of nature, as the term itself suggests, "prescribe" how nature would operate. They forbid certain routes and declare them physically impossible. Thus "Gold dissolves in aqua regia" forbids gold from staying intact when placed in aqua regia. There is only one route that gold can take once it is placed into that "royal" liquid. But "Bachelors are unmarried" does not restrict the behavior of nature at all. By definition, bachelors are unmarried. To "prescribe" that bachelors are unmarried serves no purpose because the class of bachelors is already a subclass of the unmarried.

Similarly to "prescribe" that all triangles should have less than four sides is "silly" because they, being three-angled figures, must have less than four angles, and thus must have less than four sides.

It can be seen that statements of group B, though possessing a sense of necessity, are not laws. They seem to lack informative content. Imagine a tourist guide who, introducing the peoples and customs of New Zealand, says: "First, most New Zealanders are friendly. Second, all bachelors of New Zealand are unmarried." I think the first statement is informative and the piece of information it carries probably puts the audience at ease. But what about the second statement? Does it help the tourists in any way at all?

11.3 CLASSIFICATION
OF STATEMENTS

To understand further why only statements of group C qualify as laws of nature, I think we should study the traditional classification of statements in philosophy.

A statement is said to be **a priori** if its truth or falsity can be determined independently of experience, otherwise it is said to be **a posteriori**. A statement such as "It is now raining outside" is a posteriori because in order to ascertain whether it is true or false, one has to resort to experience, perhaps by looking through the window, or by listening for the sound of raindrops, or by the sense of touch such as stretching one's hand out of the doorway. On the other hand, "Either it is raining or not raining outside" is a priori because experience is irrelevant for the assessment of its truth. One is not wiser about its truth or falsity by looking through the window or by listening. Here is another a priori statement: all red cars are red.[3]

A statement is said to be **analytic** if its truth or falsity can be determined solely by the analysis of the meanings of the words in the sentence expressing it, otherwise it is said to be **synthetic**. Take the statement 'All women are female.' We can easily recognize its truth, and the reason why it is true is that women, because of the meaning of the term 'women,' must be female. The meaning of the words in the sentence determines its truth, and nothing that has happened in the world, or can happen, or will happen, can change its truth status. On the other hand, even though "All chimneysweeps are male" is equally true, its truth depends not only on the meanings of words such as 'chimneysweep' and 'male,' but also depends on something other than

---

3. Some of you might object, saying that it requires experience to know the word 'red.' We surely require experience to know that word, but 'to know' in this sense is different from 'to know' when we say that we know a certain statement is true. The former 'know' means 'understand,' and we surely need experience to understand words. But understanding a statement is a long way from *knowing* that the statement is true. Think of this statement, "Some red cars have blue seats." I am sure all of you understand the statement, but do you know whether it is true or not? By the way, note that both a priori statements and a posteriori statements can be false. Here is a false a priori statement: "Some red cars are not red."

language—that is, the state of our world. In our world, it is a fact that no females have been chimneysweeps (and, maybe, no females ever will be), and this fact makes the statement true. Had the world been different, in that some females were chimneysweeps, the statement would have been false. That's why "All chimneysweeps are male" is synthetic whereas "All women are female" is analytic.

A statement is said to be **necessary** if its truth or falsity cannot but be as it is, otherwise it is said to be **contingent**. 'Analyticity' and 'a priori' are relatively easy to explain when compared to the notion of necessity, and philosophers have always been puzzled by this concept. So what I would do here is simply to appeal to your intuition. For example, you can see that bachelors, if they are really bachelors, *have to* be unmarried (to be so qualified). As a person, Jimi Hendrix[4] need not have stayed unmarried, for he could have chosen to get married. But as a bachelor, he *had to be* unmarried, otherwise he would not be a bachelor. Thus "All bachelors are unmarried" is a necessary statement. Similarly it is necessary that all triangles have less than four sides. There is no necessity, however, to the statement "All triangles are equilateral" even though that statement might happen to be true (accidentally, so to speak). My child has just drawn an equilateral triangle, but nothing actually prevented her from drawing a non equilateral one. On the other hand, we can see that "All copper conducts heat" is a necessary statement. Copper, somehow, has to conduct heat. It can't help but conduct heat. If one end of a copper rod is heated, the other end will necessarily get hot. There is a sense of inevitability here.[5]

So we have six classes of statements: a priori, a posteriori, analytic, synthetic, necessary, and contingent. Traditionally it is believed that the class of a priori statements coincides with the class of analytic statements. With some notable exceptions such as Kant (1724–1804) and, more recently, Saul Kripke, philosophers generally think that a statement is a priori if and only if it is analytic, and thus a statement is a posteriori if and only if it is synthetic. A posteriori and synthetic statements are informative because their truth or falsity does depend on what the world is like. Hence when an a posteriori or synthetic statement is asserted, one is committed to certain views about the world, and one knows more about the world if one is told that a certain a posteriori or synthetic statement is true. Let us say that a statement is **informative** about the world if it is either a posteriori or synthetic, and that a statement is **uninformative** if it is both a priori and analytic.

We can see that statements in group A are informative and contingent, statements in group B are uninformative and necessary, but statements in group C are "hybrids," being informative yet necessary. How can there be such hybrids? Let's leave this puzzle until Section 11.5.

11.4 COUNTERFACTUAL CONDITIONALS

Since necessity is a difficult notion to grasp, let's see if we can clarify the notion further by going into what philosophers call **counterfactual conditionals** (often simply called **counterfactuals**). A conditional is an if-then statement of the form: "If *p*, then *q*" where *p* and *q* are themselves statements. For example, we might say: "If salt is put into water, then it will dissolve." The *p* is known as the **antecedent** and the *q* the **consequent**.

A counterfactual conditional is one where the antecedent is known to be false. For example, one

---

4. Jimi Hendrix was an American rock musician who rose to fame in the 1960s. He was a bachelor.

5. 'Necessity' is a difficult notion as well as a controversial subject in philosophy. Nevertheless, two common kinds of necessity are generally recognized: logical necessity, as illustrated by 'All white swans are white,' and physical necessity, as illustrated by 'all copper conducts heat.' It is commonly assumed that statements that are physically necessary are not logically necessary. For example, even though it is physically necessary that all copper conducts heat, it is by no means logically so. It is argued that we can imagine copper *not* conducting heat without committing a contradiction. Physical necessity is also known as natural necessity as well as nomic necessity. Here and elsewhere in this chapter I will appeal only to your intuitive (preanalytic) notion of necessity in the two senses without relying on philosophical details.

might say: "If this piece of chalk were salt and were put into water, it would dissolve."

Let's now consider the following two counterfactual conditionals:

(1) If Abraham Lincoln had been a bachelor, he would have been unmarried.

(2) If Ms. Nightingale had been a chimneysweep, she would have been a male.

I think most of us would say that (1) is true whereas (2) is false. Why should it be?

The answer is that whereas one can argue quite correctly that (1) is true because all bachelors have to be unmarried, one cannot say that (2) is true because all chimneysweeps have to be male, even though as a matter of fact they are all male. To put it differently, we can say that (3) supports (1) whereas (4) does not support (2).

(3) All bachelors are unmarried.

(4) All chimneysweeps are male.

The difference between (3) and (4) is that whereas (3) is true irrespective of the state of the world, (4) is only true because the state of the world is such and such. Had the world been different as indicated by the antecedent of (2), (4) would not be true. In other words, the truth value of (4) is dependent on the truth value of the antecedent of (2), whereas the truth value of (3) is independent of that of (1).

From these considerations, we can see that necessary universal statements support counterfactual conditionals, whereas contingent universal statements do not. Since laws of nature are necessary, they should support counterfactual conditionals as well. This can be illustrated by the following example:

(5) If this piece of chalk were salt and had been immersed in water, it would have dissolved.

We can see that this statement is true because it is supported by the law:

(6) All salt is soluble in water.

In general, statements of groups B and C support counterfactual conditionals while those of group A do not. This "counterfactual conditional" test is a test of necessity.

11.5 TYPES OF LAWS OF NATURE

We can roughly classify the laws of nature that are commonly found in the sciences into the following types:[6]

Type a: **Laws of regular association of attributes**
Examples:

(7) Copper conducts heat.

(8) Sugar is soluble in water.

(9) The melting point of iron is 1,535°C.

You can see these laws claim that the two attributes (properties) they mention are regularly associated. For example, 'being copper' is regularly associated with 'being heat-conducting.'

Type b: **Laws of uniformity of development**
Examples:

(10) Most chemical reactions follow certain courses of development. For example, when electricity is passed through brine (sodium chloride solution), it will decompose into hydrogen, chlorine, and caustic soda. This process can be presented succinctly as follows:

$$2NaCl + 2H_2O \rightarrow H_2 + Cl_2 + 2NaOH$$

(11) Butterflies go through the following stages in their life time: egg $\rightarrow$ caterpillar $\rightarrow$ pupa $\rightarrow$ adult butterfly.

(12) Certain diseases when contracted by human beings will run certain characterizable courses of development—for example, chicken pox.

You can see that this type of law is quite different from the first type in that it describes stages of

---

6. The following classification is adapted from Kneale (1949, sec. 16).

development (change). Some of you might object to the idea that these "developmental laws" are real laws. Perhaps (10) is a law. However, neither (11) nor (12) seem to be strictly lawlike in that they admit exceptions. For example, some butterfly eggs may not hatch at all. Some caterpillars, because of the mutation of genes or change of climatic conditions, may develop into something that is not quite a pupa. As for (12), we all know that some of us do deviate from the *normal* course of development of a disease.

I think these criticisms are justified. However, we can still call these laws, albeit "derivative laws" and not basic laws. "Law" (11), for example, is derivable from certain chemical laws and physical laws that are basic. Such derivations are usually based on the assumption that the conditions are "normal." Should the conditions be abnormal, these derivative laws would not hold. In view of this, perhaps derivative laws should always be formulated as: "…, under conditions X, Y, and Z."[7] By the way, you can see that even "laws" (7), (8), and (9) are not really true under *all* conditions. For example, the conductivity of copper certainly changes with temperature, and so does the solubility of sugar. As for the melting point of iron, it depends on the atmospheric pressure. *Perhaps* we should qualify all our laws with the normal conditions clause, "under normal conditions (circumstances)," so as to provide a vague safety "margin."[8]

Type c: **Laws of functional relations**
Examples:

(13) The gas law: $PV = kT$ (P, V, and T stand for the pressure, volume, and absolute temperature of a fixed volume of gas, respectively, and k is a constant).

(14) Newton's law of universal gravitation: $F_{grav} = Gm_1m_2/d^2$ (where m_1 and m_2 are the masses of two objects, d is the distance between them, and G is a constant).

(15) Snell's law: $\sin a/\sin b = \mu$ (where a and b are the angles of incidence and refraction and μ is

a constant, known as the index of refraction, which differs from material to material).[9]

We can see that this type of law is a generalization of laws of *Type a*, just as the method of concomitant variation is a generalization of the joint method of agreement and difference (Chapter 3). In other words, *Type a* is a special case of *Type c*, in that laws of *Type c* correlate ranges of values, whereas those of *Type a* correlate single values.

Type d: **Causal laws**
Examples

(16) The consumption of cyanide will cause death.

(17) Vibrations of high frequencies will produce sound.

(18) Heat will melt candlewax.

We can see that the previous three types of laws only provide us with correlations, where causes and effects are not specified. For example, take (13), the gas law. It only gives you the relationship between the quantities, P, V, and T, but does not specify which factors will *cause* which other factors. In contrast, (16), for example, specifies explicitly both the cause and the effect. Example (17) specifies the cause implicitly through the use of the word 'produce,' whereas (18) specifies it through the "action" word, 'melt.' The notion 'cause,' however, is rather problematic and controversial. We shall devote more time to it in the next section.

Type e: **Probabilistic laws** (also known as **statistical laws**)

It is said that not all laws of nature are universal, in that some laws, though they do "make things happen," do not always produce the same results. In short, such statements are necessary but not universal. Here are some examples.

(19) Mendel's law: When a large number of pea plants having round, yellow seeds are crossed with a large number of pea plants having

---

7. These are the conditions under which the derivations are made.

8. Writers often prefer the expression "*ceteris paribus* clause," which literally means "other things being equal."

9. See Chapter 0.

wrinkled, green seeds, the second generation of round to wrinkled and of yellow to green thus produced is *approximately* 3:1.

(20) A law of radioactive transformation: Given a quantity of radium, after 1,620 years, *approximately* half the radium atoms in the quantity will have transmuted into radon atoms.

You can see that these laws have two unusual features. (i) The term 'approximately' occurs in both; (ii) the numerical ratios, '3:1' and 'half,' apply to the whole group of things, rather than to each individual thing itself. For example, Mendel's law does not tell you what will happen precisely if you cross *one* pea plant having round seeds with *one* pea plant having wrinkled seeds. It certainly does not tell you that the second generation *will definitely* be a pea plant with round seeds, even though from the law one can infer that the chance of getting a pea plant with round seeds in the second generation is 75 percent.

Similarly, (20) does not tell you which one of the radium atoms in the "heap" will "decay" into a radon atom. What one can know from the law is that, after 1,620 years, half of the heap will be gone. We can say that the probability of a radium atom decaying into a radon atom within 1,620 years is 50 percent. In other words, taking any single individual radium atom, all we know is that there is a 50 percent chance that it will decay within 1,620 years. This is all the law tells us. We can discern a sort of tension and even a mild sort of inconsistency here. At the group level (macroscopic level), there is certainty: in so many years, it is *certain* that approximately half of the heap will be gone. But at the individual level (microscopic level), there is no certainty but only a probability: in so many years, it is 50 percent *probable* that a certain specific radium atom will decay.[10]

Some philosophers contend that probabilistic laws are not laws at all. According to them, to be a law, the statement must be *universally* true. They conjecture that after 1,620 years, the reason why only some of the radium atoms decay is because these decayed atoms are different from the rest. It is said that there are some "hidden variables" yet to be discovered characterizing atoms. Once these hidden variables have been discovered universal laws can then be formulated. Similar claims are actually true of the pea plants of (19).

However, many philosophers think that there are truly probabilistic laws, which are irreducible to universal laws. Some even claim the following to be a probabilistic law.

(21) Most patients with a streptococcal infection when treated with penicillin will recover.[11]

We will study further the "phenomenon" of probabilistic laws in Chapter 12. However, before we move on, let me point out that *Type e* is not on the same level as the other three types. Rather, within *Type e*, there are laws of association, of development, of functional relations, and causal laws. For example, all our three examples are "laws" of development.
Finally,

Type f: **Theoretical laws**
Examples:

(22) Einstein's law of mass–energy equivalence: $E = mc^2$ (where E stands for energy, m for mass, and c for the speed of light).

(23) Newton's law of universal gravitation: as stated in (14).

(24) Ohm's law: When a steady current is flowing through a conductor, the strength of the current is proportional to the potential difference between its ends.

These are known as theoretical laws, because they come from theories, and are about unobservable entities (Chapter 8). For example, Ohm's law talks about electric currents and potential differences; all of these are unobservables and are postulational

---

10. You might be interested to know that, in the jargon of physics, radium is said to have a half-life of 1,620 years. Elements that spontaneously disintegrate are known as radioactive elements. Their half-life can be as short as a few seconds and as long as a billion years. However, most atoms are stable—that is, their half-life is infinite.

11. This example is adapted from Hempel (1965, p. 382).

products of theories. Newton's and Einstein's employ terms such as 'force' and 'mass,' which are theoretical terms.

Again these theoretical laws do not form a type on the same level as the others. Theoretical laws themselves can be subdivided into types a, b, c, d, and e. For example, (23) is a functional law. On the other hand, (20) is a theoretical law; so is (10) if we take the chemical formula as the formulation of the law.

In summary, we can say that there are two levels of laws: **theoretical laws** and **empirical laws**. This broad classification is in accordance with the classical tradition (Chapter 8). Empirical laws are sometimes known as **phenomenal laws**. They are about observables and are usually obtained through **empirical generalization** (Section 8.3). Theoretical laws, in contrast, are about unobservables and are constitutive parts of theories (Chapter 8). Within *each* of these two broad categories are **universal laws** and **probabilistic laws**. Universal laws apply universally without exceptions, whereas probabilistic laws provide only certain probabilities for the occurrence of events or association of attributes. Finally, within *each* of these two types are the types (a), (b), (c), and (d)—that is, **laws of association**, **laws of development**, **laws of functional relations**, and **causal laws**.

11.6 HUME ON CAUSATION AND LAWS OF NATURE

David Hume (1711–1776) was one of the most influential philosophers in Western philosophy. He challenged the notion of necessity as applied to laws of nature (Section 11.3). For him there can only be two kinds of statement: (i) the a posteriori, synthetic, and contingent, and (ii) the a priori, analytic, and necessary. Kind (i) is exemplified by group A and (ii) by group B (Section 11.2). Group C does not form a distinct group at all. In other words, there can be no "hybrids."

For Hume, the necessity of group B is quite understandable. The necessity is a "verbal" necessity.

It is a phenomenon of certain verbal usages. On the other hand, statements of group C are claimed to be **physically necessary** in that such necessities reside in the physical world. When one claims that gold is soluble in aqua regia, one claims that gold as a substance of this world is necessarily soluble in aqua regia. The necessity resides in the gold (and the aqua regia). Hume denies the existence of such necessities.

He produced two very convincing and detailed arguments, which I will only sketch:

Argument 1: Sense experience is the only source of knowledge. We can know of the existence of things *only through* our having encountered them via sensory experience. For example, our claim that elephants exist is reasonable and acceptable because we have encountered such animals. We can also quite acceptably claim that there were dinosaurs because we have encountered their remains. But we have no right to claim the existence of unicorns or centaurs, because no one has come upon them nor is there any physical evidence of their existence such as footprints or fossils. Since experience is the only source of knowledge, the claim of existence must be based on experience, whether direct or indirect.

However, in claiming that "Sugar is soluble in water" is a law, we are not only claiming that sugar regularly dissolves when placed in water, but also that there is a necessity to it. It is this claim of necessity that is not warranted by experience, according to Hume. At no time have we encountered, as a piece of experience, anything over and above the regularity displayed by sugar when immersed in water. The same applies to laws like "Fire produces heat." The word "produce" carries with it a message which is more than just a statement of regular association between fire and heat. The law in fact says that fire *causes* heat, and heat, being an effect of fire, has (as a matter of necessity) to occur. This claim of necessary connection between fire and heat, according to Hume, is again unwarranted as far as experience is concerned. What experience tells us is that heat is regularly *conjoined* to fire, but not (necessarily) *connected*. The distinction between two events being conjoined and being connected has been made clear by Hume. "All events seem entirely loose and separate. One event follows another; but we never can observe any tie between them. They seem *conjoined*, but never *connected*."[12] In other words, the empirical evidence we have for statements of group A is of exactly the same kind as those we have for statements of group C—that is, regular conjunctions in the form of "whenever *x* occurs then *y* will occur" or "whenever *x* is present then *y* is also present." It would thus be irrational to claim necessity for group C but not for group A. Hence members of group C should be classified as members of group A.

Hume's argument is supposed to apply to micro-levels as well. He claims that even if we should go down to such basic levels, nowhere can necessary connections be sensed over and above regular conjunctions of events. Let us illustrate with an oversimplified thought experiment. Suppose we possess a very powerful microscope (something like the electron microscope) through which we can see individual molecules and their movements. At the macroscopic level, when we heat a copper rod at one end, *A*, the other end, *B*, would eventually become hot as well. I am quite sure that you would have to concede to Hume that at this macroscopic level what we can sense is a sequence of two events: *A*'s getting hot followed by *B*'s getting hot. Nowhere can we see any "tie" or "connection" actually linking these two events. However, some of you might attempt to refute Hume by claiming that if one should examine the rod with the powerful microscope, we might be able to see the as-yet-undetected tie. I think the answer is no. What we would see through the microscope are molecules running into each other. We should see molecules at end *A* get agitated. This agitation then spreads to the neighboring molecules and eventually the molecules of end *B* start to move. The reason why end *B* gets hot is because the molecules there become agitated. (This is in accordance with the kinetic theory of heat.)[13] Where is the "necessary tie" we are looking for

under the microscope? The picture we have just described is no different from the picture of billiard balls bouncing off each other at the macroscopic level! And we have already shown that, at this level, the tie is not and never will be found: when one billiard ball collides with another, what we *actually* see is the motion of the first ball followed by the motion of the second (at the moment of impact). In other words, at the microscopic as well as at the macroscopic level, we can only sense two events, one following the other, but nothing like a tie over and above the two events.

Argument 2: Hume's second argument is even more harsh on the notion of physical necessity and the notion of necessary connection between events. According to him, experience is not only *the* source of knowledge but also *the* source of meaning (of words). The word 'red' has meaning to us only because we have the sensual experience of redness. A blind person cannot understand the word 'red.' The empirical basis of meaning applies not only to simple words like 'red' but also to words like 'unicorn.' Even though no unicorns have ever been sighted, the word 'unicorn' nevertheless does acquire its meaning through experience even though indirectly—for example, either through pictures of unicorns or through compositions from words such as 'horn' and 'horse,' which in turn are empirically rooted.

Now, since physical necessity has never been encountered, and the term 'physical necessity' presumably cannot be built up from more elementary words which have empirical roots, the expression 'physical necessity' has no meaning whatever. This claim is strong. Argument 1 only concludes that physical necessity does not exist in the world. The present argument concludes that the very term 'physical necessity' is meaningless. The same applies to 'necessary connection.'

According to Hume, the kind of necessity we see in laws of nature is an illusion. The human mind has

---

12. From D. Hume's *An Enquiry Concerning Human Understanding*, sec. 7, reproduced in *The Structure of Scientific Thought*, edited by E. H. Madden (1960, p. 219).

13. As I have warned you, this description of the transfer of heat at the microscopic level is greatly oversimplified.

been conditioned into expecting *B* to occur, given *A*, by frequent exposure to pairings of *A*'s followed by *B*'s. Lightning and thunder is such a pairing. After being exposed to a number of instances of lightning followed by thunder, the mind will expect the occurrence of thunder whenever there is lightning. To the mind, it is as if nature is such that lightning has to be followed by thunder, even though in reality the supposed necessity in nature is actually a projection of expectations in the mind. To put it succinctly, the so-called physical necessity is not in nature at all; it is created by the mind.[14]

Hume's arguments are strong, compelling, and difficult to disprove. Yet few scientists and philosophers take them seriously when engaged in the pursuit of science. Such a state of affairs is often called a **paradox**.

11.7 IMPLICATIONS OF HUME'S THESIS

Thus, for Hume, statements of group C, what we usually call laws of nature, are no different from those of group A, which are often called **accidental universal generalizations**. For Hume, it only *happens* that all gold is soluble in aqua regia just as it happens that all diamond stones are less than a certain size. If we pursue this line of thought to its logical conclusion, we can see that not only are what are usually called laws not laws at all, but what were called nomologico-deductive explanations in Chapter 10 are not explanations either. One of the requirements of a D-N explanation of a singular event is that there should be at least one law of nature to *bring about* the event given the initial conditions. For example, to explain why this floats in water, one can say:

This is ice.

All ice floats in water.

Therefore, this floats in water.

The explanation carries through because the law ensures the event's occurrence by compulsion. Should the law be just a generalization, the explanation would lose its force. Consider the following:

Bert was a chimneysweep.

All chimneysweeps are male.

Therefore, *Bert* was a male.

We can see that this is no explanation of why Bert was a male at all. In fact, the truth of the generalization "all chimneysweeps are male" (explanans) depends on whether the particular chimneysweep called Bert was a male or not (explanandum), rather than the other way round. Should Bert turn out to be a female, the generalization would have been false. On the other hand, one of the characteristics of laws is that they, because of their necessary nature, can "make" things happen. For example, the necessity that ice floats makes this thing float.

Thus Hume's thesis implies that explanation cannot be one of the aims of science, since there can be no explanation of events and happenings. Events simply occur. There are no laws to make them happen. The notion of cause-effect as we usually understand it has no place in science. We have no right to say that one event causes another. It seems that the best we can do is to make generalizations: from a few instances of *A*'s being followed by *B*'s to the general statement that all *A*'s are *B*'s, as in the case of "All chimneysweeps are male." This sort of move (inference) is called induction by simple enumeration (Chapter 3).

Unfortunately even this sort of weak science, science based on generalizations rather than on laws, is frowned on by Hume. One should not find it too difficult to work out that the absence of necessary connection between events implies that induction is rationally questionable. We will have more to say of this later in Chapter 20. Here it suffices for me to say that if events are entirely

---

14. Associationism, one of the earliest schools of psychology in the 19th century, is based on Hume's theory of association of impressions.

loose and unconnected to each other, no rational prediction is possible. No matter how often events of type *A* have been followed by events of type *B* in the past we have no grounds to claim causal connection between the two. One has a good reason to predict the occurrence of a *B* given the occurrence of an *A*, *only if A*'s are somehow instrumental for the occurrence of *B*'s. If *A*'s and *B*'s are totally unconnected, the occurrence of *A* has no significance for the occurrence of *B* whatsoever.

Thus prediction cannot be an aim of science either, if we take Hume seriously. Yet Hume's arguments are strong and compelling. This is the dilemma.

11.8 HUME'S EMPIRICISM

The term 'empiricism,' nowadays, applies to any philosophy which claims that the senses[15] play an indispensable, fundamental, and central role in the acquisition of (synthetic) knowledge. The data collected by the senses are usually called **empirical data**. Even though the role of the senses is central and indispensable, empiricism does not necessarily deny contribution from our other faculties in the acquisition of knowledge. For example, some empiricism thinks that the mind also plays a role. Thus there are shades of empiricism, depending on the relative amount our sensory experience is said to contribute to the acquisition of knowledge. **Hume's empiricism** is of the extreme form in that it claims the senses as the *sole* contributor to (synthetic) knowledge.[16] Moreover, for Hume, the senses can only perceive what he calls sense impressions—for example, *two-dimensional* color patch sensations, sounds in the form of melodies or noises, and so on. So, for Hume, strictly, what one commonly sees in a zoo are elephant-shapes rather than elephants, monkey-shapes rather than monkeys, and so on. (See phenomenalism in

Section 9.5.) However, for our purpose here, it is easier if we take a more dilute form of Hume's original empiricism, holding that empirical data consist of what we observe about "middle-sized" *three-dimensional* material objects such as elephants and monkeys. In contrast, behaviors of "theoretical objects" such as atoms, electrons, radio waves, and genes would not be considered part of our empirical data because they are beyond our direct observations. Thus the **observables** are the commonsensical objects whereas the rest are the **unobservables**. Empirical data are data about the observables (Section 9.2).[17]

Let's call this diluted version of Hume's empiricism, **commonsense empiricism**. For commonsense empiricism, unobservables do not exist. Furthermore, the very terms denoting unobservables such as 'atoms' and 'electrons' are meaningless. And, needless to say, necessary connections do not exist and the term 'necessary connection' is quite meaningless. (See conventionalism and instrumentalism in Chapter 9.)

Hume's philosophy goes well with scientific methods such as induction by simple enumeration. If one does science according to Hume's philosophy, one should never theorize, never postulate meaningless terms such as 'atom' and 'electron.' The method of theory (Section 8.8) is not an option for science. One should confine science to the phenomenal level (Section 8.1) and deal "squarely and honestly" with observables and observables alone. Many philosophers and scientists have been influenced by this "no nonsense" philosophy of certainty. For Hume, all doctrines on unobservables, including metaphysics and various kinds of religious beliefs, are obstacles to science. You can see that there is good reason why Hume is often known as a skeptic. His skepticism, in fact, does not end with the unobservables. You will find that Hume even doubts the reasonableness of inductive reasoning (Chapter 20).

---

15. We have five senses: sight, hearing, taste, smell, and touch.

16. Synthetic knowledge is what Hume calls 'matter of fact.'

17. Chapter 17 will consider the controversy over the distinction between the observables and the unobservables.

Hume's philosophy has had a lasting influence on Western scientific thought. For example, we can see that the phenomenalism of Mach (Section 9.5) was a direct descendant of Hume's empiricism (the undiluted version), and Mach's philosophy led to logical positivism, the orthodox philosophy of science of the 20th century (Chapter 23).

Is there then any hope of overturning Hume's skepticism? There have been no shortage of such refuting attempts! We will see more of Hume in Chapter 20.

KEY TERMS INTRODUCED IN THIS CHAPTER

a priori

a posteriori

analytic

synthetic

necessary

contingent

informative

uninformative

counterfactual conditional

antecedent

consequent

probabilistic law (statistical law)

theoretical law

empirical law

phenomenal law

empirical generalization

universal law

law of association

law of development

law of functional relations

causal law

physically necessary

paradox

accidental universal generalizations

empirical data

Hume's empiricism

observable

unobservable

commonsense empiricism

REFERENCES

On the nature of laws: Hempel (1966, sec. 5.3) provides a brief introduction. Kneale (1949, chaps. 17 and 18), Nagel (1961, chap. 4), and Achinstein (1971) give detailed standard presentations. Brody (1970) has a few useful articles on the subject.

On Hume's analysis of causation and necessity: Bakker and Clark (1988, chap. 3) provide a good analysis of Hume's position. Madden (1960) has a collection of articles on the subject. Mackie (1974) is an authority on the topics of both law and causation.

On the analytic and synthetic distinction: for an introductory text, see Hospers (1967, pp. 160–228).

For my view on the necessity of laws of nature, see Hung (1981b).

EXERCISES

1. Give a true statement and a false statement to illustrate each of the following terms:
(a) analytic, (b) synthetic, (c) a priori, (d) a posteriori, (e) contingent, and (f) necessary.

2. Give an example of a true counterfactual conditional supported by a universal law of nature.

3. Give an example of laws of nature to illustrate each of the following: law of regular association of attributes, law of uniformity of development, law of functional relations, causal law, probabilistic law, and theoretical law.

4. Compare and contrast the nature of natural laws with that of statutory laws.

5. Hume argues that since the necessary connection between cause and effect has never been observed, it does not exist. Is it reasonable to infer nonexistence from imperceptibility?

6(a) On a sunny day, stretch out your hand to form a shadow on the ground. Each time you stretch out your hand a shadow is formed. Here is a regularity of the co-occurrence of two (types of) events. Is it reasonable to claim that your hand *causes* the shadow?

6(b) The constellation Orion moves across the sky side by side with the constellation Gemini each night, at the same rate and in the same direction, as if the two are tied together. Is it reasonable to claim that the movement of one causes that of the other, or that there is an invisible tie between the two? How is this case the same as or different from the case of the hand and its shadow?

Based on the discussions of (a) and (b), evaluate Hume's thesis on the nonexistence of physical necessity.

7. The numeral '7' is meaningful and understandable by all of us. However, the number 7 is abstract and imperceptible. This seems to be a case where a meaningful symbol can stand for something imperceptible. Yet Hume argues that since physical necessity is imperceptible, the expression 'physical necessity' cannot be meaningful. How can Hume justify this disparity? Would this be a case of reductio ad absurdum, implying that Hume's theory of meaning must be wrong since one of its implications is absurd?

8. It is said that a universally true statement, S (of the form 'All X are Y'), is a law of nature if and only if it is supported by a theory, T, through being a logical consequence of T. (See Chapter 8 for theoretical support.) Since S is deducible from T, S is necessary relative to T. It is said that S obtains its necessity through this relationship to T. Discuss with respect to the empirical generalizations:

   (a) All creatures with livers have hearts.
   (b) All diamond stones are less than 20 pounds in weight.
   (c) All copper conducts heat.

9. Compare the following explanations:

   (a) The movements of the planets are (imperceptibly) caused by the (invisible) law of gravity and others.
   (b) The movements of the planets are (imperceptibly) caused by the (invisible) hand of God.

How would Hume react to these explanations? Is Hume justified?

Chapter 12

Probabilistic Explanation and Probabilistic Causality

12.1 INTRODUCTION

Having spent some time on natural laws and their problems, let's return to Hempel's covering-law thesis of scientific explanation. As I pointed out earlier, for Hempel, laws play the pivotal role in science. Indeed the twin aims of science—truth and explanation—are simultaneously achievable through laws if the covering-law thesis is correct. What a neat solution to the aims of science: laws in providing links between initial conditions and explananda yield explanations, and laws being necessary and universal yield predictions.

However, problems in philosophy are seldom so simple. The covering-law thesis, also known as the covering-law model of explanation, was proposed in detail by Hempel and Oppenheim (1948).[1] Even at its inception, Hempel and Oppenheim were aware of a number of difficulties their thesis would face:

(a) The logical status of laws of nature is not clear, and Hempel and Oppenheim were aware of Hume's criticism of the notion of physical necessity (supposedly a property of laws).

---

1. Popper's proposal in *Logik der Forschung* (1935) was probably the earliest proposal of the thesis, even though he had not developed it in detail.

(b) Many explanations in the social sciences and the inexact sciences such as medicine employ *probabilistic* statements rather than *universal* laws in explanation. More significant, in subatomic physics, laws of nature seem to be essentially probabilistic.

(c) In the biological sciences (including psychology), explanations are often made in terms of purposes and goals rather than in terms of causes or laws. In view of these matters, it is important and necessary that the covering-law thesis be further developed. This chapter will discuss Hempel's effort in dealing with (b). We'll leave (c) for Chapter 13.

12.2 PROBABILISTIC EXPLANATION: INDUCTIVE-STATISTICAL AND DEDUCTIVE-STATISTICAL EXPLANATION

Hempel observes that we often make explanations of the following type:

(I)   *A* is an *X*.

Most *X*'s are *Y*'s.

A is a *Y*.

It is plain that this argument is invalid and hence cannot be a D–N explanation. However, according to Hempel, this type of explanation is respectable and adequate as long as the general statement "Most *X*'s are *Y*'s" is a law. An example could be:

(II) John, a patient with a streptococcal infection, was treated with penicillin.

Most patients with a streptococcal infection when treated with penicillin recover.

John recovered from a streptococcal infection.[2]

For Hempel the general statement (second premise) is lawlike, even though not universal; hence II is an adequate scientific explanation. He calls this an **inductive-statistical explanation (I-S explanation)**, because the logic used here is induction and the law concerned is a statistical law. I-S explanation is said to be one of two types of **statistical explanation**. Many authors employ the term '**probabilistic explanation**' instead, and I will adopt this practice.

The general form of I-S explanation is:

(III) $C_1, C_2, ..., C_m$

$S_1, S_2, ..., S_n$

$\dfrac{(L_1, L_2, ..., L_k)}{\text{Therefore } E.}$ $[r]$

Here *E* is the statement to be explained (the explanandum), the *C*'s are the (initial) conditions, the *S*'s are the probabilistic laws (also known as statistical laws), and the *L*'s are universal laws, which may or may not be present. The double lines indicate that the inference is inductive rather than deductive. The *r* following the double lines indicates the strength of the induction.[3] One of the requirements for (III) to be an explanation is that *r* should be large, at least larger than 0.5. The closer *r* is to 1, the better the explanation. When *r* is 1, (III) becomes a valid deduction. We can see that D–N explanation is thus a limiting case of I-S explanation.

According to Hempel, I-S explanations abound in the more complex physical sciences such as medicine and in the social sciences, where universal laws of nature are few. It would be methodologically unfruitful if such explanations were not allowed. In the case of subatomic physics, it is claimed that the laws there are irreducibly probabilistic in nature. At least this is one of the interpretations of the laws of quantum mechanics.

---

2. Adapted from Hempel (1965, p. 394).

3. In Section 4.8, we discussed the logical interpretation of probability. By this interpretation, probability is a logical relationship between a set of premises and a conclusion. When the premises entail the conclusion, the probability of the conclusion based on the premises is 1. In all other cases, the probability is a number less than 1. The *r* here indicates this probability relationship.

A rather superficial example in this area can be as follows:

(IV) This atom was a radon atom.

Most radon atoms break up (disintegrate) within a week.

This atom broke up within a week.[4]

I-S explanation is the probabilistic counterpart of D-N explanation of singular facts. Hempel suggests a second type of probabilistic explanation in parallel to the D-N explanation of universal laws (Section 10.4). He calls it the **deductive-statistical explanation (D-S explanation)**, which has the following form:

$$S_1, S_2, \ldots, S_n$$

(V) $(L_1, L_2, \ldots, L_k)$

Therefore S.

Here S is a statistical law to be explained (the explanandum). $S_1, \ldots, S_n$ are statistical laws, forming the explanans with or without additional universal laws $(L_1, \ldots, L_k)$. Note that the relationship between the explanans and the explanandum is that of logical entailment. In other words, the argument should be a valid deduction for it to be an explanation.

According to Hempel, both I-S explanation and D-S explanation are cases of covering-law explanation, in that they both explain in terms of laws, and, given knowledge of the explanans, the truth of the explanandum is to be expected, even though here the expectancy is less than certainty for the case of I-S explanations. I am sure you can appreciate how well Hempel has managed to "generalize" his notion of D-N explanation so that his thesis now covers apparent difficulties (b) mentioned in Section 12.1. However, this move of Hempel's has encountered serious objections.

12.3 FIRST OBJECTION TO I-S EXPLANATION

You can see that both types of probabilistic explanation employ what Hempel calls **statistical laws**, alternatively known as **probabilistic laws**. But it is counterintuitive to have laws of nature that are not universal. Universality and necessity seem to be the two main characteristics of laws, each of which by itself would imply that laws should be applicable at any time and at any place. How can there be laws of nature that, under the same conditions, sometimes hold and sometimes don't, as in the case of probabilistic laws?

For example, when we say that it is a law of nature that most radon atoms break up (disintegrate) within a week, we imply that under the same conditions some radon atoms do break up and some don't, even though they are supposed to be identical and *ex hypothesi* the conditions are the same. This has been a much debated subject in relation to the study of causality at the subatomic level. Here I can only point out the counterintuitive aspect of nondeterministic laws.

It is said that nature must know how to behave, and laws of nature supposedly provide such prescriptions. That's why nondeterministic laws are counterintuitive apart from the fact that they are contrary to the well-entrenched metaphysical principle of "same cause same effect."

Many prominent scientists and philosophers, including Albert Einstein, doubt that we should admit nonuniversal general statements as laws. According to them the dictum that the same cause leads to the same effect should be taken seriously. If two atoms in the same circumstances should behave differently, then they cannot be qualitatively identical.[5] For example, if one breaks up while the other does not, the dictum of "same cause same effect" would imply that the two are different in some respect. That the observer has not been able to perceive any differences does not imply that the dictum is faulty. There may be what the quantum physicists call "hidden variables" that underlie the atoms' apparent

---

4. The half-life of radon is 3.82 days.

5. Two things are said to be qualitatively identical if they are identical in all qualitative features.

similarity.[6] In other words, some variables may have been overlooked when those atoms were characterized, and, in terms of these variables, the two atoms are not identical at all.

Let's take a simpler example. In the case of treating streptococcus-infected patients with penicillin, two similar patients John and Peter may be such that after treatment John recovers whereas Peter dies. The dictum of "same cause same effect" implies that John and Peter must be different in some respects. If they look superficially the same, "hidden" variables must account for the difference in outcomes.

So, instead of putting forth II as an explanation, the "hidden variables" theorist will recommend the following:

(VI)   John, a patient of streptococcal infection, was treated with penicillin.

All patients with a streptococcal infection when treated with penicillin recover, if their physical constitutions are of type X.

John's physical constitution was of type X.

John recovered from a streptococcal infection.

'X' is the hidden variable. On the other hand, to explain why Peter did not recover, we only need to point out that after all Peter's constitution was not of type X.

Alternative (VI) can be seen to be an explanation sketch (Chapter 10). The reason (VI) is preferable to (II) is not confined to our earlier discussions. Employing (VI) has methodological advantages over and above metaphysical reasoning about causality and laws of nature. We can see that (VI), being only an explanation sketch instead of a full explanation, encourages further research to find the missing information indicated by the variable X, whereas (II), being a complete explanation, gives no encouragement to further research.

12.4 THE HIDDEN VARIABLES THESIS

The hidden variables thesis sounds reasonable, as illustrated by (VI). This reasonableness does not seem to be confined to inexact sciences like medicine. Physics has been taken as the most advanced and most exact of all the sciences, and hidden variables theories have been proposed in subatomic physics to account for some curious facts. The radioactive decay (disintegration) of certain kinds of atom such as radon and radium has been discussed in the last two sections. Let's consider another simplistic example here. It has been discovered that when electrons are shot through a tiny hole (aperture) in a screen toward a "collecting" screen, they do not all land at the same spot on this collecting screen. Rather they will spread around a central spot. Even though most of the electrons will land at the central spot, quite a few will end up relatively far away from the center. To be more exact, there is a gradual thinning off of electron impact from the center. This "thinning-off" distribution of the electron around the central spot, in fact, follows an exact formula provided by current quantum physics. To put it differently, electrons behave like light that diffracts when passing through a tiny aperture (Section 0.7). But electrons are not supposed to be waves. How can they diffract?

One version of what is known as the **Copenhagen interpretation** is that the laws governing the propagation of electrons are not universal but probabilistic in nature. Let's focus on a single electron that is on the point of going through the aperture. According to this interpretation of the laws of quantum physics, the trajectory of the electron is not determined by the setting so that it *has to* take a certain definite path. The electron "has a choice," so to speak; it may go straight ahead in a straight line, or it may turn at an angle (angle of deviation).

6. The theory of hidden variables in quantum mechanics was first suggested by David Bohm in 1952.

Indeed the electron may even make an angular turn of almost 90°. However, in spite of all these possibilities, the laws still prescribe a certain amount of regularity. They impose a definite probability for each of the possible angles of deviation, so that even though we cannot say with certainty where a single electron will strike, the laws will predict a definite pattern of electron impact on the collecting screen when a huge number of electrons go through the aperture.[7]

This probabilistic interpretation, however, is problematic: How is it that identical electrons when passing through the same aperture can behave differently? Shouldn't the same cause in the same setting bring about the same effect? To solve this problem, the hidden variables theorist explains thus: There are features of the electron-cum-setting yet to be discovered. These are the hidden variables. In other words, we have not yet completely characterized the situation. The electron-cum-settings so far look identical, but in fact they are not. This accounts for the different outcomes from apparently identical situations. Once these hidden variables are identified, the laws of electron propagation can be made exact and *universal*. In other words, the present probabilistic "look" of the laws is due to our ignorance rather than to reality. In reality laws are always universal and necessary. But sometimes we do overlook certain characterizing variables and can only produce incomplete laws, which appear to be probabilistic.

Many of you will probably find such arguments plausible and even convincing. Unfortunately reality does not seem to want to "cooperate." Experiments done up to the present are mostly unfavorable to the hidden variables theorists. In 1964 John S. Bell produced a mathematical result that implies that, in certain experimental settings, hidden variables theories will predict certain statistical outcomes very different from those predicted by

traditional quantum physics. Quite a number of experiments have been carried out since, and most have been found to be in agreement with traditional quantum mechanics (thus refuting the hidden variables theories)!

Bell's mathematical results are now known as Bell's theorem. To do justice to the hidden variables theorists, I would like to make three qualifications here: (i) Bell's theorem applies only to hidden variables theories that satisfy a certain very reasonable condition.[8] (ii) Not all the experimental results are against the hidden variables theories, though most are strongly unfavorable. (iii) There can be experimental errors, and so on. In general, the Poincaré-Duhem-Quine thesis (Section 9.3) does allow for the retention of a theory in the face of unfavorable results. Having said all this, I would like to report that the general opinion among both scientists and philosophers is that the hidden variables thesis is very unlikely to be applicable to subatomic phenomena.[9] It is dead in practice.

But then, how should we take the probabilistic nature of the laws of quantum physics? Most practicing scientists seem to have taken a pragmatic attitude: they are happy as long as the laws give them accurate statistical predictions, and they do not ask for more. This agrees well with what is known as the Copenhagen interpretation.[10]

Einstein, the great mind behind the theory of relativity, was one of those who opposed the Copenhagen interpretation. He was a realist and a determinist and believed that every object, be it an electron or a chair, must have a definite position (and a definite momentum) at any time. Moreover, laws should be universal and deterministic. Since quantum theory provides us only with probabilistic laws, it cannot be the "end of the story." In other words, it cannot be complete, as the hidden variables theorist would say. However, unlike the latter, who tries to amend

---

7. This version of the Copenhagen interpretation originated with Max Born. According to another version, the electron has *no* definite position (and momentum) until it is being measured.

8. The condition is known as locality condition, which essentially says that there is no action-at-a-distance.

9. See Mermin (1985) and Shimony (1978).

10. See Footnote 7 for 'Copenhagen interpretation.' I will return to this in Chapter 23 when I discuss logical positivism.

the situation from "inside" by adjoining to the existing quantum theory new (hidden) variables, Einstein, according to Arthur Fine, advocated a reform from "outside."[11] In other words, Einstein thought that quantum theory had not employed the correct variables for the description and explanation of the observed phenomena. He wanted to see a totally new theory built on a totally new framework of an entirely new set of concepts. What concepts? Unfortunately he did not specify. For Einstein, "God does not play dice." Probabilistic "laws" cannot be ultimate laws of nature! Let's, therefore, study the possibility of probabilistic laws in detail.

12.5 PROBABILISTIC CAUSALITY

Let's state the **principle of uniformity of causation (PUC)**: Events of the same type will bring about (if at all) effects of the same type. To put it succinctly, we can say: "Same cause, same effect." To admit the possibility of probabilistic laws is to deny the truth of this doctrine. Is PUC true or false? Many think that it is not only true, but is necessarily true. In other words, they think that it is *impossible* to have events of the same type causally producing effects of different types.

How can we know whether it is possible or impossible?

We know that it is impossible to have a square circle (that is, a square that is also a circle), because it involves a contradiction. We also know that it is impossible to square a circle (that is, to construct, with a ruler and a compass only, a square having the same area as a given circle).[12] Mathematicians have worked this one out and have conclusively demonstrated that it is impossible. Finally, experience tells us that we cannot lift ourselves by our bootstraps. You can see from these three examples that there is more than one way to demonstrate impossibility.

The first two are at the conceptual level, whereas the last is at the empirical level.

Can experience tell us anything about PUC? When a coin is flipped, sometimes it lands heads and sometimes tails. Does this show that the same cause can bring about different effects? I am sure that you would answer no. You would point out that even though the same coin is used each time, the way the coin is flipped differs. Probably no two flipping acts are quite the same. Hence it is understandable that the outcome can be different. What about rifle shooting? Sometimes the bullet hits the target, and sometimes it misses. Again one can point out that even though the same person takes aim each time with the same gun, aiming is not an "exact science." Bullets are also not quite identical to one another, and the changing temperature of the gun barrel probably will affect the trajectory of the bullet as well. These two examples represent our ordinary way of thinking. However, it has been discovered, as I have mentioned in the last three subsections, that in subatomic physics PUC is likely to be false. Experiments suggest that identical atoms in identical circumstances can behave quite differently. These are the atoms of what are known as the radioactive elements, such as uranium, radium, and radon. Experiments also suggest that identical electrons when they stream through identical apertures do not move in identical trajectories. There is not much room to find fault with these experiments, which have been so exact and reliable. As I pointed out in the last section, experiments based on Bell's theorem also showed that it is very unlikely that there are factors (hidden variables) that we have so far overlooked. The general conclusion seems to be that PUC has been empirically falsified. In other words, experience seems to have told us not only that it is *possible* to have the same cause bringing about different effects, but also that as a *matter of fact* there are such cases in the realm of fundamental physics.

But the "impossible" camp is not convinced. It prefers to play the game at the conceptual level

---

11. See Fine (1986, pp. 57–63).

12. The problem of squaring the circle came from the ancient Greeks.

rather than at the empirical level. After all, experience can mislead. For members of the camp, causes are "blind." Given the right conditions they have no choice but to "act" and bring about the destined effects in a mechanical fashion. For example, when billiard ball *A* runs into billiard ball *B*, *A* will cause *B* to move. There is no option for *A*, and there is no option for *B* either. Unless there are external forces or constraints (for example, wind blowing hard or glue holding *B* onto the table top), *B*'s moving away from *A has to* occur. The essence of causation seems to be this kind of deterministic compulsion.

Of course one can argue, with Hume, that deterministic compulsion is unobservable, hence it does not make sense to employ such a notion (Section 11.6). Ironically, however, Hume's analysis does support the impossibility thesis, albeit in a different manner. Let me explain.

In ordinary usage, when one says that *A* causes *B*, one means something like *A* makes *B* happen,' '*A* produces *B*,' '*A* brings about *B*,' and so on. Remember how Hume questions whether we ever have any "sightings" of this "bringing about." I think he argues convincingly that what we actually perceive is the occurrence of *A* followed by the occurrence of *B*. We say that *A* causes *B* because in the past events similar to *A* have always been followed by events similar to *B*. Hume asks us to be "honest" and mean what we can mean. Thus he proposes that we should adopt the following definition:

(1) "A cause [is] an object, followed by another, and where all the objects similar to the first are followed by objects similar to the second."[13]

You can see that for Hume the reason a single instance *A* is taken as the cause of another single instance *B* is that there is a whole class of events similar to *A* that are uniformly (without exception) followed by events similar to *B*. If this *A–B*

sequence is not uniform (that is, has exceptions), *A*, by definition, is not the cause of *B*. We can see that PUC has been built into the definition of causation. If so, it is impossible for the same cause to have different effects. At least this is so for Hume.

But then do we have to follow Hume's definition? For that matter do we have to follow *any* particular definition? Can't we adopt a definition that allows for the negation of PUC? After all, causal efficacy or deterministic compulsion is not presented to the senses. It is only a notion postulated by us, much like 'electron' and 'radio wave,' and the purpose of postulating unobservables (at least according to many) is merely for the coordination, explanation, and/or prediction of phenomena (see Chapters 8 and 9). Can't we postulate causality in such a way that it is applicable to sub atomic phenomena as understood in quantum physics, even though at a sacrifice, the sacrifice being PUC? To put it differently, though it is nice and ideal to have the kind of causality that yields uniform predictions, causality that yields only probabilistic predictions may not be too much of a concession in exchange for an acceptable way of "saving the phenomenon" in the field of quantum physics—which, by the way, deals with the most basic level of nature. This is exactly what Popper proposes with his propensity interpretation of probability, to which we now turn.[14]

12.6 THE PROPENSITY AND THE FREQUENCY INTERPRETATIONS OF PROBABILITY

The **propensity interpretation (PI)** was proposed by Popper.[15]

---

13. Hume (1748, reprint p. 220).

14. Heisenberg, one of the founders of quantum mechanics, prefers to understand subatomic phenomena in terms of "essentially probabilistic and fuzzy" events and situations "linked" by deterministic and exact universal laws.

15. Popper (1957).

Remember that we discussed the classical and the logical interpretations of probability in Chapter 4. These are often known as **subjective interpretations**, in that according to them probability is not something objective, providing a measure of certain attributes or properties belonging to the natural world. Consider the following example:

(2) The probability that it will rain tomorrow is 20 percent.

This statement is *not* interpreted as asserting that nature is somehow uncertain or indeterministic. There is nothing wrong for someone who asserts (2) and yet believes that reality is such that the atmospheric conditions determine with certainty whether it is going to rain. The probability qualification in (2) is said to reflect the ignorance of the speaker rather than the uncertainty of nature; hence it is subjective. The information the speaker possesses is incomplete. According to this (meager) amount of information, one can infer at best that the chance that it will rain is 20 percent. However, note that neither the classical nor the logical interpretation assigns probability to a person's private beliefs. Rather the probability assigned is about the degree of trust that the person *should* have, given a certain amount of information. People can be irrational, and hence usually assign probabilities very different from the proper ones. These proper or correct degrees of trust are what both the classical and the logical interpretations are about. That's why the logical interpretation theorists usually define probability without mentioning believers. For them probability is a logical relationship between a set of statements, the evidence or data, and a single statement, the conclusion. It represents the weight that the evidence bears logically on the conclusion. Since the relationship is between statements, probability, strictly speaking, belongs to the realm of objectivity. That's why many writers avoid the term 'subjective interpretation' even though the term 'subjective' does have its relevance if we take

this relationship as one between evidence and *rational* (reasonably correct) belief (beliefs being subjective). An understandable alternative term is 'epistemic interpretation.'[16]

According to Popper, subjective (epistemic) interpretations are applicable to neither the case of the radon atom nor the case of the electron. When it is asserted that

(3) The probability that a radon atom will disintegrate in 3.82 days is 50 percent (in other words, the half-life of radon is 3.82 days)

what is said, so Popper argues, is not about the relationship between one's knowledge about radon atoms and the prediction that a particular radon atom will disintegrate. Rather it is about radon atoms per se. The statement says that these atoms, being radon atoms and not some other kind of atom, have the propensity or disposition to break up within a certain time. For example, take the case of glass being brittle. Being brittle is a disposition. It is a sort of hidden quality, lying dormant, which will manifest itself when the conditions are right. When sufficient pressure is applied to brittle objects, they will break. The breakage is a manifestation of the disposition. Brittleness is a "passive" disposition in that it will manifest itself when acted on. Corrosiveness is, by contrast, an "active" disposition. It is still a sort of hidden quality. Just by looking or smelling, one cannot discern the corrosive nature of a liquid. However, it is active in that it will "act" and attack metal when the conditions are right. Most material objects have dispositions. Being elastic, being flammable, and being soluble are all dispositions. According to Popper's PI, "half-life" is a disposition. Statement (3) is interpreted as saying that radon atoms have a certain disposition that will manifest itself as disintegration. Half-lives are built-in qualities of certain kinds of atom. Some have longer half-lives, and some shorter ones. Uranium-238 has a half-life of 4.5 billion years (rather stable), whereas polonium-214 has a half-life of 1/10,000 of a second (very unstable).

---

16. (i) 'Epistemic' comes from the Greek word 'episteme,' meaning knowledge, (ii) 'Subjective interpretation' often refers to what is known as personalist interpretation, which takes probability as a measure of the degree of rational belief of individuals.

PI can be seen to be an **objective interpretation** in that probability is taken to be a measure of certain attributes belonging to certain parts of reality (outside our minds). Statement (3), for example, is about radon atoms, not about what we *think of* radon atoms, nor about how much we *know of* radon atoms. In short, for Popper, probability as used in statements like (3) is a way of characterizing certain objective types of disposition. This is not to say that subjective interpretations have no role to play. When one says that it is probably going to rain, one may well be employing a subjective interpretation, saying that one's state of knowledge is such that one thinks there is a greater than 50 percent chance that it will rain. Thus objective and subjective interpretations are complementary, each applying to its own domain. But for Popper, as far as quantum physics is concerned, his objective (propensity) interpretation should apply.

However, PI faces two major objections. First, the sort of disposition assigned to atoms and electrons is not the usual deterministic kind. For example, when we say that a substance is flammable, we mean that it has the disposition of bursting into flame *whenever* the conditions are right (such as when the temperature is high and there is oxygen around). The 'whenever' here is meant to be without exceptions, hence deterministic. But Popper's propensities are not deterministic. Radon atoms have a propensity for disintegrating. But some will disintegrate earlier and some later. There is no uniformity to the timing of the manifestation. What we can say, though, is that 50 percent of the atoms will disintegrate within 3.82 days. Thus the disposition is probabilistic rather than deterministic. The same applies to the case of the electron. Moving electrons, on approaching a minute aperture, have a propensity for going through it. The going-through behavior is uniform for all electrons. However, the directions they will take on the other side of the aperture differ from electron to electron. Some will go straight through. Some will bend left

at a small angle. Some will bend right at a large angle and so on. The electron's propensity, on encountering the same situation (aperture in a screen), does not manifest itself uniformly. All we can say is that its manifestations satisfy a certain probabilistic distribution.

This is the case we discussed in the previous section, a case of "same cause but different effects." Is this possible? Is it conceptually sound? I'll leave it to you to debate.

The second objection comes from advocates of what is known as the **frequency interpretation (FI)**, whose modern architect is Richard von Mises. The main idea of FI can be explained in terms of an example. Suppose we have a collection, C, of balls, 72 percent of which are red, the rest blue. If we are asked to draw one out of C (say from an urn), we may get a red one or a blue one (depending on our "luck"). However, if we draw out a large number *at random*, making sure that we always return the drawn ones to C each time before the next draw, we should expect that the ratio of red balls in the selection, S, will get closer and closer to 72 percent as the size of S grows bigger and bigger. This is a consequence of what is known as Bernoulli's law of large numbers. Now let us see how the FI understands a statement such as

(4)   The probability of obtaining a red ball in a draw from C is p.

If the draw is a random draw, for the FI theorist, p should be 72 percent, being the ratio of red balls in C. But of course in nature C may be infinite in size, and "72 percent of an infinite set" is not a straightforward uncontroversial notion.[17] Moreover, in most scientific investigations, we do not know the composition of C to start with. Hence how is p going to be estimated, and what can (4) mean?

Let's see what FI will say. If we draw balls, at random and one at a time, with replacement, from C, and record the ratio of red balls obtained to the

---

17. Mathematicians will tell you that 72 percent of an infinite set is itself an infinite set, which is actually of the same "size" as the "mother" set.

total number of draws, we should get a series[18] of ratios—that is, a series of relative frequencies. (For example, if we have drawn three balls, and they are of the colors RED, BLUE, and RED, in that order, then we should get a series of ratios: 1 out of 1, 1 out of 2, and 2 out of 3. If we have drawn 100 balls, then we should get a series of 100 ratios.) Now FI interprets (4) as saying

(5) Any series of relative frequencies (produced by a series of random draws from *C*) will converge to a limit, and that limit is *p*. (In other words, the relative frequencies produced by a series of random draws from *C* will gradually settle down toward a number, and that number is *p*.)

The difference between FI and PI is this. FI does not attempt to explain *why* the series of ratios converges to *p*. It merely points out a fact (a prediction). In contrast, PI postulates a propensity and claims that the convergence of the series is a manifestation of this disposition. We should often hear people referring to FI theorists as empiricists. Indeed, they are, in the sense that they are followers of Hume, who, as we should remember from Chapter 11, does not trust unobservables. For Hume, the existence of necessary connection (supposedly obtaining) between causes and effects is suspect, and the meaningfulness of the very term 'necessary connection' is doubtful. For the FI theorists, propensities are unobservables and they are ad hoc postulates, doing nothing other than to explain converging series. They do have a point, for the only evidence for the existence of such propensities is the observed series that converge. If, for example, there were one and only one radon atom in the world that disintegrated, then there would be no *justification* for the postulation of a half-life propensity of 3.82 days for radon. Such a postulation makes sense only if a large number of disintegrated radon atoms have been observed and if roughly half of them have disintegrated within 3.82 days. If so,

according to FI, why should one postulate a "redundant" propensity on top of the simple statement that in 3.82 days roughly half of any given amount of radon gas will have disintegrated (and become Radium A).[19] After all, these "redundant" postulates are unobservable. Moreover, they contravene the principle of uniform causation in that they, unlike ordinary dispositions, react probabilistically rather than uniformly.

FI is the standard interpretation used by practicing statisticians. In statistics, you are dealing with finite collections of things as populations and also as samples (Chapter 4). FI suits that sort of problem situation very well, as can be seen from our example of the drawing of balls from an urn discussed earlier. However, there is quite a big difference between the behaviors of radon atoms and electrons and those of balls being drawn at random from urns. In contrast, a lot can be said for PI in the field of quantum physics. In quantum physics basically we are interested in the nature of single atoms and single electrons. We ask, "What is the structure of *the* radon atom (*the* electron)? How does *the* radon atom (*the* electron) behave in a certain situation?" In the jargon of the literature, we are interested in single events. If there were only one radon atom in the whole universe, (3) would not make sense for FI, for FI can only explain outcomes of selections (samples) from a large collection (population). On the contrary, (3) makes perfect sense for PI. It simply says that any (single) radon atom has the propensity of disintegrating within 3.82 days, even though the time of manifestation of the propensity of this particular atom is uncertain and probabilistic in nature.

The philosophy of probability which investigates and studies the various types of interpretations of probability, is an important discipline for the philosopher, the mathematician, and the scientist. So far we can classify the proposed interpretations into two major types: the subjective and the objective.

---

18. 'Series' and 'sequence' mean different things in mathematics. In our context, the latter is more accurate.

19. Molière, a 17th-century French playwright, satirized the practice of postulating occult dispositions to explain the occurrence of observable events by claiming that opium tends to put people to sleep because it has a dormative virtue (or power).

The subjective type includes both the classical interpretation and the logical interpretation, whereas the objective type includes the PI and the frequency interpretation. Subjectivists see probabilities as measures of what one is entitled to believe on given evidence, and (human subjects') ignorance is the source of probability assertions. Objectivists, on the other hand, take probabilities as measures of "things" belonging to the objective (material) world, irrespective of human beliefs. These "things" can be dispositions or can be relative frequencies. There seems to be room for both subjective and objective interpretations, depending on situations and contexts. We can take the term 'probability' as ambiguous, having several meanings that resemble one another to a certain extent.[20] When one makes a statement of probability, one can mean different things according to which interpretation of probability one has in mind. Thus these various notions of probability can be taken as complementary rather than mutually exclusive. Of course this does not mean that we have settled the problems associated with the question of which interpretation is the *proper* one to be used for which occasion—for example, in the case of probabilities concerning the behaviors of atomic and subatomic particles.

12.7 S-R EXPLANATION: A SECOND OBJECTION TO I-S EXPLANATION

Let's refer back to Explanation (IV) in Section 12.2. There we explained why a certain radon atom disintegrated within a week by claiming that it is a law of nature that most radon atoms do so. Hempel's idea of explanation is that to explain E is to provide an argument that demonstrates why the occurrence of E is to be *expected*, and such an argument inevitably employs some laws of nature. If universal laws of nature are not available to do the job, probabilistic laws will do, *as long as these laws can ensure that E is expected to occur, albeit only with high probability and not with certainty*. I'll call this the **requirement of high probability (RHP)**. You can see that prediction with high probability plays an essential role in Hempel's S-I model of explanation. However, often adequate explanation does not provide us with prediction with high probability. Take

(VII)   This was a radium atom.

Few radium atoms disintegrate within a week.

This radium atom disintegrated within a week.

The conclusion here follows the premises with only a very low probability, yet I think few can deny that the cause of the atom disintegrating lies with its being a radium atom rather than just an atom (for most atoms are stable). Had it been an iron atom, say, it would not have disintegrated. But as a matter of fact, it was a radium atom, and even though radium atoms have a long half-life (1,620 years), they are still liable to disintegrate.

A similar example is as follows:

(VIII)   Tom had untreated latent syphilis.

Few people having untreated latent syphilis contract paresis.

Tom contracted paresis.

Paresis is a form of tertiary syphilis that can be contracted only by people who have gone through both primary and secondary stages of the disease. In other words, suffering from syphilis is a necessary condition for contracting paresis, even though only 25 percent of syphilis sufferers will actually contract it.[21] We can see, from these facts, that there can be no doubt about the cause of Tom's contracting the disease paresis, for it can only be

---

20. For example, they all obey the "laws" of probability calculus.

21. This example is adapted from M. H. Salmon et al. (1992, p. 28).

due to his having contracted syphilis in the first place. Yet (VIII) does not satisfy Hempel's RHP.

Not only is RHP not necessary in scientific explanations, it is not sufficient either. Let us illustrate with an example.

(IX) Peter contracted a common cold.

Most people will recover from a common cold in a few days if they consume large doses of vitamin A.

Peter consumed large doses of vitamin A.

Peter recovered from the common cold.

Here the conclusion does follow from the premises with a high probability. Is (IX), therefore, an adequate explanation? The answer is no, because most common colds disappear in a few days with or without vitamin A. We can say that vitamin A is a red herring.[22]

We can see that Hempel's RHP is neither necessary nor sufficient for explanations. In developing this point (as well as other points[23]) in great detail, Wesley Salmon is probably the most severe critic of Hempel's S-I explanation. He thinks that S-I explanation should be replaced by **S-R explanation (statistical-relevance explanation)**.

According to Salmon, the strength of the probability between the explanans and the explanandum is unimportant. Here is how he contrasts the two models:

I-S model: an explanation is an *argument* that renders the explanandum *highly probable*.

S-R model: an explanation is an ***assembly of facts statistically relevant*** to the explanandum, ***regardless of the degree of probability that results***. (Salmon, 1984, p. 45)

Let me explain his notion of **statistical relevance** with an example. Take the case of the

vitamin A. Let the class of people suffering from common colds be called C, the class of people taking vitamin A be called A, and the class of people recovering from common colds within a few days be R. Then the probability of people with common colds recovering in a few days is usually denoted as $\Pr(R$ given $C)$. The probability of people with common colds *and* having taken vitamin A recovering in a few days is usually denoted as $\Pr(R$ given $C \,\&\, A)$ (Chapter 4). There are three possibilities:

(6) $\Pr(R$ given $C \,\&\, A) > \Pr(R$ given $C)$

(7) $\Pr(R$ given $C \,\&\, A) < \Pr(R$ given $C)$

(8) $\Pr(R$ given $C \,\&\, A) = \Pr(R$ given $C)$

Alternative (8) represents the case where A is statistically irrelevant to R. On the other hand A is statistically relevant in both of the other two cases, being positively relevant in (6) and negatively relevant in (7).

According to Salmon, to explain an event E statistically is to collect as many statistically relevant facts as possible whether they are positively relevant or negatively relevant.[24]

In the literature, $\Pr(R$ given $C)$ is known as the **prior probability** and $\Pr(R$ given $C \,\&\, A)$ is known as the **posterior probability**. Statistical relevance requires the posterior probability to be different from the prior probability; in other words, the new fact, A, does make a difference in the expectance of R.

Let's apply Salmon's model to our examples. Since vitamin A is statistically irrelevant to the recovery from common colds, this makes it understandable why Explanation (IX) fails to do its job. Explanation (VIII) is different. Even though the posterior probability (probability of people suffering from syphilis contracting paresis) is low, it is still higher than the prior probability (probability of people contracting paresis). You can see that it is not the numerical value of the

---

22. This example is adapted from M. H. Salmon et al. (1992, p. 27).

23. For example, Wesley Salmon also developed attacks on Hempel's requirement of maximal specificity. See Kitcher and Salmon (1989, pp. 56–61, 68–70, 75–79).

24. It is controversial whether the negatively relevant cases play a role in statistical explanations. However, Salmon (1975, pp. 160–165) has put forth a spirited defense of this view.

posterior probability that counts. What counts is rather the *increase* in probability by the presence of syphilis. The increase here is actually from 0 to 25 percent, quite a significant increase. Finally, on Explanation (VII): the prior probability of atoms (in general) disintegrating is very low (because the overwhelming majority of atoms do not disintegrate at all). However, the posterior probability is much higher (because the atom is a radium atom), even though it is still low in the absolute sense. Hence you can see that the S-R model explains away the difficulties of Hempel's I-S model.

Summing up, the contest between Hempel and Salmon is between what is statistically likely and what is statistically relevant. In view of the aforementioned successes, Salmon's model does have an edge, even though the notion of statistical relevance is not without its own difficulty.

Salmon's theory of scientific explanation has two parts. S-R explanation is only the first part, the preliminary part preparing for the next. Quite correctly, Salmon points out that statistical relevance is not causal relevance. Explanation, Salmon insists, should be in terms of causation, so that the ultimate form of adequate scientific explanations will be causal in nature. Let's illustrate with an example.

To explain why it rained yesterday, we can quote the change of atmospheric pressure just before the rain occurred. However, it would be a mistake to quote the drop in level of the mercury column of the barometer instead. The level of the mercury did not and cannot bring about the rain (otherwise rainmaking would be easy). Nevertheless, the "drop in level" is statistically relevant to the occurrence of the rain. This can be easily seen as follows. The probability of rain on a fine July morning is 2 percent. This is the prior probability. The probability of raining on a fine July morning when the mercury in the barometer has dropped 20 mm is 80 percent. This is the posterior probability. Hence the "drop in level" is *statistically* relevant, even though it is *not causally* relevant. Of course you can see the reason. The "drop in level" is only a symptom of the drop in atmospheric pressure, whereas the true cause of the rain is the drop in atmospheric pressure.

We can now see the relationship between statistical relevance and causal relevance. The presence of statistical relevance indicates that factors of causal relevance are "close by." Statistical relevances are *indicators*. However, to produce genuine explanations, one must go for causes. At least, this is Salmon's thesis. And we will pursue this further in Chapter 14.

KEY TERMS INTRODUCED IN THIS CHAPTER

inductive-statistical explanation (I-S explanation)	deductive-statistical explanation (D-S explanation)	propensity interpretation (PI)	requirement of high probability (RHP)
statistical explanation	Copenhagen interpretation	subjective interpretations	statistical-relevance explanation (S-R explanation)
probabilistic explanation	principle of uniformity of causation (PUC)	objective interpretation	prior probability
		frequency interpretation (FI)	posterior probability

REFERENCES

On I-S Explanation: Hempel (1966, pp. 59–69), M. H. Salmon et al. (1992, chap. 1), and Lambert and Brittan (1987, pp. 18–25) are easy introductions. Hempel (1965, pp. 376–411) gives a detailed account.

On the hidden variables thesis: Mermin (1985) gives a crystal-clear exposition of the implications of Bell's theorem on the worthiness of the thesis. Shimoney (1978) follows up with a slightly more technical paper. Both are reprinted in Boyd et al. (1991). The introduction to the papers by J. D. Trout in the same volume is also worth reading. Nagel (1961, pp. 293–315), Hughes (1989), and Forrest (1988) provide nonmathematical introductions to quantum physics as well as discussions of various philosophical interpretations of this physics.

On probabilistic causality: "Causation" in Edwards (1967) has a useful passage on the principle of uniformity of causation. Nagel (1961, pp. 316–335) offers a more detailed exposition and discussion. Bunge (1963) is most detailed. M. H. Salmon et al. (1992, chap. 6) is on determinism in physics, which,

however, requires quite a bit of physics training to follow.

On the propensity interpretation and the frequency interpretation: O'Hear (1989, chap. 7), Skyrms (1975, chap. VII), and Salmon (1966, chap. V) are good introductions. Cohen (1989, pp. 40–57) is slightly more advanced. Popper (1957) and (1983, Part II) gives Popper's own arguments for the propensity interpretation.

On S-R explanation: for introductions, see M. H. Salmon et al. (1992, chap. 1) and Lambert and Brittan (1987, pp. 18–25). For more details, see Salmon (1975) and (1984, chap. 2).

EXERCISES

1. Give an example of an I-S explanation and an example of a D-S explanation.

2. Attempt to turn the example of I-S explanation of Exercise 1 into a D-N explanation by the introduction of hidden variables. Critically discuss the idea of the hidden variables theory.

3. Attempt to turn the example of I-S explanation of Exercise 1 into an S-R explanation. According to Salmon, S-R explanation is methodologically superior to I-S explanation. Discuss this thesis.

4. How is the thesis of S-R explanation related to the thesis of the hidden variables theory? Are they in support of or antagonistic toward each other?

5. (a) Can probabilistic statements be (physically) necessary? Can there be probabilistic laws in that these laws are *necessarily* true?

   (b) Give an example of what is usually termed as a probabilistic law. Can it serve to support counterfactual conditionals?

   (c) How satisfactory is the following explanation? "John loves cricket because he is an Englishman and most Englishmen love cricket." Would the explanation be more acceptable if the word 'most' were replaced by the word 'all' (assuming that it is true that all Englishmen love cricket)?

   (d) What sort of position would the propensity interpretation of probability take in the debates in (a) to (c)? What sort of position would the frequency interpretation take?

6. How would Hume defend the frequency interpretation? Is statement (5) in Section 12.6 analytic or synthetic, a priori or a posteriori, necessary or contingent?

Chapter 13

Teleological Explanation, Mind, and Reductionism

13.1 INTRODUCTION

Having dealt with the applicability of Hempel's covering-law thesis in the field of probability, let's now ask, "Does the covering-law thesis hold for the social sciences?"

Consider the following explanation:

(I) Mary ran down the street in order to catch the bus.

This explanation seems to differ from the kinds of explanations we encountered in the last three chapters, where explanations are in terms of causes[1] and laws. Here, however, Mary's action is being explained in terms of a goal—to catch the bus—which is introduced by the phrase 'in order to.' Goals differ from causes in many respects, one of which is that, whereas causes occur before the event, goals if achieved would occur after the action. In the present case, the catching of the bus, if successful, would occur after the running.

---

1. As noted in Section 10.5, initial conditions in a D-N explanation function as causes in a broad sense of the term 'cause.'

Compare (I) with the following:

(II) Mary fell because the branch she was sitting on gave way under her weight.

Here no goal is mentioned. The breaking of the branch was surely not what Mary wanted. The breaking is not a goal. Rather it is a cause and it occurred before Mary fell.

We say that (I) is a **teleological explanation (TE)**. A TE is apparently very different from a D-N explanation. First, the explanandum is usually an action, commonly a human action. Second, as has been mentioned, it explains in terms of one or more goals instead of causes. Third, the goals form parts of the reasons or motives of the animate agent for the action. Fourth, no laws of nature are involved. The goal is still a goal even if the action for the goal is totally irrelevant. (For example, Mary might try to catch the bus by singing her favorite song.) In the case of cause and effect, however, the two are inevitably linked by some laws of nature.

Perhaps D-N explanations are distinctive of natural sciences, whereas TEs are distinctive of the social sciences. In the former, one employs causes and laws, whereas in the latter one employs goals, reasons, and motives. Are there essentially two distinct species of scientific explanation, one for inanimate objects and one for animate objects, especially for humans? The cause-effect model of explanation can be characterized as a push model, where causes make things happen by pushing from the past. The goal-action model can be characterized as a pull model, where goals draw out actions from the future. Is it that the push model suits the physical sciences whereas the pull model suits the social sciences?

Hempel's answer is no. For him there is essentially one and only one kind of scientific explanation: the covering-law explanation. TEs are defective and unscientific because they have no predictive power. The goal and the action of a TE, as previously argued, are not physically connected by some laws of nature as in the case of cause and effect. The goal need not be relevant to the action in the sense of Hempel, who thinks that if A is relevant to B, the occurrence of A should provide good grounds for the expectation of B.

For Hempel, science does not and should not explain in terms of goals. Nevertheless (I) can be admitted into science if somehow it can be shown after all not to be a genuine TE, but a D-N explanation in disguise.

There are two recognized types of TE. Explanation (I) illustrates the type known as **intentional explanation (IE)**, which is also called **purposive explanation**. The other type is known as **functional explanation**. We will start with IE.

13.2 CAN INTENTIONAL EXPLANATIONS BE PUT INTO D-N FORM?

There have been various attempts to construe (I) as a D-N explanation. Here is one plausible attempt.

(III) C: Mary wanted to catch the bus.

    L: Whoever wants to catch the bus will run.

    E: Mary ran.

It can be seen that (III) is in D-N form with C as the initial condition, L the law, and E the explanandum. Can (I) be taken as an elliptic presentation of (III)? Here C, via the law L, makes E happen. C, the cause, brings about E, the effect. Mary's action is no longer construed as being brought about by a (future) goal. In (III), her action is determined by one of her wants in the past. That want, owing to certain laws of nature, brings about the appropriate action. In brief, the goal of (I) has now been reconstrued as a want, which acts as the cause of the action.

Is the reconstruction acceptable? There are quite a few obstacles to overcome.

(A) Is the so-called law, L, true? L seems to be a rather naive law and quite untrue. When someone wants to catch the bus, she might do all sorts of things other than running. She might walk briskly to the bus stop instead of running. She might roller-skate there. She might even stay put because when she opens the front door she discovers that the street outside is flooded.

There may even be occasions when, although one wants to attain a certain goal, one may not do anything to bring it about, simply because one has other conflicting wants. Actions certainly depend on wants, but the relationship between wants and actions is much more complicated than a one-to-one relationship. Actions seem to depend on beliefs as well as wants. If Mary should believe that by singing her favorite song, she would be able to catch the bus, she might start singing rather than running. Suppose we take all these points into account and have the following:

(IV) C': Mary wanted to catch the bus, and believed that only through running would she be able to catch the bus, and there were no other wants of Mary's stronger than this particular want.

L': Whoever wants to catch the bus, and believes that only through running will she be able to catch it, and there are no other wants of that person stronger than this particular want, will run.

E: Mary ran.

Is the amended law, L', true? I must admit that we often employ similar "laws" to make predictions and explanations in everyday business. Nevertheless they are far too naive and simplistic to be true. One's actions are governed, if at all, by one's total physical makeup as well as one's mental makeup, and the physical environment as well as the social environment. I used the guarded phrase "if at all" because it might turn out that our actions are free in the sense that we have free will.

The question boils down to this: Are there psychological laws for the explanation of actions? Should psychology be modeled after the physical sciences in terms of causes and effects? These are key questions for the social sciences. J. S. Mill, whose five methods of induction we studied in Chapter 3, saw no basic difference between psychology and physics. Anything—whether a human or a stone—is governed by laws of nature. The difference lies only in the complexity of the former compared to the latter.[2]

If Mill were right, then D–N explanations should be applicable in the social sciences. Whether psychological laws are now available or not is not the point. The ideal of explanation of actions rests with laws and deduction, and maybe commonsensical explanations such as (I) can be turned into D–N explanations and thus made acceptable to science.

(B) However, there is another reason for doubting whether IEs can be construed as D–N explanations. The idea behind (II) and (III) is to replace the use of goals in explanations with wants, beliefs, and such other mental "activities." But what are such mental "activities"? Are they admissible to science?

(i)   We do not seem to know what these mental "activities" are. For example, if someone knows French, what can be going on in her mind? Is it some kind of activity that goes on all the time even when she is not thinking or speaking in French? Even when she is asleep? Again, someone may believe that the earth is round. What sort of activity in the head corresponds to this belief, which should be there as long as she so believes? Similarly, if someone wants to be rich, is there something going on in her mind corresponding to this want? If so, what is it? Are wants and beliefs kinds of activities that can serve as causes of actions (as indicated by (II) and (III))? If they can function as causes, they must be events that occur at specific times and places, yet it is difficult to place wants and beliefs at definite positions in space and time.[3] Are they underneath the skull? Do they "glow" as long as the wants and beliefs last?

(ii)   If there are such things as mental "activities," how do such activities interact with matter—that is, the human body? Descartes (1596–1650) thought that the world consists of two kinds of substance, **mind** and **matter**. Mind involves itself in mental activities such as thinking and sensing, whereas matter involves itself in activities such as motions and

2. Mill (1876).

3. Ryle (1949) discusses this issue in great detail.

transformations (for example, changes of color, changes in weight). The study of the behaviors of matter mainly lies with physics and chemistry. According to these sciences, the behaviors of matter form a closed system in the sense that all causes and effects of such behaviors are themselves further behaviors of matter. In other words, matter interacts with matter, and only with matter. Matter forms a complete world as far as cause and effect are concerned.

Now if there should be another kind of substance—mind—how is mind related to matter? In (II) and (III), mental "activities" seem to be producing certain material activities—for example, the motion of Mary's legs as she runs. But this contravenes the basic assumption that matter forms a closed system. Even if we give up this fundamental assumption in admitting the possibility that mind can influence matter, how mind actually does influence matter is puzzling. We should note that mind, being immaterial, has neither size nor position in space. How does this sizeless and positionless "thing" move matter—for example, Mary's legs? This is known in philosophy as the "mind-body problem."

So most philosophers and scientists tend to think that what we call mind does not exist. Human actions are controlled instead by the brain, which is just another piece of matter. This philosophy is known as **materialism**, which goes well with a school of thought in psychology known as **behaviorism**.

13.3 PHILOSOPHY OF MIND I: DUALISM AND MATERIALISM

Philosophy of mind is a challenging subject, which has fascinated numerous great thinkers since antiquity. It is the study of the true nature of mental phenomena: What could they be? How should they be understood? How should they be investigated? How, in general, do mental phenomena fit in with the phenomena of our familiar material world? Here and in the next section, we will study some of the more influential views on the subject.

Let's begin with **dualism**, which postulates that, apart from matter, there is another "stuff" called mind. Descartes, as we pointed out in the last section, was the main advocate and expositor. Dualism is very appealing and does agree with common sense, at least pre–20th century common sense. The Christian church, and most other religions, believe that each person has a soul or spirit. This soul, being made of mind-stuff, is incorruptible (immortal). When one dies, the soul leaves the body, taking away with it what is commonly called life. It is this soul that thinks and understands (the cognitive dimension), that feels happy or sad (the emotional dimension), and that smells, tastes, and suffers pain (the sensational dimension). In short, the soul seems to be real and its postulation seems to be able to explain a great many things. It is comforting "to know" that there is life after death, that, after all the sufferings and misfortunes in this world, there is a next world, which can be much more pleasant and joyous.[4] No wonder dualism is popular across nations and cultures.

However, evidence and reason are both against this philosophy. I have mentioned quite a few counterarguments in the last section. Here I will provide one more. According to the theory of evolution humans were evolved from apelike animals, which in turn came from lower types. As we climb down the tree of evolution we end up with single-celled animals such as the amoeba. If humans have souls, so should the amoeba. Is it possible that the amoeba has an immortal soul? Perhaps. But this is not the end of the story of the origin of the species. If we trace further down the tree of evolution from the single-celled animals, we'll come across the single-celled form of life, the euglena, which is neither plant nor animal. If we go even further, it is

---

4. Or that death is not necessarily the end of one's privileged and hedonistic life.

certain that life itself originated from lifeless chemicals. Shall we say that chemical compounds have souls (panpsychism)? The theory of evolution has had overwhelming support both from empirical data and from theoretical arguments. Since dualism is in conflict with the theory, I am not surprised to find many influential philosophers and scientists abandoning dualism for more plausible philosophies of mind.

The major alternative to dualism is **materialism**. There are two main types. Let's start with **reductive materialism**, which is also known as the **identity theory**. Often science claims that certain commonsensical phenomena are actually composed of certain "theoretical" entities, processes, or events. For example, it is claimed that sound, as the layperson knows it, is, in reality, trains of compression waves. The pitch of the sound corresponds to the frequency of the wave and the loudness to the amplitude. In the jargon of philosophy, we say that sound has been reduced to compression waves. Another well-known reduction concerns light. According to science light consists of trains of electromagnetic waves (Chapter 0), with color corresponding to frequency and brightness to amplitude. The general idea is that our commonsensical views are mistaken, and these views should be replaced by their scientific counterparts, such as compression waves and electromagnetic waves.

Reductive materialism claims that mental states are, in reality, physical states of the brain, each type of mental state being (numerically) identical with some type of physical state of the brain. So there is no mind stuff. All there is are brain cells and the physical states of the brain. What we commonly call mental states, mental processes, and mental events are physical states, physical processes, and physical events, all "happening" within the brain. It is said that this conclusion can be drawn from neuroscience, just as we can conclude from physics that the world is a soundless and colorless world, and what we call pitch, loudness, color, and brightness are in fact various states or processes of certain physical waves.

Reductive materialism is an attractive philosophy of mind. However, it has its own difficulties.

First, there is the general difficulty with any kind of reductionism. What is the logical and ontological relationship between the two "things" said to be identical: the reducing (physical states) and the reduced (mental states)? We will study more of this issue in the next section as well as in Chapter 16. Second, when we say that A is the same as B, we would expect B to retain all the properties of A. But here the physical states do not have the qualia of the mental states—for example, the painfulness of pain, the anguish of anxiety, the elatedness of joy, and so on. At best the physical states give rise to or are correlated with the mental states. The two types are so different in quality that it is madness to take them as identical, so it is argued. Third (and by no means the last objection), whereas light and sound have been successfully reduced to waves, the reduction of mental states to physical states is only programmatic. It is not only programmatic in practice but also programmatic in theory: How is one supposed to reduce the one type to the other (other than by hand-waving)?

The other popular type of materialism is known as **eliminative materialism**. We can take reductive materialism as a manual of translation, which sets out formulas for the translation of mental terms into physical terms. In contrast, eliminative materialism teaches that translation is a waste of time because the mental terms we are so familiar with misdescribe nature in ways that warrant neither their preservation nor their being translated. These terms do not stand for anything at all, it is said. In the jargon of philosophy, we would say that they have no reference.

Let's take an analogy. In Section 7.3, we saw how some scientists in the past misconceived and misdescribed heat as a sort of substance, called caloric fluid, which flows from hot to cold things. We also saw how people used to think that phlogiston leaves an object when the object burns. In modern science, we say that these pictures are totally false, and that 'caloric fluid' and 'phlogiston' have no reference, in the sense that there are no such things in the universe corresponding to these terms. Hence we do not try to reduce 'caloric fluid' or 'phlogiston' to some terms that are more acceptable and claim that the reduced terms stand for the same thing as the reducing terms. There has been no attempt to translate 'caloric fluid' and 'phlogiston.' These terms were simply dropped from the vocabulary of science.

Let's apply the analogy to mental terms. It is said that terms such as 'knowing French,' 'wanting to catch the bus,' 'believing the earth is round,' 'feeling pain,' 'being joyful,' and so on are vacuous just as terms like 'caloric fluid' and 'phlogiston' are vacuous. They do not have any reference. In our world, there are simply no mental states corresponding to these terms. The recommendation is, therefore, that these terms, together with folk psychology, should simply be dropped. In their place are terms from neuroscience. That's why this philosophy is known as *eliminative* materialism.

13.4 PHILOSOPHY OF MIND II: BEHAVIORISM AND FUNCTIONALISM

In this section, we introduce two more philosophies, which are neutral and noncommittal in the debate between dualism and materialism. They are dispositional behaviorism and functionalism.

Dispositional behaviorism claims that certain mental state terms such as 'want' and 'believe' should be understood as (physical) dispositional terms.[5]

Dispositional terms are common in daily as well as in scientific use. For example, we say that the vase is brittle, the liquid is corrosive, and alcohol is flammable. 'Brittle,' 'corrosive,' and 'flammable' are dispositional terms. There is nothing mysterious about such terms and what they represent. They represent certain dispositions or states, which in a sense lie dormant (unmanifested). The brittleness of the vase does not show itself until the vase is dropped onto a hard floor. When so dropped, the brittleness manifests in the form of the vase breaking into pieces. It can of course manifest in other ways under other circumstances. For example, the vase may crack when someone steps on it. Similarly corrosiveness shows itself only in certain circumstances. A corrosive liquid usually looks innocent, but if a needle or a nail is immersed in it for long, the needle or nail would be destroyed. Alcohol catching fire is a common phenomenon. However, the flammability is usually "hidden" in the fluid. It manifests itself only under certain conditions—that is, when the temperature is high and when there is oxygen around. We can say that these conditions trigger the manifestation.

Mental terms such as 'want' and 'believe' apparently behave like dispositional terms. Wants usually lie dormant. Someone might want to get rich and yet does nothing to satisfy that want until certain conditions exist. For example, he might come upon a pile of hundred dollar bills lying on a store counter unattended. The sight of the money would probably trigger him into action. The action of pocketing the money is a manifestation of the want. In less dramatic circumstances, his wanting to be rich might simply manifest itself in working overtime or in backing horses. 'Believe' seems also to be a dispositional term. Someone may believe that it is going to rain soon and yet takes no action. Her belief is "dormant" because the circumstances do not call for actions. However, if she is about to leave the house for an appointment, that belief might trigger an action, such as the taking of an umbrella with her. Dispositions are quite different from properties like colors or shapes. Colors and shapes show themselves explicitly all the time, whereas dispositions manifest themselves only when "stimulated."[6] Wants and beliefs do seem to belong

---

5. Dispositional behaviorism dated back to the early writings of Edward Tolman and B. F. Skinner toward the beginning of the century. Detailed exposition and argumentation, however, came from Gilbert Ryle (1949). This philosophy is also known as **philosophical behaviorism** or **analytical behaviorism**.

6. This, strictly speaking, is not true. However, here I would not like to go into controversial issues concerning the distinction of dispositions and other kinds of properties.

to the latter category. We can say that they are latent response tendencies.

Now if mental terms are (physical) dispositional terms like 'brittle,' 'corrosive,' and 'flammable,' then we would have a solution to the problem of mental terms. Since dispositional terms are perfectly respectable and scientific, mental terms should present no problem either.

The term 'brittle,' being dispositional, can be defined as follows:

(1) x is brittle $=_{df}$ If x were dropped onto a hard surface, it would break.

The sign '$=_{df}$' signifies that the left-hand side (often called the **definiendum**) has the same meaning as the right-hand side (the **definiens**). 'df' comes from the word 'definition' and '$=$' indicates that there is some sort of equality here. The definiens has two parts, a condition and a happening: if the condition should exist, the happening would occur.

In abstract, we can say that the definition has the following form:

(2) $Dx =_{df}$ If Cx, then M.

This can be read as:

(3) x has disposition $D =_{df}$ If x were placed under condition C, then M, a manifestation (of D), would occur.

In other words, we define the disposition in terms of its possible manifestations. I used the plural form of manifestation here, because there can be more than one kind of manifestation. We say that the disposition can be multitracked. Definition (1) is oversimplified. For example, we have not considered the object's reaction under other conditions, say, when it is pressed on, instead of being dropped. To get a precise definition, we should also specify in (1) the height from which the object is to be dropped, and how hard the surface has to be, and so on. Definition (2), in the literature, is known as an **operational definition**, but here we can call it a **dispositional definition**. We will return to this topic in detail in Section 17.4. For our purpose here, this sketch will suffice.

One can see that all the terms in the definiens (right-hand side) of (1) are physical terms. Since 'brittle' is definable in terms of physical terms, it is itself a physical term. Apparently all dispositional terms in the physical sciences can be so defined, hence they are all physical terms. Now, if the so-called mental terms such as 'want' and 'believe' can be shown to be dispositional terms no different from terms like 'brittle,' we have a solution to our problem. We need no longer worry about the legitimacy of mental terms because they are really (physical) dispositional terms in disguise and dispositional terms are perfectly respectable scientific terms. The problems raised in Section 13.2 no longer apply.

Dispositional behaviorism is attractive indeed. However, there are two major objections to it. First, there is the old qualia argument again (Section 13.3). Mental states have a sort of inner life. When we are in pain, for example, we *feel* the pain and we suffer from it. The external life may be capturable by dispositional definitions. When people are in pain, they may do certain things when confronted with certain circumstances. These behaviors are "external" and observable. At best dispositional definitions can capture these. But mental states seem to have an inner life as well. That painfulness! In short, dispositional definitions do not allow for the qualia of mental states. Second, it is argued that any mental state term is so complex that no dispositional definition(s) can ever capture its full meaning. Take the mental state term 'wanting to catch the bus' again. As was said in Section 13.2, the behavior of a person wanting to catch the bus varies from situation to situation and from personality to personality. In fact, even ignoring personality and other factors such as the physical constitution of the person, there are probably as many different types of behavior (ranging from running to doing nothing) as there are types of situation (ranging from seeing the bus approaching to hearing over the radio that the bus drivers have just started their strike). Since there are an infinite number of different types of situations (taking into account social, cultural, political, economic, and religious variants, of course), we can't expect any finite number of

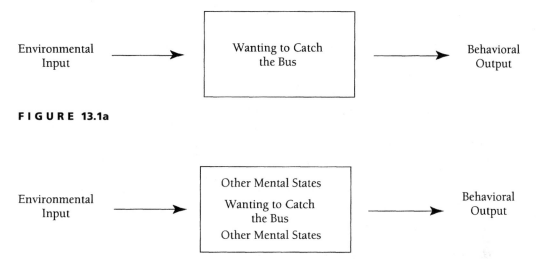

FIGURE 13.1a

FIGURE 13.1b

"If Cx, then M" sentences to be adequate in capturing the meaning of "wanting to catch the bus."[7]

Note that dispositional behaviorism is neutral and noncommittal in the debate between dualism and materialism. In saying that mental states are dispositions, one is not committed to the kind of stuff (substance) that is "supporting" these dispositions. Such dispositions can be "supported" by organic matter (for example, brain cells) or inorganic matter (for instance, metallic components and electronic circuits as in robots) or by something else (for example, mind-stuff). Similarly, when we say that the vase is brittle, we are not committed to specifying what kind of substance makes up the vase. In claiming that mental state terms are dispositional terms, we are only trying to capture the "external behavioral content" of these terms, not the "internal substantive content."

The other type of noncommittal philosophy is **functionalism**, which is a type of refined dispositional behaviorism. Dispositional definitions can be viewed as specifications of the relationships between inputs (stimuli) and outputs (reactions).

According to the functionalists, this is an oversimplified picture. One's behavior depends not only on the stimulus-inputs, it also depends on what "state of mind" one is in. Let's return to our old friend: 'wanting to catch the bus.' Whether one runs or not certainly depends on one's other wants. If one also wants to speak urgently with the doctor, one might, instead of running, pick up the telephone. Similarly, as has been mentioned before, the person might believe that by singing she could transport herself to the bus stop fast. In such a case, she might start singing rather than running. The functionalists point out that one's action depends not on a single mental state but rather on the whole lot of contemporaneous mental states. So the picture is rather like Figure 13.1b. (In contrast, dispositional behaviorism corresponds to Figure 13.1a.)

The human body has a large number of organs, each of which has its own role or function to perform. They do not operate separately, in isolation. Quite the contrary, they work as a team, cooperating and helping each other out, very much like a football team. (The implicit aims are probably growth and

---

7. I think that similar, though less complex, difficulties face the definition of physical terms such as 'brittle' or 'flammable.' I personally think that a term can be dispositional (such as 'brittle') without being able to be defined explicitly in terms of dispositional (operational) definition. We should distinguish the issue of claiming that mental state terms are dispositional from the issue that *all* dispositional terms can be defined operationally.

survival.) The heart has its own function(s) but it must work together with the lungs, the liver, the kidneys, and so on. Any piece of machinery is made up of functional parts, and it is these parts working together, each performing what is expected of it and each responding to the changes, "needs," and "demands" of the other parts, that results in the expected final output of the machine as a whole. Think of a car, a clock, or a sewing machine.

The human brain with its central nervous system is an organ of the body. It has its functional roles just like any other organ in the body. But the brain itself is composed of further functional parts. Neuroscience has made some advances in this field but there is still a lot more to learn about the brain and how it is constituted of functional parts. So, according to functionalism, mental states are functional states just as human organs are functional parts. It is these functional parts, as Figure 13.1b shows, that determine the relationship between the input and the output.

The important point to bear in mind is that corresponding functional parts of two mechanisms of the same type need not share anything in common in the building materials or the structural design. For example, compare a battery-operated clock and a clock that has to be wound. The batteries in the former correspond to the coiled spring in the latter. They both serve the *same* function of producing power to run the clock. Nevertheless, they differ both in materials and in design. The two things share little in common, both in makeup and looks. Likewise, an artificial kidney is very different from a natural kidney! But each is a kidney to its owner. We can say 'kidney' is a functional term, not necessarily referring to "flesh and blood." (That's why we often use terms such as 'robotic eyes,' 'robotic arms,' and so on, even though these items are usually made of metal or plastic.) Similarly, 'the power source of a clock' refers to a functional part, which can be fulfilled in various ways—for example, in the form of batteries, coiled springs, and so on.

Functionalism claims that mental state terms such as 'wanting to catch the bus,' 'believing that it is going to rain,' 'having a headache,' 'feeling sad,' and so forth are functional state terms. Perhaps 'functional state term' should be spelled out further. But

one thing is clear. For the functionalists it is *what* the state does that matters. How the state does it, whether in terms of "flesh and blood" or in terms of "wires and cogwheels," is irrelevant. For example, a robot can be said to want to catch the bus if it is in the same functional state as the human who wants to catch the bus. Here, of course, we assume that the robot has functional parts in a one-to-one correspondence with the functional parts of a human, and moreover the parts in the robot cooperate in ways similar to the cooperation of the parts in a human. In a similar manner, the functional states of the robot also correspond to those of the human.

If mental state terms are (when properly analyzed) functional terms, their mystique is dispelled. To say that Mary wants to catch the bus is no different in kind from saying that someone's eyes are tired, or a person's stomach is upset, or the power source of the clock is running low. (Here the someone can, of course, be a robot, and the eyes and stomach can be made of plastic, and the power source of the clock can be a nuclear reactor!)

In other words, mental states are said to be substance-and-structure-independent. They are characterized by their functions rather than by their constitutions. That's why we said at the beginning of this section that both functionalism and dispositional behaviorism are neutral in the debate between dualism and materialism. These functional parts, as far as the functionalists (and the behaviorists) are concerned, can be made of mind-stuff or of organic or inorganic matter. A corollary of functionalism is that robots resembling humans in behavior (physical, social, intellectual, religious, and all other kinds of behavior) can feel pain, can have emotions, can think, can believe, and so on. They may not have the same kind of "inner life" (if at all) as humans, because they are made of electronics and metal. Nonetheless, they can genuinely feel pain and so forth because 'feeling pain' does not refer to episodes of the "inner life." Rather, it refers to functional states that are neutral with respect to "inner life." Here let me quote Harré and Madden (1975, p. 92): "To ascribe a power is to ascribe a disposition to a specific form of behavior to something, together with an *unspecific reference* to the nature or constitution of the thing or material concerned" (my italics).

Functionalism is a popular philosophy of mind. It is an improvement on dispositional behaviorism[8] on the one hand, and it dovetails well with reductive materialism on the other. Furthermore, it provides science and everyday language with a new range of vocabulary. The functionalists can, without qualms, literally describe plants as thirsty for water or yearning for the sun, animals as caring for their young or wanting to go home, and robots as clever or obedient. Nevertheless, functionalism is not without its difficulties, which we will not study here.

13.5 REDUCTIONISM AND UNITY OF SCIENCE

In the last section, we saw how reductive materialism claims that mental states are reducible to physical states. This is only a special case of a philosophy known as **reductionism**. I think that we should spend a bit of time on this topic, because it is a major field in the philosophy of science.

Common sense tells us that societies and social organizations are, in essence, (organized) collections of people—that is, groups of individuals in certain physical, social, economical, cultural, political, religious, … relationships with one another. Hence it is claimed that sociology, the study of social groups, is reducible to psychology, the study of (the nonphysical aspects of) the individual person. If reductive materialism is correct, then psychology is reducible to physiology, the science of the physical aspects of the human body (usually in terms of the relationships between the various functional parts of the body—the organs, muscles, bones, and so on). Physiology is a branch of biology,

which in turn is said to be reduced to chemistry, since cells and organs are nothing more than complex groups of chemicals. Finally, since chemistry is about molecules and atoms, it is reducible to physics, in particular nuclear physics. You can see the ladder of reduction, leading from the high-level study of sociology down to the basic study of the atom and the elementary particles, such as the electron, the proton, and so forth.

Reductionism is attractive in many respects. First, it is most satisfying to the human spirit to see that enormously complex entities such as human societies are constructed out of simple objects such as the atom or the electron. Second, since the descending ladder of reduction takes all the sciences, no matter how complicated, to be "branches" of the basic science of physics, then, strictly speaking, there is one and only one science. This is the realization of what is known as the **unity of science**.[9] Third, since modern-day physics has a relatively small set of principles and laws, the ultimate understanding of the workings of the universe seems to be close at hand.

Reductionism and the unity of science is nothing new. More than 2,400 years ago, some ancient Greeks postulated that the world is made up of nothing but atoms. Some other Greeks thought that everything was reducible to water, earth, air, and fire.[10] Since the Greeks the history of science can be told as a story of reduction: Descartes's "empty space" theory of matter, Newton's mechanics, Dalton's theory of chemical atoms, Einstein's theory of relativity and contemporary quantum physics, to mention but a few.

Reductionism comes by degrees. The first and mildest kind is what we have just sketched: **ontological reductionism**. 'Ontology' has two senses. It originally meant the philosophical study of the nature of existence. Recently the term has also

---

8. I think that functional behaviorism would be an appropriate alternative name for functionalism, so that its relationship with dispositional behaviorism would be obvious.

9. The unity of science was a major program of the logical positivists (Chapter 23).

10. There was supposed to be a fifth element, which was the celestial matter that made up the heavenly bodies, such as the stars and the planets.

been used to refer to the basic kinds of entities assumed to exist by a particular theory. Ontological reductionism typically attempts to reduce the number of basic (kinds of) entities to a minimum.

The second kind of reductionism is **predicate reductionism**. 'Predicate' is a term adopted from logic. For our present purpose, we can take it simply to mean 'term.' Predicate reductionism is the view that terms of higher-level sciences such as sociology, psychology, and so on can be reduced to terms of lower-level sciences such as physics. How is this to be done?

There are two recommended routes. One is by definition, the other by "translation." You may recall that dispositional behaviorism attempts to *define* mental terms in terms of overt behaviors through the use of operational definitions. It is said that, for example, wanting to catch the bus is *identical in meaning* to certain types of behavior under certain types of stimulus. Functionalism is another philosophy of predicate reductionism taking the route of definition. It is helpful to note that, when one claims identity in meaning, one can mean two different things. One can mean that definiendum (the mental term) has *always* had the same meaning as the definiens (the behavioral conditional manifestation). One can also mean that one is giving new meaning to an old term, thus redefining it. Both dispositional behaviorism and functionalism intend the former.

Reductive materialism, in contrast, takes the "translation" route. I employ the term "translation" here because there are no better terms available. When scientists say that light is electromagnetic waves of wavelengths between 3,800 and 7,500 angstroms,[11] they are not claiming that the term 'light' has the same meaning as 'electromagnetic waves of wavelengths between 3,800 and 7,500 angstroms.' What they claim is rather that the two terms have the same extension in the sense that they refer to (or cover) the same things. Roughly, they

are saying that the term used by the layperson is a mistake. To describe the same thing, the expression 'electromagnetic waves and so on' is preferable. What exactly the relationship is between these two terms is a matter of controversy, which we will leave until Chapter 16.

Predicate reductionism is stronger than ontological reductionism in that the former implies the latter but not vice versa. To claim that everything is made of atoms is a weak thesis when compared to the claim that all terms—for example, 'wood,' 'water,' 'stone,' 'table,' 'dog,' and 'fire'—are definable or translatable into expressions solely constituted of terms of atoms, a much stronger thesis. In fact, it is the case that paper is made of atoms. Nevertheless, I do not think that 'paper' is definable in terms of or translatable into a single or a set of chemical formulas. On the other hand, if all the terms of Science 1 are definable or translatable to Science 2 (predicate reduction), all the entities of Science 1 must be made up of entities of Science 2 (ontological reduction). You can see that eliminative materialism is a case of ontological reductionism whereas, as has been pointed out, reductive materialism is a case of predicate reductionism.[12]

The third type of reductionism, the most demanding type, is **law reductionism**. One may be able to reduce the terms of Science 1 to terms of Science 2 (predicate reduction) without being able to reduce the laws of the former to those of the latter (law reduction). What do we mean by the reduction of laws?

Let's take an example.

(4) Light travels more slowly in water than in air.

This is a law in the field of optics, which has now been shown to be reducible to (5).

(5) Electromagnetic waves between 3,800 and 7,500 angstroms travel more slowly in water than in air (which is a law in the electromagnetic wave theory of light).

---

11. One angstrom is 10^{-8} cm.

12. For the more advanced readers, we can say that one prominent reason for this is that the natural kinds postulated by Science 1 may not coincide with those postulated by Science 2.

It is said that given

(6) Light is (numerically) identical to electromagnetic waves between 3,800 and 7,500
angstroms,

statement (4) is logically deducible from (5). Therefore, according to one popular school of thought:
reducibility is the same as deducibility. In other
words,

(LR$_1$) L$_1$ is said to be reducible to L$_2$ if the former is
logically deducible from the latter (assuming
certain identities, linking the terms
employed by the two laws—for example,
'light' and 'electromagnetic waves').

A looser version of (LR$_1$) is

(LR$_2$) Laws of Science 1 are said to be **reducible
to** laws of Science 2 if the former are logically deducible from the latter (thus allowing
for the possibility of employing more than
one law of Science 2 to deduce a single law
of Science 1).

This idea of reduction goes well with Hempel's
covering-law model of explanation, as we will see
in Chapter 15. However, there are various difficulties with this thesis, one of which concerns the
nature of the identity claim, such as (6). We will
study this topic in detail in Chapter 16.

There are many conceptions of law reduction.
Let me list three more, which are progressively
more liberal.

(LR$_3$) L$_1$ is said to be **reducible to** L$_2$ if the former
is explainable in terms of L$_2$.

This notion of reduction hinges on the notion
'explainable.' What is explanation? So far you have
studied only Hempel's covering-law model, which
is but one of the many contending theories in
the literature. Nonetheless, if we should adopt
Hempel's model, you will find that (LR$_3$) is no
different from (LR$_2$) because, for Hempel, to
explain is (roughly) to deduce.

(LR$_4$) Laws of Science 1 are said to be **reducible
to** laws of Science 2 if the former are
explainable in terms of the latter.

(LR$_5$) Laws of Science 1 are said to be **reducible
to** laws of Science 2 if whatever observable
phenomena (that is, empirical data)
explainable by the former are also explainable by the latter, and if Science 2 is better
than Science 1 (where 'better than' has quite
a number of different formulations).

Let's illustrate (LR$_5$) with law (4). J. L. Foucault
in 1850 performed an experiment to compare the
speed of light in water with that in air. His apparatus
consisted of a number of lenses and mirrors, a rotating
mirror, a tube full of water, and so on. The observed
phenomenon is that the light image generated by the
rotating mirror via the tube of water was displaced
further than the image via air. Let's call this phenomenon P, which law (4) can adequately explain.

According to Reductionism (LR$_5$), law (4) is
reducible to, say, Young and Fresnel's wave theory
of light if phenomenon P and all other phenomena
explainable by (4) can also be explained by this wave
theory, and this wave theory is (in yet-to-be-specified
ways) superior to the science within which (4) is formulated: geometric optics.[13] Note that reductionism
(LR$_5$) does not require the deduction of law (4). It
only requires that the new theory with its new
laws can explain whatever phenomena law (4) can
explain.

13.6 FUNCTIONAL
EXPLANATION

As mentioned in Section 13.1, there are two recognized types of TE: IE and functional explanation.
So far we have covered the first in detail. I think it
would be a pity if we did not at least try to provide
a rough outline of the second type before we move
on to the next chapter.

---

13. See Chapter 0 on the wave theory, and any standard physics text on light on Foucault's famous experiment.

Let me start with an example.

(IV) Human beings have lungs in order to breathe.

This is teleological because the explanation of the existence of lungs in humans is in terms of a goal—that is, to breathe. Obviously we cannot construe it in terms of wants and beliefs. It is definitely not the case that humans have lungs because they want to breathe, or because they believe that lungs can enable them to breathe. Statement (IV), however, can be construed as follows:

(V) The function of the lungs in humans is to enable them to breathe.

We call this type of explanation **functional explanation**. It explains the existence of an object, here the lungs in humans, in terms of the functions it performs. How 'function' should be understood is of course a problem. Usually it is understood as a contribution to the complex of which the object is a part. Is this a correct understanding, however, and is functional explanation scientifically acceptable under such an interpretation of 'function'? For example, can we say that the function of the sun is to hold the solar system together, thus explaining the existence of the sun in terms of its contribution to the solar system?

Functional explanation is a big topic in its own right, and it is beyond the scope of this introductory text. Here it suffices for me to point out that it is much used in biology, physiology, psychology, and sociology under the general term functionalism, which should not be confused with the functionalism that we have just studied in Section 13.4 as a topic in the philosophy of mind.[14]

13.7 SUMMARY AND CONCLUSIONS

At the beginning of this chapter, we asked, "Does the covering-law thesis hold for the social sciences?" We discovered that we usually explain human actions in terms of goals, not causes. This suggests that maybe the social sciences employ or should employ different methods of explanation. However, Hempel insists that there is one and only one type of scientific explanation: his covering-law model (including the probabilistic variant). He argues that in fact what is known as IE can be transformed into D-N form. But this project of transformation has met with seemingly insurmountable difficulties. They mainly have to do with the nature of mental terms and the availability of laws of nature involving the mental.

This led us into the philosophy of mind. We studied five main types: dualism, reductive materialism, eliminative materialism, dispositional behaviorism, and functionalism.

Dualism is emotionally appealing. (I think at heart all of us wish to be immortal in that life carries on after [material] death.) But this philosophy has made no progress at all since the dawn of civilization. On the other hand, physical sciences have advanced in leaps and bounds. So, it is no wonder that in this day and age, so many people trust Darwin's *The Origin of Species* rather than the Bible. They no longer believe that they are privileged, having a soul (mind). Nonetheless, they don't seem to think that they have lost any fundamental dignity in equating themselves with apes and monkeys. As far as they are concerned, even material beings can lead spiritual lives.

We spent some time on the two main varieties of materialism: reductive materialism and eliminative materialism. We also studied their natural allies: dispositional behaviorism and functionalism. Since these four philosophies are all reductive in nature, we went into the philosophy of reductionism in some depth.

Ontological reductionism, which underlies eliminative materialism, faces the least philosophical difficulty, and it is also the softest type of reductionism. Predicate reductionism, the next one, is the philosophy that underlies reductive materialism, dispositional behaviorism, and functionalism. It has

---

14. See Smart (1968, chap. 4).

limited success and can proudly count the reduction of substantial terms such as 'methyl alcohol' or 'water' into chemical formulas as its achievements. However, sociological terms such as 'university' and 'marriage,' and psychological terms such as 'belief' and 'joy,' seem beyond the possibility of being reduced to the next lower level. The difficulties faced seem to be more than technical; they can be logical. Finally, law reductionism is even more difficult and idealistic.

Philosophers often discuss the idea of **emergence**: **emergent properties** and **emergent laws**. An emergent property belonging to a whole (entity) is a property that cannot be predicted (deduced) from properties of its parts. Here is supposedly an example: the translucency or viscosity of water cannot be predicted from properties that belong to the hydrogen atom and the oxygen atom.[15] Similarly it is said that, even though humans may be nothing more than collections of cells and chemicals, their mental properties, especially consciousness, are emergent. Thus, even though ontological reduction (eliminative materialism) is possible, predicate reduction (reductive materialism) is not. Similarly, it is said that there are emergent laws, that laws governing the entities belonging to a higher level (say, psychology) are not reducible to laws governing the entities belonging to a lower level (say, biology). Thus you can see that the doctrine of emergence is a kind of holism, captured by the cliché that the whole is more than the sum of its parts.

Let's return to the question we asked at the beginning of this chapter: Does the covering-law thesis hold for the social sciences? Judging from what we have studied so far, the answer I think has to be: "Unlikely" I would add that even if materialism, whether the reductive version or the eliminative version, is correct, the employment of covering laws for explanation in the social sciences is still both unwise and untenable. Let me explain.

Hilary Putnam (1975, pp. 295–296) gives an analogy. Suppose one is asked why a 1 × 1 inch square wooden peg does not go into a circular hole 1 inch in diameter on a wooden board. The proper answer is that the diagonals of the peg (the peg surface) are longer than 1 inch,[16] whereas the "width" of the hole is only 1 inch (and both the peg and the board are rigid). This is a geometric answer. Of course we can attempt a physical answer. We can reason that both the peg and the board are made of molecules, which move in certain ways and are held together by certain forces, and so on. We can then *deduce*, from all these *physical* facts, that the group of molecules (known to us as the peg) cannot go through the space surrounded by another group of molecules (the space being know to us as the hole). The geometric explanation is at a "coarse" (higher) level, whereas the physical explanation is at a "finer" (lower) level. We might think that the "finer" explanation is the better one. On the contrary, Putnam thinks that the geometric one is the correct one. Worse still, the physical one is not even an explanation, at least not the kind of explanation sought.

It seems that questions for explanation can be asked at various levels. Questions at one level should be answered by explanations at the same level.[17] If we were asked why Mary ran down the street, it would not be appropriate to attempt to explain in terms of the molecules and chemicals that constitute the person Mary, even if Mary is nothing but a collection of these things. The appropriate answer is (I) of Section 13.1—that is, "Mary ran down the street in order to catch the bus."

What if the question itself is asked at the level of molecules and chemicals? I suppose the answer is that if such a question *could* be formulated, the answer should be in terms of molecules and chemicals as well. The point is: Can a question in terms of molecules and chemicals be formulated that is equivalent to the question, "Why did Mary run down the street?" Would such a question or answer be of any use to us?

---

15. This example is taken from Nagel (1961, pp. 368–369).

16. Pythagoras over 2,500 years ago worked out that the diagonals of a 1 × 1 square are the square root of 2, which is about 1.4.

17. Garfinkel (1981, pp. 49–74) makes a similar point.

KEY TERMS INTRODUCED IN THIS CHAPTER

teleological explanation (TE)

intentional explanation (IE) (purposive explanation)

functional explanation

mind

matter

materialism

behaviorism

dualism

reductive materialism (identity theory)

eliminative materialism

dispositional behaviorism (philosophical behaviorism, analytical behaviorism)

dispositional term

definiendum

definiens

operational definition

dispositional definition

functionalism

reductionism

unity of science

ontological reductionism

predicate reductionism

law reductionism

functional explanation

emergence

emergent property

emergent laws

REFERENCES

On intentional explanation: Lambert and Brittan (1987, pp. 53–59), Taylor (1970, chap. 5), Trusted (1987, chap. 10), and Kitcher and Salmon (1989, pp. 111–116).

On philosophy of mind: Churchland (1988, chap. 2) gives an excellent introduction to the various views. Lambert and Brittan (1987, pp. 53–59) provides a brief introduction. Ryle (1949, chap. V) gives the original version of dispositional behaviorism.

On reductionism: Hempel (1966, chap. 8) provides a good introduction. O'Hear (1989, chap. 8) gives a more detailed discussion. Nagel (1968, chap. 11) presents a detailed and carefully analyzed account. Popper (1982, pp. 131–175) gives an interesting view on the subject by a distinguished philosopher. Also see Oppenheim and Putnam (1958) and Garfinkel (1981) for further discussions.

On functional explanation: Hempel (1965, chap. 11) represents his view on the subject.

EXERCISES

1. Give an example of a teleological explanation. Why is it a teleological explanation? (How, for example, would you explain your joining of the protest march downtown last night?)

2. Attempt to reformulate your example of teleological explanation from Exercise 1 into a D-N explanation. Do you think it a satisfactory D-N explanation?

3. An essential feature of mind is that, being nonmaterial, it has no spatial location. Yet we often claim that certain mental events happen at certain specific places. For example, you can feel that your pain is in your leg or your tooth.

Critically discuss dualism in view of this seeming inconsistency.

4. Physics so far claims that the world is a closed material system. For example, there is the principle of conservation of energy (replaced by the principle of conservation of mass energy since Einstein), which largely says that only matter can move matter. Is it reasonable for dualism to argue that even though mind cannot move matter, thus contravening the principle of conservation of energy, mind can, nevertheless, choose the directions for certain matter (that is, the body) to move.

5. Taking dualism as a scientific theory, it has to be both consistent and empirically adequate. Furthermore, it should have high unifying power and high predictive power (Chapter 8). Evaluate dualism in terms of these properties.

6. In view of your answer to Exercise 5, how should dualism as a scientific theory deal with the following:

   (a) Can a mind exist outside a body? If so, how does it leave a body?
   (b) Can a mind control more than one body at a time? How does it manage to do that?
   (c) Can two minds control the same body? What if the wishes of the two minds are in conflict?

   Based on the answers to these questions, what should dualism predict? Can dualism make any predictions about the behavior of ghosts?

7. It is said that, while water can be reduced to collections of H_2O molecules, mind cannot be reduced to matter. The reason given is that the former is a reduction of matter to matter whereas the latter is a reduction of mind to matter, which is a reduction across substances of quite different kinds. Discuss.

8. It is said that materialism and behaviorism (for example, dispositional behaviorism) are natural allies. How is it so?

9. Would Hempel's covering-law thesis, as applied to human actions, be vindicated if any of the following is proved correct?

   (a) Reductive materialism
   (b) Eliminative materialism
   (c) Dispositional behaviorism
   (d) Functionalism

Chapter 14*

Other Theories of Explanation: The Contextual, the Causal, and the Unificatory

14.1 CRITIQUES OF THE COVERING-LAW THESIS

We have seen in the last two chapters how the covering-law thesis struggles to accommodate both probabilistic and teleological explanations, and there are serious doubts about the success of these attempts. In this chapter, we will consider more objections to the thesis, this time on the appropriateness of D-N explanation as the paradigm of scientific explanation.

Objections to the thesis of D-N explanation come from two directions: (i) Many types of argument *satisfying* the requirements of D-N explanation are nonexplanatory and (ii) many types of argument *not satisfying* the requirements of D-N explanation are nevertheless scientific explanations. Hence it is neither necessary nor sufficient for a scientific explanation to be in D-N form. This is an

---

*This chapter is more advanced and is optional.

indication that Hempel's D-N form may be ill-conceived as the ideal form of scientific explanation.

Let's consider a few well-worn examples in the literature.[1] (You will enjoy these because they are entertaining as well as philosophically enlightening.)

(a) Imagine there is a flagpole on the school grounds. The sun shining on it casts a shadow. Suppose the flagpole is 20 feet long and the shadow is also 20 feet long. Would you accept the following explanation?

(SF)   The flagpole is 20 feet long because the shadow is 20 feet long and the sun is at an elevation of 45°.

I am quite sure most of you will reject SF, claiming that to explain the length of a flagpole in terms of the length of its shadow is absurd. The explanation should be the other way around! That is:

(FS)   The shadow is 20 feet long because the flagpole is 20 feet long and the sun is at an elevation of 45°.

Why FS is acceptable whereas SF is not, you would say, is because it is the flagpole that *causes* the shadow, and not the other way around.

You should notice that the idea of causation does not play an explicit role in Hempel's D-N explanation. Instead it is the laws of nature that provide the link between the initial conditions and the explanandum. Laws of nature, unlike causation, are often symmetrical between the initial conditions and the explanandum. Let me elaborate. Let

A = the length of the shadow of the flagpole is 20 feet

B = the length of the flagpole is 20 feet

C = the sun is at an elevation of 45°

D = a set of laws including "light travels in straight lines," and certain laws of geometry

You can see that both (I) and (II) are deductively valid:

(I)   A, C, D / therefore, B

(II)   B, C, D / therefore, A

In other words, given C and D, B is deducible from A and also A is deducible from B. Since D-N explanations, in essence, require only the deducibility of the explanandum from the initial conditions (assuming certain laws of nature), both (I) and (II) should be perfectly sound scientific explanation. Yet, intuitively, (I) is unacceptable. There must be something wrong with Hempel's thesis of D-N explanation. This problem for the deductivist is known as the **problem of asymmetry**.

It is not difficult to multiply such examples. For example, Newton's laws are such that we can deduce the cause from its effect, just as easily as we can deduce the effect from the cause. Let's consider the case of two billiard balls A and B, A moving while B is stationary. Let A collide head on with B. If the two balls are identical in size and shape (and are perfectly elastic), then A will stop on collision, yielding all its momentum to B, thus making B move at exactly the same velocity as A. Newton's laws are such that, knowing the velocities of A and B after collision, we can deduce the velocities of A and B before collision. Thus, according to Hempel, we can D-N-explain the velocity of A and B (before collision) in terms of the velocity of A and B (after collision).

Many philosophers think that prediction is logically different from explanation whereas, according to Hempel, to explain is to demonstrate that the explanandum is to be expected. In the case of the flagpole, we can certainly "predict" the length of the flagpole, given the length of its shadow. But, according to our intuition, this is no explanation. Similarly, we can postdict the velocity of billiard ball A and B before collision from that of A and B after collision, but this cannot be taken as an explanation either.

For Hempel, the difference between prediction and explanation is only a matter of pragmatics, not logic. In the case of the former, we do not know the outcome, whereas in the case of the latter, we do know the outcome. But the logic is identical: both are in terms of valid deduction. It is this thesis

---

1. Consult Salmon (1989, pp. 46–50) for sources of these examples.

of logical identity between explanation and prediction (including postdiction, of course) that is under attack. It is claimed that explanation may be related to prediction, but explanation is logically *not* the same as prediction.

(b) Example of the hexed salt: Simon claimed that he could perform magic. To demonstrate that, he put on a tall hat and a dark cloak. With his hand over some salt (S) he mumbled some words. Lo and behold, when the salt was later placed in water, it dissolved. The explanation is:

(III) S was salt.

S had been hexed.

S was placed in water.

All *hexed* salt dissolves when placed in water. (law)

S dissolved.

This satisfies all the requirements of D-N explanation and hence should be acceptable. Of course one might object that the so-called law is not really a law. Common sense will certainly reject it as a law because salt, whether hexed or not, will dissolve. However, it is difficult to rule it out objectively as a nonlaw. After all it has all the characteristics of a law, being true, universal, and necessary (Section 11.20). This type of problem for the D-N thesis is known as **problem of irrelevance**.

The examples in (a) and (b) show that the requirements of D-N explanation are not sufficient to yield explanations. In other words, the requirements are not stringent enough. However, the following example paradoxically seems to show that the requirements are too stringent.

(c) Why did the automobile radiator rupture? Because the temperature overnight fell to 10°F, and the car was not under cover. According to Scriven (1962), this is a perfectly good explanation even though no law has been mentioned. For Scriven, explanations do not require laws, even though the latter may be invoked to *justify* explanations.[2]

(d) According to Scriven (1959), the theory of evolution is adequate to explain the origin of species, but is quite unable to make predictions. For example, the theory cannot predict the future shapes and sizes of animals like lions, tigers, or ravens. But most scientists seem happy with the theory as an explanatory theory.[3]

These two examples are supposedly counterexamples to Hempel's thesis of D-N explanation. Thus, if Scriven is correct, Hempel's D-N requirements are too stringent, excluding perfectly good explanations as scientific.

Trouble and dissatisfaction with the covering-law thesis are not confined to these explanations. There is at least one further type. It is concerned with the D-N explanation of laws. Let's illustrate with the following example.

(e) **The problem of law explanation**: Suppose one wants to explain the law that copper conducts heat (C). Can one D-N explain it as follows?

(IV)   Copper conducts heat. (C)

Sugar is soluble in water. (S)

Copper conducts heat. (C)

This is a perfectly valid deduction. Thus it ought to be accepted as a scientific explanation. But this is absurd! Intuition tells us that (IV) does not explain anything.

You might point out that even though the requirements of D-N explanation of laws have not explicitly stated that the explanandum should not be one of the premises,[4] it is *implicitly* understood that explanation in terms of itself, being

---

2. Hempel would consider what has just been presented as a case of elliptic explanation in that laws, even though suppressed, are still essential parts of adequate explanations (Section 10.5).

3. I think Hempel probably would say that the theory only amounts to an explanation sketch (Section 10.5). Since it is a sketch, and our knowledge of the initial conditions is not adequate, at best we can make use of it for the prediction of "trends."

4. Actually the requirement of independent testability of the explanantia implies that the explanandum itself should not be part of the explanans.

circular, is not acceptable. Fair enough. But what about the following:

(V)   Copper conducts heat and salt is soluble
      in water.
      _____

      Copper conducts heat.

You might say that the explanandum is still "embedded" in the explanans even though it is not now explicitly a separate premise. Perhaps. Now what about the following:

(VI) Copper that is electrically charged conducts
      heat, and copper that is not electrically
      charged also conducts heat.

      Salt is soluble in water.
      _____

      Copper conducts heat.

You will find that this argument is perfectly valid, and the explanandum is not present as a separate statement in the explanans. You might object that the explanandum is still "embedded" in the explanans, albeit in two "bits."

When is a statement being embedded in another? We may think that we all know when embedding has taken place. Do we? Let us look at (VII).

(VII) All humans are mortal.

       All Greeks are human.
       _____

       All Greeks are mortal.

Is the conclusion "embedded" in the premises? In Section 3.1, we pointed out that valid deductions are non-ampliative in the sense that the information carried by the conclusion is already present in the premises. In other words, the content of the conclusion is part of the content of the premises, though not necessarily explicit. The reason we perform deductions is that we would like to extract hidden information from the premises and make it explicit. If the content of the conclusion is part of the premises, wouldn't it be true that the conclusion is "embedded" in the premises? In this sense, 'all Greeks are mortal' is somewhere inside 'all humans are mortal and all Greeks are human.' Nevertheless we accept (VII) as a good explanation of why Greeks are mortal.

In sum, we can see that the covering-law thesis is far from satisfactory. Apart from problems associated with probabilistic explanations and teleological explanations, we have just seen how the requirements of D-N explanation are both too loose—as illustrated by (a) and (b)—and too stringent—as illustrated by (c) and (d). Moreover, there is the problem of explanation of laws, which is brought out by (e). On top of all these, since the covering-law thesis is based centrally and essentially on the assumption that there are such things as laws of nature, which provide necessary connections between events, Hume's skepticism, which we studied in Chapter 11, poses yet another difficulty for the thesis.

14.2 THE CONTEXTUAL THEORY OF EXPLANATION I: EXPOSITION

In view of the various difficulties faced by the covering-law thesis, just discussed, many alternative conceptions of scientific explanation have been proposed. We will study three of these: the contextual, the causal, and the unificatory. We'll start with the contextual in this section.

The contextual conception of explanation came from Bas C. van Fraassen, who thinks that the notion of explanation can only be understood through the study of the logic of why-questions, because explanations are typically answers to why-questions. Let's illustrate with an example adapted from van Fraassen (1980, p. 127).

Consider the question

(1) "Why did Bill eat the apple?"

It can be understood in at least three ways:

(2) Why did *Bill* eat the apple?

(3) Why did Bill *eat* the apple?

(4) Why did Bill eat the *apple*?

These are in fact three different questions inviting different answers. Hence van Fraassen thinks that implicit in each why-question is a **contrast class**. For example, the contrast class for (2) may consist of Mary and Lily, and the question is an expression of puzzlement why it was Bill who ate the apple rather than Mary or Lily. The contrast class of (3) can have members such as squashing the apple, putting it into the refrigerator, and throwing it into the rubbish bin. Finally, the intention of the questioner in (4) could be that of contrasting the apple with the pear, both of which happened to lie on the table. These three different questions can comfortably share the same verbal form because they have the same **topic**, which, according to van Fraassen, is the statement "Bill ate the apple."

We can see that (1) is ambiguous. Sometimes in conversation we do attempt to convey our question more precisely by mentioning the contrast class. For example, we might ask:

(5) Why did Bill eat the apple rather than the pear?

But usually we do not. How, then, do we manage to communicate unambiguously? The answer is that we rely on the **context**. For example, question (1) might be part of a longer text such as (6).

(6) I thought Bill asked for a pear. Why did he eat the apple?

'Context' covers more than just textual context. An example: On leaving for work, Mom placed on the table an apple and a pear and said to the two children, "Bill, the pear is for you, and the apple for Tom. There should be no squabbling because I know your preferences." Later that evening Tom complained to Mom that Bill had eaten his apple. Mom asked question (1). From the context, (1) clearly meant (5).

According to van Fraassen, there are no such things as adequate explanations per se. An explanation is adequate only if it is what the questioner is asking for. The (implicit) contrast class for each why-question helps to indicate the questioner's

intention. But this is not the full story. A question with an explicit contrast class can still be ambiguous. van Fraassen gave this example, adapted from Aristotle. He calls it the lantern example. "Suppose a father asks his teenage son, 'Why is the porch light on?' and the son replies, 'The porch switch is on and the electricity is reaching the bulb through that switch.' At this point you are most likely to feel the son is being impudent. This is because you are most likely to think that the sort of answer the father needed was something like: 'Because we are expecting company.'"[5]

van Fraassen thinks that "there is the respect-in-which a reason is requested, which determines what shall count as a possible explanatory factor, the **relation of explanatory relevance**."[6] What is a relation of explanatory relevance? Unfortunately van Fraassen has not defined it. Nevertheless, from his expositions and the few examples he gave, we can work out what he has in mind, albeit roughly. Every questioner would have some background knowledge about the world and also the situation that is of immediate concern. She would have some theories (scientific or not) about how things work. She would have wants and interests, long-term goals and short-term objectives, and so on. When she asks a why-question, she is soliciting information to promote her wants, interests, goals, and objectives against her background knowledge and theories. In our lantern example, the father was not interested in the mechanics of the working of electricity in the light circuit, nor was he so stupid as not to possess knowledge of basic physics. That's why the answer the son provided was inappropriate.

Here is another example provided by van Fraassen. To the question "Why does the blood circulate through the body?", there can be two answers: (a) "because the heart pumps the blood through the arteries" and (b) "to bring oxygen to every part of the body tissue." Which of the two is the appropriate answer is not dependent on the

5. van Fraassen (1980, p. 131).

6. van Fraassen (1980, p. 142).

contrast class here but rather on what the questioner wants in terms of her goals and background knowledge.[7]

For van Fraassen, the problem of asymmetry and the like can be seen to be pseudo-problems once we adopt the idea that explanations are always answers to why-questions, and proposed explanations are considered adequate only when they are of the type requested. Let's take the problem of the flagpole and its shadow (Section 14.1). The length of the shadow is explainable in terms of the length of the flagpole but not vice versa. Why the asymmetry?

van Fraassen does not see any problem here. For him, there is no asymmetry at all, for *both* can be adequate explanations. He argues that there can be circumstances when facts about the length of the shadow can be used to explain facts about the length of the flagpole! It all depends on what the questioner wants. In fact, he spins out a rather elaborate and entertaining story titled "The Tower and the Shadow" to support his claim.[8] The reason for intuitively rejecting an explanation of the length of the flagpole in terms of the length of the shadow is that under ordinary circumstances this is not what people want. But there are odd circumstances, like the case of the Tower and its Shadow, when the odd is what is asked for. At least that is what van Fraassen claims.

So for van Fraassen, the case of the flagpole and its shadow is similar to the case of the lantern example. There are occasions when the correct explanation is "Because we are expecting company," and there are also occasions when the correct explanation is "Because the porch switch is closed."

Summing up, van Fraassen's theory of explanation is that (i) an explanation is an answer to a why-question, (ii) there is nothing peculiar to scientific explanation in structure, (iii) every why-question has a topic, a contrast class, and a relevance relation, and (iv) both the contrast class and the relevance relation are indicated by context. That many suggested explanations intuitively do not sound like explanations at all is because they are not answers to questions of the expected contrast class or of the expected relevance relation.

van Fraassen's theory is a **contextual theory** because, according to van Fraassen, whether an explanation is appropriate or not depends heavily on the context in which the corresponding why-question is asked.[9] It is also known as a **pragmatic theory**. Let me explain. Three disciplines in the study of languages are of interest to the philosopher. **Syntactics** is the study of how more primitive symbols of a language can be strung together to form composite symbols such as sentences. **Semantics** studies how these symbols can mean what they mean (independent of contexts). Finally, **pragmatics** is the study of the contributions of contexts to both meaning and the actual message intended. For example, when David says, "I am tall," the message intended is "David is tall for a 10-year-old American." How do we know this? From the context, of course. David is a 10-year-old American and he is boasting in front of other American children, and, of course, since David is the speaker, 'I' refers to David. We can now see the appropriateness of 'pragmatic theory' as applied to van Fraassen's philosophy.[10]

The theory that philosophical problems have their roots in the misunderstanding or misuse of (ordinary) language came from the great Austrian philosopher Ludwig Wittgenstein (1889–1951). From him sprouted the school of philosophy

---

7. van Fraassen (1980, p. 142).

8. van Fraassen (1980, pp. 132–134). I personally do not think his example works though. His example is not about tower height or shadow length. It is about a motive for having a tower of a certain height, which is to produce a shadow of a certain length. This kind of explanation has been covered in detail in the last chapter.

9. van Fraassen (1980, pp. 134–141) gives details on the roles played by contexts.

10. van Fraassen's conception of explanation is also known as the erotetic approach, because it is based on the analysis of why-questions.

known as the **ordinary language philosophy** or **linguistic analysis**, which was at its peak during the 1950s and 1960s.[11] van Fraassen's approach to the problem of scientific explanation can be seen to be within this linguistic tradition: to understand scientific explanations properly, we should study the *actual* linguistic behaviors and properties of why-questions. His predecessors are Sylvain Bromberger, C. L. Hamblin, Nuel Belnap, and Bengt Hannson.[12]

14.3 THE CONTEXTUAL CONCEPTION OF EXPLANATION II: CRITIQUES

Salmon (1989, pp. 135–150) raises quite a few objections to van Fraassen's theory, which I will now briefly present.

First, not all why-questions call for explanations. "One might ask, in a time of grief, why a loved one had died. Such a question is not intended to evoke an explanation; it is a cry for sympathy" (p. 136).

Second, not all explanations are sought by means of why-questions. There are the how-possibly questions.[13] For example, one might ask, "How is it *possible* for a chained-up Houdini to escape from a locked strongbox totally submerged under water, and in such a short time too?" This is not a why-question, yet it is a quest for an explanation.

Third, there are the how-actually questions. For example, one might ask, "How did there come to be mammals (other than bats) in New Zealand, since New Zealand is a group of two islands in the South Pacific, far away from any land mass?" Again, even though this is not a why-question, it is a quest for an explanation.

Apart from these three points Salmon also complains, justifiably in my opinion, about the vagueness of the so-called relevance relation. "The problem is to characterize in a general way what constitutes a suitable relevance relation, recognizing, of course, that there may be more than one" (p. 143).

My own complaints are quite different from Salmon's. No doubt van Fraassen has done an excellent job in his analysis of the logic of why-questions. However, we might ask, "Does this contribute to the advancement of science?" To put it bluntly, is his contextual theory relevant to scientific methodology? One of the main aims of the philosophy of science is to study and discover correct and efficient scientific methods. To have a better understanding of how we ask why-questions and how the questioners expect such questions to be answered does not seem to contribute to methodology.

What is the problem with explanation? If we are doing linguistics or communication study, van Fraassen's theory has certainly cast some light. But in the philosophy of science we take the problem to be the problem of *scientific* explanation, which includes something like the following list: What role does explanation play in science? What sorts of things (for example, events, regularities, and laws) need explanation? What form should such explanations take? Why should they take such forms? What kind of fruitful consequences will explanations of such forms bring? Are such types of explanations achievable? What are the best ways to obtain them? How many types of explanations should science adopt? Can they be ranked as to their desirability? How is explanation related to the other aims of science? And, finally, is (scientific) explanation, as has been captured by our analysis, one of the major characteristics of science in contrast to other academic disciplines?[14]

---

11. Since linguistic analysis has been centered on Oxford, it is also known as Oxford philosophy.

12. See van Fraassen (1980, chap. 5).

13. First raised by Dray (1957).

14. See Koertge (1992, pp. 85–87) for similar complaints.

The point is: Has the contextual theory been able to provide any answers to these questions? Has it even attempted to answer these questions? To disambiguate why-questions is one thing, to explicate existing scientific methods and to improve on them is another. It is the latter that philosophy of science is about. We, as rational beings, would like to understand the workings of science better and to become more productive scientists. To be able to handle why-questions correctly is something else, quite outside the field of the philosophy of science. Having said all this, to be fair to the contextualists, I would like to say that their contributions do have some relevance. Philosophical puzzlement does sometimes arise from our misuse or misunderstanding of the use of certain linguistic items—for example, why-questions. A better understanding of them would help to dispel such puzzlement. But this is only the preliminary step, to "clear the stage," so to speak. In the philosophy of science, having dispelled such puzzlement, we still need to contribute something constructive—that is, *positive* proposals for scientific methods and the like. For example, philosophers of science are expected to suggest ways and means to explain natural phenomena.

Unfortunately, van Fraassen dismisses the problem of scientific explanation as a problem peculiar to science. For him, there is only the problem of explanation per se, including both the scientific and the nonscientific. All explanations are answers to why-questions. The understanding of how why-questions are asked and how they should be answered solves the problem of explanation, which includes the problem of scientific explanation. Thus he says, "To ask that ... explanations be scientific is only to ask that they rely on scientific theories and experimentation, not on old wives' tales" (1980, p. 129) and

> to call an explanation scientific, is to say nothing about its form or the sort of

information adduced, but only that the explanation *draws on science* to get this information (at least to some extent) and, more importantly, that the criteria of evaluation of how good an explanation it is, are being applied *using a scientific theory*. (1980, pp. 155–156, my italics)

I think van Fraassen's conception of scientific explanation is circular—that is, if we accept certain commonplace assumptions. I think we can assume that scientific explanation is an aim (or even the aim) of science, and that whether a set of beliefs is considered scientific or not depends on how well it satisfies that aim. Then, to understand scientific explanation in terms of scientific beliefs is clearly circular. Of course we can deny that scientific explanation is an aim of science, and there are prominent philosophers, including Hume (Chapter 11) and Duhem (Chapter 9), who do just that. We can also argue that for beliefs to be scientific they need not contribute toward all the aims of science. The beliefs which scientific explanations draw on could be those that have fulfilled or helped to fulfill the other aims.[15]

On the other hand, imperfect as it is, Hempel's analysis has at least attempted to provide us with a methodology: to explain is to deduce the explanandum in terms of some initial conditions and some laws of nature; if deduction is wanting, highly probable induction will do. We need not confine ourselves to universal laws either, for the universe might be (and is likely to be) probabilistic in nature. This piece of methodology may be faulty in many ways, but one must grant Hempel that (i) his theory is fruitful to a certain extent, and (ii) many historical scientific explanations can be interpreted as instantiation of this methodology. Moreover, Hempel is able to link explanation to the other (commonly accepted) aims of science—prediction and postdiction. This is, however, not to say that the proposed link is noncontroversial.

---

15. van Fraassen seems to subscribe to this line of thought. For him theories are valued for their empirical adequacy and simplicity (Chapter 18).

14.4 THE CAUSAL THEORY
OF EXPLANATION I:
EXPOSITION

The causal theory of explanation is mainly due to
Wesley C. Salmon, who, for this purpose, has borrowed heavily from the philosophy of his teacher,
Hans Reichenbach. As we saw earlier (Section
12.7), Salmon's conception of explanation falls
into two parts. The first part is his statistical-
relevance model of explanation (S-R explanation).
His causal theory makes up the second part.

According to Salmon (1978, pp. 52–53), there
are two (powerful) intuitions about explanation.
One is that phenomena are to be explained in
terms of causes, as most laypersons would see it.
The other is that all scientific explanation involves
subsumption under laws. Hempel, as has been discussed, develops the second intuition. Salmon
chooses to develop the first.[16]

Salmon, quite rightly, points out that statistical
relevance is not the same as causal relevance. Often
statistical relevance only indicates symptoms
whereas causal relevance belongs to the mechanism
that yields the symptoms. For example, since most
swans are white, being a swan is statistically relevant
to being white. But is being a swan causally relevant
to being white? Perhaps. That has to wait for scientific investigation. If the answer is yes, we can
explain why a certain bird is white by saying that
it is because it is a swan. On the other hand, if the
answer is no, such an explanation will be futile.
Here is another example. The dropping in level
of the mercury column of a barometer is statistically
relevant to the weather's turning foul. But it is not
causally relevant. (The change in level of the mercury column does not cause changes in the
weather.) Hence we cannot *explain* the change in
weather in terms of the barometric level. (The

correct explanation should be in terms of the
change in atmospheric pressure.) For Salmon,
symptoms can be used to predict but not to explain.
Only underlying causal mechanisms yield explanations, and barometer readings are merely symptoms.
That's why Salmon regards his S-R model of explanation as only a first step toward a full explication of
scientific explanation.

In many cases, we do employ laws to explain,
as the second intuition indicates. But the reason
these laws have a role in explanation is not because
they are merely laws. It is because they are *causal*
laws. A noncausal law such as the ideal gas law, $PV
= nRT$, has no explanatory power. Rather it is itself
crying out to be explained.[17] At least this is Salmon's conviction.

So for Salmon the key to the understanding
and explication of scientific explanation lies with
the understanding and explication of the notion
of causation. What are causes? What is causation?

In Sections 11.6 and 11.7, we studied how
Hume denies the existence of necessary connection
between what are commonly thought of as causes
and effects; in fact, he denies the very meaningfulness of the expression 'necessary connection.' He
warns that if we are to use the term 'causation' at
all, we should beware of its unwarranted metaphysical (and mystical) implications. Hence he recommends the following definition of causes (stripped
of its metaphysical baggage):

A cause is an object, followed by another,
and where all the objects similar to the first
are followed by objects similar to the
second.[18]

Hume's definition is unsatisfactory in many
respects. For example, nights follow days regularly,
but we would hesitate to say that the days cause
(bring about) the nights. On the other hand, many
cause-effect pairs do not have regular conjunctions.

---

16. Salmon (1978, p. 52) actually claims that his theory incorporates both intuitions.

17. Salmon (1978, p. 54). Other possible candidates for noncausal laws are those listed as laws of functional relations in Section
11.5.

18. Hume (1748, reprint p. 220).

For instance, when a moving billiard ball collides with a stationary billiard ball (an event of type A), the latter starts to move (an event of type B). We will probably all agree that the collision *causes* the second ball to move. But events of type A are *not always* followed by events of type B. Imagine the case where the second ball has been glued or nailed to the table. You might object that this is a different situation altogether: a moving billiard ball colliding with a stationary and rigidly held billiard ball (type C).

Does this get Hume out of the trouble? Hume's definition says: "all objects *similar* to the first ..." (By 'objects' here Hume means 'events.') How similar do these events have to be? I see a lot of similarity between events of type A and those of type C. This difficulty of getting the notion of similarity clarified (in the present context) has plagued Hume's definition since its proposal. On the one hand, no two events are ever exactly identical. On the other hand, any two events are similar to a certain extent. Where should we place Hume's notion of similarity in this continuum of similarity?[19]

This prompts Salmon to take 'causal process' instead as the more basic notion and try to build 'cause' on top of it.

A causal process has to be continuous in both space and time. However, not all continuous processes are causal. For example, your shadow moving across the lawn as you walk is a continuous process, but it is not a causal process because the earlier part of your shadow does not contribute to the making of the later part. What contributes to the making of the later part is your body, not the earlier part of your shadow. Had this earlier shadow been destroyed (say by light shining on it), the later shadow would have been unaffected. Salmon calls such processes **pseudo-processes**. How then can we tell causal processes from pseudo-processes?

Following Reichenbach, Salmon proposes that causal processes can transmit marks whereas pseudo-processes cannot. For example, in the case of your shadow, should your earlier shadow be distorted by a rock lying on the lawn as the shadow moved across its surface, this distortion would *not* be carried along to the later shadow (unless, of course, the rock moves along with your shadow). The distortion of your shadow constitutes what Reichenbach calls a **mark**. On the other hand, marks are carried by (true) causal processes. For example, a stone flying across the lawn carries its marks with it. If it should cross the path of a water sprinkler and hence get wet, the stone will carry the wetness with it as well. In Reichenbach's term, the flying stone transmits marks and hence constitutes a causal process.

The idea of marking came from the theory of relativity. In terms of this theory, we can say that causal processes can be used to carry signals and hence information.

Once the notion of causal process is in place, we can define causes in terms of causal interactions. What are causal interactions? In the words of Salmon (1978, reprint p. 61), "What we want to say, very roughly, is that when two [causal] processes intersect, and both are modified in such ways that the changes in one are correlated with changes in the other—in the manner of an interactive fork ...—we have a **causal interaction**." Causal interactions are events, and **causes** and **effects** are such events.

14.5 THE CAUSAL THEORY OF EXPLANATION II: CRITIQUES

Has Salmon thus given us a satisfactory analysis of causation (superseding that given by Hume)? If he had, it would be a monumental achievement. After all, philosophy has been plagued by Hume's skepticism on causation for over 200 years. Note that Salmon intends, like Hume, to provide an analysis of causation in terms of the observable only, in terms that can be empirically assessed, such as one

---

19. For detailed analysis and suggestions of improvements, see Mackie (1974, chaps. 1–3).

event temporally following another. Salmon's definition of **causal process** goes like this:

A causal process is one that is both temporally and spatially continuous, and it is able to transmit marks.

I think we can grant temporal and spatial continuity the status of being observable. But what about marks? Surely we can perceive marks, one might say. For instance, a light ray passing through a red filter will acquire a mark by becoming red and will transmit this redness to its destination. Redness can be observed both at the point of acquisition A and at the end point, Z, where the light, say, strikes a white wall. I don't think anyone will deny the observability of the two red bits at A and Z. Nevertheless, one can ask the following questions: (i) Why is the redness at A labeled as a *mark*? What does it mean by calling it a mark? (ii) What can it mean when it is claimed that the redness at A has been *transmitted* to Z?[20] The answer to (i) might be "Because the redness is *given* to the ray by the filter—that is, the filter marks the ray." In this answer, it is not difficult to see that the notion 'cause' has been smuggled in through the use of the causal term 'given,' because to say that the ray is *given* such and such is the same as saying that the ray has been *caused* to acquire such and such. Salmon's definition of causal process employs the notion of marking, and marking in turn presupposes the notion of causation. We call such definitions circular.[21]

The answer to (ii) is also damaging to Salmon's enterprise. Surely when one says that the redness has been *transmitted* from A to Z, it means that the redness at A *causes* the redness at an adjacent point B, which, in turn, *causes* the redness at the next adjacent point C, and so on till Z is reached. The notion of causation can be seen to be written all over the place.[22] This is a second circle in Salmon's definition.

You may recall that Salmon's definition is meant to improve on Hume's, while keeping strictly to Hume's empiricist prescription of disallowing unobservable entities such as necessary connection into science. We must, unfortunately, conclude that Salmon has failed in his grand scheme. However, if we do not confine ourselves to the straitjacket of Hume's empiricist prescription, Salmon's analysis is quite useful in the understanding of causation. So let's proceed with his program.

According to Salmon, once the notion of causal relevance is separated from that of statistical relevance, we can throw light on problems such as the problem of asymmetry.

Recall that we accept that the length of the shadow of a flagpole is explainable in terms of height of the flagpole but not vice versa, hence the asymmetry. Salmon points out, and common sense will agree, that it is the flagpole that *causes* the shadow, but not the other way around. That's why we have an asymmetric situation, even though we can use either to *predict* the other. In other words, the shadow is a symptom whereas the flagpole is a cause. Even though both symptoms and causes can be used to predict, it is the latter and not the former that have explanatory power. A similar solution can be given to the problem of irrelevance. For example, the reason the hexing of the salt is not acceptable as an explanation of the dissolution of the salt in water is because the hexing does not cause the dissolution.

Salmon also explains why statistical relevance (alone) has no explanatory power. He argues that statistical relevance can be and often is due to common causes. For example, the raining and the dropping in level of the mercury column in the barometer have a common cause. Events having a common cause are not causes of each other. That's why they cannot be employed to explain each other's occurrence.

---

20. See Mellor (1975, pp. 148–152).

21. The full circle is this: 'cause' is defined in terms of 'causal interaction,' which in turn is defined in terms of 'causal process,' and 'causal process' is defined in terms of 'mark,' which is defined in terms of 'cause.'

22. Salmon in his reply to Mellor (1975) concedes this point.

Salmon (1975) claims another "virtue" for his causal theory of explanation. He thinks that what we commonly call theoretical explanation in science (as was discussed in Chapter 8) can be justified in terms of causal explanation. I'll illustrate. A claps her hands, and B hears a sound. We can explain why B hears a sound in terms of A's clapping her hands, because the latter causes the former. However, scientists do not stop at that. They postulate something invisible, called sound waves, which "take" the vibrations of A's hands to B's ears. Such an explanation is known as a theoretical explanation, and we have produced quite a number of examples in Chapter 8. Why should we go for theoretical explanations? According to Salmon, the ultimate explanation of the universe is to produce a causal network linking all the events in terms of causal processes. Since causal processes are temporally and spatially continuous by definition, we have a continuous "web" of causal relationships of all the happenings in the universe. This network provides the ultimate understanding aimed for by science. Now, A's clapping of the hands and the occurrence of the sound in B's ears are two noncontiguous events, separated not only by space but also by time. According to Salmon's ideal we cannot leave these two noncontiguous events where they are. Science must provide one or more continuous causal connections for them. Hence the postulation of trains of continuous sound waves linking the two events. In a word, science aims at providing the causal underlying mechanisms that link various aspects of the universe, and these underlying mechanisms are what are postulated in theoretical explanations.[23] Hence Salmon's view is often called the **causal-mechanical theory of explanation**.

Thus Salmon sets a program both for the philosophers and for the scientists. The philosophers are asked to further their understanding of the notion of causation, so as to provide a firmer base for the explication of 'explanation.' The scientists for their part are advised to build this vast net of causal connection to link all the happenings in the world. These are inspiring programs.

However, Salmon's analysis of causal processes faces a number of major obstacles, including what we have pointed out.

Quantum physics, as you all know, is one of the two most successful theories about the ultimate nature of the world. We saw in Chapter 12 how at the quantum level causality, as far as available evidence indicates, is probabilistic (indeterministic). Salmon's theory has to face this reality. Furthermore, at the quantum level, causality is not only probabilistic but also spatially discontinuous. Is Salmon able to reconcile his notion of (continuous) causal process with these?[24]

The other most successful theory on the fundamental nature of the world is, of course, Einstein's theory of relativity. As I pointed out earlier, Reichenbach and Salmon's conception of employing marking to characterize causal process is rooted in this theory. According to relativity, "causal processes" take time to travel and the fastest causal process is that of a light signal. Cohen (1975) points out that should the theory of relativity be false and there be actions-at-a-distance, then the rug will be gone from under Salmon's feet, because his theory is based essentially on continuous "spatiotemporal worms" linking spatiotemporally distant events. Anyway, for many philosophers, the notion of causation is so fundamental that it should lead, guide, and contain the development of scientific theories rather than be dependent on or derivative of a particular scientific theory.

About 80 years ago, the great British philosopher Bertrand Russell said:

The law of gravitation will illustrate what occurs in any exact science.... Certain differential equations can be found, which hold at every instant for every particle of

---

23. Salmon (1978, p. 64) puts it as follows: "It is my view that knowledge of the mechanisms of production and propagation of structure in the world yields scientific understanding, and that this is what we seek when we pose explanation-seeking why questions."

24. Salmon (1975, p. 133) is well aware of these points.

the system... . But there is nothing that could be properly called 'cause' and nothing that could be properly called 'effect' in such a system.[25]

Perhaps we should take Russell's advice. Instead of seeking causal processes linking the events of the world, we should attempt to establish a network of laws, be they universal or probabilistic. After all, there is good evidence that the concept of law is logically prior to that of cause and thus the latter should be analyzed and understood in terms of the former. In a word, perhaps Hempel's intuition is not too far wrong. What we need is an improvement, not a change of direction. This is what Philip Kitcher is trying to do. Let's see.

14.6 THE UNIFICATORY THEORY OF EXPLANATION I: FRIEDMAN

Recall that, according to Salmon (last section), there are two intuitions about explanation: explanation by causes and explanation by laws. Philip Kitcher, whose unificatory theory we are going to study in detail, thinks that there is a third: unification. Indeed, Hempel himself points this out: "What scientific explanation, especially theoretical explanation, aims at is not an intuitive and highly subjective kind of understanding, but an objective kind of insight that is achieved by a systematic unification, by exhibiting the phenomena as manifestations of common, underlying structures and processes that conform to specific testable, basic principles" (Hempel 1966, p. 83).

What is unification? In Section 8.5, we studied how good theories are able to unify a large number of phenomena. We named Newton's theory of gravitation as an example. We pointed out that

(in the context of his mechanics) it explains diverse phenomena such as: why terrestrial objects fall downward, why they fall with uniform acceleration, why pendulums swing at a regular pace, why projectiles move in parabolas, why there are tides, why the moon perpetually circles the earth, why the planets move in ellipses, and hundreds of thousands of other kinds of phenomena. It is as if all these phenomena are stored in the single law of gravitation. In explaining, the law unifies, and in unifying, it explains. There is no doubt that unifying power is related to explanatory power, and the two could even be identical.

The intuitive idea of unification, as illustrated just now, seems obvious. However, when one tries to figure out what exactly unification is, the concept is not as plain as one might at first think. For example, shall we say that

(7)   A statement S unifies statements X, Y, and Z, if S logically entails X, Y, and Z.[26]

But then, A unifies B, C, and D.

(A)   Salt is soluble in water, and copper conducts heat, and snow is white.

(B)   Salt is soluble in water.

(C)   Copper conducts heat.

(D)   Snow is white.

You can see that each one of B, C, and D follows logically from A. Of course, you would object. You would say that A is in fact a conjunction of B, C, and D and is not different from the three taken together. However, A does satisfy criterion (7). The problem is how to strengthen (7) so that counterintuitive examples such as our present case of A, B, C, and D would not be admissible.

Shall we say that A has to be truly *one* statement? What is *truly one* statement? Is E *truly one* statement?

(E)   John is a bachelor.

---

25. Russell (1917, p. 194).

26. For logical entailment, see Chapter 2. Statement *M* logically entails statement *N* iff statement *N* follows logically from statement *M*. (Here 'iff' is short for 'if and only if.')

You will find that this has at least three statement components.

(F) John is a person.

(G) John is male.

(H) John is unmarried.

With a bit of logic, one can easily "hide" many statements in a single statement in such a way that few can detect the plurality. The intrinsic difficulty seems to be that of individuation of ideas. How much is *one* idea? How much is *one* thought? (How much is one image? one picture?)[27] We can see that this is the same problem as problem (e) (Section 14.1), which Hempel has to overcome.

Michael Friedman (1974) attempts to solve this problem. He introduces the idea of **independently acceptable sentences**. For example, there are only three independently acceptable sentences in the set consisting of A, B, C, and D, because to know whether A is true, one need only to know whether the individual sentences B, C, and D are true. According to Friedman, to "invent" A in order to unify B, C, and D is futile, because the number of independently acceptable sentences before and after the addition of A is the same—that is, three. On the other hand, Newton's theory of gravitation together with the three laws of motion does unify a great many phenomena, because by adding four independently acceptable sentences to our store of knowledge, we are able to drastically reduce the total number of independently acceptable sentences. From the four laws (plus appropriate initial conditions, of course) so many phenomena are deducible—for example, the downward motion of unsupported bodies, the swing of pendulums, the elliptical orbits of the planets, and so on. The employment of the idea of an independently acceptable sentence to explicate unification is intuitively appealing. Unfortunately it does not solve

the problem, as Kitcher (1976) and Salmon (1989, pp. 94–101) have shown.

14.7 THE UNIFICATORY THEORY OF EXPLANATION II: KITCHER

Philip Kitcher (1981) proposed a new approach. Instead of trying to show how sentences can unify sentences, he attempts to show how argument patterns can unify sentences. Since his theory requires some training in logic or mathematics to appreciate, I will give an oversimplification of it in a way that hopefully will not do too much injustice to the original. We will present the theory in two steps.

(A) Step 1: Let's look at the following argument:

(VIII)   All copper conducts heat. (I)

   X is a piece of copper. (J)

   X conducts heat. (K)

We can see that the argument is valid and, according to Hempel, the premises explain the conclusion. Indeed, the same argument can be applied to other pieces of copper and explains their conductivity equally well. Now instead of taking X as the name of a certain piece of copper, we can take it as a variable. In doing so, (VIII) becomes an **argument schema** (**schematic argument**[28] or **argument pattern**). This schema is said to have unified many, many instances of copper possessing the property of heat conducting.

I'll take a more realistic example. Newton proposes the law of motion that $f = ma$, where f is the force applied to an object, m, the mass of the object, and a, the acceleration of the object. This law, unlike the one in (VIII), is in terms of variables.

---

27. (i) Think of a picture of two cows standing in a field facing each other. Can't we take it as two pictures, each with one cow in it? (ii) The more advanced students who have done a bit of axiomatization in mathematics or science will realize that different systems can employ different sets (and number) of axioms to "summarize" a field of knowledge.

28. Kitcher uses the term 'schematic argument,' which in our context is not so helpful.

Hence it can be seen to contain many, many law-instances. Let us consider:

(IX) $f = ma$

> The force applied to H is X units.
>
> The mass of H is Y units.
>
> H's acceleration is X/Y units.[29]

According to Kitcher this schema unifies many instances of motion-behavior of objects—for example, collision of elastic bodies, projectiles, pendulums, spinning tops, and so on.

You can see from both examples that unification seems to be the application of a general idea or a formula to a variety of instances. Let's take a further illustration. What can you say about the following sequence of numbers?

(8)   0, 3, 8, 15, 24, 35, 48, 63, 80, …

Is there any unity under which they can be subsumed? No doubt most of you would be puzzled. These look like a set of random numbers, without order or justification—that is, until someone comes up with the following formula:

(9) $m = (n^2 - 1)$, where n is an integer.

We can see that the substitution of integers 1, 2, 3, and so on up to n will generate the series. Now the puzzlement is gone. The sequence of numbers can be seen to be quite orderly. They follow the pattern (9). We can say that (9) unifies the numbers in (8), and in doing so it explains. Note that unification is a global concept. You can't unify just one thing. On the other hand, we can say that formula (9) explains each individual occurrence of the numbers (and, of course, we can also say that it explains the pattern as a whole).[30]

(B) Step 2: Hempel takes deducibility (logical entailment) as playing the central role in explanation. Let's consider deduction (VIII) again. For Hempel, I and J together explain K, by logically entailing K. Kitcher, however, believes that Hempel's theory is incomplete. While agreeing with Hempel that K has been explained by being deduced from I and J, he thinks that the force of explanation of K does not lie with K's relationship with I and J alone. Deduction (VIII) per se has no explanatory power. That (VIII) explains is due to the fact that (VIII) is an instance of an argument schema that has unified lots of phenomena. In other words, deduction in isolation is not sufficient to be counted as explanation. It has to be parasitic on unification. Now, what is unification for Kitcher?

Let P stand for a collection of phenomena.[31] Let S be a collection of argument schemas. Typically an argument schema, like (VIII) and (IX), is made up of a number of schematic premises and a schematic conclusion. When the variables of these schemas are filled by constants, the argument schema will become a valid argument, which is an instance of the original schema. Suppose S has 3 members (that is, 3 argument schemas), and P has 5,000 members (that is, 5,000 phenomena as members). Further suppose that by instantiating these 3 argument schemas with different constants, each and every one of the 5,000 phenomena appears at least once as the conclusion of one of the instances. In other words, we are supposing that we can deduce all the 5,000 phenomena with just these 3 argument schemas (by instantiation). Intuitively we would say that S—that is, the 3 argument schemas—has unified P, the 5,000 phenomena. We have succeeded, in a sense, in reducing 5,000 to 3!

Based on this intuitive notion, Kitcher defines unification in two stages:

(10) S is said to be a **systematization** of P if some members of P can be deduced from S (that is, if some members of P are conclusions of instances of members of S).

---

29. This is adapted from Kitcher (1981).

30. Compare (9) with Balmer's formula: $\lambda = b(n^2/(n^2-2^2))$, where λ represents wavelengths.

31. By 'phenomenon' here, I mean 'description of phenomenon.'

Typically, given any P, there are many, many possible systematizations of P. Let's choose the best one in the following manner. S' is better than S'' if either (a) more members of P are deducible from the former than from the latter, or (b) the former has fewer members than the latter. Kitcher can see that we have to weigh the two factors (a) and (b) because some systematization may excel in one "virtue" and be short of the other "virtue." He expects that some sort of ranking can be worked out so that we can have the following definition of unification.

(11) S **unifies** P if S is the best available systematization of P.

(12) Assuming that a set of phenomena, P, has been unified by S, we say that E **explains** Q, if (i) Q is the conclusion of E, (ii) E is an instance of a member of S, and (iii) Q is a member of P.

You can see that condition (i) is what is already present in Hempel's D-N explanation, whereas (ii) is an additional condition that Kitcher thinks should be there as well. To put it differently, according to Kitcher, in order that E be able to explain anything at all, it must possess explanatory power. That power is present in E because E belongs to a set of argument schemas, which together unify P.[32] It is the act of unification that makes argument schemas explanatorily potent. Having acquired this potency, the argument schemas can then be individually employed to explain individual phenomena. In passing, note that for Kitcher it is arguments that explain, not premises of arguments.

To illustrate, let the set of phenomena, M, which requires explanation, be the set of all kinds of motions: falling objects, colliding objects, swinging objects (pendulums), rolling objects, spinning objects (spinning tops), rising tides, running water, motions of planets and comets, and so on. Suppose, in accordance with Newton's mechanics, a set, N, of 5 argument schemas has been designed such that most members of M can be deduced from instantiations of these schemas. (Argument schema (IX) could be one of the 5.) Moreover, no other set of argument schemas with fewer than 5 members can do that. We then say that N has unified M, and that each phenomenon belonging to M is explainable by at least one instance of one of the 5 argument schemas.[33]

Another example for illustration given by Kitcher himself is based on Dalton's atomic theory. To explain the observed fact that, when chemicals combine to form compounds, they only combine in certain weight ratios,[34] the following argument schema can be used:

(X) The atomic formula for compound Z is $X_p Y_q$.

The atomic weight of X is x.

The atomic weight of Y is y.

The weight ratio of X to Y in Z is $px:qy$.[35]

This is Kitcher's theory in a nutshell.[36] Let the philosopher summarize in his own words:

> Science advances our understanding of nature by showing us how to derive

---

32. To be more exact, I should have said: "E is *an instance* of an argument schema belonging to a set of argument schemas, which together unify P."

33. In these five schemas, laws such as $f = ma$, the law of universal gravitation, the law of action and reaction, the law of parallelogram of forces, the laws of geometry, and so on would be utilized. In the derivation of the phenomena of motion, idealization would be employed. For example, air resistance is ignored, bodies are perfectly elastic, the planets are round, and so forth.

34. In contrast, things can usually be physically *mixed* in any weight ratios—for example, flour and salt.

35. Adapted from Kitcher (1989, p. 446).

36. As I have said before, for easy understanding, I have oversimplified Kitcher's theory. Here are a few notable points of difference between his theory and my presentation here: (i) Kitcher takes the statements that are instantiations of the schematic premises of his argument schemas as belonging to what I call the set of phenomena, (ii) Kitcher employs a technical notion of argument pattern rather than the notion of an argument schema as used here, and (iii) Kitcher has a notion of stringency contributing to the ranking of systematizations.

descriptions of many phenomena, using the same patterns of derivation again and again, and, in demonstrating this, it teaches us how to reduce the number of types of facts we have to accept as ultimate (or brute). (Kitcher 1989, p. 432)

According to Kitcher, this unificatory theory of explanation is not only intuitively correct but can also solve some of the problems that Hempel's covering-law model finds difficult to handle. An example is the problem of asymmetry as illustrated by the case of the flagpole and its shadow. Why is it that using the height of the flagpole (together with the laws of optics and so on) to explain the length of its shadow is acceptable, whereas using the length of the shadow to explain the height of the flagpole is not acceptable? (see Section 14.1). Why is this asymmetry, even though in both approaches the conclusion follows validly from the premises? We have seen claims by both van Fraassen and Salmon as to how their pet theories handle and solve this problem; let me introduce the solution proposed by Kitcher.

According to Kitcher, to explain the physical dimensions of an artifact (for example, the length of a flagpole),

> We [normally] start with premises about the intentions of a designer and reason to an intermediate conclusion about the dimensions of the object at the time of its origin; using further premises about the conditions that have prevailed between the origin and the present, we reason that the object has persisted virtually unaltered and thus reach a conclusion about its present dimensions.[37]

This amounts to an argument schema, which can be called the *origin-and-development schema* (OD-schema). Of course, some of us might try to explain

the length of a certain flagpole in terms of its shadow. In doing so, we would adopt another argument schema, which can be called the *shadow schema* (S-schema).

Here is the essence of Kitcher's argument. It is simpler to explain the dimensions of all sorts of artifacts in terms of one single schema rather than in terms of two. It does not matter whether that single one is the OD-schema or the S-schema. However, while the OD-schema can explain the dimensions of *all* artifacts, the S-schema cannot, because many artifacts do not cast shadows. (They may be transparent or may never have been exposed to light.) So if one should choose the S-schema to explain lengths of flagpoles and the like, we would end up with *two* argument schemas, one for the shadow-throwing artifacts and the other for the nonshadow-throwing artifacts. Note that according to Kitcher there is nothing intrinsically wrong with the S-schema. It could confer explanations just as well as the OD-schema, had it been able to "take care" of all artifacts rather than just those that throw shadows. You can see that simplicity (and hence unification) is at the heart of Kitcher's theory.

From (12) we can see that E explains Q only when E comes from a set S that unifies the set of phenomena P. And S unifies P only when S is the best systematization, which in the present context means the simplest systematization. The choice of one schema to explain the physical dimensions of artifacts is obviously simpler than the choice of two schemas to do the same job. Hence, Kitcher concludes, the S-schema possesses no explanatory potency because it does not belong to the simplest set of schemas, which unifies the given set of phenomena. The problem of asymmetry is thus solved. At least this is what Kitcher claims.[38]

Let's see how Kitcher deals with the problem of irrelevance. Why is it that (III) in Section 14.1 is not acceptable as an explanation? Why can't we say

---

37. Kitcher (1989, p. 485).

38. We have again simplified Kitcher's presentation here. The more involved version can be found in Kitcher (1989, pp. 485–487), which covers nonartifact objects, and also deals (amusingly) with the counterproposal of employing the so-called dispositional-shadow pattern so as to take care of objects that do not throw or have not thrown shadows.

that the reason why the hexed salt dissolves in water is that it has been hexed? Kitcher's solution here is similar to that for the problem of asymmetry. It is simpler to explain both hexed and unhexed salt in terms of the same argument schema—that is, in terms of the same law that salt dissolves in water. To possess explanatory potency, an argument schema must belong to a set of argument schema that unify the given set of phenomena. The hexed salt argument schema does not possess this potency because it belongs to a set too "complicated" to be able to unify. You can see how Kitcher's theory differs from Hempel's. For Kitcher, being able to deduce the phenomenon is not sufficient to explain it. The argument itself must possess explanatory potency, which can only be obtained through its participation in an act of unification of the set of phenomena in question.

How satisfactory is Kitcher's theory? Salmon (1984, pp. 259–260) predictably condemns the theory: "The most severe shortcoming of the unification thesis ... is that it makes no reference to the physical mechanisms responsible for the phenomena that are to be explained." Kitcher's theory, like Hempel's, is mainly based on the mechanism of subsumption under regularities: to explain is to show that the phenomenon is expected to occur (deducible or at least inferable with high probability) because of certain regularities (laws). For Salmon there are all sorts of noncausal regularities such as pseudo-processes and regularities like "the regular relation between airplane take-off distance and the speed of drying of clothes hung out on a line."[39] Subsumption under these noncausal regularities does not explain at all. To explain, one must unveil the underlying causal mechanism that governs these regularities.

A good nonpartisan critique was given by Koertge (1989). Why is it unacceptable to explain the height of the flagpole in terms of the length of its shadow, whereas it is acceptable to explain the latter in terms of the former? Recall that according to Salmon this asymmetry comes from the asymmetry between causes and effects: whereas effects are explainable in terms of causes, causes are not explainable in terms of effects. Kitcher, however, claims that he can explicate the asymmetry without employing the (metaphysical) notion of causation. For him the asymmetry lies with the fact that the OD-schema has unifying power, whereas the S-schema has not. That the S-schema is a case of effect-cause deduction, as opposed to the OD-schema being a case of cause-effect deduction, is only incidental. Cause-effect has no role to play in explanation.

Koertge (1989, p. 157) is quick to point out that

it seems likely that there are just as many inferences from effect to cause (we might call them *semiotic* inferences) as there are from cause to effect (we could call these *production* inferences). If this is the case, then on Kitcher's unification approach, both arguments would become equally explanatory.

Let me add that whether there are more semiotic inferences or more production inferences in this world is a contingent fact. It could well be the case that there are more semiotic inferences than production inferences. If this were the case, then the S-schema would be explanatory, whereas the OD-schema would not be. This is quite contrary to our intuitions.

Barnes (1992), following Koertge's suggestions, argues in detail how one can "unify" causes in terms of effects. If these arguments are sound, we should be seeing the employment of effects to explain causes in science.

I, for one, think that there is a lot to say for the thesis that explanatory power is related to unificatory power. Whether unificatory power should be explicated in terms of 'argument schema' (Kitcher) or in terms of 'independently acceptable sentence' (Friedman) is another question. Unification, like simplicity (Chapter 9), is a very elusive notion even though it seems to be intuitively obvious.

---

39. Salmon (1984, p. 260).

Employing a single schema or pattern (or a few) to do a variety of jobs is not new. You'll probably find such practices in all sorts of activities, be it chess playing or the construction of a table. Strictly speaking, we are required to perform totally new acts and to complete totally new jobs every moment of our life, because no two situations are exactly alike and we are required to cope with these distinctively new situations all the time. How is it that we manage? We manage because we know how to generalize. Each game of chess is different, yet we can handle most of them with the same strategies over and over again. Each table required of the carpenter is different (different sizes and shapes) and yet the carpenter can manage with a small set of guidelines. I am sympathetic to Kitcher's unificatory theory of explanation. But I think 'unification' per se is not sufficient to capture the notion of explanation, because 'unification' is too general, in that it is an instrumental notion that has applications in all sorts of activities, which need not have anything to do with explanation. I think the unificationists should narrow their 'searches' within the confine of 'theoretical unification'—that is, unification by means of theories (Chapter 8). In advanced science, we explain phenomena in terms of theories. How do theories manage to yield explanations? By unification, I am pretty sure. It is this notion of unification that the unificationists should aim at. I must say that Kitcher's schemas lack features essential to *theoretical* unification.

It is too early to pass final judgment on Kitcher's program. In spite of the criticisms and doubts just mentioned, it would be interesting to see how his theory might develop from a qualitative program to quantitative reconstructions of major historical explanations.

KEY TERMS INTRODUCED IN THIS CHAPTER

problem of asymmetry

problem of irrelevance

problem of law explanation

contextual theory of explanation (pragmatic theory of explanation, erotetic approach)

contrast class

topic

context

relation of explanatory relevance

contextual theory

pragmatic theory

syntactics

semantics

pragmatics

ordinary language philosophy

linguistic analysis

causal process

pseudo-processes

mark

causal interaction

causes

effects

causal theory of explanation (causal-mechanical theory of explanation)

unificatory theory of explanation

independently acceptable sentence

argument schema (schematic argument, argument pattern)

systematization

unification

REFERENCES

On the contextual theory: The full exposition of the theory is available in van Fraassen (1980, chap. 5).

Lambert and Brittan (1987, chap. II, sec. 5) gives a clear and simple summary. For critiques of the theory, consult Salmon (1989, pp. 135–150).

On the causal theory: A good and concise presentation of the theory is given by Salmon (1978). For a full exposition, consult Salmon (1984). Salmon (1975) is probably the best single piece of work for our purpose here in that it presents not only the causal theory clearly and convincingly but also arguments for the relevance of theoretical explanations in terms of the causal theory. Moreover, the article is followed by very perceptive comments and critiques by both D. H. Mellor and L. J. Cohen, both being renowned philosophers in their own right. van Fraassen (1980), in the course of clearing the ground for his own contextual theory, has given a good summary of Salmon's causal theory, together with some fair critical comments. Part of this is reprinted in Kourany (1987, pp. 67–70). "Causation" in Edwards (1967) gives a good survey of topics on causation. Madden (1960, Part 4) provides a collection of critical essays on Hume's analysis of causality.

On the unificatory theory: Friedman (1974) and Kitcher (1981) give the original versions of their theories. Kitcher (1989) provides his latest arguments for his views as well as more examples of his (unificatory) argument schemas. Koertge (1989) and (1992) and Barnes (1992) provide useful criticisms of the theory.

For my critique of D-N explanation, see Hung (1978).

EXERCISES

1. Give an example to illustrate the problem of asymmetry.

2. Give an example to illustrate the problem of irrelevance.

3. Give an example to illustrate the problem of law explanation.

4. Suggest various ways to read the following question for explanation: "Why did Tom fly to New York?" Provide a plausible contrast class for each of the readings.

5. Explain the notion of relation of explanatory relevance in terms of the following why-question: "Why is Peter's car outside my house?"

6. Give an example to illustrate the difference between 'causal relevance' and 'statistical relevance.'

7. Give an example to illustrate the difference between 'causal process' and 'pseudo-process.'

8. Give an example to illustrate Salmon's argument that theoretical explanations are desirable in science because they are in essence causal explanations. Can you find any theoretical explanations that are not causal explanations?

9. Give an example to illustrate Kitcher's notion of an argument schema that can perform the function of unification.

10. (a) Including the covering-law thesis, we have studied four theories of explanation. Discuss each in terms of its relevance and implications to methodology. How is each going to be helpful to the practicing scientist?

   (b) Imagine that a pre-Newtonian scientist is required to explain the following five sets of phenomena, which are progressively more inclusive. Work out in detail how each of the four theories of explanation would influence his direction of research and investigation. The sets of phenomena are:

   Set 1: Magnets attract iron.

   Set 2: Set 1 plus the phenomenon that magnets do not attract wood.

   Set 3: Previous sets plus the phenomenon that similar magnetic poles repel.

   Set 4: Previous sets plus other kinds of attraction—for example, what we call electrostatic attractions.

   Set 5: Previous sets plus phenomena of collisions and rebounds of solid objects.

PART III SUMMARY

According to the classical tradition, truth and explanation are the twin aims of science. We covered the classical methodology on truth in Part II, and we have just dealt with the various theories on explanation.

One of the main activities prescribed by the classical tradition for philosophers of science is the **explication** of fundamental concepts. To explicate a concept is to make it more explicit and precise. 'Scientific explanation' is one of these fundamental concepts that, according to the classical tradition, requires explication.

Scientists, philosophers, and all sorts of laypersons have been using the term '(scientific) explanation' for centuries. Most of us have little difficulty in using the term competently, and intuitively we all seem to know what the term means exactly. We are at least as familiar with the term as we are with terms like 'understanding' and 'knowledge.' However, explaining to others what these terms mean is not easy. Perhaps after all our understanding of 'understanding' and the like is only superficial.

The term to be explicated is known as the **explicandum**, and the resulting concept after explication is known as the **explicatum**. According to Rudolf Carnap, one of the main pillars of the classical tradition, the latter should be (i) similar to the former and should be (ii) exact, (iii) simple, and (iv) fruitful.[1] Let's illustrate with an example. The biologists explicate the term 'fish' (explicandum) as 'a vertebrate that is cold-blooded, has a two-chambered heart, and breathes by means of gills' (explicatum). Let's call the biological fish a B-fish.[2] (i) You can see that the two terms, 'B-fish' and 'fish,' are very similar in that most of the one kind belong to the other kind as well. However, they do not coincide exactly. For example, the whale is normally taken as a fish (by our ancestors and by the layperson) but it is not a B-fish because it is warm-blooded and breathes with lungs. In fact, we classify it as a mammal. On the other hand, the lamprey eel is a B-fish even though many of us would hesitate to consider it a fish. (ii) The term 'B-fish' is exact. It draws a sharp boundary around a class of animals. At least there are no known animals today that cannot be discriminated by the definition of 'B-fish.' (iii) I think the definition is relatively simple. Finally (iv), is the explicatum useful? The answer is definitely yes. The common-sense term 'fish' is a phenotype term. It is based on certain observable characteristics. On the other hand, the biological term 'B-fish' is a genotype term. It is based on genetic make-up.[3] (As a genotype, the whale is closer to human beings than to sharks.) Because of this, the term 'B-fish' enables a much easier understanding as well as a much simpler presentation of Darwin's theory of evolution and the natural history of the living world.

We can consider the works of Hempel, van Fraassen, Salmon, and Kitcher as efforts toward the explication of scientific explanation. How successful are they?

Let's start with Hempel's **covering-law thesis**. In the classical tradition, logic, especially deductive logic, is the main tool employed in explication, and certainly Hempel follows this tradition. He explicates scientific explanations as arguments. For him, to explain the occurrence of an event is either to deduce a description of the event (D-N explanation) or to induce it with high probability (I-S explanation). In both, laws of nature, whether universal or probabilistic, act as indispensable premises. (Similar forms of arguments are supposed to govern the explanation of laws themselves.) This

---

1. See Salmon (1989, p. 5) for details.

2. The biological name of the class is actually pisces.

3. Compare with the fact that, in the old days, people used to classify substances in terms of their colors and smells, and nowadays we classify them in terms of their chemical compositions. Diamond and charcoal look very different, yet they are of the same substance.

explication proposed by Hempel works on the intuition that to explain is to provide reasons why the event has to happen or is likely to happen, and such reasons lie with the presence of certain circumstances (initial conditions) and the compulsion of certain laws. In other words, for Hempel, the puzzlement is dispelled once it is pointed out that a certain situation plus certain laws of nature will definitely or very likely lead to the occurrence of the event. We may have other intuitions on scientific explanations. For example, we may feel it is important that the unfamiliar should be explained in terms of the familiar or that explanations should bring about psychological satisfaction. But to explicate is *not* the same as to reproduce the original concept exactly. There would be no point to explicate if the explicandum were to be identical with the explicatum. The idea of explication is to trim and to make exact the explicandum so as to improve on it. For example, 'B-fish' can be seen to be a trimmed and regimented version of 'fish' for a good reason.

How good is Hempel's explication of scientific explanation? It is the general opinion that his theory is not able to handle a number of areas adequately, and these include probabilistic explanation, teleological explanation, the asymmetry problem, the problem of irrelevance, and the problem of explanation of laws.

According to van Fraassen's **contextual theory**, these problems are due to the fact that Hempel has taken a totally wrong line of approach. Instead of taking explanations as arguments and making laws the centerpiece in explanations, thus keeping with the classical tradition, one should study the logic of why-questions, for explanations are answers to commonplace why-questions. van Fraassen thinks that why-questions are typically ambiguous when taken out of context. They can, however, be disambiguated when the contextual contrast class and the relation of explanatory relevance are made explicit. He argues at length how his contextual theory can handle the problem of asymmetry and that of irrelevance in a satisfactory manner.

Salmon takes a less drastic line. His **causal theory** can be viewed as a modification of

Hempel's view rather than a replacement. For him the notion of subsumption under laws is not sufficient to capture the concept of explanation, as is made plain by the problem of asymmetry. He recommends that the notion of law subsumption should be strengthened, and this strengthened notion is his conception of 'causation.' Confronted with Hume's critique of the unwarranted metaphysical nature of causation, the classical traditionists tend to avoid the employment of the concept of causation in their philosophies. Instead many of them employ the notion of law of nature (and usually with it the notion of necessary connection by the back door). Salmon, well aware of Hume's critiques, attempts to develop a notion of causation without the accompanying metaphysics. He claims that his explication yields not only an improved version of probabilistic explanation (his S-R explanation) but also solutions to both the problem of asymmetry and that of irrelevance. Moreover, he argues that his notion of causation can provide a justification for the search for theoretical explanations in science.

The **unificatory approach** was taken up by Friedman and Kitcher. Again, both attempts can be seen to be well within the classical tradition, where deductive logic plays an indispensable role. However, instead of considering explanation at the local level, where each explanandum is to be explained in isolation, both of them think that explanation is basically a global concept. Kitcher thinks that an argument schema explains, not simply because it can deductively produce the explanandum, but also because it belongs to a collection of argument schemas which together can deductively produce, in the most economical manner, the total set of phenomena that requires explanation. Like the other authors, Kitcher claims that his theory solves both the problem of asymmetry and that of irrelevance.

Explanation is a notion of multiple facets. These authors probing for the true face of explanation are not unlike those four blind men who tried to discover the true nature of the elephant. The story goes like this. On hearing that the king had been presented with a precious animal known as an elephant from a distant land, these four blind folks wanted to find out what this celebrated creature was like. So they all went to the king's palace. After feeling (partly) over the animal, each blind person gave his version of the true nature of the elephant. Each answer was eccentrically different, depending on which part of the elephant the person happened to have felt.

Is there a true and correct analysis of the notion of explanation? Let me quote Noretta Koertge:

> Perhaps because of my Popperian background, I am in general dubious both about the value of asking 'What is … ?' questions and about the wisdom of basing answers to philosophical questions on our preanalytic intuitions. But I need not rest my dissatisfaction here. Carnap, who explicated the notion of *explication* in his *Logical Foundations of Probability*, emphasized that the explicatum must not only be exact, but that it must also be 'useful for the formulation of many universal statements.' What strikes me as unsatisfactory about the current philosophical discussion of explanation is not its failure to match our intuitions about flagpoles, shadows or mayors with paresis. Rather it is the paucity of explicit *theories* of explanation—the absence of systematic philosophical generalizations in which the competing explications or models of explanation play a central role. We should begin by asking what *problems* a good theory about scientific explanation might reasonably be expected to solve. Only then can we begin to sketch such a theory. (1992, pp. 85–86)

A central motivation behind the study of philosophy of science is methodology: to find out the best way to do science, the most rational and efficient way to advance science. True, the traditional way we understand and practice explanation should give us a clue as to the most desirable way to explain, the reason being that science so far has been very successful. But intuition can only provide us with guidelines. Ultimately we have to ask the question: What sort of explanation, in what particular form and satisfying what particular requirements, will be of use in the *advancement* of scientific knowledge and the understanding of the world as a whole? We should look for one or more useful notions of explanation. Whether these notions agree with our intuitions or not is only of secondary importance.

Are any of the discussed models of explanation useful methodologically? I must say van Fraassen's contextual model has little to do with methodology. Salmon and Kitcher's models, though methodologically relevant, are yet in their infancy, being sketchy and programmatic. What about Hempel's covering-law model then? In spite of all its shortcomings, it is methodologically significant. Furthermore, it is simple to use and is helpful in the formulation of scientific ideas.[4] However, I personally think that the model is still far, very far from what Koertge is urging us to search for.

Of course we can always, instead, adopt Duhem's thesis that what we take as theoretical explanations are not really explanations (Section 9.6). Rather, they are economical representations of phenomena. For Duhem, economical representation, not explanation, is the aim (or one of the aims) of science.

This leads us to Part IV, where we will study the nature and structure of theories. Do they have truth values or not? Can they explain phenomena? Or rather, are they merely economical and systematic representations that are neither true nor false? In short, we will revisit conventionalism and instrumentalism, which we have discussed in Chapter 9.

---

4. Larry Laudan (1977, pp. 184–185), for example, employs it in the discussion of explanations in intellectual history, and Laudan is one of the most influential contemporary authors. (See Chapter 29.)

The Pursuit of Reality

INTRODUCTION

Philosophers, and quite a few laypeople as well, have a natural yearning for the ultimate truth. They ask:

"What is the meaning of life?"

"Does God exist?"

"Is there life after death?"

"Where does the universe come from?"

"Why is there something rather than nothing?"

In this part we, however, will not deal with any of these awfully important questions. We are modest! We will simply be concerned with the question: "What is the world made of?"

To put it differently, we are interested in the following questions:

What are the world's fundamental building blocks?

What are its ultimate constituents?

What are the fundamental laws which bind these "blocks" or constituents together?

What is reality really like?

Let's call this question (or set of questions) the **question of ultimate reality**.

Since the time of the ancient Greeks more than 2,600 years ago, thinkers have been searching for the one true answer to this ultimate question. For example, Thales (circa 7th century B.C.) thought that the world is made of water. Heraclitus (circa 6th century B.C.) claimed that "all things are in flux," and hence the basic reality must be fire. However, Parmenides—a younger contemporary of Heraclitus—argued for the opposite, that there can be no change and no motion in the world, and hence reality is a spherical mass of uniform matter occupying the whole of space, totally motionless, changeless, indestructible, and eternal. Then, some 2,000 years later, Descartes (1596–1650), the great French philosopher and mathematician, argued that the world is made of two basic kinds of substance, mind and matter, the latter being what we would nowadays call empty space. A century and a half later, Dalton (1766–1844), the great English scientist, suggested that the world is made of indivisible atoms. In recent times, however, physicists think that the atoms of Dalton are not indivisible as Dalton thought, but are built out of even smaller things called electrons, protons, neutrons, and so on. Making the picture even more strange and more exciting, it is said that these small components of the atoms are in fact composed of extremely small vibrating "strings" residing in a nine-dimensional space (which has six more dimensions than we are perceptibly presented with).

How should we take these fantastic "tales"? Should we believe in any of them? If so, which should we subscribe to?

In Chapter 8, we pointed out that scientists invent theories to explain phenomena. These theories typically postulate unobservable entities to account for the behaviors of observable objects. Furthermore, these unobservable entities are usually taken as real, more real than the observable objects. Thus science attempts to answer the ultimate question of reality through theorizing.

Is theorizing the appropriate way to discover the ultimate nature of reality? Is it a valid method to do so? Is it the only method?

The first step toward answering these queries must be the study of the nature of scientific theories. What are they? What is their structure? What

are they supposed to do? In other words, what are their functions? How do they manage to fulfill these functions? If theories are meant to explain and to predict phenomena, how do they manage to do these things? In **Chapter 15,** we will present the classical view on these topics.

If theories are indeed what the classical view tells us, what can we say about theoretical entities— that is, the entities postulated by theories? Do they really exist, even though some are beyond comprehension? The commonsensical picture of the world usually clashes with that of science. Should we trust the senses and thus accredit reality to the commonsensical picture, which is so familiar and which we all share? Or should we trust theories, which are largely products of the mind, and believe in those strange pictures suggested to us by science? In **Chapter 16**, we will study the debate between scientific realism and instrumentalism, which is an antirealism.

The classical view of scientific theories used to be the dominant philosophy of science. However, in the last few decades many philosophers have found the view unacceptable. **Chapter 17** will be on the critiques of the classical view.

Finally, **Chapter 18** will return to the debate between realism and antirealism. However, this time we'll be on a different level. Instead of debating the ontological (existential) status of theoretical entities, we will confine our discussions to the question of what sort of epistemic attitude one should adopt toward the acceptance of theories. In other words, what sort of reasonable requirements should be expected from theories for their acceptance in the practice of science? Is it required that they be true or at least approximately true? Or is it sufficient that they be empirically adequate in the sense that they can both explain and predict phenomena correctly?

Chapter 15

The Classical View of Scientific Theories

15.1 THE TWO-LANGUAGE VIEW OF SCIENCE

According to the two-language view, science describes reality in terms of two languages, the **observation language** and the **theoretical language**.[1] The observation language consists of commonsensical terms such as color terms, shape terms, weight terms, and so on. A statement in this language can be something like "The table is red, square, and heavy." These terms are said to be directly related to our sense experience and are acquired by us through common sense. What they describe truthfully are often known as **phenomena**. Thus colors, shapes, and weights are all phenomena, which occur around us all the time, mostly familiar and unexciting.

The theoretical language, however, is quite different. It employs terms such as 'wavelength,' 'atomic weight,' 'gravitational force,' and so on. An example of a statement in this language is "The aggregate of atoms at position such and such is emitting electromagnetic waves of wavelengths 6,438 angstroms." These terms are said to be inventions of the mind for the explanation of observed phenomena (Chapter 8). What these terms portray is not directly observable and is thus quite distinct from phenomena. Let's borrow a

---

1. One of the main advocates of this view is Rudolf Carnap: see Carnap (1966, Part V).

term from the great German philosopher Immanuel Kant (1724–1804) and call these unobservable things, **noumena**.[2] Thus atoms, molecules, genes, electrons, radio waves, and gravitational forces are all noumena. According to many, noumena are the real things, whereas phenomena are only what are apparent to our senses. One of the aims of science is said to be the discovery of these noumena, which are responsible for the "production" of the phenomena. The noumena are the hidden mechanisms, so to speak, that "cause" the phenomena, and thus the noumena constitute the real nature of reality. For example, the red color of this flame belongs to the world of phenomena, whereas the electromagnetic waves of wavelength 6,438 angstroms (one angstrom being 10^{-8} cm), which "produce" the redness, belong to the world of noumena.[3]

Let's take 'color' as a variable with the specific colors such as red, green, blue, and so on as the values of the variable. Again, weight is a variable with values such as 1 gram, 2 grams, and so forth. We say these variables belong to the observation language and are used for the description of phenomena. On the other hand, we say that 'wavelength' is a variable belonging to the theoretical language with specific values such as 6,438 angstroms, 6,439 angstroms, and so on. Such variables are used for the description of the noumena.

The observation language seems to be an innate common property of the human race,[4] whereas the theoretical language is developed by scientists through the invention of abstract scientific theories. Since these theories purport to describe the real nature of things, we might call them **real–nature theories**. How do these two languages work together? Are they equivalent in the sense that sentences in one can be translated into the other (like English and French)? Or is it that they have their own fields of application that do not overlap? Why do we need two languages anyway? Is one superior to the other? In the next section, we will answer these questions by studying the structure of scientific theories (that is, real-nature theories).

15.2 STRUCTURE OF SCIENTIFIC THEORIES (REAL-NATURE THEORIES)

According to the classical tradition, a scientific theory (that is, a real-nature theory)[5] has two parts. One part consists of what are known as the **internal principles**, which are statements made in the theoretical language detailing the nature of the noumena: what they are like, how they behave, and so on. The other part consists of what are known as the **bridge principles**, which assert how the noumena are related to the phenomena. The internal principles form the core of the theory. However, since the noumena are not observable, we do need the bridge principles that relate them to the observable phenomena. For example, electromagnetic waves are not observable. A theory of such waves would therefore have to have bridge principles linking them to something observable such as colors. These principles are sometimes formulated as "p (phenomenon) corresponds to x (noumenon)." Thus, in the case of electromagnetic waves, a bridge principle could be something like: "The color 'red' corresponds to the wavelength

---

2. 'Noumena' is the plural of 'noumenon,' and note that our use of the term 'noumenon' here is quite different from Kant's original usage, though similar.

3. In Sections 14.4 and 14.5, we saw how Salmon explains his idea of explanation in terms of hidden causal mechanisms. Also note that Poincare's conventionalism is based on the distinction between the observation language and the theoretical language (Chapter 9).

4. The whole human race seems to be using this same observation language, possibly with the exception of the Hopi Indians (as reported by Benjamin Lee Whorf), and children of all nationalities manage to pick up the language with ease.

5. As pointed out in the introduction, the term 'theory' is ambiguous. In ordinary usage, by 'theory' we often mean 'hypothesis,' as when we say, "Your accusation that I did it is merely a theory. You do not have the evidence to back it up." In this chapter and, indeed, in this book, by 'theory' we mean 'real-nature theory,' as explained in the last section.

'6,438 angstroms.'" Hence some authors employ the term 'correspondence principle' instead, while others use the term 'dictionary'[6] as if the word 'red' means the same thing as '6,438 angstroms.'[7]

We have provided a number of examples of theories in Chapter 8. On top of these let's use the details of two well-known theories to illustrate the two kinds of principles.

15.3 STRUCTURE: THE CALORIC THEORY OF HEAT

The caloric theory can be attributed to Joseph Black (1728–1799).[8] It was invented to explain various heat phenomena by the postulation of a "heat fluid" that flows from hot things to cool things. This heat fluid, also known as 'caloric fluid,' is unobservable and thus belongs to the world of the noumena, whereas what it purports to explain is the observable phenomena of the temperature or hotness of objects. I will use this theory to illustrate the notions of internal principle and bridge principle, and the structure of scientific theories in general.

The caloric theory is meant to explain the following phenomena:

(i) Material objects have temperatures[9] that can be measured by thermometers.

(ii) When two objects of different temperatures are brought together, they gradually assume the same temperature, which is somewhere in between the two.

(iii) For each substance there is a definite temperature at which it freezes and a temperature at which it boils.

(iv) Each substance has its own specific heat and latent heat.[10]

These phenomena are stated in the observation language. The main observation variable is 'temperature' (T), with specific temperatures in centigrade as its values.

The theory itself consists of the following principles:

(v) Temperature is a manifestation of the amount of caloric fluid in the object. It is in fact proportional to the amount of fluid present.

(vi) Caloric fluid is indestructible and uncreatable.

(vii) When two objects are in contact caloric fluid will flow from the object with higher concentration of caloric fluid to the other until the caloric concentrations equalize.

This is a simplified version of the theory, yet from these principles we can see how a theory is organized. The first principle can be seen to be a bridge principle (correspondence principle) because it relates the notion of caloric fluid (of the noumenal world) to the notion of temperature (of the phenomenal world). The other two principles are internal principles that detail the behaviors of the fluid.

The principles are stated in the theoretical language with 'quantity of caloric fluid' (H) as the main theoretical variable. The values of H are in calories.

The theory explains the phenomena deductively. It is claimed that, from the internal principles together with the bridge principles, the phenomenon statements can be deduced. We can put it in schema form as follows:

(I) $I(H)$ Internal principles
      $B(H, T)$ Bridge principles
      _____
      $G(T)$ Empirical generalizations
                  (phenomena)

$G(T)$ are general statements of heat phenomena in terms of the temperature variable T, as illustrated by (i) to (iv), which are obtained by induction from

---

6. This term was used by N. R. Campbell (1952).

7. To be more exact, 'red' corresponds to 6,000–7,500 angstroms.

8. We touched on this theory in Chapter 7. Further details are available from Holton and Roller (1958, pp. 326–336).

9. Some would say that 'temperature' is a theoretical term rather than an observation term.

10. Those not acquainted with physics or chemistry need not worry about these terms.

specific (experimental) observations (Chapter 3). $I(H)$ are the internal principles in terms of variable H, while $B(H,T)$ are the bridge principles that link the variable H to the variable T. Remember that, according to Hempel, to explain a lawlike generalization is to deduce it from other laws (Chapter 10). We can see that schema (I) conforms to this ideal. Theoretical explanation is thus considered a case of D-N explanation, and it is claimed that our example of caloric theory here illustrates how theories in general perform their functions of explanation.

Let's call this view of theory structure, the **deductive model (view) of theories.**[11]

15.4 STRUCTURE: THE TWO-FLUID THEORY OF ELECTRICITY

Let's illustrate the structure of theoretical explanation with another theory. In the 18th century, Charles François de Cisternay Dufay (1698–1739) and Abbé Nollet (1700–1770) proposed a two–fluid theory to explain the then-discovered electric phenomena, which are as follows:[12]

(i) The amber effect: Amber when rubbed attracts bits of thread or paper.

(ii) The amber effect extended: Diamond, sapphire, opal, and glass will do the same.

(iii) The spark phenomenon: If glass is rubbed in the dark, tiny sparks are seen to pass between the piece of glass and a finger held close to it.

(iv) The communication phenomenon: The amber effect can be communicated. Some objects when connected to a piece of rubbed amber will pick up bits of thread or paper as if they themselves have been rubbed.[13]

(v) The phenomena of attraction and repulsion: There are two types of substances with respect to electric phenomena. Class A consists of glass, rock crystal, precious stones, hair of animals, and wool. Class B consists of amber, opal, gum lac, silk thread, and paper. When bodies of the same class are rubbed and placed in proximity to each other, they repel. When bodies from the two distinct classes are rubbed and placed in proximity to each other, they attract.

The theory consists of the following principles:

(i) There are two kinds of electric fluid: (a) vitreous fluid and (b) resinous fluid.

(ii) Electric fluid is indestructible and uncreatable.

(iii) Electric fluid flows.

(iv) When a body possesses an equal amount of the two kinds of fluid, it is said to be neutral, and neutral objects (if small) will be attracted by bodies possessing surplus electric fluid of either kind.

(v) A body with surplus resinous fluid will attract a body with surplus vitreous fluid and vice versa.

(vi) A body with surplus fluid will, however, repel another with surplus fluid of the same kind.

We can see that principles (i) to (iii) are internal principles, while the remaining ones are bridge principles. We can also see that from these principles the four types of phenomena can be deduced.

Here are some further examples of theories: the kinetic theory of heat, atomic theory of matter, wave theory of light, corpuscular theory of light,

---

11. Often the internal principles (and sometimes the bridge principles as well) are known as axioms. Thus what we have just presented is also known as the axiomatic model (view) of theories. Axiomatics was first introduced by Aristotle. Euclid (fl. 300 B.C.), however, should be credited with its application and development. We will hear more about this in Chapter 19.

12. Holton and Roller (1958, pp. 472–473).

13. Here is the phenomenon told in the words of its discoverer, Stephen Grey (18th century): "Having by me an ivory ball of about 1 inch 3/10 in diameter, with a hole through it, this I fixed upon [one end of] a fir stick about 4 inches long. Thrusting the other end [of the stick] into the cork, and rubbing the tube, I found that the ball attracted and repelled the feather with more vigor than the cork had done, repeating its attractions and repulsions for many times together. I then fixed the ball on longer sticks, first one of 8 inches, and afterwards on one of 24 inches, and found the effect the same" (Holton and Roller, 1958, p. 470).

and theory of gravitation. It has been claimed that each of these theories can be decomposed into internal principles and bridge principles.

15.5 THE VALIDITY[14]
OF THEORIZING

In the last three sections, we have covered the classical conception of theories. Now we should ask: Given that theories are this sort of "thing" with this kind of structure, should we theorize in science? What is the advantage of theorizing? Is it actually legitimate to theorize? To answer these questions we should make explicit what theories are for. Given such and such goals and objectives, can theories, as conceived by the classical tradition, do the job? The primary aim of theorizing, according to most, is explanation. The secondary aim is prediction. The former is to satisfy the intellect; the latter is for practical gains. Can "deductive" theories fulfill these two missions? From what we have studied so far the answer seems to be a straight yes for both: theories explain through deductively ensuring that empirical generalizations are explained, and from the theories further (often unexpected) generalizations can be deduced.

Can *all* deductive theories fulfill the two aims? Let's study the following example.

Let the phenomenon statement be: "All gold is soluble in aqua regia."

Does the following "gion" theory, (II), *explain* the phenomenon?

	All gold is amgions.	(Bridge principle)
	All amgions are bogions.	(Internal principle 1)
(II)	All bogions are cergions.	(Internal principle 2)
	All cergions are soluble in aqua regia.	(Internal principle 3)

All gold is soluble in aqua regia.	(Phenomenon)

We can see that (II) is a valid deduction, which conforms to the requirements of a D-N explanation. The theory consists of one bridge principle and three internal principles. It postulates unobservable amgions, bogions, and cergions to explain an (observable) phenomenon, just as the caloric theory postulates an unobservable fluid to explain heat phenomena, and the Dufay-Nollet theory postulates two unobservable fluids to explain electric phenomena. Nevertheless, we feel that something is wrong with this theory. Intuitively it has not explained anything. What is wrong with it?

Despite its formal correctness, the theory is, in fact, empty of content. We can see that the "device," (II), can be used to explain any empirical generalization of the form "All X are Y" simply by replacing 'gold' by 'X' and 'soluble in aqua regia' by 'Y.' Here we seem to have a magic formula for the production of theories to explain anything whatsoever! Such cheap gains cannot be taken seriously.

That's why in Chapter 8 we provided a number of criteria to draw a line between good and bad theories. Alternative (II) is a theory, all right, but it is a bad theory. The criterion of empirical adequacy for a good theory as suggested in Section 8.3 is that the theory should withstand empirical tests. The gion theory, in fact, satisfies this. However, for a theory to be really good, it must satisfy further criteria. These are the logical criteria—that is, the theory should have (i) unifying power, (ii) in-breadth predictive power, and/or (iii) in-depth predictive power. We can see that the gion theory fails according to all three logical criteria. It "explains" only one item ("All gold is soluble in aqua regia") and nothing else. It is not able to make predictions other than the very same item that prompts its invention. Indeed the gion theory is very similar to the cheon theory of chalk (Section 8.4). It is "sterile"!

In contrast, the following hydrocarbon theory of burning is good:

---

14. Note that the term 'validity' here is used as a commonsense term, not as the technical term we introduced in Chapter 2.

(III)   Phenomena:

Wood is flammable.

Gasoline is flammable.

Marsh gas is flammable.

(IV)   Theory:

Wood is hydrocarbon.	(Bridge principle 1)
Gasoline is hydrocarbon.	(Bridge principle 2)
Marsh gas is hydrocarbon.	(Bridge principle 3)
All hydrocarbon is flammable.	(Internal principle)

You can see that the three statements of phenomena in (III) can be deduced from (IV). Thus (IV) unifies and explains at least three phenomena. Further, (IV) possesses (in-breadth) predictive power. For example, it yields novel predictions such as: "Paraffin, being hydrocarbon, is flammable," "The products of the burning of gasoline would consist of hydrogen oxide (water) and carbon dioxide and no other substances," and "Gasoline probably burns better than wood (since gasoline is pure hydrocarbon whereas wood is not)."

The caloric theory, though shown to be false by experiments conducted in the 19th century, is, nevertheless, "logically" good, and so is the Dufay-Nollet theory of electricity.

Let's return to the questions we asked at the beginning of this section: (a) Should we theorize in science? (b) Is it legitimate to theorize? From the discussions so far, we can see that theorizing has its dangers. We must avoid "bad" theories. Only "good" theories are acceptable. What are good theories? Here are a few virtues: empirical adequacy, unifying power, in-breadth predictive power, and in-depth predictive power. I think intuitively we would say that the more of these virtues a theory possesses, the better the theory is. The number of virtues possessed can be measured in two dimensions: (i) How many of these four virtues does the theory possess? and (ii) how intense are each of the possessed virtues?[15]

Since (good) theories can explain phenomena and since they possess the pragmatic values of unification and prediction, I don't think anyone can doubt the value of theories, at least if she accepts the classical analysis of theory structure. Hence, to question (a), the answer is "Yes, we should theorize." But what about question (b): Is it legitimate to theorize? To answer this one, let's spell out what "legitimate" is intended to mean here.

Many of us philosophers, scientists, and laypersons take theorizing as a means to reach the "ultimate": to get to the fundamental constituents of the universe, and to get at the true picture of reality so that we can "see" and "grasp" the world as it really is. If we are just content with explanation, unification, and prediction for their pragmatic values, then theorizing for the sake of these values does not seem problematic. The question, however, is: Is theorizing a legitimate means to reach the "ultimate"? This highly controversial topic is what we turn to next.

KEY TERMS INTRODUCED IN THIS CHAPTER

observation language	noumenon	bridge principle	axiomatic model of theories
theoretical language	real-nature theory	deductive model of theories	
phenomenon	internal principle		axiomatics

---

15. See Section 8.8 for detailed explanation.

REFERENCES

General References for Part IV
as a Whole

Both Hempel (1966, chap. 6) and Lambert and Brittan (1987, part IV) give good introductions.

Nagel (1961, chaps. 5 and 6) remains one of the best classical presentations of the subject.

Brody (1970, part II) is a collection of 13 classical papers, which, though slightly difficult for the beginner, provides a detailed presentation of the main views.

Body et al. (1991, chaps. 2, 3, and 4) also present some classical papers that, however, can be difficult reading.

Brody and Grandy (1989, part I) is another anthology that provides many well-known papers.

Specific References for this Chapter

Both Hempel (1966, chap. 6) and Lambert and Brittan (1987, pp. 115–131) give good introductions.

Carnap (1966, part V) provides details as an authority in the field.

Nagel (1961, chap. 5) gives a classic presentation.

EXERCISES

1. Following Dufay and Nollet's two-fluid theory, Benjamin Franklin (1706–1790) produced a one-fluid theory. Attempt to analyze his theory in terms of internal principles and bridge principles. Is the theory a good theory? Which of the two theories is better?

2. Give one example of a scientific theory. What phenomena is it meant to explain?
   (a) Try your best to locate its internal principles and bridge principles. Which of the concepts employed are theoretical and which are observational? Based on this example, comment on the classical view that every theory can be neatly divided into internal principles and bridge principles.

   (b) Does the theory possess (i) unifying power, (ii) in-breadth predictive power, or (iii) in-depth predictive power?

3. Attempt to analyze the corpuscular theory and the wave theories of light (presented in Chapter 0) in terms of internal principles and bridge principles. Is it possible to have the theories neatly analyzed into these two sets of principles? Make explicit those phenomena the theories are meant to explain.

4. Taking theories as deductive systems, is it possible for these theories to be discovered through induction? How about through deduction?

Chapter 16

Realism Versus Instrumentalism

16.1 WHAT IS THE WORLD REALLY LIKE?

We, as humans, are all keen to know what the world is really like, and we seem to be able to distinguish between the real and unreal very well. For example, I have yet to meet anyone who takes dreams seriously—that is, who takes the contents of dreams as depicting reality.[1] We all seem to have realized since childhood that dreams somehow are creations of the mind and are not direct "pictures" of the real world. The real world, sometimes called the outer world, is the world that exists "outside" and independent of our mind. One may be dreaming of being pushed over a cliff, yet the dreamer may in fact be lying safely in bed. This is an instance of our common notion of the contrast between imagination and reality. The mind can indulge in all sorts of imaginings that have little resemblance to reality.

In Chapter 8, we pointed out that abstract scientific theories are products of the mind. It is we who invented notions such as caloric fluid, atom, electron, electromagnetic wave, and gravity. Being products of the mind, these notions need not correspond to anything in reality. They can be like objects in dreams. We feel sure of the reality of things like tables, chairs, trees, and grass because they are accessible to our senses. But theoretical entities such as atoms are not observable. Worse still, many of these theoretical entities seem strange,

---

1. There is one notable exception. ZHUANG Zhou, a great philosopher from ancient China (4th century B.C.), confessed that he could not tell dreams from reality. He once wrote that he was not sure whether he was a man, who dreamt of being a butterfly the night before, or a butterfly, who dreamt of being a man writing out his philosophical thoughts.

incomprehensible, and unpicturable. Yet the scientists and many philosophers seem to think that the world as presented by science is the true picture of the world, whereas the world of common sense is a deception of some kind. For example, Einstein thinks that space is actually curved. Young and Fresnel think that light rays are trains of waves. Count Rumford thinks that heat is matter in micro-motion.

The entities postulated by abstract scientific theories are known as **theoretical entities**. What we would like to investigate here is the question of whether theoretical entities in general exist. If they do exist, are they more real or less real than the objects of common sense such as tables and chairs? Is it coherent to say that both theoretical entities and objects of common sense exist side by side? Or are we forced to take the unpalatable position that the objects of common sense, with which we are so familiar, do not really exist?

One obvious answer seems to be that theoretical entities postulated by *true* theories exist, whereas those postulated by false theories do not. But then, how do we know when a theory is true? Are we not begging the question if we should say that a theory is true if the things it presents really exist? So this simplistic answer does not work.

16.2 THE EXISTENCE OF THEORETICAL ENTITIES

Somehow we intuitively would like to say that cheons (Section 8.4) and gions (Section 15.5) do not exist whereas atoms and light waves exist. Caloric fluid and Dufay–Nollet's electric fluids do not exist either, but the reasons for their nonexistence seem to be different from those for the nonexistence of cheons and gions. In Chapter 8, we introduced the idea of the goodness of a theory, which we elaborated in terms of internal principles and bridge principles in the last chapter.

The caloric theory is not a good theory, we said, because it has failed a number of empirical tests, including the friction tests conducted by Rumford (Section 7.3). According to the theory, heat is an uncreatable substance, yet when objects are rubbed together, they inevitably rise in temperature. In other words, one of the internal principles of the theory has been contradicted by empirical experiments. So the theory is not empirically adequate (empirically good). For this reason we conclude that caloric fluid does not exist. Similarly the theory of Dufay and Nollet has been shown to be empirically unacceptable, hence for us neither vitreous fluid nor resinous fluid exists.

On the other hand, the gion theory is empirically adequate. For what it predicts has been empirically verified, because the only prediction it makes is the phenomenon that gold is soluble in aqua regia. There is no empirical reason to deny the existence of gions. Nevertheless, intuitively it seems fantastic to believe in their existence around us. In the chapters previously mentioned, we pointed out that the gion theory lacks the logical characteristics of a good theory in that it neither unifies a significant number of phenomena nor produces any novel predictions in depth or breadth. For this reason, both the gion theory of gold and the cheon theory of chalk are in fact empty theories. The terms 'gion' and 'cheon' are mere words with no substance—they have no reference, as philosophers would say. Hence we say that neither gions nor cheons exist.

I think a *necessary* condition (though not a sufficient one) for the existence of theoretical entities is that the theories responsible for the introduction of these entities must be good both empirically and logically in the senses that we have specified.

Here are some theories that pass the "goodness" test:

(a) The water-droplet theory of rainbows, which roughly says that rainbows are water droplets (Chapter 8), is a good theory.

(b) The electromagnetic wave theory of light is another good theory. Roughly it says that colored light rays are trains of electromagnetic waves of different wavelengths (Chapter 0).

(c) The atomic theory of matter is another. Under this theory, it is said that copper is made of

(2,8,18,l)-atoms, and water is a collection of H_2O molecules where H is a 1-atom and O is a (2,6)-atom.

(d) At this point I think you would enjoy a parable. Imagine a group of children living in a room with a huge wall mirror. They can see that there are two types of people: those who live in front of the mirror and those who live behind it. They call the latter kind people-in-mirror, PIM for short. These children are keen scientists, and they record minutely all kinds of phenomena that occur around them. They make generalizations as well. Here are a few:

(i)   All PIMs are left-handed.
(ii) For each person in the room, there is a PIM that looks exactly like him or her. (The PIM is known as the person's partner.)
(iii) Whenever a person in the room smiles, the partner also smiles.

One day one of the children has a bright idea. He proposes that the PIMs are really light images. This theory is known as the light image theory of PIM.

Note that, for the children in this parable, terms such as 'people-in-mirror,' 'left-handed,' and 'smile' are observation terms. 'Light image,' by contrast, is a theoretical term. The light image theory is proposed to explain phenomena as described by (i) to (iii) (just as the water-droplet theory was proposed to explain the features of the rainbow arches).[2]

I think the light image theory is good (and I am quite sure you would agree with me).

Since all these theories are good, should we conclude that light images are real whereas PIMs are not? That H_2O is real whereas water is not?

That trains of waves of various wavelengths are real whereas light rays of different colors are not? And that rain droplets are real whereas (colored) rainbows as colored arches are not? I think most of us would answer yes to all these questions. However, life is never that straightforward, at least not philosophical life.

16.3 THREE VIEWS OF REALITY

Remember that the four theories respectively state that:

(a) Rainbows *are* water droplets.[3]
(b) Colored light rays *are* trains of electromagnetic waves of different wavelengths.
(c) Water *is* H_2O.
(d) PIMs *are* light images.

How should we read the verb 'to be' in each of the four statements?

Let's take (c) first: "Water is (a collection of) H_2O." What can this mean? Water, as we know it, is a homogeneous fluid, continuous, transparent, smooth, and usually cool to the touch. It is drinkable and thirst-quenching. Above all it is substantial, weighty, and bulky. On the other hand, H_2O is a molecule too small to be perceived and is composed of three atoms—two hydrogen atoms and one oxygen atom. A bucket of water is said to consist of billions and trillions of these molecules all buzzing around incessantly at exceedingly high speeds. The most amazing thing, however, is that the distances between the molecules are so enormous when compared to the actual sizes of the molecules (and the distances between the nuclei and the electrons of the individual atoms are also so enormous) that

---

2. This parable is not farfetched at all. It is comparable to the present situation where most of us take human beings as having minds and describe their behaviors in intentional terms. You see, we may very well be mistaken. In such a case, the taking of certain "organic robots" as free intentional agents is comparable to children's mistakes in thinking that certain light images are people.

3. Strictly speaking, rainbows are not water droplets *per se*, but water droplets of a specific kind when viewed under certain conditions.

most of what we call water is in fact empty space.[4] Which is the true picture of reality? We cannot say that both pictures are correct, for they are very different and, in fact, incompatible.

When we say "The Morning Star is the Evening Star," we mean that the two "stars," though appearing at different times of day and at different positions in the sky and looking different, are really one and the same star.[5] However, do we want to say that, when one says that water is H_2O, it means that water and H_2O are one and the same thing even though water presents itself differently at different times and places? Surely one can say that owing to our "crude eyesight" we see water as a homogeneous liquid even though in reality it is an aggregate of buzzing molecules. But then we are really denying the accuracy and correctness of the commonsense picture. We are not really using the verb 'to be' as in the case of "The Morning Star is the Evening Star."[6] In the case of the stars, there is no claim about correctness. In our case, there seems to be a bias in favor of the scientific picture.

Philosophies that favor the scientific picture are generally known as scientific realism. Though the basic idea of scientific realism is simple, the formulation of it is not so straightforward. In fact, there are many possible as well as competing formulations. Let's start with a simple and tentative one.

Scientific realism (SR) is the philosophy that (i) claims that (real-nature) theories that are both empirically good and "logically" good in the sense that they have both high explanatory power and high predictive power are likely to be true or at least approximately true, and thus (ii) claims that their theoretical terms are likely to refer to real entities (that is, the theoretical entities they postulate do exist).[7]

Under the broad classification 'scientific realism,' let me mention two subtypes: **radical scientific realism (RSR)** and **conservative scientific realism (CSR)**.[8]

In addition to what SR claims, RSR asserts not only that the scientific picture is largely correct but also that the commonsense picture, in contrast, is misleading, incorrect, and should be *relinquished*. RSR would not interpret "Water is H_2O" as "Water is *identical* with H_2O." For the reformist there is not a drop of that homogeneous, continuous stuff called water in our oceans. On the contrary the oceans are full of buzzing and vibrating molecules called H_2O. There is simply no water for the H_2O to be identical to. What the reformist advocates is *replacement*. She champions a reform—that the commonsense concept 'water' be *replaced* by the scientific concept 'H_2O.'[9]

I'll come to CSR later. For the moment let me take up a philosophy that is the polar opposite of RSR. This is **instrumentalism (INS)**, which we touched on in Section 9.6. For INS, the commonsense picture, which is the picture given by the senses, is the correct and true picture of reality, whereas the so-called scientific picture is only a "mental construct." The germinal idea of this philosophy came from the ancient Greeks,[10] and it was

---

4. This way of bringing out the difference between the layperson's picture of water and the scientist's picture is due to A. S. Eddington's *The Nature of the Physical World* (1929).

5. This example comes from G. Frege (1848–1925). A similar example could be "Dr. Jekyll is Mr. Hyde."

6. Note that in "The Morning Star is the Evening Star," identity is asserted about particular objects, whereas in "Water is H_2O," identity is asserted about substances.

7. In the literature, 'mature theories' is usually employed instead of our 'theories that are empirically adequate and "logically" good.' See, for instance, Laudan (1981). Also see Laudan (1984, p. 105) on the point that the realist claims that "a theory that exhibits certain explanatory and predictive virtues can warrantably be presumed to be true (or nearly true)."

8. These are my terms. You might prefer replacement scientific realism and improvement scientific realism, respectively.

9. See eliminative materialism (Section 13.3).

10. In the 1st century B.C., Geminus of Greece made the distinction between physically true theories and hypotheses that "save the appearances." He advocated that in the study of celestial phenomena, physicists should pursue physically true theories, whereas astronomers should only be concerned with the latter. With this Geminus laid down the foundation for INS.

later reiterated by the Lutheran theologian Andreas Osiander in the 16th century. In Chapter 7, we discussed the "debate" between Ptolemy and Copernicus, the former being in favor of the geocentric system and the latter in favor of the heliocentric system. In his preface to Copernicus's *De revolutionibus*, Osiander argued that Copernicus's system can be taken merely as a mathematical model of the universe irrespective of whether the earth actually moves around the sun. Since then there have been many philosophers who think that scientific theories should be taken as mere calculating devices, and this philosophy is the philosophy of INS. The main idea is that the world as given by the senses—that is, the commonsense world—is the real world. That is what the world is really like. However, to make predictions and descriptions, sometimes it is preferable to set up mathematical models, which, if strictly interpreted, may present unfamiliar, unpalatable, sometimes alarming, and often puzzling pictures of the world. The H_2O model of water is an example, and the wave theory of light is another (Chapter 0).

Therefore, INS takes seriously the reliability of our senses in the presentation of the world. Our senses are likened to a camera (a good camera of course), which yields an exact likeness of reality, with perhaps an occasional mistake or two. Where then are we left with the scientific theories? It is said that they are worthy of pursuit, though not because they produce true or better pictures. Rather they are calculating devices for our convenience. Thus a geocentric instrumentalist can without qualms employ the heliocentric theory (as an assumption) to work out the position of the planets as seen at certain times from earth, the dates of the next eclipse of the sun, the year of the next return of a certain comet, and so on, even though for her the earth is truly fixed at the center of the universe. The commonsense instrumentalist can consistently employ the H_2O model to make predictions on the emission of

hydrogen gas from water should certain electric currents be made to pass through it, yet at the same time believe sincerely what common sense suggests—that water is a homogeneous and continuous substance.

Scientific theories for the instrumentalists are sometimes likened to mathematical symbols such as the number zero and the square root of minus one. Even though these symbols do not stand for anything in reality, they nevertheless have their uses in calculation, and that is why they appear in mathematical texts.[11]

INS works fairly well with examples like H_2O, electromagnetic waves, and quantum mechanics. However, it is difficult to apply it to cases like the light image theory of PIM. The instrumentalist would have to say that in reality there are PIM because that is what her eyes suggest. This does not prevent her from employing the theory of light images as a device to make predictions about their movements and behaviors. As for the rain droplet theory of rainbows, the instrumentalist has to say that there are really solid colorful arches in the sky, whereas the postulated rain droplets are mere fictions for the benefit of prediction.

Let's introduce a third philosophy, a sort of middle position, that one can take. It is what I have called **conservative scientific realism (CSR)**. CSR recognizes the reality of both phenomena and noumena—the reality of what is presented to the senses as well as the reality of what is postulated by good scientific theories. In the case of water, CSR would say that the layperson's picture of water is true and so is the H_2O picture. It would be difficult to convince people that something is simultaneously a homogeneous continuous liquid and a host of buzzing particles. However, CSR can say that one is a macroscopic view and the other a microscopic view. Such a dual picture of reality seems acceptable. For example, rainbows in the distance are colored arches, while at close range they are rain droplets.

---

11. A more sophisticated case is when mathematicians find it convenient to talk in terms of "points at infinity" (where parallel lines meet) in analytic projective geometry. A comparable case is the notion of virtual image in optics.

This is comparable to the "Morning Star-Evening Star" scene, where 'the Morning Star' denotes a different view of the same object from 'the Evening Star.' It works better in cases such as the water–H_2O case, and not so well in cases such as the light–electromagnetic waves case. Is it that light when examined closely, say with a microscope, can be seen as electromagnetic waves? The case of PIM is even worse for CSR. From this viewpoint there would have to be PIM *as well as* light images.[12]

16.4 INSTRUMENTALISM AND SCIENTIFIC REALISM

Instrumentalism (INS), as pointed out earlier, came from the ancient Greeks as well as from Osiander. In more recent times, it was championed by Ernst Mach (1838–1916), whose **phenomenalism** (Section 9.5) was based on the philosophies of Berkeley (1685–1753) and Hume. (Hume was the philosopher who denied the existence of necessary connections; see Chapter 11.) Mach, a great physicist to whom Einstein owed much in his invention of the theory of relativity, thinks that what we are empirically given are merely various kinds of sensations, which Hume called **sense impressions** and which some contemporaries call **sense-data**. These are patches of color sensations, sounds of various pitches, smells of different kinds, and so on. What we can assert the existence of are these sensations, which we are immediately aware of. These are the things that we know—knowing in the sense of being acquainted with, as when we say that I know my friend Mary. (In contrast, I can only claim that I know *of* Napoleon because I don't

really know him.)[13] Other than these things with which we have immediate cognitive contact, we have no right to assert the existence of any other things. Hence for Mach theoretical entities such as atoms and gravitational force are mere *memoria technica* (technical memory aids). There are no such things. The words do not refer. The words are mere instruments for calculations.

INS is a viable and consistent doctrine (that is, within the classical conceptual framework).[14] Mach, being one of the outstanding physicists of the 19th and 20th centuries, was by no means eccentric. In Section 9.5, we saw how, with the conventionalists, he argues that economy of thought, not truth, is the aim of theorizing. The goal of theory production is to save labor, to organize the multiplicity and complexity of the given data into coherent and economic systems. The truth or falsity of theories does not come into it because, as mere instruments, theories are neither true nor false, even though they can be judged according to their usefulness. You can see that INS goes well with another philosophy known as **pragmatism**, which, in an oversimplified form, equates truth with usefulness—usefulness for us humans.[15]

INS provides a simple way out of many philosophical problems, hence its attractiveness. For instance, it explains why we should employ theories that we know to be false or whose truth we have little ground for claiming. We need not worry about inconsistent theories, either those that are formally inconsistent or those that are conceptually "inconsistent," such as quantum mechanics. We can ignore requests for (comprehensible) interpretations of some of the more abstract and complex theories such as relativity. We also need not bother about how theoretical terms acquire their meanings, a

---

12. A more vivid example would be the case of holograms. A CSR realist would have to say that holograms of people are real people and light images at the same time.

13. Bertrand Russell (1912) makes the distinction between the two senses of knowing: knowing by acquaintance and knowing by description.

14. The classical framework is being disputed by constructivism (Chapter 31).

15. Bakker and Clark (1988, chap. 7) provide an excellent introduction to this philosophy.

problem that has plagued philosophers of science for almost a century and that we will study in the next chapter.

Theories come and go. Aristotle's mechanics dominated the Western world for almost 2,000 years. Newton's mechanics took its place and reigned for 200 odd years, and then in turn was overthrown by Einstein. You can see, from history, that theories replace each other, almost like clothing fashions. On the contrary, observation data are stable, at least seemingly so. This is the strength of INS: what is important for the scientist (and the layperson) is the truth of observation statements and accurate predictions of the observable. Whether theoretical entities exist or not is of no concern to them. Indeed for INS it is illegitimate to claim or assert their existence (for lack of "substantial" evidence, evidence of "direct contact" through the senses).

I will have more to say on INS, especially on its fallacies, in Chapter 31, where we deal with constructivism. But for the moment it suffices to point out that emotions probably play a significant role in the rejection of INS by both philosophers and laypeople.

Conservative scientific realism (CSR), at first glance, does not seem to be a tenable position to hold. It seems silly to say that both phenomena and noumena are real, and that both the common-sense picture and the scientific picture are largely correct. Implausible as it seems, this philosophy has been made respectable and even appealing by a theory of reference known as the **causal theory of reference (CT)**.[16] According to CT, general terms like 'water,' 'gold,' 'tiger,' and 'lemon' denote natural kinds. Other terms such as 'yellow things,' 'round things,' 'bachelor,' 'table,' and 'furry animals' do not. It is we humans who give names to the natural kinds around us. For instance, when our ancestors first came across gold, they "christened"

that substance (that stuff) 'gold.' (Philosophers would say that the naming is by ostension.) The term 'gold,' according to the intention of our ancestors, is not meant to apply to the few gold nuggets they happen to have found. That term was meant to apply to anything of the *same natural kind* as the gold nuggets in their possession. We do not need to know much about the properties of gold or its inner structure to be able to use the term 'gold' correctly as long as we intend it to mean whatever natural kind our ancestors employed it to denote. CT is antagonistic to the traditional theory—the **descriptivist theory of reference (DT)**. According to DT, the term 'gold' is an abbreviation of a list of descriptions of gold. For example, for the average person, 'gold' probably means the substance that (i) is a metal, (ii) is yellow in color, (in) melts at 1,064°C, (iv) is ductile, (v) is malleable, and (vi) has a density of 19.3. For the specialist, 'gold' may mean the element with atomic number 79 and atomic weight 197.0. Either way, the term 'gold' stands for a list of properties. Should anything turn up with that sort of properties it would be gold by definition.

You can see the difference of approach of the two theories: CT relies on the "baptism" ceremony where something is "baptized" 'gold,' and then all other bits of matter will automatically acquire the name 'gold' by virtue of belonging to the same natural kind as the bit that has been so called in the first place. You can see that no descriptions are present in the definition of gold at all. If you like, a piece of matter will be gold if it is a "sibling" of the original piece of gold, irrespective of what it is like. On the other hand, for DT there is no naming "ceremony," or, if there is one, that ceremony is irrelevant. Whatever has certain properties is gold.[17]

DT is what common sense suggests and what we are used to. CT has become popular only since the 1970s.

---

16. The causal theory of reference was originally proposed by Saul Kripke as a theory of meaning for proper names. It was later extended by Hilary Putnam (1970, 1973) to cover a category of general terms known as natural kind terms.

17. Martin (1987, chap. 21) provides an easy-to-follow account of CT. Why is the theory called *causal* theory of reference? Because it is said that once the natural kind—say 'gold'—is named, subsequent uses of the term 'gold' will be able to refer to the substance gold through a certain kind of causal chain. See Martin (1988, p. 173).

Let's see how CT can be employed to support the philosophy of CSR. Let's take

(1)   Water is H_2O.

This can be the CSR-CT account: 'Water' is the term given to a certain natural kind by our ancestors. Our ancestors (and many of us), however, mistook it to be a homogeneous and continuous liquid. According to the modern scientist, *that natural kind* is in fact a collection of H_2O molecules, and the scientist expresses these findings as (1). So if you like, the 'water' in (1) is used to *indicate (refer to)* what we are talking about. It is used as a sort of name and is not used descriptively to say that it is a homogeneous liquid. Thus we say that 'water' in (1) is used *referentially*. On the other hand, 'H_2O' in (1) is used *descriptively*, describing a certain molecular structure. I think most of us will say that (1) under this interpretation is true and is not self-contradictory as it would have been had both 'water' and 'H_2O' been interpreted descriptively. To put it another way, (2) is seemingly false but is in fact true.

(2)   Water is not a homogeneous liquid.

And even (3) is true if you read the first 'water' referentially and the second 'water' descriptively.

(3)   Water is not water.

So for the CSR-CT theorist both the scientist and the layperson are talking about the *same* thing, the *same* natural kind. The only difference is that the former thinks that it is a collection of molecules and the latter thinks that it is a homogeneous liquid. Even though these two descriptions seem antagonistic to each other, they can coexist. Here one can employ the notion of approximate truth for the defense of coexistence. For the realist, theories can be approximately true without being exactly true. The realist can claim that both the H_2O picture and the homogeneous liquid picture are approximately true of the natural kind that has been named 'water,' even though most likely the former picture is closer to the truth. Earlier, in Section 13.5, we discussed reductionism, how the human individual is reducible

to a collection of cells, and how each cell is reducible to a collection of molecules, and so on. We can see that CT fits in well with reductionism. For CT, it is acceptable to describe human beings as a collection of cells. This is the gross picture. It is also acceptable to describe human beings as collections of molecules. This is a finer picture. Whichever picture we adopt, we are talking about the same thing: the natural kind that our ancestors called 'human being.'

Indeed, for CT, it is acceptable to describe human beings as free agents with souls, which exercise free will, and at the same time concede that humans are nothing more than a group of molecules. Again the defense of this thesis of coexistence is that both pictures are probably approximately true even though the latter is probably better than the former. For convenience on many occasions we would prefer to use the less accurate description. A similar case is that of Newton's mechanics as compared to Einstein's relativity. The former is less accurate, but in everyday life it is preferable to the "cumbersome" theory of relativity. Here is another similar case. Even though we all know that mechanical robots have no free will and do not have intentions, and would not be able to make statements, we usually prefer to describe their behaviors intentionally, as if they were humans. Thus we talk about robots making choices, aiming at certain targets, and talking to us. (The children in the mirror-room may prefer to continue to talk in terms of PIM even after the acceptance of the light image theory.)

You can see that CSR is a reasonable philosophy—that is, on the assumption that CT is valid. But is it valid?

Radical scientific realism (RSR) differs from its conservative ally in that it denies the causal theory of reference, and thus denies that you can refer to the same things through different theories. The RSR theorist is descriptivist as far as reference is concerned. For this theorist, terms like 'gold,' 'water,' and 'tiger' refer in terms of a list of properties as I explained earlier. 'H_2O,' for instance, embodies a list of property descriptions very different from 'water.' Hence the two terms cannot refer to the same thing. So by "Water is H_2O," the RSR theorist means that we should relinquish the use of the term 'water' and replace it with 'H_2O,' for 'water' refers to nothing since there is no substance in the world answering to its list of property descriptions. There is simply no homogeneous, continuous liquid, which is transparent, smooth, and usually cool to the touch. In the jargon of the philosopher, the term 'water' is vacuous. That's why it should be taken out of circulation and be replaced by 'H_2O' (assuming, of course, that 'H_2O' is not vacuous as well). In short, according to RSR, the scientific picture, and not the commonsense picture, is the true or approximately true picture, and thus the terms of science refer and those of common sense do not. You can see that RSR favors science just as INS favors common sense. In between lies CSR.

I'll further illustrate the difference between the two types of realism. Let's refer back to the four examples (a) to (d) at the beginning of Section 16.3. For the conservative realist, the following pairs *refer* to the same things:

(a') 'rainbow arches' and 'water droplets (of certain descriptions positioned at certain places)'

(b') 'colored light rays' and 'trains of electromagnetic waves (of certain wavelengths)'

(c') 'water' and 'H_2O'

(d') 'people-in-mirror' and '(certain) light images'

This is so even though the commonsense picture differs from the scientific picture in *description*. Thus both phenomena and noumena exist, even though the noumena story is more accurate.

For the radical realist, the first member of each of the pairs of (a') to (d') does not *refer* at all. The second member does *refer*, because the scientific picture is the correct or nearly correct picture while the commonsense picture is quite off the mark. Thus phenomena do not exist. Only noumena are real. (Instrumentalism, by the way, thinks that phenomena exist whereas noumena do not.)

With reference to the four examples, we can see that the conservative realist has difficulty claiming that 'people-in-mirror' in (d') does refer, whereas the radical realist would find it hard to disclaim that 'water' does refer. Other examples that would prove difficult for the conservative realist are 'caloric fluid,' 'phlogiston,' and 'ether.' On the other hand, terms such as 'gold,' 'wood,' and 'clay' would pose difficulties for the radical realist.

To sum up, if we let p stand for a certain phenomenon and let x stand for a certain noumenon, the bridge principle of a theory would have the form:

(4) p is x.

(Here p and x can be taken as variables of the observation language and the theoretical language respectively.) For the conservative scientific realist, (4) should be read as

(5) The object we usually call p would be more correctly described as x (even though it is also describable as p, albeit less correctly or even incorrectly). (Thus both p and x exist, where p and x employed in the first five words of the present sentence are used referentially.)

For the instrumentalist, (4) should be read as

(6) The object we usually call p is already correctly described as p but would be more conveniently and fruitfully described as if it were x. (Thus only p exists.)

For the radical scientific realist, (4) should be read as

(7) There are no such objects describable as p. So p does not refer. Hence p should be replaced by x, which does refer because in reality what we describe as x does exist. (Thus only x exists.)

We will see more of the debate between various realisms and antirealisms in Chapter 18 and again in Chapter 31. In Chapter 31, we will see how RSR takes a sharp turn into the exciting philosophy known as constructivism.

KEY TERMS INTRODUCED IN THIS CHAPTER

theoretical entities

scientific realism (SR)

radical scientific realism (RSR)

conservative scientific realism (CSR)

phenomenalism

sense-datum

sense impression

instrumentalism (INS)

phenominalism

pragmatism

theory of reference

causal theory of reference (CT)

descriptivist theory of reference

REFERENCES

Lambert and Brittan (1987, pp. 148–159) gives a good introduction.

Scheffler (1963, pp. 182–224) provides a detailed discussion.

Nagel (1961, chap. 6) presents a classic account.

Hempel (1966, chap. 7) and Martin (1987, chap. 21) provide good introductions of the causal theory of reference, whereas Hilary Putnam's "Explanation and Reference" in Boyd et al. (1991, chap. 9) gives the original presentation. Hacking (1983) provides good summaries of various viewpoints and suggests that experimentation should play a more significant role in the debate.

EXERCISES

1. Give a few examples of theoretical entities that satisfy the following:

    (a) Probably most (well-informed) people will think that they exist.

    (b) Probably most (well-informed) people will think that they do not exist.

2. The modern atomic theory came from Dalton (1766–1844). According to him, atoms are indivisible, and water is HO (not H_2O). For the radical scientific realist, does the following exist?

    (a) water

    (b) HO

    (c) the Daltonian atom H

3. Look around your kitchen. Try to discover theoretical entities that, according to the instrumentalist, do not exist. Are there any borderline cases whose existence the instrumentalist will find it difficult to ascertain?

4. Both diamond and coal are constituted of carbon. Suppose our ancestors came on diamonds first and named these stones 'diamonds.' Since coal belongs to the same natural kind as diamond, according to the causal theory of reference, coal is diamond. Discuss the causal theory of reference in terms of this "story."

5. The causal theory of reference is based on the assumption that natural kinds have well-defined nonoverlapping boundaries. In view of this assumption,

    (a) Do isomers belong to the same natural kind? (Isomers are compounds that, while sharing the same atomic compositions, have their atoms differently arranged in space. Enantiomers are isomers that are mirror images of each other.)

    (b) Do isotopes belong to the same natural kind? (Isotopes are atoms with the same atomic number but different atomic weight.)

(c) Do species form natural kinds? (Note that genes can be changed by both mutation and genetic engineering.)

6. One of the weaknesses of the descriptivist theory of reference is that often objects belonging to a natural kind may not have *all* the definitional properties of that kind. For example, being sour may be one of the definitional properties of lemon, yet most of us would not hesitate to acknowledge a certain fruit as a lemon if it has all the properties of being a lemon, except that it tastes sweet. Why, in view of this, is the causal theory of reference superior? Find out the typical rejoinder offered by the descriptivist, known as the cluster descriptivist theory (for example, see Martin [1987, pp. 197–198]).

7. Imagine that a certain philosopher of the 20th century came upon a bar of gold. (Sometimes even philosophers can strike gold!) How would he describe his object of discovery if he were a sincere

(a) radical scientific realist?
(b) instrumentalist?
(c) phenomenalist?
(d) conservative scientific realist?

Chapter 17

Critiques of the Classical View

17.1 INTRODUCTION

In Chapter 15, we introduced the classical deductive model of scientific theories. According to this model, science employs two languages, the observation language and the theoretical language. The former is employed to describe what we observe and what we can observe (the realm of phenomena). The latter comes from theories (real-nature theories). A theory is a set of statements divided into two kinds: internal principles and bridge principles. Together they can explain generalizations about phenomena through deduction. Schematically the logic can be represented as follows:

(1)   Internal principles

    Bridge principles
    _____

    Empirical generalizations

The **deductive model** is also known as the **axiomatic model**, and such an approach to understanding theories is called the **syntactic approach**.[1]

---

1. Syntax is the study of the manipulation of symbols according to formal rules, usually taken as a branch of metalogic. The deductive model is an attempt to reduce theories to a form to which techniques developed in the science of syntax can be applied.

This model has a number of significant "virtues":

(i)   'Theory' is an abstract notion. The layperson would understand a theory as a set of ideas. But what are ideas? The deductive model reduces theories to statements, which are represented by sentences. Sentences can be studied as concrete objects because they have components, they have structures, and they are logically related to each other. For example, "Newton was human" has three components (words), and it shares a structure similar to "Galileo was human." From either of these we can logically conclude that "Someone was human." We say that the conclusion is validly deducible from the premise (Chapter 2). You can see that once theories are reducible to statements, we can apply our knowledge of logic and metalogic (including syntax) to theories. Logic is big business in the 20th century, as you will see in Chapters 23 and 24.

(ii)   The second virtue is that the deductive model has been in circulation for over 2,400 years. Aristotle (384–322 B.C.) first proposed it. Euclid (fl. 300 B.C.) later demonstrated its power and clarity to systematize geometry. Many scientists subsequently employed the model, including the great Newton. Theories presented as such are usually known as axiomatic systems. The deductive model of the classical tradition we have studied is simply a refinement of axiomatics.

(iii) The deductive model of theories goes well with Hempel's covering-law thesis of explanation, one of the great pillars of the classical tradition. In terms of the model, theoretical explanations can be understood as special cases of D-N explanation, and thus the employment of theoretical explanation in general is justified.

(iv)   The deductive model, as has been pointed out in (ii), agrees with historical practices. It seems to agree with intuition and common sense as well.

Notwithstanding these points, contemporary philosophers are skeptical of the deductive model, which was taken as the standard before 1970. Let me detail three types of critiques.

17.2 THE OBSERVATIONAL-THEORETICAL DICHOTOMY

The deductive model faces (at least) three major difficulties:

(i)   The observational-theoretical dichotomy
(ii)   The distinction between internal principles and bridge principles
(iii) The meaningfulness of theoretical terms

I'll deal with (i) here and leave the other two points for later sections.

According to the model, terms used in science are either observational or theoretical. It is a dichotomy. The question is: Is the dichotomy tenable? Is it possible to make a clear distinction between observational terms and theoretical terms?

Let's consider bacteria. Is the term 'bacterium' observational or theoretical? Surely bacteria are too small for the naked eye to see. However, with the aid of a microscope we can easily see them. If we grant bacteria the status of being observable, and thus take 'bacterium' as an observational term, then what about viruses and some large molecules? Virus particles became detectable by Barnard's ultraviolet microscope in 1919. In 1934, the Belgian physicist Maraton built the first electron microscope, which could show up the virus particles, not simply as dots, but with well-defined shapes. Nowadays, the electron microscope is so powerful that it can show up the structure of some big molecules. Where do you stop with observability? If observability is granted to bacteria, surely it should be granted to molecules (at least to the big ones).

On the other hand, if observability is denied to bacteria because they can only be observed through the use of instruments, then perhaps the term 'ant' would be theoretical for some, because without the aid of spectacles some of us cannot see ants. Shall we take 'observability' as 'observability for the normal person'? But the normal person employs the eye to see. Surely the eye then is a sort of instrument for the normal person.

What is wrong with our notion of observability? First, it is anthropocentric, meaning that it is defined in terms of human abilities (that is, normal human abilities). If we were smaller, had better eyesight, had more senses (such as a sixth sense), or had fewer senses (losing the sense of sight, for example), the boundary of observability would accordingly change. Second, it is difficult to draw a line between instruments we are born with, such as eyes and ears, and instruments that are manufactured but that can nevertheless be taken as an extension of our senses (for example, hearing aids). Third, individuals are different from each other. If we should define observability in terms of the *average* individual, that is only a matter of convenience. It has no theoretical or ontological justification whatsoever. Recall that the **observational-theoretical distinction** has bearings on the claim of existence both for the instrumentalist and for the scientific realist. The distinction is supposed to be intrinsic. It is not supposed to be a matter of convenience for the practicing scientists.

Perhaps observability simply means detectability (with or without the use of instruments)? In this case, gravitational force is observable because every time you drop a stone, you "see" the force in operation. Radioactivity is also observable because the Geiger counter will register "clicks" when confronted with radioactivity. Radio waves, electrons, and even vacuous space are then all observable, because they are all detectable. If so, I wonder if there is anything left that is unobservable?

Let's try this. Galileo (1564–1642), Descartes (1596–1650), and Locke (1632–1704) introduced and developed the distinction between **primary** and **secondary qualities**. Primary qualities are basic properties of material objects whereas secondary qualities are derivative. Traditionally, primary qualities include volumes, shapes, motions, solidity and impenetrability. Other than being derivative, secondary qualities of an object are dispositions which, under appropriate conditions, produce in (human) observers sensory experiences, bearing the same name. For instance, take a green leaf. Its greenness is a secondary quality in the sense that this leaf would produce certain "green sensations" in the "head" of the observer if viewed under white light. (Note that the greenness of the leaf and the greenness of the observer's sensations are two different things.) We can say that secondary qualities are *sensorily dispositional*. Traditionally, colors, tastes, smells, and sounds are considered secondary qualities. Shapes and sizes, though sensorily dispositional as well, are however not secondary because they are considered basic properties of objects.

Brittleness, though derivative as well as dispositional, is not secondary either, because it is not *sensorily* dispositional.

Can we make use of this distinction between primary and secondary qualities to throw some light on the observational-theoretical dichotomy? Shall we take (2) as our criterion of observability?

(2) An entity is observable if some of its primary qualities are observable with or without the use of instruments.

By this criterion, bacteria, viruses, and certain large molecules would be observables because their shapes, which presumably are primary qualities, are detectable through the use of the electron microscope. On the other hand radio waves are unobservables. Why? Even though we can detect radio waves through the use of a radio, the sound produced by the radio is not a primary quality of the waves. Radio waves would be observables if the "shapes" or "sizes" of them were observable. But surely, you will say, their shapes and sizes are detectable. How otherwise can we come to know that a certain train of radio waves has a wavelength 9.6 meters, for instance? I think there is a slight misunderstanding of (2) here. It will help if we make a distinction between observable properties and detectable properties. When we say that a certain shape, say a triangular shape, is *observable*, we mean that that shape can be sensed (with or without the use of instruments) as a shape of similar quality (that is, as, more or less, a triangular shape).

Detectability requires less. I think triangularity can be observed by sight or by touch. This should not be in dispute. Now it may happen that when sheets of metal of a *triangular shape* are struck they usually produce a note of a certain pitch. Is triangularity therefore observable through sound? This is a controversial issue. But I think it would be reasonable to say that triangularity in this case is detectable rather than observable. The reason is that even though from the note we can infer about the shape, the note does not "look" like the shape. It does not bear a qualitative resemblance to the shape. (Probably you can say that triangularity is, for the same reason, only detectable and not observable through touch.)

Similarly, even though electrons, photons, and quarks are all detectable, none are observable. Indeed, most entities are detectable because detectability is nothing more than "inferable through some of the effects produced by the entity (possibly in conjunction with other entities)."

We can now define observation terms as follows:

(3) A term is an observational term if it stands for observable entities, otherwise it is theoretical.

But then what about terms such as color terms, shape terms, terms of temperature, terms of magnitude of forces? These terms do not stand for *entities*. We probably should have the following:

(4) A term is an observational term if either (i) it stands for observable entities or (ii) it stands for observable qualities, primary or secondary; otherwise the term is theoretical.

Will (4) do in clarifying the distinction between observational terms and theoretical terms? I think not.[2] Nevertheless, it will be both interesting and useful for you to discuss the acceptability of (4) as an exercise. But before you start doing so, I would like to make it clear that contemporary philosophical discussions around the observational-theoretical distinction largely arise out of concern about the meaningfulness of theoretical terms. The question is: Are theoretical terms meaningful, and if so how do they manage to acquire their meaning? According to the classical tradition, the way observation terms acquire meaning differs from the way in which theoretical terms do so. Hence the distinction between the two kinds of terms is important. Let's therefore turn to this topic of meaning and meaningfulness.

17.3 MEANINGFULNESS OF THEORETICAL TERMS I

In this section, we will deal with the other two difficulties with the deductive model: (i) the distinction between internal principles and bridge principles and (ii) the meaningfulness of theoretical terms.

Can a clear distinction be made between internal principles and bridge principles? Let's take (II) of Section 15.5. There we classified "All cergions are soluble in aqua regia" as an internal principle. But this statement has both a theoretical term—that is, 'cergion'—and an observational term—that is, 'aqua regia.' Is it a bridge principle, then? It does not look like one of these, either, because it is about the behavior of cergions.

Let's look at (IV) of the same section. Here again "Hydrocarbon is flammable" is classified as an internal principle, but 'flammable' is supposed to be an observational term. It does not look like a bridge principle either. Perhaps we have been unfair, because these two are both artificial cases. Let's then look at a real case, the case of caloric theory (Section 15.3). One of the principles is: "When two objects are in contact caloric fluid will flow from the object with higher concentration of caloric fluid to the other until the caloric concentrations equalize." Prima facie this is an internal principle because it is

---

2. Many philosophers of the classical tradition have conceded to the arguments against the observational-theoretical distinction. Hempel (1966, pp. 75, 88), for example, in place of the observational-theoretical dichotomy, talks about pretheoretical (or antecedently available) terms versus theoretical term.

about the behavior of caloric fluid: how it will behave under certain circumstances. But then there are observational terms in the statement—that is, 'object' (which means 'objects of all sizes') and 'in contact' (which means 'in spatial contact').

The original idea of a bridge principle is that bridge principles fulfill two functions: (i) they complete the deduction schema ((I) of Section 15.3), so that the inference from the internal principles to the empirical generalization (the explanandum) becomes valid, and (ii) through the bridge principles the theoretical terms in the internal principles acquire their meaning. (The purported reason is that, whereas the observational terms can acquire their meaning directly through the observable "things" they stand for, the theoretical terms can only acquire meaning indirectly, via the observational terms.) It is apt, therefore, to call these principles 'bridge principles,' because they do form a sort of bridge between the theory proper (internal principles) and the empirical explanandum. So there have to be bridge principles! So it seems.

We might ask: What form should the bridge principles take in order for them to fulfill those functions? For function (i) the answer is simple: "There are no definite forms. Any that will complete the deduction will do." However, for function (ii) the answer is not that simple. According to logic and semantics, the bridge principles have to be of certain forms before they can "transmit" meaning from the observational terms. What are these forms?

N. R. Campbell in 1919[3] proposed to call the set of bridge principles for a theory, the dictionary of the theory. Here is the argument for the dictionary idea. The terms of a (real-nature) theory—that is, the theoretical terms—somehow have to be defined. Obviously they cannot be defined by ostension.[4] For instance, we cannot define 'electron' by pointing at an electron and saying, "This is what an electron is." Electrons are simply too small and too elusive to be pointed at. On the other hand, we can presumably define, say, 'red'

by pointing at something red, and saying, "This color is what I mean by 'red.'" In short, the idea is that theoretical terms cannot be defined directly and can thus only be defined in terms of observational terms. According to Campbell, the bridge principles serve as such definitions. Hence the term 'dictionary.'

What form should bridge principles take? Usually definitions take the form of equations. For example, we can say

(5) x is a pentagon = x is a linear figure with five sides.

Some of you might not know the word 'pentagon,' but from (5) you can read that it means a five-sided figure, no more and no less. And in fact you can avoid the use of the term 'pentagon' if you are prepared to employ the rather lengthy 'linear figure with five sides' when required. Definitions such as (5) are known as **explicit definitions**. At one time it was thought that bridge principles should take the form of explicit definitions. For example, we can have the following:

(6) Temperature = average kinetic energy

Or, more accurately,

(6a) The temperature of x is m degrees Celsius = the average kinetic energy of the ensemble x of molecules is n joules.

(7) Wavelength = color

Or more accurately,

(7a) Light of wavelength such and such = light of color such and such.

Unfortunately this simple form does not work for bridge principles. We need only think of terms like 'magnetic,' 'electron,' and 'gravitational force.' Can these be defined explicitly in terms of observational terms? It would be a good exercise to try, and you'll find how limited the application of explicit definition is. As a matter of fact explicit definition does

---

3. *Foundations of Science* (Mineola, N.Y.: Dover), 1952. This was originally published as *Physics: The Elements* in 1919.

4. By pointing.

not work even for wavelengths. Alternative (7a) looks fine but is in fact seriously defective. For example, 'yellow' corresponds to the *range* of wavelengths from 5,700 to 5,900 angstroms. By (7a) there should be no difference between any of the 200 wavelengths between 5,700 and 5,900 angstroms. They all, by (7a), mean 'yellow.' Besides, a wave is a complicated thing. Its wavelength is one of its features. It has other features as well. Wavelengths work in terms of these other features to produce various kinds of phenomena.

Definition (6a) does not work either. In fact, it is formulated the wrong way around. Usually 'temperature' is taken as an observational term. The motional behavior of molecules is unobservable so that it is the 'average kinetic energy of molecules' that requires definition. But no physicist in her right mind will define the latter in terms of the former because 'kinetic energy' is a much more fundamental concept and is understandable independent of 'temperature.'[5]

Because of these difficulties, instead of taking bridge principles as explicit definitions, the term '**correspondence rules**' was coined. The requirement is not that the theoretical term is to be synonymous with an expression constructed out of certain observational terms. Only a loose kind of "correspondence" is now sought. What does the term 'correspondence' mean in this context? Nobody seems to be quite clear. Nevertheless there were quite a few suggestions on improving the form that bridge principles should take. Most of these were built on Bridgman's notion of operational definition, to which we now turn.

17.4 BRIDGMAN'S OPERATIONALISM

Most of us think that simultaneity is a very straightforward concept. It simply means 'happening at the same time.' However, the truth is that we don't really know exactly what it means. In 1905, Einstein published his special theory of relativity. He surprised the world by pointing out that our usual understanding of the term 'simultaneity' was both faulty and muddled. To remedy the situation, he gave the term an "operational" definition.

Percy Williams Bridgman (1882–1961), a Nobel laureate physicist, taking up where Einstein left off, asked, "What do we mean by the length of an object?", as if we do not really know what 'length' means! Indeed according to Bridgman, our idea of the notion is at best murky. He has clarified it for us as follows:

> We evidently know what we mean by length if we can tell what the length of any and every object is, and for the physicist nothing more is required. To find the length of an object, we have to perform certain *physical operations*. The concept of length is therefore fixed when the operations by which length is measured are fixed: that is, the concept of length involves *as much as and nothing more* than the set of operations by which length is determined. (Bridgman 1927, reprint pp. 58–59, my italics)

This passage summarizes his idea of operational definition. Every meaningful concept, according to him, should be either "measurable" or at least "detectable." The set of operations required for the measurement or detection of the presence of the property corresponding to the concept is what the concept means. This is exactly what Einstein proposed when he redefined simultaneity. He asked, "How do we know that two distant events are simultaneous?" (Do you know the answer?) Then he pointed out that, for two events E_1 and E_2, which occur close to each other, say both in the same room, simultaneity poses no problem. It is when they occur at a great distance apart—for

---

5. For example, it makes sense to talk about the kinetic energy of this falling stone, which has nothing to do with the temperature of the stone.

example, one on earth and one on the moon—that the concept becomes problematic. Here is one way to define simultaneity in the spirit of Einstein:

(8)   Two events, E_1 and E_2, are simultaneous if two light signals emitted from E_1 and E_2 reach an observer stationed halfway between E_1 and E_2 at the same time.[6]

Why is light signal chosen rather than other kinds of signal? For example, E_1 and E_2 may be explosions. They will both produce a big flash as well as a big bang. Why aren't sound signals employed in (8) rather than light signals? We all know that the speed of sound is not constant. It depends on many factors, including wind speed. But then how are we to know that the two light signals will travel at the same speed?! Science must start with some assumptions. Einstein boldly took the constancy of the speed of light (in vacuum) as a basic assumption of nature, and made use of it in (8) in the definition of simultaneity![7]

Note that definition (8) is in terms of a set of operations (employing light signals and so on), and you can see that Bridgman applied the same technique with regard to the definition of length.

Bridgman generalizes this idea of defining concepts in terms of a set of operations and applies it to all terms, especially to those which we call theoretical terms. Theoretical terms are especially in need of such definitions because what they "denote" is not observable. Here is Bridgman's **operationalism**:[8]

(9)   All terms should be operationally defined, and the meaning of a term is the same as the set of defining operations.

Let's discuss the notion of **operational definitions** in detail.

Suppose the term to be defined is 'electric charge,' which is a theoretical term, denoting "something" neither visible nor audible. It produces no smell or taste, no shape, and no color. Based on certain phenomena, scientists claim that there is electricity. But what can 'electric charge' mean? What can it stand for if whatever it stands for is not perceptible? (Note that, according to Hume, to understand 'red,' we must have been exposed to the color redness through experience [Section 11.6].)

In the 18th century, an instrument known as the leaf electroscope was invented for the detection of electrical charge. It consists of a horizontal metal plate, under which a thin vertical metal rod is attached. At the bottom end of the rod are two metal leaves loosely hanging side by side facing each other. When a charged object is brought near the plate, the two leaves will diverge, the amount of divergence being roughly in proportion to the amount of charge in the object.

Given this instrument, we can have the following operational definition:

(10) x is electrically charged $=_{df}$ If x is brought near a leaf electroscope, its leaves will diverge.

The left-hand side of the equation is known as the definiendum; the right-hand side is known as the definiens. The "df" following "=" signifies "definition." We can see that in (10) the definiens has two parts: an operation followed by an expected response. In general, an operational definition has the following logical form:

(11) x is $p =_{df}$ If O is performed on x, then R.

O stands for an operation to be performed on x, and R is the expected response. If we place a requirement that both O and R be formulated in observational terms, the operational definition can be taken as a means of reducing theoretical terms to observation terms. (We can also say, in a manner of speaking, that operational definitions reduce the unobservables to the observables. We have been

---

6. You can see that this definition attempts to define simultaneity between two *distant* events in terms of simultaneity between two proximate events (the two light signals arriving at the eye of the same observer).

7. This is an oversimplified definition of simultaneity.

8. Operationalism is also known as **operationism**.

over similar ground under 'dispositional behaviorism' in Section 13.4.)

Another example might be the following:

(12) x has an excess of hydrogen ions $=_{df}$ If x is placed in the mouth, it will taste sour.[9]

This definition of the theoretical term '(the excessive presence of) hydrogen ions' has the correct logical form of an operational definition, and the terms employed in the definiens are certainly observational. However, "tasting sour" is subjective in that different people tasting the substance might report different kinds of tastes.

The following is more acceptable:

(13) x has an excess of hydrogen ions $=_{df}$ If a litmus paper is placed in x, then x will turn red.[10]

Operational definitions purport to render theoretical terms objectively measurable. The operations involved in an operational definition can be viewed as an act of measurement in a generalized sense, whereas the response yields a value of the measurement. The philosophy of operationalism can thus be viewed as a philosophy that champions the grounding of all terms (theoretical or otherwise) in objective measurements. This movement has had a great impact on psychology. Associationism in the 19th century took psychology as the study of mental phenomena that are neither objective nor measurable. The advent of behaviorism brought an end to that. Psychologists have since been busy designing measurements for such unobservables as intelligence and aptitudes in terms of observable behavior.

To summarize, operational definitions must be such that:

(a) they have the right logical form

(b) they contain only observation terms in the definiens

(c) their terms in the definiens are objective, and finally

(d) they should be faithful in that the definiens must give a correct and full equivalent of the definiendum. One way to test equivalence is to see whether, for each substitution of x, the two sides of the equation share the same truth value—that is, the left-hand side is true if and only if the right-hand side is.

It would be useful for the reader to practice giving operational definitions to common terms such as "being brittle," "being deaf" (especially for animals), "being color-blind," "being alive," "being courageous," and "having a temperature of 20 degrees Celsius." Check whether your definitions satisfy the four conditions listed earlier.

Operational definitions are not meant only for property terms but also for relational terms.[11] For example, "heavier than" can be defined as follows:

(14) x is heavier than y $=_{df}$ If x and y are placed on the left and the right pan of a beam balance respectively, the left pan will descend whereas the right pan will ascend.

"Heavier than," though a common term, is, strictly speaking, not a pure observational term. If x is much heavier than y, usually we can feel the difference. But when the two are not that different in weight, direct test is not available. Definition (14) grounds the unobservable property to something that can be observed.

Operational definition is a special kind of explicit definition. But it is quite different from the simplistic kind we studied in Section 17.3—for example, (5). Another example of a nonoperational definition is (15).

(15) x is a bachelor $=_{df}$ x is an unmarried man.

It does not have the right logical form.

---

9. Chemistry tells us that the excessive hydrogen ion concentration in a liquid accounts for its acidity.

10. 'Red' is still subjective to an extent because our sense of redness is not uniform. The best kind of response for R in (10) is probably a digital printout. You can hardly imagine two scientists arguing over whether a certain printout numeral is a '2' or a '3.' We call experiences **intersubjective** if almost all of us agree on their identification.

11. Logicians would call property terms '1-predicates.' Relation terms are known as 2-predicates.

Two points are noteworthy about operational definitions.

(i) Operational definitions are of two kinds, qualitative and quantitative. What we have been studying is the qualitative kind. A quantitative operational definition corresponding to (10) is the following:

(10a) x is electrically charged to degree $H =_{df}$ If x is brought near a leaf electroscope, its leaves will diverge by amount K.

A quantitative operational definition corresponding to (14) is:

(14a) x is heavier than y by z amount $=_{df}$ If x and y are placed on the left and the right pan of a beam balance respectively, and z number of peas (assuming them to be all identical with each other, as peas usually are for us humans) are further added to the right pan, the two pans will stay leveled.

We can say that qualitative operational definition gives us means of detection whereas quantitative operational definition yields measurement. Measurement is a step forward from detection, and operationalism surely helps to promote and develop the science of measurement.

(ii) The second point worth noting is that very often operational definitions transform the (already) observable into something even more observable. Let's take (14). Given a stone and a piece of wood of the same size and shape we can probably tell that the former is heavier by balancing the two, one on each hand. But it does involve a bit of guesswork. In other words, the observability of the difference in weight is not sharp. However, (14) improves the observability to such an extent that a sensitive beam balance can tell a difference as small as the weight of a grain of sand. You can see that operational definition is useful not only in converting the unobservables into observables but also in improving observability in many

cases. Further, the improvement of observability can be such that qualitative concepts can be turned into quantitative concepts. For example, a weighing scale yields numerical weights, thus quantifying the qualitative concept 'heavy.' Thermometers yield degrees of temperature in place of 'hot' and 'cold.' Spectrometers "turn" colors into pointer readings. You should see that the notion of operational definition is closely related to the use of instruments for detection and measurement. All these should remind you of the role played by indirect tests in science (Chapter 6).

We have covered the notion of an operational definition. And according to operationalism, as stated in (10), all terms should be operationally defined, and the meaning of a term is the same as the set of defining operations. Historically, operationalism has proved fruitful in science, especially in young sciences like psychology. However, it is one thing for a philosophy to bear fruit (for example, being able to stimulate fruitful thinking in certain directions), and another thing for it to be correct and acceptable. Unfortunately, according to current opinion, operationalism is defective in more than one way and is considered both philosophically and methodologically unacceptable. The usefulness of (11) as a formula is not in doubt. It is its interpretation as a definition that is questionable. In the next section, we will see some of the commonly observed conceptual difficulties that operationalism faces.

17.5 DIFFICULTIES WITH OPERATIONALISM

Here are some of the difficulties commonly attributed to operationalism.

(A) First, it is doubtful if any term can be operationally defined at all. Take for instance the term "electrically charged." Definition (10), under close scrutiny, will be found to be inadequate. It surely has the correct logical form, and only observational terms appear in the definiens. However the equation is "unbalanced," so to speak. It is easy to think of an x such that the two sides of the equation have different truth values.

For example, let's take x to be genuinely charged with electricity. So the left-hand side is true. But when x is presented to the electroscope the leaves would not part (because the experimenter holds the leaves together with his fingers). This is not meant to be an arrogant counterexample to the definition. It is for the illustration of the following point. To make the definition faithful (so that the two sides share the same truth values), we must add a clause to the right such as: "provided that there are no other forces influencing the leaves." But then 'force' is an unobservational term. It denotes an abstract influence, which takes on forms such as magnetic force, gravitational force, nuclear force, wind force, "finger force," and so on. Such a clause is sometimes known as a **ceteris paribus clause**.[12] The addition of ceteris paribus clauses, while necessary, will inevitably break the constraints characterizing operational definitions.

Even if we should overlook such ceteris paribus clauses, the equation can still be unbalanced. What we know about the world so far is meager. There may well be other kinds of entities that when brought near an electroscope will open up the leaves. In such a case, the right-hand side of the equation is true whereas the left-hand side is false.

(B) Second, there is the case of multiple operational definition for a single concept. Hempel (1966, p. 93) points out that there are many ways to measure lengths. We can use a ruler to measure the length of a table. This operation obviously would not do for the length of the circumference of a cylinder. There we might employ a piece of string wound around the cylinder to get its length. For distant objects like distances between mountaintops or distances between celestial objects we need yet a third kind of method, perhaps employing light beams. So we end up with a number of concepts of length: tactile length, optical length, and so on. Which of these notions of length is the true length? We cannot simply say, "Pick one," because each one of these has a limitation as to the range of its applicability. What we need is a single way to measure all lengths, if all these lengths are meant to be "manifestations" of one and the same concept.

Another example that Hempel gives is the case of the measurement of temperature. There are many different kinds of thermometers. Each with its own peculiar use (operation) would constitute a distinct operational definition. Similarly there are a great many kinds of instruments for measuring weights: the beam balance, the spring balance, and so on. Which is the defining instrument?

Nevertheless, this difficulty of multiple definitions is not as unsurmountable as it seems. What science typically does is to take one of the measuring operations as basic. In the case of length, the Parisian meter rod used to be taken as the standard.[13] Whatever makes the same span as that rod is considered 1 meter. In other words, the operational definition for the meter is:

(15) x is a meter long $=_{df}$ If x is placed side by side with the Parisian meter rod, the two ends of x will coincide with the two ends of the rod.

But then how can we use (15) to measure the height of a tall building or the height of a mountaintop? We cannot very well take the Parisian rod and try to span the heights! Let's see.

In fact, there are many ways to measure the height of a tall building. Here is one. Measure the length of its shadow by spanning it with an ordinary meter rule. Knowing the angle of elevation of the sun, we should be able to work out the height of the building with a bit of trigonometry. Of course this procedure assumes a few things (auxiliary hypotheses, Chapter 6). These include:

(i)   the laws of geometry,

(ii) that light travels in straight lines,

---

12. It would be instructive to relate ceteris paribus clauses to the employment of auxiliary hypotheses (Chapter 6).

13. Nowadays a meter is defined as the distance traveled by light in vacuuo in 1/299,792,458 of a second.

(iii) that the ordinary meter rule employed has been checked with the Parisian meter rod and has not changed its shape since

What I try to point out is that we do not need to have a different operational definition for each type of length. What we need is one basic operational definition. All other measuring methods can be interpreted in terms of this single basic operational definition. In brief, we can have one basic method of measurement and a number of derivative methods. The so-called problem of multiple operational definition is not really problematic.

(C) Third, you sometimes hear people say that no amount of operational definitions can define a "continuous" concept. For instance, in between two lengths, say 1.2 meters and 1.3 meters, there is always another length—for example, 1.25 meters. So there are an infinite number of possible lengths. If each of these possible lengths requires an operational definition, we need to design an infinite number of operational definitions.[14] Obviously this is impossible! However, I think this is a fallacious argument. In defining length, we really need only one operational definition. We do not need separate definitions for 1.5 meters, 2 meters, 2.5 meters, 3 meters, and so on. By postulating that length is a scalar quantity, we can work out the lengths of objects other than 1 meter long by physical procedures such as spanning, partitioning, and projecting, together with mathematical procedures such as addition, subtraction, multiplication, and division. This sort of procedure should cover lengths of all magnitudes. (To convince yourself, just follow the methods employed by scientists or technicians in the art of length measurement.)

(D) Fourth, there is considerable concern over the interpretation of the term 'if' in an operational definition as expressed by (11). You would be surprised how philosophers spend their time arguing seemingly trivial matter. I have yet to find any ordinary English speaker puzzling over the meaning of the word 'if.' Yet the exact meaning of 'if' is one of the major topics in contemporary philosophy. I think you should tolerate the philosopher and hear her out (not because I am a philosopher myself). (Haven't you heard the story of the great scientist who was puzzled as to why apples fall downward?)

The term 'if' has occurred a number of times in this book. It was present in (2) of Section 13.4 under the topic of dispositional behaviorism. It was also present in Popper's propensity interpretation of probability (Section 12.6). It surfaced in (5) in Section 11.4 where we discussed counterfactual conditionals. If you look way back, you will find it playing key roles in Section 2.5 in the two logical forms: modus ponens and modus tollens. The term 'if' also has much to do with the notion of necessity, which according to many underlies the notion of law of nature and the notion of causation.

There is a general consensus among philosophers that unless the term 'if' has been clarified and made rigorous, operational definitions are suspect. It is beyond the scope of this chapter to go into the issue. However, we will have an opportunity to follow it up in Chapter 23, where we study the movement known as logical positivism.

17.6 MEANINGFULNESS OF THEORETICAL TERMS II

You may recall that in Section 17.3 we asked what form the bridge principles of a theory should take in order that they can transmit meaning from the observation terms to the theoretical terms. We have examined the possibility that they take the form of an explicit definition (of the common kind). We have seen that this form does not seem to work. How about letting the bridge principles take the form of an operational definition (a special kind of explicit definition)? This does not seem to work either. Since Bridgman there have been quite a number of well-known attempts to improve

---

14. Actually the situation is worse, because there are *uncountably* infinite numbers of possible lengths.

on the notion of operational definition to make it work. Unfortunately, none of them has had much success. We will follow up this story in Chapter 23.

How do theoretical terms obtain their meaning? This is a big question. Indeed, even for observational terms no one seems to be able to work out an acceptable theory of meaning.[15] The great philosopher Ludwig Wittgenstein (1889–1951) proposed that the meaning of a term is a function of its use. By saying that, he opened up a radically new avenue to explore meaning. But this theory of meaning is controversial as well. Anyway traditional philosophy of science does not take that path.

The trend in philosophy of science is that of **holism**. You may recall the holistic thesis of conventionalism and the Duhem-Quine thesis (Chapter 9). According to Quine, the truth or falsity of a statement cannot be assessed on its own. It is the totality of statements together that face the "tribunal of sense experience." It seems that we should understand not only truth holistically but also meaning as well. Terms, whether theoretical or observational, cannot be understood individually. Terms work together, rather like the organs of the human body. The meaning of each term depends on the meaning of many or even most of the other terms. The degree of dependency is not meant to be uniform, though. Let me give a simple example. The term 'red' depends on the meanings of terms such as 'orange,' 'green,' and so on. It cannot be properly understood without being both contrasted and related to these other color terms. You might think that the meaning of a color term is related only to the meaning of other color terms. "Surely it is not related to the meaning of shape terms!", you might say. Let's see.

Suppose you want to teach a young child the word 'red.' So you draw a red triangle on a piece of paper and say, "This is red." How does the child know that 'red' is not meant for the shape of the figure? So you draw another red figure, this time a red square. But the child might think that 'red' means linear figure. You can see that if the child knows what triangles and squares are, then you can simply teach her by saying, "This is a red triangle, and that is a red square."

Why is 'red' related to 'orange'? Because 'red' covers a range of similar color, and degree of similarity can only be appreciated by contrasts.

We have just been discussing very simple terms: color terms and shape terms. 'Electrically charged' is, in contrast, far more complex and advanced. To understand it properly we have to relate it to the general notion of force, and to notions of specific forces such as gravitational force. We also have to relate it to terms such as positional terms, volumetric terms, shape terms, mass terms, temporal terms, energy terms, momentum terms, and many more. That's why 'electrically charged' cannot be defined in isolation in terms of an operational definition, in which 'electrically charged' occurs neatly on the left-hand side of the equation as the definiendum, and the definiens has only observation terms. Some have suggested the use of a number of operational definitions together to cope with the complexity. I don't think this will do either.

Hempel (1966, p. 94) talks about what I will call **network definition of terms**. All terms are related, more or less. To define a term (the definiendum), we should do two things, (i) Relate the definiendum to other terms by means of what have been called internal principles or bridge principles, or other kinds of sentences. The "tightness" of the relationships between terms will vary, from strong to weak. (ii) Relate the definiendum to sense experience, not as an isolated item, but in cooperation with the other terms, so that from these relationships we can say something like: "Under certain circumstances, when A, B, C, ..., and Z are such and such, we can expect sense experience of certain types," and the definiendum is but one of the terms in the list of A, B, C, ..., and Z. That's why Hempel (1966, p. 94) says: "Thus, the concepts of

---

15. Hume was naive when he thought that these terms can be defined by ostension.

science are the knots in a network of systematic interrelationships in which laws and theoretical principles form the threads." Let's call this philosophy the **network theory of meaning**.

It would be interesting to compare this holistic theory of meaning with Quine's holistic theory of truth.[16]

We can take holism as a matured reaction against "individualism." This is certainly the case with that holism which we studied in Section 13.4. There we talked about the failure of dispositional behaviorism, a philosophy that attempts to analyze mental state terms such as 'want' and 'believe' into dispositional terms. Dispositional behaviorism takes each mental state—for example, 'wanting to catch the bus'—individually as an isolated item and tries to define it in terms of behavioral responses. Functionalism was later proposed as an improvement, and it is a holism. This holistic philosophy takes into account the interrelatedness of all the mental states in a way very similar to the network theory of meaning. The latter takes into account the interrelatedness of all the terms that occur in a science.

17.7 SUMMARY

The classical deductive model of theories takes theories as composed of a set of internal principles and a set of bridge principles, and it views theoretical explanation as a matter of deduction. It has quite a number of virtues: (i) It reduces theories to sets of statements, to which the well-developed science of logic can be applied. (ii) It has a long and well-tested history dating back to the axiomatic systems of Aristotle and Euclid. (iii) It dovetails well with Hempel's D-N model of explanation. (iv) It agrees

with many practices in the history of science, notably Newton's *Principia*.

However, the model also faces many difficulties. (a) The dichotomy between observational and theoretical terms is hard to justify. (b) The statements of theories do not seem to fall into two neat, clear-cut classes: internal principles and bridge principles. (c) No satisfactory theory of meaning has been found for the theoretical terms within the confines of the deductive model. I think I should amend this last point. If one takes to instrumentalism, then (c) does not arise.[17] In other words, (c) is only problematic for the scientific realists.

We spent quite a bit of time on the plausible forms that bridge principles can take so as to fulfill the function of transmitting meaning from the observational terms to the theoretical terms. We talked about operational which were popular once. However, they face a number of serious difficulties. It seems that the way to understand the deductive model is: (i) not to make the distinction between internal principles and bridge principles, and instead (ii) treat all the statements of a theory both as factual statements about the world and as definitions of the theoretical terms of the theory (and perhaps as definitions of the observational terms as well). This is what the network theory of meaning would recommend.

Not surprisingly, there have been a number of alternative proposals for the analysis and understanding of scientific theories. For instance, Sneed (1971) and Stegmuller (1976) propose a structuralist view. Suppes (1967) and van Fraassen (1970)[18] suggest a semantic view. In Chapter 14, we considered the view of Salmon, taking theories as providing underlying causal structures, and also the view of Kitcher, taking theories as unifying schemas.

---

16. As a matter of fact, Quine thinks that there is only one (huge) holistic "whole," which includes both meaning and truth.

17. Instrumentalism takes theories as instruments. Hence the theoretical terms in a theory are not supposed to possess any meaning (in the usual sense).

18. Sneed and Stegmüller's views are difficult to grasp for beginners. A simplified version is available in Stegmüller (1979). The semantic view has had readable introductions in Lambert and Brittan (1987, pp. 141–147) and in Giere (1991).

KEY TERMS INTRODUCED IN THIS CHAPTER

deductive model
(axiomatic model,
syntactic approach)

observational-
theoretical distinction

primary and secondary
qualities

explicit definitions

correspondence rules

operationalism
(operationism)

operational definition

ceteris paribus clause

holism

network definition of
terms

network theory of
meaning

REFERENCES

Both Hempel (1966, chap. 6) and Lambert and Brittan (1987, pp. 115–131) give good introductions.

Carnap (1966, part V) gives details as an authority in the field.

Both Nagel (1961, chap. 6) and Scheffler (1963, pp. 127–181) are classic presentations.

Edwards (1967, "Primary and Secondary Qualities") gives a good introduction to the subject.

Suppe (1977, pp. 3–118) provides a very detailed account of the evolution of the classical view of theories in response to various criticisms.

My own view on the structure of theories can be found in Hung (1981a).

EXERCISES

1. Give examples to illustrate the difficulty in making a sharp distinction between observational and theoretical terms such that the distinction is based on some objectively justifiable basis.

2. Critically discuss (4) as a definition for observation terms (which is based on (2)). Test the adequacy of the definition on the following terms:

   (a) pollens
   (b) gravitational force
   (c) caloric fluid
   (d) Newton's light corpuscles (Chapter 0)

   Which of these are observation terms and which are theoretical according to (4)? Are these conclusions intuitively correct?

3. Is it possible to define the following in terms of explicit definitions where all the definitions are observational terms? (a) Being magnetic, (b) gravitational force, and (c) caloric fluid.

4. Give operational definitions to the following:

   (a) being magnetic
   (b) being deaf (for a person)
   (c) being color-blind (for a chicken)
   (d) being alive (for a person)
   (e) being courageous (for a person)
   (f) having a temperature of n degrees Celsius for a liquid (where n ranges from 0 to 50)

   Check whether these definitions conform to the four requirements:

   (i) the definitions have the right logical form
   (ii) the definitions have only observational terms in the definiens
   (iii) the terms in the definiens are objective, and
   (iv) the definitions are faithful (Section 17.4)

   Would your definitions be useful in the practice of science?

5. Give a number of plausible operational definitions for the following concepts: (a) mass (or weight, if you prefer) and (b) time.

   Discuss, with respect to the definitions you have just proposed, whether there is a real problem with operationalism in view of the fact that the same property or same set of properties can usually be measured by more than one type of operation.

6. Assuming that the notion of 1 meter has been defined with an operational definition, attempt to define 1.5 meters without inventing a further operation.

Chapter 18*

Antirealism I: The Empiricist Challenge

18.1 SEMANTIC INTERPRETATIONS OF THEORIES

In Chapter 16, we presented three views of the existential status of theoretical entities. According to instrumentalism, theoretical entities do not exist. Theoretical terms are mere symbols or calculating devices facilitating the prediction of phenomena. They do not denote objects or types of objects in the world, and they should not be taken as referring symbols. Scientific realism, on the other hand, claims that theoretical terms are meant to denote (that is, have reference), and they will succeed in denoting if the theory introducing these terms is good in the sense that it agrees with empirical data and has high explanatory and predictive power. There are two types of scientific realism. Conservative scientific realism holds that terms employed in commonsense theories for the description of the world have references even though the theories themselves could be far from being correct. This philosophy employs the causal theory of reference for justification. Radical scientific realism begs to differ. For it, the causal theory of reference is faulty. Instead, based on the descriptive theory of reference, it argues that only terms employed in good theories (usually those that occur in mature sciences) denote. In other words, it denies that terms employed by commonsense theories have reference, the reason being that these theories are not only incorrect but seriously incorrect.

---

*This chapter is more advanced and is optional.

So far this is the story on the three positions taken on the reality of theoretical entities.

Leucippus (490–430 B.C.) and Democritus (circa 460–360 B.C.) *theorized* that the world is made of indivisible atoms. John Dalton (1766–1844) developed the idea into the modern theory of chemical atoms. To both scientists and philosophers (and laypersons, for that matter), it is satisfying to think that human wisdom has been able to reveal the ultimate secret of nature: that there is no mystery behind those millions and millions of types of substances with their idiosyncratic properties, and that all these are merely products of combinations of a relatively small number of types of atoms. The atomic theory embedded in Newton-Maxwell's mechanics seemed to be the ultimate picture of reality. Thus the scientific world was full of confidence and optimism toward the turn of the 19th century into the 20th. Even though the full details of the ultimate had yet to be grasped fully, its bold outline seemed to be all there and it seemed to be but a matter of time before the finest details were completely revealed.

Then came the totally unexpected negative result of the Michelson-Morley experiment and the inexplicable phenomenon of the photoelectric effect. The Newtonian atomic picture was found to be wanting and anomalous. The scientific world realized that the ultimate was still quite a distance away. Then came the triumph of the special theory of relativity and that of quantum mechanics. The horizon brightened once more. Could these two distinct theories, based on quite different assumptions, eventually be unified, leading us to the ultimate? A yes-answer seemed to be on hand when Paul Dirac successfully "relativized" quantum mechanics, resulting in what is now known as quantum electrodynamics.

There is still one major outstanding issue, however. In 1916, Einstein generalized the special theory of relativity into the general theory of relativity, which is a geometric theory of gravity. The new theory was exceptionally beautiful and elegant. More important, it was empirically successful. Nevertheless, it was this theory that proved to be the stumbling block for the program of the search

for the ultimate. The reason is that general relativity stood out on its own, refusing to be "dovetailed" into quantum electrodynamics. In the meantime, the field of nuclear physics saw the proliferation of subatomic particles. On top of the three familiar types—the electron, proton, and neutron—hundreds more were discovered. The ultimate cannot be that complicated! Further, instead of just two kinds of forces (gravitational and electromagnetic) governing the motions of the particles, it was discovered that there are at least four kinds of forces, the two additions being the strong and the weak nuclear forces.

The race for a grand unified theory was on. So many of the brightest minds in physics have dedicated themselves in search of a theory that could unify both the hundreds of kinds of particle and the four forces. The vogue is to "invent" more dimensions for our familiar three-dimensional space so as to provide sufficient "room" for the "generation" of these forces and particles. The latest "fashion" is the superstring theory (the supersymmetrical string theory), which, among other things, (i) postulates that space has nine dimensions (six of these nine dimensions have somehow "rolled" themselves up to such an extremely small size that they are beyond observation), and (ii) postulates that the fundamental particles such as the electron and the quark are in reality minute vibrating "strings," whose sizes are of the order of 10^{-33} cm. What a strange and incomprehensible world it is claimed to be!

Philosophers have been skeptical about the reality of what theories purport to convey. In the 18th century, there were great philosophers such as Berkeley and Hume, and then in the 19th century there were celebrated scientists and mathematicians such as Mach and Poincaré. They all doubted the reality of Newton's mechanics and the atomic theory. But the "strangeness" of these two theories is nothing compared to contemporary fundamental particle physics.

Is theorizing a valid means to arrive at the ultimate nature of the world? Can theories reveal what the world is really like? Can they tell us what the fundamental building blocks of nature are? How should we take it when scientists tell us the world is made of atoms (electrons, quarks, or superstrings)? or, for that matter, that space has nine dimensions?

We have just seen how instrumentalism and the two types of scientific realism give their answers. Are these answers justified? How are these answers to be assessed on their relative merits and trustworthiness? Which of these three schools of thought is closest to the truth? To deal with these questions let me introduce you to the field of semantics.

Semantics is a field of language study concerned with the meaning of linguistic expressions. It asks questions such as: How is it that terms such as 'red' and 'table' are meaningful whereas random marks on the beach, say made by waves, are not? How do proper names—for example, 'Abraham Lincoln'—manage to denote what they are intended to denote? How do words acquire the meaning they actually possess? Do theoretical terms acquire meanings in the same way as observational terms? Are all terms meaningful by virtue of the fact that they denote (refer to) something in the real world? If so, what do terms such as 'the,' 'of,' and 'or' refer to? Are *any* terms meaningful by virtue of the fact that they denote? How do the bigger units of language such as the sentence acquire their meaning? Are their meanings derived from the smaller units out of which they are built? These are some of the questions asked in semantics, which you can see are all about meaning. Hence the field is also known as **theory of meaning**. In the 20th century, three major fields of philosophical study are related to cognition. Theory of meaning is one of the three, the other two being theory of truth and theory of knowledge.[1]

If you look back at Chapter 16 you will find that the three schools of thought are based on different theories in semantics. For example, instrumentalism holds that only observational terms are meaningful (while theoretical terms are meaningless—that is, nonreferring). This is a theory in semantics. Both types of scientific realism maintain that we should read the theoretical terms literally, thus taking them as terms that are meant to refer (to things or

features of the real world). Again this is a thesis of meaning. The two types of scientific realism differ, though. One is based on the causal theory of reference, and the other on the descriptive theory of reference. These theories of reference, of course, belong to semantics as well.

It is quite surprising! What we are interested in is what really exists in the world. What does the study of meaning have to do with the discovery of the nature of reality? Nevertheless, from our study so far, **ontology** (the study of the nature of existence) seems to be derivative of semantics (the study of meaning). This is surprising. Certainly it would not strike a layperson that semantics can be the key to ontology. However, when you think deeper, it becomes quite obvious.

For instance, someone might ask, "Are there electrons in the world?" Before an answer is attempted I think it reasonable to ask what one can be talking about when one employs the term 'electron.' Linguistic expressions—for example, proper names, adjectives, nouns, and so on—are, by definition, symbols. As symbols they stand for something (usually) other than themselves. This "standing for" relationship is a sort of pointing relationship. This pointing relationship is roughly what we call meaning. Is it not that by following this pointing relationship we should be able to discover what is at the other end of the pointer? In other words, is it not that in order to know what a pointer points at one should know how the pointing is done? Misunderstanding the pointing relationship can lead us to wrong conclusions and as a result, we may come up with things that have never been pointed at. Adopting the language of this analogy, we can say that the instrumentalists think that theoretical terms are fake pointers pointing at nothing! These terms grammatically behave like pointers (not different from the observational terms), but in fact they are not pointers at all! Conservative scientific realists, on the other hand, think that both commonsense terms and theoretical terms are real

---

1. Western philosophy of the 21st century is roughly divided into **continental philosophy** and **analytic philosophy**. The latter is the mainstream type of philosophy studied in the Anglo-American world. The three fields mentioned here are the central fields of study in analytic philosophy.

pointers and do in fact point at real things. For instance, both 'water' and 'H_2O' point at one and the same type of real thing. Radical scientific realists have doubts about the pointing effectiveness of terms like 'water,' though. Terms from commonsense theories are intended as pointers, but unfortunately they fail to point at anything. Only theoretical terms of good theories succeed in their pointing.

You can now see why semantics is relevant to ontology. In fact, we should say that semantics is the main gateway to it. At least this is a thesis of 20th-century analytic philosophy.[2]

Since the ontological schools of thought we have been studying are founded on semantics, I propose to call them **semantic instrumentalism**, and **semantic scientific realism**[3] (this latter is further divided into conservative scientific realism and radical scientific realism). These "isms" can be seen to be **semantic interpretations of scientific theories**, and the contention between them can be considered a *semantic* debate between realism and antirealism.

Now let's turn to the *epistemic* debate between realism and antirealism.

18.2 EPISTEMIC ATTITUDES TOWARD THEORIES

The debate between realism and antirealism has always been interesting and stimulating. In recent years, it has become a hot issue in the philosophy of science. What else can you expect when so many "strange" results have been discovered in the field of quantum physics! It is difficult for the novice not to get confused—there are so many authorities on each side of the debate, and there are so many ways to formulate the issue. Without trying to be comprehensive, I will, in this chapter, take up one formulation that is mainly due to Bas van Fraassen (1980) and Larry Laudan (1981). This is not to say that other formulations are less important or less inspiring.

This is van Fraassen's (1980, p. 8) formulation of scientific realism:

(1) "Science aims to give us, in its theories, a literally true story of what the world is like; and acceptance of a scientific theory involves the belief that it is true."

Van Fraassen denies both parts of the statement. On the contrary he advocates that:

(2) "Science aims to give us theories which are empirically adequate; and acceptance of a theory involves a belief only that it is empirically adequate." (p. 12)

Having stated van Fraassen's position, let me now proceed to explain it in detail. To start with, van Fraassen is not interested in the semantic issue of realism, the issue we discussed in the last section. In fact, he takes it for granted that that issue is settled. He thinks that "the language of science should be literally construed" (1980, p. 10). In other words, he has settled for semantic scientific realism, that the theoretical terms are meant to denote and should be read as such.[4] So semantically he is a realist. However, epistemically he declares himself an antirealist.

---

2. Before the 17th century, philosophers used to *speculate* about the ultimate nature of reality: the nature of ultimate building blocks of the world. The 17th century saw the emergence of a new type of philosophy known as **epistemology** or **theory of knowledge**. According to it, knowledge claims—in particular, knowledge claims on the nature of things that exist—should be founded on a proper theory of knowledge. One should study how one comes to know and what one can know before one can claim that one knows. Without a proper understanding of the way knowledge can be gathered, any knowledge claim is liable to serious errors. Historically the period from the 17th to the end of the 19th century was the era of epistemology. One of the main tenets of this era is that epistemology is the key to ontology. In contrast, 20th-century analytic philosophers have replaced epistemology with semantics in the study of ontology. There are notable "dissidents," though. Karl Popper is one such. For him, theory of meaning has no role to play in ontology or in the philosophy of science. We will return to the issue of the foundational role of semantics in the study of ontology in Chapter 31, where we cover constructivism.

3. This use of 'semantic scientific realism' differs from that of Laudan (1984, p. 105), where he takes semantic realism to be "the claim that all theories are either true or false and that some theories—we know not which—are true."

4. Even though he has opted for scientific realism, he has not made clear which of the two types he advocates: conservative scientific realism or radical scientific realism.

For him it is one thing to read theoretical statements realistically, and it is another thing to take the *epistemic attitude* that (i) we can accept them without believing that they are true, and (ii) we need not and should not aim for true theoretical statements in practicing science.

Suppose the following theoretical statements have been proposed:

(3) Caloric fluid is indestructible and uncreatable.

(4) Electric fluid flows.

(5) Light waves interfere with each other.

(6) Photons have zero (rest) mass.

According to van Fraassen, we should read them realistically in the sense that we should read terms such as 'caloric fluid,' 'electric fluid,' 'light wave,' and so on as meant to refer to some (types of) things in the real world. In other words, these terms are not mere calculating devices as the instrumentalist would advocate. Whether these terms succeed in referring, whether these statements are indeed true, is of course another matter. For van Fraassen, the meanings of these statements are such that the theoretical terms should be understood literally, as referring terms. This puts him squarely in the realist camp.

However, he recommends that we take an antirealistic attitude toward the *acceptance* of theories. His concern is pragmatic:

(7) When should scientists accept a theory?

(8) What should scientists aim for with respect to theories?

These are questions about the (pragmatic) practice of science—that is, the way to do science. According to van Fraassen, an (epistemic) realist would answer (7) as follows:

(7R) (i) Scientists should accept a theory only when they believe that the theory is true.

(ii) Scientists should tentatively accept a theory only when they tentatively believe that the theory is true.

(iii) Scientists should accept a theory to a certain degree only when they believe that the theory is true to a certain degree.

The answer to (8), for the (epistemic) realist, is:

(8R) Scientists should aim for theories that are (literally) true.

In contrast, van Fraassen, as an epistemic antirealist, would answer the question as follows:

(7A) (i) Scientists should accept a theory only when they believe that the theory is empirically adequate.

(ii) Scientists should tentatively accept a theory only when they tentatively believe that the theory is empirically adequate.

(iii) Scientists should accept a theory to a certain degree only when they believe that the theory is empirically adequate to a certain degree.

(8A) Scientists should aim for theories that are empirically adequate.[5]

What does van Fraassen mean by 'empirically adequate'? Why is he recommending that attitude, the attitude that we should not, as far as theories are concerned, look for truth? Instead he recommends the replacement of truth with empirical adequacy.

You may recall that theories are invented to explain and to predict (Chapters 8 and 15). A scientific theory is said to be **empirically adequate** if it can explain all available empirical data (data through observation), and all of its predictions turn out to be correct. Of course we can relativize the term. We can say that empirical adequacy

---

5. Of course, van Fraassen is well aware of the other "virtues" of good theories—for example, high explanatory power and high predictive power (Sections 8.3 and 8.4).

comes in degrees. We can say that some theories are more empirically adequate than others because they explain more data and they predict more occurrences correctly.

It should be clear that truth implies empirical adequacy but not vice versa. If a theory is true, then, of course, it can explain all the available data, and it can make correct predictions about the future. But empirical adequacy does not imply truth. I'll give an example. There is hardly any theory that can claim as much empirical success as Newton's mechanics before the 20th century. By any standard, the empirical adequacy of Newton's theory was unsurpassed. It can explain most, if not all, the motions of the heavenly bodies and the motions of the objects on earth. It makes correct predictions of numerous types of phenomena, from orbits of comets to trajectories of projectiles. And yet it is well recognized that the theory is false, the more correct theory being Einstein's theory of relativity. A more comprehensible example is the geocentric theory of Ptolemy, which we studied in Chapter 7. Ptolemy proposed his theory in the 2nd century. With modifications and refinements, it ruled the field of astronomy for over 1,400 years, until Copernicus and Galileo came up with some better ideas. Ptolemy's theory was certainly empirically adequate to a high degree and yet it is recognized as false.

In Chapter 9, we studied the conventionalism of Poincaré, Duhem, and Quine. According to conventionalism, given a set of empirical data, there are an infinite number of possible theories that can explain them. Obviously not all these theories can be (literally) true. I think Poincaré, Duhem, and Quine have conclusively proved that empirical adequacy does not imply truth. Moreover, they have also shown that two or more theories can be **empirically equivalent** in the sense that whatever empirical data that can be explained by one can also be explained by the others and vice versa. We sometimes say that these theories are **empirically indistinguishable** or **evidentially indistinguishable**. All of these are based on the thesis of underdetermination of theory by empirical data, which has been so successfully argued by conventionalism.

According to van Fraassen, what we can know is that a certain theory is empirically adequate, in that it has successfully explained all the available empirical data. Since that theory is one among many (in fact infinite) possible theories that are equally empirically adequate in the explanation of the same set of data, we have little ground to claim that the theory is true. Of course, we can be lucky in striking at the truth with this theory. But we have little evidence of that because the chance of its being *the* true theory is small (in fact zero) when it is but one of an infinite number of possible theories. In fact, the more reasonable conclusion is that our theory is false or at least that our theory is most likely to be false (since the chance of its being true is zero).

Let's illustrate with the clock example that we gave in Section 9.2. You have a clock, on the face of which are three clock hands going round and round. Your empirical data consist of records of positions of these hands at various times of the day. What is required is a theory to explain these data. As I pointed out, there are a limitless number of possible theories to explain them. One can postulate that it is a spring-driven clock, or a battery-powered clock, or something else. The arrangement of cogwheels in the clock can vary as much as your imagination would allow. Of course, you need not postulate cogwheels at all. The means of transmission of movement can perhaps be string and pulleys. There is no reason why one particular theory out of all these possibilities can claim to be the true one. What we can claim, however, is that the particular theory you have invented can account for all the observed data, namely, that it is empirically adequate. That's all one can claim, and that's all one should claim, according to van Fraassen. Since this is the limit of our claim, and it would be irrational to claim what we are not justified in claiming, it follows that science should not aim at truth for its theories, but should only aim at empirical adequacy.

It is important to note that van Fraassen is *not* an instrumentalist, for he does acknowledge that the terms of a theory are meant to denote types of things in the real world, and theoretical statements are meant to mean what they say, and are either true or false, just as ordinary statements are.

However, he thinks that it would not be reasonable to claim any of them to be true or to try to discover those that are true. This is the kind of epistemic attitude that he recommends to the scientific world. Being a noninstrumentalist, he does believe that the world consists of more things than those that meet the eye—for example, macroscopic objects like tables and chairs, trees, and stones. However, we will never know what those "other things" are. Scientists say that there are electrons, atoms, photons, neutrinos, and so on according to their theories. But since these theories are but a few among an infinite number of other equally empirically adequate theories, the likelihood of these theories being true is slim, and it would be foolhardy to take them as true.

To sum up, for van Fraassen, semantically scientific realism is correct but epistemically his position is that of an antirealist.

18.3 REALISM VERSUS ANTIREALISM: THE DEBATE

Let me open the section by quoting Laudan (1981, p. 242):

> There is a difference between wanting to believe something and having good reasons for believing it. All of us would like realism to be true; we would like to think that science works because it has got a grip on how things really are. But such claims have yet to be made out. Given the present state of the art, it can only be wish fulfilment that gives rise to the claim that realism, and realism alone, explains why science works.

It would be nice if (epistemic) realism were defensible. However, neither van Fraassen nor Laudan is optimistic about its defensibility. Their challenge to the thesis of realism is from the traditional empiricist point of view. Let's study some traditional realist attempts to defend that position

against the onslaught followed by the empiricists' response.

A. The Theory Extension Argument

We just saw how conventionalism argues that for any set of empirical data there are an infinite number of possible theories capable of explaining the data. We illustrated the argument with the clock analogy. Given records of the positions of the clock hands, there are an infinite number of possible theories on the clockwork mechanism that can adequately explain these records. Nevertheless, one could say that surely a spring clock is very different from an electric clock. As far as the movements of the clock hands are concerned, the two types of mechanisms may be behaviorally the same. Yet if we consider these two types of mechanisms within a wider context, we may yet be able to predict behavioral differences. For instance, we may imagine the clock to be subjected to some strong magnetic force. The spring theory (ST) and the electric theory (ET) may, for example, yield different predictions on the change of speed of the clock hands. ST predicts a slowing down of the hands whereas ET predicts a speeding up. If so, by conducting an actual experiment by placing the clock near a strong magnet, we can eliminate one of the two rival theories.

In the jargon of philosophy of science, we say that ST and **ET**, when **extended** into the field of magnetism, may yield different empirical predictions. These predictions can be employed to weed out the false theories, thus indirectly isolating the true theories.[6]

There are two obvious rejoinders to this "realistic" defense. (i) Since the possible number of theories that can satisfactorily explain the data is infinite, the weeding out of one particular class of theories will still leave an infinite number of empirically adequate theories behind. This is not such a good argument, however. The realist can claim that what are now left behind are better theories, and

---

6. See the discussions in Chapter 7 on crucial tests.

such theories are probably closer to the truth. (ii) A better rejoinder is to make use of the Duhem-Quine thesis (Section 9.3). Suppose the strong magnet does slow down the clock. Do we need to give up ET in such a situation? After all, the experimental outcome contradicts ET's prediction, but, according to Duhem and Quine, we need not give up ET. We can always blame the *current* magnetic theory. After all, it is this theory that, when applied to the clock, yields the prediction. We can modify the magnetic theory in such a manner that ET predicts the slowing down of the clock. In fact, this is not the only possible line of defense. We can amend other auxiliary hypotheses. For instance, we can claim that it is not true that the clock is well insulated from other kinds of interference as assumed: a force other than the magnetic force is interfering.

Van Fraassen (1980) gives a more realistic example as an illustration. Let's give the name '$TN(v)$' to Newton's mechanics plus the postulate that the sun is moving with an absolute velocity v. It is well known that $TN(0)$ is empirically indistinguishable from $TN(v)$ for any values of v. In other words, $TN(0)$ and $TN(v)$ are empirically equivalent. Can we, by incorporating, say, a theory of electricity into Newton's mechanics force $TN(0)$ and $TN(v)$ to yield different predictions so that the two theories become empirically distinguishable? Van Fraassen (1980) gives a detailed discussion of this and his conclusion is no. Well, perhaps the realist can try the next defense.

B. The Miracle Defense

Suppose there is a theory T so powerful that it can explain every piece of available empirical data. It explains the orbits of all the heavenly bodies, planets, asteroids, comets, and whatever. It also explains the motions of everything on earth, not only motions of things like projectiles and spinning tops, but also motions of animals such as insects, birds, fish, and mammals. It also explains the growth of plants, the spread of disease, the transmission of signals like radio signals, light signals, color changes, smell changes, shape changes, and so on. Indeed T is so powerful that it has successfully explained *everything* so far observed. (Of course it is able to explain why I am typing these very words as well.) Now the miracle argument runs as follows:

Of course it is logically possible that T is false even though its explanatory power is so very high, so high that it has explained everything. But it is very unlikely to be false. For a false theory to be able to have such high explanatory power is a miracle. To put it differently, for a false theory to be so highly explanatory would require a coincidence of miraculous dimension. Note that the things that have been explained are what *actually* have happened in the real world. Unless T is also true of the real world, how can it manage to explain so many actual happenings?

If you are not convinced by this argument, let us accentuate it. Suppose T is not only able to explain every observed happening in the past, but also able to predict precisely what is going to happen in the future. Suppose T has been around for the last 10 years. Every day scientists make forecasts based on T: on the weather, of course, on the behavior of the stock market, on the traffic situation in every street, on wars, on famines, on earthquakes, indeed on every detail of life. And suppose all these forecasts have so far proved to be correct. The miracle argument claims that it would be unexplainably miraculous for a false theory to be able to do that, to be able to make such precise predictions in such a scale! (It is comparable to a blind mouse getting out of a maze without ever running into a wall or making a wrong turn![7])

The miracle argument is a strong argument. Of course we have accentuated it by pushing it to the extreme. None of the theories in science are anywhere near that sort of success. But if there were such a theory, the realist would say, won't it be reasonable to claim truth for that (perfect) theory?

---

7. You might say that there is no reason why the mouse could not have *smelled* its way out.

If so, won't it be reasonable to claim at least approximate truth for the less perfect theories, which are nevertheless quite successful? The proximity to truth can be measured in terms of the amount of success, so it is believed. Since many theories in the mature sciences such as physics, chemistry, biology, astronomy, earth science, and so on are very successful, the realist considers it reasonable to take them as at least approximately true. Since these theories are approximately true, their theoretical terms should refer to real entities. Thus, according to the realist, electrons, radio waves, and such others, all exist.

There are three commonly known rejoinders to the miracle argument. First, as the conventionalists have pointed out, there are always an infinite number of possible theories capable of explaining the same set of empirical data. In other words, empirical data can never fully determine theories. Even if there were a perfect theory T such as the one sketched, there would be an infinite number of equally perfect theories explaining the same.[8] If T is true, what about the others? Why T and not the others? Take the clock analogy. If a theory postulating a mechanism of 23 cogwheels, each having 17 cogs, can explain adequately the empirical data on the movements of the clock hands, a theory postulating a mechanism of 32 cogwheels, each having 71 cogs, can easily be concocted to explain the same data adequately. What reason can there be to conclude that the first theory is true whereas the second is false? What justification can there be to claim that the "world" is made of 23 cogwheels rather than 32 cogwheels?[9]

The second rejoinder is as follows. Before Darwin proposed his theory of evolution, it was believed that the wonderfully harmonious and orderly organization of the natural world can only be the product of an extremely intelligent creator.

For instance, the human body is a wonderful machine. (No one can deny that.) The highly organized societies of the bees and the ants have always been a source of wonder. Every living thing, plant or animal, fits in (almost) exactly with its ecological environment. As the seasons proceed in annual cycles, so do plant lives and animal lives. The whole natural world follows the progress of time as smoothly and effortlessly as clockwork. What can be a better proof of the existence of a creator! It would be a miracle of incredible coincidence if the natural world were not the product of a grand design! And yet Darwin and his followers were able to show that given time (millions and millions of years) the exquisite organization of the natural world can be the product, not of a conscious act of creation but the outcome of blind chaos. The motive force of evolution is chance and randomness. The emergence of orderliness is explained as the product of competition, adaption, and selection. According to the theory, progress toward order is slow. But given sufficient time, the closeness of fit of the living things to their temporal and spatial environment can be amazing. The mechanism is actually quite simple (if we do not demand details). Competition leads to the elimination of the unfit, leaving the fit. After millions of years, what we encounter are the "leftovers"—that is, the fit. No wonder everything fits in so well, as if by design.

Let's apply the theory of evolution to theories. Scientific theories have been competing for over 2,300 years. It is not surprising that theories of the mature sciences are empirically very successful, that they fit the empirical data well. The unsuccessful ones have simply been eliminated, and the successful ones have been improved on. We need not postulate a "grand design" to explain the fit. We need not conclude that the world has to be made

---

8. In recent years, there has been great optimism that the superstring theory could be developed into a "theory of everything," a theory that can explain everything. Granting that the optimism is justified, it is interesting to note David Gross, a leading theorist in the field, reporting, "And remarkably enough for the heterotic string, we have found a whole class of solutions, in fact millions and millions of possible solutions" (Davies and Brown, 1988, p. 142).

9. In science, there is a practice of preferring the simpler of two equally adequate theories. But this is a pragmatic move. There is no linkage between simplicity and truth. Anyway, no one has produced a satisfactory criterion of simplicity yet (Section 9.4).

exactly the way the theories foretell in order for the theories to fit the data. According to van Fraassen, the exactness of fit is simply the result of competition, selection, and adaptation. There is no plot. There is no mystery. And there is no miracle.

There is a third rejoinder. It is by Larry Laudan, an important historian and philosopher of science. Let me quote him:

> Now, what the history of science offers us is a plethora of theories that were both successful and (so far as we can judge) [yet] nonreferential with respect to many of their central explanatory concepts.... Let me add a few more prominent examples to the list: ... the phlogiston theory of chemistry, the caloric theory of heat, ..., the electromagnetic ether, the theory of circular inertia. (Laudan, 1981, p. 232)

Altogether he listed 12 theories from the history of science. According to him, all these were once empirically successful in both explanation and prediction, and yet they are all false and their central terms do not refer to any (types of) entities. If false and nonreferring theories can be successful, won't it be rash to conclude that successful theories are either true or approximately true?

C. Salmon's Causal Theory of Explanation

Recall that, as we saw in Sections 14.4 and 14.5, Salmon argues that statistical relevance needs to be explained in terms of causal relevance, and causal relevance is typically provided by theories that postulate underlying mechanisms. These underlying mechanisms have to be *real* in order to produce the observed statistical regularities. The short answer to this is that even if we accept that statistical regularities need to be explained in terms of underlying mechanisms, the correct kind of mechanism need not be the kind postulated by the theories of the day. The theories of the day may be extremely

adequate, but as argued before there are an infinite number of other theories that can do the same. What justifies the particular claim that this one rather than that one is the true one?

D. The Problem of "Theoretical" Truth

What is meant by truth? When the realist claims that the aim of science as far as theories are concerned is to produce *true* theories, what can she mean by true theories? The problem of truth has puzzled philosophers since Aristotle. What is truth? We do not have space here to go into this topic, which is both exciting and intriguing. It is sufficient to point out that most realists (in the context of our discussion so far) subscribe to a theory known as **the correspondence theory of truth**.[10] Briefly, it says that a statement is true if and only if it *corresponds* with the facts. Here is a statement, S. There is the real world with all its facts. S is true if and only if there is a fact F in the real world that corresponds to the statement. Which is the fact that corresponds to the statement? Where is it? How is it to be located? It is said that the sentence underlying the statement in the particular context in which it is uttered should lead us to the fact if there is one. Each sentence means something. It is through this meaning (when applied to a certain situation) that the sentence leads us to the fact. For instance, if Mary says to Peter:

(9) The person behind you is smiling.

This sentence plus the context will enable the listener to see that it is the person behind Peter that is being talked about. Following this direction, the listener can check whether the statement is true. It is true if there is really a fact "positioned" at the back of Peter. In short, the sentence through its meaning (and context) will "point" in the direction where we can find the corresponding fact. If that fact is there, then the statement is true. This is the correspondence theory of truth in a nutshell.

Let's give another example. Is the statement (10) true?

---

10. We touched on this theory before in Section 9.6.

(10) Galileo trained his newly invented telescope at the moon in 1609.

According to the correspondence theory, (10) is true if and only if there is a certain fact corresponding to it. Which fact? To find this fact, we can follow the "direction" of sentence (10). That sentence says that there should be a person known as Galileo who in 1609 trained his newly invented telescope at the moon. So following this "direction" if there is a fact where the sentence "points," then (10) is true, otherwise (10) is false. Of course you and I cannot trace the route from the sentence to Galileo because Galileo is no more. But suppose an angel can. Then, if the angel, following the route, arrives at the astronomer Galileo and "sees" him training his telescope at the moon, then we say that (10) has been proved to be true. Unfortunately we do not have such angels around. Nevertheless, we can rely on other humans to find the fact for us. For example, some of Galileo's contemporaries may have witnessed the event. They may have recorded their findings on paper, which we can take advantage of. In short, we can say that *in principle*, (10) can be empirically checked.

What about (11)? Can it be empirically checked?

(11) There is a gravitational field in this room.

We learned in Chapters 1 and 6 that (11) cannot be tested directly but can be tested indirectly. 'Gravitational field' is a theoretical term and it denotes an abstract theoretical entity. Abstract theoretical entities cannot be seen directly. Nevertheless, their presence can be tested indirectly. For instance, we can drop a pen. If the pen should fall downward, we say that this is a piece of evidence that there is a gravitational field pointing downward.

It is here that the empiricist antirealist would raise the following difficulty. It is reasonable to employ the correspondence theory of truth for (9) and (10). After all, these sentences are made up of observational terms, and you can identify the kinds of objects referred to by them. But (11) contains a theoretical term, and there is no way to match that term with the corresponding entity by observation.

It is here she doubts that it makes sense to try to assign a truth value to (11). A modest antirealist, like van Fraassen, while accepting that (11) has a truth value, will deny that we can ever have any good reason to assign one to it. Let me repeat the antirealist's argument here. Since the falling of objects downward can equally well be explained by an infinite number of theories other than the theory of gravitation, there is no good reason why we should believe that (11) is true. Were we able to "see" gravitation directly, we would be able to ascertain the truth value of (11) irrespective of how many rival theories there are.

Let's return to the original question. Can (11) be empirically checked? The answer is yes. But the kind of empirical check it allows is quite different from the kind allowed by (9) and (10). Since the latter two are couched in observational terms only, it makes sense to give them truth values. On the other hand, it is unreasonable to assign a truth value to (11) since it contains a theoretical term.

There are many versions and interpretations of the correspondence theory of truth. We are here adopting an empiricist interpretation, which requires one to know *empirically* what sort of entities (11) is dealing with before one can reasonably say that it is true. Since theoretical terms refer to unobservables, and (11) contains a theoretical term, it is beyond good reason to claim truth for (11). That's why the empiricist antirealist considers it unreasonable to hold that science aims to give us, in its theories, a literally true story of what the world is like. She suggests, instead, the more modest aim that requires science to give us only empirically adequate theories.

E. The Problem of Approximate Truth

Related to the problem of truth is the problem of approximate truth. Up to the present, there is no remotely viable notion of **approximate truth** (sometimes called **verisimilitude**) in the literature. A realist, however, requires not only the notion of truth, but also the notion of approximate truth as shown in the third clause of (7R). The realist knows from experience that the most she can hope for is that the present theories in science are *approximately* true. It is very unlikely that any of these theories, including those in the so-called mature sciences, are exactly true. That's why the realist requires an acceptable notion of approximate truth in order to talk about realism as an epistemic attitude: to accept a theory to a certain degree is to accept it as true to a certain degree. But how is approximate truth to be measured? For example, is the caloric theory of heat approximately true? What about the phlogiston theory? What about Newton's mechanics?

Comparatively it is much easier to define approximate shape. We can say that the shape of Italy is approximately that of a boot, and that the letter 'S' looks like the numeral '5.' We can even be quantitative on the notion of approximation of shape. For instance, we can say that the regular hexagon is more like a circle than the square is, and the regular polygon with 100 sides is even more like a circle. Since the circle can be considered a regular polygon with an infinite number of sides, we can establish a measure, measuring the proximity of a polygon to a circle. But can we do anything remotely similar in the case of approximate truth? It is very unlikely, since truth has more, many more "shapes" than shapes.

The measure of proximity to truth is actually made even more difficult, if not impossible, by the fact that we do not know, and cannot know, what "shape" truth itself takes. Let me explain. We know that a regular polygon with a hundred sides is approximately a circle. How? We compare the two. We have knowledge of the shape of the hundred-sided polygon as well as of the circle, and thus we can compare. Note that it is the knowledge of the shape of *both* items that enable us to compare. However, in the case of the assessment of the proximity to truth of a theory, (i) we do not know what the theoretical entities postulated by the theory look like (see D), and (ii) we certainly do not know what true reality is like (otherwise we would not need to theorize). For example, we cannot say how close the caloric theory is to reality, because (i) we do not know the "physical look" of the fluid, and (ii) we certainly do

not know the true nature of heat. In such a situation, how can we know how close the theory is to truth? In short, if we want to measure the distance between two points we need to know where these two points are. In our case, we know vaguely the position of one point and have no knowledge at all of the position of the other. How can we know how far the points are apart?

F. The Observational-Theoretical Distinction: The Achilles' Heel of the Antirealist?

It looks as though realism has been cornered. Neither the theory extension argument nor the miracle defense seem to work. On top of this, realism is facing the problem of theoretical truth and the problem of approximate truth. Has the antirealist, therefore, won the war? Let us see.

In Section 17.2, we discussed whether the observational-theoretical distinction (OT distinction) is tenable. If it turns out to be untenable, this may then be the Achilles' heel of antirealism.

Antirealism of van Fraassen's variety is based on

(12) Conventionalism la: Given a set of empirical data (in the form of observation statements), there are available many possible theories to "cope" with them (Chapter 9).

You can see from (12) how antirealism depends on the tenability of the OT distinction.

According to van Fraassen, the aim of theorizing is **to save the phenomena**—that is, to produce theories that can explain what is observable (the observable being the phenomena). The distinction between what is observable and what is not is therefore crucial to his thesis. If that distinction is indeed untenable then that thesis should collapse. Can van Fraassen "wriggle" his way out of this quandary? Let's look at his defense.

The OT distinction was originally proposed as a foundational assumption of the deductive model of theories (Chapter 15). This is a structural thesis. Through the bridge principles theoretical terms supposedly acquire their meaning from the observation terms. This is a semantic theory. If the OT distinction is not tenable, both the structural thesis and the semantic thesis will collapse. Instrumentalism is an ontological thesis (Chapter 16). It is also based on the OT distinction. You can see the pivotal role played by this distinction in various issues on the understanding of theories. The question is: does epistemic antirealism rise and fall with the OT distinction as well?

Van Fraassen argues that there is a basic difference between his epistemic thesis and the other three theses. His is a pragmatic thesis whereas the other three are absolutist theses. Let me explain. Take instrumentalism. Being an ontological thesis, it relies on the absolute distinction between observational and theoretical terms on the ground that things either exist or do not exist. There is no such thing as partial existence. According to instrumentalism, observational terms stand for (types of) things that exist, whereas theoretical terms, being instrumental in nature, do not refer. The boundary between the observational and the theoretical marks the boundary between existence and nonexistence. Since the latter boundary is absolute, the former should also be absolute. In Section 17.2, we saw how such an *absolute* distinction has been challenged. The distinction, if there is a distinction, is at best relative, depending on the physiology of human beings, which varies from individual to individual, from culture to culture, and from time to time. In other words, instrumentalism is not just based on an OT distinction but on an *absolute* OT distinction.

Similarly, the tenability of the structural thesis and the semantic thesis is also dependent on the OT distinction being absolute.

But the epistemic thesis, according to van Fraassen, is quite different. A relative OT distinction will do. The epistemic thesis argues that it is extravagant to aim for truth through theories. The reasonable and achievable aim of theorizing is not truth, but empirical adequacy. Here 'reasonable' and 'achievable' are relative terms. They are relative

to *us*. 'Observability,' for van Fraassen, is also a relative term. Things are observable relative to *us*. In practice, we classify things as observable and unobservable, roughly of course, and van Fraassen's thesis does not require exact or absolute distinction. It is a pragmatic thesis, remember.

The manner in which we are physiologically constituted enables us to see tables and chairs with our naked eyes. These are clearly observables. On the other hand our physiology does not enable us to see atoms and molecules. These are clearly unobservables. In between, some of the "unobservables" can be made visible by a simple magnifying glass while others require stronger devices. There is no clear line between the observable and the unobservable. But, as a pragmatic notion, the distinction is useful[11] and we do, in the practice of science, make such a distinction. Based on this rough and vague pragmatic distinction, van Fraassen. argues that science, in its theories, should aim for empirical adequacy instead of truth, and acceptance of a theory should imply the belief that the theory is empirically adequate rather than that it is true. Since these are the epistemic attitudes recommended for us *humans*, it is reasonable that these attitudes are tailor-made for *humans* with their characteristic human physiological constitution. Had we been Martians or some other kind of being, the epistemic attitudes recommended might be different. For example, angels may be able to see theoretical entities. In such a case, van Fraassen might recommend to the angels the epistemic attitude that science, in its theories, should aim at truth.

Let me conclude by referring back to Larry Laudan's comment made earlier (beginning of Section 18.3): "There is a difference between wanting to believe something and having good reasons for believing it." It would be nice if realism were true. But the empiricists seem to have succeeded in showing that epistemically we should be antirealists. In Chapter 31, we will take up the debate between realism and antirealism again, but from a different direction. There the challenge is made by constructivism.

---

11. There is no sharp boundary between being smooth and being rough (as applied to surfaces), yet the distinction is useful.

KEY TERMS INTRODUCED IN THIS CHAPTER

semantics

theory of meaning

ontology

semantic instrumentalism

semantic scientific realism

semantic interpretation of scientific theories

epistemology

theory of knowledge

empirically adequate

empirically equivalent

empirically indistinguishable

evidentially indistinguishable

theory extension

correspondence theory of truth

approximate truth

verisimilitude

save the phenomena

REFERENCES

Van Fraassen (1980, chaps. 2 and 3) can be taken as the basic text, a condensed version of which appears as van Fraassen (1976).

Laudan's view is presented in Laudan (1981).

Kourany (1987, Part 5) has a collection of four representative papers on the debate, which are all readable.

Boyd et al. (1991, chaps. 10–14) is a further collection of papers on the subject.

Churchland and Hooker (1985) is an anthology of articles on van Fraassen's antirealism. Chihara's (1993) critique focuses on van Fraassen's observational-theoretical distinction.

On the correspondence theory of truth: Edwards (1967, "Correspondence Theory of Truth") gives a good introduction, and Austin (1950) makes a significant contribution to the subject.

EXERCISES

1. Assess whether the following theories are empirically adequate, and whether they are acceptable to van Fraassen.

    (a) The caloric theory of heat (Section 15.3)
    (b) The two-fluid theory of electricity (Section 15.4)
    (c) Newton's particle theory of light (Chapter 0)

2. Assess whether the following pairs of theories are empirically equivalent. If not, can one or both members of the pair be modified resulting in empirical equivalence?

    (a) The two-fluid theory of electricity (by Dufay and Nollet) versus the one-fluid theory of electricity (by Franklin). (You may want to consult Holton and Roller, 1958, pp. 472–474.)
    (b) Newton's particle theory of light versus Huygens' wave theory of light.

3. Imagine a lightbulb and three switches sticking out of the top of a box (which happens to be painted black and is known as a blackbox). The lightbulb glows when and only when switches A and B, or switches A and C, are on. (Let's call this the phenomenon.)

    Design an electric circuit with a single battery (positioned inside the blackbox) to account for the phenomenon. (Your design of circuit and battery can be called a theory.)

    How many possible positions can there be for the single battery in your design?

    If more than one battery is employed, how many more possible positions can there be for these batteries?

    In view of these cases, discuss van Fraassen's antirealism.

4. Continuing from the last exercise, do you think it possible to produce a measure of truth or of approximate truth to assess the degree of truth of the various theories corresponding to the various positions of the batteries? (Assume the validity of the correspondence theory of truth.)

PART IV SUMMARY

What are theories? Can they yield reasonable answers to the question of ultimate reality? Can they reveal to us the ultimate constituents of the world?

In **Chapter 15**, we presented the classical view of theories. According to this view, science is written in two languages, the observational language and the theoretical language. Every theory has two parts: a set of internal principles and a set of bridge principles. The former purports to describe the "ultimate reality" in theoretical terms, whereas the latter forms a sort of bridge linking the theoretical terms with the observational terms. It is claimed that this represents the logical structure of theories. Such a structure "dovetails" well with Hempel's covering-law thesis of explanation. According to Hempel, theories explain phenomenal generalizations through deduction employing both internal and bridge principles as premises. Moreover, the same process should enable the prediction of further phenomena. Since deduction plays the main structural role, it is appropriate that this conception of theories should be called the deductive model of theories.

But ought we to take the "tales" given by scientific theories as literally true? Are the theoretical entities postulated meant to be taken as real entities that exist in the world? Scientific realism answers yes to both questions, thus affirming that theories are means, if not the means, to the solution of the riddle of ultimate reality. There are two types of scientific realism. The conservatives, relying on the causal theory of meaning, think that both the theoretical language and the observational language refer to the same things. Hence both commonsense objects and theoretical entities exist. However, the picture painted by the theoretical language is more accurate, whereas that given by the observational language is usually crude and approximate and can even be totally wrong. The radicals, on the other hand, think that only the theoretical language refers. Thus, for them, only theoretical entities exist. Their convictions are based on the descriptivist theory of meaning.

Opposing scientific realism are the instrumentalists. According to them the terms of the theoretical language are mere calculating devices and should not be taken as referring. Common sense provides us with a correct picture of reality. We perceive the world as it really is through our senses. It is thus both futile and senseless to try to reach "ultimate reality" through theorizing. What we see, what we hear, what we feel, what we taste, and what we smell are the ultimate reality. We need go no further. This debate between scientific realism and instrumentalism is the subject of **Chapter 16.**

Chapter 17 returns to the study of the classical analysis of theories. In the last few decades, there has been much dissatisfaction with it. Objections have been made against the distinction between internal principles and bridge principles, and strong arguments are directed toward the observational-theoretical dichotomy. Besides these two issues, Chapter 17 also examines the question of meaningfulness of theoretical terms: Can bridge principles perform the function of "conveying" meaning from the observational terms to the theoretical terms? If so, how do they manage to do it? One suggestion is that the bridge principles take the form of operational definitions. The theory of operational definition has been found to be too simplistic. In its place, the network theory of meaning has been suggested.

The last chapter, **Chapter 18**, returns to the debate between realism and antirealism. There is a difference, however. Instead of having the debate at the ontological level, Bas van Fraassen and Larry Laudan challenge realism at the epistemic level. They assert that empirical adequacy should be the criterion for the acceptability of theories. It is unreasonable to aim for true (or approximately true) theories. In other words, for them, theories should be judged by their abilities to save the phenomena, because there is no way to know whether a theory is true or approximately true. They base their arguments on the thesis of underdetermination of theories by empirical data, which the conventionalists Poincaré and Duhem propounded almost a century ago. In short, antirealism claims that science should and can only aim at empirically adequate theories, whereas realism holds that it is not extravagant to aim for true theories and science should do so.

But this brand of antirealism is based on the observational-theoretical distinction, which seems untenable. However, van Fraassen thinks that his antirealism does not depend on a sharp and objective distinction between the observational and the theoretical. He claims that since acceptance is a human action, it is perfectly reasonable to have criteria of acceptance based on a notion that is relative to humans. The vague notions we humans have of the distinction is quite adequate for the practical purposes of doing science. In other words, his is a pragmatic thesis.

So, How Does Science Work?

Book I is now drawing to a close. Its 18 chapters should have given you a fairly detailed picture of most, if not all, the fundamentals of the philosophy of science. Let's pause for a while, look back, summarize, and ask these questions: Do we now have a better idea of what science is and how it works? Is science in general trustworthy?

The **classical tradition** represents the orthodox view in the philosophy of science. According to it, truth and explanation are the twin main aims of science. And our presentation so far is based mainly on that tradition.

Book I has four parts. **Part I** covers the basic **types of reasoning** in science: deduction, induction, statistical reasoning, and probabilistic reasoning. **Part II** is on **methods of truth**, mainly methods of discovery and methods of justification of hypotheses. That section is mostly concerned with the logic of indirect tests and the ways hypotheses are supported and warranted by theories. The methods of tests and theories have been standard practices in science since Galileo. Historically they have proved to be extremely effective and successful. However, according to the conventionalists, given any set of empirical data there are an infinite number of theories that can satisfy and explain them. In fact, they argue convincingly that one can hold onto whatever theory one may prefer irrespective of any amount of unfavorable empirical discovery. This argument applies not only to high-level theories, but to low-level hypotheses as well. The simple reason is that in any indirect test auxiliary hypotheses have to be employed, and we can always alter the auxiliary hypotheses to protect the hypothesis under test.

If we can really hold onto any theory or hypothesis (as true) come what may, truth would become meaningless, at least with respect to the practice of science. The search for truth would be a farce.

Here is a serious conflict between practical science and theoretical philosophy. If our philosophical analysis of practical science leads to controversial results such as the meaninglessness (or relativity) of 'scientific truth,' should we give up the traditional methods of science or should we look for better philosophical analyses so that we can understand the workings of science better? Perhaps there is some flaw in the conventionalists' arguments. Or perhaps the classical tradition is basically misguided in that its analysis of indirect tests and scientific theories is fundamentally mistaken.

The second aim of science is **explanation**, which we studied in detail in **Part III**. According to the classical tradition, explanation is a kind of deductive argument with laws of nature playing a pivotal role as premises. This is the famous covering-law model. Is this a correct description of explanation? Does it represent the kind(s) of explanation traditionally practiced in science? The general opinion is that this deductive theory is certainly useful, but it provides only a partial picture of explanation at best. There are quite a few rival analyses of explanation. The better-known ones are contextual theory, causal theory, and unificatory theory. These three theories as well as the covering-law model are all formulated within the framework of the classical tradition. What if the classical tradition is fundamentally faulty? For instance, according to the conventionalists, the classical analysis of theoretical explanation cannot be right because scientific theories are not meant to explain. They are merely economical representations of phenomena.

Part IV is on truths of a special kind. Truths come in all sorts, from mundane truths such as truths about what you had for breakfast this morning to truths about the mysteries of life and the beginning of the universe. There is, however, one special kind of truth that kindles deep interest, curiosity, and concern in the philosopher. It is the truths about the basic constituents of the world. What is the world made of? What is the world really like? Part IV is on this question of ultimate truths about **reality**.

It is generally believed that scientific theories will yield us reasonable answers to this question of reality. However, the instrumentalists are skeptical. The epistemic antirealists are also skeptical, albeit to a lesser degree.

Is theorizing a legitimate means to the true nature of reality? Obviously it all depends on what theories are. According to the classical tradition, theories are deductive systems in the form of internal principles and bridge principles. There are serious doubts about the correctness of this analysis. If this classical analysis is a mistake—a serious mistake—the debate between realists and antirealists could be in vain. Perhaps the classical view should be replaced.

This was what Thomas Kuhn and Paul Feyerabend suggested in the 1960s. Their Weltanschauung analyses heralded in what is now known as constructivism, which, though controversial, is interesting, exciting, and enlightening in many respects. It throws new light on many of the old problems and has become very influential. This revolutionary philosophy will occupy the larger part of Book II, the second half of this book.

Book II presents a digest history of the philosophy of science. We start with **rationalism**, which dates back to the time of the ancient Greeks. It was the dominant philosophy of science right up to the 17th century. Then **empiricism**, led by Francis Bacon (1561–1626) in philosophy and by Galileo (1564–1642) in science, gradually took over. It reached its climax in the first half of the 20th century with the rise of **logical positivism**, which, in simple terms, is empiricism formulated in modern logic. Together with Popper's falsificationism, logical positivism set down a rigorous, detailed, and viable philosophy of science, which has become variously known as the **classical tradition**, the orthodox view, the standard view, or the received view. It is in terms of this classical tradition that Book I approaches the problems of truth, explanation, and reality.

Constructivism and other post-positivist philosophies arose in the 1960s out of dissatisfaction with the classical tradition. It was a revolution, whose end is not yet in sight and whose merits are difficult to assess. Perhaps the picture will become clearer with the rapid development of artificial intelligence, which should have significant implications for the philosophy of science.

I broadly divide the field of philosophy of science into **macro-philosophy** and **micro-philosophy**. In macro-philosophy we study broad perspectives, which are often called schools of thought. Rationalism, empiricism, logical positivism, and constructivism are typically broad perspectives. These schools offer basic philosophical ideas and principles. In contrast, micro-philosophy studies problems and (proposed) solutions framed and formulated typically within a chosen philosophical perspective or school of thought. You can see that Book II is on macro-philosophy, while Book I—which covers the major problems and (proposed) solutions within the classical perspective—is in the field of micro-philosophy.[1]

---

1. I think the perspectives studied in macro-philosophy correspond to Kuhn's paradigms, whereas the problems and solutions studied in micro-philosophy within a chosen school of thought correspond to what Kuhn describes as activities of normal science. We will study Kuhn in detail in Part VII.

Schools of Thought

(Rationalism, Empiricism, Positivism, and Constructivism)

Book II can be read independent of Book I in the sense that anyone who has already acquired some background in the philosophy of science from anywhere can follow it. There are two ways to read Book II.

A. AS MACRO-PHILOSOPHY OF SCIENCE

The philosophy of science can be studied through problems and solutions. In Book I we studied the twin problems of truth and explanation. The problem of truth includes the problems of how to discover plausible hypotheses, and how to evaluate these hypotheses. The problem of explanation covers the quest for the right kinds of explanation in science, their logical forms, and their empirical requirements. The study of problems as such belongs to what I will call the **micro-philosophy of science**.

We can, however, study the philosophy of science differently. We can study the main schools of thought in this field. Each school attempts to provide a global view of the structure of science (logic of science) and the paths of its growth and development (dynamics of science). It studies the source of scientific knowledge, the foundation of the meaning of scientific terms, and the methodology of science in general. All these belong to what I will call the **macro-philosophy of science**. You can see that the macro-philosophy and the micro-philosophy complement each other.

Book II is on the macro-philosophy, complementing the micro-philosophy of Book I.

B. AS A SUPPLEMENT TO THE CLASSICAL TRADITION PRESENTATION OF BOOK I

In Book I we covered the central topics in the philosophy of science. We studied them mainly in terms of the classical tradition. In doing so, however, we also drew attention to its deficiencies.

The starting point of philosophy of science should no doubt be the classical tradition, which is relatively simple and clear. More important, it provides many of the fundamental and useful concepts as well as enlightening views on science. Nonetheless, this great tradition has been declining. The downturn was brought about mainly by

Thomas Kuhn's *The Structure of Scientific Revolutions* (1962), which ushered in the *Weltanschauung* view. Since then philosophy of science has steered toward the history and sociology of science. Imre Lakatos, Larry Laudan, and David Bloor are three of the many prominent names heading in that direction. Furthermore, advances in artificial intelligence will no doubt have a monumental impact on the philosophy of science.

We can take Book II as an introductory study of the Kuhnian revolution and its aftermath so as to complement the classical tradition of Book I. However, revolutions cannot be understood out of context. Hence the book starts with the very first philosophy of science—that is, **rationalism**, which dates back to the ancient Greeks. Then we move on to its successor, (Baconian) **empiricism**, which naturally leads to the **classical tradition** in the 20th century. The **Kuhnian revolution** is a revolt against this great tradition.

PART V

Rationalism and Empiricism

INTRODUCTION

Rationalism, dating back to the ancient Greeks, was the first philosophy of science. It stresses the mind as the source of knowledge. The great works of Euclid and Archimedes were written in accordance with this philosophy. It dominated scientific methodology for almost 2,000 years. Then in the 17th century, Galileo with his telescope and his epochmaking experiments in dynamics brought about a revolution. Science was liberated from the constraints of rationalism. The works of Galileo and those of the great philosopher Francis Bacon marked the formal entry of empiricism into Western thought. This new philosophy, in contrast to rationalism, takes the senses as the main source of knowledge.

Part V has four chapters. **Chapter 19** covers the history of rationalism, its difficulties, and its eventual downfall and replacement by empiricism. However, the latter is not without its own difficulties. The main methodological problems of empiricism are discussed in detail in Chapters 20–22. Every philosopher loves puzzles, for puzzles challenge the intellect. Hume's problem of induction (**Chapter 20**) has been the "scandal" of philosophy for over 200 years. Goodman's and Hempel's paradoxes (**Chapter 21**) are more recent. You would enjoy all three "puzzles." They pose serious challenges to the philosophy of empiricism.

Chapter 22 poses a different kind of difficulty for empiricism. The previous three problems were about the rationality of certain types of scientific reasoning. The present one is about the nature of observation. It claims that empiricism has misrepresented the mechanism of observation, and hence cannot be correct in its understanding of the status and true nature of observational data. This is serious for empiricism because empiricism maintains that knowledge is founded on observation.

Chapter 19

Rationalism and Then Empiricism

19.1 RATIONALISM

The history of the philosophy of science can be told as the story of a prolonged struggle and rivalry between two schools of thought, **rationalism** and **empiricism**.[1] Whereas rationalism (in its extreme form) trusts the mind with its power of reasoning and insight as the only source of knowledge, empiricism (in its extreme form) holds, on the other hand, that only the senses can yield knowledge. The faculties of sight, hearing, smell, taste, and touch have been compared to collecting devices in the acquisition of knowledge by the empiricists, who think that no knowledge can be obtained without them. Contemporary philosophy of science generally favors empiricism over rationalism. Nonetheless the foundations of science were laid down by the rationalists, without whom science would not be as we know it today. So let's start the story with the rationalists.

Even though rationalism can be traced further back, Plato (428–348 B.C.) was the first systematic rationalist. According to him, there are two distinct worlds, the familiar world of sensible objects, which we know through sight, hearing, touch, and so on, and the (abstract) world of what Plato called Forms, which is accessible only through the intellect. The visible and tangible world of material objects is in a sense less real. It is imperfect, always changing and in flux, and things are what

---

1. More accurately, it is a contest between three schools of thought: rationalism, empiricism, and Kantianism. (See Section 19.4.)

they are only because they reflect their corresponding Forms, which are the real things. For example, the moon is a round object because it is a copy of the perfectly round spherical Form that exists in the supranatural world. No copy of the real thing is ever quite perfect, and the moon is no exception. True knowledge consists not of our sensible comprehension of material objects around us, be they spheres, triangles, horses, or roses, but of our intellectual appreciation of those immaterial Forms—the Form of the Sphere, the Form of the Triangle, the Form of the Horse, the Form of the Rose, and so on. Thus, even though the senses can be an aid to knowledge, it is the mind, the intellect that through its power of insight and reasoning can yield true knowledge. In this way, Plato set down the foundations for rationalism.

Euclid (fl. 300 B.C.), no doubt heavily influenced by Plato, was the next important rationalist. His major contribution to science was his 13 volumes on geometry, *Elements*. Even though, before Euclid, the ancient world already had a large number of geometric facts in its grasp, it could not be said to have comprehended them as genuine knowledge. To the ancients these brute facts were unexplained and unrelated to each other. They were mainly discovered by induction and generalization. It was Euclid who brought deduction and proof into geometry.[2] He organized the geometric facts into a rational system through the use of **axioms** and theorems. The following four axioms are his:

(1) Between two points there is a straight line.

(2) Straight lines can be extended indefinitely.

(3) Given a fixed point and a distance, a circle can be described with that point as center and that distance as diameter.

(4) All right angles are equal.

He also formulated a fifth axiom, the Axiom of Parallels.[3]

From these five axioms, Euclid was able to deduce hundreds of **theorems**. The most famous of these is probably what is now known as Pythagoras's theorem, which says that the square of the hypotenuse of a right-angled triangle is equal to the sum of the squares of the remaining two sides. It was claimed that these axioms are self-evident and do not require proofs. They can be seen by any clear mind to be true because they are so simple and obvious. And since valid deductive inferences preserve truth, the theorems deduced from these axioms should thus be true. Since the time of the Greeks, it has been well known that it is impossible for the conclusion of a valid deduction to be false if the premises are true (Chapter 2). In the present case, the premises are the axioms that, as claimed, are self-evidently true. Hence the truth status of the theorems cannot be in doubt.

Let's take a few examples of deduction of theorems from the five axioms. Before we proceed further it would be appropriate to define what a right angle is, since Axiom 4 talks about right angles.

Definition 1: If a straight line *CD* meets another straight line *ACB* so as to make the two adjacent angles equal, each angle is called a right angle. Line *CD* is said to be perpendicular to *AB*, and *C* is the foot of the perpendicular (Figure 19.1).

We now have:

Theorem 1: If a straight line intersects with another straight line, the sum of the adjacent angles so formed is equal to two right angles.

Let *AB* be a straight line and let *EC* intersect with *AB* at *C* (Figure 19.2). Our aim is to prove that angle *ECA* + angle *ECB* = 2 right angles.

---

2. The method of deduction and proof had been practiced to some extent by some Greek geometers even before Euclid. Aristotle certainly had conceived the idea of a deductive science consisting of axioms and theorems before Euclid, but it was Euclid who put this idea into practice.

3. The Axiom of Parallels says that if a straight line falling on two straight lines makes the interior angles on the same side together less than two right angles, the two straight lines, if produced indefinitely, meet on that side on which the angles are together less than two right angles. It was doubts about the self-evident nature of this axiom that led to the discovery of geometries other than Euclidean geometry (that is, the one propounded by Euclid).

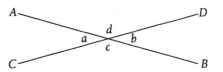

FIGURE 19.3

Let AB and CD intersect forming angles a, b, c, and d (Figure 19.3). Our aim is to prove that $a = b$, and $c = d$.

Proof:

(1) $a + c = 2$ right angles. (Because of Theorem 1.)

(2) $b + c = 2$ right angles. (Because of Theorem 1.)

(3) $a + c = b + c$. (Applying Axiom 4 to (1) and (2).)

(4) $a = b$ (By subtraction in (3).)

(5) $c = d$ (By similar reasoning.)

Q.E.D.[5]

These two are very simple proofs of simple theorems, and yet from them you should be able to notice three points: (i) The proofs are strict and rigorous in the sense that each move from one line of the proof to the next line has to be shown to be valid (the justifications are enclosed in brackets). (ii) Once a statement has been proved it can be used as a premise for further proofs (for example, Theorem 1 was used in the proof of Theorem 2). (iii) What can be used in the proofs is confined to the axioms, definitions, and theorems already proved.[6]

As more and more theorems are accumulated, we can construct more complicated proofs for the more advanced theorems. Maybe you would like to try to prove theorems such as "The sum of the angles of a triangle is equal to two right angles,"

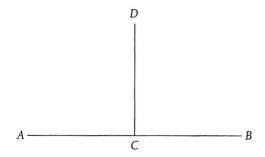

FIGURE 19.1

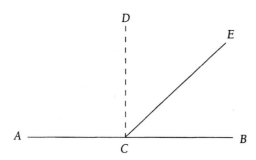

FIGURE 19.2

Proof:

(1) Construct straight line DC perpendicular to AB. (See Definition 1 for 'perpendicular.')

(2) Angle DCA + angle $DCB = 2$ right angles. (By Definition 1.)

(3) Angle ECA + angle ECB = angle DCA + angle DCB. (By superposition.)

(4) Angle ECA + angle $ECB = 2$ right angles. (By (2) and (3).)

Q.E.D.[4]

Theorem 2: If two straight lines intersect, the vertically opposite angles are equal.

---

4. "Q.E.D." is short for 'Quod erat demonstrandum,' which means 'which was to be proved.'

5. Euclid actually called the five axioms 'postulates.' The term 'axiom' was reserved for more general truths such as: "If equals be subtracted from equals, the remainders are equal." You can see that this general truth was employed in line 4 of the proof.

6. In these two simple examples, the axioms are hardly used. Only Axiom 4 seems to have played a role (that is, in the proof of Theorem 2). However, as we progress further and further into more complicated theorems, you will find that the other axioms will be employed.

and "If two sides of a triangle are equal, then the angles opposite to those sides are equal."

This Method of Axioms and Deduction became the standard practice of theoretical science right up to Newton and beyond.[7] Descartes (1596–1650), the first great rationalist of modern philosophy, describes the method clearly and convincingly in claiming that there are only two means to knowledge, namely, intuition and deduction. Whereas intuition supplies the starting points of knowledge—that is, the axioms—deduction propagates knowledge far beyond this limited beginning. Descartes describes intuition thus:

> By *intuition* I understand, not the fluctuating testimony of the senses, nor the misleading judgment that proceeds from the blundering constructions of imagination, but the conception which an unclouded and attentive mind gives us so readily and distinctly that we are wholly freed from doubt about that which we understand. Or, what comes to the same thing, *intuition* is the undoubting conception of an unclouded and attentive mind, and springs from the light of reason alone.[8]

Descartes then makes it known why intuition alone is not sufficient:

> Hence now we are in a position to raise the question as to why we have, besides intuition, given this supplementary method of knowing, viz., knowing by *deduction*, by which we understand all necessary inferences from other facts that are known with certainty. This, however, we could not avoid, because many things are known with certainty, though not by themselves evident, but only deduced from true and known principles by the

continuous and uninterrupted action of a mind that has a clear vision of each step in the process. It is in a similar way that we know that the last link in a long chain is connected with the first, even though we do not take in by means of one and the same act of vision all the intermediate links on which that connection depends, but only remember that we have taken them successively under review and that each single one is united to its neighbour, from the first even to the last.[9]

You can see that Descartes's method has two steps: (i) Intuit simple and self-evident truths and (ii) deduce from these truths further (more complex) truths. His method is primarily a method of discovery (Chapter 5). However, it can also be interpreted as a method of theoretical justification (Chapter 8). For example, Pythagoras's theorem was known long before Euclid. However, it remained unjustified until Euclid proved it from his axioms. We can say that the axioms of Euclid (theoretically) justify Pythagoras's theorem (as the empirical generalization "All rainbows have seven colors" was justified by Newton's corpuscular theory of light).

Descartes believed that the world is made up of two kinds of substance, mind and matter (Chapter 13). But as far as the acquisition of knowledge is concerned, it seems that matter doesn't matter, and only mind matters. According to Descartes, (true) knowledge comes from intuition and deduction, and both are activities of the mind.

To summarize, rationalism (in its extreme form) is the view that appeals to reason as the only source of (real) knowledge, hence rationalistic science is a priori. (In opposition, empiricism (in its extreme form) appeals to sense experience as the only source of knowledge, hence for the empiricists science is *a posteriori*.) In the jargon of

7. It would be instructive to read Archimedes' (287–212 B.C.) works on equilibrium and floating bodies, which, like Euclid's geometry, were presented in axiomatic form. See Knedler (1973, vol. 1).

8. "Rules for the Direction of the Mind" in *The Philosophical Works of Descartes* (edited and translated by Elizabeth S. Haldane and G. R. T. Ross, 1931, p. 7).

9. Ibid., p. 8.

artificial intelligence, rationalists advocate the top-down approach, starting with highly general and abstract axioms, deducing downward to more concrete and more detailed theorems. Empiricists (usually) advocate the bottom-up approach, starting with items obtained through observation, and work upward to highly general and abstract principles and laws.

19.2 DIFFICULTIES WITH RATIONALISM

Rationalism had its greatest success with geometry in the hands of Euclid, and later in the study of hydrostatics and of levers by Archimedes (287–212 B.C.). However (outside pure mathematics), rationalism achieved little after the Greeks. Intuition did not seem to be able to supply the expected flow of ultimate self-evident principles. On the contrary, rationalists often ended up with misleading and damaging results through their a priori approach. For example, Grosseteste (circa 1168–1253) claimed that the law of refraction (for water and any other media) must be such that the ratio of the angle of refraction to the angle of incidence is 1 to 2. He argued that since the simplest ratio of 1 to 1 has already been taken up by reflection, the law of refraction has to be in accordance with the second simplest ratio: 1 to 2. Since Snell (1591–1626) we all know how wrong Grosseteste was (Section 0.1). A second example can be found in the case of Aristotle, Ptolemy, and Copernicus, who all worked with the "self-evident" axiom that the orbits of the planets are circular. For them it was self-evident that the circle is the perfect figure, and since the heavenly bodies are perfect they must all move in circular orbits. The shapes of these perfect heavenly bodies should be perfect as well, hence they must be round, perfectly round. It was Kepler (1571–1630) who showed that the orbits of the planets are not circular, and, at about the same time, Galileo's telescope revealed that the moon's

surface was by no means round, being full of mountains, valleys, and craters.

One can see the folly and unreasonableness of rationalism in Descartes's ambitious project of trying to deduce all truths from the single axiom, "I think, therefore I am." This single axiom is supposed to be the one and only indubitable axiom, and hence it is essential that rationalist science should be organized around this supreme axiom through deduction. Descartes claimed from this supreme axiom that he could demonstrate the existence of God, and also that the material world exists. However, he found it difficult to prove the laws of mechanics, and he certainly could not prove the laws of optics and the laws of heat. I do not think he would even attempt to prove contingent and "trivial" matters such as the fact that Plato gave the name *Timaeus* to one of his works, that Aristotle died in 322 B.C., and that Galileo was appointed professor of mathematics at the University of Padua in 1592.

With hindsight, we can see that the axiomatic method, so admirably applicable to geometry, is quite unsuitable for sciences such as physics, chemistry, biology, and geology. It is certainly not suitable for the social sciences—for example, psychology, sociology, and economics. Is it possible to deduce from a few (intuitive) axioms all the social and physical facts about each and every one of us? To deduce the whole history of the evolution of human civilization? To deduce the past and present existence of the incredibly large number of species and varieties of plants and animals? I think not.

Galileo (1564–1642) has been hailed as the father of experimental science. Instead of relying on intuition and Aristotle's authority in matters of mechanics, he advocated the use of experiments to ascertain truths about the material world. Perhaps he was best known as the scientist who simultaneously dropped two lead balls of different weights from the top of the Tower of Pisa to demonstrate *experimentally* that Aristotle was wrong in speculating by means of intuition that heavier objects fall faster than lighter objects.[10] The empiricists think that

---

10. There is some dispute about whether Galileo did perform the experiment himself.

only through observation and experimentation can we come to know how things are and how they behave. Intuition is barren. What intuition can give us is at best truths such as "all bachelors are unmarried" that are analytic and hence deprived of content (Chapter 11). Even the axioms of Euclid are said to be analytic and noninformative in the sense that they are true by the very meaning of words like 'point,' 'line,' and 'angle.' In fact, the axioms of Euclid, if taken as synthetic statements about the world, have been falsified by Einstein's theory of general relativity. If the axioms are to be upheld as true nonetheless, we should qualify the words of Euclid by employing words such as 'Euclidean point,' 'Euclidean line,' and so on. These new terms are then understood in such a way that the five axioms become analytically true, true on account of the meaning of these new terms. Let me explain further.

Besides inventing concepts, the mind can "play" with them. For example, having invented the concept 'pentagon,' the mind can then reason out (deduce) that every pentagon, besides having five sides, has five angles. It can further reason out (deduce) that the angle sum of these five angles is six right angles. The mind is gifted with the faculty of reasoning and, indeed, reasoning can bring knowledge. Wonderful as it is, it nevertheless cannot tell us whether there are any pentagons in the real world, be they in the form of pentagonal table tops, pentagonal tiles, or other objects.[11] To know whether the world has these, the mind alone is powerless. We require the faculties of the senses. Our vision, hearing, and so on are required for us to know whether certain concepts such as 'pentagon' have any realizations in the real world. The mind can reason that *if* the tabletop is a pentagon *then* it would have five angles, and that the angle sum of these is six right angles. But it cannot by reason alone know that the top of my dining table is a pentagon,[12] nor can it know by reason alone that

the angle sum of the top of my table is six right angles.

We say that the kind of knowledge the mind can provide us is analytic knowledge. Without the assistance of the senses, the mind cannot know anything synthetic (about the real world).

Again the mind can "dream up" an image of an animal, which it calls a kangaroo. It can assign the animal a certain physique. The mind can even deduce from this physique that the animal does not run but hop, and that it is a vegetarian, so that the mind now possesses the *analytic* knowledge that kangaroos hop and are herbivorous. Nonetheless the mind does not have *synthetic* knowledge whether the world has kangaroos or not. Even if the mind were to know that the world does have kangaroos, it still cannot tell us where these animals live, without the assistance of the senses. Can Plato, Euclid, or Descartes (sitting in their armchairs) deduce from their a priori axioms that kangaroos can be found in Australia? That's why we need a Captain James Cook, the great explorer and navigator of the 18th century, to be physically present in that southern continent to acquire the *synthetic* knowledge of the existence of kangaroos. The same argument applies to other concepts such as 'unicorn,' 'centaur,' 'dinosaur,' 'electron,' 'magnetic monopole,' and 'quark.' Indeed the argument applies to all concepts.[13]

We see that intuition can only yield analytic statements, and deductions from these statements can only yield further analytic statements. Thus the Method of (a priori) Axioms and Deduction has been considered by the empiricists as infertile in that it is incapable of yielding truths about our world.[14] According to them, science should not start with a priori axioms but with sense experience through observation and experimentation. For them sense experience is the source of synthetic knowledge. Let's now turn to Francis Bacon and

---

11. Or pentagonal buildings, one of which might be called 'The Pentagon.'

12. Or that it is *not* a pentagon.

13. Excluding concepts such as 'if,' 'or,' 'the,' and so on, of course.

14. Empiricists would not object to the use of axioms as long as they are not taken as a priori self-evident truths. Indeed Newton presented his mechanics in terms of axioms, and contemporary sciences such as quantum mechanics and relativity can be axiomatized. Karl Popper has important things to say on the use of axioms as empirical hypotheses, as we'll see later in the chapter.

J. S. Mill, probably the best-known empiricists in the history of scientific method.

19.3 THE RISE OF EMPIRICISM

Francis Bacon (1561–1626) rejected speculation (intuition) as a means to acquire truths. For him the (correct) scientific method consists of four steps:

(a) Observation and experimentation: we should start doing science by collecting data with our senses either by passive observation or by active experimentation. The ancients observed the movements of the planets and the stars. Great astronomers like Ptolemy and Tycho Brahe meticulously recorded their changes of positions. These are paradigm cases of observational science. However, there are circumstances when we need to force nature to yield an answer through experiments because nature, left to herself, may not readily produce one. For example, Roger Bacon (1214–1292) mentioned that a certain "master of experimentation" (probably Petrus of Maricourt) severed a magnetic needle crosswise into two fragments and discovered that each of the two fragments was a complete magnet by itself. Francis Bacon believed that only the senses can tell us what the world is like. Hence the starting point of science must be sense experience.

(b) Classification: the data collected should then be collated and classified into tables, mainly to show when certain phenomena are always concurrent and when certain other phenomena are never concurrent.[15] For example, it might be noted that observed swans are always white, that observed fires are always hot, and that observed pieces of copper always conduct heat.

(c) Generalization: from the observed cases of association or disassociation of phenomena, empirical generalizations are then made. For example, from the results of (b), one should conclude that all swans are white, all fire is hot, and all copper conducts heat. This process is, of course, our old friend, induction by simple enumeration (Chapter 3). The process applies not only to observational and experimental data but also to generalizations themselves, thus starting a (recursive) chain of operations gradually ascending to principles of ever higher generality. For example, from "all copper conducts heat," "all iron conducts heat," and "all silver conducts heat," one can generalize further to "all metal conducts heat."[16]

(d) Testing: the generalizations obtained should then be tested further to make certain that there are no exceptions. Here experimentation plays a significant role (Chapters 6 and 7).

Bacon claimed usefulness and success for his method. For him, his is *the* method of science. He tried out this method in his study of the nature of heat and claimed that through the use of the method he arrived at the true nature of heat: heat is a kind of motion.[17]

We can see that, as in the case of the Axiomatic Method, Bacon's empirical method also sees the organization of the statements of science as forming a kind of pyramid. The difference between rationalists and empiricists is that the former think scientific discovery should start from the apex (top) and work its way down by deduction, whereas the latter think scientific discovery should start from the base (bottom) through sense experience and work its way upward by induction (Figures 19.4a and 19.4b). The contrast is obvious even though both schools of thought believe that science should start with truths, not truths *simpliciter*, but truths that are certain and indisputable. They disagree on whether

---

15. Note that this is a much simplified story.

16. Compare the method so far with SIM, the simple inductive method (Chapter 5).

17. In fact, some 200 years later Count Rumford confirmed Bacon's finding. The question, however, is whether Bacon truly arrived at this amazing result through his method, thus demonstrating the efficacy of this method, or whether it was a matter of exceptional insight.

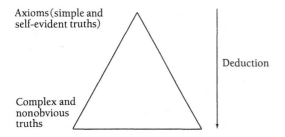

FIGURE 19.4a Rationalism

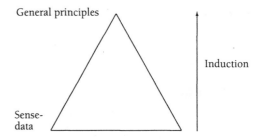

FIGURE 19.4b Empiricism

it is the mind or the senses that provide us with such assured and indisputable truths. The rationalists think that the mind is much more trustworthy and can provide us with clear and unclouded views of the world, whereas the empiricists think that sight, hearing, the sense of smell, the sense of taste, and the sense of touch are the proper vehicles for the collection of initial truths.

The other renowned empiricist in the history of scientific methodology was J. S. Mill. In the 19th century, he argued with great clarity and conviction for empiricism. His five methods of induction were derivative of Bacon's (Chapter 3).

I have thus far painted a sharp contrast between rationalism and empiricism. In fact, there are many possible intermediate positions between the two extremes. I will now sketch a well-known one for illustration.

19.4 POPPER'S DEDUCTIVISM

Karl Popper (1902–1994), one of the leading philosophers of science of the 20th century, thought that the kind of empiricism advocated by Bacon and Mill is naive.[18] For him induction plays no part in science. The only logic science requires is deductive logic.[19] The method of science advocated by Popper is known as the **hypothetico-deductive method**, which consists of the following steps:[20]

(a) Formulate a hypothesis, H. For Popper science does not and should not start with empirical data derived from sense experience, so that observation and experimentation should not form the first step of scientific investigations. The first step is always the formation of a hypothesis (Chapter 1), sometimes called a theory, which is a conjecture about the world and which can be false and is very often false.

(b) Deduce an empirical consequence C from the hypothesis, H (usually together with the aid of some auxiliary hypotheses (Chapter 6)). H is usually at a high level of abstraction, hence it cannot be tested directly (Chapter 1). In this step, through deduction, an empirically testable consequence is obtained.

(c) Test the empirical consequence C directly. At this step sense experience plays a role in the direct test of C. In other words, sense experience is employed not as the starting point of science, but rather as a means to check the empirical acceptability of H.

(d) If C is acceptable under the scrutiny of sense experience, return to step (b) and obtain another empirical consequence C' for the further testing of H.

(d′) If, on the other hand, C is rejected, then H should be rejected as a consequence of *modus tollens* (Chapter 1).

18. We have studied Popper's philosophy before, in Chapter 7.

19. We will study Popper in detail in Chapter 24.

20. Popper's methodology is given in detail in Popper (1959). A digest of his view can be found in Magee (1975).

This is a crude summary of Popper's methodology and has obviously not taken into account various kinds of complexity such as the involvement of auxiliary hypotheses.

Popper thinks that what he calls the Bucket Theory of Knowledge is impossible. One cannot simply collect observational data (as if with a bucket). Any act is intentional so that, even in collecting data, the scientist has to be selective and her action must therefore be directed. She has to make a decision as to what to collect, where to collect, and when to collect. The only way she can make such decisions is in view of a hypothesis. The hypothesis guides and prompts her as to what to look for, and this is precisely step (c). Popper calls his own theory of knowledge the Searchlight Theory of Knowledge. The searchlight is directed only at places where the object being looked for is thought to be (for example, an enemy's aircraft). In brief, for Popper, observation serves only in the empirical assessment of hypotheses and not as their generator. Hence its place should be toward the end of scientific investigations rather than at the beginning (Chapters 6 and 7).

When compared with the Axiomatic Method, we can see that Popper's method agrees with the rationalists' view that deduction is the main and only tool of logical reasoning for science. The difference is that for Popper there are no self-evident axioms to be obtained by intuition or otherwise. All statements are fallible, and it is folly to try to start with indisputable statements. Yet Popper's hypotheses are products of the intellect. They are invented freely by the mind. In this respect, Popper is a rationalist.[21] However, his emphasis on empirical tests of hypotheses through observations and experiments places him squarely with the empiricists. It is empirical evidence which has the last say as to the acceptability of hypotheses. The main difference between him and the empiricists is that, whereas the empiricists' main

tool of reasoning is induction, Popper aligns himself with the rationalists in advocating the use of deduction and deduction alone. We will return to Popper's philosophy in detail in Chapter 24.

Popper's methodology belongs to empiricism, and yet we can see that rationalism has a role to play in it. It is like mixing colors. We can have shades of empiricism. Thus, for easy identification, let us give labels to the better-known empirical methodologies as follows.

Baconian empiricism: let's employ this name to label the kind of methodology advocated by Bacon and Mill.[22] It is characterized by the following attributes: (i) scientific discovery starts with the collecting of empirical data through observation; (ii) through the use of inductive methods such as induction by simple enumeration and Mill's methods, general laws and principles are inferred.

Modern statistical methods (Chapter 4) are both empiricist and inductive. They can be taken as improvements on and refinements of Bacon's and Mill's methods.

Logical positivism (also known as **logical empiricism**): this type of empiricism is championed by the logical positivists, whom we will study in Chapter 23. Logical positivism can be considered formal improvements on Bacon's and Mill's methodology, relying heavily on modern deductive and inductive (formal) logic (Chapters 2 and 3).

Inductive empiricism: this covers Baconian empiricism (including statistical methods) and logical positivism. It advocates the bottom-up, data-driven approach.

Deductive empiricism: contrary to inductive empiricism, Popper champions deduction as the main mode of inference to be employed in science. Thus I think it should be called 'deductive empiricism.' In Chapter 24, we will study Popper's philosophy in detail. It advocates the top-down, hypothesis-driven[23] approach.

---

21. There is no reason why we can't call Popper's hypotheses axioms—that is, as long as these "axioms" are not taken as a priori and certain. In fact, according to Popper, Euclid's axioms and Newton's axioms (the three laws of motion and the law of gravitation) are hypotheses about the world, just like any other hypotheses.

22. Lakatos (1970a, p. 94) calls it 'classical empiricism.'

23. The usual term is 'theory-driven.' However, the term 'theory' so used can be confused with the term 'theory' as used in 'scientific theory' (Chapters 8 and 15).

Let's summarize these various types of empiricism as shown in the box below:[24]

Let's start with Baconian empiricism. Bacon's and Mill's methods are useful but only in a limited

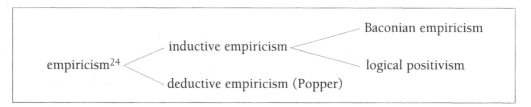

At odds with empiricism is, of course, rationalism. However, there is a well-known third position. It was proposed by the great German philosopher Immanuel Kant (1724–1804). He claimed that the mind plays an essential and indispensable role in perception (observation). Thus, even in the most elementary step of science, the step of data collection, the mind plays a key role. There is an intrinsic rational element in science. Kant's philosophy is often known as **transcendental idealism**. The modern form of this philosophy is known as **constructivism**, which we will study in detail in Parts VII and VIII. **Kantianism**' is probably the appropriate term to cover both transcendental idealism and constructivism. As a matter of fact, constructivism is often called **neo-Kantianism**.[25]

In Section 19.1, I said that the history of the philosophy of science can be read as a contest between the two schools of thought: rationalism and empiricism. To be more accurate, we should take in Kantianism as the third contending school.

19.5 ASSESSMENT AND PROSPECTS

Rationalism, at least in its original forms as advocated by Plato, Euclid, and Descartes, can be said to be dead. This is the general opinion of the philosophical community. What about empiricism?

way. We have discussed this in both Chapters 3 and 5. Let me summarize their shortcomings.

(a) Very often these methods lead to wrong conclusions. (However, since there are no such things as foolproof methods, the possibility of leading to mistakes cannot be taken as a major flaw.)

(b) These methods can only deal with "tidy" cases. They are only applicable to situations with no exceptions. (However, modern statistical methods have scored significant successes in remedying this weakness.)

(c) I think the most serious defect with Baconian empiricism is that the inductive methods employed are "flat" inferences. They are essentially methods of correlation: from given data on some existing (known) concepts, they infer the relationships between these concepts. For example, in terms of existing concepts 'white' and 'swan,' one collects data about white swans and then infers that all swans are white (or most swans are white, or 74 percent of swans are white, depending on the available data). Bacon's and Mill's methods do not enable one to arrive at novel concepts. In our case of swans, these methods cannot bring about concepts such as 'chromosome' or 'gene' so that one can, for instance, conclude that animals with genes X, Y, and Z will be white. Thus science, if confined to Bacon's and Mill's

---

24. (i) This diagrammatic summary is not meant to be exhaustive of all types of empiricism. (ii) Since inductive empiricism and deductive empiricism together make up what is known as the classical tradition (Part VI), it would be appropriate to name the "union" of these two schools 'classical empiricism.' See also Note 22.

25. I think Kantianism can alternatively be called subjective empiricism.

methods, will stay at the observation level, constituting what we called phenomenal science (Chapter 8).

Statistical methods are great improvements on Bacon's and Mill's methods. However, these types of inferences remain "flat." They do not yield novel concepts.

In Chapter 8, I pointed out that science grows in two stages: the phenomenal stage and the theoretical stage. Baconian empiricism (including statistical methods) seems to be the best methodology we have for the development of the phenomenal stage. For further results, we have to rely on theoretical science. It is those numerous scientific theories developed since Galileo and Newton that have brought scientific knowledge forward in leaps and bounds. The **method of theories (theorizing)** seems to be the right way of doing science: theories that claim to give us the real nature of things, hence called real-nature theories (Chapter 15).

Logical positivism has a lot to say about theories, their structures, and their uses. Has logical positivism, therefore, given us the right methods of science? In Chapter 23, we will see.

According to Popper both Baconian empiricism and logical positivism get the procedure of science the wrong way around. Science should be hypothesis-driven, not data-driven. The correct method is the top-down approach, not the bottom-up approach. However, Popper's deductive empiricism has little to say on the nature and structure of scientific theories.

What about constructivism then? If anything, it is a philosophy that places great emphasis on the role played by theories in scientific practices and growth. Has it provided us with the correct picture of theories? Has it given us an acceptable analysis of theories? I hope we can form better ideas on these questions by the end of Book II.

In the meantime, let's study why inductive empiricism is unsatisfactory. It faces two serious (generic) problems. These are (i) the problem of rationality of induction (Chapters 20 and 21) and (ii) the problem of objectivity of observation (Chapter 22).

KEY TERMS INTRODUCED IN THIS CHAPTER

rationalism	hypothetico-deductive method	inductive empiricism	neo-Kantianism
empiricism		deductive empiricism	method of theories (theorizing)
axiom	Baconian empiricism	transcendental idealism	
theorem	logical positivism (logical empiricism)	constructivism	
		Kantianism	

REFERENCES

For an introduction to the general philosophy of rationalism and empiricism, read the articles 'rationalism' and 'empiricism' in Craig (1998).

Melchert (1991) provides surveys of the philosophies of Plato, Descartes, and Kant. This can be read together with Ackermann (1965), which provides critiques of these philosophies.

Landesman (1970) has a relevant and easy-to-understand excerpt from Descartes' writings.

Eves and Newsom (1965) gives a detailed digest and critique of Euclid's geometry.

Madden (1960) contains good descriptive articles on the methodologies of Descartes, Bacon, and Mill.

There are lots of books on Popper. A handy one is Magee (1975). For Popper's original presentation, see Popper (1959).

Chapter 20

Problems of Empiricism IA: Hume's Problem

20.1 INTRODUCTION

In the last chapter, we saw how empiricism triumphed over rationalism. However, empiricism itself faces two serious problems. For our present purpose, by 'empiricism' I will mean 'inductive empiricism.' Whether Popper's deductive empiricism can evade these two problems remains to be seen in Chapter 24.

Inductive empiricism, as detailed in Section 19.4, covers all those methodologies that (i) take the collection of empirical data as the starting point of scientific discovery and (ii) take inductive logic (including statistical methods) as the main mode of inference to arrive at general laws and principles. Inductive empiricism thus includes both Baconian empiricism and logical positivism. It advocates the bottom-up, data-driven approach.

What is so sad about this almost common-sense approach is that both steps (i) and (ii) are apparently problematic. The problem facing (i) is the doubt about the objectivity and reliability of the empirical data. This we will leave till the next chapter. Here we study the problem with (ii): the rationality of inductive inferences.

Are inductive inferences reasonable and reliable, so that we can rely on them to further our knowledge about the world, and so that we can depend on them to make predictions?

20.2 PROBLEM OF INDUCTION

The great 18th-century philosopher David Hume (Chapter 11) raised the problems of induction, arguing convincingly that induction is both rationally unjustified and unreliable. Since then, this problem has plagued philosophy, so much so that it has been called the scandal of philosophy.

There are many forms of induction, which we studied in Chapter 3. 'Induction' is just another name for ampliative inference (whereas deduction is non-ampliative inference). It is this ampliative characteristic that, according to Hume, makes induction rationally suspect. Even though Hume's arguments are mainly about induction by simple enumeration[1] and induction by analogy (Chapter 3), they apply to induction in general.

Is induction rational (reasonable)? Do the premises in an inductive argument give logical support to the conclusion? Is the conclusion reliable (given that the premises are true)? Do the premises increase the probability of the conclusion? These are some of the ways Hume's questioning of induction can be formulated.

Let's illustrate with a modern-day example.

Suppose a friend of yours told you that her telephone number starts with six 8's in a row. Would it be reasonable to conclude that the seventh digit of her telephone number is going to be an 8 as well? Would it be more likely to be an 8 rather than another number? The answer is an obvious "No," the reason being that the digits of a telephone number are independent of each other. In Hume's terminology, there is no necessary connection between one digit and another. Even if your friend had given you a row of twenty 8's instead of six, it would still be unreasonable to think that the next digit is more likely to be an 8. But then, Hume would argue, our inference from the observation of a finite number of swans being white to the conclusion that the next swan is white should similarly be unreasonable. Nonetheless we seem to be making such irrational inferences all the time. For example, having encountered slippery ice a number of times, we take precautions when walking on ice. Having been burned by fire (once), we try hard to avoid being burned again. The Chinese have an idiom, "shouzhudaitu," which is based on the story that a certain peasant, on finding a rabbit that had accidentally knocked itself out when it ran into a tree, waited daily at the same spot for another unconscious rabbit to take home for his meal.

According to Hume, I and II (and Ia and IIa) are just as reasonable or as unreasonable:

	Swan$_1$ is white.	Swan$_1$ is white.
	Swan$_2$ is white.	Swan$_2$ is white.
I	....	II ....
	Swan$_n$ is white.	Swan$_n$ is white.
	The next swan is white.	The next swan is red.

	Swan$_1$ is white.	Swan$_1$ is white.
	Swan$_2$ is white.	Swan$_2$ is white.
Ia	....	IIa ....
	Swan$_n$ is white.	Swan$_n$ is white.
	All swans are white.	All swans, other than these n ones, are red.

Counterintuitive as it is, Hume cannot see any good reason for preferring I over II (or Ia over IIa). It might be suggested that usually animals of the same genetic makeup will share the same feather color. Hence I is more reasonable. This defense, however, suffers from an essential defect. When one considers whether an inference is reasonable or not, one should only consider what is given in the premises (and nothing else). If we are going to take account of further information, that piece of information should be explicitly added to the premises. So let us add the premise:

(1) "Birds of the same genetic makeup share the same feather color."

---

1. It is useful to note that people often use the term 'induction' to mean 'induction by simple enumeration.'

With this additional premise, we can see that I is now not only reasonable; it is actually valid (given that all swans are birds and they all share the same genetic makeup).

But then how do we know that (1) is true? It is a general statement about *all* birds, yet the number of birds that we have so far encountered is relatively small and finite. Premise (1) could only have been obtained by induction. Without induction being used somewhere previously, we could not have reasonably concluded that the next swan is white!

According to Hume's argument, the following three inferences are on the same level of rationality:

III	IV	V
My cat is blue.	My cat is blue.	My cat is blue.
My dog is red.	My dog is blue.	My cat's kitten is blue.

The reason most of us think that V is the most reasonable of the three is because we implicitly employ the premise that

(2) The fur color of the offspring of cats resembles that of the parents.

But (2), as I have pointed out earlier, could not have been obtained without the use of induction. Thus the reason an inductive inference like V appears reasonable is that induction has been used somewhere before. That particular step of induction surely requires justification.

Hume's convincing argument that induction is rationally suspect is unsettling for two reasons. First, common sense tells us that induction is reasonable. Second, induction has proved to be so extremely useful in science and everyday affairs that we use it all the time. Yet on the other hand, Hume's argument seems to be flawless. Here is an analogy. Water has been so useful and essential to our health. What if someone demonstrated convincingly to us that water was in fact poisonous! This is the dilemma. What Hume has generated for us is known as the **problem of induction**.

20.3 THREE ATTEMPTED JUSTIFICATIONS OF THE PRINCIPLE OF INDUCTION

Let's study the problem of induction further. This time I suggest that we confine ourselves to induction by simple enumeration, which works on what is known as the **principle of induction**:

(3) If a large number of A's are examined (under a variety of conditions and in a variety of situations) and are found to be B's, then it is likely that all the A's throughout space and time are B's.

A more general and more reasonable version of (3) is

(3a) If a large number n of A's are examined (under a variety of conditions and in a variety of situations) and m of these n objects are found to be B's, then it is likely that the proportion of B's among all the A's throughout space and time is close to m/n.

We can see that, if (3) is true, Inferences I and Ia are preferable to Inferences II and IIa. Obviously (3) would not be able to make I and Ia valid (Chapter 2). Still it would make I and Ia reasonable.

Is (3) true? Hume argues that it is not. Are there any sound arguments to beat back Hume's anticommonsense skepticism? Hume's argument appears to be pure arrogance. Somehow philosophy and common sense must be salvaged from Hume's "insanity"! This "crusade" in defense of common sense has taken up a significant part of the central stage of philosophy for the last 200 years. We will soon see various efforts in this direction.

Let's start with three comparatively simple defenses against Hume's skepticism.

A. The Inductive Justification of Induction

I am quite sure that all of us have often employed the principle of induction, (3) or (3a), to make predictions. We talked about this in Section 3.2. Anyway I think that's how our ancestors arrived at conclusions such as "Ice is slippery," "Wood burns," and "Water quenches thirst." They observed a large number of instances and then generalized. That's why induction by simple enumeration is also known as **universal generalization**. As history has shown, the human race has had quite a large number of successes with this mode of inference. So let us conclude that, since the principle of induction has been successful many times in the past (for prediction), it is likely that it will be successful in the future. In other words, (3) is likely to be true.

This defense of (3) unfortunately does not work. We should see why, once the defense is presented as Argument VI:

> The principle of induction worked on occasion 1.
>
> The principle of induction worked on occasion 2.
>
> VI ....
>
> The principle of induction worked on occasion n.
> _____
> The principle of induction will work on the next occasion.

You can see that the structure of this argument is exactly the same as that of Argument I—an induction. In other words, what we have tried to do was to support (3) with past successes of (3). But why should the past successes of (3) have any bearing on the future success or failure of (3)—that is, unless we assume some sort of argument which is based on (3) itself? In short, we have been attempting to support the principle of induction with the principle of induction. This is surely circular! In the literature, this defense is known as **inductive justification of induction**.

In fact, when you come to think of it, this defense is not only circular but also "cheats" to a certain extent. The principle of induction certainly had its successes in the past, but I think it had its failures too. In fact, it probably had many more failures than successes. Simply think of the discovery of swans that are not white (Australian swans), stones that do not sink (pumice stones), and suns that do not set in the west (the Arctic and Antarctic suns). The common saying that all rules have exceptions does have a point. So in all fairness, if we are true inductivists, we should have instead concluded that the principle of induction will *not* work in the future, because there have been more failures than successes in the past.

B. The Mathematical Justification of Induction

The above defense is an empirical defense, an a posteriori defense. Now let's study an *a priori* defense.

In the theory of probability, there is a well-known law called the **law of large numbers**, which says

(4) If a random sample of a sufficiently large size is taken from a population, there is a high probability that the proportion of members of the sample having a certain attribute resembles closely the proportion of members of the population having that attribute. In fact, the probability can be made arbitrarily high by increasing the size of the sample.[2]

Let me illustrate with an example. Suppose 4,000 swans are examined and 2,634 are found to be white. The proportion of members of this sample of 4,000 that are white is therefore 2,634/4,000, which is approximately 65 percent. According to the law of large numbers, the proportion of members of all the swans in the world (the population) that are white is likely to be close to 65 percent

---

2. (l) For the notion of sampling, see Sections 4.2 to 4.5, and for statistical inferences based on the law of large numbers, see Section 4.4. (2) Here is a mathematical formulation of the law of large numbers due to Jakob Bernoulli: Let p be the proportion of members of a population having the attribute B. Let a random sample of n members be taken from the population. Let m of these n members have the attribute B. Then for an arbitrary positive number ε no matter how small, the probability of m/n differing from p by less than ε is greater than or equal to $1 - 1/(4\varepsilon^2 n)$. You can see that this probability can be made arbitrarily close to 1 by simply increasing n.

(provided, of course, that the sample of 4,000 is a random sample).

Here's a second example. Suppose 30,000 lumps of common salt are placed in water and all the lumps are found to dissolve. The law of large numbers says that it is very likely indeed that all—at least almost all—common salt is soluble in water (provided, again, that the 30,000 lumps are randomly selected).

The astonishing thing is that this law of large numbers is a *mathematical* law. It has been proved to be true a priori just as "$2 + 2 = 4$" has been proved to be true a priori. You can see the close resemblance of (4) to (3a). One might be tempted to say that, if (4) is true, then certainly (3a) is true as well. Both are about sampling. Both say that if the sample size is large enough then it is very likely that the sample will resemble the population closely.

I don't think there are any truths more secure and certain than mathematical truths! Since (4) is a mathematical truth, and (3a) is just like (4), why is (3a) dubious? Why are philosophers so afraid of David Hume?

Let's read (4) more carefully. You should notice the word 'random' qualifying 'sample' at the very beginning of the law. Law (4) applies only to *random* samples! What is a random sample? It is, roughly speaking, a fair sample, a representative sample. Its technical definition is:

(5)   A **random sample** (also known as a **fair sample** or a **representative sample**) is a sample obtained by random selection. A selection is random if each member of the population has the same chance (probability) of being selected.[3]

Let's take the case of our swan example. For the law of large numbers to be applicable, the 4,000 swans should be selected randomly. It would not do if we select all the 4,000 swans from the United States, because those in Europe, say, would not have a chance to be selected, let alone having the same chance. To be a fair sample, its members must be selected at random all over the world! By 'the

world,' I do not mean the planet earth. I mean the whole wide world.

But you might rebut: "There are no swans elsewhere in the world. Anyway we are not interested in swans other than those living on our earth." Fair enough, but then you would not be interested in whether whiteness is related to swanhood as a law of nature, because laws of nature are supposed to hold throughout space and time (Chapter 11). This point can be brought out more obviously using our salt example. Surely the 30,000 lumps of salt constitute a large sample. But "All common salt is soluble in water" is supposed to be a law of nature. It is supposed to hold throughout the universe. I don't think we can deny the possibility of the existence of salt outside our earth. Hence the sample of 30,000 lumps of salt all from our own planet is certainly not a fair sample.

Strictly speaking, in order for the sample to be a fair one its members should not be selected all from a short period of time, say between 10,000 B.C. and 2,000 A.D. The universe has been in existence for billions of years, we are told, and will exist for perhaps an infinite number of years to come. Our 12,000 years of recorded history is short indeed in comparison to the lifetime of the universe. A sample of swans confined to these 12,000 years is certainly a biased sample.

As a matter of fact, the formulation of (3a) does intend to rule out the employment of unfair samples. That's the intention of the clause "under a variety of conditions and in a variety of situations." Nevertheless it remains a fact that no matter how varied our observations are we are still confined to select members of our sample from an insignificantly tiny corner of the universe, in both space and time. At best we can say that our sample is a fair sample of a population made up of things on earth in the period of recorded human history. Shall we therefore amend (3a) to (3b)?

(3b) If a large number n of A's are examined (under a variety of conditions and in a variety of situations) and m of these n objects are found to be B's, then it is likely that the proportion of B's among all the A's on earth during the period, say 10,000 B.C. to 2,000 A.D., is close to m/n.

---

3. For the notion of sampling, see Chapter 4.

I am afraid even (3b) is unacceptable to the skeptic, David Hume. (3a) is a universal generalization. (3b) can be described as a **local generalization**. Hume denies not only the rationality of universal generalizations but also that of local generalizations. Indeed he denies the rationality of any kind of induction.

But you might object: "(4) is a mathematical law. The denial of (3b) amounts to a denial of an application of (4). But mathematical laws are necessarily true!"

Hume was neither mad nor simply stubborn. He had an excellent reason for the denial of (3b). You have to put yourself in Hume's reasoning framework if you want to appreciate his very clear and logical argument. Recall that for Hume (and for all inductive empiricists), what is directly available to the scientist as knowledge is what is directly observed—that is, observational inputs about particular things such as trees and flowers, tables and chairs.[4] Note that she has *no* knowledge whatsoever about anything else. In such a situation, what justifies the claim that the sample consisting of the observed is a *fair* sample of a yet-to-be determined and totally unknown population? To put it bluntly, if the scientist's knowledge is confined to the observation that out of 4,000 observed swans 2,634 of them are white, is it possible for her to know that it is a fair sample of all the swans in the United States? Take note that *ex hypothesi* she has no knowledge about anything other than knowledge about the color of those 4,000 swans. Is it then possible for her to know that the sample is taken in a fair manner (that is, at random) from a country known as the United States? Does she know that there is such a country? Does she know its geography? Does she know that she should not confine her observations to swans kept in zoos even though these zoos are distributed quite evenly across the States? Does she know that observations done at night tend to favor white swans over black swans? To claim fairness for her sample, she requires a great deal of knowledge that by assumption is not available to her.

To be able to make use of the law of large numbers, (4), one must know (even with a very low degree of probability) that the sample taken is fair or roughly fair. However, for Hume, no such knowledge (even probable knowledge) is available to the observer, for by assumption the observer is confined to what is actually observed. Here is an analogy. A person lost in a desert may be wandering for days and days without knowledge of where she is or where she is heading. If she should start collecting sand during her wandering, she has no right to claim that she has collected a fair sample of the sand in the desert. She might, by luck, have collected a fair sample. The point, however, is that it would be unjustified for her to claim that the sample is fair.

Similarly it would be unreasonable for us to claim that what we have observed so far is a fair sample of a region known as earth, which *ex hypothesi* is beyond our knowledge. Our knowledge about the size of the earth, its global geography, and so on is inductive knowledge, not observational knowledge. To use inductive knowledge to justify the principle of induction is circular, and we have discussed such arguments in detail in Subsection A.

Hume's main point is that every observational instance is independent of any other observational instance. 'Independence' here carries two senses: (i) no two observational instances are ontologically related and (ii) the way each observation is made has no implication on the way any other observation is made. However, fair sampling requires the scientist to break (ii), for, in order to obtain a fair sample, she must design the collection of observational data in such a manner that the collection *as a whole* is fair. In other words, the manner in which an observation is made will have to be related to the manner in which other observations are made in such a way that the whole shall constitute a fair sample. Hume thus denies that we, as observers, can ever claim that our collections of observational data constitute fair samples. Thus (4) is not applicable in support of (3a) or (3b).

---

4. Strictly speaking, Hume would only admit the "perception" of sense-data as knowledge inputs, what he calls sense impressions. The argument that is presented here applies even more strongly to knowledge about these transient and nonrepeatable sensory inputs.

It should be obvious to those who are more advanced in their philosophical training that (3a) or (3b) being about the world cannot be a logical consequence of (4) alone. Statement (4) is a mathematical truth and is thus analytic.[5] It is a demonstrated philosophical thesis that no synthetic statements (about the world) are deducible from analytic statements.

C. The Uniformity-of-Nature Defense

The reason the mathematical defense fails is that we have no way to know whether our sample consisting of the observed is fair or not. It would be a different story if nature were uniform. A defense of (3a) can then be mounted, for (3a) seems to follow logically from the uniformity of nature.

But what does 'uniformity of nature' mean exactly? There are a number of plausible formulations of the **principle of uniformity of nature**. Let's start with:

(6a) Nature is uniform in the sense that any portion of the universe (any one block of space in a period of time[6]) is more or less like any other portion of the universe.

If (6a) is true, any portion of the universe will be a representative (fair) sample of the whole universe. It can easily be seen that (3a) follows logically from (6a) and (4).

But is it true that any portion of the universe is more or less like any other portion? Is the universe like a carpet with a repeating design pattern? Do you expect another earth similar to ours repeating itself say, every five light years apart? Anyway, the term 'portion' is so vague. How often do we expect a repeat? Worse still, how do we know the portions will repeat themselves?

Let's try a second formulation:

(6b) Nature is uniform in the sense that any two attributes A (for example, swanhood) and B

(for example, whiteness) found associated together a number of times will most likely be associated together all the time throughout the universe.

But this is really just another way of formulating (3) itself. Of course (3) will follow from (6b).

Let's take a formulation from one of the leading philosophers of the 20th century, Bertrand Russell (1912, p. 63):

(6c) Nature is uniform in the sense that "everything that has happened or will happen is an instance of some general law to which there are no exceptions."

This is actually a reformulation of Kant's principle of universal causation, which says that all alterations take place in conformity with the law of the connection of cause and effect. Kant attempts to prove that his principle is a synthetic a priori truth. And from this principle he claims that the principle of induction follows. I don't think we have time to go into Kant's philosophy here. So let's deal with (6c) as it is.

Does (3) follow from (6c)? I think not. Let me illustrate with an example. Suppose 10,000 ravens have been observed and that they are all black. Does it therefore follow from (6c) that it is likely all ravens are black? Does it follow that the fact that these 10,000 ravens are black is likely to be a consequence of a certain law that says, "All ravens are black"? Think carefully. Couldn't the blackness of these 10,000 ravens be a consequence of more than one law, and that none of these laws are in terms of ravenhood and blackness? We spent some time on the distinction between observation terms and theoretical terms in Chapter 15. Both 'raven' and 'black' are observation terms. However, the history of science has shown that most laws of nature are in fact stated in theoretical terms such as 'electron,' 'gene,' and 'light wave.' In other words, the causal link between ravens and blackness may be indirect.

---

5. This is not to say that philosophers are unanimous on this point. A well-known dissident is the great 18th-century German philosopher Immanuel Kant.

6. In the jargon of the theory of relativity, we can say that a portion is a four-dimensional space-time block.

There may be a whole complex of laws that yield the blackness in these 10,000 ravens including laws involving diet, weather, mutation, radioactivity, and so on. Because there are so many laws involved, a change of initial conditions can result in non-black ravens. Furthermore, we have to take in the possibility that the blackness of these 10,000 ravens may not be due to the same causes and laws. That can complicate the situation even further. Thus it would be simplistic to adopt (3) even if (6c) is true.

Of course, even if (3) did follow from (6c), we still have no justification for the truth of (6c). This is Hume's very point. We have contact with only one part of nature. We have no right to claim that the other parts are similar. To assume that the universe is governed by laws of nature is to assume a certain uniformity. How are we to justify this assumption of uniformity if not by some sort of induction? That's why Kant attempted to prove his version of (6c) a priori. Unfortunately it is beyond the scope of this chapter to go into Kant's arguments here.

20.4 THE PRAGMATIC JUSTIFICATION OF INDUCTION

Hans Reichenbach, one of the main pillars of logical positivism, in his 1938 work proposed a very interesting justification of induction by simple enumeration. Here is Wesley Salmon's comment: "Of all the solutions and dissolutions proposed to deal with Hume's problem of induction, Hans Reichenbach's attempt to provide a pragmatic justification seems to me the most fruitful and promising" (1967, p. 53). Two points should be noted at this stage. First, Reichenbach does not attempt to justify methods of induction in general. He confines himself to the justification of the method of **statistical generalization** (Section 4.4). Universal generalization, also known as induction by simple enumeration, corresponds to the principle of induction (3). Statistical generalization is more general than universal generalization, and it corresponds to principle

of induction (3a). Thus any justification of statistical generalization is also a justification of universal generalization. Since Reichenbach confines himself to statistical generalization, in the rest of this section by 'induction' I will mean 'statistical generalization.' Second, Reichenbach's attempted justification does not take the form of demonstrating that induction will definitely bring success. It does not even take the form of showing that induction is *likely* to bring success. What Reichenbach attempts is more modest. He tries to show that (i) induction, if nature is "cooperative," will bring results, and (ii) if any other method of prediction brings results, induction will as well. Hence induction is the best method available as it can at least match and perhaps outperform all other methods. Since this is the best method available, it is perfectly rational to adopt it, even though it may, as a matter of uncontrollable bad luck, not give us any correct predictions whatsoever.

You can see that his objective differs from those three justifications that we studied in the last section. Reichenbach is not attempting to show that (3a) is true, but only to show that it is reasonable to adopt (3a) as a tool for inference and prediction.

Reichenbach (1938, sec. 39) presents his defense of induction in terms of the frequency interpretation of probability (Section 12.6), which involves the mathematical notion of the limit of a sequence. In order that most of us can follow his argument, I will present his case differently, in terms of the idea of a fair (random) sample and the law of large numbers, that is, (4).

His arguments can best be illustrated in terms of an example. Imagine that we are provided with an urn of marbles and are asked to draw 4,000 marbles out of it. (A large urn indeed!) Suppose that, out of the 4,000 marbles drawn, 2,634 of them are red. Our task is to guess what proportion of marbles in the urn is red before the rest are drawn.

The marbles in the urn constitute the population. The 4,000 drawn marbles constitute a sample. Let 'S' denote the proportion of marbles in the sample that are red. (S is often known as the relative frequency; see Chapter 4.) Let 'P' denote the proportion of marbles in the *population* that are red. Here is the task:

Given:

(i)   The sample size is 4,000.

(ii) S is 2,634/4,000 (which is roughly 65%).

To guess:

(iii) What is P?

Note that we know nothing other than (i) and (ii). For instance, we do not know how many marbles there are in the whole urn, and we do not know how well mixed the marbles are in the urn.

Given this meager information, what can and what should we say about P? Reichenbach concedes to Hume that the population size may be anything between 4,000 and infinite. There may be one billion undrawn marbles and they are all red. On the other hand, this billion undrawn marbles may all be nonred. Thus you can see that P may be anything between 0 and 1. Nevertheless, if we are asked to make a guess about P, what sort of guess should we make as the most reasonable? Reichenbach argues that the best bet is to guess P to be in the vicinity of S. In other words, he recommends that we guess that

(iv) P = 65% or thereabouts.

Here is his argument. The sample is either fair (that is, random) or not fair. If it is fair then the law of large numbers, (4), can be applied. According to (4), it is likely that P is close to S because the sample size, being 4,000, is sufficiently large. On the other hand, if the sample is not fair, then P can be anything, and no method can give us a reasonable or reliable answer. Hence the best guess must be (iv).

This argument seems convincing. Nonetheless, its structure resembles the following:

"Where is Peter's watch?"

"Why don't you look under his bed?"

"Why should I?"

"The reason is this. Either his watch is under his bed or it is not. If it is, then you will find it by following my advice. If not, then no other methods (other than trying out all possible

places at random) will enable you to find it. Hence the best place to look is under his bed."

This argument seems bizarre to me.

Suppose I do not have any idea of where Peter's watch is, and I know nothing about Peter's habits; nor do I know anything about the house or the watch. So really anywhere in the house is as probable as any other place. (It may not even be in the house!) So there are really no better methods of finding the watch. But still, why should I look under his bed? The argument can easily be seen to be unsound if we replace 'under Peter's bed' with the phrase 'on Peter's desk' throughout in the argument. You can see that this second argument, being parallel to the first, should be sound as well. But it has a contrary conclusion, for it recommends that we look for the watch on Peter's desk.

Let's return to our example of the marbles in the urn. A similar argument parallel to Reichenbach's can easily be made. Let us first recall the definition of a fair or random sample from Section 20.3.

(5) A random sample (also known as a **fair sample** or a **representative sample**) is a sample obtained by random selection. A selection is random if each member of the population has the same chance (probability) of being selected.

Let's define a half-random sample (a half-fair sample) as follows:

(5a) A half-random sample (also known as a half-fair sample or a half-representative sample) is a sample obtained by half-random selection. A selection is half-random if those members of the population that possess the designated property have twice the chance of being selected over the rest of the population. (In the case of our urn example, the property 'red' is the designated property.)

Now we can construct the following argument of the dichotomy parallel to Reichenbach's: The sample is either half-fair or not half-fair. If it is half-fair then the law of large numbers, (4), can be applied. According to (4), it is likely that P is close to *half* of S because the sample size, being 4,000, is sufficiently large.[7] On the other hand, if the sample is not half-fair, then P can be anything, and no method can give us a reasonable or reliable answer. Hence the best guess must be:

(v)   P = 32.5% or thereabouts (32.5% being half of 65%).

Obviously you can construct a parallel third-fair argument, a parallel quarter-fair argument, and so on. In short, for any numerical value for P that you fancy, you can construct an argument exactly parallel to Reichenbach's. This is similar to the example of the watch. There, for any place you fancy, you can construct an argument to support your claim that the best bet is to look for the watch at that place.

Hume's whole point is that we have absolutely no idea of how representative or fair our sample of observed things is! Hence it is as reasonable or unreasonable to assume that the sample is fair, half-fair, and so on.

There is a second part to Reichenbach's argument. He claims that, should we keep on drawing marbles from the urn, and should these further draws be consistently fair, then our samples will resemble more and more closely the population. Again I think a parallel argument can be made in terms of half-fairness. Should our further draws from the marbles be consistently half-fair, then our samples will "half-resemble" more and more closely the population. Thus we should consistently take half the value of S to be P.

There is a third part to Reichenbach's argument. He claims that, should *any* method succeed, the method of induction will. When applied to our case, the claim is that, if the "half-fair" method should succeed, then the method of induction will. Here is Reichenbach's argument: If the consistent application of the half-fair method brings results, then the method of induction will enable us to discover that this half-fair method is a good method.

In other words, if there are any good methods at all, the method of induction will reveal them.

I think this argument contains three fallacies:

(i)   Until we have exhausted the whole population (of marbles from the urn), we have no way of knowing how good our method is, be it the half-fair method or another. By assumption we do not *know* P. Our consistent guess that P = half of S can neither be verified nor falsified.

(ii) Here it seems that the argument is about second-order induction rather than about first-order induction. It is about the virtue of using induction to discover the choice of methods for predictions rather than about the virtue of using induction directly to make predictions.

(iii) This argument does not establish that second-order induction is reasonable anyway. For instance, even if we knew that the "half-fair" method has been successful for the case of the urn, it is still unreasonable to recommend its use for other urns. Our half-fair method may fail miserably when we are asked to guess the P of the urn of biscuits sitting next to the urn of marbles. Anyway, as pointed out in (i), we would not have known whether any method has succeeded or not until the whole population is *known* to have been exhausted. I have stressed the word 'known.' Even when the sample actually equals the population, we still will not *know* how much the sample resembles or does not resemble the population unless we *know* that the sample is the same as the population. But in empirical science, this is impossible. Even if we have studied the last swan in the universe, we still would not know for a fact that it is the last swan in the universe. (It is possible that the supposedly extinct dinosaur still lives, or the species could be "resurrected" through genetic engineering. The conjecture that the dinosaur is extinct is arrived at through induction anyway!)

---

7. The reason is this: If the sample were fair, then P should be close to S. But since the sample favors the red marbles by a factor of 2, to convert the sample into a fair sample, what is required is to divide the number of red marbles by 2.

Before we move on to the next section, I think it useful to point out again that Reichenbach's justification is only for statistical generalization, whereas Hume's argument is so general that it applies to any kind of ampliative reasoning. In Section 3.1, we pointed out that valid deduction is non-ampliative in the sense that the conclusion is always "part" of the "sum" of the premises. We can actually say that valid deduction is by definition the only kind of non-ampliative reasoning. Inferences other than valid deduction are always ampliative. Thus we can say that induction, including statistical generalization and all other kinds of induction, is by definition ampliative. What Hume has shown is that *no* ampliative reasoning is ever rational, be it statistical generalization, universal generalization, Mill's methods, or whatever. This is a strong thesis, to say the least. No wonder philosophers are so much troubled by Hume's proof that they call it the scandal of philosophy!

Let's now proceed further to see what other responses have been made to this "scandal."

20.5 OTHER RESPONSES

Here are three more well-known opinions on the status of induction.

A. "Dissolution of the Problem of Induction"

P. F. Strawson (1952) thinks that the so-called problem of induction has been blown out of proportion for, according to him, there is no problem at all. Recall that the question is: "Is induction rational?" Strawson recommends that we study the term 'rational' to find out what exactly it means before we make any attempt to answer the question.

What can 'rational' or 'reasonable' mean (as applied to inferences)? In Chapter 2, we saw that there are two kinds of inferences: deductive and inductive inferences. A deductive inference (argument) claims that if the premises are true, then the conclusion has to be true. In other words, it claims that the premises provide conclusive and compulsory grounds for the acceptance of the conclusion. On the other hand, an inductive inference (argument) claims only that the premises provide *some* grounds for the acceptance of the conclusion. We judge deductions by the criterion of validity: a deduction is valid if, given that the premises are true, then the conclusion has to be true. Valid deductions are rational and acceptable while invalid deductions are irrational and unacceptable.

The question is: How are inductions to be assessed?

According to Strawson,

(7) Inductions are assessed by the amount of evidential support from the premises. The more evidential support there is the stronger is the argument. An induction is rational or reasonable if there is sufficient evidential support.

Let's illustrate with the example of the urn of marbles of the last section. There 4,000 marbles are drawn. Out of these, 2,634 are found to be red. Hence $S = 2,634/4,000$ (which is roughly 65%). The method of statistical generalization recommends that we conclude that P, the proportion of marbles in the urn that are red, is close to 65 percent (on the condition that the sample is fair). According to Strawson, this inductive inference is rational because it has plenty of evidential support (the number being 4,000). Had the number of draws been increased by 1,000 and S is still found to be in the vicinity of 65 percent, then the inference to the conclusion that P is around 65 percent is even more credible. "How otherwise should one assess inductive inferences," Strawson would ask, "if not by the strength of their evidential support?" So induction, *by definition*, is rational (reasonable).

It is an analytic proposition that it is reasonable to have a degree of belief in a statement which is proportional to the strength of the evidence in its favour; and it is an analytic proposition, though not a proposition of mathematics, that, other things being equal, the evidence for a generalization is strong in proportion as the number of favourable instances, and the variety of circumstances in which they have been found, is great. (Strawson, 1952, p. 256)

Strawson goes into some lengthy arguments to support (7). His arguments are based on the common use of terms such as 'good grounds,' 'justification,' and 'reasonable.' (This sort of strategy is known as 'ordinary language analysis.') We will not go into details here.

For Strawson, Hume's arguments against the rationality of induction are based on the wrong criterion of rationality. Hume is assessing inductions as if they were deductions. Of course inductions are (by definition) invalid. We shouldn't say that induction is irrational because it is invalid, for validity is only applicable to deductions. Inductions should be measured by another criterion. In fact, Strawson thinks that induction (based on sufficient evidential support) cannot be assessed at all for, *by definition*, induction (based on sufficient evidential support) is rational (according to (7)). To ask whether induction (based on sufficient evidential support) is rational is similar to asking the question, "Is the law legal?" (Strawson 1952, p. 257).

Here are a few comments you might like to entertain:

(i)   Even if it is granted that (7) is the criterion of rationality for judging inductive inferences, one should note that there are many ways to do induction, some good and some bad, and some applicable only in special circumstances. Take our example of the urn of marbles again. We have a choice of many inductive conclusions. Here are a few possibilities: that $P = 65\%$, that P is 32.5 percent (that is, half of 65%), that P is 21.8 percent (that is, a third of 65%), and so on. For example, if we think that the sample is only half-fair, then we might infer that P is 32.5 percent. All these conclusions satisfy the criterion (7). All of them are based on evidential support. They differ in their various interpretations of the support.

(ii) Strawson probably has the law of large numbers (4) in mind when he argues that induction by definition is rational. Law (4) is certainly analytic. It is even a mathematical truth. However Hume is not doubting (4). He is critical of (3) and (3a). It is quite correct to say that induction requires evidential support. But the amount of support the evidence gives and the kinds of conclusion the evidence supports depend very much on the interpretation of the evidence. Laws (3) and (3a) naively assume that the collection of the examined or observed is a fair sample—that is, that the evidence is collected at random. This assumption is unjustified according to Hume. However, without this assumption, (3) and (3a) do not follow from (4).[8]

(iii) Strawson claims that (7) underlies how the terms 'rational' and 'reasonable' are commonly used. "That's what one means by 'being rational'!" he would say. Let us, for the sake of argument, grant that the layperson does use these terms the way Strawson claims. So what! The layperson also uses the terms 'up' and 'down' in such a way that by definition the sky is up above and earth is down below. (Of course Australia and New Zealand are down under.) Should we therefore keep these terms for use in world geography and in astronomy? If Strawson's analysis of the lay term of rationality is really correct, what is required is a better idea of rationality to replace the lay term. Herbert Feigl (1950) points out that there is a difference between validation and vindication. Maybe induction does not require validation, but it certainly requires vindication. Induction is a mode of inference to serve certain purposes. To vindicate it is to show that it does serve those purposes as claimed.

The general opinion is that Strawson has not succeeded in "dissolving" the problem of induction.

---

8. One might argue that, since one does not know whether the sample is fair or not, it would be rational to assume that it is fair. This is similar to the case of throwing a die. If we have no knowledge about the die, then it is rational to assume that the die is fair. See 'classical interpretation of probability' in Chapter 4.

B. Psychological Analysis of Induction

Hume is well aware that we all make inductive inferences. In fact, we all make such inferences daily, if not by the minute. We seem to have a natural urge or tendency to make inductions. Hume gives an explanation. When the mind has been exposed to a number of pairings of two attributes, A followed by B, the mind will acquire a habit. The mind will automatically expect B when exposed to A. This is the very first **associative theory of learning** in psychology.

The renowned 19th-century Russian physiologist Pavlov demonstrated this kind of habit formation with his dogs (Section 3.4). Pavlov would ring a bell as he brought along the food to feed one of his dogs. On the sight and smell of the food, the dog would salivate. After pairing the food and the ringing of the bell a number of times, Pavlov discovered that the dog would salivate on hearing the bell alone. This experiment thus confirmed Hume's associative theory of learning, which says that when A (ringing of the bell) has been followed regularly a number of times by B (the appearance of food), the presentation of A will evoke the expectation of B.

Here are Hume's own words:

> After a repetition of similar instances, the mind is carried by habit, upon the appearance of one event, to expect its usual attendant, and to believe that it will exist. This connexion, therefore, which we feel in the mind, this customary transition of the imagination from one object to its usual attendant, is the sentiment or impression from which we form the idea of power or necessary connexion. (Hume, 1748, sec. 7)

You may recall that Hume argues against the existence of necessary (causal) connection between events (Chapter 11). If there is such a connection

between two types of events A and B, then, on the presentation of A, we can, through that connection, infer (with good reasons) that B will follow. But as Hume argues there can't be such connections. Yet all of us still regularly make inductive inferences: from a number of pairings of A and B to infer that the next A will be followed by a B. This, according to Hume, is due to the nature of the mind: the tendency to form (unreasonable) associative habits.[9]

Thus, according to Hume, it is quite understandable why we make inductions. It is simply a psychological fact that we do so. But the mind's habitual practice of induction is one thing. It is quite another thing to condone such practices. For Hume the mind is unreasonable in making inductions. Thus Bertrand Russell cautions: "It is important to distinguish the fact that past uniformities cause expectations as to the future, from the question whether there is any reasonable ground for giving weight to such expectations" (1912, p. 63).

Let Strawson (Subsection A) take note: The layperson may *feel* that it is absolutely rational to make inductions, so much so that she understands rationality itself in terms of inductive support, yet this feeling can be misguided.

C. Abandonment of Induction

Karl Popper thinks that Hume's arguments are flawless. We should acknowledge that induction is unreasonable and abandon it as a mode of reasoning. However, he thinks that there is no loss in such an abandonment. He argues that deduction alone is sufficient for the practice of science. In Section 19.4, we studied his philosophy of deductivism, which is a blend of rationalism and empiricism. Prima facie, this deductivism does not employ induction at all. Has Popper been successful in demonstrating that science can proceed without inductive reasoning? If so, philosophy would be "de-scandalized." We will study and assess Popper's claim in detail in Chapter 24.

---

9. Hume's psychological explanation of the practice of induction incidentally laid down the foundation of two schools of psychology, the school of associationism in the 19th century and the school of behaviorism (which takes conditioning as its central tenet) in the 20th century.

20.6 CONCLUDING REMARKS

We have been discussing Hume's problem of induction mainly in terms of universal generalization and statistical generalization (see (3) and (3a)). Obviously Hume's skepticism applies to all kinds of induction—all kinds of ampliative reasoning. If ampliative reasoning is ruled out, what is left of science? Prediction is a kind of ampliative reasoning. So for Hume it would be unreasonable for science to make predictions! Our knowledge is thus confined to directly given facts—that is, empirical data. Can we have explanation? According to the covering-law thesis (Chapter 10), adequate explanations depend essentially on the availability of laws of nature. But such laws being general (synthetic) statements can only be arrived at by induction. So explanation is unavailable to science as well.

We are thus lodged in a dilemma: a choice between "infertile" rationalism (as exemplified in Plato, Euclid, and Descartes) and "irrational" empiricism (as preached by Bacon, Mill, and the logical positivists).

Is Popper able to save science from the horns of the dilemma?

Before leaving the subject I think I should mention another possible way out. Constructivism, a contemporary school of thought, has quite a lot to say about observational knowledge—that is, knowledge acquired through observation. According to constructivism, our observational knowledge is not at all as Hume presumes. The mind is not like a camera which collects knowledge through its lens (for example, the eye) in a passive manner. The mind has an active role to play in perception. It is claimed that perception is theory-laden (Chapter 22). In other words, empirical data are partly shaped by the mind. This line of thought originated from Kant, hence constructivism is also known as neo-Kantism. Maybe Hume has made a faulty basic assumption about observational knowledge. Hume could have misdescribed the nature of empirical data, which form the premises of an induction, with the result that both his arguments against the existence of causal connections and his arguments against the rationality of induction could be mistakenly prejudiced. It will be interesting to see what solutions constructivism can offer for Hume's problem (Chapter 31).

In the meantime, as if Hume's problem is not sufficiently serious for empiricism, let's turn to yet a second problem of induction.

KEY TERMS INTRODUCED IN THIS CHAPTER

problem of induction

principle of induction

universal generalization

inductive justification of induction

law of large numbers

random sample

fair sample

representative sample

local generalization

principle of uniformity of nature

statistical generalization

associative theory of learning

REFERENCES

Both Skyrm (1975, chap. 11) and Salmon (1966, chaps. I–III) give good detailed introductions to the problem of induction as well as to all the well-known "solutions." M. H. Salmon et al. (1992, chap. 2) provides a summary.

Brody (1970) and Swinburne (1974) are collections of classical papers on the subject.

For the law of large numbers, see Ayer (1972, pp. 40–43).

The original presentation of the pragmatic justification can be found in Reichenbach (1938, pp. 348–363).

Strawson (1952, pp. 256–260) gives the original version of the "dissolution" of the problem.

Chapter 21*

Problems of Empiricism IB: Goodman's Paradox and Hempel's Paradox

21.1 INTRODUCTION

I think it's time to have some fun, even in the philosophy of science.

This chapter is about two paradoxes. Paradoxes are proven truths that, however, intuitively or otherwise, cannot be true, hence paradoxical. The "grue" paradox was raised by Nelson Goodman (1955)[1] and the ravens paradox came from Carl Hempel (1945). These are fun paradoxes. The results are so ridiculous, yet the proofs are so simple and straightforward. Since both paradoxes apparently undermine induction as a means of extending our knowledge, we can say that they constitute what can be called the **second** and **third problems of induction**.

As I said, these are fun paradoxes. However, they are meant to be serious even though the way they are presented may sound outrageous.

Let's start with Goodman's paradox.

---

*This chapter is more advanced and is optional.

1. The paradox was actually first raised by Goodman in 1947.

21.2 GOODMAN'S PARADOX

Suppose a large number of emeralds (say, six million of them) have been examined before 2500 A.D. and they are all found to be green. The principle of induction ((3) of Section 20.3) would advise us that it is reasonable to induce that

(1) All emeralds are green (throughout space and time).

Now let there be a tribe (of humans). They speak a language known as "U," hence they are the U-speakers. (In contrast, we speak the language E—that is, English, and, therefore, we are E-speakers.) These U-speakers use the following terms instead of 'green' and 'blue' according to the following definitions.

(2) Definition: Any thing X is said to be grue at a certain time t if and only if
(i) X is green at t and t is before the year 2500, or
(ii) X is blue at t and t is during or after the year 2500.[2]

(3) Definition: Any thing X is said to be bleen at a certain time t if and only if
(i) X is blue at t and t is before the year 2500, or
(ii) X is green at t and t is during or after the year 2500.

Now since the aforementioned emeralds are all examined before year 2500, the U-speakers will describe them as grue in color. Thus according to the principle of induction they would induce

(4) All emeralds are grue (throughout space and time).

Imagine that in the year 2501 an emerald is brought back from the moon. Let it be called the Moonstone. No one has examined the emerald yet because it is collected by a robot and is brought back in a sealed box. There is, of course, great excitement. From the chemical analysis done on the stone while it was still on the moon, the scientists know that it is an emerald. However, they do not know what color it is. All the scientists are inductivists. They all trust the method of induction. But half of these scientists are E-speakers and the other half U-speakers. You can see that the E-speakers naturally predict that

(5) The Moonstone (in the year 2501) is green. (Based on (1))

On the other hand, the U-speakers, as a matter of course, predict that

(6) The Moonstone (in the year 2501) is grue. (Based on (4))

The E-speakers, eager to know what the others are predicting, look up the definition of 'grue' and find (2). Since the year is 2501, what is grue (for the U-speaker) is blue (for E-speaker). So (6) amounts to:

(6a) The Moonstone (in the year 2501) is blue.

But (6a) is contrary to (5)! At most one of them can be true.

We can see that the prediction (6) is counterintuitive. And yet (6) is arrived at through induction based on exactly the same set of data as (5). If (6) is unacceptable, (5) should also be. This is paradoxical and puzzling. Goodman calls it the **new riddle of induction**. We can call it the **second problem of induction**.

The lesson we can learn from this "grue" story seems to be that there are many ways to describe the same set of data. For the E-speakers, the collection of the six million green emeralds examined before 2500 is described by

(7) These six million examined emeralds are all green.

But for the U-speakers, the same collection is described by

(8) These six million examined emeralds are all grue.

Predictions (7) and (8) through induction yield different conclusions—(1) and (4)—which, in turn, lead to (5) and (6) respectively.

2. This is not Goodman's own formulation. I have adopted that of Skyrm (1975, p. 62).

Everybody loves a riddle. Many solutions to this paradox have been offered. I will briefly mention two.

21.3 "SOLUTIONS" TO GOODMAN'S PARADOX

Here are two of the well-known opinions on "grue."

A. Carnap's Solution

Carnap (1947) attempts to solve the paradox by pointing out that 'grue' and 'bleen' are not **purely qualitative predicates**, whereas 'green' and 'blue' are. 'Predicate' belongs to the terminology of logic. Here, for simplicity, we can take predicates to be the same as adjectives (for example, tall), adjectival phrases (such as six feet tall), or common nouns (for instance, tall person). A purely qualitative predicate is a special kind of predicate. Roughly speaking, it is one that does not have 'proper names' embedded in it, nor does its meaning change with time. Here are a few purely qualitative predicates: hot, magnetic, square, horse, and house. 'Grue' and 'bleen' do not seem to be purely qualitative predicates. For example, 'grue' has got a proper name mentioned in its definition—that is, 'year 2500.' In addition, 'grue' seems to change its meaning with time. If the statement "Lake Taupo is grue" is made before 2500, it means "Lake Taupo is green," whereas if it is made during or after 2500, it means "Lake Taupo is blue." According to Carnap, only purely qualitative predicates are projectible. One cannot employ induction on "eccentric" predicates like 'grue.' Hence he concludes that (1) and (5) are the proper inductive conclusions to make, not (4) and (6).

However, Goodman was quick to point out that if 'grue' and 'bleen' are "eccentric," so are 'green' and 'blue.' Imagine yourselves to be U-speakers. How would you understand 'green' and 'blue'? The definitions of 'green' and 'blue' must be something like the following:

(8) Definition: Any thing X is said to be green at a certain time t if and only if
  (i) X is grue at t, and t is before the year 2500, or
  (ii) X is bleen at t, and t is during or after the year 2500.

(9) Definition: Any thing X is said to be blue at a certain time t if and only if
  (i) X is bleen at t, and t is before the year 2500, or
  (ii) X is grue at t, and t is during or after the year 2500.

You can see the symmetry of the situation. For the E-speakers, 'grue' and 'bleen' are not purely qualitative. But for the U-speakers, it is the other way around. It is 'green' and 'blue' that are not purely qualitative. Both 'green' and 'blue' have proper names in their definitions—that is, 'year 2500'—and, worse still, they change their meanings with time. For instance, 'green' changes from meaning 'grue' to meaning 'bleen' at the beginning of year 2500. To favor one language over another is a kind of language discrimination, which should have no place in the methodology of science.[3]

But you might say that almost all grue things will suddenly change from being grue to bleen at the stroke of midnight on December 31, 2499, whereas almost all green things would stay green. For example, your grue car will suddenly turn bleen as year 2499 is replaced by year 2500, even though its look stays the same. But your green car (which is of course the very same car since you can only afford one car at a time) will stay green through the coming of the new year. Perhaps you would like to offer a counterargument in defense of 'grue' and 'bleen' by making use of definitions (8) and (9). Can it be demonstrated that 'green' and 'blue' are true colors whereas 'grue' and 'bleen' are not?

3. Here is another example of a Goodman-type predicate: 'Whack' meaning 'white in Europe or black in Australia' (Gardenfors, 1990, p. 80).

There has been quite a bit of controversy over this (see, for example, Barker and Achinstein (1960)). I'll leave this for you to debate as an exercise.[4] Let's now turn to Goodman's own "solution."

B. Goodman's Solution

Goodman thinks and argues that logically there is no difference between 'grue' and 'green.' One can be defined in terms of the other. Logically the E-language and the U-language are on a par. Why 'green' is projectible whereas 'grue' is not has nothing to do with logic or semantics. It is, according to Goodman, a matter of pragmatics. 'Green' has been projected successfully a large number of times in the past. For example, we have successfully projected from instances of green leaves to the generalization "All leaves are green."[5] On the other hand, there is no record of any successful projection of 'grue.'[6] Hence according to Goodman, 'green' is much more entrenched.[7]

Here is Goodman's theory of projectibility. A predicate is projectible if there are no other competing predicates that are more entrenched. Inductions should be made only with projectible predicates. Since 'grue' is competing with 'green', and 'green' is more entrenched, 'grue' is not projectible. Hence neither (4) nor (6) should be inferred.[8]

You can see that Goodman's theory amounts to the justification of induction by induction (Section 20.3). It amounts to the recommendation of employing predicates that have been successful in the past for future projections. 'Green' is such a successful predicate, hence it should be employed in preference over 'grue.' To be more technical, Goodman is using a second-order induction to justify the choice of a first-order induction. The second-order induction is about words—for example, 'green'—whereas the first-order induction is about things, such as emeralds and green objects.

In Section 20.3, we dismissed the justification of induction by induction as a circular argument. However, recently this kind of circularity seems to be acceptable to many. The justifying philosophy is known as **naturalized epistemology** or **naturalistic epistemology**, which, in a nutshell, says that epistemology is part of empirical science.[9] Let me explain.

Traditionally it is taken for granted that epistemology is an a priori subject. It is supposed to study the nature of knowledge, in particular scientific knowledge, without relying on any scientific knowledge. Otherwise it would be circular. The results of epistemology are then used to justify or to condemn or to improve on current scientific methods as well as their products.

Now suppose Darwin's theory of evolution, which is part of scientific knowledge, is employed to justify induction, in particular to justify Goodman's theory of projectibility. Since the study of induction belongs to epistemology, we are employing the products of science to justify epistemological theses, which in turn are used to justify general scientific results such as Darwin's theory. The circularity is obvious.

Nonetheless there have been very strong and convincing arguments claiming that such circularity is justified. The movement is known as naturalistic epistemology. Let me quote W. V. Quine:

---

4. For example, you could challenge the presumption that almost all green things would stay green with the start of the year 2500. How are we to know that? Isn't it by induction based on the E-language (rather than on the U-language)?

5. Let's ignore the minor point that strictly speaking this projection is not quite successful because it is not true that all leaves are green.

6. As a matter of fact, 'grue' has been as successful as 'green' because before year 2500 the two terms are identical in extension (that is, applicable to exactly the same things).

7. Note that being entrenched is not the same as being familiar. A term is familiar if it has been used (in talking and in referring) often. A term is entrenched if it has successfully been employed in projection often.

8. This is an oversimplified version of Goodman's theory. For his own presentation see Goodman (1955), which has a more recent edition: 4th edition, 1983.

9. This philosophy originates from Quine (1969).

At this point let me say that I shall not be impressed by protests that I am using inductive generalizations, Darwin's and others, to justify induction, and thus reasoning in a circle. The reason I shall not be impressed by this is that my position is a naturalistic one; I see philosophy not as an a priori propaedeutic or groundwork for science, but as continuous with science. I, philosophy and science are in the same boat—a boat which, to revert to Neurath's figure as I so often do, we can rebuild only at sea while staying afloat in it. There is no external vantage point, no first philosophy. All scientific findings, all scientific conjectures that are at present plausible, are therefore in my view as welcome for use in philosophy as elsewhere. (1969, p. 165)

The philosophy of naturalistic epistemology is both challenging and interesting. Sadly we have to turn from it lest we should wander too far afield.

21.4 SOME COMMENTS ON "GRUE"

I personally think that Goodman's paradox, important and interesting as it is, is not a problem of induction. It is a problem and it is a challenging philosophical problem. But it has nothing to do with induction. To call it a new riddle of induction or the second problem of induction is misleading. Let me explain.

Recall that induction is any mode of inference which is ampliative. Our discussions of induction have centered mainly round universal generalization (that is, induction by simple enumeration) and statistical generalization. So for easy presentation, let us take 'induction' to mean these two types in what follows.

Induction, as pointed out in Section 20.3, is based on the mathematical theorem, the **law of large numbers**. For clarity let's repeat it here.

(10) If a random sample of a sufficiently large size is taken from a population, there is a high probability that the proportion of members of the sample having a certain attribute resembles closely the proportion of members of the population having that attribute. In fact the probability can be made arbitrarily high by increasing the size of the sample.

Let's unpack this in simpler terms:

(i)   A population is a set of individuals. Its size can be finite or infinite. In fact, the statistician need have no knowledge of its size.

(ii) A sample is a subset of the population. If the members of the sample are chosen at random from the population, then it is a random sample (also known as a fair sample).[10] The size of the sample is usually known to the statistician. It is common practice to denote it by 'n.'

(iii) When we do sampling, we are always interested in at least one attribute.[11] Let's call it the attribute of interest (AOI). Let m be the number of individuals in the sample that has AOI. 'm' is known as the frequency (of occurrence of AOI). The ratio 'm/n' is known as the relative frequency (of occurrence of AOI), n being the size of the sample. We can abbreviate the relative frequency as 'S,'[12] which is often expressed as a percentage.

(iv) The aim of the sampling is to try to estimate the proportion of members of the population that has AOI. Let this proportion be known as 'P.'

(v)   The law of large numbers says that if (a) the sample is large, and (b) the sample is fair, then P is very likely to be close to S.

---

10. See Section 20.3 for "random sample."

11. We are simplifying things quite a bit here. For more depth see Chapter 4.

12. 'S' signifies that it is a characteristic of the *sample*.

(vi) To infer from S to P is a statistical generalization, which is the kind of induction that concerns us here.

The law of large numbers is a mathematical truth, much like "$2 + 2 = 4$." It can be rigorously demonstrated. So there should be little doubt about its truth.

So much for (10), the law of large numbers.

According to (v), the law of large numbers is applicable if and only if (a) the sample size is large and (b) it is a fair sample. Condition (a) is easy to fulfill: just a few hundred instances constitute a sufficiently large sample. The (first) problem of induction, as was explained in the last chapter, is a problem with (b): there is no reason whatsoever to claim that any collection of observed instances is a fair sample. But *suppose* our sample is both large and fair, then even Hume should have to agree that induction is rational and unproblematic. So what is the problem with Goodman? Of course one can doubt the law of large numbers itself. One can even doubt "$2 + 2 = 4$."[13] But that is a different problem. Granted that the sample is both large and fair, induction on that sample should be reasonable and reliable. So where does Goodman's complaint fit in?

Let's discuss the issue in terms of the example of the emeralds. Six million emeralds have been collected and examined according to the story, and they have all been found to be green. The standard move is to infer that all emeralds are green. Here

(a) The population is the set of all emeralds.

(b) The sample is the six million examined emeralds.

What is AOI, the attribute of interest?

Recall that in any sampling exercise, at least one AOI has to be nominated. In the present case

(c) AOI is the attribute 'green.'

(d) The sample of six million is certainly large, and, for the sake of argument, let's assume that the sample is fair.

So the application of the law of large numbers should be straightforward. What is the difficulty? The reasonable conclusion is that

(1) All emeralds are green.

There is nothing problematic with this conclusion or with the reasoning. The conclusion is as reasonable as mathematics itself, since it is a logical consequence of a mathematical theorem.

Nevertheless, Goodman thinks that there *is* a problem for it would be just as reasonable to conclude that

(4) All emeralds are grue.

But does (4) follow from (a) to (d)? This is the point. To conclude (4) one needs to replace (c) by

(c′) AOI is the attribute 'grue.'

We have the following situation:

	(a)		(a)
	(b)		(b)
(I)	(c)	(II)	(c′)
	(d)		(d)
	(1)		(4)

This is not a case of the same set of premises leading to contrary conclusions. These contrary conclusions, (1) and (4), can be seen to be consequences of rather different premises. In logic, different premises leading to different conclusions is perfectly normal (and expected).

What one can and should complain about is the choice of 'grue' as AOI. In other words, one can challenge the reasonableness of the third premise of Inference II—that is, (c′). You might say that 'grue' should not be employed in scientific investigations. You might complain that 'grue' is an "eccentric" predicate, totally unnatural. But these complaints have nothing to do with induction. It is a different issue altogether. What sort of terms or predicates should be employed in the pursuit of

---

13. Historically Descartes doubted even mathematical truths such as "$2 + 2 = 4$," and Leibniz, Frege, and Russell all attempted to prove once and for all that mathematics is beyond doubt. Interesting!

science is a big issue indeed. But important as it is, it has absolutely nothing to do with induction (in support of it, or in criticism of it).

Thus Goodman's paradox can be seen to have nothing to do with the rationality of induction. What it has brought up is a different problem: the **problem of predicate choice** in science. Let me explain.

Science is both descriptive and explanatory. What sort of predicates should be adopted for these activities? Phenomenalists such as Hume and Mach (Section 16.4) think that only terms directly descriptive of sense-data (sense impressions) are admissible— for example, 'red,' 'square,' 'bright,' and 'loud.' On the other hand, physicalists (for example, logical positivists of the later period) will admit only observational terms descriptive of macroscopic objects such as 'table,' 'cat,' and 'tree' (Chapter 23). For them, the nonobservational terms (theoretical terms) are either instrumental in the roles they play (Chapter 16) or are logical constructs, reducible to observation terms (Chapter 13). You can see that ruling on legitimacy in the choice of predicates in science depends very much on one's "larger" philosophical background. Various schools of thought have their own reasons for giving blessings to certain choices of terms in the practice of science.[14]

What philosophical justification can there be for the use of normal words like 'green'? What philosophical reasons can there be for the banning of abnormal words like 'grue'? I feel that these are *not* the questions to be settled under the topic 'induction.' They belong to a much more general field. Perhaps we should settle on the choice of metaphysical schools such as realism and instrumentalism first. Perhaps we should try to understand the structure of scientific explanation to start with, since description is closely related to explanation according to some schools of thought. How the problem of predicate choice is to be handled is difficult and puzzling. But it has little to do with our subject, the rationality of induction.

Some of us might still feel uncomfortable over the paradox. We might ask, "If induction is really rational, how can it be that, starting from the same set of data—that is, the set of the six million examined emeralds—through induction one can arrive at inconsistent results: (5) and (6a)?"

(5) The Moonstone (in year 2501) is green.

(6a) The Moonstone (in year 2501) is blue.

It is a common mistake to take a set of objects as a set of data. Data are statements. Being statements, they say something and they should, therefore, be true or false. A set of objects, such as a set of emeralds, is not a set of data. The emeralds can be very valuable. But they are neither true nor false. Moreover the same set of objects can prompt many different sets of data. For example, on seeing the emeralds one may make one or more of the following true statements:

(10) They are green.

(11) They are beautiful.

(12) They are of different sizes.

(13) They are precious stones.

Inferences, in particular induction, operate on statements, not on objects. Each inference is made up of a set of statements known as premises and a single statement known as the conclusion (Chapter 2). When we assess inferences, we examine these *statements*. I think you can see now that (5) and (6a) are not conclusions from the same set of data. They are induced respectively from

(14) These six million emeralds are all green.

(15) These six million emeralds are all grue.

And these are very different statements.

We might still feel uncomfortable. One might say, "The set of emeralds might not be a set of data. Still it seems paradoxical that we obtain inconsistent inferences from the same set of objects."

---

14. In mathematics too. The legitimacy of the use of terms such as the number zero, the empty set, the irrational numbers, and certain infinite numbers have been debated from time to time.

Let's consider an analogy. Here is a set of words that you find written on the left part of a blackboard: HUT, NORMAL, KITTEN, HALT, MARK, and KIND. The game is to guess what sort of words should be found on the right-hand side of the blackboard. You are advised to use induction (of course). I can think of at least two very reasonable answers.

(16) The remaining words on the blackboard are all English words (because all the words on the left are English words).

(17) The remaining words on the blackboard are all German words (because all the words on the left are German words).

Here is a case of the same set of objects leading to inconsistent conclusions. You can see that we do not require Goodman-type predicates to yield Goodman's paradox.

21.5 HEMPEL'S PARADOX OF CONFIRMATION

Every philosopher loves a paradox, and most paradoxes are invented (or discovered) by philosophers. The ancient Greek Zeno (5th century B.C.) with his paradoxes of space and time more or less marked the beginning of Western philosophy.[15]

Following Hume's problem of induction and Goodman's "grue" paradox, let's move on to a third paradox, Hempel's paradox of confirmation. It runs as follows:

Let's consider the hypothesis

H: All ravens are black.

It is generally considered that the discovery of any black raven will support H. In technical terms, the existence of a black raven is known as a **positive instance** of H, and positive instances are considered supporting evidence for a hypothesis. We say that it **confirms** the hypothesis (Chapter 1). On the other hand, the existence of a nonblack raven is known as a **negative instance**, and negative instances **disconfirm** the hypothesis. What about nonravens? They are generally considered **irrelevant instances**, irrespective of whether they turn out to be black or nonblack. This piece of common sense on positive, negative, and irrelevant instances is known as Nicod's criterion.[16] In general, **Nicod's criterion** says that given any hypothesis of the form "All P are Q," then

(i)   Anything that is both a P and a Q confirms the hypothesis (called a positive instance).

(ii) Anything that is both a P and a non-Q disconfirms the hypothesis (called a negative instance).

(iii) Anything that is a non-P is irrelevant.

Intuitively we can see that this criterion is reasonable and unproblematic.

However, letting H' be

H': All nonblack things are nonravens,

Hempel (1945) argues as follows.

(18) H' is logically equivalent to H.[17]

(19) Hence whatever confirms H' should also confirm H.

(20) But, by Nicod's criterion, a nonblack nonraven would confirm H'.

---

15. Zeno's paradoxes have exotic names: the racecourse, Achilles and the Tortoise, the Arrow, and the Relativity of Motion. They are very interesting, and their study belongs to the philosophy of space and time, which is part of the philosophy of science.

16. The first explicit formulation of this criterion was in Jean Nicod's *Foundations of Geometry and Induction*, London: 1930, p. 219.

17. If you are not convinced, reason as follows: H means the same thing as: "There are no nonblack ravens." (Let us call this Z.) In general, "All P's are Q's" means the same as "There are no non-Q P's." So by the same token, H' should mean the same as "There are no non-nonravens that are nonblacks." But this last sentence is the same as "There are no ravens that are nonblacks." But this is the same as Z. In predicate logic, H is "$(x)(Rx \supset Bx)$" and H' is "$(x)(\sim Bx \supset \sim Rx)$." Their equivalence can easily be shown.

(21) Hence, by (19), a nonblack nonraven would confirm H.

Statement (21) is paradoxical because, according to Nicod's criterion operating on H, a nonblack nonraven should be irrelevant to H. Intuitively it is outrageous to claim the discovery of a red star, or a green leaf, or a white swan (all of which are nonblack nonravens) as confirming the hypothesis that all ravens are black. But this is exactly what (21) claims.

There has been no shortage of attempts to solve this paradox. Unfortunately none seem to be satisfactory.[18] Here is Hempel's own response.

For Hempel, there is nothing wrong with the proof (18)–(21). The proof does demonstrate that red stars, green leaves, and white swans all confirm the hypothesis H. He suggests that Nicod's criterion is defective and should be amended. He replaces it with his own criterion for the confirmation of "All P are Q":

(i) Anything that is both a P and a non-Q disconfirms the hypothesis (called a negative instance).

(ii) Anything else, including a non-Q non-P, confirms the hypothesis (called a positive instance).

In short, whatever is not inconsistent with the hypothesis confirms it. Let's call this criterion, **Hempel's criterion**.

Why should we feel uneasy in admitting white swans as confirming instances of hypothesis H then?

According to Hempel, there are two prejudices that have clouded our judgment, bringing about this uneasy feeling.

PREJUDICE 1

Because of the grammatical structure of H, we think that it is a statement *about* ravens. In grammatical terminology, we say that the subject of H is 'raven,' implying that the subject matter is ravens. Similarly we think that H' is about nonblack things. But this is wrong, according to Hempel. Grammar has misled us. For example, "Peter is taller than John" is about both Peter and John. Both 'Peter' and 'John' are the sentence's *logical* subjects. In content, the sentence is no different from "John is shorter than Peter." In fact, by analyzing H in terms of standard predicate logic, Hempel can be shown to be right. According to predicate logic, H is about everything whatsoever in the universe including stars, leaves, and swans. What H says is that:

H″: There are no nonblack ravens.[19]

You can see that, as one goes through the objects of the universe, the only instances that would be against H″ are nonblack ravens. Everything else is agreeable to H″. They are all on a par. They all confirm it (to the same degree). Since H″ is about everything in the universe, no wonder white swans are as good as black ravens in confirming H.

PREJUDICE 2

There is a further reason why we do not feel that white swans confirm H. According to Hempel, in any testing of a hypothesis, the experimenter assumes plenty of background knowledge. This background knowledge probably includes knowledge that swans are not ravens. Hence, when she is asked to test H, she is not interested in swans because *she already knows* that any swan, being a nonraven, would confirm H″ (which is equivalent to H). That's why swans, whether white or black, are not taken as relevant in the testing of H. However, if the experimenter does not have this piece of background knowledge she might spend considerable time ascertaining whether swans are nonblack ravens.

How convincing are Hempel's arguments? Let us consider this analogy. Around 1910 Ernest Rutherford, a New Zealander, proposed the following hypothesis.

(22) All atoms are structurally miniature solar systems (with the nucleus at the center and the electrons revolving around it).

---

18. For various attempts of solutions, see Swinburne (1973, pp. 55–58) and Scheffler (1963, pp. 256–294).

19. In predicate logic, $\sim(\exists x)(Rx \, . \sim Bx)$.

This is a very important hypothesis. It represents an epoch-making step in the understanding of the atom, and thus of matter in general. It has now been taken as a piece of common sense. Yet in the early 20th century, it was quite an incredible hypothesis. It certainly needed experimental confirmation. But to test (22) was not easy and required very sophisticated and expensive instruments. However, there is a very cheap way to do it, according to Hempel. To convince the scientific community, Rutherford could simply point at all the books, the pens, the tables, and chairs in his room and claim that each one of these confirms (22), because all of them are nonminiature solar systems and nonatoms.

I don't think Hempel's criterion of confirmation is reasonable.

21.6 SOME COMMENTS ON THE "RAVENS"

Let's go back to the law of large numbers, (10). I think Hempel's paradox arose because we have not taken sufficient care in the application of this law. A number of mistakes have been made in reasoning with the idea of sampling. The law of large numbers is a mathematical law (theorem). If we can rely on anything, I think we can rely on mathematical truths. Law (10) is a very simple mathematical truth. If we apply it carefully I don't think we can land with a paradox.

To start with, let me clarify the relationship between confirmation and induction. Roughly, induction is a mode of discovery (Chapter 5). It includes inferences from empirical data to a hypothesis (often a general principle or law[20]). So, temporally, the data come first, and then the hypothesis. Confirmation is also concerned with the relationship between empirical data and a hypothesis. But the temporal order is in reverse. We are first given a

hypothesis and then are asked to compare it with the data. This is the process of justification or evaluation (Chapters 6 and 7). For our present purpose, we can take the logical relationship between the data and the hypothesis as the same for induction and confirmation. In other words, as a matter of logic the two modes of inferences are the same. They differ in application. In discovery, the logical relationship is known as induction, whereas in justification it is known as confirmation. This is by no means a generally accepted opinion. But for our present purposes, it would be expedient to base our expositions on this assumption. Anyway, since we have so far confined 'induction' to mean either universal generalization or statistical generalization, in this narrow interpretation of induction I think the identity of induction and confirmation is exact.

So let's consider Hempel's paradox as a problem of induction. Here is the paradox again:

Remember that H and H' are the following hypotheses:

H: All ravens are black.

H': All nonblack things are nonravens.

Now here is Hempel's argument in terms of induction.

(23) Given a large number of nonblack nonravens, we can induce H'.

(24) H' is equivalent to H.

By (23) and (24), we can conclude:

(25) Given a large number of nonblack nonravens (for example, white swans), we can induce H, that all ravens are black.

Surely (25) is paradoxical.

We agree that (25) is paradoxical and unacceptable. But there are a few flaws in the reasoning leading up to it. Once these flaws are exposed I don't think the paradoxical result can be demonstrated as claimed by Hempel. Let's see.

---

20. This does not exclude the possibility of using induction to infer hypotheses that are not general—for example, "The earth is round."

FLAW A: We can detect the flaws more easily if, instead of dealing with universal generalizations, we consider the more general type of reasoning—that is, statistical generalization. Corresponding to H and H', statistical generalization will yield something like:

K: m/n of ravens (in the universe) are black.

K': m/n of nonblacks (in the universe) are nonravens.

(where m/n represents a percentage that is equal to or less than 100%; in the limiting case where $m/n =$ 100%, K and K' become identical with H and H' respectively).

If Hempel's argument is sound, it should be applicable to K and K' as well. But in fact you can see that K is *not* equivalent to K'. Hempel's argument (23) to (25) holds when and only when $m/n = 100\%$. It seems that Hempel has demonstrated his paradoxical results only for universal generalizations but not for the more general case of statistical generalization. Universal generalization is a limiting case of statistical generalization. Why should the paradox hold only for the limiting case? Why does it not apply to the general case?

As pointed out at the beginning of Section 20.4, when we infer from a sample to the population, we need to specify

(i)   a set of individuals as the population;

(ii) a fair (random) sample of a large size, n;

(iii) an AOI. If m is the number of individuals in the sample having AOI, then m/n is the relative frequency.

(iv) The law of large numbers prescribes that P, the proportion of individuals in the population having AOI, should be close to m/n.

Let's ask the question Q.

Q: In the reasoning (23)–(25), which are the population, the sample, and the AOI?

These are not clearly stated, are they? When we practice an exact science such as mathematics, we should be precise; otherwise we may get funny results. So let's be precise. We have to decide, for example, whether the population is

(a) the set of all nonblack things,

(b) the set of all nonravens,

(c) the set of all black things,

(d) the set of all ravens, or

(e) the set of all things.

I think Hempel would have chosen (e), because for Hempel H is equivalent to H'', which is

H'': There are no nonblack ravens in the universe.

Let's leave this rather unusual interpretation aside till later. For the moment, let us work with common sense.

I suggest that we consider hypotheses K and K', which are the more general versions of H and H'.

According to common sense, I would suggest that K is arrived at through an inference, which I will call Inference III. This inference takes

(i)   the set of all ravens as the population,

(ii) the set of examined ravens as the sample (which has n members),

(iii) blackness as the AOI (m members of the sample being black, yielding m/n as the relative frequency).

By virtue of the law of large numbers, Inference III concludes that

(iv) P, the proportion of black things among all the ravens in the universe, is close to m/n (assuming, of course, that the sample is large and fair).

In parallel, I suggest that K' is arrived at through Inference IV, which takes

(i)   the set of all nonblack things as the population,

(ii) the set of examined nonblack things as the sample (which has n members),

(iii) nonravenhood as the AOI (m members of the sample being nonravens, yielding m/n as the relative frequency).

By virtue of the law of large numbers, Inference IV concludes that

(iv) *P*, the proportion of nonravens among the nonblack things in the universe, is close to *m/n* (again, treating the sample as large and fair).

You can see that Inferences III and IV are very different inferences. They have different premises and that's why they have such different conclusions.

Are the two conclusions *K* and *K'* in any way connected? I think not. The knowledge of one has no bearings on the truth or falsity of the other—that is, unless it happens that *m/n* is 100 percent.

What I am trying to show is that given any fair and large sample, the law of large numbers will guarantee a reasonable inductive inference from the sample to the population. This is a mathematical truth, which is beyond any reasonable doubt. But, as pointed out in Section 20.3B, we can have no good reason to believe that any sample consisting of observed objects is a fair sample. Hence, to use the law of large numbers to make inductive inferences is unjustifiable. This is Hume's argument (as reformulated by me). This is Hume's problem with induction. I think that it is a genuine problem. However, Hempel thinks that in addition to that problem there is another. I simply cannot see how this other problem can arise. As I said, the law of large numbers is a mathematical law and is necessarily true.

But I do concede that when *m/n* = 100%, Hempel does have a prima facie case. It is actually quite a mystery. Even when *m/n* = 99.99%, Hempel's argument does not apply. But when *m/n* equals exactly 100 percent suddenly his argument seems to work, bringing with it the paradoxical result (25). Why?

However, this sort of phenomenon is not uncommon in mathematics. For example, we all take it as common sense that

(26) For any number *x*, half of *x* is always smaller than *x*.

This is in fact true for every number—that is, except for the number 0. You see the result of halving 0 is still 0, and 0 is not smaller than 0.[21] We can say that (26) applies to any number other than 0. In fact, (26) applies to any number *x*, no matter how close it is to 0. When you halve it, the result is always smaller, in fact always smaller by half. Now imagine that *x* moves closer and closer to 0, (26) continues to hold. Then suddenly when *x* coincides with 0, (26) breaks down. There is a sharp discontinuity here. Following mathematics, we can call such a "point" a singular point or a **singularity**. We can also simply call it an anomaly or an irregularity. Of course, giving names to a phenomenon is not explaining the phenomenon. However, here at least we can see that singularities in mathematics are not usually taken as matters of concern. They are not paradoxical, even though they may be intuitively surprising.

Here is yet another example in mathematics. We expect that

(27) When a number *y* is divided by another number *x*, the result is always a number.

But this is not true when *x* is 0. Again you can see that there is a discontinuity here. For example, *x* may be very very small, say 0.0000006. When we divide another number, say, 392 with it, we get a meaningful number. But as *x* becomes smaller and smaller, and finally becomes 0, suddenly at that very point (27) does not hold: 392/*x* suddenly becomes meaningless. Here is a discontinuity. 0 is a singular point.

Can we say that division is problematic because there are singularities in its operations? Can we say that induction is problematic for similar reasons?

Here is the more correct picture of the situation.

(i)   Inference III leads to *K*.

(ii) Inference IV leads to *K'*.

(iii) *Incidentally* when *m/n* = 100%, *K* = *H*, and *K'* = *H'*.

---

21. The infinite numbers share this feature with 0. It can be easily demonstrated that half of infinity is equal to itself.

(iv) Even though H and H' are logically equivalent, they are *essentially* very different hypotheses. They draw support from different samples based on different courses of reasoning. So even though the existence of nonblack things supports H', it does not support H, and there is no paradox.[22]

I said that Hempel's arguments have a few flaws. We have just covered Flaw A. Let us move on to Flaw B.

FLAW B: As I said before, the law of large numbers is a mathematical statement. As a mathematical statement it is precise, and we are expected to scrutinize every word in it. Error could arise if some words were overlooked. Here is the law from (10) again:

(10) If a random sample of a sufficiently large size is taken from a population, there is a high probability that the proportion of members of the sample having a certain attribute resembles *closely* the proportion of members of the population having that attribute.

Care should be taken with the qualifying adverb "closely." The law does not claim exact resemblance between the sample and the population. It only claims *close* resemblance. For example if m/n of a (large fair) sample of ravens are found to be black, the law says that it is very likely that the proportion of black ravens in the universe is *close to m/n*. If we let S stand for the relative frequency of ravens in the sample that are black, and let P be the proportion of ravens in the universe that are black, then the law says that:

(28) The probability that P is in the *vicinity* of S is very high.

In mathematical symbols, the law says that

(28a) The probability that $|P - S| < \varepsilon$ is very high (where ε is a very small number) depending on the size of the sample and on the magnitude of the probability that we require.

It is important to note that the law of large numbers never states that

(29) The probability that $P = S$ is very high.

In fact, it is easy to demonstrate mathematically that

(30) The probability that $P = S$ is zero.

Bearing these in mind, we can see that induction through sampling will not give us hypotheses such as K and K'. Instead it will give us respectively:

$K^\star$: Approximately m/n of ravens (in the universe) are black. (To be more exact: That the probability of ravens being black in the vicinity of m/n is very high.)

$K'^\star$: Approximately m/n of nonblack things (in the universe) are nonravens. (To be more exact: That the probability of nonblack things being nonraven in the vicinity of m/n is very high.)

In the limiting case when m/n equals 100 percent, $K^\star$ and $K'^\star$ become respectively:

$H^\star$: Approximately 100 percent of ravens (in the universe) are black.

$H'^\star$: Approximately 100 percent of nonblack things (in the universe) are nonravens.

You will find that $H^\star$ is by no means equivalent to $H'^\star$. Hempel's argument works only for H and H'. However, in sampling induction—that is, statistical generalizations—we never claim H and H'. What we claim are $H^\star$ and $H'^\star$. This is Flaw B in Hempel's argument.

FLAW C: There is indeed a third flaw in his argument. Actually by sampling induction we can never arrive at H', or K', or $K'^\star$. At the beginning of the

---

22. Here is an analogy. Imagine a north-south street crossing an east-west street, overlapping at A. Even though A belongs to both streets, it is actually part of two distinct streets. The traffic at A goes north-south when A is taken as part of the north-south street. It goes east-west when A is taken as part of the other street.

discussion under Flaw A, we asked the question Q, which is

Q: In the reasoning (23)–(25), which are the population, the sample, and the AOI?

We then suggested that K' is probably arrived at by Inference IV, which takes the set of all nonblack things as the population. Is this possible? Is it possible to have the set of all nonblack things as the population and then have a subset of it as the sample?

Is a population a set of individuals? What is a set of individuals?[23] A set is well-defined only if: (a) given any individual, there are explicit principle(s) or means to tell whether that individual belongs to the set or not (principle of demarcation) and (b) there are explicit principle(s) governing when something (in the set) is one individual or more than one individual so that the members of the set can be identified, reidentified, and counted (principle of individuation). In other words, it is required that members of a set can be counted so that for any set there is a definite number representing exactly the number of individuals in the set (even though this number may not be known to anyone).

For example, the set of all books in this room is a well-defined set. "Books in this room" provides the principle of demarcation of the set, and "Book" provides the principle of individuation, by which we can easily tell whether a "lump" of matter constitute one book or two. The number of books in this room is a well-defined number, even though it may remain unknown to anyone (say, no one bothers to count them up). On the other hand, the set of red things in this room is not a well-defined set. For instance, we cannot tell how many red things there are in this room. There is no definite number here. On my desk is a lump of red clay. Is there one red *thing* lying on my desk or as many red things as you can imagine each forming part of the lump? Take the red shirt lying on the floor. Is it one red *thing*? There is no reason we can't say that there are at least four red

things there: two red sleeves, one red collar, and one red shirt. You can see that "red thing" does not provide a principle of individuation. There is nothing wrong with the term 'red.' What is wrong is the word 'thing.' How many *things* are there in this room? There is no definite answer. In technical terms, we say there is no explicit principle of individuation for *things* or for red *things* but there are such principles for *books*, for red *books*, red *shirts*, and so on.

Terms such as 'book,' 'cat,' 'electron,' 'raven,' 'bar of gold,' and 'bucket of water' are known as **sortals**.[24] They can be used to characterize sets. On the other hand, terms such as 'things,' 'gold,' 'water,' and 'nonraven' are nonsortal. They do not mark out individuals. Hence they cannot be used to define sets. For instance, it does not make sense to ask for a set of water. We have to say something like "three *buckets* of water."

You can now see why Inference IV is unacceptable. That inference is based on the set of all nonblack *things* as the population. But there is no such thing as the set of all nonblack things (and there is no such thing as the set of nonravens either).

Which is the population for the reasoning (23)–(25) then? We listed five candidates (a) to (e). Of the five, only (d)—that is, the set of all ravens—makes sense!

Hempel insists that H is equivalent to H''.

H'':   There are no nonblack ravens in the universe.

And he thinks that H'' is arrived at with the population of all things in the universe, (e), in mind. But this cannot be because there is no such thing as the set of all things! 'Thing' is not a sortal.

21.7 CONCLUDING REMARKS

In these two chapters, we have covered three problems of induction: Hume's problem, Goodman's paradox, and Hempel's paradox.

---

23. 'Set' is a technical term in mathematics. The nature of sets is presented in a discipline known as set theory. For our purpose, however, we can take 'set' as meaning something like a collection of things.

24. See Strawson (1959, p. 168).

Hume formulated his problem in terms of independence of events from each other. The knowledge of one event has absolutely no bearing on the knowledge of other events. Thus justifiable ampliative inference is impossible. In Chapter 20, I preferred to formulate Hume's problem in terms of the law of large numbers and argued that the problem of inductive reasoning lies with the unjustifiable assumption that our sample (consisting of the observed) is fair. This formulation proved fruitful. It helped to clarify a lot of ideas. Since the law of large numbers is a mathematical law, from it we can read off readily what can be disputed and what cannot be. The law itself, especially in its quantitative form given by Bernoulli,[25] is so clear and precise that hidden assumptions and muddled thinking are at a minimum. I think the law of large numbers makes it clear that Hume's problem, at least within the kind of framework we have been using, is a real problem.[26]

On the contrary, neither Goodman's paradox nor Hempel's is a real difficulty for induction. Again I found that formulation of these problems in terms of the law of large numbers is very helpful. This formulation showed that Goodman's paradoxical findings have little to do with inductive reasoning. What the "grue fable" has revealed to us is the problem of predicate choice in the practice of science.

Similarly, formulation of inductive reasoning in terms of the law of large numbers has helped us to see that Hempel's arguments leading to the paradoxical results of the "ravens" is faulty. We pointed out three flaws. Flaw A was exposed when we consider the general case K—m/n of ravens are black—instead of considering the limiting case H—All ravens are black. Flaw B consists of taking H as a possible conclusion of a sampling induction. As a matter of fact we are only entitled to conclude $H^\star$. Approximately 100 percent of ravens are black. The last flaw, C, is that Hempel assumes that it is possible to take the set of all *things* as a population for sampling induction. We pointed out that 'thing' is not a sortal, and sets,

in particular populations, cannot be defined in terms of nonsortals (alone).

One might object to my treatment of Hempel's paradox in terms of induction for it was originally presented as a problem of confirmation. At the beginning of Section 21.6, I pointed out the logical identity of the two relationships between data and hypotheses. The difference between induction and confirmation is a temporal difference, not a logical one. However, one might point out that when Hempel discusses his paradox, he takes single cases of black ravens as instances of confirmation of H—All ravens are black. It makes perfect sense to consider one raven at a time and ask the question whether it confirms the hypothesis. We, however, did it quite differently. We formulated the problem as a problem of induction, and we considered only cases where a large number of ravens are involved.

I think this is a general misconception of the logic of confirmation. Most of us consider single ravens as candidates for the confirmation or disconfirmation of H. I think this is wrong. We need only consider the more general case, K (m/n of ravens are black). Suppose the actual hypothesis is

(31) 3/5 of the ravens are black.

Now a black raven has just been observed. Would this instance of a black raven confirm or disconfirm (31)?

I think when we talk about confirmation, we should not consider new data in isolation. New data should always be considered together with old data. We should ask: "Do the new data increase the probability of the hypothesis with respect to the old data?" In other words, which of the two probabilities is higher, $\Pr(H$, given $N + O)$ or $\Pr(H$, given $O)$? Here '$\Pr(H$, given $N + O)$' denotes the probability of H relative to the sum of the new and the old data, and '$\Pr(H$, given $O)$' represents that of H relative to the old data alone. If the former is higher then we say that the new data confirm H.

---

25. See Footnote 2 of Chapter 20, p. 276.

26. It may not be problematic within a Kantian type of framework.

On the other hand if the latter is higher, we say that the new data disconfirm H.[27]

You can see that even confirmation makes sense only in terms of a large number of instances because the law of large numbers works on large numbers. The new data alone do not constitute a sample. It is the new data plus the old data together that play the role of a sample. Hence our construal of Hempel's paradox in terms of induction (via the law of large numbers) is correct.

Confirmation theory is an important as well as a useful topic. We have studied it in various places: (i) in Chapters 3 and 4 under inductive and statistical reasoning, (ii) in Chapters 6 and 7 under empirical evaluation, and (iii) here in Chapters 20 and 21 under the problems of induction. However, what we have studied so far consists of only the more popular and nontechnical parts. We have regretfully passed over some important theories— for example, the Bayesian theory, the bootstrap theory, and Carnap's quantitative theory of confirmation.[28]

Before we leave the subject, I should like to signal, as I did at the end of the last chapter, that the school of thought known as constructivism may be able to throw some further light on the problems of induction. Constructivism is an interesting philosophy (Chapter 31).

KEY TERMS INTRODUCED IN THIS CHAPTER

second problem of induction	naturalized epistemology	positive instance	Hempel's criterion
third problem of induction	naturalistic epistemology	confirm	singularity
new riddle of induction	law of large numbers	negative instance	sortals
purely qualitative predicate	problem of predicate choice	disconfirm	
		irrelevant instance	
		Nicod's criterion	

REFERENCES

General: See Lambert and Brittan (1987, pp. 75–87), M. H. Salmon et al. (1992, chap. 2), and Achinstein (1983, pp. 1–9).

On Goodman's Paradox:

Skyrms (1975, chap. III) and Scheffler (1963, pp. 295–326) provide comprehensive introductions as well as more detailed discussions.

For Goodman's own statement of the paradox, see Goodman (1955, chaps. III and IV).

Brody (1970, pp. 510–538) is a collection of classical papers on the subject.

For naturalistic epistemology, see Quine (1969).

On Hempel's Paradox:

Scheffler (1963, pp. 236–294) gives a comprehensive account of the subject. Swinburne (1973, pp. 53–58) provides a brief introduction.

Hempel (1945) contains Hempel's original statement of the paradox.

Brody (1970, pp. 383-438) is a collection of classical papers on the subject.

On Bayesian and Bootstrap Theory of Confirmation, see Lambert and Brittan (1987, pp. 88–112). Edidin (1988) has a good bibliography on the latter.

---

27. See 'logical interpretation of probability' in Section 4.8.

28. Carnap's theory was briefly introduced in Chapter 4. As for the other two, see the references for this chapter.

Chapter 22

Problems of Empiricism II:
Problem of Observation

22.1 INTRODUCTION

Inductive empiricism, as detailed in Section 19.4, covers all those methodologies that (i) take the collection of empirical data as the starting point of scientific discovery and (ii) take inductive logic (whether qualitative or quantitative) as the main mode of inference to arrive at general laws and principles. Inductive empiricism thus includes Baconian empiricism[1] and logical positivism. It advocates the bottom-up, data-driven approach.

As observed before, what is so sad with this almost commonsensical approach is that both steps (i) and (ii) appear problematic. We have discussed the alleged problems facing step (ii) in the previous two chapters. Now we will study those facing step (i).

If science is to be fruitful, obviously we should start with reliable and objective empirical data. Once we have collected reliable and objective data, step (ii) can enable us to make inferences and thus amplify our knowledge. At least, this is the methodology of the inductive empiricists. But what if the data are faulty?

---

1. Note that we have taken Baconian empiricism to include statistical methods.

No matter how sound step (ii) is as a way of inference, what we end up with could be just junk. (Garbage in, garbage out!) We should surely start with authentic data. But what if the nature of our senses is such that we can never attain reliable and objective empirical data?

For the layperson, to observe is to open one's eyes and look.[2] One simply has to be careful and precise, noting exactly what one sees. The record of what one sees forms the collection of data. What is problematic about that? Unless one's eyesight is defective, what one sees should be authentic, and the data should be reliable.

22.2 THE PHOTOGRAPHIC ACCOUNT OF OBSERVATION

I think the authenticity assumption of observation is based on the folk theory that, since the eye works like a camera, seeing is similar to taking photographs. When an observer opens her eyes, say in her study, the full view of the room appears in front of her. Here is a desk, on which is a telephone, two pens, and a writing pad. There is a bookshelf standing against the wall, on which are three rows of books of various colors and sizes. Between the desk and the bookshelf is a chair, and so on. The view is no different from a photograph. To open one's eyes is no different from taking a photograph.

According to the layperson, what one sees depends on:

(a) The object being observed (whether it is a table or a chair)

(b) The physical constitution of the observer (whether she has normal vision, is nearsighted, or is color-blind)

(c) The relative position of the observer and the observed (including the relative positions of the

light sources and so on) and the nature of the environment (say, how foggy the place is)

(d) Nothing else.

This is sometimes known as the **photographic account of seeing** in that the eye is likened to a camera lens and the mind is likened to the film behind the lens. What the mind is conscious of is similar to what the film will record when the camera shutter opens to take a photograph. Since a photograph taken with a camera depends on the three conditions listed earlier, what one sees with one's eyes should also depend exactly on these three conditions.

This account is both simple and appealing. If true, the mind through observation can usually get at the truth about the object observed. It requires only simple (optical) geometry to work out the (approximate) shape, size, orientation, and so on of the observed object from the image it projects onto the mind.

Is the mind passive in observation, behaving like a blank slate?[3] Is seeing the same as receiving images from the observed objects through the eye?

22.3 FALLACY OF THE PHOTOGRAPHIC ACCOUNT

If this simplistic account of seeing is correct, when different observers under similar conditions look at the diagram in Figure 22.1, they should all see the same thing. However, experiments have shown that what people see when exposed to this figure can vary from person to person. Some see a "tunnel" going into the page. Others see a truncated pyramid as viewed from the sky. Yet others may see only an arrangement of straight lines. What one sees seems to depend not only on the amount of light, the relative position of the object, and so on; it also depends very much on the mentality of the observer. A child, unacquainted with abstract drawings, will not see the figure as a three-dimensional

---

2. In the present chapter, for simplicity of presentation, I will take observation as *visual* observation, even though what is going to be discussed applies equally to observations through the other senses.

3. Here we are borrowing an analogy from Francis Bacon.

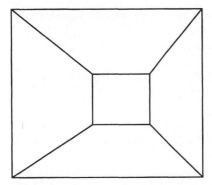

FIGURE 22.1

FIGURE 22.2

object. On the other hand, adults, who are used to seeing things around us as three-dimensional objects, will find it hard to see the figure merely as an arrangement of lines.

Figure 22.2 is the rather well-known reversible figure—ground that may be perceived as either a goblet or as two profiles. Here is a clear case of the same "thing" under the same conditions being seen differently as quite different things. What makes different observers see different things?

22.4 THE THEORETICAL AND SUBJECTIVE NATURE OF SEEING

What one sees depends not only on the three conditions listed in Section 22.2; it also depends on the theories the observer entertains. In the literature this thesis has been formulated in a number of ways. Sometimes it is said that observations are theory-laden. At other times it is said that what one sees is theory-laden. The general idea is certainly there. However, it would help if we can find a more exact formulation of the thesis.

Let's try the following:

T: Observational contents are theory-laden.

This statement is rather condensed. Let's unpack it. In this section, we'll examine the notion of

observational content. In the next two sections, we'll try to understand the exact meaning of theory-ladenness.

What are those "things" that are said to be theory-laden? What can '**observational content**' mean?

(a) I think in the present context 'observational content' cannot mean the physical object being looked at (such as a table). The existence and constitution of that physical object cannot be in any sense dependent on the theory entertained by the observer. By looking at a physical object, we can neither bring about its existence (or its nonexistence) nor impose on the object any of our wishes or fantasies (unless we possess magic power!).

(b) Some people might interpret 'observational content' as the subjective experience of the observer: her feelings as she gazes at the physical object, her conscious experience of the physical object's color, solidity, and so on. Agreeing with Popper,[4] I, however, think that science has little to do with private experience. It would be wrong to root science in private experience for the following reasons:

(i) Private experience is difficult, if not impossible, to describe in words. Poetry

---

4. Popper (1959, chap. V, esp. sec. 25).

supposedly can describe feelings. I, however, doubt very much that this is the case. What poetry does is probably the *evocation* of feelings of certain types, which the poet concerned wants to share with her audience. Titchener's structuralism of the 19th century failed miserably in promoting psychology as the description and study of sensations and images. Wittgenstein (1958), the great philosopher of the 20th century, gave convincing arguments against the possibility of private languages (for the description of one's private inner feelings).

(ii) Private experience is subjective, in that no other person can check on one's experience. Natural science is not interested in private experience, whether it is yours, mine, or anyone else's. Science is and should be about the public world expressible through public languages even though the public world might only be accessible through private experience.

(c) I think 'observational contents' should be taken as meaning the contents of (public) statements made to express what has been observed. For example, on looking into the garden through her lounge window, Mary might remark,

(1) "That's a rabbit running across the lawn."

This is what is usually called an **observational statement** or an **observational report** (Sections 15.1 and 17.2). I prefer to call it an **observational *judgment***. Obviously observational contents need not be expressed in speech. Mary might just have made the judgment silently to herself. Observational judgments are usually about the public physical world. They are purportedly descriptions of reality based on observations. It is on such descriptions that science should be founded, and it is such descriptions that inductive empiricists take as the objective and reliable starting point of science. The question is: Are these observational judgments really objective and reliable? You might think that I am trying to knock down a strawman. Obviously (1) need not be objective or reliable, because the rabbit disappeared under the hedge before Mary had time to blink. However, according to current philosophy *all* observational judgments are theory-laden. This theory-ladenness renders them subjective and unreliable. Thus not only statement (1) but all other observational judgments are subjective and unreliable.

But what can **theory-ladenness** mean? I think in current philosophy 'theory-laden' means 'theory-dependent,' and 'theory' in the present context, should be taken to mean either a set of hypotheses or a system of concepts (a network of concepts). So Thesis T is the same as T′:

T′: Observational judgments are dependent on (influenced by) (i) the hypotheses that the observer believes in and (ii) the system of concepts that the observer employs for the description of the world.

I will argue for these two subtheses, (i) and (ii), separately in the next two sections.

22.5 HYPOTHESIS-DEPENDENCY OF OBSERVATION

Let's see how our observations depend on our beliefs—that is, on the hypotheses we believe in (since our beliefs need not be true).

Let's consider the famous ambiguous figure of the duck-rabbit (Figure 22.3).[5] It can be a duck looking up to the right, but it can also be a rabbit looking horizontally to the left. The number of people seeing it as a duck would probably be about the same as the number of people seeing it as a rabbit. However, if we colored the figure brown, I think the number of people seeing it as

---

5. The duck-rabbit figure came from Wittgenstein.

FIGURE 22.3

Н
FIGURE 22.4

SCHOOL
FIGURE 22.5

SCAR
FIGURE 22.6

a duck would increase because most people have the prior belief that ducks are usually brown, while rabbits are usually taken as white.[6] These prior beliefs are hypotheses (Chapter 1), and we can see how they influence our observation.

In certain psychological experiments, subjects are asked to identify certain playing cards. In one experiment, an ambiguous ace, shaped partly like a spade and partly like a heart, was flashed to the subjects briefly. About half the subjects identified the card as an ace of spades whereas the other half said it was an ace of hearts. However, when the figure on the card was colored red, more subjects identified the card as an ace of hearts than as an ace of spades. In making their judgments they had been influenced by the prior belief that all hearts are red whereas all spades are black. Again we can see how these hypotheses (beliefs) influence judgments.

Magic works according to this same principle: that observation is theory-laden. Owing to our experience in the past, we tend to expect certain things to occur or to have occurred when we are given certain cues. Magicians typically make use of such cues to mislead the audience into thinking that something has occurred. 'Illusion' is the word for the description of this kind of phenomenon. All illusions arise from the entrenchment of certain hypotheses in the subject.

Let's look at Figure 22.4. It is ambiguous between an A and an H. However, when the symbol is placed among other letters, as in Figures 22.5 and 22.6, the choice becomes clear. Our knowledge of spelling of the words 'school' and 'scar' has affected our judgment. The hypotheses concerned are: "SCHOOL" spells with an H, whereas "SCAR" spells with an A. For a non–English speaker, the embedding of the ambiguous letter in an English word would have made no difference to the identification.

We can see that observational contents are theory-laden in the sense that our observational judgments are influenced by our beliefs in certain hypotheses. Let's now turn to the other factors influencing our observations. These are the concepts that we carry ("in our head") for understanding and describing the world.

22.6 CONCEPT-DEPENDENCY OF OBSERVATION

When laypeople employ the term 'theory,' they seldom mean a system of concepts. A theory for the layperson is a sort of abstract "story" about electrons, genes, molecules, and so on. In Chapters 8 and 15, we have elaborated this use of 'theory.' 'Theory' also is quite often used to mean some sort of "ideas" proposed but not yet confirmed.

---

6. As a matter of fact, most wild rabbits are brown. Nonetheless, because pet rabbits are usually white, and rabbits in children's stories are usually white as well (for example, the White Rabbit in *Alice in Wonderland*), we tend to associate rabbits with whiteness.

This use corresponds to what we termed 'hypothesis' (Chapter 1).

In this section, I will introduce a new use of the term 'theory': a theory is a **system of concepts**. There is a very important distinction between a *sentence* and a *word* in any language. A sentence is usually made up of a number of words. It is commonly taken as carrying a complete idea, called a *proposition*,[7] which is either true or false. Words on the other hand are neither true nor false. Words are said to denote concepts. For example, "The sun is hot" is a sentence made up of four words, and it expresses a true proposition. On the other hand, each of the four words by themselves is neither true nor false. 'The,' for instance, is neither true nor false.

Concepts (expressed by words) usually come in systems. For instance, 'animal,' 'person,' 'plant,' 'dog,' 'cat,' and so on are all related, forming part of a large system of concepts. 'Red,' 'green,' 'blue,' 'bright,' 'dark,' 'brilliant,' 'dazzling,' 'glittering,' and so forth also form a system. In this section, I would like to show how systems of concepts affect our observations.

It is said that Eskimos have seven words for different kinds of snow. When confronted with snow, they will use the appropriate word to describe the situation. Those living in more temperate regions must be missing out on a lot in looking at snow. The fine distinctions that Eskimos can make would not be obvious to us. It is not because their eyesight is superior. Rather, the concepts they possess enable them to see what others cannot see. In other words, seeing needs to be taught. With a bit of patience, anyone can probably be taught numerous concepts of snow, and, having acquired this linguistic ability, would be able to see as much as the Eskimo can.

Some concepts can be learned, but others cannot be. A blind person, for instance, cannot learn color concepts. I wonder how many can acquire the concepts of major and minor in music? Those without the concepts of major and minor will be "blind" to certain features in a piece of music. They may be able to replay or recite the piece of music exactly, yet they would miss out on something that the person possessing those concepts can pick out. Seeing involves classification. But one can only classify in terms of concepts—for example, 'major,' 'minor,' 'snow$_1$' 'snow$_2$,' and so on. Hence one can see (or hear) certain features only if one possesses concepts for the descriptions of those features.

The same thing happens in watching a game of soccer. The two of us can be seeing apparently the same thing—people running around after a leather ball. But my friend, not knowing the rules of soccer, would have missed out on so much that he would find the game senseless and boring. I, on the other hand, can pick out all sorts of tactics. I can tell when a goal has been scored, and I can spot off-sides. 'Off-side' is a concept, just as 'major' and 'minor' are concepts. This concept has to be grasped in order to perceive an off-side.

Figure 22.7a shows a Chinese character. An ordinary English person would not recognize it as other than a jumble of lines. This is similar to the case where some people would only be able to describe Figure 22.1 as a plane figure of 12 lines.

Would an ordinary Chinese person know how to segment Figure 22.8 into its component words? Would he be able to segment Figure 22.9? Similarly, if a non–Chinese-speaking person were asked to segment the Chinese character of Figure 22.7a into two radicals (the basic components of Chinese characters), most likely a large number would partition it wrongly as in Figure 22.7b, whereas the correct segmentation is as in Figure 22.7c.

To see is not merely a matter of receiving stimuli, otherwise not only would a camera be able to see, but tables and chairs, not to mention mirrors, would all be able to see. To see is to be able in some way to make sense of the stimuli (correctly). Some people call this process of making sense 'an interpretation.' One of the fundamental steps one

---

7. (i) This is only a rough presentation of the idea of a sentence, (ii) For our present purpose, 'proposition' can be taken as meaning the same as 'statement,' which has been explained in Section 1.1.

FIGURE 22.7a[8]

FIGURE 22.7b

FIGURE 22.7c

THEBOYSEESANOWL

FIGURE 22.8

WOISTMEINHUT

FIGURE 22.9[9]

must perform in the course of interpretation is the segmentation of the "scene" at the right joints. For example, to understand the message in Figure 22.8 one has to see it as "THE BOY SEES AN OWL." In other words, the string of letters has to be correctly segmented. What enables us to segment scenes or phenomena presented to us through the senses? It is our system of concepts. That's why concepts play such an important role in seeing and in other kinds of perception. The concepts 'table,' 'chair,' 'book,' 'telephone,' and so on, for example, enable me to see tables, chairs, books, telephones, and so forth. Martians with different categories of concepts will see the room differently. We would say that they have seen it wrong, and that they have carved up the "scene" at the wrong places. They might even "see" such unfamiliar scenes as a newborn baby would, or as a blind person who had suddenly acquired sight would. As far as Figure 22.9 is concerned, the non-German speaker would find it as puzzling as a Martian would. It doesn't make sense.

Here is another way concepts can affect our seeing. Let's now consider Hanson's bird-antelope (Figure 22.10). When viewed on its own, it looks both like a bird and like an antelope. However, when placed among birds the same figure looks like a bird rather than like an antelope (Figure 22.11). On the other hand, when it is placed among antelopes, observers tend to see it as an antelope (Figure 22.12). The company that the

figure-animal keeps has done something to our seeing. It is not because we lack the concept 'bird' or the concept 'antelope' that we tend to see one thing rather than the other. The background animals in the pictures act as prompts that suggest the kind of concepts we should use to make sense of the picture. Figure 22.11 suggests that we should use the concept 'bird,' hence we tend to see the figure as a bird. When Figure 22.12 suggests the concept 'antelope,' our seeing follows that suggestion instead.

In observation the mind is not passive. What is presented to the observer acts rather like clues. The mind picks up these clues and, by putting them together, attempts (actively) to make sense of them, ending with a judgment, such as: "That is a circle" (Figure 22.13), "That is a triangle,"

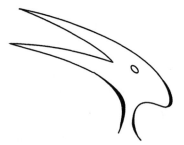

FIGURE 22.10   The bird-antelope

Figures 22.10, 22.11, and 22.12 from Norwood Hanson, 1965, *Patterns of Discovery*, pp. 13–14; reprinted with the kind permission of Cambridge University Press.

---

8. Chinese character TAO, meaning peach.

9. This is the German sentence "WO IST MEIN HUT."

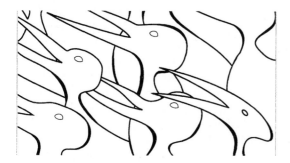

FIGURE 22.11 The bird-antelope among birds

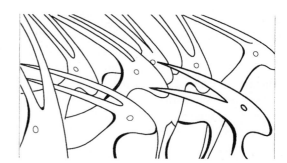

FIGURE 22.12 The bird-antelope among antelopes

(Figure 22.14), and "That is a crane in flight" (Figure 22.15).[10] The clues can sometimes be rich and plentiful, but at other times can be quite "gappy," fragmentary, or untidy with "noises." The mind, when confronted with such clues, "fills in the gaps," links up the fragments, and blocks out the noises.[11] (That's why some of us manage to read doctors' handwriting.) In performing this "act" of interpretation, the mind relies on both the hypotheses (theories, Sense 1) it entertains and the concepts (theories, Sense 2) it possesses. That is how theories enable and shape observation. It is in this sense that we should understand the statement T, that observational contents are theory-laden.

We have so far framed our discussions mainly in terms of seeing. Observation is, however, not restricted to the sense of sight. One can observe through hearing, smell, and so on. The theory-ladenness obviously applies to all modes of observation.

22.7 THE PROBLEM OF OBSERVATION FOR EMPIRICISM

If, as argued, observational contents are shaped by the theories we carry in our minds, what we claim to have seen can be far from reality. Our minds can be "bewitched" and we can see all sorts of things that are not there. Our observations can be distorted. They can be mere illusions (mirages). Inductive empiricism claims that science should start with observations and then proceed to construct the magnificent building of science upward through induction. If observations are, however, so unreliable, is it wise to build science on observations?

"Why don't we de-theorize our observations?" you might ask. One obvious way to do it is to reduce the kind of observation necessary for science to very simple acts such as the taking of pointer readings.

FIGURE 22.13

FIGURE 22.14

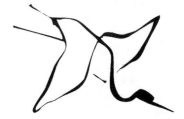

FIGURE 22.15

---

10. This is one in a series entitled 'The Crane' by the great Japanese painter Hokusai in 1823.

11. For example, the "cross" on the back of the crane in Hokusai's drawing (Figure 22.15) is a noise.

Since these acts are so simple, their "theory-load" would be minimal. Moreover, since these are more or less basic acts required of us humans, we should not differ too much from each other in the outcome of the performance of these acts.

Let's take an example. The task is to measure the speed of a moving car. I can think of three ways to do it: (i) to make a judgment directly by watching the car move past, (ii) by measuring the distance traversed by the car and divide that distance by the time taken (the distance is measured by a measuring tape and the time by a stopwatch), and (iii) by reading the speedometer on the dashboard of the car. What act (i) required of the observer is by no means simple. Trying to estimate the speed of a moving car is a complex act. Hence it should not be surprising that the outcome is highly subjective and unreliable. The theories carried by the observer in this case are significantly responsible for the subjectivity. On the contrary, act (iii) is not demanding of the observers at all. The theories carried by individual observers can hardly influence their readings. Their beliefs and concepts may differ widely. Yet these beliefs and concepts are probably irrelevant. All the observers see the same thing, a pointer moving across a dial surface. Aristotelians, Newtonians, and Einsteinians differ in their conceptions of space and time; they argue about the meaning of simultaneity; and they measure speed and acceleration differently. Yet no one would seriously expect them to give significantly different results when they are asked to read a speedometer.

Nowadays most scientific measurements are based on pointer readings. The laboratory is full of meters: the voltmeter, the ammeter, the thermometer, the barometer, the photometer, the spectrometer, and so on. As far as observation is concerned, what is required of the scientist seems to be little: just tell us which number the pointer is pointing at! (Many meters now have a digital display. That makes the task even simpler.) Where is the subjectivity? Where is the unreliability?

Our arguments based on ambiguous figures like the duck-rabbit (Figure 22.3) or the A-H (Figure 22.4) do not seem to be applicable here. Meter reading is a far cry from looking at ambiguous pictures. It is hardly comparable to the difficult and intelligence-demanding task of reading foreign languages. If all observations are theory-laden, certainly it seems that meter reading is only minimally theory-laden, and anyway the kind of theory involved in meter reading seems to be carried and employed universally by all scientists. Where are the subjectivity and unreliability that give rise to the problem of observation?

Of course, not all scientific observations consist of meter reading. Botanists have to report on the shapes, sizes, colors, and textures of leaves, for example. Astronomers are expected to study photos of planets sent back by space probes. Surely these kinds of observations are theory-laden enough to get us worried. Looking over close-up photographs of planets is no different from examining X-ray photographs of the human body. Interpretation of such photographs relies heavily on theories. That's why the phenomenalists (Sections 9.5 and 16.4) think that scientific observational reports should strictly speaking be in terms of sense-data. Here's a sample: "Here round red patch now," and "Here a squeaking noise of short duration." (Some would formulate them as: "I saw a round red patch at time x," and "I heard a squeaking noise of short duration at time x.") The idea is that sense-data reports are direct and theory-free. Let me give an example.

On looking over the horizon, one sees the moon rising. Here are three possible reports on that observation:

(a) The (round) moon is rising over the horizon.

(b) An orange round disk is rising over the horizon.

(c) An orange round disk-shaped patch is moving away from a straight line.

Report (a) can be seen to be very theoretical. First it claims that there is a three-dimensional object—that is, a sphere—thousands of miles away moving across a three-dimensional "container" known as space, and that we are watching it from a "platform" that "creates" the illusion of a line in the distance. Report (a) could not have been made by our ancestors, who knew little of our astronomy.

But both our ancestors and we ourselves can make the far less theoretical (b).

Of course (b) is still theoretical. At least it is theoretical about space, about a disk moving across this three-dimensional space.

Finally, it is said that (c) is atheoretical and purely descriptive. Of course, this is not true. The geometry involved may not be three-dimensional geometry, yet the notion of roundness and the concept of a straight line are geometrical, albeit two-dimensional. One need not be employing commonsense (Euclidean) geometry for the description either. One could have assumed one of the non-Euclidean geometries. Having said these things, I think we can agree that the theories involved in (c) are minimal, perhaps even minimal enough so that observation (c) is quite objective and reliable.

At one time, the phenomenalists thought that by reducing all observation statements to sense-data statements, they can avoid both error and theoretical prejudices. Hence such statements are able to form a solid starting base for the grand mansion of scientific knowledge.

Why don't we follow the phenomenalists' advice then? What's wrong with building science on sense-data statements? We will study the problems facing phenomenalism in detail in the next chapter (on logical positivism). Suffice it to say here that the three main difficulties are that (i) sense-data statements are subjective, (ii) our sense-data language is too impoverished to yield descriptions rich enough for the enterprise of science, and finally (iii) no one is able to devise a satisfactory logical link relating sense-data statements to ordinary statements such as "There is an apple on the table." A fortiori, no logical link has been developed between sense-data statements and scientific theories, such as the chemical atomic theory. It is suspected that such links are impossible (Sections 17.3–17.6).

What then of meter-reading statements? Can't science be built on this kind of minimally theory-laden observational statements? At least they are not subjective, and we seem to have a rich enough vocabulary to produce the necessary meter-reading statements for the construction of science.

Perhaps the problem of observation can be solved in terms of sense-data statements. Perhaps it can be solved in terms of meter-reading statements. I propose to leave this topic until Chapter 31, where we study the radical new philosophy known as constructivism. In anticipation of that philosophy, let me quote Kant: "Intuition without concepts is blind,"[12] which, when translated into our terminology, reads: "One cannot observe without concepts."

KEY TERMS INTRODUCED IN THIS CHAPTER

photographic account of seeing	observational report	hypothesis-dependency of observation	system of concepts
observational content	observational judgment	concept-dependency of observation	
observational statement	theory-ladenness		

REFERENCES

General introductions: Chalmers (1976, chap. 3), Anthony O'Hear (1989, pp. 82–94), and Pratt (1978, chap. 6).

More advanced: The problem of observation owes much of its origin to Hanson (1965, chap. 1). It can be read with Kordig (1971, chap. 1).

Anthology: Klemke et al. (1980, Part III).

---

12. Kant (1933, p. 93). By 'intuition,' Kant meant roughly what we mean by 'sense-data.'

PART VI

The Classical Dynasty

INTRODUCTION

The beginning of the 20th century was a time of great excitement in science and in philosophy. Einstein proposed his theory of relativity, portraying the world as a four-dimensional space-time manifold. Niels Bohr et al. introduced quantum physics, according to which subatomic particles usually do not have a definite position or momentum and causality is probabilistic. In philosophy, Gottlob Frege and Bertrand Russell invented a new logic, known as the predicate calculus, which proved far superior to the entrenched syllogistic logic of Aristotle. Centuries-old idols of thought fell one after another. New horizons appeared in every corner of the learned world. It was in this atmosphere of change and advancement that logical positivism was born.

Logical positivism (**Chapter 23**) represents the best and the most mature version of empiricism in the Baconian and Humean tradition. Founded on the newly invented predicate calculus, it was systematic, precise, and rigorous. It was meant to be the ultimate philosophical wisdom inasmuch as Newton's mechanics was revered as the ultimate truth in science.

Karl Popper (**Chapter 24**) was, strictly speaking, not a positivist. Yet his falsificationism shared the same sort of basic assumptions as logical positivism. For sure, Popper employed 'deduction' and 'falsification' as opposed to 'induction' and 'verification,' which the logical positivists used. Nonetheless, contrasted with Thomas Kuhn's Neo-Kantianism (Part VII), Popper's philosophy and logical positivism were clearly allies, albeit quarrelsome comrades.

The two philosophies, logical positivism and Popper's falsificationism, are usually taken together as forming what is known as the classical tradition. Sometimes the term 'positivism' is used. At other times, it is called the standard or the orthodox view. These latter expressions are apt. The classical tradition provides the philosophy of science with a simple, basic, and clear view that is useful and, in a limited sense, roughly correct. It also provides a fundamental vocabulary for the pursuit of the subject.

You might recall that Book I covers the topics of truth, explanation, and reality as viewed from the standpoint of the classical tradition. It is an essay on micro-philosophy. Here we present the classical tradition historically as a macro-philosophy. We trace the development of the main tenets of the tradition, its basic views, and its fundamental justificatory arguments. Thus this part is complementary to Book I.

Chapter 23

Logical Positivism

23.1 INTRODUCTION: COMTE'S POSITIVISM

Having studied various problems facing empiricism, let's return to the history of the philosophy of science, taking up where we left off in Chapter 19.

You may recall that Galileo's scientific successes in the 17th century marked the beginning of the triumph of empiricism over rationalism (Chapter 19). To be sure, empiricism dated back to antiquity. For example, Aristotle methodically opened fertilized eggs of chickens on successive days so as to discover the temporal development of the embryo of the chicken through observation. Hipparchus of Alexandria (160–125 B.C.) carefully charted the motions of the planets across the night sky, and his data were later employed by Ptolemy in his famous geocentric theory (Chapter 7). Nonetheless, empiricism before Galileo was overshadowed by the prominent achievements of the rationalists, predominantly by those of Euclid and Archimedes.

Galileo's works marked the turning point for empiricism. His astronomical observations with the telescope and his innovative experimental results in kinematics woke the scientific world. At about the same time Francis Bacon of England published his *Novum Organum*, laying down the methodological foundations for empirical philosophy. From then on science progressed in leaps and bounds. Here are some examples of the fruitfulness of empirical methodology: Torricelli and Boyle's experimental results on air pressure, Newton's empirical studies of light phenomena, Priestley and Lavoisier's laboratory investigations on gases, Gay-Lussac's observations on volumetric combination of gases,

Rumford's study of heat, Gilbert's contributions to magnetism, Gray's discoveries of various electric phenomena, and so on. A whole new world had been opened up by the methods of empiricism.

Encouraged by these successes, Auguste Comte (1788–1857) of France surveyed and summarized the development of science in his famous "law" of the three stages. According to Comte, every branch of science passes through the following three stages: (a) the theological stage, (b) the metaphysical stage, and finally (c) the positive stage. At the theological stage, science sees the occurrence of natural phenomena as the products of actions of supernatural agents, be they gods or devils, ghosts or spirits. The next stage is the metaphysical stage, which represents an advance. Yet this stage, in Comte's opinion, is merely a modification of the theological stage. Instead of employing humanlike agents in explanation, it employs occult powers residing in inanimate agents. For example, mass in Newton's mechanics is said to be such an agent. It is inanimate, hence not a god. Yet it possesses an occult power called gravity. Through this power it can make things move, be they large bodies such as planets or tiny objects such as dust particles. Apart from Newton's mass, quite a number of such "metaphysical" agents were employed in the sciences in the period between Galileo and Comte. Let me name some: Newton's light corpuscles, Huygens's light waves (Chapter 0), the phlogiston, Dalton's chemical atoms, the caloric fluid, Dufay and Nollet's electric fluids, and Faraday's magnetic fields. For Comte these metaphysical (occult) agents are inadmissible in proper scientific practice. Inanimate occult agents are not really that different from animate spirits. Neither metaphysical notions nor theological notions are scientific. Hence they should be eliminated from science.

According to Comte, every branch of scientific study would historically start with the theological stage, then move into the metaphysical stage and then finally enter the mature stage, known as the positive stage, where science is practiced according to the philosophy of positivism. **Positivism** (i) denies that nature is governed by any purposes or ends,[1] (ii) condemns the employment of theological or metaphysical agents in scientific explanations, and (iii) argues that the only legitimate practice in science is the observation and generalization of constant conjunctions of natural phenomena or events. It can be seen that Comte's positivism is firmly in the tradition of Bacon's and Hume's empiricism. For Hume, occult notions such as 'cause' have no role to play in science (Section 11.6). What makes sense are notions that represent observables. Hence metaphysical notions such as 'gravity' and 'caloric fluid' should be banned from science, which should deal exclusively with observables. Having observed a large number of happenings concerned with observables, and realizing that certain types of events are always followed by certain other types, the positivist can and should generalize in accordance with Bacon's inductivism (Chapter 3). This is what science expects of us, and this also marks the limit of science. In brief, the practice of science (as opposed to the practice of magic, say) is to observe, record, and generalize.[2] Let me illustrate. A number of lodestones have been observed to attract iron filings. Here are two events. Event Type A: A lodestone is placed near some iron filings. Event Type B: The iron filings move toward the stone. Type A has been observed to be followed by type B many times. By induction we can generalize it to "All events of Type A are followed by events of Type B," which, if true, is a law of nature. Establishing such laws of nature is the ultimate aim of positive science. In contrast, metaphysical stage scientists might conjecture that there are occult agents such as magnetic fields or electric currents at work. For these "metaphysicians" the aim of science is to uncover such occult agents (see Chapter 16).

Belief in the existence of supernatural animate agents is often branded as superstition. For Comte it is equally superstitious to believe in the existence of

---

1. In Chapter 13, we discussed how teleological explanations attempt to explain in terms of purposes or goals.

2. This is a bit of an oversimplification. Comte does endorse the use of inductive methods other than generalization, such as Mill's five methods (Chapter 3).

metaphysical agents. Positivism is the only correct way to practice science. According to this school of thought, science is meant to be only descriptive (descriptive in terms of observation terms) and predictive (predictive in terms of laws of constant conjunctions, discoverable by induction). It is never meant to be explanatory, let alone explanatory in terms of occult metaphysical objects or supernatural agents.[3]

Comte's positivism was presented with massive support from his interpretation of the history of science in the celebrated *Course of Positive Philosophy*, published in six volumes between 1830 and 1842. It had great influence in the philosophical thinking of the time. Thus his contemporary, the renowned British philosopher John Stuart Mill (Chapter 3), counting himself as a positivist, echoed Comte as follows:

> We have no knowledge of anything but phenomena, and our knowledge of phenomena is relative, not absolute. We know not the essence, nor the real mode of production, of any fact, but only its relations to other facts in the way of succession or of similitude. These relations are constant; that is, always the same in the same circumstances. The constant resemblances which link phenomena together and the constant sequences which unite them as antecedent and consequent, are termed their laws. The laws of phenomena are all we know respecting them. Their essential nature, and their ultimate causes, either efficient or final, are unknown and inscrutable to us.

Ernst Mach (1838–1916), a Vienna-educated physicist and mathematician of great standing, was another who took up Comte's positivism with enthusiasm. Not only did he not trust what Comte condemned as metaphysical entities such as the atom and the caloric fluid (what we would call theoretical entities), he went to the extreme of trying to rebuild physics in terms of sense-datum terms. Thus, for him, even 'stone,' 'stick,' 'table,' and 'chair' are metaphysical. They should be purged from science.

For the scientist, the only given are the sensations (Hume's sense impressions) that one obtains through the senses. These sensations when recorded (uninfluenced by the intervention of theories (Chapter 22)) become sense-data. Mach believed that science should be built out of these data. This philosophy is hence known as **sensationism** or **phenomenalism** (Section 9.5). Thus Mach went one step further than Comte. Nonetheless Mach realized that science requires the employment of theoretical terms such as 'atom,' 'gravitational force,' 'mass,' and so on. Science simply cannot work without theories. The question is therefore: What role(s) do theories (and their terms) play in science?

Concerning empiricism, we have so far pointed out three major problems. They are Hume's problem of induction, the problem of confirmation (as illustrated by Goodman's and Hempel's paradoxes), and the problem of observation. Positivism leads on to a fourth and a fifth problem.

In Chapters 15 and 17, we introduced and discussed the **observational–theoretical distinction (OT-distinction)**. Common sense suggests such a distinction, and practicing scientists assume it. (Scientists usually depict the distinction in terms of 'data' and 'theory.') Yet no sound theoretical basis has been found to support such a distinction, and there is no consensus as to where to draw the line between observational terms and theoretical terms. So here is the dilemma. On the one hand, it seems that the OT-distinction is obvious and is indispensable for empiricism. On the other, there seems to be no theoretical justification for it. This dilemma points to two problems facing empiricism.

(i) The **problem of (demarcation of) observational terms** (of observable entities, of observational statements): What is the theoretical basis (and the practical criteria) for the distinction between observational terms and theoretical terms?

(ii) The **problem of the (missing) OT-link**: What is the logical relationship between

---

3. This should remind us of the philosophy of conventionalism (Chapter 9) and of that of instrumentalism (Chapter 16).

observational terms (statements) and theoretical terms (statements)?

Mach tried to solve the first problem by confining observational terms to sense-datum terms. These terms somehow are "safe" and "nonmetaphysical," being terms representing the immediately given. But what about the second problem? Here, as I mentioned earlier, in Section 9.5, Mach takes all theoretical terms (that is, those that are not sense-datum terms) to be nonrepresentational. Thus terms like 'oxygen atom,' 'gravitational force,' 'caloric fluid,' and 'mass' are not meant to represent real (types of) entities in the world. They are pure symbols. They do not stand for things nor do they convey messages (as traffic signs do). These symbols are said to be instrumental in nature. They are calculation, inference, and memory devices (*memoria technica*). Just as in mathematics terms such as the square root of minus one are not supposed to be representational, so theoretical terms, for Mach, should not be taken as representational. In fact, for Mach, commonsensical terms such as 'dog,' 'cat,' 'table,' and 'chair' are nonrepresentational as well. Only sense-datum terms are proper in that they are representational. But what is the logical relationship between these sense-datum terms (which we never use) and all other terms (which we use daily)? In general, what is the logical relationship between theoretical and observational statements? To say that theoretical terms are instrumental in nature is merely an analogy. In philosophy and logic, and in fact in science as well, we require the answers to be more precise.

The conventionalists Poincaré and Duhem (Chapter 9), who were junior contemporaries of Mach, did not deal with problem (i) but had quite a lot to say on problem (ii). For them theories are neither true nor false. They are not meant to be explanatory either. They are just devices for the coordination of data collected from observations. Their functions are to organize and to predict. Thus the choice of theories is governed by consistency, elegance, and simplicity. Truth and explanatory power do not belong to the vocabulary of assessment of theories (Section 9.4). You can see

the instrumental slant in their philosophy. Yet in spite of their lengthy eloquence on the function of theories, Poincaré and Duhem were not able to give us a less-than-vague answer to problem (ii). How do theories manage to *coordinate* observational data? What does it mean when theories are said to *organize* data? What is the justification for predictions in terms of such "coordinators" and "organizers"?

Let me summarize. Comte reiterated and developed Bacon and Hume's inductive empiricism in the context of the history of science. He summed up his findings in his law of the three stages of development of science: the theological stage, the metaphysical stage, and the positive stage. The last stage is characterized by the practice of positivism, which (i) denies the presence of purposes in nature, (ii) condemns the postulation of theological or metaphysical agents for explanation in science, and (iii) confines science to description in terms of observational terms, and to prediction in terms of laws of constant conjunction of (types of) phenomena. His philosophy had a strong following in the 19th century, notably in the philosophies of Mill, Mach, Poincaré, and Duhem.

But positivism faces five major problems:

(i)   Hume's problem of induction (Chapter 20)

(ii) The problem of confirmation as represented by Goodman's and Hempel's paradoxes (Chapter 21)

(These two problems are concerned with the rationality of induction. Together they constitute the **problems of the rationality of induction**.)

(iii) The problem of objectivity of observation (Chapter 22)

(iv) The problem of observational terms

(v)   The problem of the OT-link

(These last three problems are concerned with the distinction between observation and theory, and their relationship. Together they constitute the **problems of the logical role of theories** [in science].)

With this survey of positivism I think we are now ready to move on to logical positivism, which can be taken as a continuity of Comte's positivism with a special interest in the problem of the logical role of theories.

23.2 THE VERIFICATION PRINCIPLE OF MEANING

Logical positivism is popularly seen as a movement against metaphysics. As such you can see that it was a continuation and development of Comte's positivism.

Antimetaphysicalism dated back to Hume, who, in his celebrated *Enquiry Concerning Human Understanding*, declares:

> When we run over libraries … if we take in our hand any volume; of divinity or school metaphysics, for instance; let us ask, *Does it contain any abstract reasoning concerning quantity or number?* No. *Does it contain any experimental reasoning concerning matter of fact and existence?* No. Commit it then to the flames: for it can contain nothing but sophistry and illusion.

Hume based his rejection of metaphysics on his theory of meaning (and his epistemology).

Hume's theory of meaning is simple, appealing, and even commonsensical, as can be seen from the brief introduction in Section 11.6. He thinks that the contents of the mind (what we think, what we feel, and so on) can be classified into impressions and ideas. Impressions are distinguishable from ideas by their strength and vividness. Let me illustrate. Try to *recall* the first few bars of Beethoven's Fifth Symphony (or any of your favorite tunes). Go through them in your head. They sound nice and you enjoy the melody. These "sounds" are, however, quite faint. You wish that they were louder. But they remain faint all the same. Hume classifies these as **ideas**. Now insert Beethoven's disc into your CD-player and start to play it. There, the opening bars of the Fifth come out loud and clear. (You might even start to mock-conduct.) These clear and vivid sensations are what Hume calls **impressions**. In general, ideas are copies of impressions. (That's why they are faint.) Since ideas are derived from impressions, you might conclude that the types of ideas that one can evoke are limited by the types of impressions that one has encountered. How come then we can have ideas of unicorns and centaurs even though we have never had any direct impressions of these animals?

Here is Hume's explanation. Impressions and ideas can be simple or complex. The complexes are made up of the simples. For instance, the idea of a horse is complex because it is made up of horse parts—a horse head, a horse torso, four horse legs, and so on. On the other hand, the idea of redness is simple. It is not made up of something else. Now simple ideas can only arise as copies of simple impressions. But complex ideas are different. They need not be copies of complex impressions, for they can be built out of simple ideas. Take the case of the idea of a unicorn, which is complex. This idea could not be a copy of some former "unicorn impression" that we had, for we have never encountered any unicorns. Somehow, all of us have no difficulty in conceiving the idea of a unicorn. According to Hume, this feat could be achieved by building the idea up from simpler ideas—for example, the idea of a horse and the idea of a horn.[4] This also explains why blind people cannot produce the idea of redness. The idea of redness, being simple, can only be produced as a copy of a red impression, which blind people do not have.

In sum, ideas are either (direct) copies of impressions or are made up of simpler ideas.

Based on this simple psychological theory, Hume builds his theory of meaning as follows. Words (and other linguistic expressions that function as words) have meaning because they stand for ideas. They are (external) symbols, representing ideas (internal in our heads). For example, the

---

4. Of course some of us might have obtained the idea of a unicorn from pictures of unicorns.

word 'red' stands for the idea of redness and the word 'unicorn' stands for the idea of a unicorn. A word, therefore, is meaningful if and only if it stands for an idea. Hence, in order to demonstrate that a word has a meaning, we must locate the idea it stands for.

Here is the main argument by Hume for the rejection of metaphysics. Words such as 'electron,' 'radio waves,' and 'gravity' cannot be meaningful because there cannot be any such ideas for these words to stand for. If there were such ideas, they would have to be derived from corresponding impressions. But where can we get these impressions? Electrons, radio waves, gravity, and so on, being unobservables, cannot supply us with such. Thus for Hume any statements containing these "metaphysical words" are mere sounds without "substance." You may recall that that is exactly how Hume rejects the possibility of existence of necessary connection in nature (Section 11.6).

Hume's theory of meaning is too simple to be correct! One fundamental mistake of his is to take words as the units of meaning. If words were the units of meaning, then (1) and (2) should have exactly the same meaning.

(1) Albert is taller than Bill.

(2) Bill is taller than Albert.

These two sentences should be synonymous because they are both composed of the same words: 'Albert,' 'Bill,' and 'is taller than.' Again (3) and (4) should be synonymous.

(3) Mary is happy and Nancy is sad.

(4) Nancy is happy and Mary is sad.

Consider the following seemingly paradoxical sentence.

(5) Big ants are not big.

'Big' occurs twice here. It is the same word, yet it seems to have different meanings. If words mean the ideas they stand for, then (5) could not be

true since the two occurrences of 'big' would mean the same.

The great philosopher Gottlob Frege (1848–1925) in his *Die Grundlagen der Arithmetik* (1884) (*The Foundations of Arithmetic*) advises: "Never … ask for the meaning of a word in isolation, but only in the context of a proposition." Under the influence of Frege (and Russell and Wittgenstein), the logical positivists got wiser and shifted from taking the word to taking the sentence as the unit of meaning, and replaced Hume's theory with the famous verification principle of meaning.

Logical positivism was a philosophical movement originating in the 1920s from two groups of scholars, composed mainly of philosophers, mathematicians, logicians, and scientists. One group was based in Vienna and known as the **Vienna Circle**. It was led by Moritz Schlick, a physicist-cum-philosopher. The other group, the Society for Empirical Philosophy, was based in Berlin and was led by Hans Reichenbach, a mathematician-cum-philosopher.[5] This latter group employed the name '**logical empiricism**' for their philosophy rather than the name 'logical positivism' as used by the first group. The great Austrian philosopher Ludwig Wittgenstein (1889–1951), though not a member of either group, had an inspirational influence on the movement from its inception.

As popularly known, the logical positivists' main task is the advancement of Hume and Comte's program for the demolition of metaphysics. Well aware of the shortcomings of Hume's simplistic theory of meaning, they proposed, instead, their famous **verification principle of meaning (VPM)**, which can be summarized by the slogan:

(6) The meaning of a proposition is its (empirical) method of verification.[6]

You can see that VPM differs from Hume's theory fundamentally in two respects: (i) the unit of meaning is now the proposition—for our present

---

5. He contributed substantially in the development of the frequency interpretation of probability (Section 12.6).

6. The verification principle of meaning actually came from Wittgenstein. See Munitz (1981, p. 228).

purpose we can take 'proposition' as just another term for 'sentence' or for 'statement'—and (ii) ideas of the mind have been replaced by methods of verification.

Let me explain (6) with some examples. Consider

(7) This (my vase) is fragile.

How do I know whether (7) is true or not? One way to find out is to drop it onto the floor and see if it breaks. (A rather expensive way, I concede.) The dropping of the vase onto the floor is a method of verification. Proposition (6) claims that the meaning of proposition (7) is no more and no less than the method of verification. We can convert this claim into a "meaning statement":

(8) 'This is fragile' means that if this is dropped onto the floor it will break.

Alternatively we can write it as a sort of equation,

(8a) This is fragile $=_m$ If this is dropped onto the floor it will break. ('$=_m$' can be read as 'means')

This should look familiar for this corresponds exactly to what is known as 'operational definition' (Section 17.4). Here are three more examples.

(9) This is magnetic $=_m$ If this is placed near some iron filings, the filings will move toward it.

(10) x is electrically charged $=_m$ If x is brought near a leaf electroscope, its leaves will diverge.

(11) x has an excess of hydrogen ions $=_m$ If a piece of litmus paper is placed in x, then x will turn red.[7]

According to the logical positivists, when someone claims that my vase is fragile, she claims no more and no less than that if it is dropped onto the floor, it will break. You can see that this is a clever way of handling the problem of metaphysics. One can now employ what Hume would call metaphysical terms such as 'being brittle,' 'being magnetic,' and 'having an excess of hydrogen ions' freely as long as we do

not intend them to mean literally. For example, you can tell your friend that your cup of coffee has an excess of hydrogen ions without committing the "sin" of metaphysics as long as you do not mean that there are invisible tiny things called hydrogen ions swimming in your coffee, and all you mean is that if a piece of litmus paper should be inserted into the coffee it would turn red (that is, if it has not been browned by your coffee already).

Being Humeans, logical positivists are wary of unobservables. Terms employed in science should be confined to observational terms. That's why the right-hand sides of (8) to (11) are in observational terms. Since the left-hand side means exactly the right-hand side in these "meaning statements," the "metaphysical" terms on the left-hand side can be eliminated. We can avoid their use if need be, for we can always employ the right-hand sides instead. Thus these "metaphysical" terms (on the left) are but abbreviations of more lengthy observational expressions (on the right). Thus theoretical terms are harmless as long as they are so reducible to observational terms.

It is an ingenious move. Now under VPM we can employ theoretical terms such as 'gravitational force,' 'atom,' 'electron,' 'radio wave,' and so on without "sinning" against a basic tenet of Humean empiricism, that only observational terms and their derivatives are meaningful. At the same time VPM is able to get rid of "genuinely" metaphysical propositions such as

(12a) Physical objects are ideas in the mind of God. (Berkeley)

(12b) Things-in-themselves are unknowable. (Kant)

(12c) Time is unreal. (McTaggart)

(12d) The Nothing itself nothings. (Heidegger)

These propositions are well-known metaphysical pronouncements in the history of philosophy. They are Hume's main targets. VPM rules them out as meaningless by challenging their advocates

---

for methods of verification. Is it possible to design experiments to test, for example, that the Nothing itself nothings? How can the unreality of time be empirically verified? What can count as empirical knowledge of things-in-themselves if they are unknowable? Would our experiences be different if physical objects are not ideas in the mind of God? If no empirical methods of verification can be produced, according to VPM, statements (12a)–(12d) are meaningless, and thus we need not worry about their truth or falsity (and certainly governments should not provide funding for philosophical debates over their truth and implications!).

Thus VPM seems to be the right kind of weapon to fight metaphysics. On the one hand, it destroys the "evil" and the pretentious. On the other, it preserves the "good" and useful.

As I said before, VPM differs from Hume's theory in two major respects. First, the unit of meaning for VPM is now the proposition, not the word. Second, propositions are meaningful, not because they stand for ideas (some sort of imagery in the mind) but because there are methods for their verification. Since these methods are meant to be *empirical* methods, Hume's tenet is upheld. Meaningful statements are all rooted to experience, while those which are not so rooted are declared meaningless.

Thus a sound theoretical basis for Hume and Comte's antimetaphysics campaign is established, so it seems.

23.3 THE PROBLEM OF OBSERVATIONAL TERMS

The VPM has not specified what counts as *empirical* methods of verification. In other words, it has not made a ruling on what sort of observational terms are allowed on the right-hand side of meaning statements such as (8) to (11). We saw in Section 23.1 that Mach thought the observational terms should be sense-datum terms. Rudolf Carnap (1891–1970), probably the most outstanding logical

positivist, thought similarly in his early years. There were two major reasons for such a choice.

(i) It was thought that science should be built on firm foundations—that is, on statements that are certain to be true or at least very unlikely to be false. Sense-datum statements (statements written in sense-datum terms) seem to fill the bill, for these statements are records of sensations, our immediate experience. What can one be more sure of than the ascertainment of one's immediate experience! For example, if I experience a pain then I would know for sure that I have a pain. The pain may be imaginary. It is a pain-feeling nevertheless. If I experience a double image of a beer bottle, then I do have a double image of a beer bottle. It would be wrong for someone to point out to me that there is in fact only a single bottle in front of me, for what I claim is about my *private* experience, not about the public physical things "outside" me. You can see that it is quite reasonable and obvious for the logical positivists to attempt to interpret observational terms as sense-datum terms.

(ii) It was thought that sense-datum terms are purely descriptive and are atheoretical. Thus sense-datum terms are exactly what the logical positivists are looking for. They do not want theories to creep into the firm basis of science. In Chapter 22, we saw how observation in general is theory-laden. As Bacon would urge, an objective science should not be prejudiced by theories and preconceptions. The employment of a sense-datum language for the description of observation will ensure that we record what we actually observe.

Thus early logical positivists were enthusiastically committed to phenomenalism. However, they eventually found out that all is not well with such an extreme philosophy.

First, since sense-datum statements are about private experience, and each piece of private experience is only "felt" by one single person and no others, sense-datum statements made by different scientists must be about different "things." In other words, no two scientists can be investigating and reporting about anything in common. Each person has her own private science, strictly about the "behaviors" of her own private experience. For instance, both A and B may report experiencing (visually) a red round patch. They may be looking in the same direction when they so report. But this does not mean that they are seeing the same thing (say, the sun). In fact, each would be reporting about her own piece of private sensation. There are two distinct pieces, A's piece and B's piece. (In fact, when A says that her patch is red and B says the same, they need not be sensing the same color.) But this is counterintuitive, for science is supposed to be public and objective. What one scientist claims should be assessable by other scientists. Anyway, I don't think many of us are interested in other people's private experience. If science were about private experience, there is not much incentive to do science.

Second, the sense-datum language is a private language. (Strictly speaking, there are as many sense-datum languages as there are people.) It is highly doubtful whether such a language is a possibility. Wittgenstein (1958), for example, provides strong arguments against such a possibility.

Third, it seems that the actual implementation of phenomenalism is not only impractical but impossible. In the 1920s, Carnap and others were highly enthusiastic about the actual implementation of phenomenalism. In 1928, Carnap published his *Der Logische Aufbau der Welt* (*The Logical Structure of the World*), which was supposed to be a piece of foundational work demonstrating how the phenomenalistic program (to reduce all scientific talk to sense-datum talk) can actually be done. However, soon afterward he realized he was mistaken. By 1931 he had abandoned the program and instead advocated the use of the "physical-thing language" in place of the sense-datum language. The physical-thing language is nothing other than our ordinary commonsensical language,[8] which employs commonsense terms to talk about macroscopic material things and their observable properties. 'Table,' 'chair,' 'dog,' 'cat,' 'round,' 'square,' 'hot,'

'cold,' 'heavy,' and 'light' are some of the terms of this language. This switch from sense-datum talk to physical-thing talk was a great compromise on Humean empiricism.

The employment of the physical-thing language as the observational language on which to build theoretical science was given the dignified name of '**physicalism**.' Under physicalism, the observational terms are what the common person takes as those terms that represent the observables (observable things and observable properties). Sadly, the compromise was not able to save the program of logical positivism. This is our next topic of study.

23.4 THE PROBLEM OF THE OT-LINK

You may recall from Section 23.1 that empiricism faces the problem of the logical role of theories. What sort of role do theories play in science with respect to prediction, explanation, and description? And how do theories play out these roles in such a way that theories can be seen to be relevant to empirical observation? Hence, what sort of logical relationship obtains between theories and observation?

We have termed the problem about this relationship between theories and observation, the problem of the OT-link.

Given that the observational language is our ordinary commonsense language, what is the logical relationship between observational terms and theoretical terms? This is our present problem.

Toward the end of the 19th and at the beginning of the 20th century, Frege and Russell developed a new logic, the predicate calculus, that proved to be far superior to Aristotle's syllogistic logic. With this new tool, the logical positivists were confident that they could find the OT-link, the link between observational statements and

---

8. To be more accurate, it is the "physical part" of our ordinary commonsense language—that is, the part that deals exclusively with observable physical objects. Thus words like 'heaven,' 'angel,' 'kindness,' and 'honesty' would have been excluded.

theoretical statements. Recall that in Chapter 15 we presented the classical view of scientific theories, which is one of the main tenets of logical positivism. Let me briefly redescribe it.

According to this view, science operates in two languages: the observational language and the theoretical language, each with its own vocabulary: the observational terms and the theoretical terms. The scientist does science in three steps: (i) she records her observations in the observational terms; these are the empirical data (for example, "This piece of copper conducts heat"); (ii) she then generalizes her data into empirical generalizations (for instance, "All copper conducts heat"); and (iii) she explains these generalizations in theoretical terms.

Each theory has two parts. The first part, which is the theory proper, consists of internal principles, which are statements in purely theoretical terms. The second part consists of bridge principles, which are mixed statements, having both observational terms and theoretical terms. If a theory works, the empirical generalizations should be deducible from the conjunction of the internal principles and the bridge principles. This is a case of Hempel's deductive-nomological explanation (Chapter 10). The question is: What form or forms should the bridge principles take? This is the OT-link that we are after. Originally the term 'correspondence rule' was used instead of 'bridge principle.' Since the present chapter is meant to be historical, let us keep to the original term in the following presentation.

A. Explicit Definitions as Correspondence Rules

The earliest attempt at the OT-link was to take correspondence rules as explicit definitions. An **explicit definition** has the following form:

(13) x is $T =_{df} x$ is $f(O_1, O_2, O_3,...)$

where T is the term to be defined, known as the **definiendum**, and $O_1, O_2, O_3,...$ are terms in

terms of which T is to be defined, and they collectively are known as the **definiens**. The segment '$f(O_1, O_2, O_3,...)$' reads 'a function of O_1, O_2, O_3,...'. For example, we can have the following explicit definition:

(14) x is a bachelor $=_{df} x$ is an unmarried man.

Here 'unmarried man' is a function of 'unmarried' and 'man,' and the definiendum is 'bachelor.'

The early logical positivists thought that all theoretical terms can be defined in terms of explicit definition. A well-known example is:

(15) The light beam x consists of electromagnetic waves of wavelength between 6,100 angstroms and 7,500 angstroms $=_{df}$. The light beam x is red.

But this simplistic thesis soon ran into trouble. The logical positivists found that terms such as 'magnetic,' 'electrically charged,' and 'having an excess of hydrogen ions' are more difficult to manage than they had thought. It is questionable whether (15) is an adequate definition of wavelengths anyway.

B. Operational Definitions as Correspondence Rules

Carnap in the 1930s realized that at least some of the correspondence rules have to take the form of operational definition, thus agreeing with Bridgman's operationalism (Section 17.4). According to Bridgman (1927),

(16) All terms should be operationally defined, and the meaning of a term is the same as the set of defining operations (Section 17.4).

Operational definitions take the following form:

(17) x is $p =_{df}$ If O is performed on x, then R.

O stands for an operation to be performed on x, and R is the expected response, and both O and R are in observational terms.[9]

---

9. Operational definition is a special kind of explicit definition.

You might observe that this is nothing new, for (16) is but a variant of (6), the VPM. Indeed, even though (8)–(11) were meant to be illustrations of VPM, they can be taken as examples of operational definition as well. It is no coincidence that the two are so close to each other, for verificationism was the spirit of the era.

The thesis that correspondence rules should take the form of operational definition therefore faces the same sort of difficulty that confronts operationalism. Here let me recount a few of the common criticisms against operationalism as listed in Section 17.5.

(i)   It is doubtful if any theoretical term can be operationally defined in such a manner that the definiendum statement (left-hand side of the definition) is true if and only if the definiens statement (right-hand side) is true.

(ii) Most concepts have more than one possible operational definition (the problem of multiple definitions).

(iii) It is said that "continuous" concepts cannot be operationally defined.

(iv) The term 'if,' the key term in an operational definition, is not well understood.

Points (i) to (iii) have been explained and discussed in detail in Section 17.5. Let's therefore confine ourselves to (iv). What can 'if' mean in (17)?

What a strange question to ask! Nevertheless, this is not a trivial problem. You might wonder what sort of answer is being sought—what sort of answer can be considered adequate? Let's see. Take (R) to be the sentence:

(R)   If P, then Q (where P and Q are sentences).

Instances of (R) can be:

(Ra) If today is Friday, tomorrow will be Saturday.

(Rb) If this is heated, it will expand.

(Rc) If today is Friday, she should be here by tomorrow.

(Rd) If you lend me the money, all my problems will be solved.

(Re) If this is pepper, that must be salt.

Contemporary analytic philosophy finds that there is no unique meaning attached to all of the if's in (Ra) to (Re). The meaning of 'if' seems to vary from example to example. Nevertheless there is a common denominator between all of them. The common denominator is that if P should be true, and Q false, then R must be false. Thus predicate calculus, the logic of Frege and Russell, construes 'if' as what is known as the **material implication**, which is usually symbolized by '⊃' with R written as '$P \supset Q$.' The symbol '⊃' is often read as 'implies,' and its meaning is defined by the following rules:

(i) R is true, when P and Q are both true.

(ii) R is false, when P is true and Q is false.

(iii) R is true, when P is false and Q is true.

(iv) R is true, when P is false and Q is false.

The logical positivists, greatly influenced by Frege and Russell, adopted the predicate calculus in their formulation of the correspondence rules and construed 'if P then Q' as '$P \supset Q$.'[10] But this poses a problem for the thesis that correspondence rules are generally operational definitions.

Take, for example, (8a) as an operational definition. Should the 'if' be construed as '⊃', (8a) would be

(8b) x is fragile $=_{df}$ (x is dropped onto the floor) ⊃ (it will break).

Applying this to one of my tennis balls, we get

(8c) My tennis ball is fragile $=_{df}$ (My tennis ball is dropped onto the floor) ⊃ (it will break).

---

10. In fact, it is one of the logical positivists' main tenets that scientific theories should be formulatable in (first-order) predicate calculus.

Let's abbreviate this to:

(8d) $C =_{df} A \supset B$

Now my tennis ball is certainly not fragile. So C is false. But suppose before anyone could drop it onto the floor, it was destroyed (say, torn up by a dog). In such a case, A is false. By Rules (iii) and (iv), we can see that '$A \supset B$' is true. But C is false. Hence (8d) is "unbalanced" (with one side of the equation true and the other side false).

This is related to the well-known problem called the **paradox of material implication**. To remedy the situation, Carnap in his 1936–1937 work proposed the employment of reduction sentences instead.

C. Reduction Sentences as Correspondence Rules

A **reduction sentence** has the following form:

(18) $A \supset (C \equiv B)$

For example, the term 'fragile' could be defined as:

(19) $(x)(t)[Dxt \supset (Fx \equiv Bxt)]$

where

(x) and (t) are universal quantifiers,[11] and t is to range over time

Dxt stands for "x is dropped onto the floor at time t"

Bxt stands for "x is broken at time t"

Fx stands for "x is fragile"

$\equiv$ is the sign of material equivalence, so that '$(Fx \equiv Bxt)$' is the same as '$[(Fx \supset Bxt)$ and $(Bxt \supset Fx)]$'

'$\equiv$' is often read as 'iff' or 'if and only if'

Thus (19) reads:

(19a) If x is dropped onto the floor at time t, then (x is fragile iff x breaks).

Carnap thinks that terms like 'fragile' can be defined in terms of reduction sentences. Definition

(19) says that for anything that has been dropped, we can say that it is fragile if it should break when dropped. What about those that have not been dropped? Statement (19) is inapplicable for that situation. The clause 'Dxt' defines the scope of the application of the definition. When Dxt is true, then '$Fx = Bxt$' applies; in all other cases, the truth value of '$Fx = Bxt$' is unspecified. That's why Carnap only claims that reduction sentences can be employed to **partially define** theoretical terms such as 'fragile.' Let's try it on another theoretical term, say, 'electrically charged.'

(20) If x is brought near a leaf electroscope at t, then (x is electrically charged iff the leaves of the electroscope diverge at t).

Again you can see that (20) can make a ruling on objects that have been thus brought near leaf electroscopes. If an object is brought near a leaf electroscope, the divergence of the leaves of the electroscope will tell us exactly whether the object is charged or not. As for those that have not been brought near any leaf electroscopes, (20) has nothing to say.

It will be helpful to our understanding if we compare (17) and (18). Let's write (18) in the language of (17).

(18a) If O is performed on x, then (x is p iff R).

Compare this with a slightly reformulated (17):

(17a) x is p iff (if O is performed on x, then R).

The difference seems to be a matter of reordering the clauses, yet it makes a great difference. Whereas the paradox of material implication poses a problem for (17), it does not affect (18a).

In shifting from (17) to (18), a sacrifice has to be made though. Full definition cannot be claimed for (18). This should be obvious. (17), though an operational definition, is still an explicit definition, with the definiendum on the right-hand side of the "equation." On the other hand, reduction

---

11. The universal quantifier (x) is roughly equivalent to the English expression "for all x" so that '$(x)(x$ is mortal)' can be translated into English as 'For all x, x is mortal,' which is another way of saying 'Everything is mortal'.

sentences are no longer explicit definitions. Their "equation" is subordinated under the operational clause (as if saying that the "equation" holds if this operational clause is satisfied). Thus Carnap observes that reduction sentences can only provide partial definitions for theoretical terms.

"Every dark cloud has its silver lining!" In Section 17.5, we pointed out that operationalism faces the difficulty of multiple operational definition: What if the same concept when applied to different situations can only be measured by different operations? It seems that this difficulty no longer applies if reduction sentences are employed in place of operational definition. Let me explain.

Suppose for one reason or another there is no floor for us to drop our tennis ball or vase on to test whether it is fragile. Thus (19) is not applicable. Nevertheless, we can introduce additional partial definitions such as (21) and (22):

(21) If x is stepped on at time t, then (x is fragile iff x breaks).

(22) If x is struck sharply at time t, then (x is fragile iff x breaks).

You can see that a concept having multiple definitions is now a virtue. Each definition covers a certain situation where the concept can be tested. Several reduction sentences together would therefore cover a wide range of situations; the wider this range is, the more defined the concept becomes.

Both (22) and (23) employ breakage as an indicator of fragility. This need not be the case. Suppose it is discovered that fragile things when exposed to X-rays of wavelengths W will turn red. We could then have:

(23) If x is exposed to X-rays of wavelengths W at time t, then (x is fragile iff x turns red).

You can see that (23) no longer relies on breakage as a sign of fragility.

Each one of these partial definitions is said to give more substance to the term 'fragile'; thus the meaning of fragility is made sharper with each additional partial definition. Ironically this suggests that there is something wrong with the idea of reduction sentences as partial definitions. As far as we can foresee, reduction

sentences like (21–23) can be multiplied indefinitely, thus implying that we can never achieve a full definition of fragility. This seems strange, for fragility appears to be a common notion that everybody understands fully. The *Oxford Encyclopedic English Dictionary* defines 'fragile' as 'easily broken; weak; of delicate frame or constitution; not strong.' It is counterintuitive to say that fragility requires an indefinite number of reduction sentences to define it. It is even stranger that reduction sentences such as (23) should play the role of a partial definition, for all of us seem to understand the notion 'fragile' fully even though none of us have knowledge of the type exemplified by (23).

For Carnap these reduction sentences are analytic, being definition-like. Yet we suspect (23) and the like are synthetic, having been discovered through experiments. Probably even (21) and (22) are synthetic, for it is not true that understanding the concept of fragility will enable us to infer that a fragile object when dropped onto the floor will break. That dropping fragile objects onto the floor will generate a strong impact (thus causing fragile objects to break) has to be discovered by empirical means.

D. Network Theory of Meaning

Can theoretical terms in general be defined (albeit partially) in terms of observational terms through reduction sentences? In practice, few theoretical terms are found to be so definable. Hempel (1952) was not optimistic about Carnap's project. Thus he observes:

> Terms of this kind are not introduced by definition or reduction chains based on observables; in fact they are not introduced by any piecemeal process of assigning meaning to them individually. Rather, the constructs used in a theory are introduced jointly, as it were, by setting up a *theoretical system* formulated in terms of them and by giving this system an experimental interpretation, which in turn confers empirical meaning on the theoretical constructs. (p. 32, my italics)

This is what we called the **network theory of meaning** in Section 17.6. According to this theory, theoretical terms are not introduced individually, each by its own reduction sentences. A theory cannot be partitioned into internal principles and correspondence rules. Rather, the theory as a whole defines all the theoretical terms in it wholesale. It is a holistic philosophy. The statements of a theory form a network, with the theoretical terms forming the nodes. By anchoring the whole theory into experiments and observations, all the theoretical terms are given meaning together, as was detailed in Section 17.6.

Correct as it seems, this network theory is but a sketch of a plausible theory of meaning. A lot more work needs to be done. Here are a few queries that must be addressed:

(i) Should the network theory be developed on the assumption that scientific theories are axiomatizable? Is the "network" for a given theory to be constructed in terms of axioms?

(ii) If so, what sort of logical constraint and conditions are the axioms required to satisfy? Other than the requirement of consistency, can any set of sentences whatsoever be considered axioms of a *single* theory?

(iii) Hempel requires that this network be given an experimental interpretation. How is this done? If the network consists of a set of axioms, how is this set of axioms to be interpreted experimentally? Are they to be related to experience (or to empirical data or to empirical generalizations) through correspondence rules? If so, what sort of shapes should these rules take? Aren't we back to the same old problems that confront Carnap's correspondence rules? In sum, how is Hempel going to solve the problem of the OT-link?

23.5 MISCELLANEOUS

Logical positivism is a unified philosophy, yet it is difficult to say what exactly it is. We have tried to describe it as a continuation and development of Hume's empiricism and Comte's positivism: how it attempts to demolish metaphysics through its analysis of meaning and how it tries to solve the

problem of the OT-link. Even though these provide the fundamentals of logical positivism, we would miss out on many other exciting features and achievements of this great movement if we stopped here. The present section titled 'Miscellaneous' is a partial attempt to remedy the situation—not that it can do justice to this epoch-making philosophy.

A. Ontological Interpretations of Theories

As we have just seen, logical positivism takes theories as an axiomatic system, partitioned into internal principles and bridge principles (correspondence rules). How are these axioms to be interpreted ontologically?

You may recall that in Section 16.3 we discussed the three views of reality: radical scientific realism (RSR), conservative scientific realism (CSR), and instrumentalism (INS). RSR favors scientific theories. These theories give us largely true pictures of reality. CSR thinks that both scientific theories and our commonsense pictures are approximately correct, though not correct to the same degree. Finally, INS takes our commonsense pictures as what truly depict reality, albeit approximately, and scientific theories as merely instrumental devices for prediction and systematization. Though later versions of logical positivism remain neutral to these three interpretations of theories, both phenomenalism and physicalism definitely take the position of INS. Phenomenalism takes sensations as the basic constituents of reality, whereas physicalism opts for commonsense objects.

B. Reductionism and Unity of Science

Both phenomenalism and physicalism are reductive in nature, and reductionism goes hand in hand with the unification of the sciences. We studied these topics in some detail in Section 13.5.

The logical positivists—equipped with Frege's and Russell's new logic, the VPM, and results of their logical analyses of scientific theories—were quite optimistic about the prospect of unification of all the sciences. In 1938, they changed the title of their journal, *Erkenntnis*, to *Journal of Unified Science*. And later arrangements were made for the publication by the University of Chicago of a series of brochures ambitiously titled the *International Encyclopedia of Unified Science*. Regrettably, the project of reductionism and unified science was not much of a success. In fact, the *Journal of Unified Science* soon ceased publication due to the outbreak of the Second World War.

C. Foundationalism

Rationalism and empiricism have one thing in common. Both aim at providing knowledge and meaning with a firm foundation. This is **foundationalism**. For example, Descartes attempted to provide an axiomatic system for all (genuine) knowledge. Around the beginning of the 20th century, Frege and Russell rekindled the enthusiasm for foundationalism by making a heroic and impressive attempt to provide a foundation for arithmetic known as logicism. Logical positivism carried their program over to science. Carnap's ambitious 1928 *Der Logische Aufbau der Welt* is one of the better-known attempts in this direction.

D. Philosophical Analysis

Again owing to the influence of Frege and Russell, the logical positivists proposed a revolutionary view of philosophy. As we saw earlier, they rejected the possibility of metaphysics. Indeed, for them metaphysics is meaningless. But then what is left for the philosopher to philosophize on? The logical positivists took the historic "analytic" turn. For them the task of philosophy is confined to **philosophical analysis**. This is how Carnap puts it:

> But what, then, is left over for *philosophy*, if all statements whatever that assert something are of an empirical nature and belong to factual science? What remains is not statements, nor a theory, nor a system, but only a *method:* the method of logical analysis. The foregoing discussion has illustrated the negative application of this

method: in that context it serves to eliminate meaningless words, meaningless pseudo-statements. In its positive use it serves to clarify meaningful concepts and propositions, to lay logical foundations for factual science and for mathematics. The negative application of the method is necessary and important in the present historical situation. But even in its present practice, the positive application is more fertile. We cannot here discuss it in greater detail. It is the indicated task of logical analysis, inquiry into logical foundations, that is meant by *"scientific philosophy"* in contrast to metaphysics. (1932, p. 77)

From this passage you can see that Carnap rejected the traditional view that philosophy consists of statements, (i) some claiming to give us first principles (very general truths) about the world (that is, metaphysics), (ii) some purportedly informing us of the correct ways of reasoning (logic), (iii) some providing us with moral principles (ethics), and (iv) some asserting the available means and ways to obtain knowledge (epistemology). Logical positivism holds that synthetic (informative) statements are, by definition, statements about the world, and hence must be empirical. The search for true empirical statements belongs to the field of science. Hence it is none of the business of philosophy to seek empirical truths. If, however, philosophers think that they can somehow know (synthetic) truths that are more general, more fundamental, and more important than empirical truths (for example, metaphysics), they must be mistaken, for there are no such statements to be found. (The so-called statements of traditional philosophy are in fact meaningless pseudo-statements.) But then what is left over for philosophy?

Carnap suggests that three tasks are left for the philosopher: (a) to purge philosophy of meaningless pseudo-statements such as metaphysical statements, (b) to clarify concepts and statements, and (c) to give foundations to science and mathematics. These three tasks are philosophical, not because they aim at statements of certain nature (because philosophy does not produce statements) but because they share the same method, the method of analysis.

Points (a) and (c) have already been covered in Sections 23.2–23.4. Let me briefly explain (b) here. One way to clarify concepts and statements is known as **explication**. For example, Hempel's covering-law model of explanation (Chapter 10) can be taken as an explication of the notion of scientific explanation, as pointed out in the Summary of Part III. This model was meant to bring out the inner structure of explanation and to make it more exact and fruitful.

E. The Discovery-Justification Distinction

The distinction between the context of discovery and the context of justification came from Herschel. We have studied these two notions and their distinction in Chapters 1 and 5 to 7. The logic of discovery aims at the generation of plausible hypotheses, including laws of nature and higher principles of science. The logic of justification consists of means and methods for the evaluation of hypotheses proposed. This distinction was historically fruitful and important. It provided the positivists with a background philosophy for their logical analysis of scientific theories.

F. Inductive Logic and Probabilistic Reasoning

Under logical positivism, elaborate systems of inductive logic and probability have been designed for the evaluation (justification) of hypotheses. In these areas, Carnap and Reichenbach were most notable.

G. The Logic of Explanation

The logic of explanation was also one of the main topics of the movement. As noted previously, the greatest contributor here is probably Hempel (Chapter 10).

H. 'Logical Positivism'

The name 'logical positivism' is apt. The philosophy can indeed be taken as (Comte's) positivism made logical. We owe this name to Herbert Feigl, a member of the Vienna Circle. Logical positivism can also be viewed as a regimentation of Hume's empiricism through the use of modern logic. Hence the other name, 'logical empiricism' (due to Reichenbach), is equally appropriate.

23.6 CRITIQUES

Logical positivism was a great movement. It was inductive empiricism (Section 19.4) at its best. It dominated Anglo-American philosophy for almost half a century up to the 1960s, when Thomas Kuhn introduced a new philosophy, the Weltanschauung view, which will be our focus in Part VII. The decline of logical positivism was partly due to exhaustion, partly due to Kuhn, but mainly due to a number of major difficulties that the philosophy could not manage to overcome. Let's go through them briefly.

A. The Verification Principle of Meaning (VPM)

As we saw in Section 23.4, some terms like 'fragile' seem to be verifiable by many methods. You can attempt to verify an object's fragility by dropping it onto the floor, by stepping on it, by striking it sharply, and so on. So if, as VPM suggests, the meaning of a proposition is its method of verification, then 'My vase is fragile' should have as many meanings as there are methods of verification, which can run into hundreds. This seems absurd, for, as far we know, 'fragile' seems to have only one meaning. This, of course, is related to the problem of multiple definitions, as was discussed in Section 17.5.

On the other hand, there seems to be no method that can verify 'My vase is fragile.' For example, the breaking of the vase on its impact with the floor does not necessarily mean it is fragile. The breakage may not be due to the impact at all. It could be due to some unknown force (such as a sonic boom) operating at the moment of impact. In Section 9.3, we discussed the Duhem-Quine thesis, which points out that in tests of hypotheses, auxiliary hypotheses are usually assumed. One can always deny the outcome of a test by blaming one or more of the auxiliary hypotheses. In our example here, we blamed the (hidden) auxiliary hypothesis that the only force in operation was the force of impact.

General statements (usually of the form 'All X are Y') are not verifiable. No matter how many X's we have studied and found to be Y's, we still cannot be sure that *all* X are Y. We have discussed this in connection with Hume's problem of induction (Chapter 20).

Because of this reasoning, the VPM was later modified into the **verifiability principle of meaningfulness**, which states that

(24) A proposition is meaningful if and only if it is (empirically) verifiable.

Since (practically) no propositions are verifiable, (24) is still too strong. A further modification was therefore made, resulting in the **confirmability principle of meaningfulness**:[12]

(25) A proposition is meaningful if and only if it is (empirically) conformable.[13]

An alternative formulation of (25) is the **testability principle of meaningfulness**:[14]

(26) A proposition is meaningful if and only if it is (empirically) testable.[15]

But what about the meaningfulness of analytic propositions such as 'All bachelors are unmarried'? Are these testable? Following Hume, the logical positivists dichotomize the class of propositions into (a) those that are analytic (and a priori), and (b) those that are synthetic (and a posteriori) (Section 11.3).

Examples of analytic propositions (which can be either true or false) are:

(27a) All fragile things are fragile.

(27b) Triangles have five angles.

(27c) $2 + 2 = 4$

Examples of synthetic propositions (which can be either true or false) are:

(28a) This vase is fragile.

(28b) The triangle on the blackboard is colored red.

(28c) There are two people in this room.

The principle of testability of meaningfulness is supposed to be applicable to synthetic propositions only. Hence even though analytic statements are not *empirically* testable they can still be meaningful.[16]

Ethical statements pose another obstacle to logical positivism. Here are a few examples of ethical statements.

(29a) Killing is immoral.

(29b) Honesty is good.

(29c) One ought to help one's neighbors.

(29d) It is wrong to steal.

Surely the logical positivists would not like to deny meaning to these moral pronouncements. We employ such statements daily. No society seems to be exempt from their use. But none of them are empirically testable. Would the logical positivists therefore reject them as meaningless just as they

---

12. This is not its historical title.

13. In Section 1.9, we defined 'confirmation' as follows: "A hypothesis H is said to be (partially) confirmed by evidence E, if E provides some grounds for the truth of H." And in Chapter 21, we discussed the notion of confirmation during the course of study of the paradoxes of confirmation.

14. This is not its historical title.

15. We spent some time on the notion of empirical tests in Chapters 6 and 7.

16. The logical positivists seem to have overlooked propositions such as 'Things-in-themselves are things-in-themselves.' Are analytic propositions that employ metaphysical terms meaningful?

have done with metaphysics? Can a place (of honor) be found for them outside the domain of science?

To get out of the dilemma, Carnap suggested that ethical statements, though meaningful, are not really statements. They are imperatives. A version of that theory, as popularized by A. J. Ayer, held that statements of value (29a and 29b) are not descriptions that are true or false but rather expressions of emotion about their subjects, and statements of obligation (29c and 29d) are imperatives (that is, commands). Note that neither expressions of emotion such as "hurrah" nor imperatives like "go!" are true or false. However, since you can make acceptable unimportant moral claims about things you do not care about, moral claims need not be expressions of emotion. Further, no one has yet been able to word statements of obligation about the past as imperatives. Hence R. M. Hare improved the theory by claiming that statements of value are commendations or condemnations, and statements of obligation are prescriptions. For example (29b), for Hare, is an expression of the speaker's commendation of honesty. The speaker is *not describing* honesty as a good kind of object, even though the words in the sentence do suggest that. Rather she makes it known that she approves of honest conduct. Statements of obligation, on the other hand, are prescriptions. They are directives. For instance, (29c) directs people to help their neighbors. Thus neither statements of value nor statements of obligation are really statements.

Since ethical pronouncements are not statements, they are incapable of having truth values. Being neither true nor false, they are obviously neither verifiable nor refutable, neither confirmable nor disconfirmable. Thus the untestability of ethical pronouncements is explained, not in terms of meaninglessness, but in terms of their being nonstatements.

Thus the logical positivists were able to preserve honor for both analytic and ethical statements, which, unlike metaphysics, are not meaningless, and are thus worthy of utterance, for one reason or other. But then, what about the verification (testability) principle of meaning itself? Since it is not verifiable or testable, is it meaningless? Or is it a nonstatement, similar to ethical pronouncements?

Wittgenstein (1961, Proposition 6.54) was rather candid about it:

> My propositions [which would include the verification principle of meaning] serve as elucidations in the following way: anyone who understands me eventually recognizes them as nonsensical, when he has used them—as steps—to climb up beyond them. (He must, so to speak, throw away the ladder after he has climbed up it.) He must transcend these propositions, and then he will see the world aright.

B. The Problem of the Observational Terms

In Section 23.3, we pointed out how at first the logical positivists settled for sense-datum terms as observational terms, and then, due to insurmountable difficulties, retreated to commonsense physical terms. But that still leaves the problem of the OT-link unsolved.

C. The Problem of the OT-Link

This is probably the most difficult problem of all, and no wonder it remains unsolved. Popper, as you will soon see, tries to bury the problem under the carpet. On the other hand, the constructivists, in denying the existence of the OT-distinction, think, wrongly, that the problem does not exist.

D. The Two-Tier Axiomatic-Deductive Model of Theories

The problems classified under (A), (B), and (C) are not unrelated problems. We should see that the logical positivists' theses on observational terms and on correspondence rules (the OT-link) are attempted refinements of their VPM. The latter is qualitative, whereas the former are "quantitative." The former are supposed to provide detailed logic for the VPM. How is this detailed logic to be provided? The logical positivists adopted the two-tier view of science and the axiomatic-deductive model of theories (Chapter 15). But both the two-tier view and the axiomatic model are problematic.

The two-tier view is built on the controversial observational-theoretical distinction, while the axiomatic view has been challenged, with good reasons, by the structuralist view, the semantic view, and Kuhn's paradigm view of theories.[17]

E. The Discovery-Versus-Justification Distinction

Sadly this distinction has also been seriously challenged. We will study this in some detail in Part VIII.

KEY TERMS INTRODUCED IN THIS CHAPTER

positivism

sensationism

phenomenalism

observational-theoretical distinction

problem of observational terms

problem of the OT-link

problem of the rationality of induction

problem of the logical role of theories

(Humean) ideas

(Humean) impression

logical positivism

Vienna Circle

logical empiricism

verification principle of meaning

physicalism

explicit definition

definiendum

definiens

material implication

paradox of material implication

a reduction sentence

partial definition

network theory of meaning

foundationalism

philosophical analysis

explication

verifiability principle of meaningfulness

confirmability principle of meaningfulness

testability principle of meaningfulness

REFERENCES

For general references, see Oldroyd (1986, pp. 230–255), Stumpf (1971, pp. 437–448), Munitz (1981, pp. 221–269), Ayer (1946, pp. 5–26); (1959, pp. 3–30).

For an anthology, see Ayer (1959), which is a collection of classic papers on logical positivism.

On Comte: Oldroyd (1986, pp. 169–175).

On Mach: Oldroyd (1986, pp. 176–182).

On Poincaré: Oldroyd (1986, pp. 189–194).

On Duhem: Oldroyd (1986, pp. 194–203).

On Carnap: Oldroyd (1986, pp. 234–248).

On Reichenbach: Oldroyd (1986, pp. 238–255).

On Hume's theory of meaning: Melchert (1991, pp. 343–344).

On the verification principle of meaning: Ayer (1946, pp. 5–16).

On the problem of the OT-link: see Lambert and Brittan (1987, pp. 115–131) for an introduction; Suppe (1977, pp. 3–118) gives a very detailed account; Boyd (1991, chap. 3) includes a classic paper by Hempel.

On ethical statements: Melchert (1991, pp. 509–511), Ayer (1959, pp. 21–23).

On the status of the verification principle of meaning: Munitz (1981, pp. 265–268).

---

17. For the structuralist view, see Stegmüller (1979). Lambert and Brittan (1987, pp. 141–147) provide an introduction to the semantic view. We will study Kuhn's view in Part VII.

Chapter 24

Popper's Falsificationism

24.1 INTRODUCTION

Karl R. Popper (1902–1994) was a charismatic writer and speaker on the philosophy of science and attracted a large following. Despite his protests, he was usually grouped with the logical positivists. This is paradoxical, for he explicitly denied that he had anything to do with logical positivism. His philosophy, he would explain, is on the contrary most critical of that philosophy. "If anything I am a "negativist," not a positivist. The method of science is not to prove, as the logical positivists advocate, but to disprove," he once declared.[1] Let's briefly summarize his philosophical position in relation to logical positivism.

(A) Popper shows no interests in the following areas, which are, however, central to the interests of the logical positivists. This is in fact an understatement. To put it frankly, he is disdainful of philosophical pursuits in these fields:

(1) Theory of meaning and meaningfulness (as exemplified by logical positivists' verification principle of meaning, and their various formulations of correspondence rules).

---

1. Made during one of his public lectures.

(2) Structure of scientific theory (in this field, the logical positivists proposed the axiomatic-deductive model of theories, and the formalization of theories in terms of internal and bridge principles).

(3) Inductive logic (as exemplified by the works of Carnap and others).

(B) The following theses formulated by Popper are critical of logical positivism and have prompted a number of amendments to the latter:

(1) Scientific statements can be falsified but not verified. (This prompted the logical positivists to replace their verification principle of meaning with their testability principle of meaningfulness.)

(2) Metaphysical statements, though nonscientific, play an important role in the development of scientific theories and are certainly not meaningless. (The logical positivists have since shown more respect for metaphysics.)

(3) Subjective experience can never justify a scientific statement, and statements that describe our experiences do not enjoy favored status in science. (This contributed to the replacement of phenomenalism by physicalism.)

(C) Nevertheless, Popper does share quite a few fundamental views with the logical positivists. These views include:

(1) Observational statements play the decisive role in the acceptability of theories. (Popper's basic statements correspond to logical positivists' (physicalistic) observational statements. Popper makes it clear that basic statements are not about experience but about physical things.) Hence Popper's philosophy is firmly empiricist.

(2) Hume's problem of induction is genuine and requires serious attention.

(3) The context of discovery and that of justification are distinct issues and should be studied separately.

(From these three items, you can see that Popper is firmly committed to empiricism, just as the logical positivists are.)

This, I think, is a fair summary of the "antagonism" between Popper and the logical positivists,

which is by no means trivial. Nevertheless I think there are good reasons for classifying Popper's philosophy together with logical positivism. You should find, after going through this chapter, that Popper's falsificationism is best seen both as a complement and also as a *friendly* critique of logical positivist philosophy. The two philosophies are complementary because, whereas logical positivism worked on and contributed significantly in area A (semantics and syntax), Popper had nothing to do with it. On the other hand, Popper contributed significantly in area B (epistemology, including methodology), and as a consequence brought about quite a few changes in the views of the logical positivists in area A. Historically the two together form the classical tradition, laying down a detailed, articulate, and relatively precise foundation for the philosophy of science. The real antagonism came from the Weltanschauung views of Kuhn and others, which we will study in detail in Part VII. In political terminology, the relationship between Popper and the logical positivists can be likened to that of the opposition party and the government, but the shift from the classical tradition to the Weltanschauung views is a revolution involving a total replacement of the nation's constitution. Hence, in this larger picture, Popper and the logical positivists are simply quarrelsome colleagues rather than adversaries.

24.2 HUME'S PROBLEM OF INDUCTION

Popper takes the problem of induction seriously. For him Hume's proof of the irrationality of induction is both valid and sound. Induction cannot be rationally justified. However, in Popper's opinion, Hume's problem does not pose any obstacle or difficulty for the scientist, because induction plays no role in (proper) scientific reasoning (Section 20.5).

Popper states that there is a fundamental logical asymmetry between falsification and verification. Let I be a logical consequence of hypothesis H.

(i) From the truth of I, we cannot infer that H is definitely true. (Since Popper does not believe in induction, nor in inductive logic, we cannot even infer that *H* is true with a certain probability.) But

(ii) From the falsity of *I*, we can infer that *H* is definitely false.[2]

Thus hypotheses can be falsified but cannot be verified or confirmed. This is the asymmetry between falsification and verification that Popper exploits. Whereas the logical positivists build their methodology and analysis of science on verification, Popper builds his on falsification. (Popper repeatedly underscores this difference.)

The nice thing with "falsification tests" is that they employ only deduction in their reasoning: From a given hypothesis *H*, one *deduces* an implication *I*, and from the falsity of *I*, one *deduces* the falsity of *H*. Nowhere is induction employed. Thus, though Hume's argument against the rationality of induction is valid and sound (and according to Popper, final), it poses no obstacle or difficulty for scientific methodology. Scientific reasoning, for Popper, employs deduction through and through. Thus Hume's problem is circumvented and rendered harmless. (The dog has lost its bite.)

Archimedes, the great ancient Greek mathematician who developed the theory of levers (and the theory of flotation), once said that if he were given a fixed point, he could move the earth (using a sufficiently long lever). Popper attempts to develop a full scientific methodology on a single mechanism, that of falsification.

24.3 POPPER'S FALSIFICATIONISM

Popper rejects both rationalism and empiricism, and in general the idea of building science on a foundation of certainty. It is not reasonable to start science from intuitive axioms (classical rationalism) or from observational data (inductive empiricism). There are no a priori axioms about empirical matters that can be known with certainty, and as we have seen from Chapter 22, observational data are not necessarily veridical either. For Popper science should start with **conjectures**, a conjecture being what we call a hypothesis (Chapter 1). Popper often calls these conjectures **theories**. For historical reasons we will adopt this terminology of Popper's in our discussion.[3]

How are theories arrived at? For Popper this is a matter of psychology and does not belong to the field of scientific method. Some discovered significant theories through dreams. For example, it was said that Kekulé (1829–1896) when sitting by the fire dreamed about atoms dancing, and as the atoms danced they gradually turned into snakelike chains, which then joined to form a ring. That was how the idea of the benzene ring[4] came about, thus solving one of the main puzzles of organic chemistry. Others obtained their inspiration from metaphysical beliefs. For example, Aristotle, Ptolemy, and Copernicus presumed that the orbits of the planets must be circular, since the circle is the perfect figure. Grosseteste argued that the coefficient of refraction for all substance is 1:2, because this is the second simplest ratio, the simplest, 1:1, having been given by God to reflection. Popper firmly believes in the separation of the context of discovery and that of justification. For him the former lies outside the logic of science. Discovery is a process for the psychologist to study. Some people are clever and gifted. They are born to discover great hypotheses. The way they achieve such feats, even if known, is not learnable. These "gifts" are not transferable. They are beyond the study of logic.[5]

---

2. This inference is known as modus tollens (Chapter 1).

3. I do not expect any confusion between Popper's usage of 'theory' and our usage, as in Chapters 8, 15, and 23.

4. The molecular formula for benzene was discovered by Faraday in 1825 to be C_6H_6. But it remained a puzzle as to how these 12 atoms are arranged spatially so as to form a unit whole until Kekulé proposed to arrange them in the form of a "ring."

5. Ironically, the English translation of Popper's classic is titled *The Logic of Scientific Discovery*. The original German title is actually *Logik der Forschung*, where 'Forschung' means 'research' or 'investigation.'

So scientific investigations start with theories, whose origins are not the philosopher's concern. However, it is another story once a theory has been proposed. That theory needs to be evaluated (justified). For Popper the method of evaluation is based mainly on the mechanism of falsification. From the theory an observational consequence is deduced. This consequence is then compared with reality (test). If it agrees with reality (success), more tests should be made. If not (failure), the theory is rejected. As pointed out earlier, success in passing a test does not mean that the theory is true. However, failure does mean that the theory is false. You can see that the reasoning tool employed is that of deduction. First, deduction is used to obtain an observational consequence from the theory. Second, deduction is used to refute the theory if the observational consequence is found to be false. This is commonly known as the **hypothetico-deductive method**.

For Popper science is not the product of a cumulative process based on induction. He thinks that Bacon, Mill, and the logical positivists before him made the mistake of taking induction as the main tool in scientific method and that they misconceived scientific method as a matter of accumulation (collection) of knowledge. For him science advances through the elimination of inadequate and incorrect theories by deductive falsification. Thus it is deduction and not induction that should be the main tool of science. In this way, Popper circumvents the problem of induction, for induction is not relevant to the workings of science, so he argues.

Popper's methodology is comparable to Darwin's theory of evolution as opposed to Lamarck's. The latter thinks that species evolve by accumulating *acquired* characteristics through inheritance. On the other hand, Darwin thinks in terms of the eliminative rather than the cumulative. He sees the unfit being eliminated through competition and nonadaptation, leaving behind the superior and the adequate.[6] Popper's methodology is an eliminative methodology.

24.4 DEMARCATION OF SCIENCE

For Popper it is important to demarcate science so as to be clear about what science is and what science is not. In the 1930s, great upheavals occurred in the scientific world. Fantastic theories had been proposed all over the place: the "incomprehensible" theory of relativity, the "illogical" theory of quantum mechanics, and the "fanatical" psychoanalytic theory of Sigmund Freud, to name just the more prominent ones. Are we to trust and believe all these? Some of them may just be "fairy tales." A demarcation criterion was therefore in order. The world of science needed such a criterion to sort out the sheep from the goats, the scientific from the unscientific. Popper thought that he could provide one, according to which Freud's theory of psychoanalysis was a pretender.

According to Popper, a statement is **scientific** if and only if it is (empirically) falsifiable. A statement is (empirically) falsifiable if in principle there are ways to demonstrate that it is false through the use of the senses. Nonscientific theories are said to be **metaphysical**. Thus the hallmark of science is falsifiability. Take for example the statement "Swans have dreams." Scientists need not be concerned about its truth or falsity unless it can be shown that it is falsifiable empirically. This definition of science was proposed out of dissatisfaction with the verification principle of meaning proposed by the logical positivists. Popper pointed out, quite rightly, that no statements in science can be verified empirically (Section 23.6). However, due to the Duhem-Quine thesis, no statements can be empirically falsified either (Section 9.3). Thus a more reasonable definition of science should be that a statement is scientific if and only if it is empirically testable (see Chapters 1, 6, and 7).[7]

6. The analogy has its limitation. Mutation is the mechanism that generates new characteristics. Popper does not have a corresponding mechanism for the generation of new theories. See Section 32.6 for a more detailed presentation of Darwin's theory of evolution, where we discuss creativity.

7. For more on this point, see Section 24.7.

Popper thinks that science enjoys a unique characteristic, that of empirical falsifiability. However, he makes it absolutely clear that his term 'scientific' is not meant to be an appraisal term. There is nothing wrong with nonscientific (metaphysical) statements. They are not meaningless, as the logical positivists would say. Only we should not treat them as if they were scientific. While scientific statements are to be evaluated through empirical tests, nonscientific ones should be evaluated via some other criteria. Philosophers and scientists should benefit from his definition of science. They would save themselves many useless arguments and misunderstandings once they distinguish science from metaphysics. Religious theories, for instance, are typically metaphysical. There may be angels and demons. There may be heaven and hell. However, unless these claims are empirically falsifiable, it is not the concern of science to ascertain or argue about their truth or worth. How they are to be taken is up to the theologians, not the scientists. It can be seen that this campaign for the banishment of metaphysics from science can be traced, via the logical positivists and Comte, right back to Hume. Popper is steeped in the Humean tradition.

Beginners often confuse Popper's criterion of scientificity with the verification principle of meaning. There are two major differences: (i) Popper's criterion is not about meaning or meaningfulness and (ii) his criterion is based on falsification, not on verification. Popper time and again made these differences absolutely clear and exploited them, quite successfully, as critiques of logical positivism.

24.5 FALSIFIABILITY

Having established falsifiability as the hallmark of science, Popper attempts to quantify this notion. Can falsifiability be measured? Can there be degrees of falsifiability? Would some statements be more falsifiable than others? In his view, scientists should aim for highly falsifiable statements. There is no point asserting that

(1) Tomorrow it will rain or it will not rain.

even though this assertion is guaranteed to be true, being analytic (Section 11.3). It is slightly more acceptable to predict that

(2) Tomorrow it is going to rain, or going to be cloudy, or going to snow.

But this sort of assertion is still too cautious for Popper. He thinks that science should take risks. It should make strong and bold statements such as

(3) It is going to rain tomorrow.

(4) It is going to rain for five-and-a-half hours tomorrow.

It can be seen that (1) is unfalsifiable, (2) is slightly falsifiable, and (3) and (4) are progressively more falsifiable. For Popper the **empirical content** of a statement is in proportion to its falsifiability, and science aims at statements with high empirical content.

A corollary of this is that science aims at precision and clarity. It is easy to conclude that

(5) The water is hot.

But science aims for more precise statements such as

(6) The water is 70.5°C.

Scientists, afraid of having their theories refuted, could try to make vague or cautious statements, both being of low content. This however is not the spirit of science according to Popper. It is easy to make true statements, (1) and (2) being good examples. But such true statements would not help in the development of knowledge. Science should take risks and should aim at bold and risky (and precise) theories.

Since statement contents are proportional to their falsifiability, it would be desirable to quantify the notion. Popper introduces the notion of a **potential falsifier** of a given theory (hypothesis). First, a potential falsifier is a singular statement (Section 6.2). Second, it is an observational statement in the sense that it only contains observational terms.[8] Third, it must be such that if it is true, then the given theory is false.

Suppose the given theory is:

(7) All swans are white.

Then here is a potential falsifier:

(8) Johnny is a swan and he is black.

Theory (8) is only *potentially* a falsifier because it need not be true. Should it be true, then (7) has to be false.

The **degree of falsifiability** of a statement can be based on the class (set) of all its potential falsifiers. The larger the class, the more falsifiable the statement is. This seems to be a reasonable notion of falsifiability. Unfortunately all universal statements have an infinite number of potential falsifiers. For example, indefinitely many potential falsifiers of (7) can be generated by replacing 'Johnny' in (8) with other names. Because of this, it is difficult to compare the falsifiability of (7) and (9).

(9) All swans fly.

Having said this, some universal hypotheses (Section 7.1) are actually comparable in falsifiability. For example,

(10) All swans are white or black.

(11) All swans are white.

(12) All swans are snow-white.

Even though they all have an infinite number of potential falsifiers, it is clear that they are in order of increasing falsifiability. The reason is simple: (12) entails (logically implies) (11), which in turn entails (10), so that whatever falsifies (10) also falsifies (11), and whatever falsifies (11) also falsifies (12).[9] Intuitively we can see that the three statements are increasing in content, thus supporting Popper's idea that content is proportional to falsifiability.

Let me summarize.

(13) A theory (that is, a hypothesis) is **falsifiable** if it has at least one potential falsifier.

(14) A **potential falsifier** of a theory is a singular observational statement that contradicts the theory.

(15) A theory T is **more falsifiable than** a theory T' if either

(i) T has more potential falsifiers than T', or

(ii) The set of potential falsifiers of T' is a proper subset of that of T.[10]

We also say that the **degree of falsifiability** of T is greater than that of T'.

(16) The **empirical content** of a theory is directly proportional to its falsifiability.[11]

24.6 PATH OF SCIENCE

According to Popper, scientific investigations start with a problem. It is not clear what he means by 'problem,' even though he usually illustrates with cases that require scientific explanation.[12] For example, "Why do apples fall downward when unsupported?" is a problem for Popper. A posed problem, P, will usually lead to a number of theories for the solution of that problem. One of these

---

8. Popper chose to employ the term 'basic statement' instead of '(singular) observational statement.' It made good sense in the days when logical positivists were in pursuit of phenomenalism. Popper wanted to make it clear that his basic statements are not about sense experience, that they are fallible, and that they are about macroscopic physical objects. However, the distinction between Popper's 'basic statement' and the logical positivists' '(singular) observational statement' vanished once the latter opted for physicalism. See 'basic statement' in Section 24.9.

9. In logic, we say that A entails B if the inference from A to B is logically valid (see Chapter 2).

10. Set A is a proper subset of set B if any member of A is also a member of B, but not vice versa.

11. See Popper (1963, pp. 385–388).

12. The notion of problem also plays a central role in Larry Laudan's philosophy. He, unlike Popper, provides us with a bit of detail (Chapter 29).

theories, T, is chosen and an observational test consequence is derived from it. The consequence is then checked against reality.

(a) If the consequence agrees with reality, we say that T is corroborated.[13] On T''s being corroborated, more tests can be proposed for the theory, or a new theory $T^\star$, with higher content, is proposed to replace T, thus starting another cycle of tests. On the other hand:

(b) If the consequence disagrees with reality, we say that T is falsified. In such a case, T would be rejected, thus posing a new problem P'. A new theory T' with higher content would be proposed to solve this problem, again starting another cycle of tests.

According to Popper this is how science grows, and how it should grow.

Thus it can be seen that for Popper the aim of science is to obtain corroborated theories with ever-increasing contents.[14] This thesis is rather unconventional. Traditionally it is thought that science aims to produce *true* theories—*true* pictures of reality. However, the notion of truth does not come into this thesis. Paradoxically Popper is proclaimed as a staunch realist. He is one of the vanguard of the correspondence theory of truth. In Section 24.8, we will study Popper's view on truthlikeness. Perhaps we will gain a better understanding there.

24.7 AD HOC MODIFICATION AND THE DUHEM-QUINE THESIS

Popper's methodology, as you have just seen, is built solely on the mechanism of falsification. However, properly speaking, no theories are ever falsifiable. The reason is simple. In an indirect test of a theory, we deduce an observational consequence from the theory *with the assistance of some auxiliary hypotheses*. Should that consequence turn out to be false, it could be the auxiliary hypotheses that are at fault. In other words, the theory itself is not falsified by the falsity of the observational consequence. This is the famous Duhem-Quine thesis that we studied in Section 9.3. Popper realizes that to make his falsificationism work, it is essential for him to cope with this difficulty posed by Duhem and Quine.

That's why he suggests the two criteria of ad hocness, one for the modification of the main hypothesis (the theory to be tested) and one for the modification of auxiliary hypotheses (Sections 7.5–7.7). He claims that no ad hoc modifications are admissible. With this move he hopes to salvage his falsification thesis from Duhem-Quine's skepticism. He argues that, since science aims for statements of ever-increasing content, and since ad hoc modifications decrease the content of the original theory, it is reasonable to ban such modifications from science.

Let's illustrate with an example.

Suppose the original theory is T.

T: Water anywhere boils at 100°C.

However, it is found that water does not boil at that temperature on the top of Mt. Cook. Scientists might modify T into one of the following theories:

T_1: Water anywhere, except perhaps on the top of Mt. Cook, boils at 100°C.

T_2: Water anywhere, except on the top of Mt. Cook, boils at 100°C.

T_3: Water boils at 100°C at and only at sea level.

T_4: The boiling point of water varies proportionally with the atmospheric pressure.

For Popper, both T_1 and T_2 are ad hoc modifications of T, whereas T_3 and T_4 are both acceptable as replacements of T.

---

13. More will be said on this important notion later.

14. See Popper (1959, pp. 276–281) for details.

Unfortunately the general opinion is that this ingenious move by Popper has not been able to block the nullifying effect of the Duhem-Quine thesis on falsification (Section 7.7).

24.8 CORROBORATION, VERISIMILITUDE, AND HUME

The Duhem-Quine thesis is not the only blemish on Popper's otherwise beautiful philosophy of falsificationism. The requirement of positive appraisal of hypotheses is another. Falsification is a criterion of negative appraisal. It advises us when to drop a theory. But surely we require some kind of criterion of positive appraisal. If there were, say, only five possible hypotheses to explain a phenomenon, the elimination of one of these five by falsification would certainly increase the likelihood of the other four. However, as a matter of fact, for any phenomenon there are an infinite number of possible hypotheses to explain it. The elimination of a finite number of these by falsification will not provide us with any information about the remaining hypotheses as to their truth or likelihood. Positive criteria of appraisal are therefore required. We have to be able to say: "Of these unfalsified hypotheses, this one or that one has a higher score of likelihood than others, and that's why we recommend it for action."

Popper is well aware of the requirement for positive appraisal. However, being in agreement with Hume's argument against the rationality of induction, he cannot employ the notion of confirmation (Chapter 21), nor can he employ inductive logic (Chapter 3). That's why he had to invent an altogether new concept for positive appraisal: the notion of corroboration. A theory is said to be **corroborated** if it passes an empirical test—that is, if an observational consequence of the theory agrees with reality.[15] This does not sound excitingly

new. However, in the able hands of Popper it can be quite a different story.

For Popper, corroboration can be measured in degrees.

(17) The **degree of corroboration** is proportional to (i) the number of tests the theory has passed and (ii) the severity of these tests.

What does he mean by the **severity of a test**? If, according to the background knowledge at the time of the test, the predicted outcome of the test is considered to be very unlikely then the test is considered to be severe. In general, the severity of a test is proportional to the *improbability* of the predicted outcome (that is, inversely proportional to the *probability* of the test statement). For instance, according to Young and Fresnel's wave theory of light there should be a bright spot at the center of the shadow cast by a small circular disk (Section 0.13). During the 19th century, this phenomenon of a bright spot in the middle of a dark circular shadow was considered to be most unlikely. So for Popper, employing this phenomenon to test the wave theory of light in the 19th century amounts to a very severe test. Historically, Fresnel did successfully demonstrate the existence of the bright spot and, as a consequence, French resistance to the wave theory softened.

The wave theory also predicts that light will be reflected by mirrors. However, nobody in the 19th century performed any experiment to check this. Indeed even though probably thousands of scientists noticed that light was reflected by their mirrors daily, they did not bother to record their findings and certainly did not take these findings as supporting the wave theory. Here is Popper's explanation. Scientists of the 19th century expected mirror reflection, with or without the wave theory. Since the degree of corroboration is inversely proportional to the *increase* in probability as predicted by a theory, the observation of reflections by mirrors yields only a tiny amount of corroboration, so tiny that it is quite insignificant.

---

15. As we saw earlier, this observational consequence is usually deduced from the theory with the help of auxiliary hypotheses. Popper is well aware of this.

Why should mirror reflection have enjoyed high probability in the 19th century? Popper thinks that there are two reasons. According to the prevailing theory of the time, which is Newton's corpuscular theory, mirrors should reflect. In other words, Newton's theory lent credibility to the phenomenon of mirror reflection.

The second reason is that mirror reflections had occurred millions of times before. In psychological terms, we say that people had gotten used to the phenomenon and hence expected the phenomenon anyway, irrespective of the truth or falsity of the wave theory. More observed reflections do not add anything to the significance of the phenomenon. In other words, mirror reflection was very much expected in the 19th century. Its degree of probability was not increased significantly by predictions based on wave theory.

We have explained how the severity of a test depends on the background expectation of the scientific community. Popper suggests an additional factor: the severity of a test is proportional to the empirical content of the theory, all other things being equal. Let me illustrate.

Let's consider the following hypotheses:

(18) All swans are white.

(19) All swans are either white or black.

Suppose in testing these hypotheses, a swan is caught in New Zealand and is found to be white. This finding would corroborate both (18) and (19). However, since (18) has a higher content than (19), the degree of corroboration for (18) is higher, even though it is the very same test result that contributes to the corroboration in both cases. In other words, the study of the color of a swan in New Zealand can be considered two tests, Test A for (18) and Test B for (19). Test A is more severe than Test B, because (18) is more improbable than (19). In Popperian terminology, we say that (18) is more risky. It is a bolder hypothesis. It is less probable than (19). That makes the testing result more significant.[16]

In sum, Popper has provided two criteria for assessment of hypotheses. Falsification is a criterion of negative appraisal whereas corroboration is a criterion of positive appraisal. A proposed theory is tested. If it should fail the test, we consider it as falsified, and the theory is to be rejected. On the other hand, if it should pass the test, it earns a credit, and that credit is added to all the credits already earned from previous tests, culminating in the total degree of corroboration of the theory up to that time. With these two criteria, Popper hopes that any theory can be assessed. It is either rejected through falsification or graded through corroboration.

But what does corroboration mean in terms of acceptance? Are corroborated theories better than uncorroborated ones? Are the more corroborated theories more trustworthy, and hence more acceptable? It is all very well to bestow a grade on a theory, but what does the grade signify? Is the grade informative with respect to the acceptability of the theory? Does the grade tell us how trustworthy the theory is? If the more corroborated theories are no more trustworthy or acceptable than the less corroborated ones, what is the point of grading theories according to their degrees of corroboration?

This is a difficulty for Popper. Since he thinks Hume has conclusively demonstrated that knowledge of past instances has no bearing on the probability of occurrence of future instances, past successes in tests should add no weight to the expectation of future successes either. Degree of corroboration is a term descriptive of *past* performances, to the effect that a certain theory has passed a certain number of severe tests. But this information about the past can tell us nothing, absolutely nothing, about the probability of success of the theory in future tests. What Popper needs is a measure of trustworthiness of a theory. To this end, the logical positivists developed inductive logic together with notions of confirmation for hypotheses. For them, the more confirmed a theory the more trustworthy it is. But Popper, taking Hume seriously,

---

16. For details of Popper's position see Popper (1959, pp. 267–268). See also Popper (1963, pp. 390–391) for a quantitative definition of severity of tests.

can have none of this. That's why he ridiculed the logical positivists for their efforts in inductive logic and their theory of confirmation. That's why he proposed to replace 'confirmation' with his 'corroboration.'

'Confirmation' is mainly based on the *quantity* of past successes.[17] Popper, agreeing with Hume, drops 'quantity' and replaces it with 'quality,' resulting in the notion of corroboration. Corroboration is mainly based on the severity of tests, and 'severity' is a qualitative term. Unfortunately the switch from quantity to quality does not enable Popper to escape from Hume's "curse." The degree of corroboration is still a measure of *past* successes even though it is now based on the quality rather than the quantity of past successes. But according to Hume knowledge of the past lends absolutely no weight to expectation of the future. To take corroboration as a measure of trustworthiness is to assume the trustworthiness of induction surreptitiously.

Thus Hilary Putnam writes:

If 'this law is highly corroborated,' 'this law is scientifically accepted,' and like locutions merely meant 'this law has withstood severe tests'—and there were no suggestions at all that a law which has withstood severe tests is likely to withstand further tests, such as the tests involved in an application or attempted application, then Popper would be right; but then science would be a wholly unimportant activity. It would be practically unimportant, because scientists would never tell us that any law or theory is safe to rely upon for practical purposes; and it would be unimportant for

the purpose of understanding, since on Popper's view, scientists never tell us that any law or theory is true or even probable. Knowing that certain 'conjectures' (according to Popper all scientific laws are 'provisional conjectures') have not yet been refuted is *not understanding anything.* (1974, p. 122)[18]

Related to the notion of corroboration is Popper's notion of **verisimilitude**, which means truthlikeness. After defining a theory's truth-content as the set of all its true consequences, and a theory's falsity content as the set of all its false consequences, Popper proposes:

Assuming that the truth-content and the falsity-content of two theories t_1 and t_2 are comparable, we can say that t_2 is more closely similar to the truth, or corresponds better to the facts, than t_1, if and only if, either (a) the truth-content but not the falsity-content of t_2 exceeds that of t_1, (b) the falsity-content of t_1, but not its truth-content, exceeds that of t_2. (Popper, 1963, p. 233)

Popper hopes that this will give him a measure of how close to truth a theory is even though the theory may be false. This measure, however, does not work, as has been demonstrated by Miller (1974, pp. 170–172) and Tichy (1974, pp. 156–157).[19] Even if this measure of verisimilitude did work, however, we would still have to possess some methods to ascertain truth or falsity for at least *some* statements before we could apply the criterion to measure the verisimilitude of a given theory. But it is these very methods of truth-falsity

---

17. See, for example, the law of large numbers in Section 20.3. See also Chapter 21 for more information on confirmation theory.

18. Actually the very notion of severity of a test is based on induction. According to Popper, repeating a well-worn test confers little further corroboration on the theory (for example, observing yet another white swan after having observed one million white swans does not yield much further corroboration of "All swans are white"). Surely what Popper is assuming here is that past successes raise the probability of future successes, and hence that repeated tests are governed by the principle of diminishing returns.

19. They have shown that, for *any* two false theories A and B, A does not have less verisimilitude than B, and B does not have less verisimilitude than A. But this is absurd.

ascertainment that we lack. It would have been all right if, alternatively, verisimilitude were correlated with degree of corroboration. But this is not the case either. Corroboration cannot tell us whether a theory is true or not; it cannot tell us how close to truth the theory is either.

This is rather sad for Popper's falsificationism, for it is both innovative and insightful. In fact, Popper's notion of corroboration agrees well with the famous theorem in statistics known as **Bayes's theorem**, which states that:

(18) $\Pr(h \text{ given } e.k) =$

$$\frac{\Pr(e \text{ given } h.k) \times \Pr(h \text{ given } k)}{\Pr(e \text{ given } k)}$$

(where, for example, '$\Pr(h \text{ given } e.k)$' reads 'the probability of the hypothesis h on the strength of the evidence e and the background knowledge k').

You can see that $\Pr(h \text{ given } e.k)$ is inversely proportional to the probability of e given the background knowledge k—that is, $\Pr(e \text{ given } k)$. In other words, the more probable e is in view of k, the less weight it lends to the credibility of h. The degree of corroboration that h gains from e is inversely proportional to the probability of e in view of k.

24.9 EMPIRICAL BASIS AND THE PROBLEM OF THE OT-LINK

Difficulties with Popper's philosophy do not stop with the Duhem-Quine Thesis and Hume's problem. It faces further difficulty with the problem of the OT-link and the problem of what I will call the SS-link.

If statements in science are empirical, they must somehow be linked to our sense experience. To put it differently, if our sense experience plays a role in assessing the veracity of statements in science, these statements must be related to sense experience in one way or other. This is the **problem of the empirical basis**. The early logical positivists were phenomenalists. They believed that (i) our sense experiences can be described—infallibly, some believed—in terms of a sense-datum language and (ii) ordinary commonsense language as well as theoretical languages can be reduced to this sense-datum language. This was how the phenomenalists attempted to solve the problem of the empirical basis: the set of all (singular) statements that describe the occurrence of sense experience (sense-data) forms the empirical basis.

Popper rejected phenomenalism from the very beginning. As early as 1934, he had already pointed out that all terms are theoretical. He gave the example of a simple everyday statement such as "Here is a glass of water." He explained how both 'water' and 'glass' are theoretical in nature, and this simple statement cannot be verified by direct observation. Terms in a sense-datum language presumably would be theoretical as well, if there was one. "For we can utter no scientific statement that does not go far beyond what can be known with certainty 'on the basis of immediate experience.' ... Every description uses *universal* names (or symbols, or ideas); every statement has the character of a theory, of a hypothesis" (Popper, 1959, pp. 94–95).[20] So for Popper there are no infallible statements describing sense experience, and he certainly does not believe that statements in science can be reduced to the sense-datum language. Phenomenalism was thus rejected from the very start. But then how is he going to solve the problem of the empirical basis? How are statements in science linked to experience?

To this end, Popper introduces the notion of a basic statement. **Basic statements** are what have been called **potential falsifiers** (Section 24.5), and in practice they are simply what the physicalists (latter-day logical positivists) took as (singular)

---

20. By 'universal name' Popper means terms such as 'table,' 'atom,' and 'horse.' 'Universal name' contrasts with 'proper name.' In fact, 'universal name' covers adjectives, adverbs, and so on as well.

observational statements: commonsense statements about (observable) macroscopic physical objects.[21]

Popper makes it clear that his basic statements are not about sense experience, but are theoretical and fallible. But then how can they constitute the empirical basis? To allay misunderstanding, he states explicitly that he does not intend the basis to be a firm basis: "In introducing the term 'empirical basis' my intention was, partly, to give an ironical emphasis to my thesis that the empirical basis of our theories is far from firm; that it should be compared to a swamp rather than to solid ground" (Popper, 1963, p. 387).

You may recall that Popper's methodology consists in the testing of theories. To test a theory, a basic statement (potential falsifier) is deduced from the theory with the help of background knowledge (auxiliary hypotheses). Should the basic statement turn out to be false, we generally either reject the theory or attempt to find fault with part of the background knowledge. If the basic statement turns out to be true, we can say that the theory has been corroborated. However, according to Popper, basic statements themselves are not sacrosanct. They are theories themselves, albeit rather low-level theories. They themselves can be subjected to tests against other basic statements. But then, where and when should the testing stop? Here is Popper's reply:

> Thus every statement (or 'basic statement') remains essentially conjectural; but it is a conjecture which can be easily tested. These tests, in their turn, involve new conjectural and testable statements, and so on, *ad infinitum*; and should we try to *establish* anything with our tests, we should be involved in an infinite regress…. Thus our 'basic statements' are anything but 'basic' in the sense of 'final'; they are 'basic'

only in the sense that they belong to the class of statements which are used in testing our theories. (1963, p. 388)

Popper does not think that the infinite regress is in any way vicious. In such a case, you might ask, when should one stop testing?

> This procedure has no natural end. Thus if the test is to lead us anywhere, nothing remains but to stop at some point or other and *say we are satisfied, for the time being*. It is fairly easy to see that we arrive in this way at a procedure according to which we stop only at a kind of statement that is especially easy to test. For it means that we are stopping at statements about whose acceptance or rejection the various investigators are likely to *reach agreement*. And if they do not agree, they will simply continue with the tests, or else start them all over again. (Popper, 1959, p. 104, my italics)[22]

Both the classical rationalists and the traditional empiricists (including the phenomenalists) think that there is and should be an objective basis to building knowledge. The rationalists take the basis as consisting of axioms, whose truth is obvious to the mind. The empiricists opt for observational statements, whose truth is ascertainable by the senses. Thus both kinds of basis are supposed to be objective in that the constituents of the basis are true statements that are known to be true. Popper's 'empirical basis' differs from them both. He makes no secret that his empirical basis is in fact no basis in the usual sense of the word. Whereas the bases the rationalists and the empiricists hope to provide are likened to solid ground, his is likened to a swamp. This analogy is apt.

It can be seen that Popper's empirical basis is a swamp in two senses: (i) It is not solid. Popper does

---

21. Popper (1963) presents the concept of basic statement as follows: "(i) Basic statements state (truly or falsely) the existence of observable facts (occurrences) within some sufficiently narrow spatio-temporal region. (ii) The negation of a basic statement will not be in general basic…. (iii) The conjunction of two basic statements is always basic if (and only if) it is logically consistent" (1963, p. 386).

22. I think Popper is advocating a type of coherence theory of truth even though explicitly he always declares himself to be a realist working from the correspondence theory of truth.

not believe any statements in the basis can be knowable as true with certainty. (ii) It is not a fixed "mass of matter." The scientific community can change its consensus on the constituents of the basis.

Popper thinks that his "swamp" theory has solved the problem of the empirical basis. However, I think not.

First, he has not provided us the *link* between members of the empirical basis and sense experience. Let's call the problem of the relationship between statements (in general) and sense experience the **problem of the SS-link**. Popper quietly swept this problem under the carpet (i) by "allowing" the scientist to keep on testing his basic statements with further basic statements, thus forever postponing the requirement of contact between statements and sense experience and (ii) by asserting that "statements can be logically justified only by statements [and not by sense experience]" (1959, p. 43).[23]

Second, the logical positivists were at pains to discover the logical link between observational statements and theoretical statements: the **problem of the OT-link**. It seems that Popper is unaware of this problem. For him, the link between what we normally call theoretical statements and what we normally call observational statements is a mere matter of straightforward deduction: for testing, observational statements are deduced from theoretical statements (with the help of background knowledge). You will find, however, that the true story is not so simple. Apart from the lessons we have learned from the logical positivists in their search of adequate forms for their correspondence rules, Kuhn and Feyerabend, for example, point out that theoretical statements (of science) and (commonsense) observational statements are incommensurable and there is no deductive relationship between them (Part VII).

Third, Popper has not been able to solve the problem of observation (Chapter 22). The inductivist thinks that science starts with observational data. In contrast, Popper insists that science starts

with conjectures (which he calls theories). Observation enters into science only in the "last" step, for checking against test consequences drawn from theories. In spite of this move, the problem of observation remains. If observation is "contaminated" by theories, the observation employed to check a theory would naturally be prejudiced in favor of that theory.

24.10 THE JUDGMENT OF HISTORY AND ARTIFICIAL INTELLIGENCE

Let's see what the judgment of history has been on Popper's work and how it has fared in light of advances in artificial intelligence.

A. Popper's philosophy was very popular and influential up to the 1960s. Its decline can be attributed mainly to the critiques of Kuhn. Instead of approaching the subject from a logical point of view as Popper and the logical positivists did, Kuhn took a historical turn. Having amassed an amazingly large amount of historical evidence he was able to show that the historical scientist, at least in most cases, did not follow the Popperian methodology. In a sense, these *historical* records are irrelevant to the *logical* study of methodology. What Popper claims to have done is to provide us with a set of rational rules by which to do science. His contribution is, therefore, *prescriptive* as to what a good scientist *should* do. On the other hand, history is *descriptive*. That the historical scientist has not followed his set of prescriptions does not show that Popper is necessarily wrong. The historical scientist could be a poor scientist. It is generally recognized that one cannot argue from 'is' to 'ought.'

But can most, if not all, of the great scientists in the long history of science be bad scientists most of the time? Can these great scientists be irrational and

---

23. Popper, of course, is right in asserting that statements can be *logically* justified only by statements. But other than being *logically* justified, they have to be justified by something else in order to get out of the circle of statements. That something else, for empiricism, is sense experience.

yet have succeeded in bringing about such impressive results? Isn't it simpler and more reasonable to conclude that it is the philosopher who is wrong? We will study the relationship between the history of science and the logic of science in detail in Parts VII and VIII. For now, we can say that *prima facie* history is not on the side of Popper. From the Stone Age to the current century, humans seem to have been making inductions all the time: from predicting that the sun will rise tomorrow in the east to avoiding the flames of fire. Great scientists like Copernicus and Priestley were interested only in protecting their pet theories (to the extent of performing ad hoc revisions) rather than attempting to falsify them. And we should add that the widespread use of statistics in the applied sciences and the social sciences in the present century has added further weight to the important role played by induction in scientific reasoning. On the other hand, falsificationism seems to be seldom practiced.

B. Recently a lot of research has been done on the study of creativity and the logic of scientific discovery in artificial intelligence. We can take these researches as attempts to show that Popper is wrong, that the phenomenon of scientific discovery can be studied outside psychology, namely, in the field of methodology and logic. We are still talking about the early days. Yet even in "these early days," results seem to indicate that there are learnable methods of discovery, and that creativity is not necessarily a "nonrational" intuitive process reserved for the gifted. Indeed you, I, and machines can all be creative. We will go into this topic in detail in Chapter 32.

C. Popper stresses again and again that one cannot make observations without the guidance of a theory. He derides the suggestions of Baconians that unprejudiced observation should be the first step of science. That's why for Popper the scientist should always start with a hypothesis (theory). From the hypothesis, one can deduce what to expect. That expectation, in turn, will guide the scientist to selective observations. The hypothesis is like a searchlight that directs the observer to where things are expected to happen. This point by Popper has, in general, been well taken. Science should not and cannot start with random observation. There are simply too many directions to direct one's "gaze." There has to be a decision on where to look!

But then a similar argument applies to Popper's first step in science: the proposal of a hypothesis. There are an infinite number of possible hypotheses. One cannot simply test them at random. Some hypotheses are more plausible than others. Some are more manageable. Some are simpler, and so on. To test hypotheses without preselection is silly and in fact just as impractical as to observe without the guidance of a theory.

Anyway hypotheses are not simply lying around for us to pick up and test. One of the major challenges to the practicing scientist is the creation or discovery of powerful hypotheses that are at the same time plausible. Maybe such hypotheses simply *occur* to the (genius) scientist out of the blue. Maybe these occurrences are totally nonrational. However, no methodology can be considered complete if the very first step in the enterprise is left to chance. It is here, I think, that artificial intelligence is relevant. The problem of constructing creative machines will provoke research that will throw light both on the psychology as well as on the methodology of creativity.

Having said all this, Popperism is by no means dead and buried. Later, in Chapter 28, you will find how Lakatos, a disciple of Popper, presents an interesting revised version of Popper's deductive empiricism that has proved to be very influential, to say the least.[24]

---

24. Popper was a very resourceful philosopher. Regrettably we cannot cover many areas where he has contributed significantly—for example, the interpretation of quantum physics, the ontological theory of the three worlds, the body–mind problem, and problems concerning the social sciences.

KEY TERMS INTRODUCED IN THIS CHAPTER

(Popperian) conjectures

(Popperian) theory

hypothetico-deductive method

scientific

metaphysical

falsifiability

empirical content

potential falsifier

degree of falsifiability

falsifiable

corroboration

degree of corroboration

severity of a test

verisimilitude

Bayes's theorem

problem of the empirical basis

basic statement

problem of the SS-link

problem of the OT-link

REFERENCES

For general references, see Oldroyd (1986, chap. 8), Chalmers (1976, chaps. 4–6), O'Hear (1989, chap. 3), Newton-Smith (1981, chap. III), Gillies (1993, chaps. 2 and 9), and Ackermann (1976).

Popper's own works: (1959), (1963), (1972), and (1983).

Anthologies: Boyd (1991, chaps. 5 and 6), Kourany (1987, pp. 139–158, 235–252).

On falsifiability: Popper (1959, chap. VI).

On corroboration and verisimilitude: Newton-Smith (1981, pp. 52–65), Popper (1959, chap. X), and Putnam (1974).

On empirical basis: Popper (1959, chap. V).

On the judgment of history: Chalmers (1976, pp. 63–72).

PART VII

The Weltanschauung Revolution

INTRODUCTION

We saw in Part V how empiricism replaced rationalism in the 17th century mainly due to the works of Galileo and Bacon. In Part VI, we detailed the classical tradition of the 20th century, which represents the best of empirical philosophy of science.

The classical tradition, indeed empiricism in general, is based on the following:

(a) There is an objective reality, independent of thinking and thought. The highest aim of science is to capture that mind-independent reality, to give it as accurate a description as possible.

(b) Contact with that objective reality is through the senses, which can be employed to collect data about that reality. The observer is a passive receiver of information.

(c) These data, known as empirical data, form the basis of acquisition of truth about that objective reality. The inductive empiricists (logical positivists) see these data as the basis for inductive inferences, through which further truths about reality can be obtained. Thus science starts with the collection of empirical data. On the other hand, deductive empiricism (Popperism) favors the use of the hypothetico-deductive method.

(d) Empirical data may not be veridical. Nevertheless they are objective in the sense that trained scientists in similar situations should largely perceive the same "thing," and hence would arrive at the same empirical data when performing the same experiments.

347

In Chapter 22, we saw how observational contents are theory-laden, and that the observer is not a passive receiver of information. Thomas Kuhn (1922–1996) develops this theme further. Based on his findings in the history of science, he introduces the notion of a paradigm, a sort of *Weltanschauung*.[1] He argues that scientists can work only within paradigms, in observation and in reasoning, in problem formulation and in problem solving. Moreover, people operating in different paradigms do not share the same empirical data or the same empirical problems. They do not share the same standards or the same rules. Kuhn thus denies all the four tenets of empiricism.

Kuhn's paradigm view and its variants are a type of Neo-Kantianism or constructivism. Knowledge is not something that can be obtained through the mind alone. Nor is it something that belongs to the preserves of the senses. It is not even something that can be arrived at through the cooperation of the mind and the senses, each faculty doing part of the task, as factory workers would at a conveyer belt. Rather, according to Kuhn—and Kant before him—the mind and the senses are not two distinct faculties working in cooperation. They are so inextricably entwined in their operations that it would be wrong to describe them as separate parts. The correct picture is that knowledge is the end product of a constructive-cum-collecting process by a unified cognitive faculty composed of the mind and the senses.

Constructivism has brought about a revolution in the philosophy of science. It has spread into general philosophy, psychology, sociology, and education. This part of the book is devoted to this innovative philosophy of Kuhn's.

---

1. 'Weltanschauung' is a German word meaning 'worldview.'

Chapter 25

Introduction: Two Paradigm Theories

25.1 INTRODUCTION

According to Thomas S. Kuhn (1922–1996), both logical positivism and Popper's falsificationism have missed an essential component in their analyses of the structure and workings of science. This component was named 'paradigm' by Kuhn in his celebrated *The Structure of Scientific Revolutions* (1962), now a classic. The notion of paradigm has revolutionized the philosophy of science. We may find the notion vague and, at times, confusing. We may not be able to stomach the implications that that notion brings with it. We may dispute many of the "proofs" brought by Kuhn. Nevertheless, as philosophers of science, we cannot afford to ignore Kuhn's paradigm view or its reverberations, not only in the philosophy of science, but also in fields as disparate as education, sociology, psychology, and general philosophy.

For Kuhn, paradigms play a definitive role in the practice of science. Science must operate in some conceptual or theoretical framework.[1] Kuhn calls these

---

1. The terms 'conceptual framework' and 'theoretical framework' are not Kuhn's own terms.

frameworks **paradigms**. A conceptual framework, loosely speaking, consists of a set of concepts and hypotheses.[2] Once a scientist adopts such a framework these concepts and hypotheses will form a mental set in her mind so that she can only perceive and understand in terms of these concepts and hypotheses. She lives within her framework rather like a person wearing glasses. If the glasses happen to be red in color, then to the wearer everything is red and she behaves accordingly. In this sense, the framework shapes the world for the scientist and dictates her practices. Even theory formation (Popper's first step in scientific investigations) is 'colored,' 'prejudiced,' and guided by a paradigm. The scientist is as free as a goldfish in a fishbowl and yet, paradoxically, it is this lack of freedom, this situation of being under constraint, that enables the scientist to make progress. Perhaps taking paradigms as railway tracks would be a better analogy. The rails in one sense constrain the movements of the train, but in doing so guide it smoothly in a definite direction.

The notion of a paradigm is a difficult and complicated one, not to speak of its vagueness and its controversial nature. It will take a bit of explanation to put you in the picture. That's why I will start with the historical case of the replacement of the phlogiston theory with the oxygen theory. These two theories can roughly be taken as two paradigms. From these two cases, we will proceed to a more rigorous and detailed presentation of the notion of a paradigm. Usually attached to a high-power telescope is a low-power telescope known as a guidoscope. The astronomer looks through the guidoscope first to locate the star she wants to examine. Only then does she study the star in detail through the high-power telescope. In the rest of this chapter, I will introduce you to the quasi-historical story of the phlogiston theory and its replacement by the oxygen theory. These two theories will guide us, much as guidoscopes would, to

a proper understanding of Kuhn's revolutionary idea of a paradigm.

25.2 SCIENCE IN THE 18TH CENTURY

In the 18th century, scientists were interested in two areas of study: kinematic changes and qualitative changes.

In the field of kinematic changes, they studied motion: how motions occur, what sort of trajectories things take when they move, and why they move in such ways. This is the field of mechanics, forming the major part of physics at the time.

In the field of qualitative changes, the scientists studied transformations of things in their sensual qualities. For example, wood, when burned, turns into ashes. In doing so it changes in smell, in taste, in color, in texture, in hardness, and so on. Sugar dissolves into water forming a solution. In doing so, it changes from a solid state into a liquid state. Other examples of qualitative changes are: ice changing into water and then into steam, chameleons changing colors when moving from one part of a tree to another, and caterpillars turning into butterflies.

In the 18th century, qualitative transformations were understood and explained in terms of the phlogiston theory.

25.3 THE ALCHEMO-PHLOGISTON THEORY[3]

The phlogiston theory of the 18th century was based on alchemy, a collection of vague beliefs and crude sciences built on Aristotle's metaphysics of the 4th century B.C. Primitive as it was, alchemy

---

2. For 'set of concepts' and 'set of hypotheses' in this context, refer to Sections 22.6 and 22.5 respectively.

3. The presentation of the alchemo-phlogiston theory is an oversimplified "clean" version of the actual theory. The presentation is meant for the illustration of Kuhn's notion of a paradigm in later chapters and is certainly not meant for historical accuracy.

fulfilled its function as the precursor of modern-day chemistry. Since the phlogiston theory was based on it, I think the title "alchemo-phlogiston theory" is accurate.

According to the alchemo-phlogiston theory substances are made up of four elements: water, air, fire, and earth. Phlogiston is the "essence" of fire. By 'essence of fire,' I think the phlogistonists meant fire in its purest form, without those contingent properties like color or smell, which differ from particular fire to particular fire. Phlogiston is fire per se.[4] These are called elements because they are the fundamental building blocks of nature in that they cannot be further broken down and they are immutable.[5] A quantity of water, for example, will always remain as water and can never change into fire or air, earth, or anything else. There are four and only four such fundamental building blocks, out of which all substances are said to be formed.[6] This idea of the four elements originated from Empedocles of ancient Greece over 2,400 years ago.[7]

Each element is said to have its own specific (sensual) qualities. Fire is supposed to be hot, dry, yellow, bright, and it tends to ascend. Earth is dry and cold. Water is cold and wet whereas air is wet and hot. Figure 25.1 shows how the elements share the sensual qualities. Out of these four elements, substances of all sorts with all kinds of (sensual) qualities can be built, simply by mixing these elements in the correct proportion. Qualitative changes can be seen as simply a remixing of the four elements in the changing object with other objects. If things should get hotter and wetter, for example, a portion of air must have been added to them (for air is wet and hot), or perhaps some of the

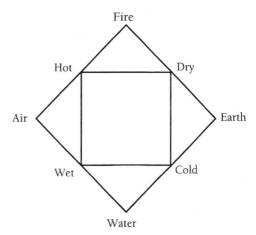

FIGURE 25.1

earth has been taken out (for earth is dry and cold). The change of water into steam can be explained as the addition of fire to water as steam is hotter and drier than water. This explanation can be seen to be reasonable.

The idea that all substances come from the combination of the four elements brought about the idea of artificial transmutation. This promised to be a useful technology. For example, since lead resembles gold in many respects, gold should be able to be derived from lead by adding or subtracting the right kinds of elements. Let's compare lead and gold. They are both heavy, malleable, and stable, and both have a low melting point. The major difference between them is that gold is yellow and bright while lead is gray and dull. Since fire is yellow and bright, it was conjectured that gold can be obtained from lead through heating (and perhaps with the addition of yellow and bright substances

---

4. Terms in alchemo-phlogiston theory are usually vague and ill-defined. Often commentators differ in their understanding of them.

5. I have simplified the notion of an element here. Opinions on whether the alchemist's elements are immutable or not differ. Certainly they are not immutable for Aristotle, who thinks that the elements can pass into one another through the medium of the quality that they possess in common.

6. There is supposedly a fifth element, celestial matter, of which the heavenly bodies are made. We can however ignore it here, since we are only interested in terrestrial qualitative changes.

7. It can be seen that 'earth,' 'water,' and 'air' correspond to our notions of solid, liquid, and gas.

such as sulfur and mercury). (If ruby were to be manufactured, the phlogistonists would probably suggest the mixing of glass and blood!)[8]

Such ideas seem strange to those of us who have been brought up in the atomic tradition. This is exactly Kuhn's point. Different scientific communities are "ruled" by different paradigms. Practices within one's own paradigm are always taken as normal and standard. Actually the phlogistonist's idea of transforming substances by mixing them with others that have the desirable qualities should not be too strange to us. Isn't it the case that when we want our coffee to be sweet, we add something sweet to it and then stir? Isn't it true that the way to produce shades of colors is by mixing colors that have those particular color qualities? For the phlogistonists, substances are mere bearers of sensual qualities. The primary bearers are the four elements. To obtain new substances, therefore, it is a matter of obtaining the right proportion of qualities by mixing up the right amount of elements. In other words, they look at substances as physical mixtures and not as what the chemists would call chemical compounds. The whole should be equal to the sum of the parts. The phlogistonists were yet to acquire the notion of emergent property.[9]

25.4 SUCCESSES OF THE PHLOGISTON THEORY

The phlogiston theory was proposed by Becher (1635–1682) and developed by Stahl (1660–1734). It was essentially a theory of combustion. Phlogiston is the "combustible principle." It is present in all combustible objects and is given up by them on combustion. By itself, phlogiston is unobservable, having no color, no smell, and no taste. However, when it resides in material bodies, it may give those bodies observable properties. For example, the sheen of metals is said to be due to their possession of large amounts of phlogiston. The brightness of fire is also said to be due to phlogiston leaving the burning objects. The phlogiston theory was rather successful in the 18th century in explaining many phenomena. Here are a few examples:

(a) Combustion:
   (i) Phenomenon: Charcoal when burnt turns into ashes, water vapor, and fire.
   (ii) Explanation: Charcoal is made up of earth, water, and lots of phlogiston. In burning, while the phlogiston escapes as fire, the water comes out as water vapor, leaving the ashes behind, which is earth. In symbols:

$$EWPPP \longrightarrow E + W + PPP$$

(Charcoal $\longrightarrow$ ashes + water vapor + fire)[10]

It is obvious that this explanation of charcoal burning can be extended to other kinds of burning—for example, candle burning, wood burning, and so on. In general, burning is the phenomenon of phlogiston escaping "with rigor" from the burning object.

This phlogiston theory of burning also explains why, in a confined space, fire will not sustain burning for long. The reason is that the space will soon be saturated with phlogiston so that no more phlogiston can escape from the burning object. In those days, it was said that the air has thus become fixed.[11]

Assuming that respiration is a kind of burning, the theory also explains why lime water turns milky when one blows into it through a straw. The air

---

8. The presentation here is for pedagogical purposes rather than for historic accuracy.

9. Carbon monoxide—that is, CO—is poisonous, yet neither C (carbon) nor O (oxygen) is poisonous. We therefore say that being poisonous is an *emergent property*, which is not obtainable by "summing" the qualities of the parts. See Section 13.6.

10. Modern chemistry explains charcoal burning as the combination of the carbon in the charcoal with oxygen, yielding carbon dioxide (CO_2).

11. Modern chemistry explains this as being due to the exhaustion of available oxygen in the confined space by the burning. The oxygen has been turned into carbon dioxide.

expelled from one's lungs is supposedly full of phlogiston, which turns the clear lime water white.[12]

(b) Smelting (the turning of metallic ore into metals by heating):
   (i) Phenomenon: When metallic ore is mixed with charcoal and heated, it starts to burn, resulting in various metals.
   (ii) Explanation: Metallic ore is a kind of earth, whereas charcoal, as has been pointed out previously, is a mixture of earth, water, and phlogiston. When metallic ore is mixed with charcoal, the phlogiston from the charcoal attaches itself to the ore, yielding metal. The idea that metal is earth plus phlogiston is supported by the fact that metal is usually shiny, an indication that it contains phlogiston (fire), which possesses the quality of brightness. It is further confirmed by the phenomenon that when sulfuric acid is poured onto zinc, a flammable gas (phlogiston) is emitted with great rigor.[13] Briefly, the explanation of the phenomenon of smelting given by the phlogistonists can be symbolized as:

$$EE + EWPPP \longrightarrow EEPP + E + W + P$$

(Metallic ore + charcoal $\longrightarrow$
      metal + ash + water vapor + fire)[14]

(c) Calcination (rusting):
   (i) Phenomena: When iron rusts, it turns into a kind of reddish-brown dust.
   (ii) Explanation: Rusting is a kind of slow burning. In burning, phlogiston is liberated from the metal leaving behind its earth. In symbols:

$$EEPP \longrightarrow EE + PP$$

(Metal $\longrightarrow$ rust + phlogiston)[15]

25.5 THE DOWNFALL OF THE PHLOGISTON THEORY

In 1772, Antoine Laurent Lavoisier (1743–1794) discovered that phosphorus when burned gains weight, whereas if, in burning, objects do give up their phlogiston the phosphorus should have lost weight. This is an anomaly that requires explanation. When phosphorus is burnt, it turns into a white fume that can be condensed and weighed. The increase in weight is actually quite phenomenal, being almost twice that of the original phosphorus. A similar result was obtained in burning sulfur. Such unexpected results call for explanation.

Various avenues were explored to find an adequate explanation of the discrepancy so as to preserve the phlogiston theory. One avenue was to postulate that phlogiston has negative weight instead of positive weight. To try to patch up an existing theory in the face of discrepancies is a conservative move, and such moves can be ad hoc, according to Popper (Chapter 7).

However, Lavoisier made an innovative and revolutionary move. Instead of keeping to the existing idea of phlogiston *coming out of* a burning object, he reasoned that something must have *gone into* the burning substance, and that something was later called 'oxygen.'

For Kuhn the change from the phlogiston theory to the oxygen theory is a change of paradigms, from the phlogiston paradigm to the oxygen paradigm. The conservative move can be likened to a change of government (say, the Democrats replacing the Republicans [in the United States]). The innovative move is comparable to the change of the *forms* of government or the replacement of the

---

12. Modern chemistry explains this as the solution of carbon dioxide from our lungs in the lime water, representable by the following equation: $CO_2 + Ca(OH)_2 = CaCO_3 + H_2O$. $Ca(OH)_2$ is soluble in water. Thus lime water is clear. On the other hand, $CaCO_3$ is insoluble in water, hence it appears as a milky white precipitate in the solution.

13. Modern chemistry explains this as: $H_2SO_4 + Zn = ZnSO_4 + H_2$. The flammable gas emitted is hydrogen H_2.

14. Modern chemistry takes metallic ore as oxides. It explains the process of smelting as the "absorption" of the oxygen present in the ore by the carbon of charcoal forming CO_2, thus turning the ore into pure metal.

15. Modern chemistry takes rusting as the oxidation of metal.

constitution with a radically new one (say, from communism to capitalism, as in the former Soviet Union in 1991).

25.6 THE CHEMICAL ATOMIC THEORY

With due respect for Kuhn, I think the story of paradigm change here would be better told as a change from the alchemo-phlogiston theory to the chemical atomic theory. The oxygen theory of Lavoisier was but the first step toward the chemical atomic theory. It was John Dalton of England (1766–1844) who completed the revolution.

Dalton's epoch-making treatise *A New System of Chemical Philosophy* was published in two parts, in 1808 and 1810. This is how he conceived the basic building blocks of the universe (the atoms):

(a) Matter consists of indivisible atoms.

(b) There are many different kinds of atoms. Atoms of the same kind are identical in every respect: shape, size, weight, and so on. Each kind forms what is known to us as a chemical element. (There are hydrogen atoms, oxygen atoms, carbon atoms, iron atoms, and so forth.)

(c) Atoms are indestructible and uncreatable.

(d) There are strict laws governing the combination of atoms forming larger units known as molecules.[16] Just as each kind of atom constitutes an element, each kind of molecule constitutes a compound.

(i) Atoms of certain kinds can combine while others cannot. For example, whereas atoms of iron can combine with atoms of oxygen to form molecules, they cannot combine with atoms of copper.

(ii) When atoms do combine to form molecules, they do so in definite ratios in terms of the numbers of atoms of each kind. For example, one hydrogen atom combines with one chlorine atom to form one molecule of hydrochloric acid (HCl);[17] one carbon atom combines with two oxygen atoms to form one molecule of carbon dioxide (CO_2); and one sodium atom combines with one oxygen atom and one hydrogen atom to form one molecule of sodium hydroxide (NaOH).[18]

(iii) Quite often, though, the same kinds of atoms can combine in more than one ratio. For example, carbon can combine with oxygen to form CO and CO_2, but cannot form CO_3. Iron can form three oxides: FeO, Fe_2O_3, Fe_3O_4.[19]

(iv) Most of the substances of the world are compounds rather than elements. For example, water is a compound, not an element.

Dalton's atomic theory formed the foundation of modern chemistry.

25.7 APT VERSUS CAT

Let's compare and contrast the alchemo-phlogiston theory (APT) with Dalton's chemical atomic theory (CAT).

A. Sensual Qualities

According to APT: The four sensual qualities, dryness, wetness, hotness, and coldness, are considered explicitly as *basic* properties of matter by APT. Presumably other sensual qualities such as colors,

---

16. 'Molecule' is not Dalton's term.

17. 'Cl' stands for chlorine.

18. 'Na' stands for sodium.

19. 'Fe' stands for iron. Dalton actually thought that the oxides of iron were FeO, FeO_2, and Fe_2O.

tastes, and smells are considered basic as well. If these are basic, it makes sense to assume, indeed it is obligatory to assume, that (i) the elements do possess these properties and (ii) the whole is equal to the sum of its parts—that is, familiar substances such as wood, charcoal, iron, and gold are mixtures of various elements in the right proportion, resulting in their familiar sensual qualities as the additive sums of their component elements. Briefly, the sensual qualities we perceive in those material objects around us come from components bearing similar properties.

In sum, (a) sensual qualities are basic, (b) the elements actually possess these properties, and (c) when the elements are mixed they produce new substances bearing the properties of their component elements in direct ratio to their constituent amounts.

According to CAT: The sensual qualities are *derived* (emergent) properties. They are not basic. The atoms of CAT are neither wet nor dry, and neither hot nor cold. They are colorless, tasteless, and without smell. Sensual qualities are anthropocentric properties in that they are defined in accordance with human interests and human perception. To put it crudely, they represent relationships to the (human) observer rather than something intrinsic in the object. In traditional philosophy, these sensual qualities are known as **secondary qualities**, whereas size, shape, weight, and motion are known as **primary qualities**. Primary qualities are considered basic, whereas secondary qualities are only derivative.[20]

That CAT takes the sensual qualities as derivative marks one great difference between it and APT. Since the sensual qualities are not basic, the **mixture principle** that the whole equals to the sum of the parts does not hold for chemistry. For

example, if atoms are neither wet nor dry, no matter how they are mixed they cannot produce wetness or dryness. Hence another principle must be at work. This is the **principle of emergence**.[21] For example, neither hydrogen nor oxygen are transparent liquids (at room temperature) and neither can quench thirst, yet when they combine to form H_2O, the result exhibits the aforesaid properties. We call these **emergent properties** or derived properties (Section 13.6). Thus CAT brought about the modern distinction between chemical compounds and physical mixtures. For example, air is a *mixture* of mainly nitrogen, oxygen, and hydrogen. Being a mixture, its proportions can vary. Indeed the ratio of hydrogen to nitrogen in the upper atmosphere is different from that at sea level. On the other hand, the notorious laughing gas is a chemical *compound*. It is composed of nitrogen and oxygen in a fixed proportion. Modern chemistry represents it as N_2O (nitrous oxide).

B. Structure of the Elements

According to APT: The elements are spatially shapeless and nomologically unstructured. The four elements can occur in parcels of any amount and in any shape. This makes them "spatially shapeless." Since there is no law governing the "aggregation" of these elements to form new substances, these elements are nomologically unstructured.

In sum, the four elements are unstructured both spatially and nomologically.

According to CAT: The atoms are both spatially and nomologically structured. The atoms of a kind (belonging to a single element) are all of exactly the same shape, size, and weight. Hence the atoms are spatially structured. Since the atoms obey exact laws

---

20. The distinction between primary and secondary qualities is due to Galileo and John Locke (1632–1704). For example, a yellow flower that looks yellow to an observer is in itself not yellow at all. It rather possesses a certain power to generate the sensation of yellowness in the human observer. This power is the secondary quality that we are talking about, and this power is generated out of the primary qualities such as size, shape, and motion. Hence it is the primary qualities that are basic and are really "there in the world." (See Reductionism in Section 13.5.)

21. Both the terms 'mixture principle' and 'principle of emergence' are mine.

of combination both in kinds and in number, they are nomologically structured as well.

We can say that APT is a syrup-and-vinegar model of nature, according to which *any* amount of "syrup" can be mixed with *any* amount of "vinegar" and the resultant "taste" is the additive sum of the contributive "sweetness" of the "syrup" and the "sourness" of the "vinegar." On the contrary, CAT is a lock-and-key model of nature, according to which only certain "keys" fit certain "locks" to form bigger units, and these "keys" and "locks" are "tasteless."

You can see the sharp contrasts between the two theories APT and CAT in their conception of the ontology and structure of nature. With these in mind, we should find it much easier to appreciate Kuhn's paradigm view of science, which will occupy the next two chapters.

KEY TERMS INTRODUCED IN THIS CHAPTER

paradigm

alchemo-phlogiston theory

chemical atomic theory

secondary quality

primary quality

mixture principle

principle of emergence

emergent property

REFERENCES

Holmyard and Palmer (1956, Part I) give an excellent brief history of development of chemistry from antiquity to the chemical atomic theory.

McCann (1978) devotes a whole book to the paradigmatic shift from phlogiston to oxygen.

On the alchemo-phlogiston theory, see Gale (1979, chap. 5) for an introduction. Read (1939, chap. 1, secs. 4 and 5), Stillman (1960, chap. XI), and Taylor (1951, chap. XIII) give more details.

On Dalton's atomic theory, Holton and Roller (1958, chap. 22) and McKenzie (1960, chap. 11) give excellent summaries.

On primary and secondary qualities, see Edwards (1967, "Primary and Secondary Qualities").

On emergent properties, see Nagel (1961, pp. 366–398).

Chapter 26

Kuhn I: Normal Science and Revolutionary Science

26.1 THE EXEMPLAR THESIS

"How do scientists attach symbolic expressions to nature?" Kuhn (1974, p. 467) asks.

In Section 23.4, we saw how the logical positivists struggled to solve the problem of the OT-link: the problem of the logical relationship between observational terms and theoretical terms. According to Carnap later, the observational terms should be terms about macroscopic physical objects and their observational properties (physicalism). The problem is to show how to link the theoretical terms with the observational terms.

The logical positivists conceive theories as made up of a set of internal principles and a set of bridge principles, together forming a set of axioms (Sections 15.2 and 19.1). The internal principles are stated purely in theoretical terms, whereas the bridge principles employ both observational terms and theoretical terms. The bridge principles, also known as correspondence rules, are expected to provide the sought-after logical link between the observational and theoretical terms.

But to fulfill the role of linking the theoretical terms with the observational terms, what forms should the correspondence rules take? In Section 23.4, we discussed how the logical positivists tried to formulate these correspondence rules first as operational definitions and then as reduction sentences. Unfortunately these efforts have been shown to be unsuccessful. Hence the problem of the (missing) OT-link remains unsolved.

Besides this problem of the OT-link, there is the problem of the SS-link. Popper, as you may recall, dismisses the necessity of linking the statements of science to sense experience. For Popper statements can only be justified with statements. If one is not happy with certain statements, be they theoretical or observational, one can always test them against other statements. As I pointed out in Section 24.9, unless one opts for the coherence theory of truth, one is required to anchor statements of science eventually outside the circle of statements—for example, to sense experience. I called this linkage problem the problem of the SS-link.

Kuhn, in asking the above question, attempts to solve both the problem of the OT-link and the problem of the SS-link in a radically novel way. In this context, he produces his **exemplar thesis**.

The exemplar thesis is at once a theory of meaning and a theory of learning. In pointing out how one learns to understand scientific concepts (theoretical terms) and their accompanying scientific theories, Kuhn thinks that he has discovered a theory of meaning that can solve the two linkage problems without employing correspondence principles.

Kuhn proposes his exemplar thesis in *The Structure of Scientific Revolutions* (1962, 1970). He argues that scientific theories are attached to nature not through correspondence rules, but rather through what he calls **exemplars**. Exemplars of a theory are the standard applications of the theory for the solution of standard problems. Kuhn (1974) gives an example. Newton's equation of motion, $f = ma$, is abstract and, by itself, devoid of empirical meaning. Its contact with reality is through various applications. For example, through its application in solving the problems of free fall, the simple pendulum, and coupled harmonic oscillators, the meaning of the equation manifests itself in specific cases.[1] Newton himself applied that equation to explain and predict the paths of the planets, the orbit of the moon, the trajectories of comets, and the movements of the tides.[2] It is through the

multitude of such applications that the notions of force, mass, and acceleration acquire their *empirical* meaning. These applications, which purport to provide solutions to problems, are what Kuhn terms exemplars.[3]

In the case of the phlogiston theory, the notion of phlogiston takes on its empirical meaning through the application of the theory to the explanation of phenomena, such as combustion, smelting, and calcination (Section 25.4). These were historically standard solutions offered by the phlogiston theory to solve standard problems. The apprentice scientist learned the theory, not through a set of axioms composed of internal principles and bridge principles. Rather he learned it through these standard solutions. Having worked through these solutions themselves, both theoretically and experimentally, he might understand other problems in a similar manner and apply similar techniques to solve these other problems. For example, he might try to solve the problem of why methylated spirits and paraffin are flammable whereas vinegar is not. It can be seen that, according to Kuhn's theory of learning, one learns (in most cases) by imitation—as an apprentice would imitate his master—rather than by studying abstract rules such as correspondence rules. His theory of understanding (and therefore, of meaning) takes the same line of approach. For him understanding is reflected by the ability to "carry on in a similar manner." When one manages to digest the given standard solutions and is able to apply similar techniques of solution to new problems, then one can claim understanding of the theory concerned.

This philosophy of understanding and learning is claimed to be instantiated by the way university students learn and understand science. A student might know all the formulas and equations of science. She might even be able to mathematically deduce complicated consequences from these

---

1. Kuhn (1974, p. 465).

2. Newton (1962, vol. II).

3. Note that exemplars are more than *theoretical* solutions to theoretical problems. They involve experimental setups, methods used, instruments employed, and observations made, and everything else that contributes to the solutions of standard problems.

formulas. Nevertheless she cannot claim any understanding of that particular field of science until she can apply these formulas to specific situations. In the case of Newton's mechanics, to help her to see the *empirical* significance of Newton's formulas, the teacher might ask her to solve problems of the conical pendulum, the governors of steam engines, the motions of objects suspended by a spring, the gyrations of spinning tops, and so on. Confronted with these problems, she would endeavor to "see" these problems as similar to the standard problems whose solutions have been provided for her through books and lectures. She can then claim understanding when she succeeds in "driving the Newtonian vehicle" through these new fields.

In short, one learns through the study of exemplars, and understanding is the ability to model new solutions after these exemplars. A scientific theory can still be conceived to be composed of internal principles (that is, the formulas and principles), but these principles are not taken as anchored in nature through correspondence rules or other kinds of rules. Rather they are attached to reality through exemplars, which provide the abstract principles with empirical meaning. Since it is such exemplars that provide empirical meaning to a theory, the only way to learn and to understand a theory is through exemplars.

This philosophy of learning and understanding is supported by findings in cognitive psychology. It is observable that many concepts such as 'bird' and 'fruit' are learned, not through definitions, but through prototypes. We all know what a bird is and what a fruit is. But we have never been given definitions of birds and fruits. We have never asked for such either. Yet somehow we have all learned and understood the terms 'bird' and 'fruit.'

According to standard cognitive psychology, we learn the word 'bird' through prototypes such as the pigeon, the robin, the eagle, and the starling.[4] When a new instance—for example, a woodpecker—is presented to us, we would compare it with the prototypes and judge whether it is a bird or not according to how similar it is to the prototypes. (We do not ask, "Does the new instance satisfy the definition of a bird?") Sometimes we have difficulty making up our mind. For example, we might be presented with a chicken or a kiwi. You can see that prototypes in psychology correspond to Kuhn's exemplars, and definitions correspond to correspondence rules. Concepts like 'bird' have been found to be learned and understood through "exemplars," not through "correspondence rules."

Similarly we learn the concept 'fruit' through prototypes such as apples, oranges, and peaches. We perceive the "fruitiness" of other plant products in accordance with the "similarity-distances" that obtain between these products and the central "prototypes." For instance, the pumpkin, though recognized as a fruit by many, has been found to be denied the status of being a fruit by almost 50 percent of the subjects in a psychological experiment. It is not because the pumpkin does not satisfy a given definition of fruit. Rather it is so dissimilar to the "standard" cases such as apples and oranges that people cannot quite see it as a fruit. The peanut fares even worse, because its "similarity-distance" from the prototypes is greater.[5]

In sum, cognitive psychology finds that many terms acquire meaning through "exemplars" and not through "definitions." This lends support to Kuhn's exemplar thesis.[6]

(In the first edition of *The Structure of Scientific Revolutions*, Kuhn employed the term 'paradigm' to mean (at least) two kinds of "things": (i) what we call exemplars as mentioned earlier and (ii) what we call paradigms in the next section. Because of this ambiguity, in the Postscript to the second edition of the book he proposed that these two kinds of "things" be called (i) exemplar and (ii) disciplinary matrix.

---

4. Here I am talking about laypeople such as you and me, not biologists.

5. For reference see Anderson (1985, pp. 126, 130).

6. It can be seen that both Kuhn's exemplar theory and the prototype theory were derived from Wittgenstein's family-resemblance theory of meaning.

We have adopted 'exemplar' and will retain 'paradigm' for the second kind.)

26.2 THE WELTANSCHAUUNG THESIS

Popper's methodology, as we saw in Chapter 24, can be caricatured as one for perpetual revolutions: always attempt to overthrow proposed hypotheses! Kuhn, however, finds that, as a matter of fact, scientific revolutions are few and far between in history.[7] Most of the time scientists practice what Kuhn calls normal science. Normal science is routine and unexciting—it does not mean it can't be fulfilling or challenging though—a far cry from Popper's image of science as conjectures and refutation.

Normal science is research carried out within overall theoretical frameworks that Kuhn calls 'paradigms.' These frameworks somehow eluded the classicists—that is, the logical positivists and Popper. According to Kuhn, paradigms play a decisive role in the practice of science. They determine the relevance of data, the content of observations, the significance of problems, and the acceptance of solutions. No, much more than just these. Paradigms supply values, standards, and methodologies. In brief, each paradigm determines the way science should be practiced; it is a *Weltanschauung*. But then how come the classicists missed this all-important element in their analyses?

According to Kuhn, the classicists' findings would in many cases be correct if they are interpreted as being about scientific practices *within*

paradigms. For example, within paradigms classicists' logic of confirmation (and disconfirmation) does apply (Chapters 6 and 7). If only the classicists could see the paradigm encasing their logic!

So here is Kuhn's second major thesis: the **Weltanschauung thesis**[8] or the **paradigm thesis**.

A. Theories can roughly be classified into two types: generic theories and specific theories.[9] Each **paradigm** is essentially a generic theory. **Generic theories** are comprehensive theories[10] such as Aristotle's mechanics, Newton's mechanics, quantum mechanics, the theory of relativity, the alchemo-phlogiston theory, Dalton's atomic theory, Darwin's theory of evolution, Lyell's uniformitarianism, Newton's corpuscular theory, and Huygen-Young-Fresnel's wave theory of light (Chapter 0). They are comprehensive in two respects: (i) each generic theory covers a wide field, providing an ontology and a methodology for the field of study and (ii) generic theories are general. In itself, such a theory is too general to make any predictions. What produce predictions (and hence are testable) are **specific theories** that can be developed within these generic theories. For example, within the generic theory of alchemo-phlogiston one can postulate that paraffin is rich in phlogiston. One can postulate that steam is water plus phlogiston. These are specific theories. Dalton postulated that water is made up of one atom of hydrogen and one atom of oxygen (that is, HO). Again this is a specific theory, specific within Dalton's (general) atomic theory. Dalton also proposed another specific theory, that the atomic weight of oxygen is 6.[11] According to Kuhn, it is these specific theories that are testable, not the generic theories. As can be seen, the relation of the generic theories to the

---

7. Kuhn started his career as a theoretical physicist, then turned historian of science, and only later in life took up philosophy. Recently he returned to history of science. Thus his knowledge of the history of science should be respected.

8. 'Weltanschauung' is a German word meaning 'worldview.'

9. These are my terms. Larry Laudan (1977, pp. 73–74) opts for the terms 'maxi-theory' and 'mini-theory.'

10. Maxi-theories are also described as global theories.

11. When Dalton synthesized water from hydrogen and oxygen, he found, incorrectly, that the weight ratio of the two is 1:6. Since he thought HO is the formula for water, he concluded that the atomic weight of oxygen is 6 if 1 is taken as the atomic weight of hydrogen.

specific theories is the relation of genus to species. In rather simplistic terms, generic theories provide the outlines, whereas the specific theories are instances of fleshing out these outlines.

B. A generic theory develops into a paradigm only when it has achieved convincing successes in the explanation of natural phenomena and in empirical predictions. The alchemo-phlogiston theory, for example, became a paradigm because of such successes (Section 25.4). Dalton's atomic theory, for the same reason, developed into a paradigm as well. Let's call the generic theories that have developed into paradigms '**paradigm theories**.'[12] Let's call the specific theories that are specific articulations of paradigm theories '**subparadigm theories**.'

C. Paradigm theories constitute the core of paradigms. Each paradigm theory usually has a number of explicitly stated formulas and/or principles in a technical vocabulary, together with an unknown number of implicit ideas and views. These formulas, principles, ideas, and views are anchored to nature[13] through exemplars as explained in the last section.[14] Generic theories are not finished products with sharp boundaries. They are not "frozen." They grow and change. First, their empirical interpretations change with additional applications taken as exemplars.[15] Second, the explicit formulas do not exhaust the content of the theories because there are implicit ideas not expressible in formulas. Third, the contact of the theory with nature is through exemplars rather than through correspondence rules. These are the main reasons given for the claim that paradigm theories cannot be axiomatized.

Let's take some examples. The alchemo-phlogiston theory possesses explicit principles such as "The world is made of four elements," and "The

element water is wet and cold whereas the element fire is hot and dry." These principles are given empirical meaning through their proposed solutions to the problems of combustion and so on. Later this initial empirical meaning is gradually augmented and articulated by further experiments and applications of the theory. For example, Priestley in 1775 obtained a new gas by heating calx of mercury (mercuric oxide) with a magnifying glass and *interpreted* the gas as dephlogisticated air.

The explicitly stated principles in Dalton's atomic theory are such as: "Matter consists of indivisible atoms," and "Atoms are indestructible and uncreatable." This theory was initially rooted empirically in Dalton's and others' experiments. It was then further developed and amended in the able hands of scientists such as Gay-Lussac and Avogadro through their experiments and theoretical articulation. It can be said that such developments and articulations have continued right up to the present day.

D. Paradigm theories are *not* the same as paradigms, even though the former constitute the core of the latter. Whereas paradigm theories are abstract entities,[16] paradigms are social constructs. Paradigms are generic theories shared by members of a scientific community. For example, a generic theory entertained by a single individual is not a paradigm. Paradigms have a sort of life which is sustained by a scientific community. At the preparadigm stage, there may be a number of generic theories competing for domination. Eventually one takes over because of its notable achievements and successes. The victor then becomes the paradigm of the community. Consequently,

the members of a scientific community see themselves and are seen by others as the men uniquely responsible for the pursuit of

---

12. See Kuhn (1970, p. 26).

13. I would think it more appropriate to say: "These formulas and/or principles are anchored in *experience* and/or nature."

14. Strictly speaking, paradigm theories can only be anchored in nature through subparadigm theories, since only the latter are testable.

15. This resembles the case of statutory laws. Each new court ruling (exemplar) adds or alters the meaning (interpretation) of the laws concerned.

16. In Popper's terminology, they are in World 3. At best they are in World 2, the world of the mental.

a set of shared goals, including the training of their successors. Within such groups communication is relatively full and professional judgment relatively unanimous.[17]

This kind of communication and unanimity in professional judgment sustain paradigms as "living" things. Thus paradigms are often likened to languages, because every language is a social construct, a live entity sustained by a community, the members of which share a common culture, similar goals, and similar views.

E. Scientists of the same community perceive and think in terms of the community's paradigm theory. They recognize problems, propose solutions, perform tests, collect data, and perform all other kinds of scientific activities in accordance with this paradigm,[18] so much so that often the paradigm becomes invisible and uncriticizable. Just as those who wear glasses are often oblivious of the presence of the glasses, scientists usually take their paradigms as given, natural, unproblematic, and transparent. Paradigms more or less rule the scientific lives of those who embrace them. This pervasive feature of the paradigm in the practice of science makes it so important and, ironically, so elusive. Paradigms provide *Weltanschauungen*, worldviews and conceptual frameworks, which, according to Kuhn, are necessary for the pursuit of science—that is, normal science.

26.3 NORMAL SCIENCE

As pointed out earlier, for every field in science, there is a period when no paradigm exists. As time passes, a number of (usually vague and ill-conceived) generic theories are proposed. They compete for supremacy. In doing so, they are sharpened and articulated. Eventually one generic theory makes a certain breakthrough. It scores

some outstanding successes in explanation and/or prediction. Scientists are drawn to it. As its competitors drop out of the arena of contest one after another, the theory takes over as the one and only left in the field. Now this generic theory becomes a paradigm, with more or less unanimous support from members of the scientific community.

According to Kuhn, during the preparadigm stage little or no progress is made in explanation and prediction. The field is in disarray and chaos. There is a lack of direction. Most scientists are confused. However, once a paradigm is in place, things are quite different. The paradigm guides thought and reasoning. It supplies inspiration, means, and methods. It provides rules of practice. There is now a definite direction to follow, and a uniform way of understanding the world. Under a paradigm, members of the community work in unison, cooperating both in theoretical articulations and in experimental explorations. Such a setup is conducive to progress, and indeed conspicuous progress is usually made during this period, which is what Kuhn calls the period of **normal science**.[19]

The term 'normal science' is to be contrasted with the term 'revolutionary science.' According to Kuhn, revolutionary science rarely occurs. Most of the time scientists practice normal science. Normal science, in political terms, is a time of peace and prosperity, which is occasionally interrupted by revolts and revolutions. How and why these revolutions occur will be explained later. In the meantime let us enjoy some "peace." Let us see how normal science is practiced.

For Kuhn there are four main types of normal science:

A. Factual scientific investigations. It sounds counterintuitive to say that the nature of facts depends on the adopted paradigm theory and that each paradigm creates its own type of fact. Most of

---

17. From, "The Structure of Scientific Revolutions, 2nd Ed." Kuhn, Thomas S. (1970, p. 177) Reprinted with permission from the University of Chicago Press.

18. In the literature, authors often mean 'paradigm theory' when they use the term 'paradigm.' I will for the sake of lucidity follow this practice when there is little risk of confusion.

19. From, "The Structure of Scientific Revolutions, 2nd Ed." Kuhn, Thomas S. (1970, p. 18) Reprinted with permission from the University of Chicago Press.

us would have thought that facts are somehow objective and independent of us and our theories. However, according to Kuhn, paradigms not only determine the kind of facts there are in the world but also generate problems: the problems of how to find and determine these facts. Let me illustrate with a few examples.

Within the paradigm of alchemo-phlogiston theory (APT) it makes sense to inquire about the nature of phlogiston: What is its weight? Has it a definite density? How fast does it flow from one substance to another? Is there just one kind of phlogiston or are there many kinds? *We* would not ask such questions, because we 20th-century scientists do not work under APT. Had APT been our paradigm, to say that these questions are fair and sensible would be an understatement. Indeed these would have constituted the central problems for science of the 20th century. Furthermore, we would probably like to determine the relative abundance of phlogiston present in charcoal as compared to its presence, say, in gold. We would like to know how to extract pure phlogiston from charcoal. We might even like to know if it is possible to turn charcoal into gold by the manipulation of the relative amount of phlogiston in the two types of substance. These are examples of the problems generated by APT.

In contrast those working under Dalton's chemical atomic theory (CAT) would search for the atomic weights of elements such as hydrogen and oxygen[20] and would try to ascertain the atomic constituents of compounds such as carbonic oxide, carbonic acid,[21] and water.

For Newton there is no such thing as wavelengths of light. But wavelengths for Huygens, Young, and Fresnel were real (Chapter 0). For example, it not only made sense to search for the wavelengths of red light; the wave theorists were in fact required to ascertain these facts. For each paradigm, certain classes of facts are significant because they reveal the nature of things. Wavelengths are significant for the wave paradigm of light. Atomic weights are significant for CAT, whereas the properties of phlogiston are significant for APT.

You can see that these problems are all fact-finding problems. We want to know, under a particular paradigm: What is X made of? How much Y is present? How many Z's are there? How big is L? How can M be turned into N? and so on. This category of (significant) fact gathering takes up the major part of normal scientific activities.

B. Paradigm support.   The second type of normal scientific activity is the search for supporting facts for the given paradigm. Often this involves the invention of new instruments. Kuhn (1970, p. 26) gives the following examples: "Special telescopes to demonstrate the Copernican prediction of annual parallax; Atwood's machine, … , to give the first unequivocal demonstration of Newton's second law; Foucault's apparatus to show that the speed of light is greater in air than in water …— these pieces of special apparatus and many others like them illustrate the immense effort and ingenuity that have been required to bring nature and theory into closer and closer agreement."

Let's now take an example from APT. It was discovered that when sulfur is heated it will burn and yield a copious vapor. When the vapor is later dissolved into water, the resultant solution is acidic and will not burn further. In view of this the phlogiston paradigm naturally prompted that sulfur is a combination of phlogiston and acid. If sulfur is indeed so composed, then it would be logical to predict that sulfur would be formed by adding phlogiston to the acid of sulfur. Indeed when acid of sulfur was boiled with charcoal (which is full of phlogiston), sulfur was formed! This verification of the prediction was seen as a strong support of APT.

C. Paradigm articulation.   The third type of normal science is the articulation of the given paradigm. There are three subtypes.

---

20. The atomic weight of an element is the weight of each of its (identical) atoms, usually expressed as weight relative to the weight of the hydrogen atom. The atomic weight of hydrogen is usually given the value 1.

21. Carbonic oxide is our CO, and carbonic acid is our CO_2.

(i) Determination of physical constants. For example, Newton's gravitational theory is incomplete without an explicit value for the gravitational constant. It was Cavendish who supplied the first value in the 1790s. Since then more accurate values were constantly proposed. The determination of the true value of the gravitational constant contributes toward the articulation of Newton's paradigm. This belongs to the third type of normal science. Other constants that Kuhn mentions are: the astronomical unit, Avogadro's number, Joule's coefficient, and the value of the electronic charge.[22]

(ii) The determination of quantitative laws—for example, Boyle's law and Coulomb's law of electrical attraction.[23]

(iii) The resolution of ambiguity in the application of the paradigm theory in new areas.[24]

D. Solving of theoretical problems.   Often the theory itself can be conceptually simple, yet its application to certain types of problems can require the development of complicated mathematics. Kuhn mentions the application of Newton's mechanics to the planets. The mathematics involved in the explanation and prediction of the orbits of the planets is relatively simple and straightforward if we treat the planets as point particles, and if we ignore the mutual attractions between the planets. However, the results obtained under these simplifications do not agree exactly with observations. To improve on them, one is faced with what is known as the many-bodied problem, which is complicated enough even for three interacting bodies. Kuhn thinks that much of normal science is occupied with such theoretical work.

It can be seen that each paradigm theory generates problems for the scientists to solve, thus providing work for its scientists. Such work is almost routine and nonexciting. That doesn't mean that it is easy and nonchallenging. It often requires scientists of great ingenuity to pursue such work. Nonetheless, normal science is nonexciting in the sense that the paradigm, in generating its problems, has usually determined what sort of solutions are to be expected. Furthermore, the very nature of a paradigm is such that it (truthfully or otherwise) always explicitly guarantees that solutions exist. For instance, APT guarantees that phlogiston will have a certain weight. The scientist might not be able to determine it for the time being, yet that number allegedly exists. The problem of the weight of phlogiston is expected to have a definite answer. Again, according to CAT, each atom must have a definite atomic weight. The answer to the problem of atomic weight is guaranteed by the theory itself. Whether oxygen, for example, is 6, 8, or 16 is disputable. (Dalton thought that it was 6.) Nonetheless CAT guarantees a unique solution. It is this guarantee of a solution together with the provision of the type of solution to be expected that renders normal science nonexciting.

Kuhn pictures this nonexciting nature of normal science as **puzzle solving**. Let me develop this analogy in terms of a jigsaw puzzle. The task of the puzzle solver is to make sense of a collection of colored pieces of cardboard by putting them together to form a "sensible" picture. This is comparable to the aim of science, which is to put together the empirical data (collected or to be collected) to form a "complete" and "rational" picture. At the start of the game, one has no idea what the picture is going to be like.[25] So one fumbles one's way along until one strikes upon some sort of idea

22. From, "The Structure of Scientific Revolutions, 2nd Ed." Kuhn, Thomas S. (1970, p. 28) Reprinted with permission from the University of Chicago Press.

23. From, "The Structure of Scientific Revolutions, 2nd Ed." Kuhn, Thomas S. (1970, p. 28) Reprinted with permission from the University of Chicago Press.

24. From, "The Structure of Scientific Revolutions, 2nd Ed." Kuhn, Thomas S. (1970, p. 29) Reprinted with permission from the University of Chicago Press.

25. For the sake of argument, let's assume that no picture of the solution has been printed on the cover of the box or package.

about the picture to be.[26] This idea will then prompt the formation of a sort of master plan that is comparable to the emergence of a paradigm in science. Suppose it strikes the player that the completed picture is going to be a house. Then instead of trying to fit random pieces together to form a picture, she would look positively for pieces "predicted" or required by the master plan. Thus she would adopt what AI theorists would call a top-down search.[27] For example, if she suspects that the completed picture is going to be a house, she will look positively for the typical items present in a house—for example, windows, doors, perhaps a chimney, and so on. Top-down searches guided by a master plan (if the master plan is relevant) are much more efficient than the bottom-up approach of blind trial and error.

We can see that solving a jigsaw puzzle involves two kinds of activities: (a) proposing a master plan and (b) fitting together the pieces in accordance with the master plan.

The practice of science is similar in that one can only grope one's way along before the advent of a paradigm. Then an idea will occur to the scientists that the world is organized in a certain way. They then try it out. If the idea works significantly in a number of places, the scientists adopt it as a "master plan." In other words, the idea has become a paradigm. Once the paradigm is in place, the practice of science is a matter of course, being both guided and constrained by the paradigm. To put it figuratively, science then progresses like a train gliding forward on its rails. This is the period of normal science.

You can see how the master plan for solving the jigsaw puzzle provides direction for the search for the missing pieces. For example, doors and windows will be some of the missing pieces if the jigsaw puzzle is thought to illustrate a house. You can also see how the master plan indicates what sort of solutions are to be expected. For instance, only certain kinds of doors will (usually) go with certain types of houses. Moreover, the master plan promises that such solutions exist.

In short, according to Kuhn, the activities of normal science are comparable to puzzle solving.

26.4 ANOMALIES, CRISIS, AND REVOLUTION

Normal science prospers under a paradigm. It is the routine science of the day until it encounters difficulties, which Kuhn calls **anomalies**. The concept of an anomaly (to a paradigm) is rather vague. In its weakest and vaguest sense, it means some sort of difficulty. However, it is often taken as an empirical phenomenon that shows that the paradigm theory is incorrect, even though no theories are, strictly speaking, falsifiable according to the Duhem-Quine thesis (Chapter 9). Paradigm theories, being generic theories, are even less falsifiable. Having said this, let me illustrate this concept of anomaly as best as I can with an example.

In 1774 Joseph Priestley (1733–1804) experimented with the following chemical reactions:

He heated liquid mercury in air, and it turned into a red powder, known as the red calx of mercury. When the calx was further heated to a higher temperature it turned back into mercury.

In 1775 Lavoisier, on repeating Priestley's experiment, noticed an additional phenomenon—that is, the mercury derived from the calx during the second part of the experiment had weighed less than the calx. In other words, when mercury turned into calx in the first part of the experiment, it *increased* in weight. This is an anomaly because, according to the phlogiston theory, mercury (a metal), being earth plus phlogiston, should *decrease* in weight on burning, having given up its phlogiston to form calx (which is just earth).[28] This

---

26. Again, for the sake of argument, I am ignoring the obvious tactic of starting from the edges of the puzzle board.

27. 'AI' is short for 'artificial intelligence.'

28. This experiment was elegant and simple, for the burning of mercury does not require the presence of charcoal, hence the difference in weight between the calx and the mercury can easily be detected. For a more detailed story of Lavoisier's experiment, see Wolf (1962, pp. 368–369).

result reinforced Lavoisier's findings in 1772 when he discovered that both phosphorus and sulfur when burned increase in weight (Section 25.5).[29]

When an anomaly (potential empirical falsification) arises, something must be done. It is not, however, a straight case of contradiction or inconsistency. Had that been the case, either the experimental result or the paradigm would have to be given up. As pointed out in Chapters 6, 7, and 9, such adverse implications can usually be circumvented by modifying either the main hypothesis (paradigm) or some of the auxiliary hypotheses involved.

In the present case, the phlogistonists attempted to explain away the anomaly in a number of ways. Here are a few:

(a) As has been mentioned, some postulated that phlogiston has negative weight (levity).

(b) Some proposed that the density of the calx is more than that of the metal. Hence when they are respectively weighed in air, the buoyancy of the air will render the former heavier.

(c) Robert Boyle suggested that some fire particles must have been trapped in the calx, thus making it heavier.

(e) Others suggested that water could have been absorbed by the calx.

It can be seen that (a) is a case of modification of the main hypothesis (the paradigm) whereas (b) to (d) are cases of modification of some of the auxiliary hypotheses.

According to Kuhn, scientists should not and usually do not give up their paradigms when confronted with a single or even a number of anomalies. As many have pointed out, theories, especially in their infancy, are usually plagued by unfavorable empirical data. It is unwise to give up a major theory so easily. As a matter of fact, Priestley defended the phlogiston theory right up to his death. However, as more and more anomalies accumulate, and more and more amendments to the paradigm or their auxiliary hypotheses have to be made, a **crisis** develops.[30] Scientists will then search for a new paradigm. In the case of the phlogiston theory, Lavoisier proposed to explain the loss in weight when the red calx turned back into mercury as due to the escape of oxygen (rather than to an absorption of phlogiston). This, according to Kuhn, amounts to a change of paradigm, which is a **revolution**.

Ptolemy's geocentric theory has been taken as an example of a paradigm. Under it, apparent motions of the planets are to be explained in terms of deferents and epicycles around the earth. The mapping of the apparent motions onto epicycles belongs to the field of normal science. As more and more data on the movements of the planets were collected and analyzed, it was found that more and more epicycles were required to accommodate the data. The number, in fact, went beyond 80. If we take each requirement of change in the number of the epicycles as an anomaly, we can say that the Ptolemaic theory was in a state of crisis by the 16th century when Copernicus replaced the geocentric theory with his heliocentric theory. This amounted to a change in paradigm, which is again a revolution.

However, not all anomalies end up with a change of paradigms. The planet Uranus was discovered by William Herschel in 1781. Thereafter its motions were continually tracked and cataloged by astronomers. It was found that they agreed well with Newton's law of gravitation—that is, until 1830. Evidence started to accumulate indicating that the planet's motions were not as they should be. These misbehaviors were anomalies to the paradigm of Newton's mechanics. However, instead of

---

29. The presently accepted explanation is that things when burned combine with oxygen to form an oxide. For example, carbon combines with oxygen to form carbon dioxide, and the red calx of mercury is in fact mercury oxide that, due to the presence of oxygen, is of course heavier than the mercury metal.

30. Sometimes amendments are made even before the paradigm enters into a crisis. "Yet the net result of their experiments was a variety of gas samples and gas properties so elaborate that the phlogiston theory proved increasingly little able to cope with laboratory experience. By the time Lavoisier began his experiments on airs in the early 1770s, there were almost as many versions of the phlogiston theory as there were pneumatic chemists" (Kuhn, 1970, p. 70).

abandoning Newton, J. C. Adam and U. J. J. Leverrier independently explained the misbehaviors as due to the presence of a yet-to-be-discovered planet in the vicinity. This was later confirmed by the observatory in Berlin, with the discovery of the planet Neptune. Newton's paradigm was upheld.[31]

26.5 SUMMARY

According to Kuhn, the notion of a paradigm is central to the understanding of science and its growth. Science takes off from the groping stage once a paradigm is adopted. Under the guidance and constraint of the paradigm science prospers. This is the period of normal science, the constructive and blissful stage. Anomalies will occasionally arise, but they are either ignored or explained away. At this stage they are nonthreatening. However, as anomalies accumulate, the scientific community feels the pressure of a crisis. The taken-for-granted paradigm will be reassessed and reexamined. The scientists will become philosophical and critical. Proposals of new theories will be made and tried. Eventually one of these will be adopted and become a new paradigm.

KEY TERMS INTRODUCED IN THIS CHAPTER

exemplar thesis	paradigm	subparadigm theory	crisis
exemplar	generic theory	normal science	revolution
Weltanschauung thesis	specific theory	puzzle solving	
paradigm thesis	paradigm theory	anomaly	

REFERENCES

Kuhn's own writings: Kuhn (1970) is a reprint of his original *The Structure of Scientific Revolutions* (1962) with an added lengthy postscript, which provides clarifications and minor amendments, especially on the notion of paradigm. Kuhn (1970a) and (1970b) resulted from the famous 1965 debate at London between him and Popper. Kuhn (1974), (1977), and (1983) are later clarifications and defenses of his view. Both Kourany (1987) and Boyd (1991) have representative excerpts from Kuhn's works.

General: Trigg (1973, pp. 99–118), Chalmers (1978, chap. 8), Newton-Smith (1981, chap. V), Oldroyd (1986, pp. 318–327), and Lambert and Brittan (1987, pp. 132–140) all provide good summaries of Kuhn's philosophy.

On incommensurability and internal realism, see Sankey (1997) and Hacking (1983, chaps 5–7).

Critiques of Kuhn: Suppe (1977, pp. 191–221, 633–649) gives a good detailed overview of most of the significant critiques of Kuhn. Scheffler (1982) represents typical counterarguments from the classicists. Further discussions can be found from references under "General."

For my view on the notion of incommensurability, see Hung (1986, 1987, 2006).

---

31. According to Kuhn, paradigm theories are invented only when science enters a crisis. This is not quite true. For instance, the superstring theory that has commanded much interest in recent decades was not proposed in response to a crisis. It was devised to satisfy the desire for a unified theory in fundamental physics.

Chapter 27

Kuhn II: Incommensurability and Relativism

27.1 STAGES OF SCIENTIFIC GROWTH

According to Kuhn, science progresses through the following stages in a sort of spiral: (a) prescience, (b) the emergence of a paradigm, (c) the practice of normal science, (d) the accumulation of anomalies leading to a crisis, (e) the emergence of a new paradigm replacing the old, (f) the practice of normal science under the new paradigm, (g) crisis, and so on.

Pre-science is the period when there are many schools of thought around. Each scientist (or small group of scientists) has her own metaphysics, her own ontology, her own theory, and her own view about the correct way of practicing science. Because of this kind of idiosyncrasy, scientists will tend to make different observations, perform different kinds of experiments, and place different weights on the relevance of experimental data collected. They would even give different interpretations and descriptions of the same phenomenon. They argue, they talk through each other, and they compete. Thus, during this period of prescience, there is little progress for lack of consensus.

Eventually one of the schools, because of its successes, triumphs over the others. It becomes accepted as a paradigm. With the paradigm in place, science progresses at "a steady pace." This is the period of normal science, where scientific knowledge is "collected" and accumulated through study and research under the guidance and constraint of the paradigm. It is a period of accumulation of knowledge, as if the scientist-workers can now proceed to build the great cathedral of science according to an architectural plan (the paradigm). Bit by bit the scientist-workers put the blocks and pillars together, erecting their building, and overcoming occasional difficulties (anomalies) that only cause brief delays. However, when more and more difficulties accumulate, a sense of crisis emerges. A different architectural plan is sought, and finally the old one is replaced. According to Kuhn, since the new architectural plan (the new paradigm) is so different from the old, the half-completed building now has to come down, and work according to the new plan has to start afresh—from scratch. It can be seen that science is cumulative only within a paradigm. The new science under the replacing paradigm cannot be built on the existing edifice. Science starts all over again, from the ground level. This is what Kuhn calls a **scientific revolution**.[1]

The thesis of noncumulation of scientific knowledge *across* paradigms is counterintuitive and difficult to accept. Students of science have all along been taught that scientific knowledge has gradually been built up over the last 2,000 years. We read about the accumulation of inventions and discoveries by the great scientists: inventions such as the telescope, the steam engine, the lightbulb, the telephone, and such discoveries as oxygen, electromagnetism, X-rays, the microbes, new comets and stars, and so on. The exhibits in a museum of science also graphically demonstrate the cumulative character of science. Yet according to Kuhn, each paradigm change brings about a new science that is built on its own foundation, sharing little with the past.

Controversial as it is, Kuhn has good reasons for his claim. Is it not true that modern-day textbooks of chemistry seldom mention the phlogiston theory or any of the results obtained under it? In the preceding two chapters, we reported many results obtained by the phlogistonists: how charcoal is composed of earth and phlogiston, how phlogiston escapes when charcoal is being burned, how phlogiston combines with metal ores resulting in

pure metal, how spirit of wine is composed of water and phlogiston, and how sulfur can be obtained by adding phlogiston to acid of sulfur. Have any of these results ever found their way into our modern-day chemistry textbooks? Are they of any help at all to our chemistry research? Would it matter if these results had never been "discovered"? None seem to be of any relevance to us in this age of the chemical atomic paradigm.

Let me give another example. According to Aristotle, the universe consists of the terrestrial world and the celestial world. The former consists of everything on earth, which is the center of the universe. The latter consists of all the heavenly bodies: the sun, moon, and planets and stars, which move around the earth in circles (or in epicycles according to Ptolemy). Terrestrial objects are made out of the four elements, whereas the celestial objects are made out of the celestial substance, a sort of crystalline material. By nature the four elements move in straight lines toward their natural places of rest, and that is why earthly objects when unsupported fall straight downward. (Fire, however, by nature seeks its natural place upward.) On the other hand, the nature of the celestial substance is such that it necessarily moves in circles. This is a rough sketch of Aristotle's conceptual framework. It was the paradigm underlying Western mechanics until Galileo and Newton, who introduced a new paradigm. It can be seen that, after the Galileo-Newtonian revolution, results obtained under the Aristotelian paradigm have been either denied (for example, that heavier objects fall proportionally faster than lighter objects) or ignored (for instance, that the natural place of water is the center of the earth). Contemporary students of mechanics universally start with Newton's three laws of motion. The once-dominant Aristotle has no place in modern science at all. His results have been reduced to naught.

Let's consider one further example, the paradigm change from Ptolemy's geocentric theory to Copernicus's heliocentric theory. Ptolemy and his

---

1. It is significant that Kuhn called his book *The Structure of Scientific Revolutions*.

followers painstakingly worked out their epicycles to accommodate those thousands and thousands of observational data on the positions of the planets accumulated through the centuries. Where have they all gone now? Few science students, I am sure, have ever heard of the great Ptolemy, let alone his epicycles. None of them have contributed to contemporary astronomy. Hasn't Kuhn proved his point that scientific results are noncumulative across paradigms? Science starts anew with each new paradigm.

Psychology students might like to ponder the change of paradigm from associationism to behaviorism at the beginning of the 20th century. Does this change support Kuhn's claim?

Nevertheless, we somehow do feel that science is cumulative, even across paradigms. At least we feel that all the work done under Newton's mechanics is still useful for the Einsteinian as well as for the quantum physicist. Perhaps experimental and observational data are neutral to paradigms. What a phlogistonist observes and sees in the laboratory is exactly the same as what a chemist observes and sees. If a phlogistonist and a chemist were side by side performing the experiment on the red calx of mercury, they would both record the same data. What would differ would be their *interpretations* of these data, one in terms of phlogiston and the other in terms of oxygen. Lavoisier in his famous Easter Memoir described how he obtained 45 grains of red calx by heating mercury just below its boiling point for 12 days. Then he heated the red calx to a higher temperature and obtained 7 to 8 cubic inches of gas, whereas the 45 grains of red calx turned into metal mercury that weighed only 41.5 grains. These experimental observations seem independent of the phlogiston theory prevailing at the time and also independent of the oxygen and atomic theories later proposed. We can even repeat the experiment today. Our record of the happenings should be similar to that mentioned earlier. It has been claimed that raw data of this sort are independent of

paradigms.[2] Paradigms, theories, and interpretations come and go, yet raw experimental and observational data remain. It is the latter that accumulate. They grow in volume, anti-Kuhnians would say.

Another good example would be the collection and recording of specimens of plants and animals. These collections represent raw facts about the living world. They are of value per se, independent of whether Darwin is right or wrong in his evolutionary explanation of the origin of the species.

Aristotle and Newton, if both were repeating Galileo's "tower experiment" by dropping metal balls of unequal weights from the top of the Leaning Tower of Pisa, would observe the same phenomena (assuming of course that they both are careful observers and both employ the same measuring instruments). For example, Galileo reported that "if an observation is made, the lighter body will, at the beginning of the motion, move ahead of the heavier and will be swifter" (Cohen, 1985, pp. 194–195). Aristotle probably would have experienced exactly the same phenomenon had he cared to observe (instead of speculating).

Again, even though Ptolemy's epicycles are of no value to contemporary astronomy, the raw data collected by him were of great significance to later astronomers like Brahe and Kepler. These records of observed relative positions of the planets in relation to the stars eventually forced Kepler toward his elliptical orbit theory of the planets.

Notwithstanding all this, according to Kuhn, paradigms are incommensurable. There are no such things as neutral raw data independent of paradigms to be recorded. Observations are always theory-laden, as was argued in Chapter 22. Scientists' observational records under a paradigm are inevitably "colored" by the conceptual framework (theory) of the paradigm, so that what they see are data framed by that particular paradigm and that simply would not make sense when viewed from another paradigm. This of course is an extreme

---

2. Take Lavoisier's own words: "Afterwards, having collected all the red particles, formed during the experiment, from the running mercury in which they floated, I found these to amount to 45 grains." This record of happening seems to be independent of the controversy between the phlogiston theory and the oxygen theory. It is just a piece of "raw" datum.

view of the theory-ladenness of perception. Not too many philosophers can swallow it.

Nevertheless Kuhn's arguments are strong. Let's take the jigsaw puzzle analogy again. Under the master plan (paradigm) that the completed picture is going to be a house, one might spend hours putting together pieces forming walls, windows, doors, and so on. Suppose she somehow replaces this master plan with the plan that the picture is going to be a wagon towed by a donkey. Obviously what she has assembled so far has to be thrown out, and the game has to be started afresh (even though part of the "house" can be reused: for example, the round windows can be turned into wheels).

Thus science, according to Kuhn, goes in cycles: paradigm—normal science—crisis—(new) paradigm—revolution—normal science—crisis—(new) paradigm—revolution, and so on. Scientific results are cumulative only during the periods of normal science. After each revolution, science starts from the ground anew.

27.2 INCOMMENSURABILITY

In the last section, we pointed out that normal scientific results obtained within a paradigm have to be relinquished when the paradigm is replaced. The main reason is that paradigms in general are incommensurable. **Incommensurability** is a difficult notion to comprehend as well as a controversial thesis to accept. It was independently proposed by Thomas Kuhn and Paul Feyerabend. The word itself came from the ancient Greeks. Pythagoras demonstrated that the square of the hypotenuse of a right-angled triangle is the sum of the squares of the other two sides. This implies that the diagonal of a unit square, being the square root of 2, is not a rational number.[3] In other words, no matter how small a unit of measurement is chosen, no unit exists such that it will span the diagonal an integral number of times as well as spanning each of the four (equal) sides an integral number of times. Differently put, there is no common measure that will yield a whole number for both the diagonal and each of the sides. The Greeks would say that the diagonal and the sides are incommensurable, while we nowadays say that the ratio between the diagonal and each of the sides is an irrational number. Kuhn and Feyerabend borrowed the term to express their thesis that there is no common measure between paradigms.

I will attempt to explain and make sense of this difficult thesis as well as I can, at times with exaggeration.

A. Paradigms are Constitutive of Nature[4]

(1) Each paradigm imposes its own ontology on scientific thinking. For example, the alchemo-phlogiston theory's ontology consists of the four elements with their (sensual) qualities, whereas the atomic theory's ontology is very different, being the collection of discrete atoms, each with its own distinctive primary qualities and each with its distinctive ways of combining with other atoms. The ontology of Newton consists of absolute time, absolute space, inertial mass, and acceleration-causing forces, whereas the Aristotelian ontology (vaguely) consists of absolute time, directional space,[5] weight, and speed-causing forces.

(2) Each paradigm has its own empirical data: as has been explained in Chapter 22, perception is theory-laden. When presented with a duck-rabbit picture, some would see it as a duck and others would see it as a rabbit. According to Kuhn all perceptions are paradigm-dependent. Phlogistonists would "see" phlogiston leaving burning candles, whereas the atomic scientists would "see" oxygen entering into them. There is no such thing as raw

---

3. A rational number is equivalent to a fraction.

4. This expression is Kuhn's own: Kuhn (1970, p. 110).

5. From, "The Structure of Scientific Revolutions, 2nd Ed." Kuhn, Thomas S. (1970, p. 110) Reprinted with permission from the University of Chicago Press.

data (independent of paradigms) to be collected by the scientists. A person wearing red-tinted glasses would see everything red, whereas someone wearing green-tinted glasses would see everything green, and figuratively speaking, no one can avoid wearing glasses!

Kuhn (1970, pp. 118–129) discusses at length how Aristotle saw constrained falls whereas Galileo saw pendulums when both looked at swinging stones. He denies that the phenomenon under discussion can be described in some neutral language, neutral between Aristotle's and Galileo's paradigms. The observational data of these two (great) scientists are not, as one would have thought, different interpretations of some stable extra-paradigm empirical data. Each person's observations would be *the* only (recognizable) data for him. Each would work on his own data and would neither understand nor recognize the other's. For Kuhn, seeing, understanding, and recognizing are all done within some paradigm. It is impossible for someone working within one paradigm to understand data obtained via another paradigm—that is, unless he leaves his own and takes on the other instead.[6]

(3) Each paradigm has its own facts: let's for the sake of explanation employ the jargon of the logical positivists. If "observational facts" are paradigm-dependent, "theoretical facts" should be even more so. From this, we can conclude that *all* facts are paradigm-dependent. Thus scientists subscribing to different paradigms live in "different worlds."[7] Kuhn puts it as follows:

> Led by a new paradigm, scientists adopt new instruments and look in new places. Even more important, during revolutions scientists see new and different things when

looking with familiar instruments in places they have looked before. It is rather as if the professional community had been suddenly transported to another planet where familiar objects are seen in a different light and are joined by unfamiliar ones as well.[8]

Kuhn denies the correspondence theory[9] of truth: "There is, I think, no theory-independent way to reconstruct phrases like 'really there'; the notion of a match between ontology of a theory and its "real" counterpart in nature now seems to me illusive in principle" (1970, p. 206). According to Kuhn, facts—that is, what makes statements true—are partly determined by the mind (theories). This line of thinking came from the great philosopher Kant (1724–1804), who developed it into a full philosophical system. That's why Kuhn's philosophy has been dubbed neo-Kantianism. An alternative label for it is 'constructivism.' We will have an opportunity to study this interesting topic in detail in Chapter 31.

This is the first thesis of incommensurability: paradigms do not share any facts in common.

B. Paradigms are Constitutive of Science[10]

As we have seen in Section 26.3, each paradigm defines its own type of normal science:

(i) Each paradigm poses its own fact-finding problems. For example, the alchemo-phlogiston theory asks: What sort of weight does phlogiston have? The chemical atomic theory asks: What is the atomic weight of oxygen?

---

6. This sort of situation is parallel to the original meaning of 'Verstehen': one can only understand the other person's feelings and thoughts if one "steps into the other person's shoes."

7. From, "The Structure of Scientific Revolutions, 2nd Ed." Kuhn, Thomas S. (1970, p. 150) Reprinted with permission from the University of Chicago Press.

8. From, "The Structure of Scientific Revolutions, 2nd Ed." Kuhn, Thomas S. (1970, p. 111) Reprinted with permission from the University of Chicago Press.

9. See Section 18.3.

10. This expression is Kuhn's: Kuhn (1970, p. 110).

(ii) Each paradigm asks for its own kind of supporting facts. For example, the heliocentric theory asks for the confirmation of the annual parallax.

(iii) Each paradigm inspires work for its own articulation. For example, Newton's gravitational theories require the determination of the value of the gravitational constant.

(iv) Each paradigm poses its own theoretical problems. For example, Newton's theory requires the solution of the many-body problem.

(v) Each paradigm prescribes its own methodology.

Thus it can be seen that each paradigm defines its own problem field. Each paradigm also has its own standard of solution. Kuhn puts it thus:

> In the first place, the proponents of competing paradigms will often disagree about the list of problems that any candidate for paradigm must resolve. Their standards or their definitions of science are not the same. Must a theory of motion explain the cause of the attractive forces between particles of matter or may it simply note the existence of such forces? Newton's dynamics was widely rejected because, unlike both Aristotle's and Descartes's theories, it implied the latter answer to the question. When Newton's theory had been accepted, a question was therefore banished from science. That question, however, was one that general relativity may proudly claim to have solved.[11]

Another case that Kuhn has in mind is the fortunes of Maxwell's electromagnetic theory of light. Initially it was widely rejected simply because it did not provide a medium to support these electromagnetic waves. Later, when this theory achieved the status of a paradigm, the attitude of the scientific community changed.[12]

Since scientists belonging to competing paradigms "disagree about what is a problem and what is a solution, they will inevitably talk through each other when debating the relative merits of their respective paradigms."[13]

This is the second thesis of incommensurability: Paradigms do not share any of their problems and their standards of solution.

C. Paradigms are Constitutive of Meaning

It is not uncommon to find terms shared by the old and new paradigm. It might be thought that this would provide common grounds for the two paradigms, thus resulting in commensurability. Kuhn, however, argues that this is an illusion. The terms shared, though typographically the same, are not in fact identical terms for they have different meaning. Take for example the case of the alchemo-phlogiston theory versus the chemical atomic theory. They both employ the term 'element,' yet they mean different things. In APT, 'element' means air, earth, water, and fire (phlogiston), which are characterized by their sensual qualities, whereas in CAT it means the chemical elements such as oxygen, which combine in terms of atoms to form molecules. Kuhn would deny that 'element' means simply 'fundamental building block,' so that its meaning might be shared by both theories.

Another example is the case of 'space' and 'time' shared by Newton's mechanics and Einstein's relativity. However, Kuhn thinks that the two terms mean quite different things in the two theories. For the Newtonian space is necessarily flat, homogeneous, isotropic, and unaffected by the presence of matter. Yet Einstein declared that space is curved, and its curvature is dependent on

---

11. From, "The Structure of Scientific Revolutions, 2nd Ed." Kuhn, Thomas S. (1970, p. 148) Reprinted with permission from the University of Chicago Press.

12. From, "The Structure of Scientific Revolutions, 2nd Ed." Kuhn, Thomas S. (1970, p. 107) Reprinted with permission from the University of Chicago Press.

13. From, "The Structure of Scientific Revolutions, 2nd Ed." Kuhn, Thomas S. (1970, p. 109) Reprinted with permission from the University of Chicago Press.

the distribution of matter in space.[14] Again, part of what the geocentric theorists meant by 'earth' is fixed position. Hence they could not understand how the earth could move, as Copernicus argued.[15]

The philosophy behind this assertion is that many or even all of the principles of a paradigm theory contribute to the meaning of the terms of that theory. Since the principles of APT differ (drastically) from those of CAT, the term 'element' has different meaning in each. The same applies to 'space,' 'time,' and 'earth.'

Not only does the meaning of the "theoretical" terms depend on its paradigm, but Kuhn claims that the meaning of the "observational" terms also depends on the paradigm under which the observations are made. The reason is that all observations are theory-laden (Chapter 22). A geocentric theorist and a heliocentric theorist may both report: "An apple has fallen down," but they would mean different things by 'down.' Similarly a Newtonian and an Einsteinian would not mean the same thing when they both say: "That stone is moving in a straight line."

This is the third thesis of incommensurability: paradigms do not share any terms (with the same meaning) in common.[16]

D. Paradigms are Constitutive of Subject Matter of Discourse

Statements made under different paradigms are about different things. There is no common subject matter between discourses under different paradigms.

Let's consider the following pair of statements:

(1) A quantity of caloric fluid is flowing toward the end of the bar.

(2) Waves of molecular vibrations are traveling toward the end of the bar.

According to the thesis of incommensurability, these two statements are about different events comparable to:

(3) People are running down the street.

(4) Rocks are rolling down the street.

There is no neutral statement that can mediate between (1) and (2) such as:

(5) The temperatures of the two ends of the bar are equalizing.

Most of us would take (5) as the actual record of what is observed and (1) and (2) as mere interpretations, which are incompatible (that is, both can be wrong but both can't be right). Statement (5) plays a mediating role between the two, being the common measure for evaluation of the two competing interpretations. However, according to Kuhn, (1), (2), and (5) are all on the same level. They are all about different subject matter and each is embedded in its own paradigm. There are simply no paradigm-free statements.

At best we can say that (1) and (2) are *corresponding*[17] statements, whereas (3) and (4) are not necessarily so. But other than corresponding to each other they are about different things altogether. In fact, not only do (1) and (2) have nothing in common, they have nothing in common with (5) either. The idea of incommensurability is not that of incompatibility. The latter implies comparability, whereas the former implies the absence of common ground to compare. Let's consider two more statements.

(6) The sun is setting in the west.

(7) The earth is spinning eastward.

Again it is claimed that the two are about different things—different events. But what about (8)?

15. Kuhn (1970, p. 149).

16. This is a strong interpretation of Kuhn. A weaker interpretation is that only some of the terms of competing paradigms differ in meaning. This third thesis of incommensurability is sometimes known as semantic incommensurability. See Kuhn (1983).

17. They are corresponding in the sense that they are usually evoked by the same type of stimulus.

(8) The observed relative distance between the sun and the horizon is diminishing.

It might be suggested that (8) represents a sort of uninterpreted observation on which (6) and (7) are based. Perhaps scientific data can be reduced to statements such as (8), which can then serve as common ground between paradigms.

Remember that Kuhn meant to start a revolution with his paradigm view, and the revolution was directed toward the classical tradition: the logical positivists and Popper. You may recall how the early logical positivists tried to found scientific statements on sense-datum language (phenomenalism) and later on physicalistic language (physicalism), and how they failed (Section 23.3). Kuhn thinks that his paradigm view, being a Kantian thesis, is able to rectify his predecessors' mistakes. To admit that (8) represents the raw datum of observation whereas (6) and (7) only represent interpretations is to return to the classical tradition. According to Kuhn, (6), (7), and (8) are each in its own paradigm, and each is about a different subject matter. Statement (8) cannot serve as a common ground for the assessment of (6) and (7).[18]

This is the fourth thesis of incommensurability: paradigms do not share statements in common, nor do they share subject matter.

27.3 RELATIVISM

These four theses of incommensurability are strong assertions indeed. It can be seen that together they pave the way to relativism. Let me summarize the four theses here.

A. Paradigms do not share facts in common. Scientists belonging to different paradigms live in "different worlds."

B. Paradigms do not share problems or standards of solution.

C. Paradigms do not share terms (with the same meaning).

D. Paradigms do not share statements or subject matter.

From these four theses, we can picture scientists of different paradigms living on different "planets," solving different problems, providing solutions in their own idiosyncratic terms, and describing and recording them in their own languages. It is doubtful whether they are all practicing the same "trade," namely science. If they are all practicing science,

(i) Can they communicate with each other? Do they want to communicate with each other? What is the point of them communicating with each other? (given that they are interested in different facts and different problems and employ different standards to measure their solutions).

(ii) Are there any objective criteria to assess these scientific practices? Are some of the practices better than others? Are some more commendable? Do these practices share the same goal anyway? Can we provide objective measures of the efficacy of these practices toward the achievements of their goals?

It can be seen that a negative answer to (i) amounts to what might be called **de facto relativism** and a negative answer to (ii) amounts to what might be called **de jure relativism**.[19] A logical consequence of relativism can be seen to be: Anything goes (to use Paul Feyerabend's celebrated phrase).

But relativism as such seems both counterintuitive and disastrous. It borders on irrationality.

At one stage, Kuhn seems to be embracing relativism. He describes scientists' change from one paradigm to another as (religious) *conversion*. To induce such a change, *persuasion*, rather than proof, is in order. And the actual "transition between competing paradigms cannot be made a step at a time, forced by logic and neutral experience. Like the *gestalt switch*, it must occur all

---

18. See Chapter 31 (on constructivism) for further discussion in this area.

19. "De facto" means "in fact, in reality, as a matter of fact." "De jure" means "according to law, by rights; opposed to 'de facto.'"

at once (though not necessarily in an instant) or not at all."[20] For Kuhn, it is not unreasonable to stick to the old paradigm. In fact, many prominent scientists such as Priestley and Lord Kelvin never got converted. And Kuhn quotes Max Planck, the great quantum physicist, as saying that "a new scientific truth does not triumph by convincing its opponents and making them see the light, but rather because its opponents eventually die, and a new generation grows up that is familiar with it."[21]

Nevertheless, Kuhn has made it obvious that he does not want to be associated with relativism. He denounces relativism again and again.

First, about de facto relativism. He thinks that members of different scientific communities (working in different paradigms) can communicate. (Of course, factually they do communicate.) The way they do it is through translation. Here, by 'translation,' Kuhn does not mean 'translation of sentences from one language to another, preserving meaning' as we ordinarily presume. Here is how he puts it:

> Each may, that is, try to discover what the other would see and say when presented with a stimulus to which his own verbal response would be different. If they can sufficiently refrain from explaining anomalous behavior as the consequence of mere error or madness, they may in time become very good predictors of each other's behavior. Each will have learned to translate the other's theory and its consequences into his own language and

simultaneously to describe in his language the world to which that theory applies. That is what the historian of science regularly does (or should) when dealing with out-of-date scientific theories.[22]

This seems to be the best that Kuhn can do to explain how communication is possible between paradigms, and how we need not subscribe to de facto relativism.[23]

Second, Kuhn is more forthcoming about de jure relativism. He thinks that there are transparadigmatic criteria and values for the assessment of paradigms. These criteria and values are thought to be neutral between paradigms, and thus can serve as arbitrators between paradigms:

(i) Problem-solving ability; How many problems can the paradigm solve? Can it solve those that have led the old one to a crisis?[24]

(ii) Quantitative precision: Does the paradigm yield quantitatively more precise explanation and prediction?[25]

(iii) Predictive power: Does the paradigm yield unsuspected (and therefore surprising) predictions?[26]

(iv) Consistency: Is the paradigm theory consistent, internally and externally?

(v) Simplicity: How simple is the paradigm theory?[27]

(vi) Aesthetics: Is the paradigm "beautiful"? Does it provide solutions neater than the old one?[28]

---

20. Kuhn (1970, p. 150), my italics.

21. Kuhn (1970, p. 151).

22. Kuhn (1970, p. 202). I apologize for not attempting to present his notion of translation in my own words, for I doubt if I can make it clearer.

23. A similar passage to show the possibility of communication between paradigms can be found in Kuhn (1970b, p. 277).

24. Kuhn (1970, p. 153; 1970b, p. 264).

25. Kuhn (1970, pp. 153–154, 199; 1970b, p. 264).

26. Kuhn (1970, p. 154).

27. Kuhn (1970, p. 199; 1970b, p. 262).

28. Kuhn (1970, p. 155).

(vii) Future promise: Does the paradigm show promise in solving further problems? Is it going to be fruitful?[29]

Kuhn has pictured paradigms as all-embracing, ruling and dictating every aspect of scientific practice. Philosophers are understandably worried: that paradigms dictate their own values and standards so much so that each paradigm, based on its own values and standards, can circularly justify its own correctness and desirability. To dispel this misconception Kuhn explicitly denies that he is a relativist. He argues that in spite of the "dictatorship" of paradigms, there are transparadigmatic criteria to act as controls. These criteria are independent of paradigms. They are objective measures of the goodness of paradigms so that (a) the preference of one paradigm over another is not a matter of subjective "taste" or irrationality and (b) these criteria can provide practical guides for the choice between competing paradigms. Because of the existence of such objective criteria, there is no need to embrace relativism even though paradigms do, to an extent, control the thoughts and practices of the scientists.[30]

Nonetheless, Kuhn warns that these criteria fall far short of providing anything like an algorithm for theory choice. There is no proof (in the mathematical or logical sense) to demonstrate step by step that one paradigm is better than another. These seven criteria serve as maxims rather than formal rules. Maxims can be vague and even conflicting in their advice. To quote Kuhn, "[c]ontrast 'He who hesitates is lost' with 'Look before you leap,' or compare 'Many hands make light work' with 'Too many cooks spoil the broth.'"[31] Even though these seven criteria (and values) are all desirable, the weight to be assigned to them can vary from scientist to scientist, and the assignment of weights can vary from circumstance to circumstance. It is therefore not surprising that scientists on opposite sides of the paradigm divide can both claim rationality, because, according to Kuhn, there is no hard-and-fast rule legislating the assignment of weight to these values and criteria. For instance, it is rational to assign more weight to problem-solving ability than simplicity, and it is also rational to reverse the weighting.[32] Furthermore, some of these seven notions—such as simplicity—are vague and imprecise.

Having said these things, Kuhn does embrace a sort of relativism with respect to truth. For him there is no truth in the absolute sense. It is not that there is something real "out there" with its properties and characteristics all determinate and definite for the scientist to capture and portray. Commonly we think that a scientific theory is true if it duplicates the "shape" of reality. A theory is to be judged like a portrait: the more similar the portrait is to the real person, the better the painting. This is the traditional correspondence theory of truth (Section 18.3). Kuhn, following Kant, denies this. For Kuhn, the notion of truth has no role to play in the assessment of theories. A fortiori, the notion of verisimilitude (from Popper) is not applicable either (Section 24.8). If truth or verisimilitude is not applicable, how do we know we are practicing science in the right direction? How do we know that we are making progress?

Kuhn's answer is his evolutionary theory of scientific development.[33]

According to Darwin's theory of evolution, species do not develop toward a set goal. There is no goal to pursue. Yet through natural mutation and natural selection the world of living things progresses. Natural mutation is a productive process:

---

29. Kuhn (1970, pp. 158, 199, 262; 1977, pp. 321–322) lists and discusses in some detail five desirable values for theories: accuracy, consistency, scope, simplicity, and fruitfulness.

30. Philosophers often use the terms 'value,' 'standard,' and 'criterion' interchangeably, which leads to confusion. I will adopt the term 'standard' when I talk about paradigm-dependent standards and will use 'value' and 'criterion' in trans-paradigmatic contexts, following Kuhn's practice.

31. Kuhn (1977, p. 330).

32. Kuhn (1970b, pp. 260–264; 1977, chap. 13).

33. Popper before Kuhn also borrowed the evolution model in his description of science.

new characteristics are produced by chance. Natural selection is an eliminative process: what does not fit into the environment gets eliminated. Thus through natural mutation and natural selection, more fit species are produced and preserved at the expense of the unfit. The result is progress.

Kuhn thinks that a similar process occurs in science. There is no set goal for science. There is no objective reality for science to model. Truth is not a goal of science, for 'truth,' as traditionally understood, does not make sense. Science should not be understood as an enterprise to produce theories approximating the truth. Nonetheless, science does progress. It progresses in the evolutionary sense. The "unfit" paradigms get eliminated through competition. New paradigms are produced, not by natural mutation though, but by clever scientists.[34] Kuhn claims that, given two paradigms that share the same lineage, it is possible to tell which is older and which is more recent, hence "better." (Those seven criteria, presumably, will enable us to make the differentiation.) Thus Kuhn declares: "For me, therefore, scientific development is, like biological evolution, unidirectional and irreversible. One scientific theory is not as good as another for doing what scientists normally do. In that sense I am not a relativist."[35]

27.4 COMPARISON WITH THE CLASSICAL TRADITION

For Kuhn the logical positivists err in taking theories as axiomatic systems composed of internal principles and bridge principles. That sort of conception gives rise to the problem of the OT-link (Section 23.4) and the problem of the SS-link (Section 24.9). Kuhn proposes an alternative, namely his exemplar thesis (Section 26.1).

The logical positivists conceive science as cumulative: the replaced theories are reduced (and thus absorbed) into the replacing theory. For example, they take Newton's theory as being reduced to Einstein's theory. Kuhn thinks that the relation is a matter of replacement and displacement, not replacement and absorption.

Kuhn's paradigm view was proposed as a reaction to Popper's falsificationism. Let's therefore make a more detailed comparison.

A. For Popper the characteristic of science is that its statements are falsifiable. Thus Popper sees critical discussion as the heart of science. However, according to Kuhn, "In a sense, to turn Sir Karl's view on its head, it is precisely the abandonment of critical discourse that marks the transition to a science."[36] Kuhn illustrates his assertion with an example. Astrology is not a science, not because it is unfalsifiable, not because its statements are vague, and not because of the way its practitioners explained away its failures as Popper claims. Similar practices occur in both medicine and meteorology. The reason astrology is not a science, according to Kuhn, is that astrology does not provide normal science: it does not yield research puzzles to solve. With no such puzzles to solve there is no science. "To rely on testing as the mark of a science is to miss what scientists mostly do and, with it, the most characteristic feature of their enterprise [namely, puzzle-solving normal science]."[37]

B. Kuhn does concede that testing (resulting in falsification or confirmation) is part of the activities in science. But they occur only in normal science (Section 26.3). What are being tested are subparadigm theories (Section 26.2). The paradigm theories are not as a matter of fact subjected to tests. They are held as sacrosanct for scientists. The reason (occasionally) paradigm theories are given up is due

---

34. Paul Feyerabend's theoretical pluralism would produce exactly the kind of theoretic mutation that Kuhn's evolutionary model of scientific development requires.

35. Kuhn (1970b, p. 264). Lambert and Brittan (1987, pp. 166–170) provides a good introduction.

36. Kuhn (1970a, p. 6). 'Sir Karl' refers to Popper.

37. Kuhn (1970a, p. 10).

to an accumulation of anomalies. But, as Kuhn carefully points out, the anomalies do not amount to a refutation of the paradigm theories. On the one hand, Popper names the overthrow of the phlogiston theory, Aristotle's mechanics, Newton's mechanics, and so on as typical cases of falsification. We can fairly say that Popper is a professional revolutionary: his war cry is "Overthrow!" On the other hand, Kuhn is a conservative: his advice is "Status quo." However, Kuhn does allow for occasional revolutions, but these revolutions are forced on the scientists as a consequence of circumstances, and it is certainly not Kuhn's advice to overthrow paradigm theories as part of routine science. Constant revolutions are neither factually the case, nor are they methodologically advisable. If Kuhn's scientist is a revolutionary, she is a reluctant one.[38]

Let me illustrate. Dalton hypothesized that water is HO (not H_2O), ammonia is NH, ethylene is CH, and methane is CH_2. These hypotheses all proved wrong. However, what was considered refuted were these four subparadigm theories, not the paradigm theory of atomic theory.

Ptolemy's suggested epicycles for the planets were proved wrong again and again. Nevertheless, no one considered these as falsifications of the paradigm theory of geocentricism. Even Copernicus's new theory was proposed as a *possible* alternative, not as a replacement of a falsified theory. Anyway, for the 1,300 years between Ptolemy and Copernicus, few thought of the possibility that the geocentric theory could be false.

You can see that falsification (in the logical sense) does not occur at the level that interests Popper, the level of paradigm theories, exemplified by Newton's mechanics, relativity, and quantum mechanics. Ironically it does occur in normal science, which, however, plays no role in Popper's

methodology. In normal science, subparadigm theories are proposed and tested as a matter of routine.[39]

C. The growth of science. Popper describes the growth of science as the replacement of one (falsified) theory with another theory of greater content and greater verisimilitude. Hence in this sense science is cumulative. Kuhn thinks that science is cumulative in the periods of normal science, which are occasionally interrupted by revolutions. After each revolution, science starts afresh (under a new paradigm). According to Kuhn, history supports his description of scientific growth.

Since Kuhn, the history of science has taken on a more and more significant role in the adjudication of the rights and wrongs of philosophers in their theories of science. We will see more of this in the chapters on Lakatos and Laudan (Chapters 28–30).

27.5 CRITIQUE OF KUHN

A. Kuhn's theses have provoked strong criticisms from various quarters. Here is a summary.

We have seen how Kuhn's thesis of incommensurability asserts that paradigms determine their own facts, that there is no objective truth, and that paradigms determine their own problem field as well as standards of solution. All these ideas are highly counterintuitive and contrary to common sense. Kuhn's thesis has thus attracted loads of critics. That's why Kuhn was quick to distance himself from relativism.

Not everyone is scared of being labeled a relativist though. Paul Feyerabend was probably the most outspoken philosopher championing the virtues of relativism. In *Against Method* (1975), he argues convincingly for a relativistic methodology,

---

38. "[Popper] and his group argue that the scientist should try at all times to be a critic and a proliferator of alternate theories. I urge the desirability of an alternate strategy which reserves such behavior for special occasions," Kuhn (1970b, p. 243).

39. "Sir Karl [Popper] has erred by transferring selected characteristics of everyday research to the occasional revolutionary episodes in which scientific advance is most obvious and by thereafter ignoring the everyday enterprise entirely. In particular, he has sought to solve the problem of theory choice during revolutions by logical criteria that are applicable in full only when a theory can already be presupposed," Kuhn (1970a, p. 19). The contrast and difference between himself and Popper was vividly put in Kuhn (1970a); the present paragraph is based on pp. 4–6 of that essay.

and concludes that the method of science is no method—that is, "Anything goes." His philosophy is often labeled anarchism or pluralism. Whether correct or not, this philosophy of Feyerabend's is certainly interesting and thought provoking. Unfortunately space limitations do not allow us to pursue it further.

At the other extreme, Israel Scheffler in his *Science and Subjectivity* (1982) condemns almost every aspect of Kuhn's thesis, defending common-sense objectivity and the classical tradition. For instance, he argues that even though a paradigm theory may act as a classification or categorization system, it should not affect our perception of nature, and it certainly cannot generate its own facts. A classification system may have categories such as 'chair,' 'cheese,' 'cherry,' and 'chimney' for the purpose of sorting objects. But these categories by themselves are neither true nor false, and they certainly would not determine whether there are any objects falling within these categories. They should not influence our observational judgments either. For instance, we would not be seeing tables as chairs, or mistaking chalk for cheese, simply because we have the terms 'chair' and 'cheese' for classification. No categories are able to generate or annihilate reality. Thus it is wrong for Kuhn to claim that paradigms are constitutive of nature, so Scheffler argues.[40]

B. Kuhn's thesis that paradigms are constitutive of meaning has provoked strong reactions. There are two possible interpretations of this thesis:

(a) *All* formulas, principles, and exemplars of a paradigm theory contribute to the meaning of *all* the terms. Hence any change in formulas, principles, and exemplars will lead to a change in meaning of all the terms. This is the strong interpretation.

(b) *Some* formulas, principles, and exemplars of a paradigm theory contribute to the meaning of *some* of the terms. Hence changes in some formulas, principles, and exemplars will lead to

a change of meaning of some of the terms. This is the weak interpretation.

How are we to choose between the two? Shall we say the one that agrees with actual scientific practice should be adopted? How do we find out which agrees with scientific practice? The meaning of 'meaning' is so elusive. Has the meaning of 'element' changed after Dalton's atomic theory took over from the alchemo-phlogiston theory? Is the meaning of 'mass' the same between Newton's mechanics and Einstein's? Does Einstein use the term 'simultaneous' differently from the way we use it? It's no good to argue from intuition. What we need is a solid, criticizable, and detailed theory of meaning that can give us the required measures. Kuhn, and indeed his critics as well, are terribly vague about meaning. Kuhn certainly gives a large number of examples trying to illustrate how exemplars can link words to nature. But these are examples only. At best they provide prima facie evidence for a possible theory of meaning based on exemplars. But this is still a long way from a theory of meaning worthy of that name. A similar criticism can be directed at Wittgenstein's theory that the meaning of a linguistic expression is a function of its use. Until this 'function' is spelled out, his theory is too qualitative to serve as an arbitrator of quarrels over the issue of meaning change.

Ironically, it was the logical positivists who attempted to produce rigorous theories of meaning in terms of detailed accounts of correspondence rules: operational definitions, reduction sentences, and so on. The further irony is that these theories were "shot down" because, being detailed and rigorous, they provided a big and easy target.

Wittgenstein was responsible for two philosophical schools of thought: ideal language philosophy and ordinary language philosophy. Logical positivism belongs to the first, whereas Kuhn's exemplar thesis belongs to the second. They are complementary rather than competing. Exemplars serve to explain how ordinary language develops its meaning and

---

40. Scheffler (1982, pp. 37–42).

how it is learned. The exemplar theory is essentially a psychological and sociological thesis. On the other hand, the axiomatic theory of theories is meant to be a logical analysis of a rather elusive socio-psychological product. It is meant to be a logical reconstruction. The virtue of such a reconstruction is that it is explicit and rigorously worked out in all its details. As such it is available for discussion and scrutiny. Unfortunately the axiomatic conception of theories failed to pass the "test."

C. Another common criticism of Kuhn is that the distinction between 'generic theory' (that is, 'paradigm theory') and 'specific theory' (that is, sub-paradigm theory) is vague. It seems that the typical generic theories are: Aristotle's mechanics, Newton's mechanics, the theory of relativity, quantum mechanics, the alchemo-phlogiston theory, and chemical atomic theory. But what about the caloric theory, the kinetic theory of heat, Newton's corpuscular theory of light, the wave theory of light, uniformitarianism, plate tectonic theory, the geocentric theory, the heliocentric theory, Harvey's theory of the circulation of blood, Franklin's fluid theory of electricity, and Darwin's theory of evolution? Is the thesis of incommensurability applicable to all of these? Intuitively incommensurability applies best to the transition between Newton's mechanics and the theory of relativity on the one hand, and between Newton's mechanics and the theory of quantum mechanics on the other. Can these model cases of incommensurability be extended to cover other transitions; say between Newton's corpuscular theory and Huygens-Young-Fresnel's wave theory? Between Ptolemy's geocentric theory and Copernicus's heliocentric theory? I doubt it very much.

D. One can see that Kuhn's evolutionary model of scientific progress belongs to **naturalistic epistemology**, which has been criticized as being viciously circular.[41] Let me explain.

The model assumes the correctness of Darwin's theory of evolution (and that this theory can be adapted to the field of science). Now Darwin's theory is a scientific theory. Like any other scientific theory, it is in need of justification and assessment. How do we know that it is good? In particular, how do we know that it is better than its predecessors? According to the evolutionary model of scientific development, since Darwin's theory displaced its predecessors as a matter of fact, *according to Darwin's theory* (adapted to science) it must be a better theory. I think there is at least a prima facie circle here.

Darwin's theory assumes the later theory is always more progressive, as a matter of definition. Hence history will tell us which theory is better. I think this sounds too simplistic. The seven criteria proposed earlier sound better and more appropriate. However, they themselves require justification. Why these seven criteria? Why should they be accepted as measures of goodness?

Perhaps the evolutionary model can be amalgamated with the theory of seven criteria. Nature is such that it selects the better ones according to the seven criteria. If so, the seven criteria would provide a sort of theoretical justification for the assertion that every theory is better than its predecessors. Of course we have to justify why nature works in accordance with the seven criteria, and why the seven criteria are measures of goodness. And what is goodness if it is not meant to be "closer to the truth"? I suppose we can join the camp of pragmatism. We can assume that what is good is what enables the human species to survive and multiply and argue that the seven criteria have survival value for the human race. Thus progress (moving toward the better) is to be measured by the enhancement of conditions of survival.

E. Is Kuhn's paradigm view of science prescriptive or descriptive? Is he merely describing how science as a matter of fact develops? Or is he prescribing how science should develop (in doing so recommending a methodology by which to practice science)? Are normal scientific practices commendable? When anomalies occur, should scientists ignore

---

41. For reference, see Shimony and Nails (1987).

them, tinker with auxiliary hypotheses, or change some of the subparadigm theories, always leaving the paradigm theory alone? On the other hand, should they search for a new paradigm theory? Here is Kuhn's answer:

> Are Kuhn's remarks about scientific development ... to be read as descriptions or prescriptions? The answer, of course, is that they should be read in both ways at once. If I have a theory of how and why science works, it must necessarily have implications for the way in which scientists should behave if their enterprise is to flourish. The structure of my argument is simple and, I think, unexceptionable: scientists behave in the following ways; those modes of behavior have ... the following essential functions; in the absence of an alternate mode *that would serve similar junctions*, scientists should behave essentially as they do if their concern is to improve scientific knowledge.[42]

Notwithstanding these criticisms, Kuhn's theory has had a tremendous impact in the philosophy of science. It was instrumental in dislodging the classical tradition from the central stage. Indeed, its influence has spread far and beyond: well into fields such as general philosophy, psychology, sociology, education, and the historiography of science. A Kuhnian revolution has taken place.

KEY TERMS INTRODUCED IN THIS CHAPTER

scientific revolution

incommensurability

de facto relativism

de jure relativism

naturalistic epistemology

REFERENCES

Kuhn's own writings: Kuhn (1970) is a reprint of his original *The Structure of Scientific Revolutions* (1962) with an added lengthy postscript, which provides clarifications and minor amendments, especially on the notion of paradigm. Kuhn (1970a) and (1970b) resulted from the famous 1965 debate at London between him and Popper. Kuhn (1974), (1977), and (1983) are later clarifications and defenses of his view. Both Kourany (1987) and Boyd (1991) have representative excerpts from Kuhn's works.

General: Trigg (1973, pp. 99–118), Chalmers (1978, chap. 8), Newton-Smith (1981, chap. V), Oldroyd (1986, pp. 318–327), and Lambert and Brittan (1987, pp. 132–140) all provide good summaries of Kuhn's philosophy.

On incommensurability and internal realism, see Sankey (1997) and Hacking (1983, chaps. 5–7).

Critiques of Kuhn: Suppe (1977, pp. 191–221, 633–649) gives a good detailed overview of most of the significant critiques of Kuhn. Scheffler (1982) represents typical counterarguments from the classicists. Further discussions can be found from references under "General".

For my view on the notion of incommensurability, see Hung (1986, 1987, 2006).

---

42. Kuhn (1970b, p. 237).

PART VIII

Toward History, Sociology, and Artificial Intelligence

INTRODUCTION

Since Kuhn's introduction of the paradigm view, the philosophy of science in the Anglo-American world has taken a sharp turn. The classical tradition, which ruled for the larger part of the 20th century, has given way to a new way of thinking. The logical approach has been replaced by various historical, psychological, and sociological approaches. No longer are scientific theories taken as finished products to be studied "architecturally" (logically). The "new wave" takes science as a dynamic process powered by humans in their socio-psychological complexities. Scientific theories are viewed as historical and/or social products that can be understood and assessed only in the context of history. This is the era of post-positivism.

Part VIII starts with Lakatos, who attempts to strike a compromise between Popper, the traditionalist, and Kuhn, the reformist. No longer are theories to be assessed in isolation. They are to be evaluated only in their historical contexts. Kuhn's paradigms are reformulated as research programs (**Chapter 28**). Laudan is another prominent historicist, whose eclectic approach is an attempt to supersede his predecessors through the selective integration and modification of Kuhn, Lakatos, and the classical tradition. Corresponding to Lakatos's 'research program,' Laudan introduces the notion of research tradition (**Chapter 29**).

According to the classical tradition, the context of discovery and the context of justification are sharply distinct. The study of discovery, unlike the study of justification, belongs not to the philosophy of science but to history and psychology. Since Kuhn, however, this dichotomy of the two contexts has been generally relinquished. For Lakatos and Laudan, the relationship between the history of science and the philosophy of science is intimate. They are so interlocked that each can only be understood correctly in terms of the other (**Chapter 30**).

Kuhn's alleged relativism takes on a strong form in the hands of the sociologists. Knowledge is viewed as a social phenomenon. Scientific truths are relative to their social milieu both in their origin and in their acceptance. The sociology of science, as a study of the subject science, thus contrasts sharply with the logic of science as practiced by the classical tradition (**Chapter 30**).

Realism, as you may recall, has been attacked by empiricists such as van Fraassen and Laudan (**Chapter 18**). Their arguments are based on the underdetermination of scientific theories by empirical data. The Weltanschauung thesis of Kuhn attacks realism from yet another angle. This new antirealism is known as neo-Kantianism or constructivism (**Chapter 31**).

Just as Kuhn's paradigm view has brought about a revolution in the philosophy of science, so will artificial intelligence in the near future. The book therefore ends with a chapter on the interrelationship between AI and philosophy of science, and the mechanization of scientific creativity (**Chapter 32**). Are scientists replaceable by robots?

Chapter 28

Lakatos: The Revisionist Popperian

28.1 INTRODUCTION

Imre Lakatos (1922–1974) was a great admirer of Popper's philosophy. In 1960, he joined Popper at the London School of Economics, where he taught until his premature death. This chapter is mainly on his contribution to the methodology of science: how he attempted to graft the revolutionary ideas of Kuhn onto the Popperian tree, representing a sort of compromise and synthesis.

You may recall how Kuhn's book *The Structure of Scientific Revolutions* caused a stir in the philosophy of science community when it was first published in 1962. The book was a challenge to the classical tradition: to logical positivism and Popper's falsificationism. In 1965, the philosophers of the London School of Economics (with others) organized an international colloquium at Bedford College, London, to which Kuhn was invited to debate with the Popperians. As conference secretary, Lakatos edited three volumes of conference proceedings, the last of which, titled *Criticism and the Growth of Knowledge*, was devoted to that historic debate.[1] Needless to say, this book contains many important papers, including two by Kuhn and one by Popper. Ironically, the main contributor to the fame of this book is someone who did not participate in the debate, having been too involved in organizing the conference. That someone was Lakatos. His paper "Falsification and the Methodology of Scientific Research Programmes," finished in 1969, was an attempt to reconcile Kuhn and Popper

---

1. Alan Musgrave was a co-editor of this last volume.

through what he termed "Methodology of Scientific Research Programmes." Let's see what this methodology is all about.

28.2 POPPERIANISM TRIMMED

A. You may recall from Chapter 24 how Popper builds his philosophy on the notion of falsification. For instance, Popper thinks that science advances, not through a process of accumulation, but rather through the elimination of inadequate and/or incorrect theories through deductive falsification. However, according to the Duhem-Quine thesis, strictly speaking, no theory is ever falsifiable. Popper's ingenious device—his thesis on ad hoc modification—helps to salvage the situation to a certain extent. Nevertheless, the general opinion is that Popper's falsificationism is seriously defective. It was against this background that Lakatos entered the scene.

Lakatos proposes the following modified notion of falsification:

> [A] scientific theory T [is] falsified if and only if another theory T' has been proposed with the following characteristics: (1) T' has excess empirical content over T: that is, it predicts *novel* facts, that is, facts improbable in the light of, or even forbidden by T; (2) T' explains the previous success of T, that is, all the unrefuted content of T is contained (within the limits of observational error) in the content of T'; and (3) some of the excess content of T' is corroborated. (1970a, p. 116)

You can see that this modification is no small modification. The word 'falsified,' as commonly understood, means 'being made false,' and Popper's original definition of falsification conforms with this traditional usage. However, in the hands of Lakatos, 'falsified' has little to do with falsity. I think it would be more honest and less misleading to

employ the term 'superseded' instead, and say that T is superseded (or defeated) by T' should it satisfy the three conditions listed.[2] Nevertheless, this notion of supersession is still a Popperian notion. You may recall that, according to Popper, the aim of science is to obtain corroborated theories with ever-increasing contents (Section 24.6). If so, obviously T' is preferable to T.

Popper's falsificationism has been plagued with difficulties. On the one hand, strictly speaking no theory is ever falsifiable. This has been pointed out earlier. On the other hand, all major theories were born falsified when 'falsified' is understood in the Popperian sense. Such theories include Copernicus's heliocentric theory and Newton's gravitational theory. (Kuhn and others have argued convincingly on this.) Thus there would have been no science if we had adhered to the methodology of Popper. Even though Lakatos did not spell it out in so many words, he could be seen to be recommending 'supersession' in place of 'falsification.' In the practice of science, not only can we not demonstrate truths, we cannot demonstrate falsehoods either. However, we can always strive for better theories. If T and T' satisfy the three conditions proposed by Lakatos, he thinks that we will definitely know that T' is better than T. The aim of science is to obtain better and better theories in this sense. Whether better theories are necessarily closer to the truth has not been discussed. Lakatos is wise to avoid the issue of truth and verisimilitude, since it has been shown to be an unsurmountable difficulty for Popperian falsificationism (Section 24.8).

Since a better theory in Lakatos's sense need not be a truer theory, and he has not given us any explicit justification for the preference of such theories, I think it would help to employ the new term, 'L-better,' to present Lakatos's ideas. Let's say that

(1) T' is **L-better than** T iff T' and T satisfy the three conditions in the quote from Lakatos.

With this definition in mind, we can now reinterpret Lakatos's passage as asserting

---

2. I think Lakatos retained the term 'falsified' out of respect for Popper.

(2) Methodologically, T should be taken as **superseded by** T' iff T' is L-better than T.

You can see that I have broken his passage into two parts. Statement (1) is a definition, whereas (2) is an assertion. To assert (2) without supporting arguments is to assume that whenever T' is L-better than T, T' is better than T, the second 'better' being understood in the ordinary sense of the word. This would be a slide. Unfortunately Lakatos does just that.[3]

According to Popper, we should drop a theory when that theory does not conform to nature (having been falsified). For Lakatos, a theory should be dropped if and only if there is an L-better theory around. This is a switch from an absolute "scale" to a relative "scale" in the rejection of theories. In doing so, Lakatos is following both Kuhn and Feyerabend. It was Kuhn who pointed out that a paradigm is relinquished only if an alternative is available. Feyerabend was more radical. He positively encouraged the proliferation of theories as the only means to progress.

B. Popper introduced the idea of demarcation of science, that a statement is scientific if and only if it is (empirically) falsifiable. Since the notion of falsifiability is problematic, Lakatos proposes the following revision.

Let a series of theories, T_1, T_2, T_3, ... , be such that (i) each can explain the empirical success of its predecessor (that is, all the unrefuted content of T_{n-1} is contained in the content of T_n) and (ii) each can explain some of the empirical failure of its predecessor as well. Lakatos calls such a series a **problemshift**.

(3) Definition: a problemshift is **theoretically progressive** if each new theory has some excess empirical content over its predecessor— that is, if it predicts some novel facts.

(4) Definition: a problemshift is **empirically progressive** if some of this excess empirical content is also corroborated—that is, if some of the predicted novel facts have been corroborated.

(5) Definition: a problemshift is **progressive** if it is both theoretically and empirically progressive, and **degenerating** otherwise.

By calling certain problemshifts 'progressive,' Lakatos is intending to recommend such problemshifts. Again Lakatos is rolling together definitions with recommendations. I think he takes it as obvious that progressive problemshifts as he defines them are commendable. Indeed he writes:

(6) "We '*accept*' problemshifts as 'scientific' only if they are at least theoretically progressive; if they are not, we '*reject*' them as 'pseudoscientific.'" (1970a, p. 118)

By saying this, Lakatos departs from Popper on two counts: (a) he is not defining the term 'scientific' as Popper does; he is using it as an appraisal term and (b) he is not attempting to draw a line between statements, isolating those that are suitable for the application of scientific methods. Instead he is recommending a certain methodology: strive to construct theoretically progressive problemshifts; avoid constructing degenerating ones.

Even though Lakatos appears to be modifying Popper's criterion of demarcation, he is attempting something quite different. Of course that is not to say that what he attempts is not worth serious consideration. Far from it. It is only that quite often Lakatos's respect for Popper leads him to present his arguments in such a way that it tends to mislead.

C. It can be seen that (A) and (B) are not unrelated. Summing up we can say that Lakatos defines a **progressive** problemshift as a series of theories such that each is L-better than its predecessor. He calls a problemshift **degenerating** if it is not progressive. His methodology is that science should work toward progressive problemshifts. In this respect, he is simply touching up Popper, for this methodology of his is essentially Popper's.[4] It is based both on Popper's notion of empirical content and also on Popper's general philosophy that science should aim for

---

3. In Section 28.4, I will pursue this issue further.

4. Lakatos recognizes this explicitly when he argues that sophisticated falsificationism is Popper's (Lakatos, 1970, pp. 116–132).

theories of ever higher content. Nevertheless, he is also critical of Popper. He recommends, in fact though not in word, that we should drop Popper's notion of falsification from scientific methodology. This is no small matter, for falsification is the cornerstone of Popper's philosophy. Furthermore, Lakatos recommends that we drop Popper's idea that scientific statements can be demarcated in terms of falsifiability. What remains from Popper seems to be his conception of empirical content and his ideas on the roles played by bold hypotheses (theories) in the methodology of science.

28.3 KUHN GRAFTED ONTO POPPER

For Kuhn, normal science is what typifies science. It is research carried out (i) within the confines of and (ii) under the guidance of a paradigm theory. This idea of a guiding framework that enables scientific research is now going to be borrowed by Lakatos.

Lakatos observes that theories forming a problemshift are seldom arbitrary. They are usually connected by "a remarkable continuity." He adds: "This continuity evolves from a genuine **research programme** adumbrated at the start. The programme consists of methodological rules: some tell us what paths of research to avoid (*negative heuristic*), and others what paths to pursue (*positive heuristic*)."[5]

It can be seen that Lakatos's 'research program' corresponds to Kuhn's 'paradigm theory.'

Every research program has a **hard core**, consisting of principles characteristic of that program. The **negative heuristic** forbids practitioners to doubt or criticize these principles, which are to be

taken as sacrosanct.[6] For instance, the hard core of the alchemo-phlogiston research program would consist of, among others, principles about the essential nature of the four elements: how each element has its characteristic sensual qualities such as dryness and hotness. The hard core of Dalton's atomic research program consists of principles governing how the chemical atoms can combine to form molecules.[7]

The hard core of each research program is surrounded by a **protective belt**, which consists of "auxiliary, 'observational' hypotheses and initial conditions."[8] When the program meets with empirical difficulties (anomalies), it is these auxiliary hypotheses and initial conditions that should be questioned and altered so as to leave the hard core untouched (protected). "We must redirect the *modus tollens* to *these* [auxiliary hypotheses and initial conditions]."[9] "The **positive heuristic** [of the program] consists of a partially articulated set of suggestions or hints on how to change, develop the 'refutable variants' of the research-programme, how to modify, sophisticate, the 'refutable' protective belt."[10]

For illustration, Lakatos presents Newton's mechanics as a research program. The hard core of this program consists of the (famous) three laws of motion and the square law of gravitational attraction. As for the positive heuristic and the protective belt, I'll let Lakatos speak for himself:

> Newton first worked out his programme
> for a planetary system, with a fixed point-
> like sun and one single point-like planet. It
> was in this model that he derived his inverse
> square law for Kepler's ellipse. But this
> model was forbidden by Newton's own
> third law of dynamics, therefore the model

---

5. Lakatos (1970, p. 132). 'Heuristic' literally means 'serving to find out.'

6. How un-Popperian this is!

7. In Section 25.6, I listed four such principles.

8. Lakatos (1970, p. 133).

9. Lakatos (1970, p. 133).

10. Lakatos (1970, p. 135).

had to be replaced by one in which both sun and planet revolved round their common centre of gravity. This change was not motivated by any observation (the data did not suggest an 'anomaly' here) but by a theoretical difficulty in developing the programme. Then he worked out the programme for more planets as if there were only heliocentric but no interplanetary forces. Then he worked out the case where the sun and planets were not masspoints but *mass-balls*. Again, for this change he did not *need* the observation of an anomaly; infinite density was forbidden by an (inarticulated) touchstone theory, therefore planets *had* to be extended. This change involved considerable mathematical difficulties, held up Newton's work—and delayed the publication of the *Principia* by more than a decade. Having solved this 'puzzle,' he started work on *spinning balls* and their wobbles. Then he admitted interplanetary forces and started work on *perturbations*. At this point, he started to look more anxiously at the facts. Many of them were beautifully explained (qualitatively) by this model, many were not. It was then that he started to work on *bulging* planets, rather than round planets, etc.[11]

According to this example, the positive heuristic of the Newtonian research program consists of advice on how to develop a series of models of the solar system, each more precise than its predecessor: Model 1 consists of very simplistic assumptions—that is, the sun and the planets are mere mass points with the sun fixed. Model 2: the sun is no longer taken as fixed. Model 3: the planets are no longer treated as points but as spheres which can spin and wobble. Model 4: interplanetary forces are taken into account. Model 5: the planets need not be perfect spheres.

Lakatos in the same paper describes another research program: "Prout, in an anonymous paper of 1815, claimed that the atomic weights of all pure chemical elements were whole numbers [that is, multiples of the atomic weight of hydrogen],"[12] which presumably constitutes the hard core. The positive heuristic consists of the advice: If the result of an experiment implies that certain chemical elements have atomic weight other than whole numbers, find fault with the purity of the samples of chemicals employed. A third example that Lakatos gives is the research program of Bohr on the structure of the atom.

According to Lakatos, the hard core of principles characterizes the research program. Any tampering with the hard core amounts to an abandonment of the program. The positive heuristic gives advice both of how to develop the program (as in the case of Newton) and of how to channel away potential refutations of the principles in the hard core to auxiliary hypotheses, which form a protective belt around the core (as in the case of Prout). In Kuhn's terminology, we can say that normal science is practiced under the forbidding dictatorship of the negative heuristics on the one hand, and the helpful guidance of the positive heuristics on the other.

We can envisage how a problemshift (series of theories) can develop under a Lakatosian research program. The scientist—for example, Newton—might come upon a "wonderful" idea, which he formulates into a set of principles forming a hard core for his program. Under the "dictatorship" of these principles, he then works out a set of strategies for developing a series of ever more complex and realistic theories (see Newton). He also works out strategies for the protection of the hard core (see Prout). If the series of theories is such that each theory is *L*-better than its predecessor the series is a progressive problemshift; if not, it is degenerating. We can see how a research program provides unity and continuity for a problemshift. Thus Lakatos

---

11. Lakatos (1970, pp. 135–136).

12. Lakatos (1970, p. 138).

often talks in terms of 'progressive/degenerating research program' instead of 'progressive/degenerating problemshift.'

According to Lakatos, the history of science can and should be told in terms of competing research programs. Let's see how Lakatos differs from Popper. For the latter, the history of science is describable as a series of conjectures and refutations. In contrast, Lakatos, following Kuhn, takes the growth of science as cumulative research work done under the guidance of a research program, whose hard core is held irrefutable. Nevertheless Lakatos thinks that Kuhn is wrong in picturing "normal" science as a stable period of time when one single paradigm theory has monopolized science. As a matter of fact, Lakatos observes, there are always a few competing research programs around, each with its own champions. Methodologically, too, proliferation of research programs is a desideratum. In saying this, Lakatos agrees with Feyerabend.

Although Lakatos calls this philosophy of his the **methodology of research programs (MRP)**, it turns out to be more of a theory of historiography of science than a theory of methods. One would have thought a methodology should consist of rules of practice. A methodology of science should advise the scientists what to do. Does MRP give such advice? Yes and no.

MRP does advise the scientist to aim for progressive research programs (progressive problemshifts): (i) invent a research program with its positive and negative heuristic, (ii) within this program produce theories that are ever *L*-better. Thus MRP does give advice.

When should one abandon a research program? Should a degenerating program be abandoned? As pointed out earlier, following Kuhn and Feyerabend, Lakatos acknowledges that one cannot do science in a "vacuum." There must be always a guiding idea, be it called a paradigm theory or a research program. But when should one switch guiding ideas? Surely if MRP is a methodological theory it should give advice here as well. How otherwise is the scientist to know what to do? Surprisingly Lakatos declines to give any advice:

> My 'methodology,' older connotations of the term notwithstanding, only *appraises* fully articulated theories (or research programmes) but it presumes to give advice to the scientist neither about how to *arrive* at good theories nor even about which of two rival programmes he should work on. My 'methodological rules' explain the rationale of the acceptance of Einstein's theory over Newton's, but they neither command nor advise the scientist to work in the Einsteinian and not in the Newtonian research programme.... When it turns out that, on my criteria, one research programme is 'progressing' and its rival is 'degenerating,' this tells us only that the two programmes possess certain objective features but does not tell us that scientists must work only in the progressive one.[13]

Strange as it may appear, his refusal to advise can be understood for at least three reasons: (i) In the face of the Duhem-Quine thesis, he has abandoned falsification as an instrument for rejection of theories; anyway, for him research programs are irrefutable by fiat.[14] (ii) Being basically a Popperian, he has learned to distrust induction. A program that has been degenerating in the past need not be so in the future. Indeed the past carries no weight whatsoever as to the expectation of the future, (iii) History has more than once demonstrated this point, Lakatos argues: he points out how Prout's degenerating research program was resurrected by Rutherford's school and became the cornerstone of modern atomic theory since 1911.[15]

---

13. Lakatos (1971b, p. 174).

14. "*There are no such things as crucial experiments*, at least not if these are meant to be experiments which can *instantly* overthrow a research programme" (Lakatos, 1970, p. 173).

15. Lakatos (1970a, pp. 139–140).

Many critics have pointed out that a methodology that does not give advice on the choice between competing research programs is no methodology. Lakatos, however, seems to be content to offer his so-called methodology, not as *practical* methodology, but rather as a framework or theory of historical appraisal: when we look back into history, we can judge whether a program is progressive or degenerating—that is, we can employ MRP to classify historical events. Indeed the term 'appraisal' is too strong because, according to Lakatos, it is not irrational to stick to a degenerating program. (For example, Priestley stuck to the alchemophlogiston theory to the very end of his life.) There is nothing wrong with pursuing a degenerating program.[16]

28.4 APPRAISAL OF LAKATOS

Lakatos is a revisionist Popperian: one who attempts to absorb Kuhn's paradigm view into a Popperian framework.[17] For Popper philosophy of science is normative: it should provide a (prescriptive) methodology for science, independent of the history of science. However, this view of the philosophy of science seems to be indefensible in the face of Kuhn's historical findings, that major scientific episodes do not conform to Popper's falsificationism. Thus, Lakatos pays much more attention to actual history than Popper does. Lakatos thinks that a methodology is acceptable only if it agrees with most of the practice of what is generally acknowledged as successful science. In short, the history of science plays a role in the appraisal of methodology.

For Lakatos, Kuhn has demonstrated conclusively that every scientific practice is guided by a theoretical framework. Kuhn calls it a paradigm.

Lakatos calls it a research program. Nevertheless, Lakatos remains a Popperian. Whereas Kuhn's paradigm view is, in many respects, socio-psychological, Lakatos's MRP, like Popper's falsificationism, is normative and logical.[18] Furthermore, MRP is based on Poppers idea that science should aim for theories of ever-increasing empirical content.

This grafting and absorption process is ingenious, to say the least. Yet in doing so, Lakatos's compromise has missed out the perhaps greatest contribution of Kuhn to the philosophy of science: the Kantian element of his paradigm view. For Kuhn, paradigms are constitutive of nature, of science, of meaning, and of subject matter of discourse (Section 27.2). For Kuhn, scientists in different paradigms "live in different worlds." Perhaps this loss is a real gain in that Lakatos need not have to face up to the relativistic consequences of incommensurability. Certainly there are advantages in remaining within the classical tradition. This is the path of "Kuhn without Kant." Is such a compromised methodology feasible though?

Apart from the loss of Kuhn's Kantian insight, and apart from Lakatos's inability to provide a methodology for the choice between research programs, how good is MRP? How should it be received? Alan Musgrave, another Popperian, gives the following critiques in his *Method or Madness?* (1976):

(a) Musgrave scrutinizes Lakatos's Newtonian research program in detail. He points out that scientists before 1850 seldom treated Newton's law of gravitation as part of a hard core. Musgrave concludes that

> [In] the Newtonian research programme scientists did not follow Lakatos's methodology, and render Newton's laws unfalsifiable by fiat. Moreover, this methodology is clearly not one which scientists *ought* to follow. Lakatos seems to be

---

16. We will study Lakatos's MRP as a theory of historiography in Chapter 30.

17. *New* wine into *old* bottles?

18. This is how Lakatos describes the difference; "Indeed, … , *my concept of a 'research programme' may be construed as an objective, 'third world' reconstruction of Kuhn's socio-psychological concept of paradigm:* thus the Kuhnian 'Gestalt-switch' can be performed without removing one's Popperian spectacles" (1970, p. 179). See also Lakatos (1970, p. 177).

recommending that scientists select certain of their hypotheses, christen them a 'hard core,' and decide *in advance* not to modify or renounce them in the face of difficulties. He tells us little about how these hypotheses are to be chosen. And therefore his methodological rule, stated generally, gives *carte blanche* to any group who want to erect some pet notion into a dogma. But most pet notions are mistaken, and may quickly be found to be mistaken. To decide in advance that the blame for any mistake must be shifted elsewhere, is to open the door to obscurantism.[19]

So the "hard core" description of scientific practice is neither historically accurate nor methodologically desirable.

(b) Musgrave finds fault with the "positive heuristic" component of research programs as well, (i) The so-called positive heuristic of Newton's research program is not a positive heuristic in the true sense: a set of strategies for the protection of the hard core from empirical refutations. It is just a detailed plan of how to develop a full and accurate model of the solar system by successive approximation. (ii) On the other hand, Prout's program does have a positive heuristic, which, however, is rather trivial.[20] (iii) Bohr's heuristic fares better. It is built on an analogy, that the atom resembles the solar system. Musgrave concludes that "in other cases in which an elaborate positive heuristic can be laid down at the outset of a research programme we will find that an *analogy* is responsible."[21]

I think a positive heuristic is a multifaceted "thing," and some research programs contain more of it and some less. Let us, for example,

look at Dalton's research program. Dalton's main project is to determine the atomic weights of the elements and the laws of their combination to form compounds. He recommends the following rules:

(i)   When one combination (compound) of two elements can be obtained, it should initially be assumed to be a binary compound.

(ii) When two combinations are observed (for example, carbon monoxide and carbon dioxide), they should initially be assumed to be a binary and a ternary compound.

(iii) When three combinations are observed, they should initially be assumed to be one binary and two ternary compounds.

(iv) When four combinations are observed, they should initially be assumed to be one binary, two ternary, and one quaternary compounds.

There were three more such rules.

(By 'binary compound' Dalton meant a compound formed from one atom of each of the two elements. By 'ternary compound,' he meant a compound formed from one atom of one and two atoms of the other element. By 'quaternary compound,' he meant a compound formed from one atom of one and three atoms of the other element.)

As a matter of fact these rules led him to conclude (wrongly) that water was HO, ammonia was HN, and the oxides of nitrogen were: NO (nitrous gas), NO_2 (nitric acid), N_2O (nitrous oxide), N_2O_3 (nitrous acid), and N_2O_5 (oxynitric acid).[22]

As is obvious, these rules of Dalton's were not meant to protect a hard core. Nonetheless they were positive suggestions as to how to develop the atomic theory. Hence they were positive heuristics. It can be seen, however, that they were not based on analogies, as Musgrave thought. These were rules of simplicity.

19. Musgrave (1976, p. 465).

20. Musgrave (1976, pp. 469–470).

21. Musgrave (1976, p. 472).

22. Holmyard and Palmer (1956, pp. 46–47).

(c) Musgrave thinks that Lakatos is overcautious in not recommending any rule for the choice between competing hypotheses. He suggests that advice to the scientific community as a whole can be given, to the effect that it should as a whole pursue progressive programs in preference to degenerating ones. Funding should be channeled into programs that have shown promise by being progressive. This is not to say, according to Musgrave, that the *individual* scientist should not pursue degenerating programs for fear of being accused of being irrational or stubborn. For the individual any program is as rational to follow as any other.

But why should public funds be allocated to progressive programs? Is the reasoning not based on induction? What has been progressive so far is more likely to prove progressive in the future? Can Musgrave, being a Popperian, embrace induction as such? Musgrave attempts to justify the choice of the progressive programs over degenerating programs by pointing out that the former usually provide lots of open problems, with promises of solutions, whereas the latter have few such problems. Since it is the task of science to study such problems, it makes sense to fund progressive programs. I think the availability of unsolved solvable problems is reminiscent of Kuhn's 'normal science.' Musgrave is not alone here. We will find that Larry Laudan (next chapter) takes the notion of problem solving as the cornerstone of his theory of scientific progress.

(d) Miscellaneous opinions from others and myself: You might recall that the key notion in Lakatos's methodology is 'L-better than.' This concept is based on Poppers notion of empirical content. Furthermore T' is L-better than T only if T' can *explain* all the previous successes of T.

(i) 'Empirical content' is a terribly elusive concept to apply. Methodology is supposed to be practical methodology. There is no point in recommending a methodology which is inapplicable in most cases. To know whether a program is progressive we must know whether each theory is L-better than its predecessor. In other words, we need to know at least whether it has more empirical content than its predecessor. I would say that in most cases one would not know this. For instance, one would have thought that Newton's successive approximations of the solar system discussed in Section 28.3 would be such that each has more empirical content than the one before. However, if you should attempt to apply the definition of empirical content (Section 24.5) you would find it difficult to ascertain which of the five models has a higher content.

(ii) The definition of 'L-better' just mentioned involves the notion of explanation. Has Lakatos told us what that term means in this context? In Chapter 14, we studied three theories of explanation. Before that we studied Hempel's covering-law thesis in detail. Which, if any, of these theories are presupposed by Lakatos? It does make a difference, I think.

(iii) For a Popperian like Lakatos, the ultimate aim of science must be truth. In Chapter 24, where we discussed Popper's notion of verisimilitude, we found that notion defective. Would Lakatos be able to show that progressive research programs will bring us closer to the truth? When a theory T' is *L-better* than T, is T' therefore *better* than T? If so, in what sense is it better? This has a bearing on the question of choice between research programs. Why are progressive programs preferable to degenerating ones? At least the conventionalists (Chapter 9) can say that the former would probably lead to simpler and more elegant theories whereas the latter would not. This, of course, is not very helpful if the notions of simplicity and elegance are left vague and subjective.

Lakatos's methodology of research programs created a stir in the circle of philosophers of science in the 1970s. His attempt to salvage Popper's philosophy by absorbing Kuhn's criticisms and insights was ingenious, to say the least. However, I don't think the Kantian window opened by Kuhn for the philosophy of science can ever be closed again. There seems to be no return to the classical tradition, be it the tradition of the logical positivists or that of Popper.

KEY TERMS INTRODUCED IN THIS CHAPTER

L-better than problemshift

theoretically progressive

empirically progressive

progressive problemshift

degenerating problemshift

research program

hard core

negative heuristic

protective belt

positive heuristic

methodology of research program (MRP)

REFERENCES

For general introductions, see Chalmers (1978, chap. 7), Losee (1980, chap. 14), Suppe (1977, pp. 659–669), Newton-Smith (1981, chap. IV), and Oldroyd (1986, chap. 9).

For Lakatos's own writing, see Lakatos (1970).

For critiques of Lakatos, see Cohen et al. (1976).

For explorations into the application of Lakatos's methodology, see Howson (1976).

Chapter 29

Laudan: The Eclectic Historicist

29.1 INTRODUCTION

Larry Laudan (1941–), in the preface to his influential *Progress and Its Problems* (1977), wrote: "It has been my good fortune to have been student or colleague to many of the scholars whose work has done much to shape the character of contemporary history and philosophy of science: C. G. Hempel, T. S. Kuhn, Gerd Buchdahl, Paul Feyerabend, Karl Popper, Imre Lakatos, Adolf Grünbaum have all left their mark on the *eclectic doctrines* that make up this essay" (p. ix.) This sums up succinctly the background and intentions of his book, which provides the main source material for this chapter. His effort should be understood as a continuation of those of Kuhn and Lakatos. He thinks that he can provide a better framework for the understanding of science and its methodology than his predecessors.

Laudan recommends that science be viewed as a **problem-solving system**, an approach that, he contends, "holds out more hope of capturing what is most characteristic about science than any alternative framework has."[1] Thus he dissociates himself from realism at the very start. Scientific theories may be assessable in terms of truth and falsity—as to whether they represent reality correctly or not. But this is not an appropriate way to study scientific practice. For Laudan science is a dialogue of problems and theories, the latter being proposed solutions to the problems.[2]

---

1. From Progress and Its Problems: Towards a Theory of Scientific Growth, by Larry Laudan, p. 12 © 1978 by the Regents of the University of California. Published by University of California Press.

2. This should remind us of Popper.

Laudan classifies problems into empirical problems and conceptual problems. Let me elaborate.

29.2 EMPIRICAL PROBLEMS

Laudan introduces the notion of an **empirical
problem** as follows:

> Empirical problems are easier to illustrate
> than to define. We observe that heavy
> bodies fall toward the earth with amazing
> regularity. To ask how and why they so
> fall is to pose such a problem. We observe
> that alcohol left standing in a glass soon
> disappears. To seek an explanation for that
> phenomenon is, again, to raise an empirical
> problem. We may observe that the off-
> springs of plants and animals bear striking
> resemblances to their parents. To inquire
> into the mechanism of trait transmission is
> also to raise an empirical problem. More
> generally, anything about the natural
> world which strikes us as odd, or otherwise
> in need of explanation, constitutes an
> empirical problem.[3]

It is not difficult to see that by 'empirical problems'
Laudan means something like problems of explanation, even though he thinks that to equate the two
will be a mistake:

> Given that similarity, one might be inclined
> to translate the claims I shall make about the
> nature and logic of problem solving into
> assertions about the logic of explanation.
> To do so, however, would be to

misconstrue the enterprise, for problems are
very different from "facts" (even "theory-
laden facts") and solving a problem cannot
be reduced to "explaining a fact."[4]

Nevertheless, I think it would be easier to
understand Laudan's thesis if we interpret his 'empirical problems' as meaning problems of explanation,
provided that we bear the following point in mind.

For Hempel (Chapter 10) it is facts[5] that are
candidates for explanation. These facts are supposed
to be independent of theoretical frameworks such
as Kuhn's paradigms. For Laudan, however,

> problems [that is, candidates for explana-
> tion] ... *arise within a certain context of inquiry*
> and are partly defined by that context. Our
> theoretical presuppositions about the natu-
> ral order tell us what to expect and what
> seems peculiar, problematic or questionable
> (in the literal sense of that term). Situations
> which pose problems within one inquiry
> context will not necessarily do so within
> others. Hence, whether something is
> regarded as an empirical problem will
> depend, in part, on the theories we possess.[6]

Theories, for Laudan, are solutions to empirical
problems. When is a theory considered to be a satisfactory solution?

> [A] theory may solve a problem so long as
> it *entails* even an approximate statement of
> the problem; in determining if a theory
> solves a problem, it is irrelevant whether
> the theory is true or false, well or poorly
> confirmed; what counts as a solution to a

---

3. From *Progress and Its Problems: Towards a Theory of Scientific Growth*, by Larry Laudan, p. 14–15 © 1978 by the Regents
of the University of California. Published by the University of California Press.

4. From *Progress and Its Problems: Towards a Theory of Scientific Growth*, by Larry Laudan, p. 16 © 1978 by the Regents of
the University of California. Published by the University of California Press.

5. Here by 'facts,' I mean 'statements of fact.'

6. From *Progress and Its Problems: Towards a Theory of Scientific Growth*, by Larry Laudan, p. 15 © 1978 by the Regents of
the University of California. Published by the University of California Press. I apologize for the amount of quotation. But then,
if one is not able to make better sense than the author himself, one has a good excuse for not representing the point in new
wording.

problem at one time will not necessarily be regarded as such at all times.[7]

Generally, any theory, T, can be regarded as having solved an empirical problem, if T functions (significantly) in any schema of inference whose conclusion is a statement of the problem.[8]

As *a first approximation* we can take Hempel's deductive model of explanation as what Laudan has in mind for the notion of 'solution of empirical problems,' since he seems to take the relationship between the theory (explanans) and the problem statement (explanandum) as that of the entailment relationship.

For Laudan the aim of science is to solve empirical problems, which, as has just been explained, is roughly the same as explaining phenomena.[9] One common kind of phenomena that "yearn" for explanation are those that occur with "amazing regularity," as Laudan puts it—for example, the downward fall of material objects, the disappearance of alcohol when exposed, and the resemblance of living things to their parents. Other interesting regularities include ice floating on water, copper conducting heat, and the 365-day cycle of the year. So far, as you can see, there is nothing really new. We had all these before in Chapter 10. But then Laudan introduces a second kind of phenomena that require explanation. These are the anomalies.

Popper presents his falsificationist thesis in terms of counterinstances (counterexamples, refuting instances, falsifiers). In view of the Duhem-Quine thesis, Kuhn employs the term 'anomaly' instead. Anomalies, for Kuhn, are prima facie counterinstances that need not be interpreted as fatal to a theory. They are simply difficulties, perhaps annoying and even threatening difficulties. Kuhn has not elaborated further. These difficulties, however, can always be explained away if we are willing to sacrifice some of the (presumed) auxiliary hypotheses. Laudan thinks that he can make the notion of anomaly more precise and more faithful to history.

(1) Definition: whenever an empirical problem, p, has been solved by any theory, then p thereafter constitutes an **anomaly** for every theory in the relevant domain that does not also solve p.[10]

In the language of explanation, we can formulate (1) as

(1a) Definition: an accepted empirical statement p constitutes an anomaly for every theory that is not able to explain p if p has been explained by some theory.

Let's take some examples. Pendular motions are anomalies to Aristotelian physics once they have been explained by Galileo and Newton. Not that Aristotelian physics gives wrong predictions on the motions of pendulums. Rather it has nothing to say to explain them.[11]

It has been observed that the orbit of the planet Mercury displays a precession around the sun with a period of three million years. (Minutely slow!) Newtonian scientists attempted to explain the phenomenon by postulating the existence of an unknown planet nearby disturbing Mercury. The planet, christened 'Vulcan,' was never found. Normally we would have considered this an anomaly

---

7. From *Progress and Its Problems: Towards a Theory of Scientific Growth*, by Larry Laudan, p. 22–23 © 1978 by the Regents of the University of California. Published by the University of California Press. I have altered some of his italics.

8. From *Progress and Its Problems: Towards a Theory of Scientific Growth*, by Larry Laudan, p. 25 © 1978 by the Regents of the University of California. Published by the University of California Press.

9. Laudan probably would not confine science to one aim, but as far as his presentation of science as a problem-solving activity is concerned the aim of science is to solve empirical problems.

10. From *Progress and Its Problems: Towards a Theory of Scientific Growth*, by Larry Laudan, p. 29 © 1978 by the Regents of the University of California. Published by the University of California Press.

11. From *Progress and Its Problems: Towards a Theory of Scientific Growth*, by Larry Laudan, p. 31 © 1978 by the Regents of the University of California. Published by the University of California Press.

(even a refuting instance) to Newton's theory. However, according to this definition, the precession is *not* an anomaly as long as no other theories are able to explain it. Einstein published his theory of general relativity in 1916, which proved to be successful in explaining this strange phenomenon. From then on, according to Laudan, Mercury's precession is an anomaly to Newton's theory (and, a fortiori, to Kepler's, Copernicus's, Ptolemy's, and Aristotle's theories). This way of assessing theories is not altogether novel. Whereas Popper considers theories in isolation (through the mechanism of falsification), both Kuhn and Lakatos propose that theories should be appraised in comparison with other theories. Specifically, Kuhn thinks that paradigms should not and cannot be surrendered without an alternative at hand. Lakatos redefines Popper's theory of falsification in terms of theory comparison.

Is this revised conception of anomaly helpful to the understanding of science? Is it superior to Kuhn's rather vague version? The answer is yes and no. Certainly Aristotelians never considered motions of the pendulum as anomalies, and certainly Galileo's and Newton's successes in their explanations of them did bring out the weakness of Aristotelian physics. However, intuitively the precession of the orbit of Mercury did stick out as anomalous even before Einstein's general relativity. Historically it was certainly an annoying, if not a threatening, difficulty. In fact, Laudan himself slipped into the use of Kuhn's notion of anomaly at the expense of his own. He pointed out that

> it was Prout's view that all the elements were composed of hydrogen and, consequently, the atomic weights of all elements should be integral multiples of the weight of hydrogen. Shortly after the appearance of this doctrine in 1815, numerous chemists pointed to seeming exceptions or *anomalies*. Berzelius and others found that several elements had atomic weights incompatible

> with Prout's theory (e.g., weights of 103.5 for lead, 35.45 for chlorine, and 68.7 for barium). (1977, p. 31, my italics)

These anomalies were considered anomalous without the assistance of other theories!

Laudan might have taken his idea from Feyerabend, whom we have not had space to study in detail. The latter argues that there are facts that cannot be unearthed except with the help of alternatives to the theory under consideration. For illustration, he discusses the phenomenon of the Brownian movement, discovered by Robert Brown in 1827. This phenomenon is actually inconsistent with the second law of phenomenal thermodynamics. However, according to Feyerabend, this inconsistency would remain unnoticed if it were not for Einstein's study of the phenomenon in terms of another theory, the kinetic theory as interpreted by Einstein. Thus the Brownian movement becomes an anomaly to phenomenal thermodynamics only when it has been explained by another theory. This episode seems to fit in with Definition (1) very well. But, there is a difference. In Feyerabend's case, the *inconsistency* was brought out by another theory, and this inconsistency is at the heart of the anomaly. Put differently, for Feyerabend the anomaly is always there, but it is not and cannot be made explicit without the presence of the other theory. In contrast, Laudan's notion of anomaly does not depend on the existence of inconsistency at all (as in the case of pendular motion). The common ground between the two is the requirement of an alternative theory.[12]

As was said earlier, the aim of science, for Laudan, is to solve the first kind of empirical problems—that is, to explain natural phenomena, especially regularities. Anomalies constitute the second kind of empirical problems. I don't think it makes sense to say that it is an aim of science to solve these, because these, unlike the first kind, are not "given" by nature.[13] Nature does not produce

---

12. See Feyerabend (1975, pp. 39–40).

13. On the contrary, Laudan writes as if to solve problems of anomaly is also an aim of science (for example, Laudan, 1977, p. 66).

anomalies per se. Anomalies are anomalies *for theories*. They are symptoms of diseases—not diseases of nature, but diseases of theories. Therefore it is more appropriate to say that it is a *requirement* of theories to solve their own anomalies—to get rid of their own diseases. Laudan illustrates with the example of Prout's hypothesis. As mentioned earlier, the nonintegral atomic weights of lead, chlorine, and so on are anomalous to this theory. These anomalies were later solved by the discovery of isotopes.[14]

In sum, Laudan's conception of science up to this point is as follows:

(2) The aim of science is to explain (amazing or puzzling) natural phenomena by producing theories, which can explain (deductively) as many of these phenomena as possible while generating as few anomalies as possible. Both problems of explanation and anomalous problems are classified as empirical problems.

Laudan also introduces some (rather vague) means of weighting these empirical problems:

Some problems [of explanation] count for more than others, and some anomalous problems are more threatening than others. If the problem-solving approach is ever to become a useful tool for appraisal, it must be able to show how, and why, certain problems are more significant than others.[15]

The intention, then, is to develop a scale for the appraisal of theories. That scale is known as problem-solving effectiveness:

(3) The overall **problem-solving effectiveness** of a theory is determined by assessing the number and importance of the empirical problems that the theory solves and deducting therefrom the number and importance of the anomalies and conceptual problems that the theory generates.[16]

Unfortunately this "scale" is far from being a quantitative scale, able to give an unambiguous ordering of theories in terms of their problem-solving effectiveness. The reason is that the notions of "importance" (which are meant to be logical consequences of the weighting exercises) are qualitative at best. But let's see what Laudan means by 'conceptual problem' in (3).

29.3 CONCEPTUAL PROBLEMS

Laudan proposes to look at science as a problem-solving system. That's why he expends much effort in the classification and weighting of scientific problems. Apart from the empirical problems just discussed, he points out problems of another kind: what he calls **conceptual problems**.

(4) "Conceptual problems arise for a theory, T, in one of two ways: (i) When T exhibits certain internal inconsistencies, or when its basic categories of analysis are vague and unclear; these are **internal conceptual problems**. (ii) When T is in conflict with another theory or doctrine, T', which proponents of T believe to be rationally well founded; these are **external conceptual problems**."[17]

---

14. However, we cannot say that the theory of general relativity has solved the Mercury precession anomaly of Newton's theory because, according to Laudan, the phenomenon is not an anomaly until it has been explained by the theory of general relativity.

15. From Progress and Its Problems: Towards a Theory of Scientific Growth, by Larry Laudan, p. 31 © 1978 by the Regents of the University of California. Published by the University of California Press.

16. From Progress and Its Problems: Towards a Theory of Scientific Growth, by Larry Laudan, p. 68 © 1978 by the Regents of the University of California. Published by the University of California Press.

17. From Progress and Its Problems: Towards a Theory of Scientific Growth, by Larry Laudan, p. 49 © 1978 by the Regents of the University of California. Published by the University of California Press.

Often when a theory is proposed to solve some empirical problems (to explain phenomena), it brings with it conceptual problems. If the theory is internally inconsistent, it creates what Laudan calls an internal conceptual problem. If it is externally inconsistent, it creates external conceptual problems. These problems discredit the theory and must be solved. Thus while a theory may earn credits by its ability to solve empirical problems, it can generate debits by creating conceptual problems.

Here are a few examples.

Bohr's model of the atom is a well-known case of a theory suffering from internal inconsistency. The orbiting electrons of Bohr's model are classical electrons, supposedly obeying classical laws of electromagnetism. Bohr postulated, however, that these electrons do not continuously emit radiation as they circle around the atomic nucleus. They are said to emit photons (of discrete amounts of energy) when they "jump" orbits.[18] This conceptual problem was eventually solved when Bohr's "old" quantum physics was replaced by the "new" quantum physics.

A good example of a theory suffering from external inconsistency is Copernicus's heliocentric theory.[19] In the days of Copernicus, the prevailing theory of motion was Aristotle's physics. According to Aristotle, there are five substances: fire, earth, air, water, and ether. The first four are terrestrial substances, whereas the last is the celestial substance of which the stars and planets are made. All four terrestrial substances have their own natural places; the law of nature dictates that each substance moves toward its own natural place unless it is prevented from doing so by force. As for the celestial substance, ether, its natural pattern of movement is a circular orbit. The heliocentric theory is obviously inconsistent with Aristotle's doctrines. By classifying the earth as a planet, Copernicus went against Aristotle's distinction between the terrestrial and the celestial, which is fundamental to his theory of motion. For

Copernicus's theory to be acceptable, a new physics was required, and that was the contribution of Galileo and Newton.

Sometimes a theory could be in conflict with "extrascientific" beliefs—that is, beliefs outside the domain of science. Laudan calls these worldview difficulties.[20] For instance, Newton's gravitational theory is in conflict with the Cartesian mechanical worldview that actions can only be transmitted through bodies by physical contact. Critics of Newton such as Leibniz and Huygens asked: How can the sun exert a gravitational force on the earth through empty space? What carries this force through such an enormous distance? Action-at-a-distance is unintelligible within the action-through-contact worldview. The Cartesian worldview was eventually dropped, owing to the great empirical success of Newton's theory.

Quantum mechanics is another theory inconsistent with the then-prevailing worldview. When quantum mechanics was proposed in the 1920s, the accepted worldview was Newtonian, according to which: (i) causality is deterministic[21] and (ii) every piece of matter has a definite position and momentum at any given time. Quantum mechanics seemingly contravenes both doctrines. Neither philosophers nor scientists seem to have any firm idea of how this conflict is going to be resolved.

Thus we can see how external conceptual problems can come about owing to the theory's conflict with another theory or with an (extra-scientific) worldview. Laudan names a third possibility. The theory concerned may clash with the prevailing methodology, and he gives this example. By the 1720s, the dominant methodology of science was inductive empiricism (Section 19.4), which takes as legitimate only theories obtainable through inductive methods from observational data. However, by the 1740s and 1750s theories postulating unobservables abounded in the fields of electricity,

---

18. See Holton and Roller (1958).

19. See Chapter 7.

20. Laudan (1977, p. 61).

21. See Section 12.5 for a discussion of probabilistic causality.

heat, pneumatics, chemistry, and physiology. Even though variously successful in explanation and prediction, they were in direct conflict with the prevailing methodology of the day. Eventually inductive empiricism lost the war, being replaced by the hypothetico-deductive methodology (Section 19.4).[22]

As with empirical problems, Laudan attempts to provide a weighting scale for measuring the relative importance of the conceptual problems.

We can see how, from the presentation so far, Laudan classifies scientific problems into empirical problems and conceptual problems. Empirical problems are of two types: problems of explanation and anomalous problems. Conceptual problems are either internal or external. A theory earns merit by solving problems of explanation. Its demerits are the anomalies and conceptual problems it generates, unless, that is, these generated problems are somehow solved. Thus, by keeping a "score sheet" on its merits and demerits, and employing (3), it is hoped that we can calculate the theory's problem-solving effectiveness. Proposed theories can then be assessed and ranked according to problem-solving effectiveness. Laudan states that "progress can occur if and only if the succession of scientific theories in any domain shows an increasing degree of problem-solving effectiveness."[23]

29.4 RESEARCH TRADITION

As with Kuhn and Lakatos, Laudan thinks that theories come in clusters or series. For Kuhn the unity of such clusters is provided by paradigms. The corresponding notion in Lakatos is that of the research program. In Chapter 26, we contrasted 'generic theory' and 'specific theory.' Generic theories are global and vague. They provide the theoretical

and conceptual frameworks for paradigms. Under a generic theory, specific theories (subparadigm theories) can be developed. They are specific in the sense that they are precise and explicit, so much so that they are empirically testable.[24] Laudan recognizes this distinction. Attempting to improve on Kuhn's 'paradigm' and Lakatos's 'research program,' he introduces a slightly different notion, that of **research tradition**.

Here are some examples of research traditions as given by Laudan: Darwinism, quantum theory, the electromagnetic theory of light, Aristotelianism, Cartesianism, Newtonianism, Stahlian chemistry (alchemo-phlogiston theory), mechanistic biology, and Freudian psychology.

A research tradition provides an ontology and a methodology for scientific investigation in a certain domain. The ontology will specify the types of fundamental entities to be employed in specific theories in the explanation of phenomena in that domain. For example, the research tradition of the alchemo-phlogiston theory provides the ontology of the four (continuous) elements with no specific constraints on combinations (Section 25.3). In contrast, the ontology of the chemical atomic theory consists of discrete atoms with built-in combination structures (Section 25.6). In this respect, research traditions resemble paradigms. The other aspect of research traditions is that they provide methods of inquiry: methodological principles for experimental techniques, methods of theoretical testing and evaluation, and the like. This is also reminiscent of Kuhn.

How are specific theories related to their parent research traditions? Laudan finds it difficult to specify. But he is certain of one thing: the research tradition does not *entail* its "children" theories, for a research tradition can "breed" a number of mutually inconsistent theories (different competing specifications of the generic theory). This may sound strange, but in

---

22. From Progress and Its Problems: Towards a Theory of Scientific Growth, by Larry Laudan, p. 59–60 © 1978 by the Regents of the University of California. Published by the University of California Press.

23. From Progress and Its Problems: Towards a Theory of Scientific Growth, by Larry Laudan, p. 68 © 1978 by the Regents of the University of California. Published by the University of California Press.

24. That is, they are testable as far as the Duhem-Quine thesis would allow.

fact it is common and understandable. An obvious example is the historical case of the alchemo-phlogiston theory. When it was discovered that products of combustion gain rather than lose weight, one suggestion was that phlogiston has negative weight (Section 25.5). This version of the phlogiston theory contradicts the earlier version. Another ready example is that, according to Dalton, the chemical formula for water is HO, whereas our version of the atomic theory is that water is H_2O. These two versions are inconsistent.

Like paradigms, research traditions define their own empirical problems. For example, it is a problem for the chemical atomic theory to explain why one oxygen atom cannot combine with one hydrogen atom to form a molecule, even though it can readily combine with two. Obviously this is not a problem for the phlogiston theory. According to Laudan, research traditions also play a role in the weighting of empirical problems as well. Research traditions also behave like research programs in that they provide heuristics (clues) for theory construction and modification.[25]

So far, Laudan's research traditions closely resemble Kuhn's paradigms and Lakatos's research programs. Let me now proceed to a major difference. Laudan thinks paradigms and research programs are too holistic. For Kuhn the change from one paradigm to another is like a gestalt switch. The change is both abrupt and holistic. There is no middle ground, and there is no gradual transition and continuity. For Lakatos, each research program has a hard core, which works as a single indivisible unit. To give up part of the hard core is to give up the program altogether. Laudan thinks that these descriptions of generic theories are inaccurate, too neat and tidy. For him research traditions do change gradually, bit by bit. Research traditions are not undissectable wholes. To quote Laudan,

Certain Aristotelians, at times, abandoned the Aristotelian doctrine that motion in a void is impossible. Certain Cartesians, at times, repudiated the Cartesian identification of matter and extension. Certain Newtonians, at times, abandoned the Newtonian demand that all matter has inertial mass. But need it follow that these seeming "renegades" were no longer working within the research tradition to which they earnestly claimed to subscribe?[26]

Not only do research traditions "evolve" through time: they sometimes merge. Laudan gives the example of the amalgamation of Newtonianism and subtle fluid theory in the 18th century.[27]

There are two modes of appraisal of research traditions: the synchronic mode and the diachronic mode. We can assess the **adequacy** of a research tradition at a certain time, which is determined by the problem-solving effectiveness of the theories produced under the tradition at that time. This is the synchronic mode. Alternatively we can ask how progressive a research tradition is through its lifetime. This **progressiveness** is measured either by comparing the adequacy of the tradition at the beginning of its life and its adequacy toward the end (general progress) or by the speed at which the adequacy of the tradition improves (rate of progress).

Laudan notes that, at any one time, there are usually more than one competing research traditions present, and scientists need to make a choice. He recommends that we should always **accept** the most adequate research tradition, the research tradition that has produced the most effective problem-solving theory. On the other hand, even though a research tradition may not be so accepted, it does not mean that we should not **pursue** the research tradition further. To accept a research tradition is to take it as if it is true, and to employ it for all

---

25. From *Progress and Its Problems: Towards a Theory of Scientific Growth*, by Larry Laudan, p. 90–92 © 1978 by the Regents of the University of California. Published by the University of California Press.

26. From *Progress and Its Problems: Towards a Theory of Scientific Growth*, by Larry Laudan, p. 97 © 1978 by the Regents of the University of California. Published by the University of California Press.

27. Laudan (1977, p. 104).

pragmatic purposes—for example, for predictions. On the other hand, we can pursue a research tradition without accepting it. Some research traditions, even though not as adequate as others, may be promising. They have a future, so to speak. This may be indicated by their high rates of progress. They may have produced some astonishing new solutions to certain old problems very recently. Thus, stressed Laudan, it is important to distinguish between the **context of acceptance** and the **context of pursuit**. It is not irrational to pursue a research tradition that is unacceptable. While it is only reasonable to accept one research tradition at any one time, it is not unreasonable to pursue several research traditions simultaneously.

The distinction between acceptance and pursuit is clever. In this way, Laudan is able to strike a way out of the triangular entanglement between Kuhn, Feyerabend, and Lakatos. For Kuhn during normal science, the whole scientific community works under one paradigm, and it is irrational to attempt to employ an alternative unless there is an accumulation of anomalies resulting in a crisis. For Feyerabend, it is always desirable for different scientists to work in different paradigms at any time. There is no unbiased means to tell which paradigm is superior, and in fact progress would be faster under his methodological pluralism. Finally Lakatos, agreeing with Feyerabend, thinks that the proliferation of research programs is a desideratum, and that even though, prima facie, progressive programs are better, it is not irrational to stay with a degenerating program. By making a distinction between acceptance and pursuit, Laudan is able to hammer out a reasonable compromise between these three methodologists.

Note that neither the concept of acceptance nor that of pursuit is based on the notion of truth. These are pragmatic notions.[28] This is reasonable in light of the fact that, for Laudan, the aim of science is to solve problems, and not to discover truths: accept the most problem-solving-effective theory and research tradition! Pursue any that you think may turn out to be problem-solving-effective!

29.5 ASSESSMENT

Let's briefly assess Laudan's theses.

A. Aim of Science

As we have seen, Laudan's conception of science is based on the notion of problem solving. For him the aim of science is, of course, problem solving. This conception is meant to be both descriptively accurate and normatively (prescriptively) correct. Descriptively, science is said to be a problem-solving activity. Normatively, he thinks science should be a problem-solving activity as well. What are these problems? They are, as have been presented earlier, the problems of explanation, anomalous problems, and conceptual problems. The aim is to solve as many problems as possible of the first kind without creating problems of the second and third kind.

Is this descriptively accurate? Laudan is a historian of science by profession, and he named numerous historical examples to support his thesis. Yet one feels that perhaps many historical figures in science were actually after the truth, after the real structure of the world, after predictions, and so on. Perhaps what Laudan meant was that we can take scientific activities *as* problem-solving activities, looking at them from outside, so to speak. The individual scientists may have their own aims and their own ideas of what they are doing. Yet the historian can describe these activities (objectively) from an external point of view. This can be compared to our description of the activities of honeybees in their hives. In so describing, we are certainly not required to see their activities as they themselves would see them.

Is Laudan's conception of science normatively correct? Is this conception of his, when taken as a methodology of science, acceptable? Should science be practiced as a problem-solving activity as he recommends? One point that immediately comes to mind is that this methodology of his is rather empty as long as we do not know what sort of theories are supposed to be considered satisfactory

---

28. Laudan (1977, p. 120).

solutions to empirical problems. Recall that his empirical problems are effectively problems for explanation. Certain phenomena occur with (amazing) regularity (Section 29.2). The task of science is to explain them. But what is a scientific explanation? What can be considered a satisfactory explanation? How is explanation related to prediction? What is the relationship between the explaining theory and the explanandum? What is the structure of such a theory? We have explored various opinions from the classical tradition on these matters in Part III (Book 1). Is Laudan recommending that we assume the classical conceptions in understanding his methodology of problem solving? But then these classical answers are full of flaws. Are we to adopt the suggested alternatives as presented in Chapter 14? The notions of explanation and theory are fundamental to Laudan's methodology. Without making these clear, I think this methodology of his is rather empty. I understand that the persistent failure of the logical empiricists (including Popper and his followers) to furnish us with a sufficiently satisfactory account of the *logic* of science has made many philosophers of science negatively predisposed toward logic. Contemporary popular approaches are the historical and sociological, which, we will study in the next chapter. However, I think that as far as methodology is concerned we *have to* fall back on a sound logic of science if we are not to be content with intuitive and preanalytic notions such as Laudan's 'explanation' and 'theory.'

B. Rationality

Laudan argues that his conception of science as a problem-solving activity enables a better understanding of the notion of rationality. According to him there are two "levels" of rationality: the general and the specific.[29] Rationality at the general level consists of the acceptance of research traditions

that are the most effective problem solvers. This level transcends the particularities of specific periods of time. It is time-independent and culture-independent. In other words, it is absolute in that it applies to all cultures at all times, from pre-Socratic thought to the development of ideas in the Middle Ages to the more recent history of science. In brief, Laudan prescribes that science aim at problem solving, and research traditions are means to that end. To be rational is to accept the research traditions that can do the job of problem solving best. This, it is said, is valid for all times and for any background culture.

However, below the general level just discussed, there are the specific "parameters" of rationality. These are "local." They are culture-dependent and they change with time:

> The kinds of things which count as empirical problems, the sorts of objections that are recognized as conceptual problems, the criteria of intelligibility, the standards for experimental control, the importance or weight assigned to problems, are all a function of the methodological-normative beliefs of a particular community of thinkers.[30]

In Section 27.2, we saw how Kuhn claims that paradigms are constitutive of science: paradigms define their own fact-finding problems and their own methods and standards of solution. Laudan is obviously making use of this thesis of Kuhn here.

Let me attempt to describe Laudan's two levels of rationality from a different perspective.

There are two types of criteria of rationality, the agent-neutral and the agent-oriented. Agent-neutral criteria are objective and universal, whereas agent-oriented criteria are subjective and local. The same agent-neutral criteria are applicable to all scientific activities. Laudan thinks that these criteria should be based on the conception of science as a

---

29. From *Progress and Its Problems: Towards a Theory of Scientific Growth*, by Larry Laudan, p. 130 © 1978 by the Regents of the University of California. Published by the University of California Press.

30. From *Progress and Its Problems: Towards a Theory of Scientific Growth*, by Larry Laudan, p. 131 © 1978 by the Regents of the University of California. Published by the University of California Press.

problem-solving activity. They should be measures of how well a piece of science has managed to fulfill the aim of problem solving. Thus all scientific theories can be judged according to the same standard, namely, problem-solving effectiveness. On the other hand, agent-oriented criteria are subjective and local in the sense that they are measures of rationality in accordance with the methodological beliefs of a community at a certain time. For instance, if it is Aristotle's science that is to be assessed, we should apply measures that are based on the particular methodological beliefs of the practitioners of Aristotelian science. It would be unfair and irrelevant to apply measures based on the methodological beliefs of another community or of a different epoch—for example, the community of Newtonian scientists of the 19th century. Thus Laudan writes:

> Aristotle was not being irrational when he claimed, in the 4th century B.C., that the science of physics should be subordinate to, and legitimated by, metaphysics—even if that same doctrine, at other times and places, might well be characterized as irrational.[31]

Laudan thinks that this general-specific distinction of his solves the "central" problem: "How can we, with the philosophers, continue to talk normatively about the rationality (and irrationality) of theory choices in the past, while at the same time avoid the grafting of anachronistic criteria of rationality onto those episodes?"[32] Has he solved the problem? He seems to have the best of both worlds: absolutism as well as relativism. At the general level, he is an absolutist and at the specific level he is a relativist.

I think this is an expected outcome from a historian turned philosopher. As a historian he would like to understand how the scientist actually works in her social and physical milieu, and whether she behaves rationally with respect to that milieu. On the other hand, like his positivist predecessors, he

hopes to arrive at some sort of absolute and universal criterion of rationality that, on the one hand, can measure objectively the correctness of scientific practices, and, on the other hand, can provide a methodology for the advancement of science. Seen in this light Laudan is not really trying to both have his cake and eat it. The question that concerns us in this book is whether his absolute criterion of rationality provides an acceptable methodology for science. On this we have given our opinions in Subsection A.

C. Incommensurability

Laudan thinks that his problem-solving approach can solve the problem of incommensurability. He acknowledges that there does not exist theory-free observation language—for example, sense-datum language. He also acknowledges that all observation is theory-laden. Nonetheless, according to him, different theories (from different research traditions) can share empirical problems in common. These theories can all attempt to explain the same set of phenomena. Here is an example. Many different theories have been devised to solve the three geometric laws of optics. For instance, Newton proposed a corpuscular theory, Huygens proposed a longitudinal wave theory, and Young and Fresnel proposed a transverse wave theory (Chapter 0). All these three attempt to solve the same problems: the explanation of these three laws and others.

For sure, the three laws cannot be stated in a theory-free language. Their very statement presupposes some theory. But as long as this theory is different from the corpuscular theory of Newton and the wave theories of Huygens, Young, and Fresnel, Laudan can see no difficulty in the corpuscular and the wave theories all explaining the same three laws of optics. Thus he writes:

> So long as the theoretical assumptions necessary to characterize the problem are

---

31. From *Progress and Its Problems: Towards a Theory of Scientific Growth*, by Larry Laudan, p. 131 © 1978 by the Regents of the University of California. Published by the University of California Press.

32. From *Progress and Its Problems: Towards a Theory of Scientific Growth*, by Larry Laudan, p. 131 © 1978 by the Regents of the University of California. Published by the University of California Press.

different from the theories which attempt to solve it, then it is possible to show that the competing explanatory theories are addressing themselves to the same problem.

Differently put, Laudan thinks that the ubiquity of theory-ladenness does not necessarily result in incommensurability as long as there are languages neutral to the competing theories. The three laws of optics are said to be stable in some sort of neutral language, and the traditional theories of light, even though from research traditions as diverse as the corpuscular theory and the wave theory, can all have the same statements as explananda. Are there such neutral languages? How is cross-theoretical explanation possible?[33] Kuhn's theory of incommensurability argues exactly for negative answers to both of these questions (Section 27.2). Until he can provide us with some analysis illustrating the possibility of cross-theoretical explanation, I think Laudan has done nothing to counter Kuhn's thesis other than hand-waving and appealing to preanalytic common sense. In assuming the possibility that prima facie incommensurable theories are able to explain the same set of phenomena, Laudan is closer to the logical empiricists than he would like to admit.

Laudan may have foreseen this objection, for he asserts: "Even if we grant that it cannot be decided whether theories are dealing with the same problems, there is still scope for the objective evaluation and comparison of incommensurable theories and research traditions."[34] The way to evaluate and compare incommensurable theories and research traditions is to compare their problem-solving effectiveness, in terms of (3) in Section 29.2.

However, (3) is only as good as what it says, for the following reasons: (i) The content of (3) depends on what empirical problems and their solutions are. At present we do not know what Laudan has in mind for the notions of explanation and theory (Subsection A). Without these notions clearly set out, (3) is rather empty, (ii) Laudan's

weighting criteria of problems, both empirical and conceptual, are certainly too vague to be of much *practical* value for theory choice. Thus Laudan's proposal to compare theories in terms of (3) is at best programmatic.

You may recall that Kuhn, as a matter of fact, thinks that there are trans-paradigmatic criteria for theory comparison and choice (criteria independent of research traditions). One of these criteria is problem-solving ability, which is obviously of the same genre as Laudan's problem-solving effectiveness. Others are: quantitative precision, predictive power, consistency, simplicity, aesthetics, and future promise (Section 27.3). However, Kuhn makes it clear that these criteria are far short of providing anything like an algorithm for theory choice. They serve more like maxims.

But Kuhn makes it clear that such trans-paradigmatic criteria have little bearing on incommensurability. He insists that the four subtheses of incommensurability still hold, namely: (i) paradigms are constitutive of nature, (ii) paradigms are constitutive of science, (iii) paradigms are constitutive of meaning, and (iv) paradigms are constitutive of the subject matter of discourse (Section 27.2).

D. The Kuhnian Tradition

In his attack on the classical tradition, Kuhn has contributed a number of innovative ideas to the philosophy of science: (i) the two-level structure of scientific knowledge (paradigm theories versus subparadigm theories), (ii) the puzzle-solving nature of normal science, (iii) the difference of an anomaly from a refuting instance, (iv) the thesis of incommensurability, (v) the exemplar thesis, and (vi) the grounding of the philosophy of science in the history of science.

Laudan has adopted (i) without reservation. Contribution (ii) is about the kinds of problems to be solved in normal science. In Section 26.3,

---

33. See Hung (1981b) for my theory of cross-theoretical explanation.

34. From Progress and Its Problems: Towards a Theory of Scientific Growth, by Larry Laudan, p. 145 © 1978 by the Regents of the University of California. Published by the University of California Press.

I classified Kuhn's problems into: (A) factual scientific investigations, (B) paradigm support, (C) paradigm articulation, and (D) solving of theoretical problems. Laudan has overlooked (B) to (C) and has adopted only part of (A) in his problem-solving approach. For example, he does not seem to recognize "mundane" work such as the determination of the gravitational constant or the speed of light as scientific. On the other hand, it is to his credit to have acknowledged the importance of solving anomalous problems and conceptual problems in the practice of science. As for (iii), Laudan attempts to improve on the notion of anomaly. His attack on (iv), however, is not very convincing, and he avoids any discussion of (v). Finally, as a historian, Laudan has put (vi) to good use.

29.6 SCIENTIFIC CHANGE

We have so far covered Laudan "Stage 1." Let's move on to Laudan "Stage 2," which is embodied in his second influential book, *Science and Values* (1984).

According to Kuhn, when normal science develops into a crisis because of the accumulation of anomalies, the scientific community concerned may switch paradigms. The switchover is an all-or-nothing affair, the reason being that the old paradigm and the new paradigm are incommensurable. Such a changeover is what Kuhn calls a scientific revolution (Section 26.4).

Laudan thinks that this holistic account of scientific change is historically inaccurate as well as methodologically undesirable.[35] He accuses Kuhn of committing what he calls the **covariance fallacy**: when a revolution takes place, the paradigm change brings with it a change in all the following: (i) the aims and goals, (ii) the methodology, and (iii) the ontology as well as other factual principles, laws, and so on. For Kuhn, indeed, goals, methods, and

factual claims seem to come invariably in covariant clusters. If true, this will lead to radical relativism, argues Laudan, and relativism can be seen to keep company with subjectivism and irrationalism.[36]

Laudan attributes to the classical tradition what he calls the **hierarchical model of justification**, otherwise known as the **theory of instrumental rationality**. According to this model, factual claims, methodological rules, and aims and values of science form a hierarchy of three levels. Disputes over matters of fact (at the base level) can be resolved by moving one step up the hierarchy to the level of shared methodological rules. At this level, scientists can examine factual claims in terms of shared rules, which should be able to produce unequivocal judgments on these claims. However, if the scientists somehow cannot agree on which methodological rules to adopt, they can then move one level up, to the level of aims and values. According to this hierarchical model, the aims and values determine methodological rules. As long as the scientists can agree on their aims and values, they should be able to work out a set of common rules to adopt. Thus, provided that scientists of a community share the same aims and values, they should be able to agree, via the intermediate stage of methodological rules, on factual claims. These three levels are known as the **factual level**, the **methodological level**, and the **axiological level**. Each level provides evaluation for the items at the next level down. Differently put, each level is justified by the next level above.

For Laudan's description of this model, factual claims include all sorts of claims about reality, including both the observable and the unobservable. As for methodological rules, Laudan gives the following examples: (i) formulate testable and simple hypotheses (which is very general), (ii) prefer the results of double-blind to single-blind experiments, (iii) make sure to calibrate instrument x against standard y (which is very specific).[37] Finally,

---

35. Laudan (1984, p. 73).

36. We have discussed Kuhn's thesis with respect to relativism in Section 27.3.

37. Laudan (1984, p. 25). More methodological rules can be found in Laudan (1984, pp. 33–34).

'aims and values' are meant to denote cognitive aims and values such as truth, coherence, simplicity, and predictive fertility.[38]

Laudan argues that this hierarchical model is a mistake, and, by showing how this model is at fault, he paves the way to demonstrate why the "covariance fallacy" is indeed a fallacy. His ultimate aim is to "dissect" Kuhn's holistic picture of scientific change:

(a) According to the hierarchical model, aims and values determine the methodological rules. But as a matter of fact, argues Laudan, empirical discoveries about how the world operates and behaves can also affect the rational choice of methodological rules. He gives an example. Before the discovery of the so-called placebo effect, in testing the therapeutic efficacy of newly invented drugs, scientists typically prescribed to one group of patients the drug being tested, and to another group of similar patients (the control group) nothing. After the placebo effect was discovered, they changed the procedure. The members of the control group are provided with placebos, which look and taste exactly like the real drug, and moreover the subjects themselves would not know which group they belong to. In other words, they do not know whether the "drug" they are taking is the real thing or not. This is the single-blind testing procedure. When later it was discovered that the experimenter can also be affected by expectations about the therapeutic claims of the drug being tested, the single-blind testing procedure was modified into the double-blind testing procedure. Under this procedure even the experimenter does not know which patient is taking the real thing. Laudan concludes: factual beliefs thus shape methodological attitudes, every bit as much as our goals do.[39] It follows that scientific methodology is itself an empirical discipline.[40]

(b) According to the hierarchical model, aims and values occupy the top level of the hierarchical model. From there they control methodological rules, which in turn control the production and evaluation of factual claims. Aims and values are thus supreme in that they "dictate" and govern the practice of science and are themselves not subject to any higher authorities. Laudan thinks that this is a mistake. Aims and values can be subjected to various kinds of pressure, often resulting in changes. Moreover these pressures can come from empirical discoveries. He gives a few examples: Aims to achieve eternal youth, physical immortality, and perpetual machines have been abandoned because of our understanding of the laws of nature. We have relinquished the goal of seeking infallible universal knowledge because we have come to realize that the universe is infinite and that we can only know a finite number of instances. The explicit scientific methodology in the 18th century forbids the postulation of unobservable entities. It is an inductive methodology based on Bacon and Hume. This methodology is presumably Newtonian as well, since Newton made the famous remark: "I feign no hypotheses." Yet it was abandoned when the postulation of unobservables in the field of electricity, embryology, and chemistry met with obvious success. Finally the triumph of the (factual) theories of relativity and quantum mechanics in the early 20th century, as we all know, brought about tremendous changes in both methodology and axiology.

These examples, Laudan claims, demonstrate that, in contradiction of the hierarchical model, changes at the two top levels of the hierarchy can actually be initiated by changes at the bottom, the factual level. The next step for Laudan is to introduce his reticulated model of scientific rationality and change to replace Kuhn's holistic picture of paradigm change.

---

38. Laudan (1984, p. 35); Laudan makes it clear that moral values are not his concern in the present context.

39. Laudan (1984, p. 39).

40. Laudan (1984, p. 40).

According to the reticulated model, there is only one level, to which the factual, the methodological, and the axiological all belong. They all equally and mutually influence each other. Aims and values no longer occupy the lofty top position from which they "dictate" downward, without being influenced upward by new methods or factual discoveries. They are as "negotiable" as any of the other players in the game of scientific change. Indeed, on reading Laudan, everything seems to be negotiable independently of the rest. Laudan thinks that Kuhn's insistence on the *integral* character of paradigms cannot be right, and he writes: "Various components of a world view [that is, paradigm] are individually negotiable and individually replaceable in a piecemeal fashion."[41] For example, one can change part of the methodology without changing either any of the aims and values or any of the factual claims, and vice versa. Moreover, such piecemeal changes usually spread themselves out in a sizable span of time. Nonetheless, often it can look as if the Kuhnian picture is correct, Laudan grants. For instance, the shift from the Aristotelian paradigm to the Newtonian paradigm involves changes in all three "levels": the factual, the methodological, and the axiological. It looks as if there was an abrupt wholesale gestalt switch from the Aristotelian to the Newtonian à la Kuhn. However, this "Kuhnian effect" is an illusion. This is because in the writing of the history of science, authors tend to compress or telescope a number of gradual changes into what, from our distance in time, can easily appear as a discrete, abrupt, all-or-nothing "block" change.

It can be seen that Laudan is as much against Kuhn as against the classical tradition. John Worrall (1988) came to the defense of the latter.

The three "levels" are supposed to be "rationally" interlocked in that the acceptance of certain items (say certain aims) at one "level" should provide good reasons for the adoption of certain items in another "level" (say, certain methods). The difference between Laudan and the hierarchical model is that the latter takes this rational influence to be hierarchically one way, whereas Laudan argues that the influence is mutual between any of the three "levels." Now, Worrall thinks that Laudan's model is impossible if it is supposed to be a model of *rationality*. He illustrates it with an example.

In the 18th and early 19th centuries, the prevailing methodology was supposed to be (Baconian, Humean, and) Newtonian. Now Worrall argues as follows. Fresnel's wave theory of light is certainly noninductive because it postulated unobservable waves (Chapter 0). If Newtonian inductivism was really in force, then the acceptance of Fresnel's theory could not be rational. Conversely, if the acceptance was really rational, Newtonian inductivism could not have been in force. Worrall suggests that at that time Newtonian inductivism was only the *explicit* methodology. Newton did *verbally* pronounce such a methodology in his writing. Yet his *implicit* (that is, real) methodology was in fact the hypothetico-deductive method, which sanctions the postulation of unobservables.[42]

Worrall thinks that if Laudan insists that Newtonian inductivism was not only the explicit methodology at the time, but that it was the implicit methodology as well, then the reticulated model would collapse into relativism (since there seems to be no good reason to prefer one rather than another). Laudan also seems to suggest that not only does methodology change with time, but

---

41. Laudan (1984, p. 73).

42. My own explanation is this. The prevailing explicit and implicit methodologies might both be Newtonian as claimed. This, however, need not prevent someone like Fresnel from working on a theory that did not conform to that methodology. Perhaps Fresnel was being irrational. On the other hand, Fresnel might not believe in Newtonian inductivism. Anyway, once Fresnel's theory proved to be successful, it created a challenge to the prevailing methodology. In such a situation, it is not irrational to side with the successful theory rather than with the established methodology. Having said this, it is not factual discovery that prompted the methodological change as Laudan suggests. It is the success of an application of a new methodology that led to the abandonment of the old methodology. It is a case of two "things" competing at the *same* level, ending with a winner and a loser.

(rational) standards for the assessment of methodology also change with time. There is no eternal objective methodology.[43] Worrall, on the contrary, suggests that there *are* objective rules and methods, which are correct and rational for all times. These rules and methods are neither constrained by factual discoveries nor subject to the governance of axiology. They are simply rational per se. Such a conception of methodology is not new. This is the way the classical traditionists think about methodological rules. Laudan is wrong, Worrall suggests, to attribute the hierarchical model to the classical traditionists— whereby axiology governs methodology.

These eternal (and universal) methodological rules may not have been found. Nevertheless, they are there and it is reasonable to look for them. For illustration, Worrall gives as an example of such a rule: theories should, whenever possible, be tested against plausible rivals.[44] Other examples include induction by simple enumeration and Mill's five inductive methods (Chapter 3). These rules may not be genuinely eternal. Nonetheless their very proposal demonstrates the hopes of the classical traditionists. Carnap's inductive logics based on various notions of confirmation function (Section 4.8) are further evidence of such pursuits. For Worrall these efforts to discover eternal and objective methodological rules are worthwhile and are comparable to the search for valid rules of inference in deductive logic:[45]

> The idea was to do for the 'logic of science' what Boole, Frege, Russell and the mathematical logicians had done for *deductive logic*: just as the latter had articulated the general and unchanging principles of valid inference, so those methodologists were trying to find the general and unchanging principles of 'inductive logic,' and in particular of when one theory was, in view of all evidence,

better supported than another. (Worrall, 1988, p. 268)

Worrall thinks that Laudan (and Kuhn as well) has adopted a much wider conception of methodology than the classical traditionists. For Laudan, methodology ranges from "eternal" and totally general rules to "local" rules such as the double-blind testing procedure. The latter, Worrall admits, do depend on factual findings, and they do change with time in accordance with our factual beliefs. However, the former, Worrall insists, are independent of factual findings, being both totally general and eternal. When the classical traditionists talked about methodology they had only these eternal rules in mind. Thus Laudan's examples such as the example of the double-blind testing procedure are not able to demonstrate that the classical traditionists were wrong when they took methodology to be nonempirical and a priori.

Laudan, however, insists that there are no such eternal, purely procedural (that is, nonsubstantive) methodological rules:

> The general point is that *all* principles of theory evaluation make some substantive assumptions about the structure of the world we live in *and* about us as thinking, sentient beings.... Specifically, our methodological rules represent our best guesses about how to put questions to nature and about how to evaluate nature's response. Like any theory, they are in principle defeasible. And like most theories, they get modified through the course of time. (1989, p. 374)

In a compromising mood, Worrall concedes:

> Laudan is correct: no methodological principle is *purely* formal. But does it follow, as he suggests it does, that every such principle is open to revision in the light of

---

43. This issue is not at all clear. It would be helpful to consult Subsection B of Section 29.5.

44. Worrall (1988, p. 274).

45. See Chapter 2.

further discoveries about the world?

I believe that we should resist the inference from 'substantive' (and therefore 'strictly fallible') to '*seriously* corrigible.' There is evidence from the history of science of the reusability of our 'methodological principles' only if these are understood in Laudan's very broad and *highly* substantive sense. The principles from the narrower domain may be substantive, but there is no evidence that the possibility need be taken seriously that they might be revised. (1989, p. 387)

This concession, however, does not imply that Laudan's reticulated model of rationality and scientific change is necessarily correct, that science does change and should change gradually and continuously instead of abruptly and discretely as advocated by Kuhn. Nevertheless Laudan does have a strong case, especially since it is supported by a significant volume of historical materials. One point remains though: how does this reticulated model of "Stage 2" Laudan dovetail with the problem-solving model of "Stage 1"? Laudan, I think, owes us an explanation.

The logic and historiography of scientific change are both fascinating and challenging studies. So far in this book we have covered five models. They are (i) the cumulative model of the logical positivists, (ii) the eliminative model of Popper, (iii) the revolutionary model of Kuhn, (iv) the methodology of scientific research programs of Lakatos, and (v) the gradualist reticulated model of Laudan.

KEY TERMS INTRODUCED IN THIS CHAPTER

problem-solving system	internal conceptual problem	accept	theory of instrumental rationality
empirical problem	external conceptual problem	pursue	factual level
theory	research tradition	context of acceptance	methodological level
anomaly	adequacy	context of pursuit	axiological level
problem-solving effectiveness	progressiveness	covariance fallacy	
conceptual problem		hierarchical model of justification	

REFERENCES

For a general introduction, see Losee (1980, pp. 212–215).

For Laudan's own writings, see Laudan (1977, 1984). Kourany (1987) has an excerpt from Chapter 4 of Laudan (1984).

Pearce (1987, chap. 3) has a good discussion of Laudan's problem-solving model with respect to incommensurability.

Worrall (1988), Laudan (1989), and Worrall (1989) form an interesting debate over the reticulated model. Doppelt (1986) and Grobler (1990) have also made significant points on the issue.

Laudan et al. (1986) is a comprehensive study of the four theories of scientific change: Kuhn, Feyerabend, Lakatos, and Laudan.

Chapter 30*

History, Sociology, and the Philosophy of Science

30.1 HISTORY VERSUS PHILOSOPHY

What role does the **history of science (HOS)** play in the study of the **philosophy of science (POS)**? According to the classical tradition, the answer is "Little, if any." POS is an a priori study, being the investigation of how science *should* be done. Reason alone should yield the correct methodology for science. On the other hand, HOS is an empirical study. It attempts to describe how past scientists *actually* worked, and how science *actually* developed. Historical science may conform exactly to a priori methodologies. But it may not, and it certainly need not.[1]

Which of the two disciplines is logically prior then? The classical traditionists have no hesitation on this. "POS is obviously prior!" Correct reasoning alone should bring about the correct methodology for science, independent of how actual history (accidentally) behaves. The prime example is that of Descartes, the rationalist. He reasoned, a priori, that the correct method of science consists of two steps: (i) intuition (with the mind) and (ii) deduction (with the mind) (Chapter 19). More recently Popper revived and developed the hypothetico-deductive method, which, in brief, consists of three steps: (i) proposal of

---

*This chapter is more advanced and is optional.

1. Here is an analogy. Just as drivers need not drive in accordance with the traffic laws, so scientists need not follow the methodologies as proposed by philosophers.

hypotheses, (ii) deduction of empirical consequences, and (iii) testing these consequences against reality. For Popper, the empiricist, as for Descartes, the rationalist, the correctness of their methods can be ascertained by reason alone. History plays no role whatsoever in the validation of methodology. This is in accordance with the traditional philosophical doctrine that methodological oughts are not derivable from historical iss.

On the other hand, HOS is acknowledged to be dependent on POS. For clarity of explanation, let us introduce a distinction between **actual history (AH)** and **history of science (HOS)**. AH consists of all those events that have actually occurred in the past, independent of our knowledge and understanding of them. HOS is usually written in books. They are supposed to be records of AH. However, when such records are made we need, first of all, concepts. Where do we get these concepts? For example, we might describe AH in terms of concepts such as 'experiment,' 'indirect test,' 'hypothesis,' 'evidence,' 'confirmation,' 'falsification,' 'induction,' 'deduction,' 'paradigm,' 'normal science,' 'anomaly' 'crisis,' 'incommensurability' 'research program,' and 'research tradition.' Some of these concepts may come from the practicing scientists themselves. For example, Galileo employed the term 'experiment.' However, you would find that most of the influential HOS was written in terms of concepts invented by philosophers in POS. In this sense, POS is prior to HOS, for HOS is conceptually dependent on POS.

There is a second sense of dependency of HOS on POS. Obviously, when one records the past, it is impossible to record every detail that has occurred. (What would your diary be like if you attempted to record *all* that had happened to you during the day!) HOS must be selective. HOS can only be a minute, minute fraction of AH. How are events of AH selected to form part of HOS? You will find that the selection is much influenced by the historian's philosophical affiliation. Popperians usually select in accordance with the hypothetico-deductive methodology and Cartesians are usually heavily influenced by Descartes's rationalism. Kuhnian, Lakatosian, and Laudanian methodologies have all left their mark on HOS.

There is actually a third sense of dependency of HOS on POS. Historians very often pass value judgments on the practice of science. Some might praise Galileo's practice. Some might condemn the science of the alchemo-phlogistonists. Some might take Newton's gravitational theory as the model of correct science. In doing so, they rely on POS. If they are Cartesians, they evaluate in accordance with rationalism. If they are Popperians, they assess in terms of falsificationism, and so on.

The one-way dependency of HOS on POS seems obvious. This was the scenario up until Kuhn.

As was pointed out in Chapter 26, Kuhn was originally a historian of science. He found that there was a huge discrepancy between AH and the methodologies preached by the classical traditionists (logical positivists and Popper). Based on his *empirical* study of AH he concluded that (i) AH followed his paradigm view of scientific development, and, further, (ii) this view of science provides the correct methodology for the practice of science. In other words, he claimed that his methodology is both descriptively accurate and normatively correct. This claim was mainly based on the convincing amount of historical evidence that he amassed in *The Structure of Scientific Revolutions*. For the classical traditionists, methodology is an a priori enterprise. They devised their methodologies through pure reasoning and appealed to the mind for justification and support. By contrast Kuhn rested his case mainly on historical evidence. "That was how science actually behaved!" "That was how scientists practised their trade!" Kuhn's *Structure* marked the beginning of what is now known as the **historicist school**, the leading figures of which are Kuhn, Feyerabend, Lakatos, and Laudan, to name but a few. We will now study the "historicist" works of Lakatos and Laudan in detail.

30.2 LAKATOS

Lakatos (1978), like Kuhn before him, criticizes the methodologies of the logical positivists and Popper as not true to history (that is, AH). Kuhn's construal is not correct either. Lakatos argues that it is his methodology of research programs (MRP) that can do justice to history (Chapter 28).

MRP is a theory of rationality. This is how science *should* be done. It is how a perfectly rational person would do science. Just like Popper's hypothetico-deductive method, it is the product of a piece of a priori reasoning. The mind can see that this is the correct way to do science. Having settled on MRP, Lakatos proposes his famous **theory of historiography**: how history of science (HOS) should be written. He makes the distinction between 'internal history' and 'external history.' An **internal history** of science is a **rational reconstruction** of what actually happened. A rational reconstruction is always done in accordance with an adopted methodology. For instance, an inductivist will reconstruct history as a sequence of discoveries of hard facts and empirical generalizations based on these discovered facts. A falsificationist will tell his "tale" in terms of bold conjectures (hypotheses), empirical tests, falsifications, non–ad hoc revisions, and radically new conjectures. A Lakatosian, armed with MRP, will present history as the rivalry between research programs. Some of these research programs will be degenerating, and some will be progressive. The scientists make their choices. Eventually one or more of the research programs will emerge as victorious over the others.

Internal history is not meant to be a true account of actual history (AH). It is a reconstruction in two senses. First, it is AH written in terms of the concepts proposed by a certain methodology. Second, if AH should misbehave, deviating from that methodology, the historian would "rectify" actual history so that the final product would come out exactly as if the recommended methodology had been precisely adhered to. Thus internal history is partially fabricated. It is written in accordance with a certain methodology, which is taken as the norm of rationality.

Obviously internal history by itself would be misleading. Thus an **external history** is recommended to supplement the internal history. Often actual science does not conform to the norm of rationality laid down by the philosopher. These deviations are to be explained by what Lakatos calls external factors, such as the psychological, the sociological, the economic, the political, the religious, and so on. For example, a certain scientist did make ad hoc revisions to his pet hypothesis and thus behaved irrationally according to Popper's methodology. In the writing of external history, the Popperian historian should record this irrational act and, furthermore, should seek to explain it in terms of "disturbances." Perhaps the scientist was psychologically unstable. Perhaps he was living in a society where the admission of mistakes would be frowned on. Perhaps the deviation was due to the high inflation rate of the economy, and so forth.

In sum, internal history is a normative reconstruction of AH. It reconstructs an ideal world where every scientist is perfectly rational (according to that special model of rationality). External history is empirical. It records what actually happened, and at the same time points out how and why the actual events deviate (irrationally) from the internal history. Internal history is primary while external history is only secondary, because "the most important problems of external history are defined by internal history."[2] Thus "one way to indicate discrepancies between history and its rational reconstruction is to relate the internal history *in the text*, and indicate *in the footnotes* how actual history 'misbehaved' in the light of its rational reconstruction."[3]

No doubt Lakatos's notion of internal history is based on Popper's notion of objective knowledge, which resides in what Popper calls the third world or World 3. In this world, objects are abstract. They can only be appreciated by the mind. World 3 "is the world of possible objects of thought: the world of theories in themselves, and their logical relations; of arguments in themselves, and of problem

---

2. Lakatos (1978, p. 118).

3. Lakatos (1978, p. 120).

situations in themselves."[4] In contrast, World 1 is the world of material objects and World 2 is the world of mental states.[5] Internal history is history in World 3, where the mental states of the scientists do not play a role. Internal history has its own laws of development, which are the methodological rules that philosophers hope to discover. Lakatos thinks that internal history of science follows the "laws" of the methodology of research programs (MRP). Research programs are objects of thought. They have lives of their own in World 3, and they evolve and compete according to the laws of rationality. What is of interest to the scientific historian is to tell the story of the "history" of these research programs *internally*, internal to World 3. However, we mortals may be interested in external history as well, a sort of accidental occurrence in World 2, accidental due to psychological and social factors. As a philosopher of the classical tradition Lakatos has no interest in the accidental. That's why he proposes to relegate external history to the footnotes.[6]

The distinction between internal and external history is, strictly speaking, independent of the correctness or otherwise of the methodology entertained. In other words, the doctrine of internal history only advocates the writing of history according to *some* methodology. As such it is neutral between methodologies, and there are as many internal histories as there are methodologies. For instance, inductivism, falsificationism, and MRP each inspires their own internal history. At this point Lakatos makes another innovative move! The writing of internal history can in fact enable us to evaluate competing methodologies:

(1)   The best methodology is the one that yields an internal history closest to AH.

In other words, the methodology that can see AH as mostly rational and that leaves little (belonging to the irrational) for external history to explain is the sort of methodology that philosophers should be looking for. This is a thesis in what Lakatos calls **meta-methodology**. To put it differently, lack of discrepancy between internal history and external history is a measurement of the goodness of a methodology.

Thesis (1) is not, however, what Lakatos subscribes to. It can be seen to be based on Popper's falsificationism, Lakatos calls it **meta-falsificationism**.[7] If we apply this meta-methodology to Popper's methodology the latter would be rejected, because the discrepancy between Popperian internal history and AH would be intolerably great. Such an internal history would require masses of external "excuses" to explain the deviation of AH from the Popperian ideal. Thus (1) would require us to reject falsificationism. "If falsificationism is not acceptable as the correct methodological theory why should meta-falsificationism be acceptable as the correct meta-methodological theory," Lakatos asks. In short, he requires that

(2)   The correct *meta*-methodology of science should be a second order version of the correct methodology of science.

Put differently, the methodology of science is required to be applicable to itself by taking itself as just a scientific theory. This sort of reflexive application is rather new in the philosophy of science. Does it make sense to talk about a methodology as applied to itself? My mind boggles at the thought of it. Nevertheless, let's push on to see how Lakatos applies his own MRP to itself.

What happens when MRP is applied to itself? In order to apply MRP to itself, we must raise it by one level. At this higher level, Lakatos calls it the **methodology of historiographical research programs (MHRP)**. MHRP is now not a methodology of science but a methodology of historiography (a meta-methodology of science if you like).

---

4. Popper (1972, p. 154).

5. Objects of Popper's World 3 can be seen to be similar to Plato's Forms (Section 19.1).

6. See Lakatos (1978, pp. 118–120).

7. Lakatos (1978, p. 124).

Viewed downward from MHRP, MRP is now only one of many possible historiographical research programs. Other possibilities include inductivism of the logical positivists and falsificationism of Popper. To assess the worth of each of these research programs, one should judge whether they are progressive or degenerating. For a research program to be progressive, historiographical or otherwise, it must be "marked by discoveries of novel historical facts, by the reconstruction of a growing bulk of value-impregnated history as rational."[8] Put differently,

(3) Internal history in accordance with MHRP should predict an ever-growing number of historical events as conforming to MRP, thus leaving an ever-decreasing number of irrational happenings for explanation by external history.

In other words,

(4) If MRP is taken as the standard of rationality, MHRP should predict most activities in the actual history of science as being rational.

Needless to say, Lakatos thinks that an ever-growing number of historical events do conform to the thinking pattern of MRP. Thus MRP is a progressive research program. On the other hand, both inductivism and falsificationism are, according to Lakatos, found to be degenerating. In short, Lakatos thinks that most scientific activities are describable in terms of MRP.

It can be seen that by taking MRP as one of the many possible research programs under MHRP, Lakatos is treating his methodology MRP as an empirical theory, not much different from generic scientific theories such as the chemical atomic theory and the alchemo-phlogiston theory. Even though generic scientific theories are not empirically refutable, they are, nonetheless, empirically relevant (Chapter 27). We now have a curious sort of circle. Lakatos initially introduces MRP as a product of pure reason, arrived at through a priori reasoning. Then somehow by creating a higher level of MRP known as MHRP, MRP ends up as an empirical theory. Furthermore, according to Lakatos, AH has demonstrated that his MRP constitutes a progressive research program. Thus this a priori product of pure reason has been vindicated by empirical findings! Does this sort of bootstrap argument make sense? Has Lakatos produced any cogent arguments for (2)?

Lakatos's theory of historiography is interesting, to say the least. The idea of internal history (versus external history) is innovative. Thesis (2), the idea of meta-methodology being a second-order version of methodology, is ingenious. However, are these ideas and theses well supported? Why should one write internal history, even if we grant that the methodology assumed is the correct methodology? External history is meant to play only a secondary role. It attempts to provide social, psychological, and other causes to explain the deviation of actual history from internal history. Since to be rational is to follow the correct methodology, the intention of internal history is to chart out the rational course of science, and external history is meant to look after the irrational. Is it correct to assume that science following the rational course requires no social explanation, and social explanation is only required for the irrational? Thesis (2), as pointed out earlier, is a rather curious thesis. It requires reflexivity of the methodology of science. Does reflexivity here make sense? Why and how should (normative) methodology of science be supported by actual history?

On this issue of the relationship between history of science and philosophy of science, Laudan attempts to improve on Lakatos. Can he do better? Can he shed more light on the issue? Let's see.

30.3 LAUDAN ON META-METHODOLOGY

To improve on Kuhn and Lakatos, Laudan introduces his problem-solving model of science, as you may recall (Chapter 29). He argues that his model is

---

8. Lakatos (1978, p. 133).

both descriptively accurate and methodologically correct. His thesis is that the aim of science is problem solving, and that the history of science can largely be described as sequences of problem-solving activities.

Is this justifiable? Following Lakatos, he takes meta-methodology as the study of methodologies: their discovery and justification. Here is his meta-methodology for the justification of his problem-solving model.

Laudan (1977) starts with what he calls our **preferred preanalytic intuitions about scientific rationality (PI)**. He claims that there is a set of cases of theory acceptance and theory rejection about which most scientifically educated persons have strong (and similar) normative intuitions. For instance, most such people would be convinced that it was rational to accept Newtonian mechanics and to reject Aristotelian mechanics by 1800. Most of us would, nowadays, believe that it is rational to accept astronomy but not astrology. PI thus consists of the class of cases where most, if not all, of those who understand science would agree on its rationality or irrationality. This class is given a special status. Members of it will act as the touchstones for appraising and evaluating different methodologies. Here is Laudan's meta-methodological thesis:

(5)   It is a necessary condition that any acceptable methodology (that is, theory of rationality) should square with (at least some of) the PI's, and the adequacy of a methodology is proportional to the number of PI's it agrees with.[9]

He contrasts his meta-methodology with Lakatos's. Whereas the latter employs the whole history of science for the appraisal of meta-methodologies, he recommends only those cases where our intuition about their rationality is strong, clear-cut, and (almost) unanimous. He supports his view with an analogy. In the field of ethics, it is traditionally recognized that any ethical theory should square with the obvious cases of morality and immorality. For instance, no ethical theory would be acceptable if it does not conform with our intuition that the murder of a healthy child is immoral. For the moral philosopher, these intuitively obvious cases serve as the base for any sound ethical theory. An ethical theory so constructed can then be employed as a norm for the assessment of the "fuzzy" cases, such as abortion or euthanasia. Similarly the methodology of science, for Laudan, is both descriptive and normative, both empirical and a priori. It is descriptive and empirical with respect to the PI's. It is normative and a priori with respect to all the other cases. An acceptable methodology must conform with the PI's. A methodology so established can then serve as a norm for the evaluation of all other cases in the history of science. Laudan calls his meta-methodology **meta-methodological intuitionism (MMI)**.

Needless to say, Laudan argues that his problem-solving model empirically squares with the PI's. Thus, according to MMI, it is an acceptable methodology for science, and it is a satisfactory theory of rationality.

However, Laudan (1986a), in response to Daniel Garber's criticism (1986), retracts MMI. Here are the main reasons given:

(a)   The PI's are established according to *our* (present) strong intuitions about what is rational and what is irrational. But intuitions on rationality change with time. It is unreasonable to assume the present set of PI's will stay the same for ever.

(b)   Our preanalytic intuitions of rationality, which are responsible for the establishment of the PI's, can certainly be wrong. The taking of the PI's as the touchstones of rationality will not allow for the possibility of rectification of our (fallible) preanalytic intuitions.

(c)   Laudan doubts if it is true that most of us can agree on a set of cases to be typically rational or irrational.

(d)   Even if there is universal assent on the set of PI's, it is conceivable that this set of PI's can

---

9. From *Progress and Its Problems: Towards a Theory of Scientific Growth*, by Larry Laudan, p. 160–161 © 1978 by the Regents of the University of California. Published by the University of California Press.

conform to a large number of competing methodologies.

(e) MMI is apparently circular.[10]

In view of these, Laudan (1987) proposes his **naturalistic meta-methodology (NMM)** to replace MMI.

He points out that methodological rules usually appear as categorical imperatives. For example, we have such rules as

(6) Propound only falsifiable theories.

(7) Avoid ad hoc modifications.

(8) Prefer simple theories to complex ones.

These appear to be of the form:

(9) One ought to do x.

But this is a wrong way to conceive methodological rules, for they are in fact implicit hypothetical imperatives of the form:

(10) If one's goal is y, then one ought to do x.

Thus, for example, the true form of (7) is:

(7a) If one wants to develop theories that are very risky, then one ought to avoid ad hoc hypotheses.

Such hypothetical imperatives are amenable to empirical assessment. If doing x has usually brought about y in the past, we can take (9) as a good methodological rule. If you start to complain that this is a case of justifying predictions of the future in terms of similar instances in the past, you have hit the nail on the head. Recall that Hume complains that the principle of induction is unreasonable (Chapter 20). It is argued that induction can neither be justified a priori nor be justified empirically. Ironically Laudan takes the principle of induction as the supreme methodological principle, the principle that can be used to justify all other methodological rules (empirically): if we should accept the inductive principle then we can assess methodological rules

such as (7a) empirically, by studying their success rate in the past.[11]

But why should we accept the inductive principle? Laudan argues that it is the one principle that all philosophers of science—with the exception of Popperians—would accept. Is universal acceptance of a methodological rule sufficient for its soundness? Laudan apparently thinks so.

Laudan points out that scientists do differ in the goals they seek. It would not be reasonable to recommend categorical rules for them:

(11) Do x irrespective of your goal.

Methodologists can only recommend hypothetical rules:

(12) Do x if your goal is y.

But such means-to-ends rules are practical rules. Their effectiveness can be checked empirically: perform x a few times, and see how often x leads to y. Thus for Laudan methodological claims are no different from ordinary factual claims. Methodology is itself an empirical "science." For instance, (12) is as much a factual claim as:

(13) Put on some clothes if your goal is to keep warm.

Laudan concludes:

> What we thus have before us is the sketch of a *naturalistic* theory of methodology which preserves an important critical and prescriptive role for the philosopher of science, and which promises to enable us to choose between rival methodologies and epistemologies of science. What it does *not* promise is any *a priori* or incorrigible demonstrations of methodology; to the contrary, it makes methodology every bit as precarious epistemically as science itself. But that is just to say that our knowledge about how to conduct inquiry hangs on the same thread from which

---

10. See Laudan (1986a).

11. Laudan (1987, p. 25).

dangle our best guesses about how the world is. There are those who would like to make methodology more secure than physics; the challenge is rather to show that it is as secure as physics. (1987, p. 29)

In brief, Laudan replaces the quest for categorical rationality with the quest for instrumental rationality, and he argues that the latter can be discovered and checked by empirical means. He calls his thesis **naturalistic meta-methodology** because it takes methodological claims on a par with factual claims of the natural sciences. It is a species of the philosophical stance known as **naturalistic epistemology**, which in recent years has gained much support and popularity.[12]

30.4 LAUDAN ON HISTORIOGRAPHY

We have just covered Laudan's views on the role played by history of science (HOS) in philosophy of science (POS). Let's now study the "converse"— Laudan's views on the role played by POS on HOS. In short, we will study Laudan's theory of historiography.

Just as Lakatos thinks that HOS should be written in accordance with his methodology of research programs, so Laudan thinks that HOS should be written in accordance with his problem-solving model of rationality. Lakatos's internal HOS is about things in World 3, a world independent of any thinking subjects (for example, the scientists). Laudan does not subscribe to this type of HOS. For him actual history of science (AH) is made up of beliefs, real beliefs by humans that reside in World 2, not supranatural objects that reside in World 3. HOS should therefore attempt to interpret and record these actual beliefs

of the scientists in World 2, which are variously the empirical data observed, the theories invented, the laws discovered, and the reasonings employed. Laudan calls this type of history **exegetical history**.[13] It is purely descriptive. However, Laudan is personally not interested in the historiography of this type.

What interests Laudan is what he calls **explanatory history**, which attempts to explain why certain beliefs were subscribed to. Exegetical history provides us with merely a sequence of belief occurrences in chronological order. Explanatory history, in contrast, aims at providing the rationale for this sequence.

For explanatory history, Laudan introduces what he calls **rational explanation of belief**. Such an explanation has the following structure.

(14)

(a) All rational agents in situation type S will accept (or reject or modify) belief type B.
(b) Smith was a rational agent.
(c) Smith was in a type S situation.
_____
(d) Smith accepted (or rejected, or modified) belief B_1 which is of type B.[14]

You would recognize this form of argument as an instance of Hempel's D-N explanation (Chapter 10). Statement (d) is the explanandum. Statements (b) and (c) are the initial conditions. Through the law (a) they entail (d), thus explaining it by entailment. Given (a)–(c), (d) has to occur. For Laudan (b)–(d) are not difficult to establish. It is (a) that is problematic. How do we know that rational agents in situation S will accept B? To start with we lack a proper understanding of rationality. What does it mean to be rational? There are probably as many theories of rationality in the literature as there are philosophies of science. Here Laudan, needless to say, claims that his problem-solving model provides the correct theory. It is supposedly justified by history!

---

12. For various positions of naturalistic epistemology, see Shimony and Nails (1987). Quine (1969) is a classic.

13. From *Progress and Its Problems: Towards a Theory of Scientific Growth*, by Larry Laudan, p. 178 © 1978 by the Regents of the University of California. Published by the University of California Press.

14. From *Progress and Its Problems: Towards a Theory of Scientific Growth*, by Larry Laudan, p. 185 © 1978 by the Regents of the University of California. Published by the University of California Press.

The problem-solving model of rationality sub-scribes to principles such as:

(15) All rational agents will prefer a more effective research tradition to a less effective one; and

(16) All rational agents, in modifying a research tradition, will prefer more progressive to less progressive modifications of it.[15]

Such principles, according to Laudan, can play the role of laws of nature as required in line (a) in the explanation schema (14).

However, one would have thought that to explain why Smith accepts a certain belief the appropriate thing is to discover what goes on in Smith's head and what causes this "going on." The sociologist of knowledge typically thinks that the social milieu plays a decisive role in bringing about beliefs. When a person is brought up in a certain social, political, economic, religious, and cultural environment, her beliefs will be heavily influenced and shaped by that environment. For example, someone brought up in the old Soviet Union, an orthodox communist state, would have very different beliefs from someone brought up in the United States. Principles (15) and (16) may be true. They may even be analytically true, because they are true by the definition of rationality—Laudan's, that is. But then (b) is usually not true for most scientists, according to the sociologists of knowledge. Smith and Jones may both be well rec-ognized as competent scientists. Yet Smith and Jones differ in their scientific beliefs. They can't both be rational in Laudan's sense (otherwise they would have both come to the same conclusions). For instance, Einstein and Bohr, two great scien-tists, could not agree on the proper interpretation of experimental results in quantum physics. Recall that Lavoisier and Priestley believed in two theo-ries, which are as different as water and oil. Lavoisier championed the novel oxygen theory whereas Priestley held onto the well-established

phlogiston theory. Both worked more or less on the same set of empirical data (*pace* Kuhn)!

We will devote the next section to the sociology of knowledge. Here let's confine ourselves to the comparison of Laudan and Lakatos. Laudan dislikes the idea of internal history because it is not real his-tory. It is a rational *reconstruction*. At best it pictures "events" in World 3, the world of intelligibles.[16] Laudan wants his explanatory history to be about actual beliefs of real people. But are his rational expla-nations about actual beliefs of real people? Einstein and Bohr were rational people, I am quite sure. Did they, however, as a matter of fact behave in accor-dance with (15) and (16)? Did they think in terms of research traditions at all? They may not even have possessed the concept of research tradition. They may not have taken science to be a problem-solving enterprise as Laudan would have every scientist do. As a matter of fact Einstein was a realist, having an abso-lute conception of truth. He would prefer theories that are true or closer to the truth rather than theories that constitute effective research traditions, as (15) would require of a rational person.

Laudan's problem-solving model of rationality is not meant to be a psychological theory. In fact, it is supposed to be a methodologically normative theory. Psychological theories are about people, about real people and their real thoughts (for example, about real people like Einstein, Bohr, Lavoisier, and Priest-ley). On the other hand, methodological theories are about ideal people and their ideal thoughts. In spite of his explicit wordings, I suggest that what Laudan has in mind is something rather close to Lakatos's internal history: AH (actual history) should be seen as the development of rational thoughts, and rational thoughts (by definition) always develop in accordance with the problem-solving model of rationality. You may recall the two levels of rationality Laudan distin-guishes (Section 29.5). Laudan's problem-solving model of rationality belongs to the level that is agent-neutral, objective, and universal. At this level,

15. From *Progress and Its Problems: Towards a Theory of Scientific Growth*, by Larry Laudan, p. 187 © 1978 by the Regents of the University of California. Published by the University of California Press.

16. Popper (1972, p. 154).

we are not talking about real people and their actual thoughts. If we are to talk about real people, we have to move down one level, to the level that is agent-oriented, subjective, and local. Laudan's rational explanation clearly belongs to the agent-neutral level.

Nonetheless the agent-oriented level of explanation of belief does have a place in Laudan's historiography. When a belief is irrational (according to the agent-neutral standard of rationality), the historian should attempt to explain it psychologically and/or sociologically. The deviation from the norm (of rationality) could be due to psychological "disturbances." For instance, the scientist concerned may be deeply depressed, may have encountered certain traumas during childhood, or may have had his latest book rejected by the publisher. On the other hand, the cause may lie with the social milieu. The country may be under a Stalinist-type dictatorship. The economy is in recession. The government may have introduced a new funding scheme for the sciences. Thus Laudan subscribes to the **Arationality Thesis**:[17]

(17) *When a thinker does what it is rational to do, we need inquire no further into the causes of his action; whereas, when he does what is in fact irrational [according to agent-neutral standards]—even if he believes it to be rational [according to his own standards]—we require some further explanation.* (1977, p. 188)

In sum, Laudan's historiographical methodology consists of three steps of recommendation:

(i) View AH (actual history of science) as a sequence of (acceptance, rejection, and modification of) beliefs. (Exegetical History)

(ii) Attempt to explain these beliefs as the exemplification of the norm of rationality—that is, Laudan's problem-solving model of rationality. Such explanations are known as rational explanations. (Explanatory History: Type 1)

(iii) However, some of these beliefs will resist rational explanation. These are the irrational beliefs, which should then be explained in terms of social (and other kinds of) causes. These explanations are known as social explanations. (Explanatory History: Type 2)

It can be seen that Laudan's historiographical methodology is in fact very close to Lakatos's. 'Rational explanation' corresponds to Lakatos's 'internal history,' and 'social explanation' corresponds to Lakatos's 'external history.' For Lakatos, internal history is perfectly rational. There, events unfold in accordance with the "law" of rationality. When actual history (unfortunately) deviates from internal history, such deviations are taken as being brought about by external (social) causes. Hence external history complements internal history. Correspondingly for Laudan, social explanation is required where, and only where, rational explanation fails. This is the Arationality Thesis, according to which rational explanation and social explanation ride in tandem.

30.5 THE STRONG PROGRAM

Strongly opposed to the kind of historiography proposed by Laudan is David Bloor, who in 1976 proposed the **Strong Program** for the sociology of knowledge, which consists of four tenets: Causality, Impartiality, Symmetry, and Reflexivity.[18]

The Causality Tenet: [The sociology of knowledge] should be causal—that is, concerned with the conditions that bring about belief or states of knowledge. Naturally there will be other types of causes apart from social ones that will cooperate in bringing about belief.

The Impartiality Tenet: It should be impartial with respect to truth and falsity,

---

17. Laudan (1977, p. 202) employs the name 'arationality assumption' and formulates it as: sociology of knowledge may step in to explain beliefs if and only if those beliefs cannot be explained in terms of their rational merits. Brown (1984) calls it the Arationality Principle.

18. David Bloor is a leading figure of what is known as the Edinburgh School, a group of sociologists and historians of science centered in the Science Studies Unit of the University of Edinburgh.

rationality or irrationality, success or failure. Both sides of these dichotomies will require explanation.

The Symmetry Tenet: It should be symmetrical in its style of explanation. The same types of cause would explain, say, true and false beliefs.

The Reflexivity Tenet: It should be reflexive. In principle its patterns of explanation must be applicable to sociology itself. (Bloor, 1991, p. 7)

For Bloor, knowledge, including scientific knowledge, is a natural phenomenon. Philosophers commonly take knowledge as (justified) true beliefs. For the sociologist the qualification 'true' is inappropriate. Knowledge is what people take to be knowledge. Put differently, knowledge for a community is what that community believes in and accepts as true. The community lives by it. For instance, it would be true for the ancients that the earth is flat. For the phlogistonists, it is true that a candle during combustion gives off phlogiston. Knowledge is thus relative in two senses: (i) relative to a community and (ii) relative to the attitude adopted by that community.

Knowledge is a natural phenomenon, no different in kind from dreams. Just as dreams are caused and are in need of explanation, so is knowledge. This is the Causality Tenet in a nutshell. In the explanation of dreams, it would be inappropriate to make a distinction between good dreams and bad dreams, between true dreams and false dreams. All dreams require explanation, as does all knowledge, true or false, rational or irrational. This is the Impartiality Tenet. The Symmetry Tenet proposes that the same types of cause should be employed for the explanation of all kinds of beliefs, be these beliefs taken as true or false by the community. After all, knowledge, like false beliefs and dreams, is a mere natural phenomenon. It is no different from other kinds of mental phenomenon, hence the Symmetry Tenet. Finally, Bloor requires that the findings of sociology of knowledge apply to sociology itself,

for sociology is just one of the many disciplines of knowledge. Thus if certain (allegedly true) beliefs—such as the belief that Zeus exists or that the emperor is divine—could be socially "fabricated," sociology, in particular sociology of knowledge, could itself be "fabricated." This is the Reflexivity Tenet.

The four tenets make perfect sense once knowledge is taken as a psychological and social phenomenon. At the individual level it could be likened to dreams. At the community level it could be likened to customs and mores. All psychological and social phenomena are caused, *all* of them require causal explanation.

It can be seen that the Strong Program is in direct confrontation with Laudan's Arationality Thesis, (17). For Laudan, (i) rational beliefs do not seem to require causal explanations. Their rationality is self-explanatory. Rational beliefs are the natural course. They represent normal behavior for the human (the rational animal), (ii) Social (causal) explanation is called for only when the thinker departs from the normal course. Just as psychology usually only focuses on abnormal behaviors, so in sociology only "abnormal" beliefs require causal explanation. It is obvious that Laudan's thesis clashes head on with Bloor's Symmetry Tenet.

Laudan (1984), however, complains that his Arationality Thesis has been misunderstood. He makes it clear that he has no difficulty with Bloor's Causality and Impartiality Tenets. Rational beliefs, like irrational beliefs, are caused. The dispute between him and Bloor only concerns the Symmetry Tenet. Laudan insists that even though both rational beliefs and irrational beliefs should be causally explained, the type of causal explanation employed for the two cases should differ. Laudan explains in terms of his "modest notion of rational action and rational belief."[19]

A *rational* agent entertains a certain goal and engages in a process of ratiocination to obtain that goal in the context of her current beliefs about the world. This process of ratiocination is what characterizes rationality. If she eventually adopts certain beliefs in order to take a course of action to attain

---

19. Laudan (1984, p. 58).

that goal, those beliefs will be rational. She can always support their rationality by giving reasons based on her process of ratiocination. This, Laudan claims, is a *causal* theory of rationality where reasons function as causes. Such reason-like causes are characteristics of rational beliefs; they are typically absent from irrational beliefs. Laudan illustrates:

> For instance, my belief that flying [in an airplane] is highly dangerous and my belief that the earth is spherical were, so far as I can see, produced by radically different *causal mechanisms*; the evidence for that difference can be found in the fact that I sheepishly admit that I have no reasons in the one case and very convincing arguments in the other. (1984, p. 59, my italics)

Here Laudan makes it clear that he agrees with Bloor that rational beliefs are caused, just as irrational beliefs are caused. However, causes of the former differ from those of the latter in nature. The difference lies with the ratiocination process pointed out earlier, which one would find at the back of every rational belief. On the other hand, irrational beliefs are no different from knee jerks, a sort of unmediated reflex.

I do not think this is the place to discuss the psychology or physiology of rational beliefs. It would take us books! However, common sense does tell us that irrational beliefs often result from ratiocination. In other words, irrational beliefs are not necessarily unmediated reflexes. One can ratiocinate for hours and yet end up with "silly" plans of action because one (i) uses false premises, (ii) uses unreliable inductive inferences, (iii) uses invalid deductive rules, and/or (iv) cannot see certain seriously detrimental consequences the plan would imply. These "silly" plans are often regarded as irrational.

"But then these plans, even though irrational to the observer, are in fact quite rational for the subject!"

Laudan would probably rejoin. However, in doing so, Laudan is shifting from normative rationality to natural rationality in his use of the word 'rationality.' "Natural rationality refers to typical human reasoning propensities; normative rationality refers to patterns of inference that are esteemed or sanctioned. The one has reference to matters of psychological fact; the other to shared standards or norms" (Bloor, 1984, p. 84). The term 'rational' employed in the Arationality Thesis, (17), refers to normative rationality, which is supposed to be captured by the problem-solving model. In his *causal* theory of rationality, Laudan has in fact shifted to natural rationality. His 'causal mechanism' for rational beliefs refers to the psychological mechanism of the thinker and certainly could not have referred to the norm of normative rationality.

In sum, if the rationality employed in rational explanation is normative rationality, then rational explanation is not a causal explanation. On the other hand, if rational explanation is a kind of causal explanation, the rationality employed has to be natural rationality. But then the Symmetry Tenet holds: the same types of cause would explain both (normatively) rational beliefs and (normatively) irrational beliefs because both are usually (naturally) rational beliefs in accordance with the private criteria of the subject concerned.

A better defense of the Arationality Thesis is in fact available. Laudan (1977, pp. 202–203) interprets this thesis as a methodological principle and denies that he is asserting it as a metaphysical principle. "It does not assert that 'whenever a belief can be explained by adequate reasons, then it could not have been socially caused.' It makes the weaker, programmatic proposal that 'whenever a belief can be explained by adequate reasons, there is no need for, and little promise in, seeking out an alternative explanation in terms of social causes.'"[20] Thus interpreted, the Arationality Thesis would, however, deny the

---

20. From Progress and Its Problems: Towards a Theory of Scientific Growth, by Larry Laudan, p. 202–203 © 1978 by the Regents of the University of California. Published by the University of California Press. He justifies this "little promise" claim as follows: "Despite decades of research on this issue, *cognitive sociologists have yet to produce a single general law which they are willing to invoke to explain the cognitive fortunes of any scientific theory, from any past period*" From Progress and Its Problems: Towards a Theory of Scientific Growth, by Larry Laudan, p. 217–218 © 1978 by the Regents of the University of California. Published by the University of California Press.

Causality Tenet, for now he is asserting that for (normatively) rational beliefs, the sociologist should not be concerned with "the conditions which bring about [certain] belief or states of knowledge."

30.6 SOCIOLOGY OF SCIENCE

The Strong Program is one of the most influential schools of thought in the sociology of knowledge. As has been pointed out, it treats all beliefs on an equal footing, and knowledge is just that type of belief (justifiably or unjustifiably) taken as true. The findings of science are usually revered and upheld as (true and reliable) knowledge. Yet, for the sociologist, scientific knowledge should be studied exactly in the same manner as nonscientific beliefs, ranging from superstition to witchcraft, from astrology to palmistry. The sociologist should study its creation, its maintenance, its propagation, and its transformation. She should study how science is organized and categorized into different disciplines or spheres, and how science is institutionalized through universities, research institutes, education ministries, journals, books, lectures, conferences, and so on. In short, science is treated as a mere natural phenomenon. The ultimate aim is to find regularities and general principles governing this phenomenon of science. Thus the sociology of science is a kind of **science of science**. It is only that the *sociology* of science emphasizes the role played by the social factors, among other factors, in the determination of scientific knowledge. This role is often taken to be the dominant and decisive role. It is commonly considered that all scientific knowledge has social origins.

Let me illustrate with two much-quoted examples.

According to Paul Forman,[21] the rise of quantum physics in the 1920s was due to the antirationalist social-intellectual environment of post–World War I Germany. The spirit of the country was devastated by the loss of the war, which threw doubt on the general conception of science as mechanistic, rationalistic, and causalistic. Instead, thinking and conception tended toward the romantic, the irrational, and the mystical. This was how and why the new quantum physicists attempted to rid science of the traditional notion of deterministic causality, replacing it with the quantum notion of probabilistic causality.[22] Forman claims that this illustrates the social origin of scientific theories.

A second example is Shapin's interpretation of the Edinburgh phrenology debate.[23] Phrenology was founded by Franz Gall (1758–1828). Its main idea is that the brain is divided into a number of distinct parts, each of which is responsible for a particular mental faculty. Further, the size of each part is related to the power of the associated mental faculty. In the early decades of the 19th century in Edinburgh, there was a growing tension between the mercantile classes on the one hand and the landed gentry, with the professionals, on the other. Shapin noticed that phrenology was somehow well supported by the middle and working classes but rejected by the university community. The membership of the Royal Society of Edinburgh and that of the Phrenological Society were virtually disjoint. Shapin takes this as an illustration of social determination of scientific beliefs.[24]

It can be seen that this type of **sociology of science (SOS)** is hostile to philosophy of science (POS). The Strong Program treats true beliefs and false beliefs equally and attempts to explain both rational and irrational beliefs in terms of the same types of causes. Thus truth and rationality have lost their central places in **meta-science** (the meta-study of science). What one is concerned with seems to be causes only, especially social causes. For now science, as with other kinds of belief, is taken as a

---

21. Paul Forman, "Weimar Culture and Causality," in *Historical Studies in the Physical Sciences*, McCormmich (ed), 1971.

22. See Section 12.5 for probabilistic causality.

23. S. Shapin, "Phrenological Knowledge and the Social Structure of Early Nineteenth-Century Edinburgh," *Annals of Science*, *32* (1975), pp. 219-243.

24. These two examples were adopted from Brown (1984, pp. 13-16).

natural phenomenon subject to (blind) cause and effect. SOS of this kind *tends* toward an extreme kind of relativism: any belief is as good as any other. Since both the alchemo-phlogiston theory and the chemical atomic theory are socially caused, there is no reason to prefer one over the other. Again, there is no reason why Newton's mechanics should be valued above Aristotle's. We will have the opportunity to study relativism in detail in the next chapter. Here let us simply ask the question: given that part of POS is to demarcate good science from bad science, does POS have any role to play in meta-science?

A common rejoinder to the Strong Program is that since it subscribes to the Reflexivity Tenet, which requires the Strong Program to apply to itself, we need not take the Program seriously. After all, its proposal was socially caused, and it is just one out of an infinite number of equally good programs. Certainly the Strong Program would not claim truth or rationality for itself in exclusion of others!

I think that, even if we grant validity to the Strong Program, POS still has an indispensable role to play in meta-science. In fact, the role it should play is not much different from that envisaged by the classical traditionists. Let us see.

For any meta-study of science one must possess some concepts to describe this activity called science. For instance, we will describe a certain activity as an experiment, a certain proposal as a hypothesis, a certain observational result as a piece of datum, and so on. We require such concepts, which may or may not be available to the practicing scientist in question. The provision of these concepts belongs to the initial stage of POS.

Let's say that these initial concepts of POS carve up the world of science into meaningful chunks. The next thing surely is to look at these chunks minutely and analytically to discover their structures and interrelationships. I'll illustrate with an analogy. Common sense gives us descriptions of various kinds of substances: water, wood, metal, gas, and so on. Chemistry then comes in and attempts to study the fine structures and relationships of these substances, resulting in such findings as "Water is H_2O." Similarly the philosopher of science studies and analyzes "things" such as experiments, tests, hypotheses, arguments, and observations. You may note that the notions of truth and rationality have not yet entered into the picture. This stage of POS is purely descriptive and analytic. It attempts to develop a set of concepts for the fine description of the activity of science. From those crude intuitive concepts supplied at the initial stage of POS, one then advances to fine-grain concepts, which detail structures. Let's take an example.

The Florentine astronomer Francesco Sizi produced the following arguments against Galileo's claim that he had seen four satellites orbiting the planet Jupiter:

> There are seven windows in the head, two nostrils, two ears, two eyes and a mouth; so in the heavens there are two favorable stars, two unpropitious, two luminaries, and Mercury alone undecided and indifferent. From which and many other similar phenomena of nature such as the seven metals, etc., which it were tedious to enumerate, we gather that the number of planets is necessarily seven.... . Besides, the Jews and other ancient nations, as well as modern Europeans, have adopted the division of the week into seven days, and have named them from the seven planets: now if we increase the number of planets, this whole system falls to the ground.... . Moreover, the satellites are invisible to the naked eye and therefore can have no influence on the earth and therefore would be useless and therefore do not exist.
> (Holton and Roller, 1958, p. 160)

There are at least three arguments in this short passage: (i) The number seven is a sort of sacred number. "Things" have to come in sevens. If there were indeed four satellites orbiting Jupiter, the total number of "planets"[25] would be more than seven,

---

25. It is not unreasonable to take the satellites as planets since they are "wanderers" as well, not being fixed stars.

and this cannot be. (ii) Since the days of the week are named after the seven planets, any additional planets will destroy this naming system. (iii) Since the claimed satellites are unobservable (to the naked eye), they do not exist.

To understand how science comes about, and how it evolves, the first step, as I said before, must be to describe it. Initially we rely on preanalytic concepts such as 'argument' for our descriptions. Then we want to understand these "chunks" better. We want to study and investigate their inner structures. In our present case of studying Francesco Sizi, we ask ourselves: "What sort of arguments has Sizi produced? How are they structured?" With a bit of training we can detect three arguments in the passage. But what sort of arguments are they? Closer study reveals that the three arguments are of very different kinds. How different are they? Are they valid arguments? Are they reasonable? Are they satisfactory? To answer these questions, POS is called for. The sociologist cannot start with the task of finding the social causes of scientific beliefs without first understanding the structure of these beliefs, and to understand such structures she has to rely on POS.

Let's now see how Galileo arrived at the conclusion that there were four satellites orbiting Jupiter. On January 7, 1610, Galileo, with his telescope, saw little bright specks near Jupiter, two to the east and one to the west, all in a straight line with Jupiter. Then on January 8, to his surprise, he found a very different state of things, for there were three little bright specks all west of Jupiter. On January 10, he saw two specks to the east of Jupiter; on January 11, he still saw two specks to the east of Jupiter, but now at different distances from the planet... . Then on January 13, for the first time, he saw four of these little bright things, one to the east and three to the west of Jupiter. From these and further observations, he concluded that Jupiter had four satellites.[26]

What sort of argument is this: from observation of some bright specks through some glass lenses to a conclusion about the existence of satellites revolving around Jupiter, hundreds of thousands of miles away? Is the argument valid? Is it reasonable and/or reliable? How much weight have the premises on the conclusion? Again I think that POS is called for here.

As mentioned in Chapter 0, Newton explained the phenomena of light in terms of (colored) corpuscles whereas Huygens, Young, and Fresnel explained them in terms of waves. Again, what sort of arguments are these? Are they of the Hempelian kind (Chapter 10)? Are they really arguments (Chapter 14)? How do they compare to Galileo's and to those of Francesco Sizi?

It can be seen that POS is required for the description and understanding of science if for nothing else. According to the classical tradition, it is the task of POS to uncover the structures of scientific arguments, of laws of nature, of theories, of experiments, of tests, of observations, and so on. This kind of study of science is often called the **logic of science**. This name is apt for two reasons. (i) The study employs quite an amount of formal logic, both deductive and inductive (Chapters 2 and 3), but more important (ii) its method of analysis is akin to that employed by the formal logician. Pioneer logicians such as Aristotle, the Stoics, and later Frege and Russell, started with arguments from everyday life. By analyzing them, they arrived at certain structures: the logical forms of arguments. From these forms they built systems of logic. Similarly the philosopher of science either starts with or should start with or should have started with incidents from the (actual) history of science. For instance, she might take up Francesco Sizi's arguments or Galileo's arguments and attempt to analyze them. Her analysis is not confined to arguments, of course. She might study certain indirect tests or crucial tests to uncover their logic (Chapters 6 and 7). She might examine certain theories so as to discover their relationships with observational data (Chapters 8 and 9). Scientific explanations are interesting scientific "objects" of study as well. The history of science is full of wonderful explanations: ranging from the explanation of the rainbow to the explanation of radioactivity. Again the philosopher

---

26. The exciting story of the discovery of satellites round Jupiter was told by Galileo himself in his *The Sidereal Messenger*, partly reprinted in translation in Moulton and Schifferes (1963, pp. 74–76).

might analyze the structure of a number of these, hoping to arrive at a general pattern of scientific explanation (Chapters 10–14). All of these can be done independent of the sociology of science. Indeed, all of these should be done prior to pursuit of the sociology of science.

Here I am not pleading for the case of the classical tradition. What I am saying is that there is room for the logic of science (a type of POS) even if we grant full validity to the sociology of science. Whether the classical traditionists have come upon the correct logic is a different matter. Indeed, it is a serious oversight of theirs to have overlooked the ubiquitous presence of paradigms in every kind of scientific practice. It is memorably to Kuhn's credit to have pointed this out. However, I think it would be a mistake to take Kuhn's thesis as a demonstration that the study of the logic of science is misconceived. Rather, what it shows is that the kind of logic of science proposed in the classical tradition should be supplemented and rectified by the logic of paradigms. The error of the classical traditionists is to take the scientific statement and the scientific theory as the units of analysis per se. Their approaches should have been more holistic. They should have studied scientific statements and theories in the context of paradigms.

The Kuhnian revolution has brought into prominence both the history of science and the sociology of science. Nonetheless these two subjects should not be viewed as replacing the logic of science. It would be a big mistake to consider the logic of science irrelevant. The three are in fact complementary to each other.

We have just studied the role played by philosophy of science in the understanding and description of scientific practices. Let me summarize. History supplies the philosopher with scientific episodes for analysis. The philosopher comes up with concepts and tools for the description and understanding of these episodes. In terms of such descriptions, the sociologist can then proceed with her (social) cause-effect explanation of their occurrence. Are there any other roles that POS can play?

The classical traditionists conceive POS as providing norms for the practice of science. POS is meant to play a normative role. Can this role be justified in view of the advance of the history and sociology of science? The answer is a definite yes, even if we take science as a mere human activity, a natural phenomenon. Even if the notions of truth and rationality are inappropriate in the meta-study of science (according to the Impartiality and the Symmetry Tenets), it can be shown that the logic of science is still required to provide norms for the practice of science. Let's see.

Surely we would like to learn from history. We would like to know what sort of practice will lead to successful predictions and technologies, and what other sort will not. If history should reveal that certain methods employed have time and again brought about their goals, then by induction, we can take those methods as reliable tools for future use. For instance, from history we might find that arguments of the same sorts as those employed by Francesco Sizi seldom led to the desired goals, whereas those belonging to the types employed by Galileo often brought about successes. In such a situation, learning from history, we should take Galileo's methods and arguments as the norm. Note that here we are simply implementing Laudan's naturalistic meta-methodology (Section 30.3). If, for the sociologist, meta-science is simply the science of science, then since induction is one of the main tools of science, we can and should use induction in meta-science. Hence our generalization from the past successes of certain methods and arguments is certainly justified. Note that we have invoked neither truth nor rationality to justify these methods.[27]

---

27. Of course if science is purely socially caused, and these social causal factors are beyond human control (rather like the weather), there is no point in having normative methodology. In such a case, we are just puppets of our social environment. There is no real choice of methods *for us*. These social factors will implicitly determine courses of action. The social "mechanism" will create science via the puppets known as scientists. However, it is generally agreed that it is *we* who form social institutions such as universities and government agencies, banks and corporations. Since social causes are efficacious only through such institutions, we humans seem to have the final control. Thus normative methodology for the practice of science is relevant.

Having justified the normative status of the logic of science independent of the notions of truth and rationality, I would like to make it clear that this is not to say that truth and rationality have no role to play in meta-methodology. I think methods can be justified by their rationality as well as by their past successes. For example, it is not difficult to see intuitively that those three arguments of Francesco Sizi quoted earlier are unreasonable (a priori), whereas the method employed by Galileo in association with his telescope is reasonable. How exactly we can justify such intuitions is another matter. Perhaps we should adopt the kind of justificatory methodology of the classical traditionists. Perhaps, in view of Kuhn, we should invent some new methodology of justification. It is not the place here for a general discussion of the issue. Suffice it to say that prima facie we can see that methods can be justified both a posteriori by their past successes and a priori by their reasonableness. There is therefore a role for rationality to play in POS.

KEY TERMS INTRODUCED IN THIS CHAPTER

history of science (HOS)

philosophy of science (POS)

actual history

historicist school

theory of historiography

internal history

rational reconstruction

external history

meta-methodology

meta-falsificationism

methodology of historiographical research programs (MHRP)

preferred preanalytic intuitions about scientific rationality (PI)

meta-methodological intuitionism (MMI)

naturalistic meta-methodology (NMM)

naturalistic epistemology

exegetical history

explanatory history

rational explanation of belief

Arationality Thesis

Strong Program

science of science

sociology of science (SOS)

meta-science

logic of science

REFERENCES

For Lakatos's historiography and meta-methodology, see Newton-Smith (1981, pp. 92–101) and Lakatos (1978, chap. 2).

For Laudan's historiography and meta-methodology, see Laudan (1977, Part Two), Garber (1986), Laudan (1986, 1987).

For the Strong Program, see Bloor (1991) for the original statement. For the debate between Bloor and Laudan, see the anthology edited by Brown (1984). For an introduction, see Newton-Smith (1981, chap. X).

For an introduction to the sociology of science, see Oldroyd (1986, pp. 318–362). Chalmers (1990, chaps. 6–8) provides a more detailed presentation and analysis. Brannigan (1981) discusses the issue from a sociologist's point of view.

For a discussion of the interrelation between the philosophy, history, and sociology of science, see Hoyningen-Huene (1992). Thagard (1988, chap. 7) gives a useful analysis of the relationship between the descriptive and the normative.

Chapter 31*

Antirealism II: The Constructivist Rebellion

31.1 INTRODUCTION

We have just seen how the Kuhnian revolution has changed the scene in the philosophy of science. The shift was from logic to history and sociology, from the logical approach to historical and sociological approaches. The most important and serious philosophical impact, however, is that made by the Weltanschauung (or paradigm) thesis. For instance, it assumed the form of methodology of research programs in Lakatos, and the form of methodology of research traditions in Laudan.

The aim of science, as commonly understood, is to find out what reality is like. Are things made of particles or waves? Are they composed of atoms? Of superstrings? Of the four Aristotelian elements? Or are they in reality exactly as they appear to be: trees and flowers, sticks and stones, tables and chairs? The assumption that there is an objective reality and that it is the task of science to capture its real nature belongs to the philosophy of realism.

The Weltanschauung thesis, however, has raised serious doubts about this commonsensical view (Sections 27.2 and 27.3). This Kuhnian thesis is quite antirealistic. It champions constructivism in place of realism. The aim of the present chapter is to clarify and develop this Kuhnian theme further. What is constructivism? How should it be understood? What does it imply?

---

*This chapter is more advanced and is optional.

31.2 KINDS OF ANTIREALISM

The first antirealism we studied was instrumentalism (Chapter 16). It denies that theoretical terms have references, that they are meant to refer to (kinds of) entities. Only observational terms are said to refer. Instrumentalism is a theory of meaning. It belongs to the field of semantics (Section 18.1). Hence it is **antirealism of the semantic kind**. It is a **semantic antirealism**.

Chapter 18 introduces a second kind of antirealism. Both Bas van Fraassen and Larry Laudan think that it would be unreasonable to contend that science aims for true theories. Although we can tell when a theory is empirically adequate, we cannot know when it is true or even approximately true. Thus science should confine itself to the modest aim of acquiring empirically adequate theories. van Fraassen and Laudan are recommending an epistemic attitude based on a theory of knowledge of theirs. Hence theirs is an **antirealism of the epistemic kind**. It is an **epistemic antirealism**.

Theory of meaning (semantics), theory of knowledge (epistemology), and theory of truth are the three central fields of 20th-century analytic philosophy:

(a) In semantics, we ask: What is meaning? How do symbols (for example, sentences) acquire their meaning? What makes symbols meaningful? When are they meaningful?

(b) In epistemology, we ask: What is knowledge? How is it acquired? What are the sources of knowledge? What are the limits of knowledge? What can we know and what can't we?

(c) In theory of truth, we ask: What is truth? What makes some statements (theories) true and some false? When is a statement (theory) true? Under what circumstances are statements (theories) true?

We have so far discussed two kinds of antirealism, the semantic and the epistemic. There should be a third kind. Let's call this kind **truth-theoretic antirealism**. Kuhn's antirealism is antirealism of this truth-theoretic kind.[1]

31.3 KUHNIAN ANTIREALISM

The commonsensical realism of the truth-theoretic kind is what is generally known as the **correspondence theory of truth**. In a nutshell it says: a statement is true if and only if there is a fact in the real world that corresponds to the statement (Section 18.3.D). This fact in the real world is supposed to be objective, with attributes and existence independent of the observer-speaker's thoughts and ideas (that is, mind-independent). Kuhn denies this. He asserts that facts are determined by paradigms, and paradigms are invented by the mind (us). Moreover, competing paradigms are incommensurable, and hence they cannot share the same facts, so that scientists belonging to different paradigms live in "different worlds" (Section 27.3). How should such counterintuitive antirealistic statements be understood?

Since Kuhn, numerous antirealistic statements and expressions have appeared in the literature.

Here are a few such statements:

Reality is a social construct.

Reality is an intellectual construct.

The world is a socially constructed reality.

Knowledge is constructed in the mind of the learner.

Scientific knowledge is a social construct.

Scientific activity is not about nature, it is a fierce fight to construct reality.

Here are a few titles of books and articles in the same spirit:

Science and Its Fabrication[2]

---

1. This is my term. Just as 'semantics' corresponds to 'theory of meaning,' 'epistemology' to 'theory of knowledge,' I propose the term 'truth-theoretics' to correspond to 'theory of truth.'

2. The book title of Chalmers (1990).

What can these titles mean? Are they saying that what we consider reality is in fact unreal? Are they claiming that what are usually taken as facts are rather dreams of a kind? Perhaps they are simply illusions, mirages, or products of wishful thinking? Is reality made up (constructed) by us?

Expressions that philosophers, sociologists, and educationists use are often misleading. The expressions listed earlier are no exception. I do not think any Kuhnian antirealist would deny the existence of a mind-independent external world. Even for Kant, Kuhn's predecessor, there is an external reality, consisting of things-in-themselves. It is only that this reality is unknowable. But then, how are we to understand Kuhnian antirealism if it is not a denial of the existence of mind-independent reality? How are we to understand all those exotic expressions? I will try to explicate this Kuhnian antirealism in terms of **representationism**.

31.4 SIMPLE REPRESENTATIONISM

Symbols are used to represent things. The symbol is the **representer**, and the thing represented is the **representee**. Thus the portrait of Kant on the wall is a representer representing the 18th-century philosopher Immanuel Kant, the representee. The existence and character of the representee is supposed to be independent of the existence and character of the representer.

The question is: How does the representer manage to represent the representee? Why is it that the portrait of Kant represents Kant, but not Kuhn, for example? Why is it that the telephone on my desk does not represent Kant? A common answer is: "Because the portrait of Kant resembles Kant, the person!" Resemblance is often taken as the mechanism underlying representation. That's why model planes usually resemble the real plane. I once saw the model of a ship and could instantly recognize it as the QEII. This resemblance thesis seems to have strong support.

But then, if resemblance is the essence of representation, one can never misrepresent! The resemblance thesis makes it true by definition that the representer has to resemble the representee. If I did a bad painting of Kant (the figure perhaps looking like Abraham Lincoln), then by definition, it is not a representation of Kant. Hence I haven't misrepresented the great philosopher after all.

I think this resemblance thesis, commonsensical as it is, is wrong. It has mistaken the accidental for the essential. Resemblance, you will see, is only an accidental feature of representation. What underlie all representations are intentions and conventions.

First, what makes A a representation of B is that A is *intended* to be a representation of B. We also intend certain types of property of A to represent certain types of property of B. For example, we may intend this tall box to represent the Empire State Building. We say that the scale is one to a thousand, meaning that we intend that a length of one unit of the box is to represent one thousand units of length in the representee—that is, the Empire State Building. You can see how **intention** comes into representation. In this brief example, we have covered intentions of two kinds. The first kind

---

3. "Making (up) the Truth: Constructivist Contributions" by B. H. Smith, in *University of Toronto Quarterly*, 61:4, 1992.

4. *The Manufacture of Knowledge*, by Karin D. Knorr-Cetina, Pergamon Press, 1981.

5. *The Social Construction of Reality*, by Peter L. Berger and Thomas Luckmann, Penguin Press, 1966.

6. *Laboratory Life: The Social Construction of Scientific Facts*, by B. Latour and S. Woolgar, Sage, 1979.

7. *Constructing Quarks*, by Andrew Pickering, Edinburgh University Press, 1984.

is about a certain object *A*. The intention is that it should stand for a certain object *B*. The second kind is about properties (and relations as well). We intend a certain property of *A* (for example, length of a certain size) to represent a certain property of *B*. Intentions of this second kind are commonly known as conventions.[8]

Conventions are intentions to have certain properties (and/or relations) to represent certain properties (and/or relations). Frequently the representing property is of the same genre as the represented property. For example, we often use lengths to represent lengths, colors to represent colors, shapes to represent shapes, and so on. These are **natural conventions**. Take this map of Australia on my wall. The map-distance between Sydney and Melbourne is intended to represent the actual distance between the two cities in accordance with the scale of the map. The shape of the map-Australia is intended to represent the shape of the continent Australia. However, conventions need not be natural. For example, both Sydney and Melbourne appear as little circles on the map. But it would be wrong to take these round shapes as standing for the shapes of the cities.[9] Rather, the convention is that little round circles represent cities (not shapes of cities). My map of Australia is colored brown, yellow, green, light blue, and dark blue. What do these colors stand for? If the convention were of the natural kind, we would have to conclude that the continent of Australia with its neighboring seas is correspondingly colored. The fact, of course, is that these colors represent heights and depths. Let's say that these are **artificial conventions**, conventions where the representing is different in genre from the represented.

So you see, representations are based on intentions and conventions. But what do all these have to do with science? In particular, with scientific theories?

According to realism, scientific theories aim at the description of reality. How do they manage to provide such descriptions? It is often said that such descriptions are done through representations. Some would say through modeling.[10] Let's discuss this in terms of an example. The chemical atomic theory (CAT) is a scientific theory. It has postulates such as

(1) Matter consists of indivisible atoms.

(2) There are many different kinds of atoms.

(3) Atoms of specific kinds can combine to form bigger units known as molecules according to certain lawlike rules.[11]

How do these postulates represent reality? Is it through natural conventions? But certainly the atomic theory is not claiming that reality resembles those English words in (1)–(3).[12] But then how do (1) to (3) manage to represent? This is a complicated and difficult field. Shall we say, for our present purpose, that the CAT attempts to represent reality through a set of yet-unknown conventions? If it does give the correct representation, then it is true. If it misrepresents, then it is false. You can see that this is a correspondence theory of truth. It is a kind of realism. Let's give this view of scientific theories a name. Let's call it simple representationism.

(4) **Simple representationism** is the view that scientific theories attempt to represent reality through certain conventions. A scientific theory is true (to a certain degree) if its representation resembles reality (to a certain degree).

---

8. These two types of intention correspond to Austin's 'demonstrative convention' and 'descriptive convention' (Austin, 1950).

9. Actually a young boy did think that all cities were round in shape when he was first introduced to maps.

10. See Patrick Suppes's and Bas van Fraassen's semantic view of scientific theories, described in van Fraassen (1980, chap. 3) and Giere (1991, chap. 2).

11. See Section 25.6.

12. Wittgenstein once proposed that propositions are in essence pictures. Propositions manage to say what they say through pictorial representations.

It can be seen that instrumentalism denies simple representationism on semantic grounds. For instrumentalism, theoretical terms are non-referring—there are no theoretical entities for them to refer to. Hence scientific theories cannot be representations of reality. The antirealism of van Fraassen and Laudan also objects to simple representationism, not on semantic grounds but for epistemic reasons. For them even if scientific theories are meant to be representations of reality, we are not in a position to look for true theories. We should be satisfied with empirically adequate theories. Whether scientific theories are representations of reality or not is pragmatically and epistemologically irrelevant.

The third kind of objection to simple representationism is Kuhnian antirealism. It is a truth-theoretic objection. Let's see.

31.5 SOPHISTICATED REPRESENTATIONISM

What is wrong with simple representationism? I think it has overlooked one essential element in the mechanism of representation. Every representation requires a **medium**. This representational medium together with the conventions supply a representational space. It is within this space that representations take place. Simple representationism has managed to uncover the role played by conventions. What it has missed is the often-taken-for-granted medium.

Let's illustrate with a rather familiar kind of representation, namely, maps. Suppose the task is to draw an accurate map of Australia. Two methods immediately come to mind. The first is the centuries-old method of triangulation. Basically one starts with one or more base distances, and then employing the laws of trigonometry works out further distances in terms of measured angles between points of reference. With these angles and distances, one can then calculate the relative positions of these points. Cities like Sydney and Melbourne can be such points of reference. The second method is the modern method of aerial photography. One can photograph part or even the whole of Australia from space, you see. As I related these methods of mapmaking, I did not mention the medium on which the map is to be drawn. I took it for granted that the medium is some other kind of flat surface, probably a piece of paper. The kinds of medium we assume are usually those we traditionally employ. We seldom question their suitability. We rarely understand their contributions. And it would be unusual for someone to contemplate the possibility of employing alternatives. Media are usually invisible to us—that is, until we encounter difficulties.

Let me illustrate with a story: the Parable of the Four ETs.

Once upon a time, four extraterrestrials (ETs) arrived on earth. They were Paul (P), John (J), George (G), and Ringo (R). Among other interesting things, they told the Earthlings that they were great friends and lived close to each other. For instance, Paul lived only 2 unit lengths away from John. Here is a summary of the distances between their homes:

(5) $PJ = JG = GR = RP$, and all the four distances are equal to 2 unit lengths.

To understand the "geography" of the "land" where these ETs lived, a mapmaker proposed the map shown in Figure 31.1.

As the days passed, the Earthlings learned more about these four friendly beatlelike creatures from outer space. One day John complained: "You see, back home both Paul and Ringo lived equally close to me. It used to take me a long time to make up my mind which one I should go to when I ran out of milk. I suppose I am a sort of Buridans Ass."[13] Thus, apart from (5), the mapmaker now had the further information that

(6) $JP = JR$

---

13. Buridan, a 14th-century philosopher, told the story of the ass who died of hunger because it was placed at an equal distance between two equally attractive bags of corn.

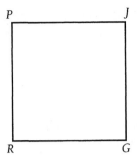

FIGURE 31.1

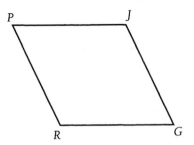

FIGURE 31.2

He reckoned that Figure 31.1 could not be right. The homes of these four ETs could not be at the corners of a square. The figure had to be something like Figure 31.2, a rhombus.

The mapmaker was quite sure that he had it right this time. Nevertheless, being a Popperian, he thought that he should test his theory with predictions. Using elementary geometry, he worked out from Figure 31.2 that it ought to be the case that

(7) $PG = 3.46$ units

Here is a scientific prediction! Moreover, the prediction can be easily checked. Thus the mapmaker asked Paul, "How far did you live from George?" To his surprise and disbelief, the answer was:

(8) $PG = 2$ units

Where had the mapmaker gone wrong? (By the way, Kuhn would call (8) an anomaly.) The mapmaker checked and rechecked his calculations. Perhaps some of the information in (the auxiliary hypotheses) (5) and (6) was incorrect. If (5), (6), and (8) were all true, we would have the situation that

(9) The four points P, J, G, and R are all equidistant from each other.

But (9) is an impossibility! The mapmaker was baffled.

"Wait a minute!" came a voice as if from nowhere, "(9) is impossible only because you are attempting to plot the four points on a flat surface.

The flat surface is what I would call a paradigm. For simplicity, we can call it a medium. In every representation, we employ a medium of some sort. The medium (together with conventions) determines what is possible and what is not possible. Why don't you try a curved surface instead?" It was the voice of Dr. K, the wise man.

Taking up the advice, the mapmaker tried to fit the four points on the surface of a spherical globe. Unfortunately that did not work either. Fortunately the mapmaker happened to be an amateur astronomer. He had read Ptolemy, Copernicus, Kepler, and Galileo, the lot. Kepler, following Ptolemy and Copernicus, first attempted to chart the orbit of Mars in terms of the circle. He changed over to the ellipse when the circle didn't work. This gave the mapmaker an idea. "Why don't I try an ellipsoid?" (An ellipsoid is a sort of three-dimensional ellipse.) Lo and behold, he found an ellipsoid such that the distance between each pole and the equator is one-third the length of the equator.[14]

"So, after all, these ETs came from an ellipsoidal planet! One of them lived at its north pole or the south pole. The other three were equally spaced out on its equator." The mapmaker was overjoyed. Everything fit.

This is not quite the end of the story. Let's pause and try to draw a moral from the story so far. In any representation, we require a medium. What seems to be impossible can be made possible by a change of the medium. The medium when interpreted according to

---

14. Such an ellipsoid would look like an American football or a rugby football.

certain conventions yields a set of possibilities. This set makes up a **representational space**.[15] Within this space, we can build models (representations) of whatever we want to portray. The mapmaker started with a plain piece of paper as the medium. He employed natural conventions such as "Lengths represent lengths," "Straight lines represent straight lines," and "Angles represent angles." Such a representational space can accommodate figures like squares and rhombuses, but not figures with four equidistant points. There are numerous kinds of curved surfaces, the spherical, the ellipsoidal, the paraboloidal, the hyperboloidal, and so on. Each defines its own set of possibilities (and impossibilities). They constitute different representational spaces.

I think Kuhn's notion of paradigm is in essence our notion of representational space here. Representational spaces are usually taken for granted and are thus invisible to most of us. We are indebted to Kuhn for having this "invisible" feature of our knowledge structure pointed out to us.

Let's return to the story. The four ETs were chatting away. They talked about their good old days when they had regular concert performances at the theater. Where was the theater?

(10) The theater was equidistant from the four homes.

That's strange. Where could the theater be on that ellipsoidal planet? Here's another anomaly. Here's another puzzle for the poor mapmaker.

It seems that **representation** consists of two steps. Step 1 is the step of **representational space construction** and it is made up of two substeps:

(1a) A **medium** is chosen (for example, a flat surface).

(1b) A set of **conventions** are adopted. (For instance, we can have lengths representing lengths to the scale of 1 to 100.)

These two substeps together yield a **representational space**.

Step 2 is the modeling step, and it is made up of three substeps:

(2a) A model is built within the representational space,

(2b) Its (empirical) consequences are checked against available data, and

(2c) If these consequences square with the data, the model is retained, otherwise it is rejected.

Step 2, the modeling step, can be seen to be the hypothetico-deductive method, much championed by Popper. Alternatively the inductivists would probably recommend the following steps: (a) record the data, (b) induce a model from the data, and (c) check the model with further data. It can be seen that the debate between deductivism and inductivism is about Step 2, the modeling step. However, the questions that concern the philosopher of science are: How should representations of reality be made? What are the steps involved? What is the logic of representation? Here is where the classical tradition falters. Both the inductivists and the deductivists, like most of us, are only aware of Step 2. They overlook the presence of Step 1, the step of representational space construction. It was Kuhn who pointed out the ever-presence of paradigms in the practice of science. Paradigm theories are simply special cases of our 'representational space.'

In the practice of science, a generic theory is first adopted. This is what Kuhn calls a paradigm theory (Section 26.2). Normal science is then practiced under such a theory, where subparadigm theories (that is, specific theories) are constructed. For example, the CAT is a paradigm theory. Under this paradigm, the following subparadigm theories have been proposed:

(i)   Water is HO (proposed by Dalton).

(ii) Water is H_2O (contemporary formulation).

(iii) Ammonia is NH (proposed by Dalton).

(iv) Ammonia is NH_3 (contemporary formulation).

---

15. In the literature, there are concepts similar in intention—for example, conceptual space, conceptual framework, conceptual scheme. Our term 'representational space' here can be taken as a construal of these concepts.

You can see that HO was proposed as a model of water (Step 2a). This model was constructed in the representational space of CAT. That model was, however, found to be wanting (Step 2b). So another model was proposed, namely, H_2O (Step 2c). This model could still be wrong. Who knows? The important point to note is that each representational space provides its own set of possibilities. Under CAT water can be HO, H_2O, HO_2, and so on. However, it does not make sense to talk in terms of HO or H_2O within the alchemo-phlogiston theory (APT) because APT constitutes another very different representational space. On the other hand, in this very different space it makes sense to say that water is an element, ice is water plus earth, steam is phlogiston plus water, and so on. Each representational space has its own possible "figures."

Kuhn argues that paradigm theories are irrefutable. In fact, the relativistic interpretation of Kuhn would say that one paradigm theory is just as good as another. They cannot be ranked in terms of merits. The choice of paradigm theories is a matter of taste. Of course we need not subscribe to this. Indeed, Kuhn has gone to great lengths to try to shake off the label of relativism.

On the logic of paradigms, Kuhn makes three fundamental claims: (i) Paradigm theories are unfalsifiable. (ii) Competing paradigm theories are incommensurable. (iii) Even though subparadigm theories can be said to be falsifiable, strictly speaking they are not, because of the Duhem-Quine thesis. All scientific theories, both generic and specific, are underdetermined with respect to empirical data. These three claims can easily be illustrated by our Parable of the Four ETs:

In our parable, there are three paradigm theories: (A) the ETs' universe is flat, (B) it is spherical, and (C) it is ellipsoidal. Two subparadigm theories were proposed under A, namely, (M) the four ETs' homes were at the corners of a square, and (N) they were at the corners of a rhombus. One subparadigm theory, L, was proposed under C—that one ET lived at one of the poles while the others were evenly distributed on the equator.

When (6) was discovered, the flat universe theory, A, was not threatened. Subparadigm theory M was simply replaced by subparadigm theory N. However, (8) did threaten A. It was an anomaly according to Kuhn. It causes the mapmaker to change his paradigm theory from A to B and then to C. But he need not have made the change. He could have just blamed some of the auxiliary hypotheses, such as one of the equations in (5). Paradigm theories are indeed unfalsifiable!

As noted in Section 27.3, Kuhn gave seven trans-paradigmatic criteria and values for the assessment of paradigms. They are: problem-solving ability, quantitative precision, predictive power, consistency, simplicity, aesthetics, and future promise. These are objective measures of the goodness of paradigms. They provide practical guides for choice between competing paradigms. Maybe the mapmaker did employ these criteria. Anyway, according to the story, he did change from paradigm theory A to paradigm theory C, and consequently the anomaly (8) disappeared (as if by magic).

In view of the Duhem-Quine thesis, we can see that the mapmaker could have stubbornly stuck even to his subparadigm theory, M. He simply had to discard some of the data supplied to him by the ETs. After all, the ETs need not be telling the truth, or they may have made measuring mistakes. They may have used the wrong laws of nature to measure the distances. For example, their instruments might have assumed that light travels in curves, or that light travels at varying speeds according to its direction of propagation.

Finally, Kuhn claims that paradigm theories are incommensurable. Indeed, the notion of straight line in universe C is different from the notion of straight line in universe A. (We would probably say that, in universe C, the straight lines are geodesics.) Kuhn claims different paradigm theories employ different ontologies. For example, universe A is a two-dimensional Euclidean space and its occupants are Euclidean objects. On the contrary, universe C is curved and non-Euclidean, and so are its occupants.[16] The facts belonging to A are distinct from those of C. There is no overlap, and the statements describing one cannot be translated into statements belonging to the other.

As pointed out in Section 27.3, incommensurability and underdetermination (of theories by empirical data) apparently lead to relativism. Kuhn denies this. However, he does reject the traditional notion of truth, that a scientific theory is true if it corresponds to some objective reality. Is this antirealism justifiable? To answer this let's try to understand Kuhn's Weltanschauung view in terms of sophisticated representationism, for which I take full responsibility:

(11) **Sophisticated Representationism (SoR) is** the view that science aims to represent objective mind-independent reality. Representation takes two steps: (1) the step of representational space construction, and (2) the step of modeling. Representational spaces are generic theories (paradigm theories). Models built within representational spaces are specific theories (subparadigm theories). Because of incommensurability the notion truth does not apply to generic theories. As for specific theories, they can be said to be true or false only within their own generic theories.

Does it make sense to say that science aims at depicting reality as it really is? This is the question posed by Kuhnian antirealism. I propose to understand Kuhn's antirealism as SoR and discuss the question accordingly.

31.6 REALISM OR ANTIREALISM

As said before, the correspondence theory of truth is commonsense realism. The thesis of SoR apparently rejects it. The common notion of truth does not seem to make sense according to this philosophy.

SoR claims that each statement has form and content. Thus each fact also has form and content since facts correspond to true statements. The form comes from the representational space.[17] The content is given by a particular model constructed within the representational space. The form, because of incommensurability, seems to be quite arbitrary. Contrary to conventional thinking, sociologists would say that the form is largely determined by social factors. It is not objective reality that determines the form. Thus the form adopted seems to be rather accidental, depending on the social milieu of the scientists concerned. Once a form has been adopted, models (contents) framed by the form can be built. Objective reality now plays the prominent role. It is objective reality rather than social milieu that determines the adequacy of the models.[18] But then this type of adequacy is relative to the form within which the model is built. Because of this relativity it seems inappropriate to call a model true per se when it is empirically adequate. For example, the model that water is H_2O has been accepted as empirically adequate for nearly 200 years. Yet according to SoR it is only adequate as a subparadigm theory of the CAT. 'H_2O' would not even make sense when viewed from another representational space, let alone be considered adequate. Hence

---

16. For the benefit of the mathematically minded, let me make clear that I have stretched the parable a bit. The four ETs, strictly speaking, were three-dimensional Euclidean objects like us, and theory C says that these three-dimensional objects were living on a curved two-dimensional surface embedded in a three-dimensional Euclidean space. However, there is no reason we cannot retell the story as if the creatures were two-dimensional creatures living in a two-dimensional non-Euclidean space.

17. The notion of representational space is roughly what people vaguely call 'conceptual space,' 'conceptual scheme,' and 'conceptual framework.'

18. Sociologists do not distinguish between form and content, representational spaces and models, generic theories and specific theories, paradigm theories and subparadigm theories. For them *all* knowledge and beliefs are socially determined (partly or totally). I am trying to improve on their thesis here by suggesting that it would be more reasonable to claim that forms are (largely) socially determined, whereas contents are (largely) determined by objective reality.

it seems absurd to say that 'Water is H_2O' is true per se.

Here is an analogy. Position, motions, size, and shape are said to be (some of the) primary qualities. It is said that these qualities belong to material objects themselves. However, colors, smells, and tastes are said to be secondary qualities. They are not really qualities of observed objects. For instance, ripe bananas only appear yellow. The objects are themselves quite colorless. They appear yellow because these objects, owing to the peculiar kinds of primary quality they possess, produce in the observer yellow sensations. Thus colors, smells, and tastes appear to be real qualities only because we are what we are. Such realities are relative to us humans. They are mind-dependent.

The case of models is similar. That water is H_2O appears to be true because we are working within the CAT. This sort of truth is relative, relative to a representational space. Since representational spaces are products of the mind (and social milieus), the truth of models is mind-dependent. Indeed SoR would claim further that perception is made and can only be made through representational spaces. Thus the (perceived) reality, so immediate and tangible to us through our senses, is in fact mind-dependent.

I think this is how we should read statements such as "Reality is a social and intellectual construct" and "Knowledge is a social and intellectual construct" (Section 31.3). These should not be taken as denials of an external reality. Rather, these are about the "shape" and nature of a reality we acknowledge to be "out there." What these statements assert is that the "shape" and nature of the reality that scientists claim to have discovered are social and intellectual constructs. The reason is this. It is the form adopted that determines the "look" of the contents. Since the form adopted is socially caused and mind-dependent, the resulting contents are social and intellectual products as well.

For example, the mapmaker first saw the homes of the four ETs as taking the shape of a square. This piece of "reality" was perceived within the framework of a flat two-dimensional space. But this flat two-dimensional space is a product of the intellect. It was freely concocted by the mapmaker. Hence the "square model" is also an intellectual construct. This is how I would understand constructivism, a name often employed by philosophers, sociologists, and educators to express this type of philosophy.

"**Constructivism**" is actually a misleading term.[19] For example, people tend to read "Reality is a social and intellectual construct" as something like: "Reality is an illusion. There is no mind-independent reality at all. It is just a social and intellectual fantasy." Hence, constructivism would have been simply and more accurately expressed as:

(12) Knowledge is paradigm-determined and paradigm-framed, and paradigms are social and intellectual constructs.

I prefer the term "**Neo-Kantianism**." Kant does not deny the existence of an objective, mind-independent reality. What he claims is that this reality, consisting of things-in-themselves, is unknowable. What we can know are the phenomena.[20] Phenomena are framed and shaped by a framework such as our representational space. Whereas SoR allows for an infinite number of possible representational spaces in the representation of reality, Kant argues that there is one and only one possible "representational space" for the mind (us). This "representational space" can roughly be called the Euclidean-materialistic-causal Framework (EMC Framework). According to Kant, this framework is innate, and the mind has no choice and no alternative but to employ it both in thinking and in perception. Thus **Kantianism** can be said to be a type of SoR. It is SoR with one possible representational space. But then this philosophy is antirealism in name only. It is in practice no different from

---

19. It can be misleading in another way. According to Popper all hypotheses, being conjectures, are constructed. But constructivists are not using 'construction' in this sense.

20. Here 'phenomenon' is not used in the same sense as in Section 15.1.

commonsense realism. When there is only one possible representational space it makes no practical difference whether that space is a product of the mind or a part of objective reality itself. Empirically it is the same, whether it is objective reality that is EMC or the attribute EMC is projected onto reality by the mind. The Kuhnian paradigm view, on the other hand, is quite different. Since paradigms can be replaced at will, they can't belong to objective reality, because objective reality is not supposed to be alterable at will by the mind. Thus Kantian antirealism is only antirealism in words, not in deeds.

Hilary Putnam argues for a form of antirealism, which he calls **internal realism**. Here is how Putnam (1981, p. 49) puts it:

> I shall refer to it as the *internalist perspective*, because it is characteristic of this view to hold that *what objects does the world consist of?* is a question that it only makes sense to ask *within* a theory or description. Many 'Internalist' philosophers, though not all, hold further that there is more than one 'true' theory or description of the world.

You can see that Putnam's internal realism, unlike Kantianism, is truly antirealistic. Like Kuhnianism, it belongs to the same genre as SoR.

Is SoR essentially antirealistic? Let me finish the Parable of the Four ETs, and see if it can throw further light on this question.

Recall that, according to (10), there was a theater equidistant from the four homes. How is this possible on a two-dimensional ellipsoidal surface? Can other types of two-dimensional surfaces cope? Are there any two-dimensional surfaces that can accommodate (10)? There seemed to be no way out. Then the mapmaker, having studied Riemann, had an idea: "Why not try a space of a higher dimension? The four ETs must have lived

on four distinct 'planets,' which were situated at the corners of a tetrahedron.[21] Being equidistant from the four homes, the theater must have been on a fifth 'planet' at the 'heart' (center) of the tetrahedron." This three-dimensional model can be seen to satisfy all the data, (5), (6), (8), and (10).[22] The mapmaker was so pleased with himself that he took the rest of the day off to read philosophy of science!

You can see from this parable that there was something driving the mapmaker to replace one representational space after another. Each replacement seemed to be for the better. Each replacement brought with it satisfaction, as if a key had been found to fit a lock. He saw progress. Though the representational spaces—that is, two-dimensional flat space, two-dimensional ellipsoidal space, and three-dimensional Euclidean space—were all so different, the mapmaker felt that he was gradually approaching reality all the time. Nonetheless, it is difficult to claim that the spaces converge toward something. The sequence is not at all like the sequence of polygons: triangle, square, pentagon, hexagon, heptagon, and so on, each of which is clearly getting closer to being a circle than its predecessor. Incommensurability seems to be in the way, and incommensurable "things" cannot be compared. Yet we feel that the three spaces can be ranked in the context of the available empirical data. Each subsequent space can handle the empirical data better, which suggests that each is getting closer to the truth than its predecessor was. Is it possible to design a notion of truth so that we can say that the sequence of spaces is gradually approximating the truth? Or is the fact that each space is more empirically adequate than its predecessor the best that we can claim? (See van Fraassen and Laudan in Chapter 18.) If such a truth notion could be designed, SoR would be antirealistic no more. Representational spaces would no longer be

---

21. The tetrahedron is a pyramid-like three-dimensional figure, with four identical equitriangular faces. It is the simplest of the five regular solids. The cube is the next simplest regular solid.

22. I know that the ETs did say that they lived very close to each other. But then they were ETs, not humans. Their transportation vehicles were so advanced that they usually considered thousands of miles as short distances. Thus it can be understood why they adopted units of length that were astronomical in magnitude.

arbitrary constructs. Some spaces would be "truer" than others. The really "true" one would represent the actual form of reality!

The question is: Can such a notion of truth be designed? Does such a notion of truth make sense? Does such a notion of truth bear any resemblance to our traditional notion of truth so that the term 'truth' can be used for both?

Perhaps the mapmaker's feeling of satisfaction, his conviction of success, and his perception of getting nearer to the truth all the time can be explained in terms of philosophies other than the correspondence theory of truth. Can we not say, as the conventionalists do, that the aim of science is to coordinate empirical data (Section 9.4)? One can take the successive proposals of representational spaces by the mapmaker as attempts to coordinate the ever-increasing amount of data—for example, (5), (6), (8), and (10). The later spaces yield more satisfaction, because they can cope with more. As said before, the mapmaker could have stuck to the two-dimensional flat space. But then he would have to invent auxiliary hypotheses to coordinate the further data of (8) and (10). He would have to claim things like: light does not travel in straight lines, measuring rods shrink in certain directions, some of the ETs are lying, some of them may not know how to handle measuring rods properly, and so on. But the addition of such auxiliary hypotheses would complicate the coordination, and simple coordinations are preferable to complicated ones.

Here I have mentioned two desiderata: power of coordination[23] and simplicity. We require representational spaces that can coordinate the maximum amount of data in the simplest way. Now, the notion of simple coordination belongs to the coherence theory of truth. Perhaps we should explain the progress of science and the mechanics of scientific theories in terms of the coherence theory rather than the correspondence theory of truth. Kuhnian antirealism is very close to conventionalism indeed.

I hope that through the notion of SoR here we have come to a better understanding of Kuhnian constructivism: how it works, why knowledge is said to be constructive, and in what sense constructivism is antirealistic.[24]

There is, however, one blemish on this reconstruction of constructivism in terms of SoR. I feel obliged to mention it before moving on. According to SoR, there is a clear distinction between 'representational space' and 'model.' They are simply two very different kinds of things. The dividing line between form and content is sharp. There are no in-betweens. However, their counterparts in Kuhnian conceptions of science are not so sharply divided. Generic theories (paradigm theories) and specific theories (subparadigm theories) do not seem to be two distinct kinds of things. They only differ in degree of generality. They shade into each other. There is no hard-and-fast line to be drawn between the two.

This difference between representational spaces and paradigm theories will surface again in the next chapter. You will find that the continuum between 'paradigm theory' and 'subparadigm theory' is an advantage in the design of machine creativity in artificial intelligence.[25]

---

23. Power of explanation, if you like.

24. If SoR is correct, it should throw new light on the problem of induction (Chapter 20). Suppose empirical data can only be collected and understood through a representational space (paradigm), and it is never the case (and perhaps it is impossible) that we perceive and conceive the world in terms of Hume's representational space where objects are sense impressions, (causally) loose, and unconnected. Further suppose that we have to conceive the world causally, as Kant insists. Under such suppositions, we can see that the problem of induction would not have arisen, because the premise that observational data are causally unconnected is simply not true. This is a Kantian solution to Hume's problem. However, does this Kantian solution work if Hume's problem is reformulated in terms of the law of large numbers (Section 20.3B)?

25. This chapter represents my personal understanding and defense of constructivism. It can be seen that constructivism is a development of conventionalism (Chapter 9).

KEY TERMS INTRODUCED IN THIS CHAPTER

semantic antirealism

epistemic antirealism

truth-theoretic antirealism

correspondence theory of truth

representationism

representer

representee

intention

conventions

natural convention

artificial convention

simple representationism

medium

representational space

representation

representational space construction

model

sophisticated representationism (SoR)

constructivism

Neo-Kantianism

Kantianism

internal realism

REFERENCES

Boyd (1983) provides a useful survey and discussion of the debate between realism and constructivism. Vision (1988) covers all the major theories of truth, and the major types of truth-theoretic antirealism. Kuhnian constructivism can be found in Vision's Chapter IX, whereas the correspondence theory of truth is covered in Chapter V.

Engel (1991, chap. 5) gives an introduction to various theories of truth. Oldroyd (1986, pp. 119–135) is a good digest of Kant's philosophy. For arguments for internal realism, see Putnam (1981). Giere (1991) is an introductory text portraying scientific theories as models.

For sociological versions of constructivism, see Knorr–Cetina and Mulkay (1983), especially the Introductory Essay. Latour and Woolgar (1979) and Knorr–Cetina (1981) give two representative sociological constructivist positions.

For constructivism in theory of education, see Bodner (1986) for an introduction.

Chapter 32*

Artificial Intelligence and the Philosophy of Science

32.1 WHAT IS ARTIFICIAL INTELLIGENCE?

Just as Kuhn's paradigm view has brought about a revolution in the philosophy of science (POS), so will **artificial intelligence (AI)**. In the last four chapters, we saw how the logical approach of the classical tradition was replaced by Kuhn's historical-cum-sociological approach. We will see how AI is starting to bring about a new approach, the computational approach. But first, what is AI?

I am sure all of us have great admiration for the electronic computer. It is smart. It can multiply 20-digit numbers in a flash. It can do square roots. It can handle complicated equations. It can store vast records, from encyclopedias to the criminal records of a whole nation. It can remote-control machinery, from robots to rockets, and it can land spacecraft on the moon. To say that computers are smart seems an understatement. Yet from the point of view of AI, these tasks are relatively simple and straightforward. They belong to the category of "number crunching" and data processing. Such "mechanical" work requires little intelligence, if any. The computer just does what it is told to do, as people would say. On the other hand, AI wants to create machines that are genuinely intelligent. We want computers that can solve crimes somewhat like Sherlock Holmes, that can do mathematics somewhat like Gauss, that can produce scientific theories somewhat like Newton and Einstein, and maybe we can even have machines that can produce philosophical ideas like Aristotle or Kant.

---

*This chapter is more advanced and is optional.

The history of AI is relatively short. The subject started only in the mid-1950s. Nevertheless in just a few decades it has yielded impressive results. AI can be divided into the following fields:

(a) **Vision**: The camera can take good pictures. But it cannot see. Seeing involves more than producing images (Chapter 22). Seeing means knowing what one is looking at, understanding what is happening, and anticipating more or less correctly what is going to happen next. A picture of a room consists of shapes of colors of various intensities. A camera can easily produce such pictures. But the camera does not see. It does not know how to interpret these colored shapes. For instance, it cannot tell us that it is a desk that produces that brown shape, that the dark patch on the right-hand corner of the brown shape is a shadow cast by a pile of books, that there is a partly obscured chair behind the desk, that the room is oblong in shape and about 20 feet wide, that a person is walking across the room, that she is going to reach the desk in the next moment or two, and so on. It requires someone—for example, us—to "read" the picture in order to arrive at this interpretation. AI is expected to be able to function as that someone.

(b) **Speech Recognition**: This is a relatively simple field compared to the others. AI is required to be able to discern the words spoken from a sequence of sound input.

(c) **Language Understanding**: To be able to transcribe a sequence of sounds into words is far from being able to understand what is being said. Think of a typist typing from a dictaphone. She can be a hundred percent accurate, transcribing what she hears into written words. Yet she need not understand the contents of what she types. She could be typing medical records, court cases, company laws, articles on microbiology, on astrophysics, on philosophy, and so on. Surely she is not required to have a mastery of all these subjects before she can be a competent typist. Thus language understanding is much more than speech recognition. In short, language understanding requires a grasp of the meaning of sentences and paragraphs over and above recognition of certain sounds as representing certain words.

(d) **Memory**: An intelligent being retains information acquired, which can later be recalled and used. Every computer of modest size has a reasonable storage capacity for data. So what is the problem? The problem, strictly speaking, is not one of storage but of retrieval. It's not much good if the stored information cannot be retrieved with reasonable ease. That's why it is not a simple matter to design an efficient library catalog system. It benefits the potential reader little with a library full of books if it takes "ages" for her to find the books she wants. To design data storage for computers that can yield information of all sorts on request can be quite a challenge.

(e) **Learning**: The above four fields—vision, speech recognition, language understanding and memory—are about the interpretation of input signals: how these input signals can be interpreted correctly as information or data. Learning is about the further step: how these data can be made use of to improve on future performances. Thus, for instance, we would like to have computers that can learn to recognize chairs in general after being shown a few examples of chairs (data). If a computer succeeds in recognizing chairs whose shapes, sizes, colors, structures, or weights have not been encountered before, we would say that it has acquired the concept of a chair. We humans are "smart" in that we can usually acquire the relevant concepts from a few examples, whether of worms or insects, cars or airplanes. Can computers do equally well?

Concept learning is only one of many fields of learning. We certainly learn facts as well from examples. For instance, from a few encounters a child can learn that dogs in general bark whereas ducks in general quack. A third kind of learning is that of skill acquisition. Let me explain by way of an example. Someone learning to play chess would, to start with, learn all the rules of the game. But knowing the rules alone does not make her a good chess player. Even the "ingestion" of established strategies would not. She has to play a large number of games. Somehow by playing games she learns to improve herself. This is skill acquisition by practice. Typists, drivers, doctors, lawyers, programmers, indeed professionals of all sorts learn to improve their skills this way. Truly intelligent computers should be able to learn in a similar manner.

(f) **Problem Solving and Planning**: Problem solving is the making use of concepts and information acquired to solve problems. Let's take an example, the River Crossing Problem:

> There is a little girl who wants to cross the river with her three belongings: a fox, a duck, and a cabbage. The boat available is small. Other than the rower, it can only hold one thing at a time. How is she going to get across with all her belongings given that (i) the fox will eat the duck if left together unsupervised, and (ii) the duck will eat the cabbage if left together unsupervised.

From this example, we can see that the order of execution of the steps is vitally important. If the little girl were to perform the steps in the wrong order, she might end up losing her duck or cabbage. Thus problem solving is closely related to (steps) planning.

Problem solving can be characterized as the development of a sequence of actions to achieve a goal state from a given initial state. This includes theorem proving (in mathematics and logic) and automatic programming.

So far we can say that AI intends to replicate human intelligence in three areas: interpretation, memory, and reasoning. Fields (a) to (c) belong to the area of **interpretation** of input signals. Field (d) is the field of **memory**. Fields (e) and (f) belong to the area of **reasoning**, deductive and inductive. Finally, there is the field of creativity.

(g) **Creativity**: We say certain artists—such as Picasso, Mozart, and Shakespeare—are creative. We also say that certain scientists—including Galileo, Newton, and Einstein—are creative. Creativity probably represents intelligence of the highest kind. Can computers be made creative? We will devote most of the present chapter to this area.

How is information stored in the computer so that it can readily be recalled, can be made use of in reasoning, and can enable the machine to be creative? This area of research is known as **knowledge representation**.[1]

Suppose the computer has recorded in its knowledge base all the works of Einstein: Does it mean that it possesses knowledge of the theory of relativity? Suppose the whole of the *Encyclopaedia Britannica* has been typed into the computer: Does it mean that it is now a "walking encyclopedia"? The answer, I am afraid, is no to both questions. Let me illustrate.

Suppose stored in the computer's knowledge base is the sentence:

(1) Captain James Cook was born in 1728.

Should question (2) be directed at the computer, I think it reasonable to expect the computer to be able to respond (correctly) with (3).

(2) Was Captain James Cook born in 1728?

(3) Yes.

The computer can arrive at the correct answer (3) through the use of an operation called matching. Here question (2) in essence is:

(2a) Captain James Cook was born in 1728?

The computer can easily locate (1) in the knowledge base to match (2a). The computer is programmed to answer yes whenever there is a matching sentence.

However, let us look at

(4) What year was Captain James Cook born in?

---

1. The term 'knowledge representation' is slightly misleading. In AI terminology, 'knowledge' means what we mean by 'beliefs.' What the computer takes for granted as true is simply the computer's beliefs, which are not necessarily (true) knowledge. Having said this, since the term 'knowledge' is now widely used, I think we should follow this usage.

By matching alone, this simple question cannot be answered. It would not improve the situation much if we reformulate (4) as

(4a) Captain James Cook was born in year_____?

For sure, the computer will find the first six words of (1) matching the first six words of (4a). But then how is the computer to deal with the word 'year'? How does the computer *know* that '1728' was the name of a year and thus transfer it to the blank slot of (4a)? The item '1728' could very well be the name of a city or a country or the name of a spacecraft.

You can see that far from being a "walking encyclopedia," the computer armed with the *Encyclopaedia Britannica* cannot supply answers even to simple questions such as (4). One reason is that the data are not stored in the right form.

One suggestion is that data should be stored in a language of logic, such as the predicate calculus. The logical language works as a sort of universal language. Whatever questions are directed to the computer will be translated into that language, and since questions and data are in the same form, answers should be easily forthcoming.

Using logic in knowledge representation has another advantage. It facilitates reasoning. For example, let (5) and (6) be information stored in the computer:

(5) All humans are mortal.

(6) Socrates is human.

Suppose the question is:

(7) Is Socrates mortal?

Since there are no sentences in the knowledge base matching (7), the answer will have to be no—that is, unless the computer can infer from (5) and (6) to

(8) Socrates is mortal.

Logic provides all sorts of rules enabling exactly this kind of inference (Chapter 2). To put it

dramatically, when knowledge is stored in the computer in the form of logical formulas, the computer can reason like a logician.[2] But you may ask: Why do we have to employ logical notations to do reasoning? Why can't we simply provide the computer with reasoning rules in English? For example we can have this rule:[3]

(9) All *X* are *Y*.

$\underline{A \text{ is } X.}$

Therefore *A* is *Y*.

The trouble with this rule is that even though it can enable the inference from (5) and (6) to (8), it would not be able to if (5) is rephrased as

(5a) Any human is mortal.

The computer does not know that 'any' has the same semantic value as 'all' here.[4] This is not the only reason we have to employ logical notations. There are many others, most of which are much more serious. Let me illustrate with an analogy.

We should find it easy to multiply 3,217 by 205. Now try to do the multiplication in terms of the English words 'three thousand two hundred and seventeen' and 'two hundred and five.' Just as the use of Arabic numerals facilitates arithmetical operations so does the use of logical notations facilitate reasoning.

Thus you can see the importance of knowledge representation. To put it briefly, in order for the computer to be able to retrieve information, to reason, and to create, the knowledge it acquires has to be stored in a suitable representational system. Many systems of logic have been employed for this purpose, and there are many nonlogical systems as well. There are many kinds of knowledge. Some systems are more suitable for some purposes than for others.

When we talk about AI we usually mean what is sometimes termed as GOFAI (Good Old-Fashioned

---

2. This is an overstatement. The computer requires more than just rules of logic to reason. It requires heuristics as well (Section 32.6).

3. See the argument from BARBARA in Chapter 2.

4. Strictly speaking, the computer has to know that 'is' and 'are' have the same semantic value as well.

AI) or classical AI. A more recent type of AI is known as **connectionism** or **neural networks**. Unfortunately we do not have the space here to introduce this exciting field.

You have probably come across the term **cognitive science** as well. Cognitive science is the interdisciplinary study of the nature of cognition in human beings and other animals. Its major contributors are philosophy, cognitive psychology, neuroscience, linguistics, and AI. The difference between AI and cognitive science is that the former is an engineering discipline, aiming at the *construction* of machines that yield cognition, whereas the latter is an empirical science, aiming at the *description* and *explanation* of the phenomena of cognition. Obviously the two disciplines are natural partners.

32.2 AI AND THE PHILOSOPHY OF SCIENCE

Science is generally recognized as representing the best kind of reasoning and creativity that human civilization has ever produced.[5] Hence, to construct AI it makes sense to look into the workings of science, which is what the POS is about.

A. Philosophy of Science as the Supplier of Ideas to AI

We saw in the last section how learning and problem solving belong to the area of reasoning. Can scientific reasoning be made use of in the construction of AI? For example, in Chapter 5 we talked about mechanical methods of discovery (of plausible hypotheses). In Chapters 6 and 7, we discussed methods of evaluation (of hypotheses). Surely we would like AIs to be able to discover and evaluate hypotheses. Thus the results of POS are of great relevance. The hypothetico-deductive method, championed by Popper (Chapter 24), should be of use as well; so should Carnap's confirmation theory (Section 4.8).

The logical positivists take scientific theories as sets of statements, sometimes known as axioms. These statements are divided into internal principles and bridge principles (Chapter 15). Can this view of theories be adopted in knowledge representation? We might like to provide the AI with the knowledge of a theory such as Newton's theory of mechanics or the caloric theory of heat. How should this piece of knowledge be stored in the computer? Accepting logical positivism, we might like to store it as a set of statements. If these statements are in logical notation, and the computer is given rules of deduction, the machine should be able to give deductive-nomological explanations (Chapter 10) as well as deductive predictions.[6]

On the other hand, Kuhn thinks that scientific theories are not sets of statements at all. First, there are no such things as internal principles. Theories are attached to nature and experience through exemplars (Section 26.1). This exemplar thesis has a bearing on the computational representation of theories (Thagard, 1988, chap. 3). Second, there are two types of theories: paradigm theories and subparadigm theories. Unfortunately Kuhn has not told us the "architecture" of their internal structures. Nonetheless, this two-level distinction will no doubt have implications for the design of knowledge representation systems. So will Lakatos's notion of research program, with its negative and positive heuristics.

The theory-ladenness of observation occupies the central stage in post-positivist philosophies (Chapter 22). This should also have implications for the design of vision in AI.

Finally, scientific creativity should be relevant to the construction of AI-creativity. We will devote much of the chapter to this area.

---

5. This is not meant to belittle great philosophical thinking. It is only that the two kinds of reasoning are so different, and philosophical reasoning is so obscure to the layperson.

6. As a matter of fact, life is not that simple. Besides logical rules, the computer requires the guidance of heuristics (Section 32.6).

B. AI as the Testing Ground of Philosophy of Science

Philosophers are often at odds about the correct methods of reasoning in science, about the structure of scientific theories, and about the nature of observation. With AI techniques, we can actually test these ideas empirically. We can attempt to implement these ideas in the construction of AIs. The performance of such AIs is a measure of the adequacy of those ideas. Thus "AI as the testing ground of POS" is simply the other side of the same coin, "POS as the supplier of ideas to AI," described in Subsection A.

C. AI as the Supplier of Ideas to Philosophy of Science

It is a two-way street. Not only can POS provide AI with ideas, but results from AI research can in turn supply POS with new insights: in the fields of reasoning and knowledge representation and in studies of the nature of observation and creativity.

I propose to study the problem of creativity in some depth. From this study, I hope the intimate relationship between POS and AI will become obvious.

32.3 MECHANIZATION OF DISCOVERY I

At the beginning of this book (Chapters 1 and 5), we introduced the **problem of discovery**. We asked the questions:

(a) How can *plausible* and fruitful hypotheses be discovered?

(b) Are there any methods to improve the chances of such discoveries?

(c) Are there any mechanical methods that will inevitably lead to such discoveries?

Let's add one more question here:

(d) If the answer to (c) is in the affirmative, does it show that mechanical creativity is possible?

As we are drawing to a close in this rather lengthy book of ours, I think it nice to return to the very first problem with which we began. It gives a sense of completeness.

As I pointed out in Section 5.7, philosophers are quite polarized on Question (c). The pessimists think that we should not expect to be able to secure partially mechanized methods significantly more sophisticated than Mill's five methods of induction and some of the methods of statistical inference. The optimists, on the other hand, think that partial mechanization can go far beyond these. Some even think that sophisticated theories such as Newton's mechanics and Einstein's theory of relativity are not beyond the reach of mechanical methods of discovery. Here are some well-known historical pessimists: William Whewell (1794–1866), R. B. Braithwaite, and Karl Popper. Here are some equally well-known optimists: Bacon, Mill, Charles Sanders Peirce (1839–1914), Norwood R. Hanson, and Herbert A. Simon. To see the issue more clearly, I propose that we study some computer programs and systems.

A. The BACON systems (versions 1 through 6) are a series of computer programs that have been designed by P. Langley et al. (1987) to discover *quantitative* empirical laws of nature[7] from sets of numerical empirical data. Let's start with BACON.1.

Around 1660, Robert Boyle discovered what is now known as Boyle's law:

(10) $PV = c$

which says that for a given amount of gas, the product of its pressure P and its volume V is equal to a constant c (Section 4.5). Can machines be programmed to do the same? According to Langley and his colleagues, BACON.1 can. Here is how it does it.

---

7. We called these laws of functional relations in Section 11.5.

BACON.1 is designed to handle only two variables. In the present case, the two variables are P and V. Given the set of data on P and V as obtained experimentally by Boyle (the first two columns of Table 32.1), BACON.1 looks out for functions of P and V that yield constants from the set of data. The strategy is to try out possible functions one at a time, starting with the simpler ones. Here are eight simple functions: P, V, $(P + V)$, $(P - V)$, $(V - P)$, PV, P/V, V/P. The first five are quickly ruled out as far from yielding constant values. For example, since the second column of Table 32.1 varies from 29.750 to 1.250, the function P cannot be a constant. Similarly, V cannot be a constant because it varies from 1.0 to 32.0. Now, what about the sixth function, which is PV? BACON.1 looks at the last column of Table 32.1 and decides that the values suggest that PV equals the constant 31.6 (which is the mean value of the last column). Even though the last column is not exactly constant, BACON.1 is programmed to ignore discrepancies as long as they are within certain acceptable limits.

In this way, it is claimed that Boyle's law has been mechanically rediscovered.

Here is a slightly more complicated example. The aim is to rediscover Kepler's third law of planetary motion (formulated in 1618):

(11) $D^3/P^2 = c$

which says that the cube of a planet's distance D from the sun when divided by the square of the planet's period P is equal to a constant c.[8]

BACON.1 is provided with a table of data, namely, the corresponding values of D and P for the six known planets, including earth. As before, it attempts to discover the presence of any constant functions. Let's confine ourselves to the multiplicative functions. The simpler ones are DP, D/P, P/D, D^2/P, P/D^2, P^2/D, D/P^2, D^2/P^2, P^2/D^2, D^3/P, P/D^3, P^3/D, D/P^3, D^3/P^2, and so on. You can see that if BACON.1 tries these out one after another, it will arrive at Kepler's third

TABLE 32.1[9]

Volume (V)	Pressure (P)	PV
1.0	29.750	29.750
1.5	19.125	28.688
2.0	14.375	28.750
3.0	9.500	28.500
4.0	7.125	28.500
5.0	5.625	28.125
6.0	4.875	29.250
7.0	4.250	29.750
8.0	3.750	30.000
9.0	3.375	30.375
10.0	3.000	30.000
12.0	2.625	31.500
14.0	2.250	31.500
16.0	2.000	32.000
18.0	1.875	33.750
20.0	1.750	35.000
24.0	1.500	36.000
28.0	1.375	38.500
32.0	1.250	40.000

law after 13 attempts. Testing 13 functions for a computer is nothing. BACON.1 has apparently also rediscovered Galileo's law of uniform acceleration and Ohm's law.

BACON.1 is the prototype. Langley and his colleagues produced six versions of BACON, each an improvement on the previous version. For instance, BACON.3 has rediscovered more complicated quantitative laws—for example, the ideal-gas law and Coulomb's law of electric attraction. You can see that these laws have more than two variables. BACON.4 has rediscovered even more *complicated laws,* including Snell's law of refraction and the law of conservation of momentum.

---

8. The period of a planet is the time it takes to go round the sun.

9. From Langley et al. (1987, p. 82). This is Boyle's original table converted to decimals from the fractional form.

From these examples, I don't think that we can deny the success of BACON in the discovery of quantitative laws. It seems to have demonstrated that there are mechanical methods of discovery, and the answer to Question (c) should therefore be yes. What about Question (d)? Has it shown that mechanical creativity is possible? Are the works of BACON really creative?

A Popperian would probably say no, and for good reason. To start with, the processes employed by BACON are not inductions at all. Take for example the rediscovery of Kepler's third law by BACON.1. What it did was to test a number of hypotheses, one after another. The 14th hypothesis was adopted because it passed the test, whereas all the earlier 13 failed. This is a typical application of the hypothetico-deductive method, the Popperian method of falsification. If BACON.1 was truly creative, it would have to create a plausible hypothesis, out of nothing, so to speak. What as a matter of fact it did was to test a series of hypotheses, fed to it from an outside source. I suppose BACON.1 can claim that it did generate the series of hypotheses itself. But that generation was hardly creative in that what it did was simply to generate a series of functions in order of simplicity. There was no insight involved. A truly creative being would be able to "leap" to a plausible function simply by looking at the set of data. The historic Kepler may have been just that. He may have had some sort of sixth sense or intuition, which enabled him to spot D^3/P^2 right away. Had he discovered this function simply by trying out all sorts of functions, he would not have been truly creative. He would certainly have been patient, hard working, devoted, and so on, but he would have been far from creative. In fact, the method of blind trial and error requires a lot of luck. For instance, the function that governs the relationship of D and P for the planets might not have been in the series of multiplicative functions at all. It could be an additive function, a logarithmic function, or even a trigonometric function. Success in terms of "blind luck" can hardly be called ingenious or creative! Can it? We will have more to say in Section 32.6.

You can see that 'BACON' is a misnomer. The series of programs was supposed to be following Francis Bacon's methods of induction (Sections 3.3 and 19.3). However, the method employed by BACON is ironically the hypothetico-deductive method of Popper, who distinguished himself as a staunch critic of Bacon.

B. STAHL is another program by Langley and associates. Unlike BACON, it aims to produce qualitative laws rather than quantitative laws. Specifically it aims to rediscover those qualitative laws proposed by G. E. Stahl and others during the development of the phlogiston theory (Chapter 25).

Data available to STAHL are of the form:

(12) (Reaction: input $\{X_1, X_2, ..., X_n\}$
output $\{Y_1, Y_2, ..., Y_m\}$)

where $X_1, X_2, ..., X_n, Y_1, Y_2, ..., Y_m$ are names of substances known. For example, the "known" substances at the time of Stahl were air, charcoal, ash, phlogiston, water, ice, steam, iron, calx of iron, lead, sulfur, gold, vitriolic acid, potash, lime, quicklime, fixed air, and so on. Examples of (12) would be:

(12a) (Reaction: input {charcoal, air} output {phlogiston, ash, air})

(12b) (Reaction: input {calx of iron, charcoal, air} output {iron, ash, air})

From the given data, STAHL aims at producing conclusions of the form:

(13) (Components of X are $Y_1, Y_2, ..., Y_k$)

Here are three examples:

(13a) (Components of charcoal are phlogiston and ash)

(13b) (Components of iron are phlogiston and calx of iron)

(13c) (Components of mercury are phlogiston and calx of mercury)

Note that no quantity is mentioned in (12) or (13). Conclusion (12) does not state the relative amount of substances involved in the reaction, and (13) does not tell us the weight or volume proportions of the component substances. This is purely qualitative chemistry.

How does STAHL infer conclusions of form (13) from data of form (12)? Here are five of the rules employed:

Rule 1:

IF A and B react to form C,

  Or IF C decomposes into A and B,

THEN infer that C is composed of A and B.

Rule 2:

IF A occurs on both sides of a reaction,

THEN remove A from the reaction.

Rule 3:

IF A occurs in a reaction,

  AND A is composed of B and C,

THEN replace A with B and C.

Rule 4:

IF A is composed of B and C,

  AND A is composed of B and D,

  AND neither C contains D nor D contains C,

THEN identify C with D.

Rule 5:

IF A is composed of C and D,

  AND B is composed of C and D,

  AND neither A contains B nor B contains A,

THEN identify A with B.[10]

Langley and associates gave STAHL as data the experimental results in the order that they were observed in the history of the phlogiston theory. Employing its rules of inference, STAHL was able to rediscover many historical results.

Again it cannot be denied that this computer program has shown that there are mechanical methods of discovery. Thus the answer to Question (c) is again yes. What about Question (d)? Can STAHL be credited with creativity?

It can be seen that STAHL's rules of inference resemble Mill's method of residues (Chapter 3). It is a matter of subtraction and addition. Surely we expect more from creativity.

In Chapter 5, we recognized the partial mechanical nature of Mill's methods. Many of the statistical inferences can be mechanized as well. In the wide sense of the word, both BACON and STAHL can be said to be creative. However, I think most would prefer to see some more impressive and astonishing results before we bestow the honorary title of creative genius on these mechanical beings.

C. What about DENDRAL?[11] This is an AI system that can propose plausible structures for complex chemical compounds.

Let me first explain the idea of an isomer. In organic chemistry, it is quite common for more than one compound (molecule) to share the same chemical formula. These are known as isomers. For instance, both *n*-butane and iso-butane share the formula C_4H_{10}, but the spatial arrangement of their component atoms is different. We say that their structures are different. The structures of the two molecules are shown in Figures 32.1a and 32.1b.

It is a relatively straightforward procedure to determine the composition of a compound by employing mass spectrography together with other methods, thus arriving at chemical formulas such as C_4H_{10}. However, even for relatively simple organic compounds the possible structures may run into thousands. Hence it is quite a task to try to work out the exact structure of an organic compound from its formula. Here is where DENDRAL comes in.

Given a chemical formula, DENDRAL possesses a mechanism to generate all the possible structures for that formula, which as I said may run into thousands. If required, it can print out all of these. But what is the point? Instead it eliminates

---

10. From Langley et al. (1987, pp. 228–229, 234).

11. DENDRAL was designed by Lindsay et al. (1980).

FIGURE 32.1a *n*-butane

structures that are improbable given the existing experimental data. For example, some structures may contain substructures that should preclude certain spectral lines. If those lines are found to exist, then those structures can be discarded. In this way, DENDRAL is usually able to reduce the number of plausible structures to a manageable few. The chemist can then attempt to further narrow the set down to one, with or without further experiments.

To say the least, DENDRAL has been of great help in finding structures for organic substances. It is certainly a mechanical process of discovery. It employs a process of systematic elimination of implausible candidates, like BACON. Again, is this creativity?

D. PI is an AI program developed by Paul Thagard and Keith Holyoak.[12] It can yield plausible hypotheses through analogical reasoning. For example, it is able to conjecture that sound consists of waves because sound propagates and reflects, just as water waves do. Here is the conventional schema of analogical reasoning:

(14) A is P, Q, R, and S.

B is P, Q, R.

Therefore, B is S.[13]

However, Thagard thinks that this is not quite right. It should be:

(15) Both A and B are P, Q, and R. A's being S explains why it is P, Q, and R. Hence B is likely to be S as well.[14]

FIGURE 32.1b iso-butane

Since sound propagates and reflects just as water waves do, it is likely that sound consists of waves as well.

Analogical reasoning has been generally recognized as an important source of creative thinking. This is evidenced by many historical cases. For instance, Dufay, Nollet, and Franklin all conjectured that electricity is a kind of fluid, on the grounds that it flows. Heat was taken as a kind of fluid by the caloric theorists for a similar reason. Huygens's wave theory of light was modeled on sound waves (Chapter 0). Newton's corpuscular theory of light was modeled on bouncing "tennis balls." And Niels Bohr's atom was modeled on the solar system. Having said this, I think I should also mention some of the great scientific theories that could not have been arrived at through analogical reasoning: Newton's mechanics, Rumford's kinetic theory of heat, the kinetic theory of gases, Dalton's atomic theory, Heisenberg's matrix mechanics, and Einstein's theory of relativity.

32.4 MECHANIZATION OF DISCOVERY II

In Section 31.5, we proposed to understand Kuhn's constructivism as **sophisticated representationism (SoR)**. The aim of SoR is to represent

12. 'PI' stands for 'processes of induction.' For further details see Holland et al. (1986) and Thagard (1988, p. 15).

13. See Section 3.2.

14. Thagard (1988, p. 93).

objective reality in two steps: (i) to construct a **representational space** and (ii) to build a model of reality within that space. In the Parable of the Four ETs, the mapmaker started with a two-dimensional flat space, then tried a two-dimensional curved space, and ended up with a three-dimensional space. The mapmaker's spaces are real spaces, the word 'space' being understood more or less as what the word usually means. However, in the context of SoR, the word 'space' in 'representational space' means something more and much more general. A representational space is simply a set of possibilities. It is important to bear this in mind as we study the notion of mechanized discovery in terms of SoR.

Let's study the notion of representational space and the logic of mechanized discovery in terms of the four great cosmological theories: (i) Eudoxus's geocentric theory, (ii) Ptolemy's geocentric theory, (iii) Copernicus's heliocentric theory, and (iv) Kepler's heliocentric theory.

A. Eudoxus's Geocentric Theory

Eudoxus of Cnidus (409–356 B.C.) took the earth as the immovable center of the universe. The fixed stars, the five known planets, the sun, and the moon, all revolve around the earth. What sort of orbit do they follow? How do they do it?

According to Eudoxus, the fixed stars are studded on the surface of a huge crystalline sphere centered around the earth. This sphere turns on a fixed axis once a day at uniform speed. That explains why the same stars return night after night to the same place. The polar star happens to be in line with the axis. That's why it does not appear to move.

Within this "starry" sphere are the spheres carrying the planets. Ideally each sphere carries one planet, and each "planetary" sphere is fixed onto the next outer one via an axis. Thus we should have a system of concentric spheres with the earth innermost at the center and the starry sphere as the outermost shell. However, this simple scheme does

not work because, as we saw in Chapter 7, the paths of the planets across the night sky are rather complicated. They do not move in (apparent) straight lines. Their speeds are not uniform. They sometimes move backward (retrograde motion). They do not follow exactly the same paths every year. The ancient Greeks called them 'planets,' meaning 'wanderers.' The problem is how to reproduce their apparent motions in terms of uniform and circular motions. This is historically known as Plato's problem, for it was traditionally believed that Plato was the first to formulate it.

Let's take Saturn, the outermost planet known at the time, and see how Eudoxus attempted to solve Plato's problem. As said earlier, ideally Saturn (S) is carried on the equator of a sphere whose axis is fixed on the inside of the starry sphere, as in Figure 32.2a. But this simple scheme does not work, and the reason is obvious. Planets such as Saturn are charted against the (fixed) stars of the night sky. In other words, the positions of planets are observed relative to the stars. If Saturn were to move as pictured in Figure 32.2a, it would be seen as moving at uniform speed in a perfect straight line across the night sky of stars.[15] But as a matter of fact the path of Saturn against the stars is far more complicated. To accommodate such complexity a secondary sphere can be added, as in Figure 32.2b. Here Saturn (S) is fixed on the equator of the

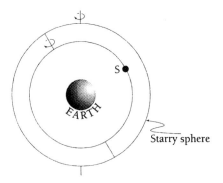

FIGURE 32.2a

---

15. Since we are talking about the relative motion of Saturn with respect to the stars, the spinning of the starry sphere on its axis is irrelevant.

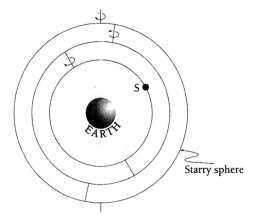

FIGURE 32.2b

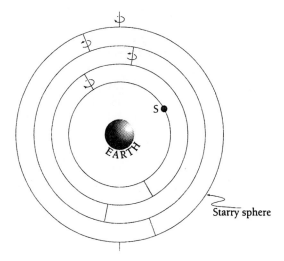

FIGURE 32.2c

secondary sphere. Relative to the starry sphere, it moves on the combination of two rotations. However, even this arrangement was found to be inadequate; a third sphere had to be added, as in Figure 32.2c.

The next outermost planet was Jupiter. It required four spheres, with the axis of the primary sphere attached to the sphere of Saturn. In a similar

manner, the orbits of Mars, Sun, Venus, Mercury, and the moon were reconstructed. To account (rather crudely) for the motions of all 7 celestial bodies, Eudoxus had to employ 26 spheres. This Eudoxian scheme was later modified and adopted by Aristotle, who ended up with 55 spheres in all—that is, not including the starry sphere.[16]

(16) The Eudoxian system is a system of concentric spheres with each planet (including the sun and moon) fixed to the equator of a chosen sphere. The inclination of the axis of each sphere is independent of that of any others. The relative speed of rotation of each sphere is uniform and is also independent of that of any others. However, since each sphere is attached to the next outer one through its axis, the resultant (absolute) motion of each sphere depends on the rotational motions of all the outer spheres. The outermost sphere is the sphere of the stars.

Scheme (16) defines the representational space of Eudoxus's theory. It defines a set of possibilities: a set of possible spheres carrying the planets (including the sun and moon). In the terminology of SoR, Eudoxus first constructed this representational space and then tried out various models within it. He ended up with 26 spheres for the planets and 1 for the stars.

This raises two questions: (a) How did he arrive at this representational space of his? (b) Having obtained this representational space, how did he arrive at the (26 + 1) spheres? Both are steps of creative discovery. Can these two steps be mechanized? We are not really interested in the historical reconstruction of Eudoxus's reasoning. What we are interested in is the theoretical reconstruction: (a) Given Plato's problem, are there mechanical methods that can enable the discovery of Eudoxus's representational space? (b) Given this representational space of the concentric spheres, are there any mechanical methods leading to the discovery of the (26 + 1) spheres?

---

16. The materials here are taken from Holton and Roller (1958, pp. 105–110) and Singer (1959, pp. 43–45, 52–54). There is quite a bit of inconsistency in Singer. In one place, he says that Saturn requires three spheres (p. 53), but in another place he says "in the explanation of the movements of the ... planets, four spheres each were demanded" (p. 44).

Leaving Problem (a) for the next two sections, let's study (b) in terms of Saturn.

The problem of Saturn is to create a set of concentric spheres so that its three-dimensional orbit round the earth will produce the observed path it makes against the two-dimensional night sky of stars. Suppose someone conjectures that Saturn is riding on three spheres. She then has to work out what inclination the axes of the three spheres should take. Here are three independent "axis" variables. She has also to decide on the rotational speeds of the spheres. This is another set of three independent variables, the "speed" variables. So altogether there are six independent variables to deal with. Is it possible to design mechanical methods to handle these six variables leading eventually to a three-dimensional orbit for Saturn that will produce the apparent motion of Saturn across the night sky?

Compare this problem of Saturn with the problem of Boyle's law. BACON.1 was asked to discover the functional relationship between P and V (Section 32.3). So BACON.1's representational space is the set of all functions of P and V. In the jargon of AI, we say that the **search space** for BACON.1 is the set of all such functions. So reasonably BACON.1 started with the simplest eight: P, V, $(P + V)$, $(P - V)$, $(V - P)$, PV, P/V, V/P. Bingo! It arrived at the right answer on the sixth attempt: "$PV = c$."

We can say BACON.1 was lucky. The target function came sixth in the list. What if the target function were a complicated trigonometric function, which came at place one million and one! Moreover, BACON.1 was asked to deal with functions of only two variables. In comparison, the problem of Saturn has six variables to cope with. In other words, the search space is six dimensional (given that Saturn turns on three spheres). Is it possible to design efficient algorithms to search through this space so as to arrive at a reasonable set of values for the six variables to yield the orbit of Saturn?

The problem of Kepler's third law for BACON.1 was also simple. The search space is the set of all multiplicative functions. BACON.1 started with the simple ones: DP, D/P, P/D, D^2/P, P/D^2, P^2/D, D/P^2, D^2/P^2, P^2/D^2, D^3/P, P/D^3, P^3/D, D/P^3, D^3/P^2. On the 14th trial, it arrived at "$D^3/P^2 = c$." It is pragmatically justifiable to search among the simpler functions first. It is a matter of economy of thought (and of cash). However, can the principle of economy be applied to the search through the six-dimensional representational space of Saturn? Without a justifiable principle of some sort, the only alternative is apparently to search blindly. But blind search is hardly efficient or creative.

The problem of Jupiter is similar. The only difference is that now it is the apparent motion of Jupiter relative to Saturn that is to be reproduced by concentric spheres. The reason is simple. The primary sphere of Jupiter is to be attached to the sphere of Saturn, not to the sphere of the stars. Similar reasoning applies to all the other celestial objects.

B. Ptolemy's Geocentric Theory

As detailed in Chapter 7, Ptolemy abandoned the system of concentric spheres. Instead he introduced the mechanism of epicycles. Let's see how many variables (dimensions) govern this representational space. Again, let's take just one of the planets, say Saturn again. Suppose the number of epicycles employed by it is 10.[17] We can adjust the size of each of these 10 epicycles. We can adjust the speed of each. (Let's ignore the direction of rotation for the epicycles.) So we have 20 variables. Is it possible to design efficient algorithms to search through this space of 20 dimensions to obtain an acceptable approximation to the

---

17. The total number of epicycles proposed for all the planets was at one time up to 80. So it is not unreasonable to assume Saturn requires 10.

apparent motion of Saturn?[18] As a matter of fact, Ptolemy employed two additional devices. (i) The earth is allowed to be placed off the center of the "universe." In other words, the deferents of all the planets, according to Ptolemy, would share the same center. But the position of the earth need not be exactly where that center is. It is allowed to be displaced slightly. That distance of displacement is an additional variable. To put it succinctly, Ptolemy has abandoned the doctrine that the earth is at the center of the universe.[19] (ii) Ptolemy invented another device, known as the equant. Originally epicenters on the deferents were supposed to move on the deferents at uniform speed. In other words, these epicenters were supposed to move around the center of the universe (not earth) at uniform rate. To account for certain discrepancies, Ptolemy, however, allowed these epicenters to move uniformly with respect to a point off the center. That point is known as the equant. The distance between the equant and the center of the universe is another variable.

With so many independent variables (for a single planet), I think it would be difficult to construct a machine that could match Ptolemy (and his followers) in the design of epicycles. Mechanization of discovery within Ptolemy's representational space can't be easy.

C. Copernicus's Heliocentric Theory

In the 16th century, Copernicus proposed his heliocentric system to replace Ptolemy's geocentric system (Chapter 7). It was a revolution. Now the sun was supposed to occupy the center of the universe, with all the planets, including the earth, revolving round it. Nonetheless Copernicus had to employ epicycles, just as Ptolemy did, to account for the irregularities of the observed paths of the planets. His system used 48 epicycles. In addition, he had

to place the sun slightly off the "center of the universe" in a manner similar to Ptolemy's system.

Thus we can see that the representational space of Copernicus is quite similar to that of Ptolemy in complexity. The average number of epicycles per planet, including the moon, is seven. Thus the representational space is a (2×7)-dimensional space. In addition, there is the variable representing the distance of the sun from the "center of the universe."

D. Kepler's Heliocentric Theory

Finally, let's study the representational space of Kepler's theory. Kepler (1571–1630), dissatisfied with Copernicus's system, suggested that the planets move in ellipses with the sun at one of the two foci. It seems to be only a minor adjustment of Copernicus's system. But in fact it was a major step forward. With the ellipse, Kepler did away with all those cumbersome epicycles. As well, he was able to justify in a natural manner the displacement of the sun from the "center of the universe."[20]

Since Kepler's system supersedes all its predecessors, one would have thought that its representational space should be the most complicated of them all. On the contrary, it is the simplest. Given that the planets move in ellipses around the sun, what is the representational space for each individual planet?

The shape of an ellipse is determined by its eccentricity, which is a function of the two axes of the ellipse. Here is therefore one variable. Since all the observations are made from the earth, the relative size of the ellipse for the planet with respect to the size of the ellipse for the earth is relevant. This ratio of sizes constitutes the second variable. Finally, the speed of motion of the planet in comparison with the speed of motion of the earth should also

---

18. I am exaggerating the problem here. The epicycles for each planet are not of equal significance. Additional epicycles are meant for fine adjustments so that each additional epicycle should, in general, be much smaller than the previous one. In other words, there is not as much freedom of choice as I have suggested. Additional constraints always make searching simpler.

19. It is of course possible to argue that the earth is still at the center, only now the celestial objects no longer revolve around the center.

20. An ellipse can be taken as a flattened circle with two centers, known as foci. These foci are as "central" to the ellipse as the center is central to the circle. Yet the foci are at a distance from the true center of the ellipse.

be relevant in order to reproduce the apparent motion of the planet across the starry night sky. So here is a third variable.[21] All together, to work out the orbit of an individual planet, it is necessary to deal with three variables. Hence the representational space is only three-dimensional. How much simpler it is when compared with the three previous systems.

Kepler's search space is only three-dimensional. Would it therefore be relatively easy to construct mechanical rules for the discovery of planetary orbits? I should think not. I doubt Kepler's ingenuity can be duplicated with ease by machines. Note that this problem is not the same as BACON.1's problem of attempting to discover the third law from observed data![22]

Thus we can see that, at least in these four cases, it is not that easy to construct mechanical rules to arrive at empirically adequate models within a given representational space. The possibility of mechanization of model construction seems to be confined to simple cases such as those mentioned in the previous section—for example, those dealt with by BACON and DENDRAL.

As mentioned earlier, SoR consists of two steps. We have just dealt with step (ii). What about step (i), the construction of representational space? Are there any mechanical methods that will enable the discovery of novel representational spaces? We have studied four such spaces in this section. Can these spaces be mechanically discovered, given the available data of the observed paths of the planets across the night sky?

32.5 MECHANIZATION OF DISCOVERY III

How did Eudoxus come upon the theory of concentric spheres to solve Plato's Problem? What gave Ptolemy the idea of epicycles to replace the concentric spheres? Then, about 1,400 years later, Copernicus turned from Ptolemy's earth-centered system to a sun-centered system. This was not, however, as original as it appears to be. Aristarchus of Samos (born about 310 B.C.) had proposed the idea of a sun-centered system long before, and Copernicus borrowed the device of the epicycle from Ptolemy. Kepler was more original though. He broke the 2,000-year-old "rule" of the circle by suggesting the ellipse. Where did he get this rather "eccentric" idea?[23]

Since we are doing neither psychology nor history here, how these ideas actually arose is not our concern. The question, rather, is: Are there any mechanical methods, which, when applied in the right circumstances, will yield brilliant ideas such as these? Are there any mechanical methods for the production of representational spaces in general? Here let's explore three candidate methods:

(a) The method of axiomatic variations (MAV)

(b) The method of hierarchical ascent (MHA)

(c) The method of hierarchical descent (MHD)

I am responsible for these names and most of the contents.

A. The Method of Axiomatic Variations (MAV)

You may recall that, according to the logical positivists, scientific theories can be taken as sets of axioms (Chapters 15 and 23). Some of the axioms act as internal principles, whereas others play the role of bridge principles. However, since the advent of the Kuhnian revolution, this axiomatic view has been shunned by philosophers. I think it a pity. In spite of its shortcomings, there is quite a lot that can be said for it.

---

21. Unlike the previous systems of circles and spheres, the speed of the planets on the ellipse is nonuniform. Thus this variable does not take a constant value.

22. The third law was published in *Harmony of the World*, 1619, 10 years after the publication of the law of elliptic orbits in his *New Astronomy*.

23. The circle is an ellipse with eccentricity 0, so ellipses are as a matter of fact "eccentric" circles.

Before Euclid, the Egyptians and the Greeks conceived space in terms of what we call Euclidean geometry. They did their spatial measurements, their spatial designs, and their spatial predictions all within this conception. The great pyramids are standing proofs. Yet their idea of that geometry was woolly and unsystematic. It was Euclid who gave that geometry a clear and definite "shape" by axiomatizing it in his 13 volumes of *Elements* (Section 19.1). His system had five axioms. Let me repeat them here:

(i)   Between two points there is a straight line.

(ii) Straight lines can be extended indefinitely.

(iii) Given a fixed point and a distance, a circle can be described with that point as center and that distance as diameter.

(iv) All right angles are equal.

(v)   The Axiom of Parallels: In any plane, through a given point there exists one and only one straight line parallel to a given straight line.[24]

This set of axioms is, by today's standards, faulty and lacking rigor. But then it was conceived over 2,000 years ago, and for the first time. In 1899, David Hilbert, the great German mathematician, reformulated it in 20 axioms divided into five groups:

I.   Axioms of connection (seven axioms)

II.   Axioms of order (five axioms)

III. Axiom of parallels (called Euclid's axiom in honor of Euclid)

IV.   Axioms of congruence (six axioms)

V.   Axiom of continuity (called Archimedes' axiom in honor of Archimedes)

These five groups of axioms are independent of each other. They thus represent distinct "units" of ideas. It is as if the holistic idea of geometric space has been dissected into five parts, each representing a particular characteristic. The greatness of axiomatization can be seen in terms of these axiom groups. For the ancient Egyptians and Greeks—and most of us, I would imagine—the idea of (Euclidean) space is an unanalytic whole. It is a seamless finished product. We possess it in a manner similar to people's possession of mechanical clocks. The mechanical clock, to us, is a holistic object and, more important, it works. We can use it to tell the time. But how does it work? What sort of mechanism does it have to enable it to keep time? What are the parts of that mechanism? What should we do if it is too fast or too slow?[25] What Euclid and Hilbert did was open up the clock, identifying the parts and discovering their functions. Hilbert's five axiom groups represent the five aspects of space. Through them the structure of space becomes obvious. It is generally understood that chemistry aims for the analytic understanding of the structure of matter. Yet few of us realize that axiomatization of geometry leads to the analytic understanding of space. And in general axiomatization of a subject leads to the analytic understanding of that subject.

But then you might ask: What do all these things have to do with the mechanization of discovery? Let me illustrate with an example. Suppose it is discovered that the angle sum of certain triangles does not add up to two right angles—that is, 180°. What should we do? For both Euclid and Hilbert, it is a theorem that the sum of the three angles of a triangle is two right angles. However, here certain triangles are found not to obey this "law."[26] Kuhn would call it an anomaly. Now what should we do? We can of course try to blame our measuring instruments. But suppose we have found good reasons not to, and further suppose we suspect we have the wrong conception of space. If geometry is not axiomatized as in the days of the ancient Egyptians and Greeks, what can we do? How should we handle the anomaly? Think, while bearing in mind that

---

24. The point is assumed to be outside the line, of course. This is John Playfair's (1748–1819) reformulation. The original is: if a straight line falling on two straight lines makes the interior angles on the same side together less than two right angles, the two straight lines, if produced indefinitely, meet on that side on which the angles are together less than two right angles.

25. I know. Most of us will simply shake the clock if it runs too slow.

26. Historically the great 19th-century mathematician Gauss attempted to check if the angle sum law of Euclid holds for large triangles such as triangles made up from three distant mountain peaks.

our conception of space is holistic and unanalytic. It's rather like the case of the clock misbehaving. If we know nothing of the mechanism of the clock and how its parts cooperate to give us the correct time, how are we able to correct its misbehaviors?

Axiomatization is the dissection of an idea into its functional parts. Only when we know the functioning of the parts can we rectify the misbehaviors of the whole.

In the face of a geometric anomaly, the logical thing to do is to examine each of the axioms—for example, each of Hilbert's 20 axioms—and see which one or more are faulty. In the present case as we all know the fault lies with Axiom III, the axiom of parallels.

So here is a method of discovery: the method of axiomatic variations. According to this method, novel ideas can be obtained by the variation of the contents of axioms (for an axiomatized subject). Such variations can be motivated by the presence of anomalies. But that need not be the case. They can be motivated simply by curiosity. For instance, Nicolai Lobachevsky in 1829 explored the consequences of a variation of the axiom of parallels. That variation reads:

IIIa. In any plane, through a given point there exists more than one straight line parallel to a given straight line.

By replacing Euclid's axiom of parallels with this, Lobachevsky discovered a non-Euclidean geometry, now known as Lobachevskian geometry. In this geometry, the angle sum of a triangle is smaller than 180°, the deviation from 180° being proportional to the size of the triangle. Some years later, in 1854, Bernhard Riemann explored another variation, which reads:

IIIb. In any plane, through a given point there exists no straight line parallel to a given straight line.

With this axiom in place of Euclid's, Riemannian geometry was discovered. This is another non-Euclidean geometry, according to which the angle sum of a triangle is greater than 180°. Again the deviation is proportional to the size of the triangle concerned.

For the production of novel geometries, the variation of the axioms of Euclid is not confined to the axiom of parallels. For instance, Max Dehn (1878–1952), again out of curiosity, varied the axiom of continuity (Archimedes' axiom) and was rewarded with a non-Archimedean geometry.

We can see how the method of axiomatic variations can bring about new ideas. It is a powerful method of discovery. The method can be summarized as:

(17) **The method of axiomatic variations (MAV)** consists of two steps to produce novel theories: (i) axiomatize the subject matter so that the axioms fall into independent topic groups and (ii) vary each topic group of axioms in turn and work out the significant implications of the variations. (There is usually more than one way to axiomatize a subject. It is advisable to try out step (ii) for each axiomatization.)

Historically we can see that the shift from Dufay and Nollet's two-fluid theory to Franklin's one-fluid theory in the 18th century is an application of MAV (Section 15.4). As we saw in Chapter 0, Young and Fresnel improved on Huygens's longitudinal wave theory of light by postulating that light consists of transverse waves. This was another example of application. MAV can be seen to be a method of modifying given representational spaces. Even though it does not yield totally new ones, it is nonetheless a method of creativity. All the non-Euclidean geometries are genuinely innovative products; so is Franklin's one-fluid theory as well as Young and Fresnel's transverse wave theory.

B. The Method of Hierarchical Ascent (MHA)

Usually theories are made within the context of some higher background theories. Let's take some examples. Let's start with Newton's corpuscular theory of light (Chapter 0). It presupposes Newton's mechanics. Newton's mechanics, in turn, presupposes Euclidean geometry. Moreover, it assumes that space is three-dimensional, time is one-dimensional, and that they are independent of each other and absolute.

When a theory is in trouble (facing anomalies), it is advisable to attempt to find fault within the theory itself. One can, for example, employ MAV to isolate a faulty axiom. However, after much fruitless faultfinding within the theory itself, one should make an ascent to the next level of assumption and try to discover faults there instead. For instance, Newton's corpuscular theory cannot cope with the phenomena of diffraction and polarization adequately. Obviously the first step is to try to amend the theory itself. However, if such a move does not bring results, I think it wise to attempt to find fault with Newtonian mechanics, within which the corpuscular theory is embedded. We can even go higher. We can doubt the adequacy of Euclidean geometry as the theory of space. Indeed, that's how Einstein arrived at his theory of relativity. He did not believe that the results of Michelson-Morley's experiment could be explained within the framework of Newtonian mechanics. So he went up one level. He doubted the then-prevailing Newtonian absolute theory of space and time, which was based on Euclidean geometry.

MAV is a lateral procedure of discovery. The method of hierarchical ascent is, on the other hand, a vertical procedure of discovery. We can take the move from Eudoxus's, Ptolemy's, and Copernicus's circular motions to Kepler's elliptic motions as such an advance. We can say that the first three astronomers had exhausted the search space (representational space) of circles as far as their imagination could go. Kepler then made the advance to the next simplest search space, the space of ellipses. He could, of course, try out search spaces of more complicated closed curves. But this would be against the principle of economy of thought.

The shift from geocentric systems to heliocentric systems in cosmology is another example. It is a replacement of search space again. Unavoidably there are competing search spaces. For example, one can take Mars or the moon as the center of the universe. There is no a priori reason why the universe is not marsiocentric or luniocentric. However,

these search spaces should not be attempted until the simpler search space of heliocentricity has been thoroughly explored. So here is the method of hierarchical ascent:

(18) **The method of hierarchical ascent (MHA)** says that to bring about novel theories, one can make variations at the next higher level of presuppositions aiming at the production of novel search spaces (representational spaces). These novel search spaces should then be investigated in order of simplicity.

C. The Method of Hierarchical Descent (MHD)

There is a third way to produce novel theories, this time by descent. Let's illustrate it with Dalton's chemical atomic theory (CAT). The axioms of that theory were introduced in Section 25.6. Some of them are unspecific. For example Axiom (b) says that there are many kinds of atoms without specifying what kinds there are. Are these kinds determined by weight, size, or some other property? Axiom (d.ii) says that when atoms do combine to form molecules, they do so in definite ratios in terms of the numbers of atoms of each kind. What ratios? The axiom has not specified.

The idea of valency was introduced by J. J. Berzelius in 1812. It was later developed by Frankland, Dumas, Thomson, and Drude. Valency theory is about the capacity of atoms for combining into molecules. A univalent atom such as H or Cl can combine with another univalent atom to form a molecule—for example, HCl. A bivalent atom such as O can combine with two univalent atoms as in H_2O. Some atoms are trivalent, quadrivalent, and so on. Moreover, when atoms link to form molecules they link through certain valency bonds, and there are three major types of such bonds. For instance, one Na atom and one Cl atom can combine by one electrovalent bond. One C atom and four Cl atoms can combine by four covalent bonds. Third, two Al atoms can combine with six Cl atoms through six covalent bonds and two dative bonds. The theory of valency can be seen to be a development and refinement of CAT. This development is representable as subaxioms to Axiom (b) and Axiom (d.ii). Thus we have the method of hierarchical descent:

(19) **The method of hierarchical descent (MHD)** says that new ideas can be obtained by refining some of the ideas of a given theory, possibly by specifying subaxioms to existing axioms.

Thus I have introduced three methods of discovery: MAV, MHA, and MHD. The first proposes to discover new ideas through the variation of the axioms of a theory. This is discovery on a horizontal plane. The second proposes to make stepwise ascent to ever higher levels in search of alternatives. The third method proposes to obtain new ideas through refinement. These methods are not as original as they appear. To start with, recall that Kuhn (Chapter 27) claims that paradigms are holistic objects. Paradigm changes are likened to gestalt switches: the transitions are abrupt and wholesale and there are no "halfway houses." Laudan (Section 29.6) argues otherwise. He proposes the reticulated model of rationality, according to which scientific changes can be piecemeal. Our methods here are obviously written in the spirit of Laudan. In place of 'paradigm,' the notion of research program was proposed by Lakatos, who describes research programs as consisting of two parts: negative heuristic and positive heuristic. The latter consists of suggestions or hints on how to develop the research program. Our third method, MHD, can be seen to be along the same line of thinking.

I'm sure you have come across the term 'lateral thinking,' be it in the context of jokes or in situations of serious problem solving. The concept of lateral thinking came from Edward de Bono (1933–). Let me quote him:

> Rightness is what matters in vertical thinking. Richness is what matters in lateral thinking. Vertical thinking selects a pathway by excluding other pathways. Lateral thinking does not select but seeks to open up other pathways. With vertical thinking one selects the most promising approach to a problem, the best way of looking at a situation. With lateral thinking one generates as many alternative approaches as one can. With vertical thinking one may look for different approaches until one finds a promising one. With lateral thinking one goes on generating as many approaches as one can even after one has found a promising one. With vertical thinking one is trying to select the best approach but with lateral thinking one is generating different approaches for the sake of generating them. (1970, p. 39)

Our three methods here do not exactly fall within the folds of lateral thinking. However, the common stress on alternatives and variations identifies them as methods of the same type.

Before we leave this topic, I think it is important to point out that the three methods of discovery are far from being mechanical. They are guidelines of practice in scientific discovery rather than algorithms which will inevitably lead to results. It took great minds like Lobachevsky and Riemann to work out the implications from alternative axioms. There is no indication that computational power can perform similar feats. Einstein made the ascent from Euclidean space and time to Minkowski spacetime, resulting in the theory of relativity. Again, I do not think machine intelligence can match that, at least not in the foreseeable future. The third method, MHD, is probably more amenable to mechanization though. To specialize is to eliminate portions of the search space (representational space). This can often be done by mechanical means.

Let's return to the question we started with: Are there any mechanical methods for the production of representational spaces? Since none of the three methods we just studied are mechanical, the answer to this question should then be no, not as far as we know. Nonetheless, these three methods can guide us to the modification of existing representational spaces. Some of these modifications are so drastic and innovative that the end products are in essence new representational spaces. Examples of such include Kepler's representational space of ellipses, the non-Euclidean geometries, and Einstein's relativity. Thus our methods are creative, even though not mechanical.

Our three methods complement Mill's methods. Whereas Mill's methods apply to phenomenal science, our methods apply to theoretical science (Chapter 8). Mill's methods deal with the correlation of data. Our methods deal with the revision and development of theories. Mill's methods are methods of discovery within given representational spaces. Our methods are methods of discovery of representational spaces themselves.

We should say something about the mechanization of justification (evaluation of theories), since justification and discovery are the twin problems we started with in Chapter 1. Regrettably, this chapter has already used up its allocated space. So let's turn to the next and last topic.

32.6 WHAT IS SCIENTIFIC CREATIVITY?

What is creativity? This is a big question. Nonetheless, having spent so much time on mechanized discovery, I think it a pity not to venture just one step further to explore this exciting field of study.

There are lots of romantic ideas and beliefs about the act of creativity and the mystique of the creative genius. We read so much about flashes of insight, creative leaps, intuitive ideas, and dramatic visions. Where do novel ideas come from? It must be from somewhere. How are these ideas obtained? Mozart believed that his music came directly from the Divine. The phenomenon of creativity is indeed puzzling and at the same time fascinating.

There are two kinds of creativity. I will call them **artistic creativity** and **functional creativity**. Artistic creativity is exemplified by the works of Bach, Mozart, and Beethoven in music; Turner,

Monet, and Picasso in art; Shakespeare, Goethe, and Hugo in literature. There is little constraint on artistic creativity. (Pure) art is expressive in nature. It is not meant to serve any practical purpose. On the other hand, functional creativity is highly constrained. It is constrained by the purposes the piece of work is meant to serve. For instance, the theory of relativity was meant to serve a purpose. Einstein did not create it for self-expression or for fun. Part of that purpose was to try to make comprehensible the negative results of Michelson-Morley's experiment. Newton's gravitational theory was meant to explain the orbits of the planets and the moon, among others. Dalton's CAT was meant to provide a foundational mechanism for chemical changes. Scientific theories differ from scientific fictions. They are judged according to how well they fulfill functions such as explanation, prediction, and truth. Scientific creativity is functional creativity.

How does scientific creativity arise? Can this phenomenon be explained? Can scientific creativity be learned? Is scientific creativity mechanizable?

Let's start with a parable. Imagine an extraterrestrial visiting earth. It might wonder at the varieties of species: millions of them, each different from the other, and each constructed in such a way that it fits exactly into its environment. The extraterrestrial would probably start to marvel at their creator or creators. And yet, according to the theory of evolution, there was no creator and there was no conscious design. Those wonderful "artifacts" are simply the products of chance! Given time, millions and millions of years of time, such products can, believe it or not, "automatically" arise out of "water" and "mud." So, what appears as clever designs need not be designed at all.

The process of scientific creativity, or for that matter artistic creativity as well, can be similar to the process of evolution! Creativity can be an illusion. An end product will appear to be the result of creativity if the process that leads to it remains obscure.

In fact, a rather popular theory of creativity has been around for some time. It models itself on the process of biological evolution and has been called the **blind-variation-and-selective-retention theory (BVSR)**.[27]

According to the biological theory of evolution, mutation yields varieties. Varieties more suited to the given environment will have a better chance to survive at the expense of others. Resources are limited in nature. These include food, shelter, and mates. All biological individuals compete for them. There are bound to be winners and losers. The winners, being winners, will be more fruitful in reproduction. (At least they have more mates and live longer to reproduce.) Through reproduction advantageous characteristics of the parents are generally retained. Thus of the many varieties generated at random by mutation, only those that suit the environment are preserved. The rest are gradually eliminated. This is known as natural selection: it is as if nature consciously selects the more suitable varieties. The change effected by each step of natural selection is minute and imperceptible. Yet given sufficient time (for example, millions and millions of years), the cumulative effect can be dramatic. That explains the diversity of the species and why each species fits in so perfectly with its environment. The main mechanism behind the theory of evolution can be summarized as blind variation (mutation) and selective retention (natural selection).

BVSR claims that creative thought arises in a way very similar to the origin of species. Let's explain BVSR in terms of sophisticated representationism (SoR) (Section 31.5). According to SoR, science aims at the representation of objective reality. Such a representation takes two steps: (i) the creation of a representational space (generic theory) and (ii) the search for a model (specific theory) within that space. Since a representational space is but a set of possible models, to search for a model is the same as to single out one among the (very many) "possibles" as the correct "picture" of reality. According to BVSR, creativity is an illusion. "Direct" or "insightful" creative thought processes do not exist, at least not in the production of scientific theories. When attempting to produce an adequate scientific theory, the mind simply runs blindly through the representational space. Implausible models are rejected. Plausible models are retained for evaluation and testing. With a bit of luck, one of the plausible models may be found to pass all the severe tests. In such a case, it would be accepted by the scientific community, and history would portray it as a product of ingenious creative thought.

Note that we are employing the "search" idiom here. It is as if all the possible models are there in the representational space, independent of us. We do not create these models. What we do in scientific thinking is to search through the representational space, hoping to find the right model. Thus the picture is "search and discover." However, we can alternatively present BVSR in terms of the "variation" idiom. We can speak as if these variations (that is, varieties of possible models) are nonexistent prior to our investigation. Since they are nonexistent, we cannot search through them. They need to be invented. They are generated by the mind just as biological varieties are generated by mutation. This is the "variation through invention" picture. When a parallel is drawn between BVSR and evolution, the "variation" idiom is obviously more appropriate. However, when BVSR is presented in terms of 'representational space,' the "search" idiom is preferable. The space metaphor agrees better with the picture of search and discover. In fact, in the study of AI, the term 'search space' is commonly employed.

For illustration, let me tell one of the memorable tales of blind search. You might remember Henri Poincaré (1854–1912), one of the initiators of conventionalism (Chapter 8). This distinguished physicist-mathematician-philosopher reported his moment of creativity thus:

> For a fortnight I had been attempting to prove that there could not be any function analogous to what I have since called Fuchsian functions. I was at that time very ignorant. Every day I sat down at my table

---

27. Campbell (1960, pp. 380–400).

and spent an hour or two trying a great number of combinations, and I arrived at no result. One night I took some black coffee, contrary to my custom, and was unable to sleep. A host of ideas kept surging in my head; I could almost feel them jostling one another, until two of them coalesced, so to speak, to form a stable combination. When morning came, I had established the existence of one class of Fuchsian functions, those that are derived from the hypergeometric series. I had only to verify the results, which only took a few hours.[28]

You can see how Poincaré's mind ran blindly through the representational space of mathematical functions. Poincaré could recall "shadows" and "images" because he was semiconscious. It is believed that this sort of search often occurs during sleep. The subject cannot recall a thing. On waking she suddenly finds the problem solved. That brilliant idea simply appears, as if from nowhere.

As early as 1855, Alexander Bain suggested that trial and error play a role in creative thinking.[29] In 1881, Paul Souriau was even more forthcoming on the factor of chance as the source of innovation. He wrote:

In this case it is evident that there is no way to begin except at random. Our mind takes up the first path that it finds open before it, perceives that it is a false route, retraces its steps and takes another direction. Perhaps it will arrive immediately at the sought idea, perhaps it will arrive very belatedly: it is entirely impossible to know in advance. In these conditions we are reduced to dependence upon chance.... New ideas cannot have prototypes: their appearance can only be attributed to chance.[30]

This much is about blind search. Let's see what Souriau had to say about selective retention:

By a kind of artificial selection, we can in addition substantially perfect our thought and make it more and more logical. Of all of the ideas which present themselves to our mind, we note only those which have some value and can be utilized in reasoning. For every single idea of a judicious and reasonable nature which offers itself to us, what hosts of frivolous, bizarre, and absurd ideas cross our mind.... It is after hours and years of meditation that the sought-after idea presents itself to the inventor. He does not succeed without going astray many times; and if he thinks himself to have succeeded without effort, it is only because the joy of having succeeded has made him forget all the fatigues, all the false leads, all of the agonies, with which he has paid for his success.[31]

Well argued and well witnessed as it is the method of BVSR is nonetheless unreasonable. Blind search will take an impossibly long time to arrive at the correct idea. Representational spaces are usually infinitely large. No blind search would have a reasonable chance of success. Imagine someone searching blindly for gold. She might just be picking through sands and stones aimlessly on the beach day in and day out. The chance of discovering gold through blind search, whether on a beach, in a forest, or anywhere except in a bank vault, is practically nil.[32] (The idiom 'searching for a needle in a haystack' would be appropriate here, if the haystack were infinitely large!) Thus Paul Thagard

---

28. Poincaré (1914, p. 52).

29. Campbell (1960, p. 385).

30. Campbell (1960, pp. 385–386).

31. Campbell (1960, p. 386).

32. See our discussion of the simple inductive method in Section 5.3.

(1988, p. 106) writes: "If variation were blind, we would be faced with the necessity of choosing among an unmanageably large number of theories, many of them irrelevant."

Thus the obvious amendment to BVSR is to let the variation (search) be methodical. Let's therefore take **MVSR (methodical-variation-and-selective-retention theory)**[33] instead.

What sort of methods can be employed in methodical variation (search)? To start with we can always group the possibilities in a representational space into groups or categories. Instead of trying out each individual possibility, we can assess the possibilities group by group. Putting it differently, we can carve up the representational space into subspaces. Instead of going through each point of space and assessing its suitability, we can move from subspace (region) to subspace (region) and assess each subspace as a whole. Let me give an example.

The problem for Kepler is to discover the orbits of the planets, in particular that of Mars. We can view the problem as a problem of search. The representational space is the set of all curves. The problem is to find within this representational space that single curve which faithfully depicts the orbit of Mars.

The method of blind search would have us "walk" through this representational space at random. We pick up a curve here and a curve there, assessing each as we "walk" along. Obviously the chance of encountering a curve of the right shape and size for Mars is practically nil. Alternatively we can search through the space methodically. We can, for instance, carve up the representational space into subspaces. One way to proceed is to partition the space into two subspaces: the subspace of all open curves and the subspace of all closed curves. With the data on hand, we can very quickly rule out the first subspace as implausible. The available data (at the time of Kepler) suggested that the orbit of Mars is a closed curve. We can further partition this subspace of closed curves into "segmented" and "smooth." The "segmented" are those that have corners such as polygons. The rest are "smooth," which include circles, egg shapes, apple shapes, pear shapes, tomato shapes, ellipses, and so on. Again the data on hand would quickly rule out the "segmented" as plausible candidates, leaving the "smooth" closed curves as the only plausible candidates.

We can proceed by further dividing up the "smooth" curves into (a) circles, (b) closed curves generatable from circles, (c) egg shapes, (d) apple shapes, (e) pear shapes, (f) tomato shapes, (g) ellipses, and so on. Again the data available would rule out (a), and there is simply no available mathematics to deal with (c) to (e). For Eudoxus, Ptolemy, and Copernicus, both (b) and (g) are mathematically manageable.[34] (The study of the ellipse was quite advanced in the time of the ancient Greeks.) However, for them, (b) was definitely easier to handle and more pleasing to work with. Thus, for pragmatic purposes, it is justifiable to search for the orbit of Mars in (b) first. Having failed to locate it in (b) after more than 2,000 years of search, it was no accident that Kepler switched over to (g), the subspace of ellipses. This step was both logical and wise. This is what we mean by 'methodical search.'[35]

Methodical search is also known as 'heuristic search.' The word 'heuristic' came from the Greek word 'heuriskein,' meaning 'to discover.' According to Newell et al. (1967, p. 78), the term 'heuristic' denotes 'any principle or device that contributes to the reduction in the average search to a solution.' In our discussion of the search for the orbit of Mars, we have implicitly introduced three heuristics:

(20a) Divide the representational space into subspaces. Reject those subspaces that, in accordance with available data, are implausible.

---

33. This is my term.

34. Recall Galileo's observation that nature is written in the language of mathematics. We may as well say manageable models are written in the language of mathematics.

35. Our portrayal of the move from circles to ellipses here as a move from one subspace into another is slightly different from our presentation in Section 32.5B. There I portrayed it as a move from one representational space into another representational space. There is no inconsistency here. How much is one representational space is a matter of convention.

(20b) Give preference to the subspaces that are mathematically more manageable.

(20c) Give priority to the subspaces that are aesthetically more pleasing.

Not all heuristics are rationally justifiable. For example, (20c) here, I think, is not. Heuristics can contradict each other when applied. For instance, there are circumstances when (20b) and (20c) conflict. Finally, heuristics certainly do not always lead to success. In fact, they seldom lead to success, otherwise we would have solved most of the problems in science. Nevertheless, we have no choice but to use heuristics. No search is manageable without employing them. The use of heuristics increases both the efficiency of the search and the likelihood of its success.

The study of heuristics is an important area of research in AI. The three proposed here are domain-independent heuristics. There can be domain-specific ones, heuristics that are applicable only to certain specific types of problems, say to problems of geometry or to the study of lung cancer. Heuristics are themselves not algorithms. They are more like maxims. Most domain-independent heuristics are vague. Nonetheless, when applied to specific problems, they can be made precise and turned into component parts of algorithms. When so applied, usually these domain-independent heuristics become domain-specific. For example, take (20a). The heuristic advises us to subdivide the representational space into subspaces without telling us how. In our discussion of the search for the orbit of Mars, we advise that the representational space should be partitioned into certain groups of curves. This could have been obtained from the following heuristic:

(20a1) If the representational space consists of curves,[36] subdivide the space into groups of curves, which are identifiable by mathematical functions—for example, the ellipses, the hyperbolas, parabolas, sine curves, and so on.

It can be seen that this heuristic is a specification of (20a). It is domain-specific because it is only applicable when the representational space is one of curves. One of the central tasks in AI research is to turn general heuristics into (component parts of) specific algorithms. This is an essential step in the mechanization of MVSR. It is hoped that mechanized MVSR can reproduce a significant part, if not all, of human creative thinking.

It has been recognized that the major obstacle to creative thinking is mind-set. Often we are used to working or thinking in a certain way. We are simply blind to the possibility of alternatives. In the terminology of representational space, we can say that the mind can be so confined to a particular representational space that it cannot envisage alternative representational spaces. Sometimes the mind can be so used to just one "corner" of the representational space that it does not realize that there is more space "just around the corner." I'll give an illustration.

Many of you have heard the "romantic" story of Friedrich August von Kekulé's (1829–1896) discovery of the benzene ring. Benzene was known to have the chemical formula C_6H_6. But how are these 12 atoms linked to form a unit? It was known at the time of Kekulé that C is quadrivalent (that is, it "has four arms") and can combine with four ("one-armed") monovalent atoms, such as H. The problem is: How do these twelve atoms "link arms" in such a way that all the arms of the 12 atoms are utilized?

Kekulé was used to "open chains" of atoms. Figures 32.3a and 32.3b show two open chains. Up to the time of the problem of benzene, he was very successful in modeling molecules in terms of open chains, and he had always employed open chains. It was thus natural for him to attempt to give the benzene molecule an open chain structure. But alas, he wrestled with the problem for months, trying out all sorts of open chains without success. Then one evening he was sitting in front of his open fire. (Let's hear the story from Kekulé himself.)

> I turned my chair to the fire and dozed.
> Again the atoms were gambolling before
> my eyes. This time the smaller groups kept

---

36. Namely, all curves in a three-dimensional Euclidean space.

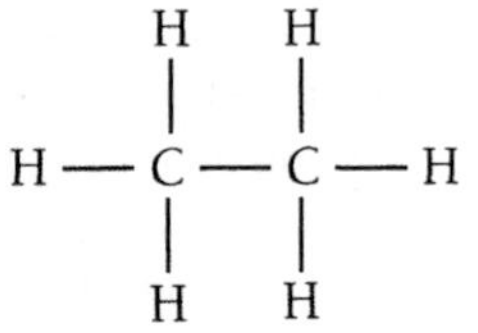

FIGURE 32.3a Ethane

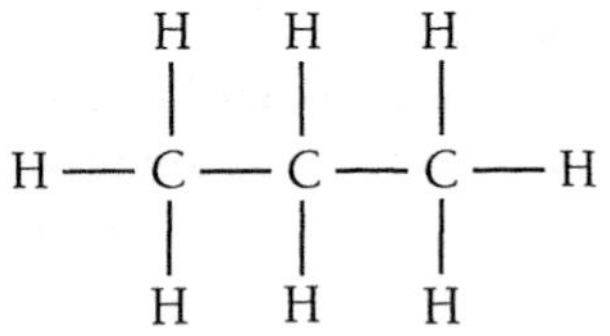

FIGURE 32.3b Propane

modestly in the background. My mental eye, rendered more acute by repeated visions of this kind, could now distinguish larger structures, of manifold conformation; long rows, sometimes more closely fitted together, all twining and twisting in snake-like motion. But look! What was that? One of the snakes had seized hold of its own tail, and the form whirled mockingly before my eyes. As if by a flash of lightning I awoke. (Boden, 1990, pp. 50–51)

It was in this way that Kekulé realized that the benzene molecule was a closed chain rather than an open chain. Thus the famous benzene ring was born (Figure 32.4). We can see how the C atoms form a ring at the center. The important point is that all the "arms" of the 12 atoms are utilized. Each C atom has four "arms" and each H atom has one "arm." There are thus 30 "arms" altogether. Yet each and every arm is linked to some other arm. There are no idle "arms" in this clever structure!

We can say that Kekulé had a mind-set for many months. He was trapped in the "open–chain corner" of the representational space. Then, on that fateful evening, stimulated by the dancing flames in the open fire—or was it due to the exceptionally good quality of his after-dinner cognac—his mind broke out of its confines into the open space of "rings"!

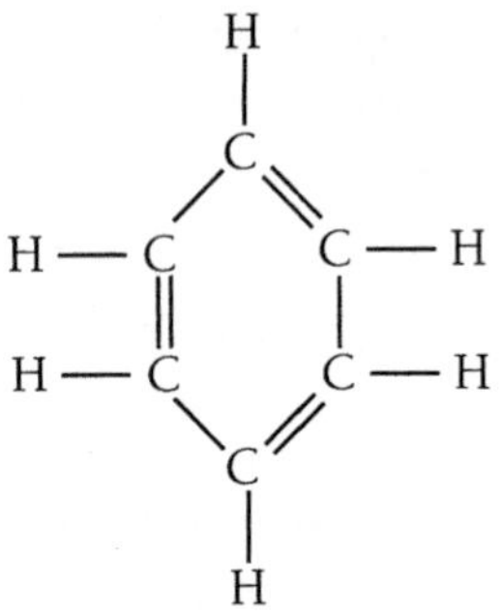

FIGURE 32.4 The Benzene Ring

That's why de Bono recommends lateral thinking. To think laterally is to attempt the unconventional. Most of our minds are set—the older we get the more set our minds usually are. This is a fact of biology and psychology. However, there are many ways to escape the confines of mind-sets. Sitting in front of an open fire is one way. Drinking coffee is another. Some prefer to take a bath. Some opt for sitting under an apple tree. As for myself, I think taking a break from the problem at hand is probably as helpful as any. All these "strategies" are, however, dependent on chance. Are there any that can provide more sure ways of success? The answer is yes. We have been studying MVSR. According to it, variations (searches) should not be blind. They should be methodical. Being methodical would prevent one from going in circles, being confined to the familiar part of the representational space.

Is creative thinking therefore nothing more than methodical search through a representational space? Has MVSR reproduced the essence of creative discovery? Let me end this rather lengthy chapter with the following observations.

In the 17th century, Descartes invented analytic geometry, often known as Cartesian geometry. He introduced the novel idea of representing geometric objects such as the straight line, the circle, the ellipse, and the parabola in terms of algebraic equations. This creativity is not simply a matter of breaking through from one subspace into another. It is the invention of a totally new way of thinking. It is the introduction of a completely novel representational space. Can MVSR enable us to make